Carl Loren Reinhold

Therapeutic Psychology

3rd edition

Therapeutic Psychology

Fundamentals of Counseling and Psychotherapy

Lawrence M. Brammer

*Professor of Educational Psychology
and Counseling, University of Washington;
Diplomate in Counseling Psychology,
American Board of Professional Psychology*

Everett L. Shostrom

*Director, Institute of Actualizing Therapy,
Santa Ana, California;
Diplomate in Clinical Psychology,
American Board of Professional Psychology*

Prentice-Hall, Inc., Englewood Cliffs, New Jersey 07632

Library of Congress Cataloging in Publication Data

BRAMMER, LAWRENCE M
    Therapeutic psychology.
    (Prentice-Hall psychology series)
    Bibliography: p.
    Includes index.
  1. Psychotherapy. 2. Counseling. 3. Self-
actualization (Psychology) I. Shostrom, Everett L.,
(date) joint author. II. Title. [DNLM:
1. Counseling. 2. Psychotherapy. WM420 B815t]
RC480.5.B7 1977   616.8'914   76–26564
ISBN 0–13–914622–9

Prentice-Hall Psychology Series
Richard S. Lazarus, Editor

Printed in the United States of America

10 9 8 7 6 5 4 3 2

PRENTICE-HALL INTERNATIONAL, INC., *London*
PRENTICE-HALL OF AUSTRALIA, PTY. LTD., *Sydney*
PRENTICE-HALL OF CANADA, LTD., *Toronto*
PRENTICE-HALL OF INDIA PRIVATE LIMITED, *New Delhi*
PRENTICE-HALL OF JAPAN, INC., *Tokyo*
PRENTICE-HALL OF SOUTHEAST ASIA PTE. LTD., *Singapore*
WHITEHALL BOOKS LIMITED, WELLINGTON, *New Zealand*

Contents

v

In the past twenty-five years counseling and clinical psychology have grown closer together. The writers, one from a university teaching and counseling background and the other from a private clinical practice emphasis, have worked together to produce this third edition. Each has contributed from his unique experience to this common general approach to counseling and psychotherapy. This third edition attempts to reassess the current status, trends, and problems in research and practice of general counseling and psychotherapy with mildly disturbed people. Professional acceptance of early editions of *Therapeutic Psychology* convinced the authors that the developmental approach and our current creative synthesis position on counseling issues is productive of research, discussion, and improved practice. Aims of this edition are updating findings and expanding topics such as counseling theory, values, and professional issues. The evolution of our actualizing counseling point of view is outlined in detail and is presented as an illustrative model in our creative synthesis approach which attempts to go beyond eclecticism.

Counseling services are in such great demand in school, college, and community agencies that every effort must be spent to order present knowledge and discover new methods in the helping professions. People everywhere are concerned not only with living more comfortably with their life problems, but also with improving their human effectiveness and becoming their true potentials. This demand puts counseling in a framework much broader than traditional solving of personal problems or planning educational and vocational futures. People want help with a broad range of philosophical concerns about the meaning and purpose of living, as well as with problem-solving skills. Mastery of their environment is important; but looking inward toward self-understanding and development is of increasing concern. Counseling and psychotherapy must tool up to meet these challenges to the human potential.

The authors wish to thank their students and colleagues who have contributed criticisms and suggestions for this revision. We are also grateful to the large number of dedicated people in research and practice of counseling and psychotherapy who put their findings and thoughts on the pages of technical journals and papers. We wish to acknowledge with special gratitude the generous permission of Robert Knapp, President of Educational and Industrial Testing Service, to quote extensively from *Actualizing Therapy*. We also thank Ms. Sharon Roberts for her careful preparation of the manuscript.

We shall use the terms counselor, psychotherapist, clinician, and therapist interchangeably. While there are some distinctions, the differences lie mainly in agency usage. We shall use the generic term "he" as a convenience to refer to a counselor or client in general. We recognize the inadequacy of our language to provide a suitable generic person term; and we wish to state that this usage does not detract from our commitment to affirmative action in all spheres.

Lawrence M. Brammer / Everett L. Shostrom

Therapeutic Psychology

Foundations

part 1

Professional Counseling and Psychotherapy

Introduction

The helping functions of counseling and psychotherapy offer great challenges, rewards, and opportunities to persons interested in helping their fellow human beings. Help is defined as providing conditions for people to fulfill their needs for security, love and respect, self-esteem, decisive action, and self-actualizing growth. Professional helpers offer their services under specified conditions described in this book. Professionals not only avoid deluding themselves that they can be all things to all people, but they are also aware of their limitations and needs to be helpful. They can see when help becomes control and when they need clients to fulfill their own needs for love, power, or prestige. Counselors need rewards for their efforts, however, and seeing clients become self-sufficient, realize their hidden potentials, and function at higher levels of effective living are such rewards.

In addition to describing the fundamental techniques of counseling and psychotherapy, this volume presents significant historical foundations, personality theory, professional issues, and special adaptations necessary for the practice of counseling and psychotherapy in various settings: schools, colleges, agencies, churches, industries, and clinical practice.

This chapter covers origins of the counseling and psychotherapeutic emphases in psychology, present status and trends, and pressing professional problems in practice.

Since counselors and psychotherapists are concerned with facilitating personality changes in their clients, an introductory discussion of the significance of theory, varied approaches, and brief descriptions of views on the nature and functioning of personality are included in Chapter 2. Prin-

1

ciples of personality growth with the special problems of each stage from birth to old age are discussed in Chapter 3, whereas an overview of the nature of the counseling and psychotherapeutic processes is presented in Chapter 4.

The principal purposes of Part 1 are to promote broad understandings of professional problems and to prepare the reader with personality theory and concepts about the development of human personality for the technique discussions in Part 2 and 3. Part 1 contains four unique key terms. The first, and the title of this book, "therapeutic psychology," encompasses much of the accumulated wisdom of the helping professions. "Creative synthesis" is our term for efforts to develop a comprehensive dynamic outlook on personality structure and change as a basis for counseling practice. "Multidimensional" refers to the varied modalities of theory underlying the helping process—philosophical, structural, functional, developmental, and research. "Actualizing counseling and psychotherapy" is our illustrative understanding and action approach described in Chapter 3.

Part 2 includes the "how to do it" aspect of counseling and psychotherapy. Beginning with Chapter 5 on preparing a client for the counseling experience, the important points of the technique description are made in Chapters 6 through 8, which are concerned with the nature of the counseling relationship, how it is established and maintained, and which factors create problems for the counselor. In Chapters 9 through 11, important techniques of interpretation, appraisal, information-giving, and group methods are described and illustrated. A basic assumption underlying Part 2 is that psychotherapeutic attitudes and skills are learned, not endowed. Hence, effective counseling methods can be acquired with conscientious study, practice, and evaluation.

It is anticipated that the reader, whatever his professional setting, may be able to choose from those techniques which have particular application to his specialty and institutional role.

Part 3 covers applications of techniques to human problems of marriage, family life, philosophy and religion, intellectual functioning, and educational and career choice. The purpose of Part 3 is to present some of the problems and methods in each area, unique materials needed, and the adaptations of general theory and technique which are required. An additional purpose is to acquaint students with the multitudinous applications of applied psychology to intimate human problems.

The overview of this volume will help the reader to understand the title of the book, *Therapeutic Psychology*. Much material has been included which is not technique, but rather knowledge and values considered necessary to the professional background of a counselor or psychotherapist. Although we do not assume that this material represents *all* that should be known for competence in this field, we hope that the student in training and the practitioner already at work will find this volume a useful attempt to describe more precisely how counseling skill is developed.

Therapeutic psychology represents a body of knowledge which gathers its data from a number of related professions. All embody the "helping function." In psychology, the clinical specialty, with its traditional emphasis on diagnostic evaluation, is concentrating more on psychotherapy and counseling. Counseling psychology incorporates traditional counseling and assessment in education, industry, and rehabilitation with newer emphases on achieving self-actualization and improving human effectiveness. School psychology is a third division of applied psychology where counseling and psychotherapy are being utilized increasingly. Psychiatry has contributed greatly to the concepts and techniques currently employed in the helping process. The field of social work has also given us a rich heritage of case-work and interviewing skills. Pastoral counseling by clergymen is one of the traditional helping areas which has contributed much to therapeutic psychology in the realm of values clarification. Community psychology is a growing field which also applies counseling and psychotherapy methods to varied institutional settings such as clinics, prisons, homes for the elderly, and drug treatment centers.

The establishment of a formal area of therapeutic psychology which incorporates contributions from many helping professions is a natural phenomenon. For many years psychology has collaborated with other professions in contributing its unique approaches to understanding human behavior. In order to succeed in counseling and psychotherapeutic efforts, it is necessary that counseling and clinical psychologists recognize and utilize the understandings of all the established helping professions in addition to capitalizing on the unique findings of their own science. Figure 1 illustrates the unique contributions as well as the interrelationship among disciplines which contribute to the viewpoints of this volume.

The study of therapeutic psychology, then, has four broad purposes: (1) to create an appreciation of the scope and depth of learning necessary for competency as a skilled counselor and psychotherapist; (2) to develop an understanding of relevant knowledge from behavioral sciences; (3) to develop skill competencies for the various specialties in counseling and psychotherapy; and (4) to understand research results and needs.

Since therapeutic psychology embraces both counseling and psychotherapy, it is necessary to comment on the similarities and differences. The authors of this book are a counseling psychologist with experience in college and school settings and a clinical psychologist experienced in agency and private-practice settings. We bring together viewpoints from our respective areas of experience to create a body of knowledge which overlaps and contributes to both counseling and psychotherapy. The result, entitled *Therapeutic Psychology*, may be defined as the body of understandings, values, research, and skills common to both counseling and psychotherapy. The substance of therapeutic psychology comes from several helping professions and is rooted in applied behavioral sciences.

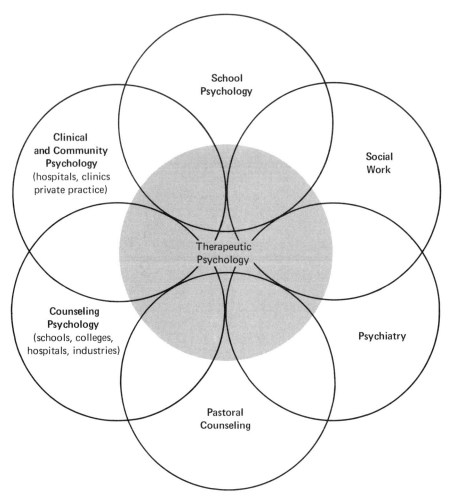

School
Psychology

Clinical
and Community
Psychology
(hospitals, clinics
private practice)

Social
Work

Therapeutic
Psychology

Counseling
Psychology
(schools, colleges,
hospitals, industries)

Psychiatry

Pastoral
Counseling

Figure 1. Relationship of Therapeutic Psychology to Selected Helping Professions

In Figure 2 the scope of therapeutic psychology is illustrated. Counseling and psychotherapy are viewed as overlapping areas of professional competence. Historically, counseling has been characterized by the following words: educational, vocational, supportive, situational, problem-solving, conscious awareness, normal, present time, and short term.

Psychotherapy has been described with terms such as supportive (in a crisis setting), reconstructive, depth emphasis, analytical, focus on the past, emphasis on "neurotics" or other severe emotional problems, and long term. In current usage, however, counseling and psychotherapy are used interchangeably. In the remainder of this volume we will use either term to encompass the other, unless otherwise stated.

We believe that one could hardly quarrel with the two lists in Figure 2

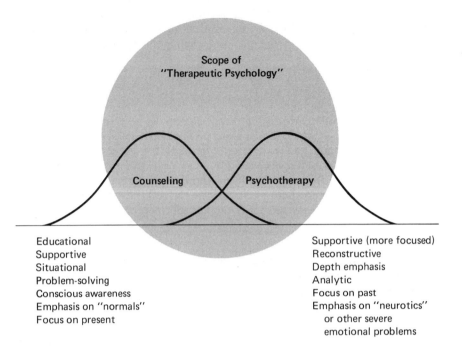

Educational	Supportive (more focused)
Supportive	Reconstructive
Situational	Depth emphasis
Problem-solving	Analytic
Conscious awareness	Focus on past
Emphasis on "normals"	Emphasis on "neurotics"
Focus on present	or other severe
	emotional problems

Figure 2. The Scope of Counseling and Psychotherapy Within the Framework of Therapeutic Psychology

which characterize the extreme ends of the counseling-psychotherapeutic continuum. An exception is the trend toward work with psychotic people on an out-patient basis in community clinics. Therapists in Veterans Administration Centers or mental hygiene clinics, for example, would call this psychotherapy; but they would also emphasize its supportive rather than personality-change features. Most people probably would not call this intensive type of activity counseling, however.

Blos (56) and Pepinsky (360) state that counseling deals with relatively nonembedded problem cases, that is, with those persons who have not developed rigid neurotic patterns, but are primarily victims of pressures from the outside environment. Thorne (474), however, who is both a psychologist and a psychiatrist, describes counseling as a type of psycho-therapy adaptable to problems of normal people. Robinson (385) contributed a useful concept to the definition of counseling, which he describes as aiding normal people to achieve higher level adjustment skills which are manifested as increased maturity, independence, personal integration, and responsibility. The phrase, increasing human effectiveness, is used frequently to describe the goal of counseling (Brayfield 69, Blocher 55).

Although attempts to formulate precise inclusive definitions of *counseling* have been difficult, Gustad (212) marshaled the published definitions into three categories: *participants,* generally two in number and with specified professional roles or affiliations, such as teachers, ministers, or psychologists; *goals*, in terms of improved adjustment, higher functioning, and greater happiness; and definitions stressing the *learning* emphases in counseling.

Gustad, from his survey, suggests a composite definition of *counseling* which includes three key elements:

Counseling is a learning-oriented process, carried on in a simple, one-to-one social environment, in which a counselor, professionally competent in relevant psychological skills and knowledge, seeks to assist the client by methods appropriate to the latter's needs and within the context of the total personnel program, to learn more about himself, to learn how to put such understanding into effect in relation to more clearly perceived, realistically defined goals to the end that the client may become a happier and more productive member of his society (212, p. 17).

Counseling, therefore, stresses more rational planning, problem-solving, decision-making, and support for situational pressures arising in the everyday lives of normal people. Counseling, consequently, is shorter in duration than psychotherapy and is defined by what professional counselors do—their roles and matching competencies.

Psychotherapy, in contrast, is defined as more inclusive re-education of the individual. The basic aims of psychotherapy are to assist the client to gain perceptual reorganization, to integrate consequent insights into his everyday behavior, and to live with intense feelings originating in past hurtful experiences. Existing defenses are modified so that readjustment is obtained. Thus, psychotherapy emphasizes intensity and length of involvement and is more concerned with alleviating pathological conditions.

To many clinicians distinctions between psychotherapy and counseling appear to be primarily quantitative rather than qualitative in nature. We have chosen for the purposes of this book to use the terms counselor, psychotherapist, clinician, psychological counselor, psychotherapeutic counselor, and psychologist interchangeably in the broad areas of overlap. Yet, we recognize that there are some differences in usage of the terms. Wherever possible, distinctions will be made throughout this book in those areas judged to be primarily the concern of either counseling or psychotherapy.

Another approach to differentiating forms of therapeutic help is to look at traditional professional roles and responsibilities. Figure 3 shows the great overlap that exists between psychology and psychiatry, as well as some of the unique functions of medical therapists on the extreme left and of psychologists and counselors on the extreme right. The re-educative or psychotherapeutic functions shared by both groups are listed in the middle with factors to be considered in determining responsibility for psychotherapy.

There are psychiatrists who claim that all psychotherapy is medicine and would crowd counselors and clinical psychologists to the extreme right of Figure 3. Some psychologists and educators would do the same

Psychiatry and Neurology (Medicine)		Counseling-Clinical (Psychology)
Treatment of Severe Neuroses or Psychoses involving, for example	Psychotherapy or Re-education (Criteria applied to determine the locus of responsibility in a medical or psychological therapist)	Planning and Problem Solution, involving, for example
		Diagnostic and predictive psychological tests
Psychosurgery Electro-shock Narcosynthesis Tranquilizers Sedatives Hormones Insulin shock Vitamins	Therapist Factors:	Informational resources Interpretation of data
		Learning Difficulties involving:
	Amount of training in psychotherapy Experience in psychotherapy Diagnostic skill and knowledge of psychotherapy Amount of therapeutic responsibility delegated by the institution Type of institutional setting (hospital or school) Legal restrictions	Remedial techniques Diagnostic psychological tests
		Feeling Problems, including:
		Working through situational anxiety, hostility, ambivalence, and their nonincapacitating, non-imbedded symptoms
	Patient or Client Factors:	Case studies and descriptions of personality functioning through use of psychometric tests
	Depth of involvement in the personality Rigidity of defense structure Strength of the ego and other personality resources Somatic Involvement Incapacitating nature of the symptoms Nature of the therapeutic goal	

Figure 3. Therapy Continuum Between Medicine and Psychology

for physicians. We feel there are logical and practical reasons for sharing psychotherapy responsibility. The answer, in our opinion, lies in making carefully defined distinctions around the middle transitional area of Figure 3. The criteria of depth, training, experience, responsibility, and institutional setting should determine who does psychotherapy and to what degree.

This introductory chapter deals with seven trends in the practice of therapeutic psychology: (1) insistence on accountability and responsible service; (2) professionalization and deprofessionalization; (3) dual emphases on the personal characteristics of the counselor combined with helping skills; (4) use of behavioral science data and research methods in the solution of human problems; (5) use of group counseling and contributions from the human potential movement; (6) the emergence of unifying constructs to reconcile conflicting viewpoints and to explain the process of change; and (7) broadening goals and wider applications of counseling.

Trend I: An Accountable and Responsible Service

The prevalence of the term *accountability* is indicative of the concern of professional helpers, their clients, and their agencies about responsibility and productivity. Counselors recognize the necessity to strive for improved competency, evaluation of expected outcomes, and cost effectiveness. When agencies tighten their budgets on human services, we are pressed harder than ever to show that our efforts help clients and agencies reach their goals efficiently as well as effectively. Increasingly, counselor training programs are incorporating a competency approach. This emphasis on counselor performance is characterized by describing counselor behavior in terms of specific competencies, assessing candidates before training to establish baseline achievement, prescribing training events to achieve minimum performance on prescribed competencies, and assessing results at the end of training to ascertain achievement of minimum performance.

Therapeutic psychology has its roots in many disciplines. The following historical sketch covers the development of therapeutic psychology as a responsible service and illustrates how each field is related to therapeutic psychology.

Counseling Psychology

Counseling psychology is a synthesis of many related trends found in the guidance, mental hygiene, psychometrics, social casework, and psychotherapy movements. A counseling psychologist assumes that it is *people*, not problems, that need help through counseling. Fractionation of the personality into problem areas, such as vocational, marital, or reading, is largely a phenomenon of the past.

Counseling psychology is at a point comparable to that of medicine at the turn of the century. Sir William Osler at that time took the medical "tower of Babel" and formulated an eclectic system of scientific medical practice from the many diffuse and conflicting therapies. "Counseling psychologist" has been incorporated in occupational titles which the Veterans Administration, for example, uses (Moore and Bouthilet 333; Super 467). Many private and collegiate counseling centers have on their staffs psychologically trained counselors called counseling psychologists. Some schools and rehabilitation centers are using this title. Yamamoto (512) surveyed the characteristics of over one thousand members of the Division on Counseling of APA. The results suggested that counseling psychology had grown into a psychological specialty with unique roles and functions.

Writers close to developments in counseling psychology, such as Brayfield (68, 69), are uncertain about the future of counseling psychology as a specialty. It may be absorbed into clinical psychology as this specialty concerns itself more with personal assets and less with behavior pathology. A new professional emphasis, such as community counselor or psychologist, may absorb both clinical and counseling psychology. The outlook generally appears optimistic about the continuing need for counseling psychologists. Their flexible open approach to meeting client needs in a variety of settings, and their emphasis upon improving normal client functioning and personal decision-making skills, are needed in the current climate of preoccupation with mental illness and irresponsible behavior.

Largely as a result of a conference of psychologists at Northwestern University in 1951, the American Psychological Association changed the designation of Division 17 from Counseling and Guidance to Counseling Psychology in recognition of the growing discreteness of the counseling branch of psychology (Super 467). Similarly, the American Board of Examiners in Professional Psychology conducts certification proceedings for counseling psychologists as one of its four areas of specialization.

The 1964 Greyston Conference (471) of psychologists interested in counselor education reconsidered the status and future preparation of counseling psychologists. The consensus of the conferees was that counseling psychology is one significant answer to the increasing social need for varied counseling services.

The Vail Conference, held in 1974, sought to examine the current trends and futures of applied psychology (240). A key conclusion was the need for counselors and psychotherapists to be more aware of racial-cultural differences between practitioners and clients and the necessity to develop more practitioners from minority groups. A second element in changing roles was the need for counselors to become not only aware of social problems and injustices, but skilled in community change and client advocacy. It appears that counseling psychology is moving more toward the concept of community psychology with its dual focus on facilitating human development and community change to make human potentials more realizable.

Hence, a growing body of terminology and usage supports the contention that counseling psychology is a full professional endeavor, but that it must revise roles constantly and encourage competencies in community change.

Other occupational designations for counselors have been made. It is quite apparent that the term "counselor" must be preceded by an adjective to be meaningful, since so many persons with differing skill levels claim to do "counseling." Other terms have been suggested to describe the psychological counseling function—general clinical counselor (Hahn 213), psychological counselor (Bordin 60, Tyler 481), psychotherapeutic counselor (Porter 367), and community counselor (Lewis and Lewis 287). Employment Service Counselor is another type of counseling psychologist serving persons in the throes of career or job changes.

Clinical Psychology

Clinical psychology grew largely out of intelligence testing efforts from 1912 to 1930. Clinical psychology and counseling psychology have much in common, since both use case study methods, evaluation instruments, and psychotherapeutic interviewing techniques. There are, nevertheless, significant historical and functional distinctions. After studying differentiations between counseling and clinical psychology at length, Gustad (211) concluded that counseling and clinical psychology are essentially the same general endeavor, but that they have differing emphases. This is substantially the same conclusion reached by Watson:

The characteristic educational setting and the fact that counseling psychologists work primarily with normal people probably are the chief lines of demarcation, not training or breadth of responsibilities. . . . Counseling psychologists and clinical psychologists are *not* engaged in a struggle of opposing camps, but rather, are seriously, and without undue heat, attempting to work through their intra-professional problems to a mutually satisfactory solution (492, pp. 9–10).

The clinical psychologist's skill in assisting with diagnostic evaluation of the mentally ill and his consequent unique role on a clinical or hospital team is another major distinction. As Super (467) has pointed out, counseling is more concerned with the "hygiology" than the "psychopathology" of behavior. Hygiology is the study of problems in normal people and the prevention of serious emotional difficulties. Clinical psychologists, on the other hand, are found mainly in hospitals and clinics where severe behavior disorders are treated.

Institutional settings for counseling or therapy determine other distinctions between counselors and clinicians. As Williamson (498) has suggested, therapeutic counseling takes its place naturally in the educational setting where the school assumes its societal function of learning and personality development. Clinical psychologists, however, are found in hospitals, clinics, and, increasingly, in private practice. Some counseling psychologists are found in hospitals and private practice (333); but the educational setting attracts counseling psychologists interested primarily in maturational problems of school-age youth. On the other hand, clinical psychologists in private or agency practice work with marital, rehabilitation, geriatric, and parental problems of essentially normal people in nonschool relationships.

Clinical psychology has had its periodic training and role-definition conferences similar to those of counseling psychology. Boulder, Miami, Chicago, and Vail have been locations for crucial conferences of leaders in the education of clinicians. These conferences have reflected a growing shift from almost exclusive concern about responsibility to the individual client to a much more widespread concern about responsibility to the broader community and the public interest.

Psychiatry

Psychiatry, a third psychotherapeutic counseling specialty, is difficult to distinguish functionally from other counseling specialties. The obvious distinction is one of differential training—the psychiatrist having an M.D. degree and the psychologist generally having a Ph.D. Medical therapies used in the treatment of severe emotional conditions contribute other clear distinctions.

Counselors and psychotherapists cannot escape the reality of the societal concept of medical responsibility. The physician has legal responsibility for care, having life or death implications for the individual. From one point of view, this concept embraces all of life's activities. From another view, the psychiatrically trained physician's responsibility covers psycho-therapy mainly to the point where the problem becomes one of ignorance or learning rather than one of illness. Mowrer offers a useful distinction between the psychologist's and the psychiatrist's view of psychotherapy:

Personality disorders are from one point of view no more disease than ignorance is a disease. Both prominently involve the phenomenon of *learning*. And if, as educators, we have any business working with the ignorant mind, we also have a right and an obligation to be interested in the confused, disordered mind (338, p. 21).

Fine distinctions between ignorance and illness, however, become very vague in practice. Szasz (412) has created considerable controversy with his emphasis upon severe emotional problems as disorders of learning and per-ception rather than illness in the traditional medical meaning. Szasz, a physician, certainly recognizes that there are brain diseases which affect behavior profoundly. He objects to the mental illness idea that all dis-orders of thought and feeling are related to some neurological defect. Problems of living, from this viewpoint, are reduced to a biochemical process which will be discovered ultimately. Such difficulties in everyday living, or differences in belief or value causing personal problems, are then by definition "mental illnesses" because they differ little from anal-ogous bodily disease. Szasz argues that this view is erroneous because it confuses a *defect* correlated with a lesion in the central nervous system with a *belief*, a learned behavior. Szasz also emphasizes the role of social value norms in making judgments about who is deviant or "sick."

Finally, the concept of *personal responsibility* for one's behavior enters this controversy. If people believe they cannot function because they are "sick," they relieve themselves of responsibility for their behavior. If they believe, on the other hand, that their beliefs and choices determine their behavior, then they carry the awesome burden of responsibility for their actions. For example, this is a critical issue in dealing with criminal behavior.

Perls (361), also a psychiatrist, expresses his disillusionment with the medical model of sickness or wellness. Perls emphasizes the person who has experienced problems of living and uses self-defeating manipulative patterns. Similarly, Glasser (193), who is also medically trained, stresses the therapist's role of teaching clients more responsible and self-fulfilling behavior. He emphasizes how this learning approach is incompatible with a conventional conception of mental illness.

Psychotherapeutic counseling, according to Mowrer, involves helping the individual whose learning is incomplete or who has more or less conscious conflicts which have as their accompaniment so-called "normal" anxiety. This, of course, places a severe burden on the counselor to distinguish "normal" from "pathological," but this recognition of pathology and therapeutic limitations has become part of the psychologist's professional training. It is important for any professional group to realize that it cannot be all things to all people.

Psychiatric Social Work

Psychiatric social work, a fourth counseling specialty, also is difficult to distinguish from psychology in terms of psychotherapeutic function. Many practitioners of this professional group feel they are doing psychotherapy in the formal sense. One principal difference, however, is the training route. Social workers generally complete a two-year graduate program, including a year of agency work, leading to a master's degree in social work. Social workers function, as do clinical psychologists, on a psychiatric team. In clinics they specialize in the intake process, deal with other agencies, and collect psychiatric histories. Often they have an assigned therapeutic role, as in the Family Service Agency system where family counseling is conducted mainly by social workers.

School Psychology and School Counseling

A fifth counseling specialty, educational counseling, differs from other specialties largely on the basis of breadth of training and experience required. The school psychologist or counselor deals with a wide variety of educational problems close to the areas of teaching and administration, in addition to working with the personal counseling problems of children and adolescents. School psychologists function very much as clinical psychologists in the school setting, with a heavy emphasis on diagnostic functions.

A significant concept in school counseling is that of levels of service. Three general counseling levels are identifiable on the basis of differences in training, competence, and counseling time. These are functional levels, not status differentials. On the first level is the educational counselor whose professional roots are mostly in teaching and who may be doing part-time counseling largely of the educational planning type. This counselor primarily gives information and suggestions. The counselors on this level are frequently called "advisers."

At the second level is the counselor whose professional affiliation is primarily in education and who generally has a masters degree or special training in counseling. This counselor deals with the majority of school counseling problems, ranging from giving simple information on college requirements, through vocational planning and social conduct, to dealing with the more emotionally involved problems concerned with maturation. The school counselor suffers from a severe identity problem, since the historical educational guidance model does not meet his needs. Since school counseling deals with the kinds of developmental problems described under counseling psychology, it appears that this model holds hope for the school counseling specialist. The American School Counselors Association, a component of the American Personnel and Guidance Association, has developed a statement on policy and guidelines for implementation of this policy on roles and functions of school counselors (19).

The counselor on the third level is the counseling or clinical psychologist, described earlier in this chapter. The school or college counselor on this level generally has experience in educational positions; but his primary graduate professional education has been psychology, psychiatric social work, or medicine.

Pastoral Psychology

Clergymen have been counseling for years. Not until recently, however, has there been an emphasis on professional preparation for clergymen to do psychological counseling. Increasingly, seminarians are taking clinical internships in counseling agencies. Many churches offer extensive counseling on marriage, divorce, widowhood, drug abuse, and family problems in line with their traditional community helping services. In Chapter 14 we describe more completely some of the specialized concerns with which all secular and religious counselors must come to grips as they deal with clients on moral and spiritual value problems.

Marriage and Family Counseling

While general counseling and clinical psychologists work with couples and families extensively, a specialty has emerged with its own professional organizations, journals, and state licensing, as in California.

Rehabilitation and Employment Counselors

With considerable national emphasis on solutions to problems of handicapped and underprivileged citizens, counseling has become a central helping function. Vocational rehabilitation counselors, working primarily in state rehabilitation offices and hospitals with the physically handicapped, have had their functions increased by law to include emotionally, mentally, socially, and economically handicapped clients. The rehabilitation counseling service with its expanding functions may become the wave of the future for massive nonschool counseling services.

In similar fashion, recent manpower and economic opportunity legislation has created expanded roles for employment counselors who traditionally have been concerned primarily with placement problems. With fast-changing economic conditions, many persons need counseling connected with retraining and upgrading of job skills. Agencies such as state employment services, government service programs, half-way houses, drug and alcohol treatment centers, and crisis clinics employ counselors to perform a wide range of counseling tasks.

Trend II: Professionalization and Deprofessionalization

The current professional scene contains many paradoxes. One relating to to professionalization is the widespread effort to train helper types in more specialized services, for which increasingly larger fees are charged. One consequence is the growing dependence on experts. Another is the formalizing of the helping process, even in law, so that helping and being helped, instead of being normal human functions, are ritualized into elaborate specialties. While few persons deny the need for behavior change specialists, many feel we have gone too far in formalizing the helping function and take the view that we should deprofessionalize counseling and give psychology away. We believe that a key function of professional counselors and psychotherapists is to serve as trainers of others in helping skills, such that a vast multiplier effect is put into motion to make helping skills widely available in the population.

As indicated earlier, many professional groups use counseling and psychotherapeutic techniques. Conflicts tend to grow among psychologists when they view themselves as *either* scientists *or* professional practitioners. Hughes (237) emphasizes the danger of "hardening an endeavor prematurely," before the techniques used by a "profession" are validated. Pepinsky (360) faces this problem neatly in his concept of the "scientist-practitioner," in which the counselor or psychotherapist is a scientist primarily, using the methods of hypothetico-deductive thinking, and a practitioner secondarily. This view is stressed because of the undeveloped state of psychological knowledge and its application to counseling. Recently, the scientist element has been deemphasized, and the social change agent role has been made more central.

The following important characteristics of a profession are discussed below: (1) socially useful services which individuals cannot render to themselves; (2) skills and procedures; (3) definite sequences and standards of training (including selection procedures); (4) professional societies and journals dedicated to advancement of the profession and its basic scientific foundations; (5) a planned research program; (6) certification and licensing; (7) a code of ethics; (8) working relationships with other professions; and (9) professional freedom.

The development of these characteristics is made from the viewpoint of the psychological practitioner. Variations will be found in the psychotherapeutic training of psychiatrists, social workers, and clergymen. The following material on training, certification, publications, and organizations is cited to illustrate the broad developments in the psychological fields. These developments are also included as a sobering reminder that reading this book and special skills training will not make a psychotherapist or counselor out of the reader. Extensive background and professional development are needed for such a complex human service.

Socially Useful Services

The first and most important value of psychotherapeutic counseling is its usefulness in helping *individuals* with problems. The military forces utilized psychological personnel extensively during World War II. The vast postwar program of the Veterans Administration is testimony to public acceptance of counseling. Flourishing public marriage and mental hygiene clinics and rehabilitation centers, as well as school and college counseling programs, are further evidence that not only are such services requested, but also that clients are satisfied that the services are effective in helping them achieve their goals. Growth centers emerging from the human potential movement utilize many counseling styles and methods.

Another socially useful service which psychotherapeutic counseling performs is that of *discovering and developing human talent*. There is talent in all segments of our social structure. Finding the talented and appraising educational need and opportunity have been special functions of counselors. Likewise, the efforts of counselors to conserve human talent and to prevent emotional breakdowns have been extended to the emotional and social areas at all age levels. Their efforts have not been limited to the potential delinquents and the social "wallflowers" alone. Many leaders in the helping professions are asking why youth must break down emotionally before they receive help. These preventive and personal development services need more attention now that the focus is moving away from "salvage" services for the pathological client.

A third value of psychotherapeutic counseling, and another example of the concept for conserving human talent, is that of *national survival*. Counseling is very much concerned with social values. Political and economic crises throughout the world make it imperative that we find talented youth, encourage them to make the most of their potentialities, and help them over the rough spots in achieving high-level productive and personal adjustment skills without sacrificing values of freedom of choice and responsibility.

Being an agent of community change is perceived by a growing number of counselors as a key value of counseling. The client is encouraged to better his circumstances and to fight injustice. Counselors even see themselves as advocates until clients are able to act for themselves. Some advocates of this broader community counseling role emphasize the active involvement of the counselor in local community change processes (Lewis and Lewis 287).

Assisting the individual to achieve his or her dream of *social advancement* is a fifth value of psychotherapeutic counseling. Although many persons find themselves hemmed in by circumstances of birth, such as race or poverty, our American democratic social organization and expanding economy still provide means for social mobility. Psychotherapeutic counseling services are ideally suited to help the individual acquire a knowledge of his needs and goals as well as to plan for the opportunities facing him.

With automation and economic abundance reducing work opportunities for many citizens, counseling offers much hope for the future. We must face the possibility that large segments of our population will not be able to find productive work, which has been the mainstay in developing personal worth and a sense of identity. A new approach to leisure, service, and personal growth must be found to take the place of previous dependence on work. Counseling programs hold great promise for this task of reorienting our attitudes toward work, leisure, and retraining for new careers.

The demand for counseling services in all areas has far outstripped the supply. Since facilities in counselor education cannot cope with this demand, a number of short courses to develop counselors and counselor aides have been organized, largely by government agencies. How to meet social demands for counseling services in high professional levels is one of the greatest problems facing the helping professions.

Skills and Procedures

One of our assumptions is that there is an identifiable body of fairly valid techniques and procedures for counseling and psychotherapy. The major portion of this book is devoted to substantiating this assertion, and to describing these techniques and procedures.

Training Sequences and Standards

Two organizations interested in counselor and psychotherapist training are the American Psychological Association and the American Personnel and Guidance Association. The American Psychological Association Committee on Counselor Training (14, 24) and the Association for Counselor Education and Supervision (347) have published recommended training standards and areas for counseling psychology, school counseling, and college personnel work.

Training programs are superimposed generally on a basic background of behavioral sciences and general education. Early graduate years contain further basic training in general psychology, experimental methods, statistics, measurement, human development, physiological and social psychology, personality theory, and behavior pathology. Advanced training leading to the doctoral degree contains, according to the APA Subcommittee on Ph.D. Training Programs (15), additional work in appraisal, counseling practicums, professional issues, and research.

The APA Committee and the Association for Counselor Education and Supervision stress the need for subdoctoral practicum training to give supervised experience in counseling and clinical psychology as well as to enable the student to synthesize many fragments of information from previous graduate work. Internships, generally half-time, have become common in training programs. There is a need for more postgraduate, including postdoctoral, education in counseling to update practices.

Competency-based programs, as described earlier under accountability, are becoming the norm in counselor training. Specified counselor behaviors in a competency program, especially when tied to client outcomes, clarify expectations and role definitions of counselors. One consequence is a strong emphasis on skills training to meet competency requirements, yet we know that counseling competence requires refined judgments on ethical, case management, and intervention issues. It is doubtful at this stage whether a strictly skills development approach is adequate for development of helping professionals.

The practice of training and of utilizing so-called paraprofessionals has become widespread. These persons function at prescribed helping tasks under the supervision of professionals who monitor their client work and provide training. Usually, the paraprofessional has competencies in basic helping skills, but does not have experience or training in complex case management skills, research competence to answer basic questions of practice, or theoretical background to conceptualize client problems.

In addition to didactic course work and practice with clients, the counselor must confront himself in order to become more aware of his strengths and weaknesses. Individual therapy is not practical for most counselors. As a result, sensitivity, or encounter, groups are fulfilling this need for self-confrontation in training programs.

Professional Societies and Publications

Another criterion of a profession is the existence of societies and publications dedicated to improving the science and practice of the profession. In psychology, for example, the American Psychological Association is one group the object of which is "to advance psychology as a science, as a profession, and as a means of promoting human welfare" (11). The

American Personnel and Guidance Association is another professional association dedicated to the improvement of counseling services, particularly in educational and rehabilitation institutions.

The vigor of professional journals is a further criterion of a profession's growth. Some of the representative publications of help to counselors and psychotherapists are the *Journal of Counseling Psychology*, the *Journal of Clinical and Counseling Psychology*, the *Personnel and Guidance Journal*, *American Psychologist*, *The School Counselor*, *The Counseling Psychologist*, *Psychotherapy: Theory, Research and Practice*, the *Journal of Marriage and Family Counseling*, and the *Journal of Applied Behavioral Science*.

Research Orientation

In a profession and science as young as psychology, research plays a significant part in discovering new procedures, validating current techniques, and resolving contradictions and theoretical confusion. A large portion of the graduate program is directed to research techniques so that the practitioner has a research orientation in whatever professional activity he performs. In addition, there is a strong social obligation to validate constantly the psychological services offered to the public.

It should be emphasized that the frontiers of knowledge in the field of psychological services are pushed back through an interaction of both practice and pure research in human sciences. One endeavor helps the other in reciprocal fashion. An example is outcome assessment in group approaches to counseling and psychotherapy.

Certification and Licensing

With the prevalence of quacks in the field of counseling and psychotherapy, it is imperative that the public as well as the profession be protected. Steiner's (455) early survey revealed astounding findings on disreputable help for troubled people. Although a certificate or license does not guarantee competence, it informs the public that the practitioner has been exposed to several years of training and supervision in the techniques he espouses.

A certificate is a document attesting achievement granted by a public or private group. It is solicited voluntarily by the individual. An example is the postdoctoral certificate or diploma granted by the American Board of Professional Psychology (9). Diplomas are issued by this Board in four areas: clinical, industrial, counseling, and school psychology. The written examination covers basic professional knowledge in the candidate's specialty. The oral examination includes questions on client relationships, professional issues, and a field situation where candidates under observation perform services in their specialties. The American Association of Marriage and Family Counselors certificate is another example of efforts to certify professional competence.

Almost all state boards of education maintain counselor certification as part of their credentialing programs. An increasing number of states, beginning with Washington, are requiring demonstration of specific competencies as a condition of certification. This approach is replacing the older bases of accumulated college credits and unevaluated years of experience.

Actual licensing of psychologists poses a somewhat different problem from certification. A license gives a psychologist a legal right to engage in psychological practice. A licensing law forbids certain practices, generally defines what a psychologist is, and describes psychological practice. Psychology certification laws, which frequently describing practice, tend to restrict the use of the title "psychologist" only. Licensing and certification which protect the public are further marks of a profession.

Code of Ethics

The opening statement in the APA *Ethical Standards of Psychologists* is, "The worth of a profession is measured by its contribution to the welfare of man" (12, p. 1). Psychotherapeutic counseling, being a welfare service, is faced with ethical practice problems. Until codes were formulated, there were few concrete guides for determining unethical practices. The presence of a well-defined code and tradition of ethical practice is a distinguishing mark of a profession.

The original APA code of ethics has undergone several revisions, the latest at this writing being the 1975 draft (143). The APGA Committee on Ethical Practices has published a similar code aimed largely at educational settings (142). These codes reflect professional and social values at a particular time, and one would expect them to change over the years as the consensus of social values undergoes revision. Codes are only rough guides and are no substitute for the disciplined judgments of socially conscious and morally sound practitioners. All professional organizations, furthermore, have ethics committees which perform surveillance functions as well as provide channels and judicial groups for complaints of unethical practice.

Section 2 of the APA Ethical Code (12, 143) pertains to client relationships and covers questions of confidentiality, responsibility, competence, and client welfare. The ethical behavior of the counselor or therapist is such an important topic that further material is given in Chapter 6.

The influence of values on the perception of people and the value context of psychology itself are important ethical topics (282, 205, 450, 245). The papers just cited contain provocative discussions on the problems of goals (such as "adjustment"), value conflicts, social forces, parochialism, and professional vanity. We feel strongly that both the professional counselor and psychotherapist need to give much serious thought to these problems. Therefore, ethical problems are covered at several points in this book.

Each profession must recognize its limitations and the role of other professional groups in rounding out its knowledge and skills. One mark of the psychology profession is its willingness to collaborate with other professional disciplines in working for the client's best interests.

Professional Freedom

The American Psychological Association (13) lists as one of the characteristics of a "good" profession the freedom to accept its responsibilities and to carry them out in ways dictated by its own wisdom. The profession willingly faces all evidence of social need for services and its own competence to fulfill these needs. The profession must not be swayed by attempts to restrict its activities which demonstrably fulfill its social function and advance human values. We feel that counseling and psychotherapy are well along in attempts to fulfill this professional principle.

Trend III: Emphasis on Counselor and Therapist Personality Factors and Skills Training

Counseling went through a decade of focus on the person of the counselor as the key variable in the change process. Recent years have revealed a stronger emphasis on behavior change and general helping skills. Current research and practice efforts appear bent on discovering the best mix of these two key approaches on attitudes and skills. Figure 4 is a representation of how we see these key relationships in a helping paradigm. The combination of personal factors and skills produces growth conditions which lead to desired outcomes for the client, agency, society, and counselor.

Most literature on counseling and psychotherapy of the past thirty years has emphasized techniques and skills—tests, records, surveys, sociometrics—as if these were central. Shoben estimates that the amount of space in early counseling texts devoted to the "modification of client behavior through face-to-face contacts" (430, p. 259) was only 8 percent of the total. One explanatory hypothesis regarding this deficit would be

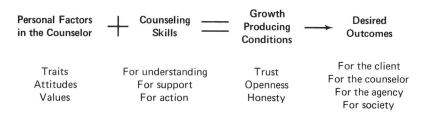

Figure 4. The Helping Process. Adapted from L. M. Brammer, *The Helping Relationship: Process and Skills* (64, p. 2).

that so little is known about this important face-to-face relationship and the related personality factors that writers fall back on the traditional test and records diagnostic approach to counseling and psychotherapeutic problems.

Trend IV: Use of Behavioral Science Data in the Solution of Human Problems

Although interest in personality factors in counseling relationships has increased, it has not appeared to overshadow or diminish the studies on the use of data in counseling. Efforts to develop new predictive and diagnostic tests, as well as to improve old instruments, have kept a steady pace of development. Interest in projective techniques is an evolving facet of this work. The use of electronic computers has revolutionized research on counseling problems and offers great hope for automating some of the prediction and planning aspects of counseling. More detailed results on counseling implications of tests are summarized in Chapter 10.

Information from the fields of anthropology, computer technology, developmental psychology, gerontology, economics, rehabilitation, and sociology is appearing in forms useful to counselors and psychotherapists. The vast resources of the Federal Bureau of Labor Statistics, for example, are producing more useful materials to aid the counselor with career planning problems. Comparative culture studies on sexual behaviors, child-rearing methods, and personality determinants are further examples. The cultural context of counseling has been given considerable emphasis by Wrenn (507).

Trend V: Groups and the Human Potential Movement

The human potential movement of the past ten years has included many human growth emphases which are related to counseling and therapy. At the center of this movement has been the small-group method applied in settings as diverse as management development, drug treatment, and family therapy. The human potential movement includes a variety of sensory awareness methods to make one conscious of the body. Skills training for special needs such as assertiveness, sexual functioning, leadership, parenting, and conflict management has been a part. Awareness training to broaden one's perception of the world and to achieve greater personal tranquillity is included in this movement to enhance the potential of every human being. In this sense the various liberation movements are included. While all of these facets relate to counseling and supplement the one-on-one focus of counseling and psychotherapy, only group counseling will be emphasized in Chapter 11.

The rapid increases in group approaches have come about partly as a result of limited access to costly individual counseling, due to costs and scarce services, but also because of increasing confidence of practitioners in the efficacy of group work. There is also a growing recognition that people need other people for help through everyday problems, and that this help can come from confreres as well as professional experts in the helping process. One serious limitation is the lack of valid knowledge about the optimum conditions for personal growth through groups and the relative permanence of growth-enhancing or growth-retarding changes effected through the group process. Participants characteristically experience much enthusiasm, often ecstatic, after a group experience. As in all learning experiences, the crucial questions are what is the transfer value to everyday life, and do learnings from the group result in effective changes in behavior over time?

Groups often function as means to behavior change without individual counseling. At other times they function as adjunctive experiences to individual counseling. In any case, it behooves persons interested in individual counseling to know these group developments, since it is becoming increasingly apparent that skills and time for individual counseling are becoming very dear, and the counselor is looked upon as a change facilitator in family, community, and work groups.

This trend is supported by a vast body of research and descriptive literature on group methods in solving human problems. In addition to the long established models for group therapy with adults and multiple counseling groups for school-age clients, family therapy structures varying from several families meeting with one or more therapists at once to intensive weekend work with a single family unit have appeared. Increasing group work in prisons, with intensive efforts with drug users such as Synanon, and group self-help methods with alcoholics attest to the vigor of this trend.

Trend VI: Unified Theoretical Constructs and Roles

Out of concern for the divorce of science from practice during the last few years, much thought has been devoted to integrating psychotherapeutic counseling practice with personality and learning data. Instead of thinking about the counseling process as a collection of cookbook recipes or miscellaneous techniques culled from experience, psychotherapeutic counseling may be viewed as the application of systematic and unified theory and principles to specialized learning situations in the interview. Some current and historical views on personality development, structure, and function, and their applications to counseling and psychotherapy, are presented in Chapters 2 and 3.

Throughout this book, we have attempted to bridge the gap between systematic theory and loose practice. This ideal is difficult to realize, however. Part of the problem lies in terminology and translation of phenomena such as transference and resistance into a meaningful theoretical framework. The counselor must strive constantly, nevertheless, to analyze what he is doing and to know what is happening in his counseling interviews. Theory often supplies the needed conceptual tools, though it is recognized that the need for technique often surpasses available verified knowledge and conceptual developments.

Counselors' awareness of their social responsibility and the welfare of their clients forces them to maintain a healthy balance between skepticism and confidence in their methods. As Shoben so aptly said, "When the chips are down, as they generally are in professional practice, skepticism about one's own resources is a luxury that few can afford" (430, p. 252). Hahn and McLean comment in pointed language also:

> The Counselor's humility of self-recognized ignorance is therefore of continuing importance. It must be a rational humility, however, an objective admission of limitation in the face of infinite complexity. It must never develop into an emotional sense of inferiority which leads to self-recrimination, depression, overtimidity, about undertaking responsibility for new cases. When this happens, the counselor himself is ready for psychotherapy (213, p. 37).

Rogers (395) has stated the mixed feelings of psychotherapeutic counselors when they perceive themselves as subjective sensitive therapists and tough-minded scientists combined.

Psychotherapy and counseling practice offer rich opportunities for formulating hypotheses and elaborating theory through applications to practical events in counseling. The Pepinskys (360) stress the role, mentioned earlier, of the counselor as a "scientist-practitioner." In this dual role, the counselor and psychotherapist continuously utilize a process of observation, inference, and assessment of behavior changes during and after counseling. Thoreson (473) speaks of the counselor as an "applied behavioral scientist" who systematically undertakes to promote specific changes in client behavior which are related to the goals set mutually by client and counselor. A growing number of counselors stress additional roles, including community change facilitator, client advocate, skills trainer, and organizational consultant.

Rotter (402) summarizes the principal values of theories in clinical work as follows: as bases for construction of new instruments and methods and of testing old ones; as tools for evaluating counseling techniques where experimental evidence is lacking; as encouragement for consistency of terminology and assumption; as evaluation devices for new ideas or unusual problems in practice; and as aids to help clinicians recognize and resolve apparent contradictions and inconsistencies in experiments, concepts, or practice.

Attempts to unify constructs have served to diminish the "school" emphasis in psychotherapeutic counseling. Wherever a parochial or segmental approach to counseling is promulgated, a "school" of counseling tends to spring up. This is not to discourage individual practitioner-scientists from launching into creative thinking or theory. Rogers (394) comments that one of the critical problems of practicing psychologists today is the climate in the profession which discourages theory construction. Rogers goes on to postulate that this lack of theorizing rests in a "real fear of grappling with the new and unconventional" (394, p. 247). There are encouraging signs, however, that we are moving toward more unity in theoretical views of counseling, even though practices vary widely.

Trend VII: Concern with Goals and Values

Another prominent trend discernible in psychotherapeutic counseling discussions is that of increasing clarification of the goals and purposes of counseling. This trend naturally takes a tack into the realm of values. This topic of goals and values is treated at several points in this volume—under ethical problems in Chapter 6, within the context of goals of psychotherapeutic counseling in Chapter 4, under relationship problems in Chapter 6, and in the discussion of values in Chapter 15.

The change in emphasis from the solution of immediate manifest problems the client may have, such as choosing a career goal, or relieving momentary situational anxiety, to more long range goals is very apparent. An example of a long range, generalized goal is the reinforcement of the self-directive capacities of the client which make him better able to solve his problems in the future without help.

Counselors with concerns about values tend to become involved in social issues such as racial injustice, status of women, reduction of poverty, and protection of children.

Summary

This introductory statement has included a survey of the trends contributing to professionalization of therapeutic psychology. The field of therapeutic psychology has many historical antecedents in clinical psychology, counseling psychology, psychiatry, social work, school psychology, and pastoral psychology. With this rich background, the profession is facing and mastering many problems of responsibility, interprofessional relationships, training, selection, scientific societies, research, certification, licensing, ethics, and freedom. Counseling and psychotherapy overlap on many topics, although they are unique entities. Psychotherapists generally aim at personality reorganization at relatively deep levels of personality, whereas the counselor is more concerned with the dénouement of incomplete maturing or learning processes.

Theoretical
Foundations
of Therapeutic
Psychology

To give precision, coherence, and promise to counseling and psychotherapy techniques, it is necessary to become familiar with certain aspects of personality and learning theory. One of our basic assumptions is that counseling or therapy becomes an impulsive application of "cookbook" recipes to human problems unless the clinician has a firm foundation in the current thinking and research of other practitioners and has a consistent set of assumptions about personality structure and function. The psychological counselor must know his medium just as the mechanic must know the intricacies of a vehicle, or as the surgeon must know anatomy and physiology.

This chapter contains, therefore, a discussion of the significance of theory, an overview of various approaches to counseling from the standpoint of western views of personality and learning theory, and an attempted integration of various historical and contemporary theories as a basis for the consistent application of techniques. The principal purposes in presenting the following materials are to provide the student with some of the concepts from various personality theories which have useful implications for counseling, and to encourage development of a personal theory of counseling using a creative synthesis approach.

2

The Significance of Theory

One model of a psychotherapeutic counselor proposed in Chapter 1 was as scientist-practitioner. The premise of this model is that the counselor can be both subject and object; that is, he can be an objective observer, hence critical, of what goes on, yet he can be a participant in the counseling process at the same time. The essences of scientific method used by this model counselor are observation, inference, and verification. Counseling practice involves the application of principles deduced from generalizations, or theories, as well as from specific experiences. One foundation of the scientific practice of psychotherapy and counseling, therefore, is theory. By counseling theory we mean a structure of hypotheses and generalizations based on counseling experience and experimental studies. Generally this theory includes four elements: goals and values, assumptions, strategies, and expected outcomes. Since these elements change, one's theories are in a constant state of development.

When speaking of the counselor as a scientist, two related meanings should be distinguished. In the first meaning the counselor acts as a careful observer of the process. The counselor describes accurately what behavior is seen, and may go to the second stage of making inferences about the meaning of his observations. In this descriptive sense everyone can be a scientist. The second is the scientific attitude which the counselor assumes so that he can verify his rough hypotheses and improve his services. This second view of a counselor as scientist is the application of the scientific process to his work. He is required, typically, to control extraneous variables and manipulate the experimental variables according to the established rules of scientific practice. This is rarely possible in a counseling situation unless a deliberate study is designed to test certain hypotheses about counseling. Therefore, the scientific approach to counseling in the latter sense remains, admittedly, an ideal.

Although the counselor is interested in the applications of scientific attitudes and methods to improve practice, he is interested also in behavioral science *qua* science. That is, he is interested broadly in the greater understanding of human behavior, whether or not it leads to any practical results in his counseling.

The Values of Theory

Theory helps to explain what happens in a counseling relationship and assists the counselor in predicting, evaluating, and improving results. Theory provides a framework for making systematic observations about counseling. Theorizing encourages the coherence of ideas about counseling and the production of new ideas. Hence, counseling theory can be very practical by helping to make sense out of the counselor's observations.

What behaviors exemplify the scientific attitude? A counselor or psycho-therapist who proceeds through daily tasks without asking the following questions is not likely to progress in therapeutic effectiveness, nor is he likely to contribute new ideas to the profession. The scientific attitude leads to questions such as: What is happening here? What is my model? What are my assumptions? What accounts for this event? What will happen if I try this? The "unscientific" counselor, who does not ask himself these vital questions, is likely to develop a dangerous feeling of smugness and certainty about his counseling methods.

The clinician, acting as a scientist, starts with a question or problem; then he *observes* what happens in the interaction between himself and his client. He examines his data and formulates hypotheses about what is happening. These hypotheses are the *inferences* based on his observations and require further testing. Sets of refined hypotheses are generally referred to as theories. Then, from his theories the counselor attempts to explain or predict further events in counseling. He must check constantly the validity of his new theories against the reality of his observations so as to bring the two closer together. The refined theories are then used to make more precise explanations and predictions of counseling events.

To illustrate this process, let us take a simplified example of the phenomenon of defense. A counselor observes that when he "pushes" a client too hard with questions or interpretations the client gets angry, stops talking, or even leaves counseling. He observes the various conditions under which the client behaves in this negativistic fashion and speculates as to why this might be so. The clinician observes similar cases and notes a pattern and a consistency. He hypothesizes that clients become negativistic or "defensive" when they are threatened, or perceive the counselor as a source of frustration and even psychological danger. The counselor may postulate an "unconscious" or a "self" in his client with feelings or attitudes which are inconsistent with the client's conscious feelings or attitudes. The client perceives the inconsistency between his own behavior and deeper attitudes as well as the discrepancy between his attitudes and the counselor's attitudes. The therapist or counselor, perhaps, may be "pushing" the client too fast, so of course he checks his hypothesis about threat and defense with further observations until he has refined the concepts and generalizations to the point where they are useful in predicting what will happen to a client under threat. The counselor is then in a better position to evaluate both his hypotheses and his techniques.

The "miniature" theories, or confirmed hypotheses, are combined with much other data and hypotheses into more consistent and larger theories about personality structure and function in general. The broader theory is then used in a deductive fashion to produce more hypotheses to be tested experimentally or through counseling experience.

Although the preceding section expresses the ideal of the scientific clinician's approach, the novelty of the scientific approach for many practicing counselors makes it difficult to use in practice. In addition, there is still no compelling evidence that counseling effectiveness in producing certain outcomes depends definitely upon the extent and explicitness of one's theoretical foundations, nor that one particular theory of personality or psychotherapy is superior to another.

Much work has been done in the last few years in the area of systematic theory construction by psychologists having the temperament and ability to do so. A really satisfactory general counseling and psychotherapeutic theory, however, is not yet available. Counselors attempt to explain what they see with their unique and limited perception. Hence, there are still a number of "schools" of counseling or therapy. This multiplicity of theories is a healthy state of affairs in a young profession; but, ultimately, it is expected that a unified theory of behavior and of counseling practice will evolve. In the meantime, counselors must examine the thinking of others as well as work on the formulation of their own hypotheses about the structure and function of the human personality and the counseling process, as in the creative synthesis below. Even though most counselors cannot be creative theoreticians, they can develop an attitude of careful critical observation of everyday practice and an understanding of formal experimental approaches to counseling problems.

One further point in reference to differential theoretical approaches should be made. Black (53) has pointed out in his comparative study of psychotherapeutic approaches that follow-up research data indicate that all "schools" get positive results. Black thinks that the ultimate resolution to theoretical differences will come about through critical analysis of the process itself rather than through the promotion of a parochial or "school" point of view. Black found that, although differing in emphasis, all approaches stress the significance of a working relationship, acceptance of the client, need for support, professional status of the counselor, and some types of limits. Fiedler (151), using Q sort methods, found that in spite of varying theoretical and methodological views among therapists there was much agreement on their conceptions of the ideal therapeutic relationship. Gonyea's (198) later study of the "ideal" therapeutic relationship and counseling outcomes used Fiedler's Q sort criteria of the ideal relationship. His study suggested that, while relationship quality is related to experience, positive outcomes and quality of relationship are not correlated for less experienced counselors. In other words, counseling effectiveness improves with experience, but not simply because of improved relationship quality. This confusion about the significance of relationship points up the need for more information on the qualities of experienced therapists who produce more positive outcomes. Counselors must recognize that practitioners of different "schools" may not agree on theory points, such as the degree of rational analysis needed, even though they might agree on the importance of the relationship. The oft-quoted Fiedler relationship studies sometimes imply that all differences diminish with experience.

Creative Synthesis Approach

Counselors and psychotherapists can take one of three positions: identify with one of the theories already published and tested in practice; develop an eclectic position; or strive for a personalized creative synthesis of theory and practice. These positions will be explored in the following sections and are summarized in Figure 5.

The Single Theory

The case for a single theoretical approach is argued in terms of having a ready-made set of assumptions, concepts, and related strategies which have been proven useful over a long period. Research productivity flowing from a single theory is offered as another advantage. While numerous practitioners state their allegiance to a single approach such as analytic, behavioral, or client-centered, their actual practice, as indicated later in this chapter, is not so parochial. They tend to move beyond their favorite theory quickly.

The single theory approach tends to promote the "great man" myth— a view that the original formulator was a genius of some kind with special gifts. While some persons, such as Freud, had special conceptualizing abilities, they were seeing events in terms of their unique life experiences and times. A highly elaborated system, such as analytic, tends over the years to become a closed system, and adherents tend to act more like disciples or hero worshippers than creative clinicians.

Eclectic Views

In one sense all theories are eclectic; but we restrict the definition to the process of selecting concepts, methods, and strategies from a variety of current theories which work. Some persons who take this position decline to theorize altogether, claiming that it is premature to identify too closely to a set of concepts or experimentally verified principles, or just that specific theorizing is not useful. The "technical eclecticism" of Lazarus (279) is an example. They prefer a kind of empirical principle of "What works for me now is valid." Some eclectic counselors choose this position out of inertia or feelings of defeatism to avoid the rigorous thinking necessary in developing a unique position. Their practice is based upon an additive process of picking and choosing among many theories, often relying on a superficial knowledge of them to suit their needs of the moment. Thus, a kind of faddism tends to develop which changes tomorrow when

Established Single Theory	Eclectic Approaches	Creative Synthesis
Main Characteristic:	*Main Characteristic:*	*Main Characteristic:*
Integrated set of assumptions related directly to strategy and method	Strategies and methods from several approaches applied selectively to clients	Application of broad and varied strategies and methods related to a synthesized theory evolved and "owned" by the practitioner
Examples:	*Examples:*	*Examples:*
Freud's Psychoanalytic (169) Rogers' Client-Centered (390)	Thorne's Integrative Psychology (474) Lazarus's Structural Eclecticism (279)	Assagioli's Psychosynthesis (23) Shostrom's Actualizing Therapy (432)
Advantages:	*Advantages:*	*Advantages:*
Ready-made system of assumptions and concepts Extensive experience and data base Consistency of theory and method	Collection of various methods Flexibility of choice on methods Wide agency application of methods	Continues synthesizing, extending, and amplifying personal system Discourages competition Fosters therapist's identity with own views
Limitations:	*Limitations:*	*Limitations:*
Tendency toward restricted view of data Often a closed system Encourages hero worship Fosters competition and divisiveness	Encourages uncritical picking and choosing Deemphasizes integrative theorizing Tends toward faddism Additive collection of what works for now Imitative, and tends toward limited creativity	A continuous lifelong task Tends to be idealistic Futuristic—ahead of its time Requires continuous creativity Requires trust in self Risky—requires standing on one's own
Illustrative Comments by Practitioners:	*Illustrative Comments by Practitioners:*	*Illustrative Comments by Practitioners:*
"Client-centered theory speaks to me" "Ellis is my hero" "I dig Freud" "I am analytic" "I stick with the tried and true"	"I use what works" "I'm flexible" "I try many methods" "I like TA methods but not the basic assumption" "Everyone says something important"	"I'm constantly reevaluating my ideas" "I develop my own theory to fit me" "I try to keep open and take some risks" "I trust my own observations and judgments"

Figure 5. Comparison of Basic Approaches to Theory Building

a more attractive method comes along. The principal limitations of the eclectic position are that it often attempts to equate opposite views, gloss over irreconcilable differences, or ignore larger philosophical issues.

To be fair to many persons who label themselves systematic eclectics, it must be stated that such persons struggle to integrate, to be consistent, to validate, and to create a unique personalized theory position. This approaches a different stage, however, which we have described in the next section as creative synthesizing. We feel this effort goes beyond what is currently regarded as eclecticism. Eclectic practitioners attempt to be flexible and open to new ideas and to apply methods as client needs demand. Eclecticism is a popular position, as indicated in a survey by Garfield and Kurtz (181). They surveyed 733 doctoral level clinical psychologists, of whom 211 were basically in teaching and research. The remaining 522 were practitioners or supervisors. Of the total group of 733, 64 percent identified their position as eclectic. Undoubtedly, many of this group see themselves in terms of what we will describe as creative synthesizers.

Developing a Unique Theory—A Creative Synthesis Approach

Each counselor and psychotherapist must ultimately develop a point of view which is uniquely his or her own. Freud was not a Freudian, Jung not a Jungian, and Rogers not a Rogerian. Each of them was himself most fully and completely, while building upon the wisdom of the past. Each practitioner must feel that his counseling practice reflects such individuality. This is the reason why no one text or school is fully adequate, and why we try to exemplify an approach which we have termed "creative synthesizing." This approach is not an arrogant attempt to put down predecessors. Ideas are rarely developed in solitary efforts. Usually, they are the results of many years of cumulative cross-fertilization of numerous minds. Isaac Newton is alleged to have said on this point, "If I have seen further, it is because I have stood on the shoulders of giants."

The "creative" element comes in when the counselor not only puts together concepts and practices from other theories in new ways, but also transforms them into ideas and methods which have continuing relevance for himself. As each new gestalt emerges, it becomes more than the sum of its parts. Each new gestalt goes a step beyond; it expands, modifies, and amplifies. Synergy is involved in that summated systems create a new whole which exceeds the power of the individual systems.

The "synthesis" element comes into the theory-building process as the counselor strives to integrate in incremental fashion what appear to be separate ideas and uncoordinated methods. He synthesizes dynamic and structural elements to form a basic personality model; he describes strategies and methods which follow from his assumptions and values. This could include culling relevant methods from psychoanalytic practices, cognitive strategies, existential viewpoints, and behavioral methods which are supported by the basic assumptions of the theorizer. In this process one must be careful about excessive conceptualizing beyond known empirical data.

It is easy to get caught up in attractive metaphors which can go well beyond explanatory functions and inject a note of mysticism. Therefore, the criteria which must be applied to such synthesizing processes are that they must be simple, based on data, consistent, open to criticism and change, and useful to explain and predict behavior.

The growing and evolving qualities of the creative synthesizing approach are illustrated by the abstractions in Figure 6. Large segments, such as cognition, feeling, action, or body strategies are integrated and then expanded with mini-segments to include concepts and methods flowing from the basic assumptions.

A number of people have attempted this difficult type of synthesis. Assagioli (23) with his psychosynthesis, Gendlin (184) with his synthesis views, Perls (361) with his Gestalt synthesis, and Schutz's work (418) in group process are some examples of efforts to integrate a wide range of psychological ideas, research findings, and methods into a consistent point of view.

Our Actualizing Counseling and Psychotherapy model is another effort at creative synthesizing. It will be described in the next chapter and will be used as an illustrative model in the remainder of the book. For a more complete statement of creative synthesizing, consult *Actualizing Therapy* (432).

Steps in Personal Theory Building. Developing one's own view is a very demanding lifelong task. In addition to knowing current theories of personality structure and behavior change, counselors must know their own assumptions about the nature of man and the process of knowing, their own values and views of the good life, and their models of the mature well-functioning person. This goal is accomplished through self-study of client-counselor relationships and personal therapeutic experiences resulting in increased self-understanding. These understandings and assumptions are then related to one's goals for counseling, which in turn are matched with strategies and methods to reach those goals most effectively. One borrows from other theorists in the sense that one stands on their shoulders to reach higher levels of understanding and effectiveness in practice. Then, one synthesizes these pieces incrementally into a unified system which is comfortable and effective in a particular setting. Finally, one tests the theory in practice and formulates hypotheses which can be tested experimentally. The results then are incorporated into one's system, or one revises the system.

Parametric Analysis

Clinicians seem to go through a process of professional growth toward a unique style with definable "parameters." We define therapeutic parameters as follows: Parameters are the dimensions of systematic counseling and psychotherapy which are adopted by a particular therapist. The

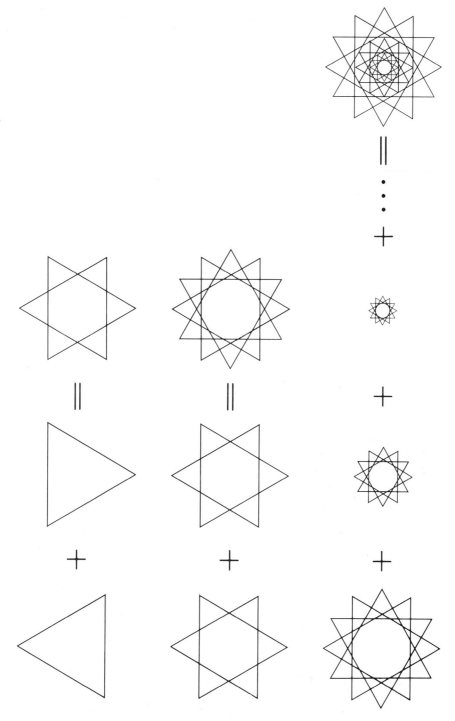

Figure 6. The Creative Synthesis Model. From E. L. Shostrom, L. Knapp, and R. Knapp, *Actualizing Therapy* (432, p. 300).

resulting combination of parameters would be descriptive of his or her unique style or approach to counseling and psychotherapy. The technique of "parametric analysis" suggests that growing practitioners commit themselves to unique combinations of therapeutic parameters and apply them flexibly to the *emerging* therapeutic situation.

Therapeutic Rating Form. A Therapeutic Rating Form with ten parameters is an example of an instrument to rate therapists on the degree to which their approaches manifest these parameters. Albert Einstein is alleged to have said, "Never *ask* anyone what he does, follow him around and *see* what he does"; so it seems that the therapist may perform differently from what he *says* he does, i.e., use different parameters.

Caring (C). It is the therapist's attitude of loving regard for the individual, whether expressed by unconditional warmth or aggressive critical caring.

Ego-strengthening (E). It is helping the person to develop his thinking, feeling, and perceptive ability so that he can cope with life more effectively.

Encountering (N). It is providing the experience of active encounter between person and therapist—each of whom is being and expressing his real feelings.

Feeling (F). It is helping the person to experience, in a psychologically safe relationship, feelings which he has heretofore found too threatening to experience freely.

Interpersonal Analyzing (I). It is the analyzing by the therapist of the person's perceptions or manipulations of the therapeutic relationship, and therefore of his other interpersonal relationships in life.

Pattern Analysis (P). It is the analyzing of unworkable patterns of functioning and assisting in the development of adaptive patterns of functioning for the individual.

Reinforcing (R). The therapist rewards behavior that is growth-enhancing as well as socially adaptive, and punishes behavior that is negative or self-defeating.

Self-disclosing (S). It is the exposing by the therapist of his own adaptive and defensive patterns of living which encourages the person to do the same thing.

Value Reorienting (V). It is the reevaluation by the therapist of the person's loosely formulated value orientations (assumptions about self and others, etc.) which enables the patient to commit himself to examined and operational values.

Reexperiencing (X). The therapist assists the person in reexperiencing of past influential learnings, and assists him in desensitizing the pathological effects of these learnings on his present functioning.

A study by Shostrom and Riley (441) confirms our general hypothesis that counselors tend to adopt a creative synthesizing approach. Each of the therapists in the study utilized all of the parameters to some degree in his work as judged by forty raters. The therapists rated were Carl Rogers, Fritz Perls, and Albert Ellis as they performed in the films "Three Approaches to Psychotherapy" (436). Even Carl Rogers, whom many feel is the most parochial, included many parameters in his work. This study revealed the following:

1. Rogers scored highest on the parameters of CARING and FEELING.
2. Perls scored highest on ENCOUNTERING, FEELING, and INTERPERSONAL ANALYZING.
3. Ellis scored highest on VALUE REORIENTING and PATTERN ANALYSIS.

Thus it is possible for a supervisor of students in counseling or psychotherapy to describe a pattern of parameters which would give a clear picture of his particular style.

Development of Major Theory Groups

The following section contains a summary of the major theories of personality with implications for counseling theory and practice. It offers the student a basis for establishing his own theoretical position.

This selection of theories reflects an arbitrary choice of basically western views which emphasize individuality and personal worth. Eastern traditions and native American cultures focus more on people as extensions of nature. They strive more than westerners, therefore, to blend with nature and return to simple natural states as a counterbalance for the complex demands of technological civilizations and supremacy of the individual.

Two historical bases for western psychological counseling theory can be traced. One, the behavioristic approach, stresses relearning more adaptive problem-solving modes of response to life's demands through use of rewards, punishments, and information. The focus of effort is on the conditions which promote behavior change. Consider, for example, a client who has difficulty concentrating on his studies. The counselor makes a rational diagnosis to determine if the client is in the right field, if his study skills are adequate, if he possesses sufficient ability to do the work, and so on. Learning conditions are created wherein the client can acquire better work habits, more information, further appraisal of the realism of his goals, or more counseling on personal problems. Reinforcement of adaptive responses is a key element.

A related view stressing behavior change comes from the phenomenological tradition, with its emphasis upon perception and Gestalt principles. The principal focus is upon the client's perception of his world at this moment in time and how this perceptual matrix can be altered. The basic assumption is that the person's perception of himself and his world is the key determiner of behavior. Historical and depth factors are minimized.

Another view, depending largely on psychoanalytic principles, stresses the more emotional, so-called dynamic, aspects of personality. Hence, although not overlooking cognitive considerations, the dynamic approach stresses attempts to elicit feelings about the problem and to understand the unconscious bases for behaving. Thus, through removing emotional obstacles to learning or "lifting of repression," the client is enabled to use more rational approaches to problem-solving. For example, if a client has difficulty concentrating on his studies and also appears to resent his parents forcing him to go to school, it may be hypothesized that he unconsciously resists his parents by "inability" to study.

A third emphasis, or "third force" in psychology, which has evolved in recent years, is labeled broadly existential or humanistic. It is partly a protest against the limitations and claims of dynamic and behavioristic views of man. Briefly, it is a way of construing man's existence largely in nonbehavioral terms such as states of being and becoming. It lacks an elaborate rationale and methodology, yet it is having a profound impact on therapeutic psychology theory and practice. The existential viewpoint has been especially influential on persons subscribing to the Gestalt and self-theory approaches, although there are also views labeled "existential analysis." The existential view emphasizes man's search for meaning and authenticity in his present circumstances. May (312), Maslow (307), Rogers (388), and Bugental (77) have written extensively on the problem of becoming an authentic person. Such persons are open and honest with themselves and others so that who they really are can be perceived clearly by others. Their observable behavior is consistent with their feelings.

To achieve the counseling goals of authenticity and meaningful existence, the existentialist counselor helps the client to become aware of and to confront the paradoxes in his existence, such as freedom-determinism and rationality-irrationality. He is encouraged to confront conditions which lead to loss of personal significance, confused identity, and anxiety resulting from threat to his cherished values. The emphasis is upon the special meaning these feelings have for him rather than on causes or rational interpretations in light of some theory. Some writers, notably May (313), assert that existential approaches do not constitute a distinctive "school" but a set of attitudes and assumptions about people and their condition which supplement traditional theories. As in all approaches, there are the dangers of using existentialism as a new type of intellectualization to avoid the experiencing of feelings—or its opposite, using existentialism as a kind of anti-intellectualism rather than as a supplement to scientific ways of viewing man.

The categories for theorists in the following sections are often arbitrary and based upon historical oversimplifications. With the decreasing emphasis upon distinctive parochial views, there is a greater blending of ideas and integration of theories. The following overview, furthermore, includes the views of those writers who have been practitioners rather than primarily personality and learning theorists.

Psychoanalytic Approaches

The psychoanalytic approach stresses the importance of the client's life history (psychosexual development), the influence of genetic impulses (instincts), a life energy (libido), the influence of early experiences on later personality of the individual, and the irrationality and unconscious sources of much of human behavior. The psychoanalytic concepts of levels of awareness are significant contributions. The conscious level consists of those ideas of which the individual is aware at the moment. The preconscious contains those ideas of which the individual is not aware at the moment but which can be recalled. The unconscious level consists of those memories and ideas which the individual has forgotten and cannot remember. Freud conceived the unconscious as making up the bulk of the personality and of having a powerful influence on behavior.

A significant psychotherapeutic issue raised by the psychoanalytic approach is this: Do we need a "depth" approach which postulates that the origin and solution of human problems lie deep within the personality, or do the explanation and solution lie more within the perceptual organization of the individual? Psychoanalytic counselors emphasize the importance of having a concept of depth in personality and postulate a series of structural elements known as Freud's "iceberg" concept, which are illustrated in Figure 7. The largest element is the *id*, which has the characteristics of being unconscious, irrational, unorganized, pleasure-

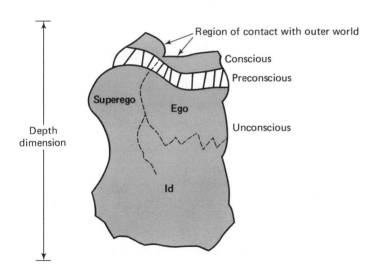

Figure 7. Psychoanalytic Conception of Personality Structure. J. F. Brown, *Psychodynamics of Abnormal Behavior* (New York: McGraw, 1940), adapted from W. Healy, A. Bronner, and A. Bowers, *The Structure and Meaning of Psychoanalysis* (New York: Knopf, 1930).

oriented, primitive, the source of "libido" or life force and energy, and the source of drives and basic wishes for life and death.

Another element of structure is the *ego*, which functions as a controlling, reality-oriented, mastery mechanism. The ego functions also as a mediating element among superego, id, and reality demands. One of the principal functions of the ego is that of controlling the id and keeping impulses and feelings, such as anxiety, out of consciousness. Ego control is accomplished through the mechanism of "defense," of which the main type is "repression." The id impulse, thwarted in direct expression, penetrates the ego barrier in a disguised and usually safer derivative form.

Although the early psychoanalytic theorists placed great emphasis upon repression of anxiety and the consequent symptoms, more recent classical or "orthodox" psychoanalytic therapists have been giving greater attention to ego psychology which emphasizes the adaptive mastery functions of personality.

The *superego* is another Freudian concept which functions as a controlling agent in the personality. It is conceived generally as parental moral attitudes and social mores learned in early years, and which become an important structural and functional part of personality in later years. In many ways, the concept is similar to the popular term "conscience."

Later students of Freud, such as Jung and Rank, not only modified, but also abandoned many of his basic postulates. Adler, a colleague of Freud, emphasized the goal-directedness or purposiveness of human beings more than did Freud, who saw clients more as blind victims of their impulses operating in a rather mechanical deterministic fashion. Adler felt that power and status motives were more significant for behavior than the broadly sexual motives of Freud. Adler saw superiority attitudes as compensations for perceived weakness or the "inferiority complex." Related to Adler's drive for mastery is his notion of the "masculine protest" of some women who envied the status and power of men.

Adler emphasized also the "social interest" or current "life style," as well as the biological determinants of behavior. One of the Adlerian therapist's devices to gain clues to his client's life style is to ask for his "first recollection." This approach gives the therapist an idea of the experiences on which the client's style of life is based.

Adler is well known for his concept of the "ego ideal" or the person's model of the kind of person he would like to be, a prelude to the now popular concept of "self-image." Helping the client become more aware of his unique life style, ideals, and self-images is one of the major goals of counseling. Adlerian concepts form the basis of a currently popular form of family counseling.

Jung stressed the uniqueness of human motives and the striving toward individuation. Jung postulated a broad "collective unconscious," consisting of inherited "archetypes" which are collections of primordial universal motives and human images. His second structural element is the "personal unconscious" which contains forgotten and repressed material. The "conscious" is the external awareness level concerned with problems of everyday living. The "persona" is a type of mask hiding the deeper personality characteristics from others. Jung felt that the persona was an important and healthy element of personality except where it tended to dominate the "real" personality, or to blind the person to what Jung called his "shadow." The shadow part of the personal unconscious is considered to be impulsive and generally not consciously nor socially acceptable. In addition to the "persona" and "shadow"—there are other examples of archetypes—"animus" (masculine aspect of women), "anima" (feminine element in men), and "self" (the achievement of oneness and unity).

Jung emphasized that the psychotherapist must help the individual get something in place of his neuroses and "build" an individual self. Hence, he placed high value on religion and the integration of religion and psychology. Jung's descriptions of the paradoxes in human personality, such as the mixed feminine and masculine components, are often useful concepts in the interpretation phase of psychotherapy. Both Jung and Adler stressed the value of the direct, face-to-face contact of the psychotherapist with the client, as contrasted with the less direct, couch-centered treatment of the Freudians.

Rank contributed much to psychoanalytic theory by his emphasis upon the traumatic events of birth and separation from the mother. These ideas were expanded to include the security-seeking efforts of people. Rank pointed out many implications from the growth and development as a child for development of independence and security as an adult, thus offering counseling theory a significant and meaningful developmental point of view. One implication, for example, is the importance of "limits." According to this concept, the client is helped to gain a feeling of security by setting limits to his behavior, such as making him stay within the time and place of the interview. With children, especially, this is a significant part of the therapeutic process.

Rank's central concept is the "will," which is a guiding, integrating, and instinct-inhibiting force. He views resistance as the operation of the will in maintaining the integrity of the personality. Rank's a-historical views placed considerable emphasis upon the positive motivations of the client and his present feelings, rather than upon the therapist and his interpretations of the past.

Rank's major contributions to counseling were his insistence on viewing the client as a person, and his casting of the psychotherapist into a more personalized role. Rank believed strongly in "ethical self-determination," implying that the counselor should be careful not to force values on the client. Rank's view sharpens another significant issue in counseling: Where should the content of the process come from, primarily—the client's field of awareness or the counselor's?

Rank's theories have influenced several American psychotherapeutic writers. In addition to Carl Rogers in the adult psychotherapy field, Jesse Taft in social work and F. H. Allen in child psychotherapy have extended Rank's special adaptations of psychoanalytic theory. Rank's will is interpreted as a positive growth force. The conflict between dependence and independence needs is seen as a tendency to regress to earlier dependent relationships when the demands of life become too overpowering. Allen perceives that the basic adjustment difficulties of clients result from excessive demands being made upon them before they have the resources to cope with them. Rank's insistence upon the therapeutic power of the relationship itself has led naturally to a strong emphasis being placed on the attitudes held by the counselor and the importance of having the client assume his own psychotherapeutic responsibility.

Implications of Classical Psychoanalytic Positions for Counseling and Psychotherapy

A significant implication for counseling is Freud's theory of defense mechanisms. Psychoanalysis has made us more aware of the unconscious bases of behavior, with the result that counselors are less concerned with the symptoms (defenses) and more concerned with the origins of the defensive behaviors. One therapeutic task is to help the client become more aware of his style of handling unconscious wishes and anxieties and to find more socially approved, as well as personally satisfying, ways of resolving tensions. The analytic counselor, furthermore, sees his task as one of making the "unconscious more conscious," that is, of helping the client to know and utilize in a mature way his psychic energies, and of becoming more aware of distorted behaviors that result from threatening unconscious impulses. Helping the client to become more aware of his unconscious feelings tends to result in more spontaneity, rationality, and other values implicit in the mature personality.

Psychoanalytic therapists use techniques such as abreaction, free association, and interpretation of resistance, dreams, and transference material. The assumptions, style, and length (usually two to five years) of psychoanalytic therapy make it of limited utility in psychotherapeutic counseling. A prominent feature of psychoanalytic technique is to encourage regression to promote exploration of early experiences. The therapist can help the client work through experiences which might otherwise have been beyond his awareness.

Counseling and brief psychotherapy, in contrast, are not as concerned with attempting *major* personality transformations through detailed interpretation of early and persistent unconscious conflicts as is psychoanalysis. Psychotherapy is concerned more with conflicts and feelings which are already in, or dimly in, awareness and with helping the client to develop resources for handling them. In other words, the psychotherapist concentrates more on the "here and now," whereas the psychoanalyst is concerned with lifting repressions of deeply unconscious material. The relevance of analytic techniques to psychotherapeutic counseling is treated in later chapters on relationship techniques.

One key implication of a deterministic system like Freud's, in which one has a blocked urge, then repression, then the neurotic symptom, is that individual responsibility tends to be de-emphasized: "It is not I who is at fault; it is my frustrated id impulses which are causing me trouble." For example, "My hunger stole the fruit, not I." Psychotherapeutic counselors operate on the assumption that the client must, sooner or later, accept personal responsibility for his behavior. Existential therapists, for example, place great stress on the client feeling a sense of "ownership" of himself.

Jung's and Adler's amplification of psychoanalytic theory includes more of the social determinants, such as cooperativeness, and the purposive character of behavior. Rank, as well, stresses the person's integrating powers and the necessity for understanding the client's feelings and potentialities. This concept paved the way for later therapists such as Sullivan, Horney, Taft, Allen, and Rogers to develop theoretical positions of even greater value to psychological counselors.

Recent Positions Evolving from Psychoanalytic Theory

Sullivan is known for his theory of interpersonal relationships, including the interaction between personality development and culture. According to the "interpersonal theory," the individual appears quite different, both to himself and to others, depending upon the particular personalities with whom he is interacting at the moment. The practical import of this view is that the individual can be understood only within the context of his family, friendships (real or imaginary), and broader social groups.

Sullivan postulates two basic goals of human behavior—physical satisfactions (food, drink, rest, sex), and security (defined as a state of pleasantness or euphoria resulting from fulfilled social expectations). The child, in the process of acculturation, finds himself in frequent conflict between need satisfaction and security. As parents use prohibitions and disapprovals in the acculturation process, he begins to feel anxiety as a result of his inability to fulfill these expectations. The child develops increased muscle tension. He excludes from his consciousness selected phases of his experience which have proved anxiety-provoking. His attempts to resolve the tensions through activity do not result in complete relief since anxiety-reduction does not tend to follow release patterns of other physiological tensions.

If the child can obtain both satisfaction and security, he gains a sense of mastery or power; hence, he begins to experience a higher evaluation of himself. This self-regarding attitude is thus determined by the attitude of others toward him. Self-attitudes, in addition, seem to determine the attitudes which he has toward others.

It is important to realize, therefore, that much anxiety originates in an interpersonal context. If considerable anxiety has been generated during the acculturation process, then useful learning, awareness, and capacity for insight will be greatly reduced. Sullivan speaks of this process as "selective inattention." When other persons in the interpersonal situation mention words or feelings which provoke anxiety in one's self, the evaluation of others tends to change in a negative direction; hence, individuals are alienated from one another. It helps, therefore, to understand that an aggressive client responds in this manner largely because he has been rebuffed in his bids for affection and understanding. Through his inability to receive as well as to give affection, he maintains hostile attitudes even toward those who attempt to satisfy his needs.

Sullivan traces self-development through a series of stages from preverbal infancy through adult maturity. The principal implications for counselors are the necessity to provide security relationships, to accept emotional outbursts which are indicative of tension buildups, and to organize learning situations which result in enhancement of self-regarding attitudes of worth and confidence. Therapists and counselors must realize that affectional growth may be poorly developed owing to disturbances in interpersonal relationships and, as a result, the client needs a treatment environment where he can develop self-esteem and confidence adequate to any situation. He needs an opportunity to develop the ability to love another person whose welfare is as significant as his own.

The counselor must be cautious, however, in interpreting the explanations of personality dynamics to the individual. He must recognize also that he too has developed through the same social processes as his client and that the present counseling relationship is changing him further through what Sullivan describes as his "participant-observer" status. This topic will be treated in Chapter 8 under "countertransference."

In summary, the principal implication of Sullivan's theory for therapists and counselors is that the individual can be understood mainly in light of his or her interpersonal history. The quality of the client's interpersonal relationships must be examined, in particular, as a key to the client's understanding of his or her attitudes. The counselor must realize that the client's responses to the counselor are affected by these past relationships and that feelings expressed are displacements of feelings from previous personal relationships. Sullivan's ideas are related to the current emphasis in counseling known as the "communications approach."

Karen Horney (232), who may be classified among the so-called neo-Freudians, differs from the earlier psychoanalysts in that she too stresses the cultural determinants of behavior and emphasizes that maladaptive behaviors arise largely from disturbances in human relationships. Horney, while remaining in the general framework of psychoanalytic theory, shifted the stress from early childhood experiences and repression of biological drives to presently existing character structure and conflicts. She does this, however, without negating the significance of early experience in personality formation. Horney feels that the totality of early childhood experiences and conflict forms a unique character structure which predisposes the person to later neurotic difficulties. This view differs somewhat from the earlier Freudian idea that adult conflicts and neuroses are essentially repetitions of isolated childhood experiences.

An example of the cultural origin of personal problems is the American emphasis on competition, which appears to produce considerable frustration and hostility. Our hostilities are projected to others who are then viewed as competitors. This creates anxiety about the potential danger of others and fear of retaliation for having hostilities of our own. This situation results in a need for security which is satisfied partially through love relationships. Since deeply satisfying affectional relationships are infrequent for many persons in our society, we are subjected to further frustration.

Horney stresses the competing and contradictory demands of our culture upon the person as one source of tensions. Examples are the conflicts between stimulation of demand for material goods and the limited means for satisfying them, independence and free choice as opposed to the limitations imposed by birth and social circumstances, brotherhood and love for your neighbor against competition and "eye for an eye and a tooth for a tooth."

The conflicts in the culture are often internalized and express themselves in various forms of aggressiveness and yielding, personal power and helplessness, self-aggrandizement and self-sacrifice, trust of people and fear of them. An implication here for psychological counseling is that these conflicts, faced by all people in our society, become accentuated or reappear as unintegrated childhood conflicts, causing feelings of distress. Individuals may then develop defense mechanisms annoying to themselves or others. The awareness of these conflicts, or the associated anxiety, drives people to seek psychological counseling. An example is the person with a self-effacement defense, so common in our middle-class culture. He feels it is important to "be nice to everyone, so they will be nice to me and will love me." He finds, however, that other people often dislike him anyway; so he is baffled, concludes that he is fighting a losing battle, and becomes even less assertive.

Another useful distinction that Horney makes is between "normal" anxiety, which is fear of concrete events such as accident and death, and "neurotic" or "basic" anxiety, which is fear that arises in early relationships when the person faces a potentially hostile world and which leads to neurotic defenses. One of the psychological counselor's jobs is to help individuals to recognize their basic anxieties and to help them build more satisfying ways of handling them.

Closely related to Horney's concept of basic anxiety is "basic hostility." Horney postulates that much neurotic anxiety stems from the presence of repressed hostility which has been projected to others. The perception of the world as a hostile place generates anxiety and further repression of hostility, and so begins the "vicious circle."

Of further interest to counselors is Horney's concept of the "basic conflict," which exists largely at an unconscious level. This conflict concerns the feelings of dependence and affection which one has for parents versus feelings of hostility toward them for having to be dependent. The conflict may not be recognized at the conscious level because one cannot easily alienate one's self from those on whom one depends. The more normal individual moves freely between the opposing tendencies of independence and dependence, whereas the more neurotic person is more compulsive about his behavior and experiences his independence-dependence feelings as being in direct conflict with one another. This condition has the effect of limiting spontaneity and of giving the victim a feeling of helplessness, indecision, and fatigue. One of the therapist's tasks, according to Horney, is to make the client aware of his basic conflicts and his attempts to solve the conflict by moving toward, against, or away from people.

One of Horney's (231) formulations of interest to therapists is her description of the basic types of personalities which come for psychotherapy. The "expansive type" gives an impression of glorified self-regard, exhibits an arrogant and contemptuous demeanor, and seems to feel that he can impress and fool others into believing he is someone he is not. This type of client is difficult to involve in a therapeutic relationship initially, but later, when his defenses are reduced, he becomes involved quite easily.

The "self-effacing type" tends to subordinate himself to others, to be dependent upon them, and to seek protection and affection. He is characterized by a strong feeling of failure, inferiority, and self-hate. He exhibits a demeanor of passivity and obsequiousness. He generally becomes involved easily in a counseling relationship.

The "resigned" type puts on an air of disinterest, reflecting retreat from inner feelings and from the rigors of life. He takes on more of a detached observer role in life's activities. He lacks a strong achievement drive and avoids serious effort. This type of client maintains an emotional distance from others and avoids pressures to get involved in any kind of close human relationship. This avoidance behavior makes involvement in a counseling relationship very difficult.

Additional utilitarian concepts for counselors are Horney's "alienation from self" and the "tyranny of the shoulds" (231). The former term refers to common client conditions involving fear of losing identity, hazy thoughts and feelings, and feelings of remoteness from one's thoughts and feelings. Horney's "tyranny of the shoulds" refers to the strong tendency in many clients to strive compulsively to be their ideal selves without due regard for reality conditions in their lives. Such a client, for example, operates on the assumption that nothing is or should be impossible for himself.

Erich Fromm (172, 173), like Sullivan and Horney, is concerned with the social influences on behavior. He, too, stresses the individuality of the client, his goal-directedness and productive possibilities.

Fromm was one of the first to use the term "self-realization" in a therapeutic context, viewing growth as an unfolding process of man's psychological powers. He places the responsibility for many personal conflicts on the economic structure and guilt formation. More broadly, Fromm conceives that the main problems of modern man center around ethical conflicts and relatedness, particularly in regard to loving and being loved. An example would be the social emphasis upon unselfishness versus social competitiveness and self-interest, both of which involve problems of relatedness and ethics. The relatedness of people to their world, particularly to other people, is an unending human problem. The counselor helps clients on these matters through improving their ability to lead creative lives and to relate to their worlds. The unifying "glue" in Fromm's discussion of human relationships is mature love, which will be elaborated upon in later chapters of this book.

Alexander and French (3), though adhering closely to more classical Freudian assumptions and techniques, have modified the practice of psychoanalytic therapy so as to reduce the time required to achieve results. The amount of time that should be spent on a client is one of the key issues of professional counseling. Alexander and French have reduced the time required for therapy by selecting carefully therapists to match the clients' particular needs, by keeping techniques flexible in order to suit individual styles, and by varying the time between interviews. They emphasize that psychotherapy is a "corrective emotional experience" achieved through forced insight and liberal use of supportive techniques. This latter approach highlights another counseling issue concerning the effectiveness of very direct therapist activity and liberal use of support.

Eric Berne has developed a position he calls "transactional analysis" (47). He postulates that each of us carries with him three basic ego states —parent, adult, and child—which we use to test reality. The main subject matters for the helping process are the defensive and gratification interactions of these states within and between individuals. For example, one person may react with his archaic "child ego" to the "parent ego" of another person in such a way that the communication is marked by manipulation or distortion. Berne calls these defensive interactions "games." He tries to help the client see more clearly the use of his various ego states and how he can strengthen his more adaptive adult ego. He does this through a progressive structural analysis of his own ego states, a transactional analysis of his communications with others, and analysis of the games he plays with others. A key activity in transactional work is reconstruction and analysis of "life scripts," which are basically life style histories.

Summary of Recent Psychoanalytic Positions

In summary, the current directions and implications of neo-psychoanalytic theory are as follows: (1) greater recognition of the cultural determinants of behavior; (2) more concern with the client's present circumstances, especially people close to him, and less preoccupation with infantile development and traumata; (3) more emphasis upon the quality of the therapeutic relationship and how the client perceives it; (4) a de-emphasis of sexual needs and aberrations, and increasing stress on other needs and feelings such as love, hostility, and ambivalence; and (5) a greater emphasis on rational ego functions in solving life problems.

Self-Theory and Phenomenological Approaches

Self-theories are relatively new in counseling and psychotherapy. Although the concept of a "self" was postulated many years ago by Jung, McDougall, and others, a counseling approach based upon this basic concept was not specifically offered until Rogers' controversial volume, *Counseling and Psychotherapy*, appeared in 1942 (391). Roger's position became known as "nondirective" because it was counter to the traditional counselor-centered methods of solving client problems. Rogers emphasized the client's creative responsibility for reperceiving his problem and enhancing his "self."

The reader familiar with the problems of classifying counseling and psychotherapy theories may note the painful difficulties in systematizing them. In the present classification, the writers recognize that some theorists would not like some of the others they are classified with. Others can be classified in several places. Self-theorists, for example, cover a wide range of persons who classify themselves as psychoanalysts. Horney is a conspicuous example with her frequent use of the concept of self.

Carl Rogers (390) is generally recognized for having collected the most systematic set of assumptions and constructs on self-theory, as well as for applying the theory to counseling and psychotherapy. His "client-centered therapy" highlights an issue in counseling; namely, how much responsibility can be placed on the client for his own problem-solving or psychotherapy? Many of the following summaries are taken from Rogers' thinking. Rogers speaks for his system of assumptions and demonstrates his methods in the film "Three Approaches to Psychotherapy" (436).

The Nature of the Self. The "self" is a construct rooted in Gestalt and phenomenological psychology. It is typically defined as "the individual's dynamic organization of concepts, values, goals, and ideals which determine the ways in which he should behave" (440, p. 8). It is the individual's consistent picture of himself and is best represented by what he calls "I" or "me." Various terms such as "concept of self," "self-images," "self-concept," and "self-structure" are used to describe this personality construct. The main sources of these personal evaluations are direct experience and the values and concepts of parents which are incorporated as if directly experienced.

As with all constructs of this type, there is great danger in thinking of the "self" as a type of homunculus, or "man within a man," having personal qualities. The next temptation is to use the concept as a universal explanation for motivation and action problems. Rogers (390) used "self" in the sense of awareness of being or functioning, not as a synonym for organism or a "place where."

The concept of self is a learned attribute, a progressive concept starting from birth and differentiating steadily through childhood and adolescence like an unfolding spiral. For example, one of the earliest manifestations of the self is the negativistic attitude of the two-year-old child when he begins to realize that he has an individuality of his own with pressing and distinctive needs and powers. This growing awareness of himself as a unique person is his concept of self. This self takes on various subjective attributes in the form of "I am" (his nature), "I can" (his capacities), "I should or should not" (his values), and "I want to be" (his aspirations) (440).

When the individual perceives himself as behaving in a manner consistent with his picture of himself, he generally experiences feelings of adequacy, security, and worth. If he acts in a manner different from the way he defines himself, he experiences what is known as "threat" and feels insecure, inadequate, or worthless. The individual, if he perceives no other alternative, may then defend himself against this threat or inconsistency via one of the commonly described "defense mechanisms."

An example of this phenomenon is the young man who comes for counseling in an anxious state. His first attempts at handling the feelings of anxiety have been to deny or distort them. The client describes his mixed feelings about going to college and continues: "My parents keep telling me I can make it; my aptitude test scores indicate I can do it; I would like to do it; but I am somehow convinced I can't. I feel caught between, so I freeze when I take exams. I would like to junk the whole idea." The client continues to describe his discomfort and other symptoms.

The client's *self-definitions*, capacity concepts, and aspirations run partially along these lines: "I am a young adult; I respect my parents' opinions; I do not have the ability to do college work; I want a college degree; I want to be liked and admired." Yet, the client experiences the fact that he is in college now; his parents have expressed themselves and he values their judgment; the tests indicate that he has the ability to do the work. He is very much *aware* of the anxiety which results and is aware that this anxiety expresses itself in "exam panic." He does not yet perceive, however, that he is experiencing *threat* because his self-concepts are so incongruent with the data. The *symptom* is anxiety which is experienced when threat occurs. He is tempted to deny (defense mechanism) the conflict by running away from the situation. This evasive action may reduce his awareness of the threat, but not the threat itself. Unless counseling or other life experience breaks this defensive chain reaction and strengthens his self-concept, the defensive behavior (exam troubles, running away) will very likely increase susceptibility to further threat and guilt, thereby creating more distortion and more mechanisms. The preceding sequence is a summary of the self-theorist's threat and defense theory. The theoretical points on defense, mentioned above, are modeled after those of Hogan (229).

Another common example of the threat-anxiety-defense sequence is that of the young woman who feels a conflict between career and marriage. If she falls in love she would satisfy the need for marriage, but it would threaten her career. However, if she does well in her grades in school and spends much time on training instead of social activities, it would support her career needs but would seriously threaten her marriage goal. The preceding analysis of threat-defense sequences could be applied to this situation where there are two seemingly opposing self-concepts. In this case, the counselor tries to help the client recognize and accept both desires.

When the person above is not acting in accord with her self-concept, we might say she is maladjusted in the sense that her awareness of threat and anxiety, and her consequent defensiveness, are high. Her concept of self and her experience as perceived by herself are dissimilar, as indicated in Diagram a of Figure 8. The student in the former illustration who feels deeply that he cannot do college work, yet denies the significance of parental judgments and test data, fits this paradigm also.

Conversely, when the person's concept of self is in relative harmony with his perceived experience and he feels that he is acting in accordance with his values, ideals, and past experiences, we might say he has good adjustment. Our student illustration recast in hypothetical terms to match Diagram b of Figure 8 would say: "I'm convinced I can make it. My

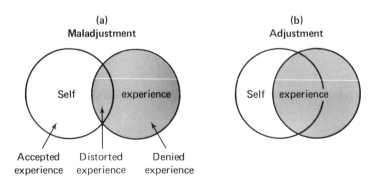

Figure 8. Maladjustment and Adjustment from the Self-Theorist's Viewpoint. Adapted from Rogers (390, p. 526).

parents expect it; my grades and test scores all point to the fact that my plans are realistic."

Congruence is a significant term used by self-theorists, particularly Rogers (390). It means the close matching of awareness and experience. If a client is aware of communicating a feeling which he is genuinely experiencing, his behavior is said to be congruent or integrated. If a client is *aware* of trying to *communicate* a feeling of love to another person, for example, yet he *experiences* hostility toward that person, the recipient of his feelings may experience an awareness of phony communication. The recipient is often aware, furthermore, of the unconsciously motivated defensiveness underlying the client's inaccurate communication. This illustration points up the clear incongruence between experience and awareness, because what the client is aware of and what he is genuinely experiencing are two different phenomena. This condition is also an illustration of the nature of defense from a self-theorist's viewpoint.

A further example of incongruence is the bored guest who insists he is having a wonderful time. Here the guest is aware of the incongruence between his real feeling of boredom and a desire to be polite. Rogers would say this is a type of incongruent behavior which is deceptive rather than defensive because he is aware that his communication is incongruent with his genuine experience of boredom.

The principal counseling implication of this theory of congruence, it would seem, is that the counselor's problem is how to help the client to face courageously the incongruence between awareness and experience so that communication of his real experiences is in full awareness and not defensively distorted.

Further Characteristics and Assumptions. Although the "self" is the key structural construct, the principal assumption or central hypothesis of the self-theory group is that the individual has a self-actualizing growth tendency or need. The organism strives not only to maintain itself, but also to enhance itself in the direction of wholeness, integration, completeness, and autonomy. Hence, the client is believed to have the capacity and the motivation to solve his own problems. The main implication of this view is that the counselor's role is to create an interview "climate" and to use techniques which allow these natural growth forces to emerge in the direction of mentally healthy and creative behaviors.

Although the "self-actualizing tendency" is postulated as being biologically determined, the direction of the growth tendencies is assumed to be culturally determined by parents, peers, teachers, and other persons significant to the child. Since the individual tends to deny perceptions which conflict with his self-concept, these growth forces often become distorted in the developmental process. This condition often gives the picture of a person devoid of positive growth motives. These seems to be a strong belief on the part of the self-theorists that the positive growth forces will ultimately triumph. For example, independence will supersede dependence; integration will overcome disintegration; social behavior will replace antisocial behavior.

A third assumption, based on the point of view called "phenomenology," is that people's "reality" is that which they perceive. External events are significant for individuals only insofar as they experience them as meaningful. The phenomenologists say that the way to understand individuals is to infer the "phenomenological field" from their behavior. In other words, to really know a person, the observer, or counselor, must know how the individual views his environment and himself. Thus, the term "internal frame of reference" has come into common use in counseling with the implication that counselors must try to perceive clients' perceptual worlds as closely as they can. This intimate understanding is a necessary prelude to "acceptance" of the client's feelings. This viewpoint explains why the client-centered counseling group focuses on deep understanding and acceptance of client attitudes. Thus, the phenomenological approach places a premium upon the empathic skill of the psychotherapist.

Rogers (388, 390) has developed a tentative system of fourteen postulates which go beyond the basic assumptions summarized above. Much current effort is being expended to clarify his propositions and to submit them to rigid experimental tests. Grummon (210) has summarized the assumptions and postulates of the Rogerian position in a form extremely useful for counselors. The research centers on how the conscious and unconscious states of the organism are organized and altered. It is a difficult problem, however, to relate the changes which are observed in client-centered counseling to the self-theory postulates, particularly the basic one of self-actualization. Examples of research efforts toward this goal are collected in Rogers' and Dymond's report (400) and Truax and Carkhuff (480).

A related group of personality theorists is the "need"-centered group. Maslow (307), for instance, combines the self-theorist's basic postulates, such as the self-actualization principle, with basic human needs. He views the human being as an integrated holistic organism with a series of basic needs organized into a hierarchy of importance dictated largely by the culture in which he is raised. The psychotherapeutic process becomes a systematic need gratification through a very special type of interpersonal relationship. Maslow feels that his need gratification theory explains why so many people are helped by persons who are well-meaning but who are untrained in counseling technique and theory.

General Implications of Self-Theories.   One of the basic contributions of this view for counseling and psychotherapy is that the experiencing individual becomes the center of focus in the counseling process. Since the client holds the power of growth and meaningful perception within himself, the responsibility for change and the "locus of evaluation" of his experience must be within the client. His internal frame of reference is generally close enough to "objective reality" so that the counsel can follow meaningfully what the client is saying. The counselor, nevertheless, constantly must ask, "What is he trying to say; and what does this mean to him?" His understanding of the perceptual world of the client is then communicated to the client in fresh language. This condition facilitates further elaboration and clarification of feelings, which leads to insight, and in turn results in positive planning and action.

Another implication of the growth principle is that the counselor's attitudes in the interview must be so genuine, caring, and transparent that the threat to the client's self is reduced to a minimum. Reduction of threat allows the client to accept hitherto unaccepted parts of himself and to express feelings never before admitted. Since he accepts more of his previously denied and distorted experiences into his self-organization, he is in a better position to accept others and to achieve the characteristics of the fully functioning person as described by Rogers (387, 388, 393).

A third implication is that the emotional quality of the relationship is the most significant therapeutic element. Wealth of information, diagnostic accuracy, and historical understanding, which are primary in some theories of psychotherapy, are secondary to the trusting "climate" created by the counselor's sincerity, warmth, acceptance, and sensitive empathic understanding. There is less concern about the *direction* in which the client will move and more concern about providing a *relationship* where he can freely and safely move in exploring his own feelings. When a "delinquent," for example, is given this type of relationship, the expectancy is that he will move in a socializing direction because he sees this as the most rewarding way to go. Thus, there is little emphasis upon changing basic motivations or habits. The self-theorist claims that these behaviors automatically change in a socially desired direction when the client's perception is more finely differentiated and when he discovers for himself more satisfying ways of meeting his own and society's needs.

A limitation of self-theory approaches is their lack of applicability to types of counseling stressing information, test results, persuasion, and environmental change. The self-concept is too narrow to encompass the full range of counseling problems. It is a confusing variable to utilize in counseling research because specific dimensions of the self are difficult to define and assess. For example, how are changes in the self-concept determined as a result of an educational-vocational counseling experience?

Summary of Self-Theory Approaches. The principal mark of the self-theory group is its postulation of a self-concept. A second distinguishing characteristic is the belief in the innate positive growth potential or self-actualizing power of the organism. The main focus in therapy is on the relationship of counselor to client. In this relationship, the counselor's attitudes of honesty, trustworthiness, and genuine concern are crucial. A main difference from other dynamic approaches appears to be the effort to build and maintain a nonthreatening, anxiety-reducing relationship in which growth can take place from the very beginning. Another difference from other approaches is the increased amount of responsibility placed upon the client compared to that ascribed to the counselor.

Behavioral Approaches

Although the dynamically oriented theorists seek to understand conscious and unconscious conditions through inference, the behavioral group concentrates on objective study of client behavior and the learning process in particular as the source of hypotheses about counseling. Since the emphasis of this group is on behavior, their primary concern is to discover how the behavior was acquired and how it can be changed. A second emphasis is on cognitive processes and how these can be altered as a precondition for behavior change. The label "Cognitive Theories" applies to this group.

Behavioral counselors are concerned about goals of counseling also, although they insist that the goals be stated in observable terms. Krumboltz (273), for example, states specific illustrative goals under three general types. They are "altering maladaptive behavior," "learning the decision making process," and "preventing problems." Goals are stated differently for each client and generally are compatible with counselor values, but the goals are stated in specific terms which different observers could agree were achieved.

The Gestalt or field theorists are a rather independent group. They are included with the broad behaviorist group since they, too, stress learning and systematic behavior observation. The differences, however, between Gestalt approaches and behaviorism are more striking than their similarities. In many ways, Gestalt views, with their emphasis upon perception and their relation to phenomenology, are significant sources for the self-theory group's views.

Learning-Theory Contributions

Historically, this group evolved from the Pavlovian conditioned-response approach to learning and the Watsonian behaviorism of the 1920s. Their objective orientation resulted in a heavy emphasis upon studying behavior in its most simple forms through the medium of animal experiments. Until recently these early experiments had little impact on counseling theory or practice. Mowrer (339), Dollard and Miller (125), Shoben (429), and Shaw (425), for example, made early efforts to integrate learning theory concepts with counseling principles. Behavioral concepts and research have had two types of impact: One is the development of a wide range of strategies to assist clients in counseling. The other is known as behavior modification—applying behavior technology to change individuals in group settings, such as classrooms.

Learning theory has become a promising source of productive experiments, and for some counselors and psychotherapists, the keystone in their theory of behavior change. Some of these practitioners who have experimented with concepts, such as operant conditioning and reconditioning in counseling are Krasner (272), Krumboltz (273), Bandura (30), Eysenck (144), Grossberg (208), Wolpe (504), and Michael and Meyerson (321). Most of these investigators follow the experimental leads of B. F. Skinner (447), the principal exponent of operant conditioning principles in learning theory.

Characteristics and Assumptions. The learning theorist assumes, first of all, that most of human behavior is learned. It is assumed also that behavior can be modified by application of learning principles, some of which are discussed below.

Strictly behavioristic explanations of client behavior are based largely upon the theoretical works of Thorndike, Hull, Guthrie, Skinner, and Tolman. Mowrer and Miller, Shaw, Rotter, Shoben, Wolpe, Bandura, Krasner, and Krumboltz are some persons who have attempted to apply these principles to counseling. All these investigators start with the assumption that the person has *drives*. These drives are primarily physiological, but through social learning a vast hierarchy of secondary *motives* is acquired. These drives and motives propel the individual toward goals. From past learning, the individual acquires *expectancies* (excluded by some reinforcement theorists) that, if he seeks a goal in a certain way, he will achieve it. A *stimulus* or *cue* sets off the *response* which propels the client toward his goals. The response is *rewarded* and tends to be repeated. This sequence is described as an S-R model (stimulus-response). The individual *discriminates* among various stimuli according to past *conditioning*. Stimuli are assumed to be interchangeable. The person learns to make a particular response to a once nonsignificant stimulus which happened to be around when he was making a response to a quite different stimulus. In an oversimplified way then, almost any stimulus can become associated with almost any response. The counselor's task becomes one of helping the client to identify undesirable stimulus-response patterns and then interfere with them or set up conditions for more desirable stimulus-response patterns. These patterns often take the form of very specific goals, such as approaching strangers to ask for information, which heretofore had been a deeply anxiety-provoking experience.

A key concept of the behavior approach is that of *reinforcement*. This is a rewarding condition which occurs when a stimulus-response sequence has been completed. The S-R pattern then tends to be repeated under similar circumstances and *generalizes* to other types of responses which are similar to the learned pattern. Also, response patterns which are not repeated and reinforced periodically tend to be *extinguished*, that is, disappear. The process of substituting one stimulus for another to get the same response, or of getting a different response for the same stimulus is called "reconditioning," or in psychotherapeutic terms, *re-education*. The concept of anxiety for the learning theorists is a type of nonspecific fear in which one is unaware of the source as well as the object of his fears.

Two principles of learning which have applicability to therapeutic processes are *operant conditioning* and *desensitization*. Operant conditioning is a procedure of rewarding behaviors as they occur so that they will be stronger and less likely to be extinguished. Examples are therapist praise, smiles, and nods for client statements which are interpreted by the client as approval. Desensitization is a process of exposing clients to increasing amounts of anxiety-provoking stimuli until they cease to elicit anxious responses. As this technique is described by Wolpe (504), it includes special training in relaxation methods so that a relaxation response is substituted for an anxiety response to the same stimulus. Salter (407) has developed a program of conditioned reflex therapy growing out of human and animal conditioning research. Emphasis is upon removing inhibiting behaviors, not symptoms, through environmental change.

An example of a learning-theory approach to counseling is Phillips' (365) "interference theory." Phillips stresses the contemporary assertive and choice-making behaviors of a person and leaves out concepts involving "depth" and "defense" in the personality. To change behavior in psychotherapy, then, the counselor sets up conditions which interfere with present behaviors and which teach the client new ways of responding to his environment. Phillips hits directly on one of the major issues of psychotherapy; namely, is it necessary to postulate a depth dimension of personality and invoke assumptions about an unconscious and defense mechanisms such as repression?

Another issue faced squarely by learning-theory advocates is that of experimental validation. The learning theorist strives valiantly to state his concepts, postulates, and hypotheses in forms which have behavioral correlates and which can be observed and studied in laboratory situations. Learning theorists criticize other theory-making efforts severely because the concepts, postulates, and hypotheses are "slippery," vague, and difficult to correlate with behavioral referents. However, learning theory does not offer utilitarian substitutes for some of the inferred structural and functional concepts of personality propounded in the dynamic and self-theories.

A key issue separating the behavioral group from dynamically oriented people is the nature of neurosis and the origin of symptoms. Neuroses were viewed historically as behaviors preventing intense anxiety from becoming conscious. Phobias and compulsions, for example, were regarded as casually learned behaviors which kept the personality intact and reduced anxiety from conflicts originating largely in childhood. Behaviorally oriented counselors look upon these so-called neurotic behaviors as learned responses in the process of drive reduction. Phobias, for example, are learned avoidance behaviors to be reduced through reconditioning methods.

Dollard and Miller (125) were among the earliest investigators to link social learning theory with psychotherapy. Their views are still considered valid for a behavioristic rationale for counseling. Basic principles are *drive*, which is motivation for action, and *cue*, which is the stimulus for provoking a *response*. Strength of response varies with the intensity of the drive and the cue. A final concept is *reinforcement*, described above as a rewarding condition which tends to fix the behavior. Conversely, when behavior is repeated without reinforcement it is *extinguished*, or eliminated. This is an oversimplified sketch of the Dollard-Miller view, an approach to behavior change involving a blend of learning principles and psychoanalytic assumptions.

Implications and Limitations of Learning Theory for Counseling and Psychotherapy. Experimental psychologists generally do not attempt to draw parallels between laboratory conditions and the interview. Clinicians, however, make attempts to define counseling variables in learning-theory terms. They reason along the following lines: An almost universal condition of clients, from those who have superficial counseling problems to those who need deep psychotherapy, is some form of *anxiety*; the counseling relationship as experienced by most clients is *anxiety-reducing*; many defense mechanisms are anxiety-reducing also and have been reinforced so many times that they become fixed; although a defense mechanism, such as sarcasm, may reduce tensions, it is paradoxically self-defeating or socially maladaptive; hence, the defensive measure itself creates more anxiety.

Learning theory may some day shed more light on why counselor characteristics enable clients to feel secure and to learn more personally rewarding behavior in place of their maladaptive defenses. Pleasure experienced from smoother interpersonal relationships, for example, appears to have a reinforcing effect on the new behavior.

We need to know why some clients fail to learn more satisfying behaviors under the same conditions. Why do some clients persist in their maladaptive defenses even when they are very much aware of their source and of the pain they cause themselves and others? Many clients can label the dynamisms and symptoms with great aplomb, yet they do not seem able to act upon this knowledge.

How impulses can be inhibited in clients with immature characteristics and so-called character disorders is another problem which may someday be helped by learning methods. How can responses considered undesirable by the client himself be extinguished so that they do not recur? How can this inhibition of undesirable responses be accomplished without resorting to conscious suppression or unconscious repression?

Learning theory has stimulated the idea that the client should be encouraged to experiment with new behaviors for the purpose of enlarging his repertoire of adaptive behavior in social situations. He is often given tryout "homework" to do, for example.

How can the client be helped, furthermore, to *generalize* or *transfer* from *response sets* (215) discovered as rewarding in the counseling relationship to situations outside of counseling? This question often plagues counselors.

Rotter (402) emphasizes that one psychotherapeutic task is to increase the *freedom of movement* of the client so that he is aware of, and can engage in, more activities which lead to satisfaction. After loosening the client's rigid perceptions of his situation, *expectancies* are built up which anticipate reward instead of punishment. Then, when the client tries out a new expectation of himself, such as speaking before a group, his feelings of success about himself are reinforced through people telling him he did a good job. The counselor's attitude of acceptance alone seems to be helpful in supplying positive reinforcements and positive expectancies. The client may come expecting criticism for his exploits, but he finds the counselor understanding and relaxed about the matter. This feeling of being understood and liked is a type of positive reinforcement which may lead to more generalized feelings of being liked by others outside the psychotherapeutic interview.

Although there is some agreement among clinicians interested in learning theory as to what learning labels can be applied to client behavior, they differ greatly regarding how active the counselor should be in promoting new learning. Some think the counselor is obliged to have the client spell out his problem so that he can perceive and redefine it accurately; then the counselor helps the client through suggestion and interpretation to build expectancies for more satisfying outcomes. The counselor tries to get the desired behavior, and then reinforces it.

Other counselors with a learning orientation feel that the first chore is to prevent the client's anxiety from generalizing to other stimuli and to allow expectation principles to operate. Next, the counselor attempts to help the client recognize distorted expectancies without using argument or pressure. Meanwhile, the counselor's accepting attitude conveys the idea that the client's difficulties are due to his confusion and lack of understanding rather than to "weak will power, orneriness, laziness, or perverseness." New behaviors are then elicited as tryout suggestions from the client rather than through direct suggestion from the counselor.

In some cases, the counselor may decide to intervene more actively, to teach the client *skills* which may be used to achieve the expected rewards. For example, the failing student may need improved study methods before he can experience the rewards of achieving his new expectancy of being the "successful student," which he will very likely generalize to being the "successful person." Thoreson and Mahoney (472) have developed a series of principles and practices of self-management whereby the person can establish change programs for himself without the intervention of a counselor or therapist.

The principle of expectancy has another implication in the phenomenon of transference. Transference, which will be described in Chapter 8, can be explained in learning terms as a series of learned client expectancies. Examples of such expectancies are that the counselor will be like other persons the client has known who are feared, disliked, or loved.

Summary of Learning Approaches. In summary, the learning approach to counseling and psychotherapy has great promise as a methodology of guided behavior change, especially since it is stimulating so much basic research on the counseling process. The participants in the Kentucky Symposium on learning theory, personality theory, and clinical research (1) concluded that learning theory, which is based on controlled and highly artificial experimental situations, has limited applicability to practical problems. They agreed also that personality and clinical theories which are based on clinical case observation do not have suitable forms for experimental testability. The Kentucky Symposium participants suggest that one way to mesh the two is to strive for more generality of learning theory and to be more concerned with finding means whereby results of psychotherapy can be measured with laboratory methods. This hope is being realized through an abundance of current experimental efforts.

Critics of the learning approach to counseling feel that emphasis on objectivity and denial of unconscious manifestations leads to sterile, mechanistic, atomistic approaches, and that the personality is too complex to study with the present methods which are designed to study lower organisms. The next criticism logically following is that theories based upon simple models have little applicability to complex human processes. Learning theorists aim to understand behavior in small, highly controlled samples and argue strongly against premature attempts to explain higher processes until methods for study of these processes are developed. The self-theory group is generally skeptical of the learning-theory approach because it tends to stress the process of learning rather than to focus on the client who is doing the learning.

Some critics are concerned that conditioning methods will be too effective and might be used to manipulate clients, as is the case with critics of behavior modification strategies. There is fear that freedom and individual responsibility will be reduced by the counselor who perceives his role as a human engineer controlling behavior in a psychologically determined utopian state.

Field Theories and Counseling

Field theorists are often classed with the behavioristic group because of their emphasis on learning as change of perception and their stress upon systematic behavior observation. They differ, however, in several ways, and particularly with respect to their phenomenological approach to perception. Among field theories, Gestalt psychology has the more formalized approach and is represented by such familiar names as Koffka, Kohler, Wertheimer, and Lewin.

The Gestalt approach was introduced to the United States from Europe about the same time Behaviorism reached full flower. The Gestalt movement was radically different from Behavioristic movements in that it tended to de-emphasize minute analysis of behavior into mechanistic stimulus-response bonds and stressed, instead, the dynamic organization of whole units of behavior.

Perls, Goodman, and Hefferline (362) have developed a therapeutic approach called Gestalt Therapy which stresses the applications of Gestalt psychology to psychotherapy. They emphasize problems of awareness, the whole self in creative contact with the environment, and the reshaping of one's sensory capacities. Perls' system of therapy claims a reintegration of Gestalt principles, Freudian structures, Reichian viewpoints, and the principles of general semantics. Perls also emphasizes the importance of the present encounter to encourage awareness of current feelings. He encourages the emerging Gestalt of personal integration and the recovery of lost potential through exposing defenses, "games," and escapes to the future. Perls does not explain or interpret to the client, but provides opportunities for self-discovery. Perls speaks for his Gestalt therapy system and illustrates his work in the film series "Three Approaches to Psychotherapy" (436).

Two principal contributions to counseling theory have been made by the Gestalt psychology group, as distinct from Perls' Gestalt therapy approach. These are principles of perceptual organization and the phenomenon of insightful learning. The Gestalt group postulates that psychological organization of the person tends to move in the direction of wholes or the "good gestalt." This means that the person tends to organize his perceptions simply and completely in order to reduce tensions arising from a state of disorganization. For example, when we see an incomplete drawing of a familiar object we tend to complete the details to make it a meaningful figure. The Gestalt group stresses the influence of the "field," that is, surrounding forces in the environment, on the organism.

Lewin, although not thinking necessarily of applications to psychological counseling, formulated some concepts of particular value to counselors. Lewin calls his theory a "topological theory" of personality because he used a mathematical model to account for the psychological field of the person (286). He pictured the personality in his psychological field with field theory terms such as *vector* (direction) and *valence* (attraction power). He conceives a dynamic system of interdependent subsystems of personality which offer a considerable contrast to Freud's more historical deterministic system.

Lewin describes the person as "differentiated life-space" organized into energy systems. In this framework, the child begins life as a relatively simple organism; as he or she grows, the processes of differentiation and integration become more rapid. Along with growth comes more rigidity of boundaries within the personality. The tensions, or needs, developing from internal conflicts and from frustrations in goal-seeking act as motivating forces. These forces impel the personality toward actions to alleviate the tensions or reduce the needs.

One implication of Lewin's theory for counseling is the importance of helping individuals to make barriers within their personalities more permeable so that they do not suffer from the dissociating effects of rigidity. Another counselor task is to help the individual keep goals within reasonable grasp in order to reduce the frustration concomitant with goal barriers; that is, help him to develop a realistic "level of aspiration." A consequence of frustration, for example, is to force the personality to make fantasy solutions. In severe cases, the individual so displaces reality with fantasy that the latter is perceived as reality.

The principal goals of the counselor, summarizing implications from Lewin, are to increase the life-spaces of clients so that they have more flexibility in living, to help them reduce the rigidity of barriers which prevent them from reaching their goals (such as achieving better reading skills so as to obtain success in job or school), and finally to reduce the rigidity within their own personalities to allow an experience of freedom and spontaneity.

Values of Gestalt Principles

Perception. The first significant contribution of field theory was the influence of perception in behavior. The main principles of perception theory are summarized as follows by Combs (106): First, the physical state of the organism determines the nature of what is perceived. Therefore, how the person behaves is a function of the state of his perceptual field at the moment. Second, perception is a function of time since the exposure must be long enough to allow sensory organs to function adequately. Third, perception cannot occur unless there is an experience, either concrete or symbolic. Fourth, the client's values and goals influence perception. In general, people perceive what they want to perceive, or are trained to perceive. Fifth, the ego and the self-systems selectively determine what is perceived. Sixth, experiencing threat (as previously defined) affects the range and quality of perception. Threat seems to narrow the perceptual field as well as to force the individual to maintain the integrity of his personality organization by various defenses.

The perceptual learning group, then, begins with the basic postulate that behavior is a primary function of the person's perceptual field at the moment. Snygg and Combs (451), for example, emphasize the importance of understanding persons in terms of their unique perceptual or "phenomenal fields." This phenomenological view is a considerable contrast to the psychoanalytic view that behavior is influenced by deeply repressed historical events in the personality. The psychoanalytic theorist is inclined to say that how people behave now is a function of the meaning automatically given to events in terms of their unique past histories of repressions and "libido," or life energy, uses. The behaviorist, in contrast, would stress the importance of past learning.

Kelly (257) has devised a system which he calls "constructive alternatism." This view is a perception theory wherein the client construes his world in a variety of ways; hence, the client is not bound to a particular set of constructs about his world. Kelly's fundamental postulate is that "a person's processes are psychologically channelized by the ways in which he anticipates events" (257, p. 46). There are many corollaries and definitions in his "psychology of personal constructs," but it reduces to a perceptual learning viewpoint incorporating the personal history of the client as a basis for understanding the perceptions of the moment. There are many implications for counseling in Kelly's formulations, including the strategy of assisting the individual to change role constructs, or pictures of himself, as a basis for planned changes in behavior. Kelly's view differs from that of Rogers and the self-theory group in the important respect that Kelly does not postulate a "growth principle" impelling the client toward a "mature self."

Self-theory leans heavily on principles of perception. For instance, a significant part of the rationale of the self-theory group is that the counselor attempts to get within the perceptual frame of reference of the client so that he can see the world in somewhat the same way the client sees it. Since the client's reality is that which he perceives, it is quite important that the counselor get a good look at the client's reality.

Related to the idea above is the client's need to "free his perception," which means making it less rigid and less subject to distortion. The counselor does this by allowing himself to be used as a screen upon which the client can project his perceptions. The counselor reflects these back in ways which help the client to see that there are other ways of looking at his problem. The counselor encourages the client to explore feelings and ideas which heretofore had been outside of his awareness. This verbalizing process helps the individual to alter and extend his perceptual world so that he has more flexibility of choice.

A significant contribution of the perception researchers to psychotherapeutic counseling has been the development of projective techniques. Although they were instigated primarily as diagnostic personality instruments, they are important aids to counseling, as will be indicated later in Chapter 10. Rorschach, Murray, Beck, and Klopfer not only pioneered the projective instruments but also added much to the perception theory of personality.

Insight. Another important contribution of the Gestalt group to counseling is that of insight-learning. Here, a process of searching for solutions leads to a "restructuring of the field," or reshuffling of relationships, which, in turn, often results in a sudden solution. Past experiences are seen in a different manner and events stand in a different relationship to one another. Insight accounts for the, "Oh yes, why didn't I realize this before," type of response heard so frequently in counseling.

Insight is achieved in counseling by helping the client review his past experiences, arrange them for clear observation, search actively for new solutions, and then wait for the perceptual reorganization to take place. In an actual counseling situation, the client usually has some form of hypothesis about causes and some tentative solutions he anticipated trying. The counselor's job is to help the client loosen his rigid ways of thinking so that perceptual reorganization resulting in insight can take place. This is done through a thorough discussion by the client of feelings and ideas about relevant aspects of the problem. It is through the process of verbalizing that he actually relives or reexperiences his past or present perceptions. Something happens within the perceptual organization of the individual when superficial knowledge about himself and others is translated into deep understanding and the increased awareness which we label "insight."

The importance of an "incubation" period must be stressed here. The counselor and client may discuss many relevant aspects of the client's problem without a satisfactory solution being presented. Then, after a period of time, the client comes back with a fresh "set" to attack the problem, or he may have a solution which he wishes to discuss in the interview. Insight often cannot be rushed. It seems to be spontaneous and sudden when it comes, but the surest way to bring it about seems to be through the counselor's success in creating an interview climate where the client can explore many relevant past experiences and present feelings with a sense of freedom and deep personal intensity. Insight is more likely to come when the client is "involved" with his problem; that is, when his feelings have full sway in the deep reexperiencing of those feelings he has tended to deny, distort, or project. There also must be an intense desire to find a solution to his discomfort.

Limitations of Gestalt Views for Counseling or Psychotherapy.   The principal limitations of Gestalt views for counseling are their incompleteness. Perception theories aid considerably in hypothesizing how attitudes are learned and changed. Insight theory gives further enlightenment to these matters. The therapist or counselor is still in the dark, however, when it comes to setting conditions whereby perceptual changes and insight are accomplished. How intellectual understanding of one's feelings and thought processes can be translated into the deep awareness called insight is still unclear. Even more baffling is how the counselor can assist the client to *act* on his insight.

Other theories have been constructed which do not claim to have the inclusiveness or systematization of some of the other approaches; yet, they help to explain the events observed in counseling. The trait theorists see personality as a system of interdependent traits or factors such as abilities (verbal, numerical, memory, spatial, and so on), interests and values, attitudes, and temperament. Social traits and adjustment types are included also. The trait approach has a long history of attempts to classify people into dominant character types, and to describe them in terms of test scores along various trait dimensions.

Trait and factor approaches have been used widely by the nonpsychotherapeutic counselor, the counselor most concerned with educational and vocational problems. The problem has been one of prediction of school and job success using an all-around appraisal of factors. On the other hand, the psychotherapeutic counselor, concerned with deep attitudes and debilitating feelings, has looked more to the dynamic and perception theories.

The trait and factor group was influenced greatly by the early measurement movement in psychology. Psychometrics was concerned with measuring the various dimensions of personality in order to make accurate diagnoses and predictions of probable success. Paterson, Bingham, Darley, and Williamson were pioneers in the early attempts to make counseling an objective measurement-centered process. Thorne and Symonds did the same for psychotherapeutic counseling. They have written profusely about integrating the procedures of testing, case study, observation, diagnosis, prediction, planning of action, and follow-up, making this a formal process which has become known as professional counseling.

Other theorists are contributing sidelights to counseling. Factorial methods of statistical analysis are being utilized to gather data on the organization of personality. Cattell (97), for example, has amassed considerable data on "trait clusters." Several major developments on aptitude factors have emerged in research centers. A number of test batteries based on factorial studies are available to the counselor and have influenced his theoretical model of personality organization and function. These developments will be explained further in Chapter 10 on testing.

Allport (5) has strongly influenced counseling groups with his views on the independent unitary trait. A large group of personality tests have been based upon the general premise that personality can be broken down into quite consistent generalized response units called "traits." Tests of traits such as social introversion, honesty, aggressiveness, cheerfulness, and self-confidence, for example, attest to the widespread infiltration of this view into counseling language. Allport's recent views have a more existential flavor. He has attempted a synthesis of many viewpoints on personality, particularly for counselors. He ties together behavioristic views about man as a reactive being with dynamic views of man reacting in depth, and man as a "being-in-process-of-becoming" (6). Allport argues for an inclusive theory which accounts for complex human motivation, aspiration, a balance between tentativeness and commitment, an adequate image of man, and a new and broader rationalism.

There is a group of theorists who emphasize that mistaken beliefs or perceptions people have about themselves are the source of their psychological problems. Representatives of this view are Kelley (257), with his personal construct theory, Ellis (136), and Raimy (372). Raimy points out misconceptions, such as "my parents never loved me," and how strategies such as identifying mechanisms for avoiding awareness and admitting mistakes can be utilized in counseling.

Rational approaches to behavior change assume that man is a rational being capable of changing his behavior by altering his belief system. Ellis is an exponent of this point of view with his rational-emotive system of psychotherapy. Ellis's rationale is that emotional distress is a result of self-defeating irrational thoughts with which the person continues to reindoctrinate himself. Change in behavior comes about when he changes his thinking. Examples of irrational premises which Ellis attacks are that one must be loved by everyone and that one must be perfectly competent to feel worthwhile.

Implications and Limitations of Trait-Factor and Cognitive Theories for Counseling and Psychotherapy. The trait-factor people are devoted to an empirical study of the counseling relationship with only modest attempts at conceptualizing these observations into broad theories. Their pragmatic concerns seem to have led them to focus on the minute-by-minute study of the interview, factors or traits which can be measured and incorporated into prediction formulas, and upon the total counseling process as a series of steps to rather specific counseling goals.

One important problem arising from this practical concern with specific goals is how to establish criteria of success in counseling and psychotherapy. How to relate events in counseling, meaningfully, to measurable criteria of success in counseling is the subject of much current research effort. For example, what is the relationship between the degree of lead assumed by the counselor and the client's subsequent ability to assume responsibility for his own life and to seek a job, raise his grades, get along more amicably with his family, or just feel happier? In this empirical method, there is little interest in the client's past except as it seems relevant in the counselor's opinion through the systematic case study.

The emphasis on objectivity, diagnosis, and prediction by this group of researchers on counseling led to some reaction and alarm. They were labeled "directivists," with the implication that this method of counseling was: "Find out what's wrong with 'em and tell 'em." Misapplication of the diagnostic and predictive techniques and avoidance of more dynamic views led to abuses and extremes which stimulated much of the vitriolic writing on the directive-nondirective "controversy" during the forties. One of the more naive followers of the trait-factor school of thought believed that if one collected enough facts about the client's various traits his behavior would make sense. We know now that mere cataloging of facts has limited value.

Process Research

Some study of counseling has been done by the process analysis approach. The process researcher focuses on the counseling process from the standpoint of procedures that work best for accomplishing a particular goal with a particular type of client in a particular institutional setting. The process approach is more empirical than eclectic. Theorists in this area have studied the interview, searching for elements which retard or accelerate interview progress and for factors which improve communication between counselor and client. Robinson (385), for example, has developed a "communications approach" which delineates the verbal dimensions of the interview. Problems are studied by means of recordings along dimensions such as "responsibility," "leading," "talk ratios," "planning statements," and "discussion units." Robinson is concerned with the effect of counselor attitude and technique on the client, without special regard to a particular systematic personality or learning theory.

Computer-Assisted and Programmed Counseling

A promising behavior-oriented development is the use of computers as a counseling adjunct or substitute. A system to conduct an automated interview is an experimental reality and is described and documented by Cogswell (100) and Loughary (293). The client faces a teletypewriter linked to a computer. The computer begins, for example, by printing a question on the client's machine: "Do you plan to continue your formal education beyond high school?" If the client types "no," the next question is likely to be: "Which of these is most like what you plan on doing after high school? 1. Join the military service; 2. Go through vocational job training; 3. Enter an apprenticeship; 4. Get a job; 5. Decide later." Additional information and questions are sent back and forth depending on the answers of the client and the previously stored information about the client in the computer.

This approach has much promise for relieving the counselor of routine kinds of readiness work with clients. The system is programmed so that unusual responses needing individualized attention will be referred to a professional counselor through direct suggestion from the computer.

Computers have been programmed such that student data can be screened by the computer and brought to the attention of the counselor like the warning light on a car instrument panel. Programs were developed to simulate counselors going through record folders. For example, printouts contain responses such as: "Student's grades have gone down quite a bit. Ask about this in interview. Possibly there are personal problems." Other possibilities include: "Student is a potential dropout"; "Low counseling priority. No problems apparent."

It is possible to link computer systems containing student data to other systems programmed with prediction data on college entrance, admission, and retention probabilities, scheduling, and other decision-making aids. Monitoring systems ensure that clients needing special attention are singled out. Unusual output indicating machine malfunction or inadequate programming also is brought to the attention of the counselor through monitors.

Validation for computer-assisted counseling comes from the Cogswell and Estavan and the Loughary, Friesen, and Hurst studies (100, 293), and a comparison of programmed face-to-face counseling by Gilbert and Ewing (191). Loughary and associates studied the similarities between automated school counseling systems and human counselors in terms of pre- and post-interview assessment, and similarities in output, such as course selection. Client feelings about the computer were found to be favorable, although they preferred the human counselor. Some clients felt the computer was more helpful with certain kinds of prediction data, but they felt the human counselors had a greater amount of information to offer. The automated counseling system performed in a manner similar to human counselors in choice-making and prediction such that the investigators see automated counseling as a valuable counselor adjunct of the future rather than a replacement.

The Gilbert and Ewing study in a college counseling service compared programmed counseling with highly trained and experienced counselors. Programmed counseling was compared to simulated programmed counseling (with counselor personal factor present) and normal counseling. Results indicated that, in terms of learning about one's self, each of the three methods produced some significantly greater performances. Generally, students preferred normal counseling, but they learned as much from programmed counseling. Studies of automated counseling have demonstrated the value of programmed assistance in certain kinds of planning and decision-making interviews. While the personal factor is still a relevant consideration in this type of counseling, apparently it is not as necessary as previously thought.

Decision and Choice Theory

While computers are aids in making predictions and plans, they also contain possibilities for developing models of the decision-making process. Programming is difficult unless objectives and a predictive system with alternatives and relevancy weights for each choice are determined. Gelatt (183), for example, holds high hopes for counseling applications from decision and games theory developed in economics and mathematics. Counseling, especially of the planning type, needs more precise concepts and steps whereby significant life decisions are made.

A number of theories about how vocational choices are made by school-age youth have been developed. These are special variations of choice theory and will be reviewed in Chapter 14 in the context of educational and career counseling. Greenwald developed the view that all counseling focuses on decisions, even though feelings are important foci also. He has evolved an elaborate set of principles and strategies based on what he calls "decision therapy" (207).

Summary

This chapter maintains the view that counselors and psychotherapists should have a consistent and explicit theory of personality to guide their practice as scientist-practitioners in therapeutic psychology. Although there is no one theory of personality which is suitable to frame the practice of counseling and psychotherapy, each position has unique implications for practice. The various dynamic, behavioral, and existential models of personality can be drawn upon to help understand this unique client in this particular setting. Each counselor must assume responsibility for developing his own approach to counseling.

Actualizing Counseling and Psychotherapy: A Multidimensional View

This chapter title summarizes our views on a creative synthesis approach to counseling theory and human growth. The whole point to growth is to become one's true personhood, to realize all the potentials within one's self, that is, to continue actualizing into a responsible, fulfilled human being. In the preceding chapter we surveyed a variety of theories intended to achieve the goals of counseling and psychotherapy and described our creative synthesis approach. We emphasized that any one theory is not yet sufficiently comprehensive or systematic enough to guide the counselor through the multitudinous problems met in everyday practice. Therefore, a multidimensional view is described.

As counselors grow, their theory progresses. The intuitive dynamic and existential theories become integrated with objective rational action approaches. The historical depth model of personality, which stresses inner drives and impulses to action, becomes reconciled with theories which emphasize the individual's present perceptual matrix, rationality, and conditioned behaviors.

We have struggled with the problem of devising a parsimonious, yet multidimensional, approach to counseling which involved selection of concepts that would hold up with growth, crisis, and prevention models, or which were at least workable for the majority of our clients. The selection of a personality model which had consistency for the universe in which we worked, and the selection of techniques which fitted our personalities, gave us a vocabulary and a frame of reference within which to verbalize, communicate, and test our observations about counseling relationships.

This chapter is our effort to make the events of counseling and psychotherapy more understandable to us, and we hope more understandable

3

to the reader. We have discovered that it is much easier to develop a point of view for a restricted clientele in a special setting than a theory for counseling in general. Yet we know from our teaching and conferring with colleagues that most counselors work in settings with wide varieties of human problems requiring a multidimensional dynamic theory and a flexible approach to methods.

Other theories have made their unique and rich contributions to our thinking, for which we are grateful. We have added reflections, however, from our combined experiences in counseling and psychotherapy over a broad spectrum of clients and settings. Figure 9 represents perceptions of the current state of our thinking in reference to other wide and over-lapping categories of theory. Major conceptual contributions to actualizing counseling flow from Gestalt psychology, an aspect of the phenomenological view. Perls' ideas about perception, awareness, and encounter in the present moment are examples. The humanistic contributions of Maslow on self-actualization, May on human encounter, Rogers on sensitivity to feelings, and Jourard on transparency and self-disclosure are central also. Behavioral views such as those of Krumboltz,

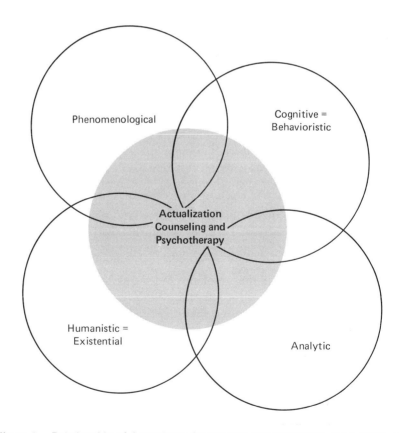

Figure 9. Relationship of Actualizing Counseling and Therapy to Four Overlapping Historical Approaches

Lazarus, and Bandura emphasize behavior reinforcement and specificity of client goals. These views are important for actualizing counseling because they focus on problem-solving and actualizing goals desired by clients. Analytic views have made their impact in the form of levels of functioning, with special focus on the ego, and the phenomenon of defense.

Counseling and Psychotherapy

Introduction

The principal tenet of actualizing counseling is progressive awareness and growth toward the actualized person. This growth process stresses responsible social action within a self-fulfilling framework. The term "actualization" was used originally by Goldstein (197) to describe the becoming process of the organism. We use Maslow's and Goldstein's concept as a departure point, emphasizing the process term "actualizing."

Multidimensional Scope of the Actualizing Model

A *developmental* or *historical* approach is a facet of actualizing counseling. As indicated in Chapter 2, there is considerable disagreement on the necessity for including an historical depth approach in one's conceptual framework; but we feel that even though our focus is on the present and the future, inclusion of a time dimension is very important to help the client understand the present and predict the future.

Each developmental stage has its unique problems and learnings which form the seeds of future problems. The counselor may work with the client at a particular historical level of development in the actualizing process in addition to immediate concerns. Thus, diagnostic statements are more meaningful as they are viewed in the context of a continuous growth process.

A *contemporary perceptual* approach is equally important, since we must know the client's unique outlook on his or her life at this moment in time. We need to know not only their current world view, but also perceptions of their immediate life space—not others' interpretations of it. Actualizing counseling, therefore, has a here and now phenomenological quality as a fulcrum on which the actualizing process turns.

An *action* or *behavioral* focus is central to actualizing counseling also, since it is behavior we wish to change, and not an illness we wish to cure. With this key assumption it behooves the actualizing counselor to become knowledgeable about behavior change concepts such as conditioning, reinforcement, generalizing, and others outlined in Chapter 2 to mobilize the client into constructive action. Actualizing counselors work with data in the solution of human problems and must have a rationale for including significant behavioral data from tests, for example, in helping the person predict and plan directions for actualization.

Because of the broad context in which most counselors and psycho-therapists perform their helping functions, we feel strongly that a multi-dimensional approach must be utilized in maximizing their helpfulness. Frequently counselors must approach clients on a wide front, utilizing many interacting modalities of feeling, cognition, sensation, imagery, and action. For maximum effectiveness, however, it appears that counselors must focus on one or two modalities at one time, drawing on numerous techniques to reach client goals. For example, a counselor may focus on expression of feeling during the early stages, use fantasy to facilitate expression, move to a desensitization method to assist with management of specific fears, model new behaviors through role playing, interpret growth goals according to the polarity hypothesis, and set up a schedule of rein-forcement to perpetuate new adaptive behaviors over the next few months. We are fully aware of the difficulties in attempting integration of the broad spectrum of theoretical views of personality and behavior change, but we are convinced that this task needs continuous effort by every counselor.

We see five dimensions comprising the actualizing point of view. A *philosophical* dimension is an essential consideration because of the em-phasis on goals of actualization. We have a model of the kind of person who evolves in this growth process. This model incorporates a series of value judgments about the human condition and the nature of reality. The *structural* dimension, a schematic conceptualization of personality organization, is a kind of cognitive map for viewing the actualizing process in a given moment of time. Closely related is the *dynamic* dimension, which emphasizes basic processes of growth and motivation. A *develop-mental* dimension includes much of what we know about human develop-ment.

Finally, a *research* dimension is essential to an enterprise as new and dynamic as actualizing counseling and psychotherapy. The actualizing counselor is a true scientist as described in Chapter 2. Counselors are curious, critical, truthful, logical, objective, and precise in this role, as opposed to their more subjective emotional functioning as a participant in the client's actualizing process. The actualizing counselor must strive to reconcile these frequently contradictory roles through employing them in a kind of synergic alternating of awareness, or as a check and balance system. We feel strongly that an overemphasis in either direction is not appropriate at this stage of development in actualizing counseling. Maslow has approached this problem in depth through his extended essay *The Psychology of Science: A Reconnaissance* (308), recommended to the reader for more ideas on reconciling these conflicts.

The Philosophical Dimension

Counseling and psychotherapy, being such deeply human growth processes, constantly face questions of what values and goals to promote, how free the individual is or should be, and how much influence the actualizing counselor should have on client values. These questions will be discussed more extensively in Chapter 6 on the actualizing counselor as a valuing person. The purposes of this section, however, are to emphasize the importance of the counselor's philosophy and to present some philosophical assumptions underlying actualizing counseling. The vastness of this subject requires restating that this discussion is illustrative and does not do justice to the importance and complexity of this topic.

Assumptions of Actualizing Counseling. Actualizing counseling is based in part upon the following assumptions:

1. Each person is a *unique human being* seeking actualization, even though he shares much "human nature" in common with others. A better term is Buber's "particularity" principle, a unique "thou" seeking to be realized.
2. While the actualizing principle has a futuristic quality in the "becoming" sense, it takes place in the *moment-to-moment growth* process. Hence, the "here and now" becomes the temporal focus of the process.
3. While much of man's behavior is determined by his personal history and forces beyond his control, the actualizing process assumes that his future is largely undetermined and that he has wide ranges of *freedom to choose.*
4. The assumption of freedom places corresponding *responsibility* on the person for his own actualizing. He cannot depend upon others or blame others for his growth or lack of it. Even though growth takes place in a social context, he alone is responsible for his life.
5. While some primitive behaviors are reflexive, hence largely genetically determined, and some are the result of chemical or neurological changes, a fundamental assumption of actualizing counseling is that *social behavior is learned* and changes in behavior follow an active learning process.
6. Actualization is not achieved by direct determined thinking, meditation, or reading about the goals of growth, but in *social interaction* with a counselor, teacher, minister, group, friend, or family. The social interaction becomes the vehicle for the conditions of actualization such as honesty with feelings, awareness of self, freedom of expression, and trust in one's self and others. We must press beyond awareness into action.
7. Each personality contains the paradoxical state of *polar opposites* which are expressed and forced to awareness and action in the actualizing process. Examples are dependence and independence, affection and aggression, support and criticalness.

Goals of Actualizing Counseling and Psychotherapy. A philosophy of counseling must contain some indications of outcomes expected from the growth process. The following statements of personality growth are just that—ideals of the ongoing actualizing process and not fixed quantitative end points. While some of these goals are preludes to more remote growth stages and could be organized in a hierarchy such as Allport's and Maslow's schemas, we prefer at this point merely to list and describe some of our objectives of Actualizing Counseling and Therapy.

There are three kinds of goals. The first is a category of *process goals,* which are means toward broader actualization. Examples are free spontaneous verbalization, and continued working through of problems. *Client goals* are the manifest purposes of the client's initial search for help. Examples are reduction of anxiety, desire for information, removal of annoying symptoms, making a crucial decision, or easing a situational pressure. Clients do not come initially asking to be "actualized." *Actualizing goals*, however, are broader, more generalized growth outcomes than solutions to immediate problems. It should be emphasized that these actualizing goals are tied closely to social values and the kinds of behaviors required to live effectively in Western culture. In another sense, these goals are characteristics of a theoretical model personality which would seem to "fit" Western cultural settings. This statement does not imply that psychological counseling or therapy leads necessarily to passive adjustment or to conformity. The principal emphasis is upon developing the individuality of the client, at the same time helping him to see his social responsibilities for contributing to, and possibly changing, the culture about him.

1. Independence. The end point of any counseling effort is to help the client to become self-sufficient and to minimize his dependence on his physical and social environment. The client should be able to act decisively on the basis of increased awareness.

2. Spontaneity. Various phrases are used as synonyms for this goal, such as freedom to be, flexibility in meeting change, openness to one's own and others' experience, and reduction of rigidity. Spontaneity may be construed as the polar opposite of defensiveness. Rogers (387) describes this characteristic as "increasing openness to experience." The world of experience for the client is no longer threatening. His picture of himself is more congruent with the way he is seen by others; therefore, he need not defend himself as strenuously as he did before counseling.

There are objective indices of such a characteristic as spontaneity on psychological instruments. Rorschach protocols, for example, show how spontaneity follows as the constrictive control indices decline. Flexibility takes its place. Shostrom's *Personal Orientation Inventory* (435) has a spontaneity scale which measures this quality.

As a result of the decrease in defensiveness, the client is better able to perceive reality as defined by others. There is less rigidity of perception and less need to distort or narrow perceptions in the direction of delusions. As Rogers says:

He sees that not all trees are green, not all men are stern fathers, not all women are rejecting, not all failure experiences prove that he is no good, and the like. He is able to take in the evidence in a new situation, *as it is*, rather than distorting it to fit a pattern which he already holds (387, p. 16).

A close relative of spontaneity is a concept called "tolerance for ambiguity." One can live comfortably with value and factual conflicts or unclear situations. One can hold beliefs in a tentative fashion while sifting conflicting evidence. One is not compulsively bound to seek definiteness in all things.

Another related term used by Rogers is "getting behind the mask." Successful counseling results in dropping the facade, the mask, or the role. One becomes more genuinely one's true self. In Jungian terms the "persona" decreases. As one of Rogers' clients put it, "I haven't been really honestly myself, or actually known what my real self is, and I have been just playing a sort of false role" (387, p. 11). It should be emphasized that one retains some of one's defenses and roles.

Counselors are not trying to "standardize" personalities in psychological counseling. Actualizing counselors strive to help the individual appreciate his uniqueness, providing the unique qualities are not maintained at too high a price. There is also value in the client's appreciation of the other person's "particularity" and realization that people are basically alike in many ways. They have similar hopes, feelings, and thoughts, though their various roles and "persona" characteristics often make them appear to be vastly different.

Creativity is one consequence of spontaneity. Analytic psychotherapists, especially Jungian ones, place great stress upon developing a creative personality. According to analytic therapists, the client is able to use more of his unconscious feelings as servant rather than as master. Much of the energy heretofore used to defend feelings is now released to the other systems for the client to use more creatively. Maslow (307) postulates that all humans are given this creative potentiality at birth, but that they lose it through the process of acculturation. The creative impulses must not be thought of necessarily as being applied to the arts, as in writing or music, but in more humble circumstances of everyday life. One can be a creative clerk, craftsman, teacher, or homemaker.

3. *Living Here and Now.* By this phrase is meant an increasing tendency to live each moment fully. The client tries to live so as to extract the richness of every moment. One does not try to anticipate life with too many ready-made answers. Rather, each moment is new; what one will do with that moment is something creative, hence, unpredictable. His value structure, which is part of his basic individuality, will assist him to act appropriately. As Rogers says in his reflective paper on the *fully functioning personality*, the individual is "dependable but not predictable" (393, p. 11).

The client, in terminating psychological counseling or psychotherapy, feels as if the job is not done, but just beginning. It is as if he were on the right train, not exactly knowing where he was going, yet feeling that he was moving in the right direction. One is in closer contact with one's own feelings and goals, and is more aware of social values and goals. One does not, however, approach a new situation with a rigidly preformed structure. One's personality is flexible and the defensive walls permeable. One can, thereby, make possible modifications of inner structures from each new experience. One is satisfied in the feeling that one never quite "arrives."

Rogers (393) points out in his discussion of the fully functioning person that such a person enjoys an activity for the pleasure of doing it, not necessarily because it is a means to an end. Our American culture puts great stress on the value of *means* toward ends, and not enough stress, in our opinion, on the *ends* themselves. Some people, for example, feel it is necessary to rationalize golfing because it is good for their health—they get sunshine and air—and do not admit that the act of golfing itself is pleasurable.

Rogers' summary of his philosophical paper entitled A *Therapist's View of the Good Life* emphasizes the significance of a philosophy based on awareness and acceptance of one's own nature:

I believe it will have become evident why, for me, adjectives such as happy, contented, blissful, enjoyable, do not seem quite appropriate to any general description of this process I have called the good life, even though the person in this process would experience each one of these feelings at appropriate times. But the adjectives which seem more generally fitting are adjectives such as enriching, exciting, rewarding, challenging, meaningful. This process of the good life is not, I am convinced, a life for the faint hearted. (It involves stretching and growing, becoming more and more of one's potentialities. It involves the courage to be. It means launching oneself fully into the stream of life. Yet the deeply exciting thing about human beings is that when the individual is inwardly free, he chooses as the good life this process of becoming) (399, p. 13).

4. Trust. Clients terminating successful psychotherapy have certain attitudes toward themselves which may be characterized as "self-confidence" or "self-worth." One trusts one's self and one's judgment. In deciding what course of action to follow in any question, one does not necessarily rely on rules, common-sense aphorisms, or mandates laid down by institutions or "Emily Post." Rather, one trusts one's judgment and does what feels right or appropriate—all things considered.

The last phrase, "all things considered," should be emphasized. The confident, self-directive individual does not just act impulsively or whimsically. As Adler points out, one considers consequences. One thinks, for example, of one's social responsibility. One trusts one's own inner promptings rather than depending exclusively upon external motivation to behave. One believes in one's self, as well as in other persons and institutions.

The stringent controls of the character level are relaxed so as to make their modification more possible. The authors incorporate the concept of "conscience" or the Freudian "superego" as part of the character level. The earlier learnings from parents regarding social values are more amenable to critical examination and alteration after a course of successful psychotherapy.

The authors are indebted to Rogers (399, p. 8) for an illustration of how the process of achieving self-trust and confidence might work in a client. We can compare the personality to a gigantic computing machine. Since the client is now more open to his experience, more data from his present situation as well as the extensive data from his past learnings are available to him. Since he is interacting more completely with his environment at any point, he has more access to data from within and without. The client can more properly evaluate and select relevant data for the solution of his present problem. We feel that one reason people err in judgment is that they include data which do not belong to the present context and exclude data which do. Thus, people who exclude data from their present situation and react only in terms of memories and stereotypes from previous learnings, as if they were this reality, are in trouble. Prejudice functions this way. Or, conversely, people who react to present situations without the benefit of past experiences may be in trouble as well. The present data may be "punched on the tape" in distorted form. All reliable data are needed to produce the most appropriate answers to life problems.

Operating in the spontaneous, self-trusting manner cited above does not mean a client will avoid errors. But it is hypothesized that such a client will correct errors due to omitted or distorted data without guilt or self-punishing defenses. Learning to trust one's feelings, as well as one's intelligence and experience, is a difficult state to achieve. Many people tend to want direction from without, to be dependent upon someone else to tell them what to do and how to do it.

Learning to express one's feelings—to live them—is stressed by many writers of psychological literature. Fromm (172), for example, emphasizes that the client "becomes alive" to his feelings. Knowing one's real feelings, expressing them in individually and socially satisfying ways is an extension of the psychotherapeutic process of uncensured emotional experiencing when the client *is* his anger, his fear, or his love. This experience of learning to like and trust one's self is one meaning of self-realization—of becoming a real person.

5. *Awareness.* A primary objective of actualizing is increased awareness, a sense of aliveness and responsiveness. One can perceive and appreciate one's environment freshly and more deeply. One has more of what Maslow (307) calls "peak experiences," those intense emotional experiences accompanying life activities. This awareness includes experiencing the full range of behavioral possibilities in each of the polarities of existence. An especially troublesome polarity in human experience is the masculinity-femininity dimension. In Western, particularly American, culture the male is expected to behave in special stereotyped ways, and females likewise. Bem (42) cites her research to validate the numerous

ways this dichotomy creeps into our culture; and she gives her rationale for androgynous behaviors where males can exhibit traditional female traits such as tenderness and females can be assertive in the traditional male fashion.

After becoming more aware of their innermost feelings over a long period of time, clients experience a greater range and a finer differentiation of feelings. They find that they do not live merely in terms of their intellects, but that they can experience feelings also. They can courageously and joyfully experience communication with more varied feelings. Again we quote Rogers' observations on this point:

> It seems to me that clients who have moved significantly in therapy live more intimately with their feelings of pain, but also more vividly with their feelings of ecstasy; that anger is more clearly felt, and so also is love, that fear is an experience they know more deeply, but so is courage. And the reason they can thus live fully in a wider range is that they have this underlying confidence in themselves as trustworthy instruments for encountering life (399, pp. 13–14).

Occasionally the phenomenon is called "freedom from emotional constriction." This means the capacity to experience a greater range of feelings without consequent threat.

Brown (72) expresses the experiencing of increased range of feeling in another way. He suggests that one goal of psychotherapy is to help the client to love more easily and to hate more wisely. Occasionally clients come who can express only positive feelings, having been forbidden to express hostile feelings at home. It has been our observation that the necessity to suppress expression of the negative feelings tends to have a constricting effect on the expression of positive feelings also.

Finally, the reduction of painful anxiety is a criterion of successful psychotherapy. The client is relieved of incapacitating guilt and anxiety so that the uncertainty and insecurity he felt formerly are replaced with more certainty and optimism.

6. Authenticity. Being one's genuine person in relations with others is a way of expressing authenticity. Becoming more authentic through actualizing counseling is one way to overcome the alienation, loneliness, and meaninglessness felt by many people.

7. Responsible Action. Actualizing persons make judgments which enhance their own welfare and that of others. Their spontaneity, freedom, and expressiveness are controlled and limited to the extent that they live in a real social world where consideration of others, commitment to family and work, and contribution to social good become a large part of their lives. They have the courage to resist social demands and trends which run counter to their own lives, however, and do not blame others for their adverse conditions. They take responsibility for their own choices and utilize their own style of problem-solving.

The mature client can postpone and modify decisions about others at this moment in this situation. The latter idea is often called a "time-binding" facility with which the client is better able to postpone pleasures and goals. For example, the graduate student undergoes much immediate sacrifice and strain to reach the satisfactions of a distant professional goal.

While much actualizing behavior is concerned with inner development of pleasure and fulfillment, active outgoing interpersonal contact is equally significant. This focus includes an activist stance which concentrates on enhancing others' welfare and serving as an advocate for the weak, helpless, alienated, and deprived. This role also means functioning as a force for community change by attempting to transform community norms, attitudes, and behaviors to those more in line with the actualizing goals cited above.

8. *Effectiveness.* While overlapping and summarizing many of the actualized characteristics above, the goal of increased human effectiveness is central to actualizing counseling. Effectiveness in living is related to developmental stages to be described later in this chapter, since effectiveness is defined in terms of the expectancies and skills the person possesses at his or her particular stage in life. The actualizing person meets life's demands effectively at each of his or her developmental stages.

The list above is not exhaustive of actualizing goals. Empirical studies of ideal growth have been made by investigators such as Maslow (307), with his "self-actualized young persons," and Shostrom (435), with his *Personal Orientation Inventory* with dimensions of self-actualizing. Much of the counseling, mental hygiene, and existential literature is replete with statements of ideal maturation for our culture. Mental health is a term to describe this ideal mature state. Jahoda (244) developed six key criteria after reviewing the extensive literature on mental health. These are:

1. Attitude toward himself.
2. Degree of realizing self-actualization potential through action.
3. Integration of personality function.
4. Autonomy or independence of social influence.
5. Perception of reality.
6. Taking life as it comes and environmental mastery.

Key problems for counselors are to find empirical indicators of the above criteria and then to specify the conditions for achieving them.

The Structural and Dynamic System of the Actualizing Model

The following outline of personality structural and functional dimensions is presented as an example of a way of conceptualizing the actualizing process. Several basic concepts characterizing this model will be described, followed by a detailed listing of functions and actualizing goals for each of the levels. The personality model which we espouse is from the original work entitled *Actualizing Therapy* (432) by Shostrom, Knapp, and Knapp. Readers interested in a more complete analysis should consult that volume.

Levels in a System. Five levels—¹facade, ²actualizing, ³manipulative, ⁴character, and ⁵core—are shown in Figure 10. They are hypothesized as interlocking energy systems with their unique functions to perform for the person. They represent rough levels of awareness from high awareness on the exterior to low awareness at the core level. The term "system" is used to denote the dynamic interactive characteristic of these functional levels, rather than to imply a static and rigid hierarchy of functions, or a structured topographical personality "map."

Dynamic. This is a key concept because it denotes the unstable changing character of the personality system. There is constant movement along

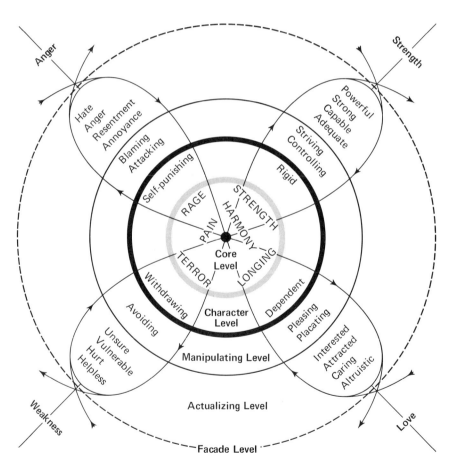

Figure 10. An Actualizing Model. Adapted from E. L. Shostrom, L. Knapp, and R. Knapp, *Actualizing Therapy* (432, p. 137).

the polarities in an interweaving fashion among the various levels. This idea is represented in Figure 10 as arrows moving across levels. The rhythmic flow through the levels of the model means that one can move freely from one level to another or begin awareness processes at one level and move to another, according to client need or situational demand. This idea does not imply a depth conception, as in psychoanalytic models, but rather the client's freedom to work at the most relevant level of the moment.

Another dynamic aspect, furthermore, is the current skepticism regarding the validity of the idea of stable traits of personality. It appears from Mischel's (328) extensive review of the personality literature and his own research that personality is such a determined function of the person and his situation of the moment that we cannot make valid generalizations about the stability of traits.

The term "dynamic" implies the action element so central to the Actualizing model. We assume that awareness is moving continuously from vague experiencing into active behavior change in the direction of the client's specific goals and the general actualizing goals cited earlier.

Energy. It is assumed that energy is a characteristic of all personality levels and provides the motivational force impelling the person to action. It is predicated upon a biologically based need system. It is postulated that energy flows freely among the levels in the system. All levels are "grounded" in the body where feelings are expressed in the musculature.

Polarities. The Actualizing model attempts to come to grips with one of the baffling issues in counseling, *viz.,* the paradoxes inherent in the idea of feeling polarities. The idea of polarities in existence is an old one— for example, the idea that if dependence is a pronounced characteristic, a dormant independence opposite is present also. Leary (280) brought the concept of polarities and continua of polar characteristics to the center of personality theory. This concept of polarities is central to Actualizing Counseling and Therapy because we think that helping the client to become more aware of these polar traits and to accept their seemingly contradictory functions in our lives is a key actualizing goal. One of the additional goals, furthermore, is to develop both poles in the service of the person. In Maslow's research on self-actualizing people (307), he found that they could express anger or tender love with ease. They were competent and strong, yet were aware of their weaknesses. In Figure 10 only four polar points, with illustrative feelings, are included for the sake of simplicity and because we regard these four points of anger-love and strength-weakness as key polarities. Others, such as dominance-submission, masculinity-femininity, dependence-independence, are significant also. The descriptive terms along the polar continua express the polar characteristics for that level of personality, for example, actualizing on the weakness pole has unsure and helpless feeling qualities.

Facade Level. This level is defined as a permeable boundary between the actualizing level and contact with the interpersonal world. This permeability, indicated by a dotted line in Figure 10, varies with the person's needs for defense or freedom of contact. Openness to others, for example, can be thought of in terms of permeability of the facade.

The principal functions of the facade level are to *defend* the person from psychological threats from without; to "hide" feelings at the other personal functioning levels from others and to present a "public image" or impression. The facade functions are controlled largely by the manipulating or managing level. Here, the defensive functions, such as projection, deception, denial, and manipulation, are initiated. These defensive functions are learned in the process of development and become quite automatic, even though partially under the control of the manipulating level. They are part of our "programming" for survival.

An objective of the actualizing process is to make the person more aware of facade level functions, to make defensive maneuvering functions more serviceable to the person, and to place them more under the control of the actualizing level. For example, "game" behavior, as Berne (47) defined it, has a deceptive or manipulative effect on others and has many "payoffs" for the person, such as social advantage and satisfaction of aggressive needs at the expense of others. Actualizing processes attempt to put these functions in juxtaposition with actualizing behaviors so the person can make some basic adaptive and rational choices and achieve some balance in expression of his polarities. Another goal is to achieve some measure of congruence between the public image put forth at the facade level and the private images one has of one's self at other levels. An example of such a discrepancy would be the person's behavior at a cocktail party. Here, the manipulative type of person responds in terms of what others expect rather than in terms of his private feelings. In other words, open, flexible, and congruent facade functions are the basic goals.

Actualizing Level. This is the first level of awareness in the system. First, it serves an *objectifying function* such that the person can look at himself as both subject and object. That is, he can get outside of himself to observe himself as an object. Thus, it has many functions of an ego system in the analytic models. It is the equivalent of the "I" or "me" of everyday language. In the objectifying function, the actualizing level also is the locus of rationality and ordering of experience.

Through its rational functions, the actualizing level performs a type of filter effect for selecting stimuli to which the person will attend. This actualizing function includes symbolizing and externalizing much of the feeling which comes from the other levels within the system. As a symbolizing agent, the actualizing level helps the person to rationalize conflict by attempts to reduce apparent inconsistencies. Hence, the actualizing level contains the major integrating force.

1.Thus, one of the important related functions of the actualizing level is construing the world in a manner so as to make perceptions "fit." Following the above-mentioned symbolizing and filtering functions, this system organizes and attaches meanings to current sensations in light of past experiences. The actualizing system also compares perceptions with past experiences and data from the other levels.

When the actualizing level is functioning in the ways described above, which are effective and satisfying for the person, it is said that one has a "strong" actualizing system. The person is perceiving events as accurately as possible with his unique experience background. He is aware of a feeling of competence to master both internal and external pressures and to reconcile polarities. He is also aware of a feeling of value and individuality which is a goal in the actualizing process.

2. A second important function of the actualizing level is *action*. Many of the problem-solving, decision-making, and energy-mobilizing functions of the person have their locus here, as well as in the manipulating level, to be described next. The actualizing level is the locus of activity in the person, where actualizing behaviors are focused and find expression in interpersonal contacts.

3. A third function is serving as a vehicle for *expression of feeling*, usually in contact with others. In Figure 10, it may be noted that these feelings follow the axis of the polarities and are characteristic in both kind and intensity of the actualizing level. The aim in the actualizing process is to facilitate the active expression of basic polar feelings freely and appropriately. A function of the actualizing level is to translate the feelings in nonfunctional or dysfunctional forms from other levels such that the actualizing goals of the person are achieved. This is accomplished in the rhythmic style described earlier and illustrated with arrows in Figure 10.

Manipulating Level. The chief function of this level in the system is to manage or control the person for purposes of protecting the person, manipulating others, gaining support from the environment, or coping with environmental demands. A key synonym for manipulating would be "managerial," since one consequence of this level of functioning in interpersonal events is that the other person feels controlled. The manipulator functions without much feeling. This nonsensitivity to others is understandable, since the main function of the managing level is to protect the person. An overemphasis on this function leads to a "thick-skinned" protective reaction which is perceived by others as insensitive and rigid. A counselor may say, for example, "Are you aware that your need to defend yourself sometimes hurts people and shuts off their caring about you?" (From here the counselor works on specific actions the client can take to loosen his behaviors and increase his contact skills.)

Character Level. This level functions as an identity base for the person. The basic personal styles, or character patterns, are stylized ways of responding to the world. For example, in terms of the basic polarities of the Actualizing model, a character style would be the typical personal patterns of handling hostility, dependency, and rejection or acceptance of others. Much of the reaction is experienced by the musculature in the form of tenseness or by organ dysfunction, such as colitis. Holding back on feelings, for example, is associated with muscular rigidity.

Another function of the character level is to provide a definition of self, that vague, undifferentiated part of the person which one defines as the "real me" or the "self." It is a learned pattern of responses to characteristic life situations which are expressed in the form of stereotyped responses along the polarity dimensions. As in the manipulating level, the character level performs essentially negative protective functions. The challenge of actualizing is how can one's basic character structure be made over sufficiently to act in the service of actualizing the whole person, instead of maintaining essentially stereotyped responses? The level of awareness of the person in regard to the character level is usually low. One of the goals of the actualizing process is to loosen the boundaries between the core and actualizing levels so that the basic character of the person can be modified sufficiently to serve the actualizing goals of that person. This process means taking risks so that the manipulating level can release sufficient controls to allow change to take place. This loosening process can be monitored to a limited degree by keeping in touch with body developments. For example, as the control and caution needs lessen, the body can loosen. Muscular rigidity is the body's way of communicating that the person does not consider that release of feelings or revelation of core polarities is safe.

Core Level. This center of the person is the locus of basic feelings and what the man-in-the-street calls "human nature." Paradoxically, the core has the common elements of feeling polarities which characterize all human beings; at the same time, it defines the uniqueness of a person. It is the center of one's existence and has the function of providing a harmonious and satisfying home in a world of loneliness and isolation from others; or it can be a living "hell on earth" of accumulated painful feeling experiences of which one is only vaguely aware.

We have been impressed over the years with people's basic need for privacy—a place in their existence which is uniquely their own. We view the main function of the core, then, as providing this center of one's existence where the vectors of many polar feelings cross. It is here that much of the painful hurt of the past is experienced. It is often expressed in deep longing for contact as, "Why wasn't I loved?" or in a form of rage as, "Why wasn't I given the freedom to be?" Sometimes, an awareness of being rejected is experienced as betrayal. Core pain is thus a basic reaction to the denial of the person's fundamental right to exist as a person. The actualizing process consists, in part, then, of aiding the person to be aware of those feelings of hurt and denial, to own them, and to take responsibility for actualizing himself or herself to the point of effective and satisfying living.

The core level is the locus of experiencing positive and strong qualities also. These qualities are expressed frequently as awareness of well-being, harmony, peace, confidence, worth, beauty, oneness with nature or with the universe. One goal of the actualizing process is to bring these feelings to awareness and to reinforce them with actualizing level behaviors which validate the positive core feelings.

We view the core level, therefore, as being neither positive nor negative from an external judging point of view. It is much like Fromm's description of the unconscious, which he describes as follows:

In Freud's thinking the unconscious is essentially that in us which is bad, the repressed, that which is incompatible with the demands of our culture and of our higher self. In Jung's system the unconscious becomes a source of revelation, a symbol for that which in religious language is God Himself. In his view the fact that we are subject to the dictates of our unconscious is in itself a religious phenomenon. I believe that both of these concepts of the unconscious are one-sided distortions of the truth. Our unconscious—that is, that part of our self which is excluded from the organized ego—*contains both the lowest and the highest, the worst and the best* [italics ours.] We must approach the unconscious not as if it were a god whom we must worship or a dragon we must slay but in humility, with a profound sense of humor, in which we see that other part of ourselves as it is, neither with horror nor with awe. We discover in ourselves desires, fears, ideas, insights which have been excluded from our conscious organization and which we have seen in others but not in ourselves (175, p. 97).

The core level is a powerful motivating agent in the person, since it is from here that much of the energy for action stems. If our hypotheses are correct—i.e., that basic drives for security, sexuality, and aggression originate here through learned life experiences—then it is understandable what a dominating force the core could be in the personality. This is the case particularly in times of threat or crisis. The biological and anthropological evidence on the inferred nature of the core level is fragmentary and conflicting. Generally, people seem to come into this world with basically outreaching, cooperating, security-seeking need systems. In the normal processes of family life many frustrations and learnings are experienced which affect the person's basic outlook on life and himself. It is assumed, therefore, that the feeling propensities and characteristics of the core level are learned rather than inherited.

Since core feelings are learned, and work in such individualistic ways to influence the behavior of persons, it is difficult to generalize about "human nature." While some people seem motivated by "blind" pleasure and seek to minimize pain and effort, others appear to be motivated by challenge and search. One goal of the actualizing process is that persons seek meaningful activity and meaningful relationships to fulfill complex longings for worth and dignity. This goal and the value premise underlying it have profound political implications as we visualize a society which makes possible full actualization of its members.

A basic principle of the actualizing process is to open communication between the core and the actualizing levels of the person. One of the main methods is release of affect through talk, body sensory work, fantasy, or other projective method. The safety of a counseling relationship offers the person an opportunity to face the frightening feelings of rage, deep longing for contact, terror, or rejection and betrayal by trusted persons. This relationship offers opportunities for release of these feelings to awareness and the companion approach of taking responsibility for constructive action to change one's behavior. This awareness serves to prevent use of these past experiences and feelings as excuses for not realizing one's potential for growth. Often the labored expression of these painful core feelings with a caring helper results in feelings experienced as harmony, peace, and well-being. In terms of our postulate of system energy, this energy that was so bound to the core feelings is now released for constructive use at the actualizing behavior level. A basic principle of many therapy models, the Actualizing model included, is that release from emotional conflict equals available emotional energy for actualizing pursuits. This release of energy coupled with action methods for behavior change offers clients a wide spectrum of actualizing possibilities.

Developmental Dimension

In the following sections, significant events in the life of man are traced in order to place the process and goals in developmental perspective. This survey is not intended to be a comprehensive digest of growth and development literature. It has a strong psychoanalytic flavor because this group of theorists has given considerable attention to developmental stages and problems.

General Periods of Growth. Psychological growth occurs in two general stages: from birth to about thirty-five years, and from age thirty-five to death. The first mastery stage is one in which the individual has broad capacities for learning and adapting to his external environment and his internal needs and drives. His unfolding intelligence and his physical and emotional maturation are in his service to pursue countless goals which are both created and limited by his physical and cultural environment. In this stage, the individual develops habits to cope with parental demands; then pressures often mount to develop rational skills, acquire an education, enter and progress on a career.

At the end of this first stage, the individual's intellectual, physical, and emotional potentials have taken direction; habits have been formed; choices have been made; both mastery skills and a way of life have been developed. Following this stage of activity, the person begins to think of ways to consolidate his gains. He has in some fashion mastered the economic and social environment. Learning efficiency and physical strength begin to diminish. The goals of youth begin to be replaced by the goals of maturity and old age. He finds himself beginning to scrutinize his values and to look for a way of life that will support and reward him and those he loves until the end of life.

Basic Principles of Growth. Psychological growth has several general underlying principles. Growth is *progressive* and *cumulative;* that is, it moves by steps and through stages. Growth is *integrative* and *disintegrative;* that is, growth is a building- and fitting-together process as well as a tearing-down process. For example, childhood patterns must be disrupted before adult patterns can become operative. Psychological growth depends upon the twin principles of *maturation* and *learning.* Maturation implies a potential for development which unfolds under the proper stimulating conditions when the organism is ready to respond. Restrictive environments and restrictive adaptations of the individual, such as overly intense psychological threat and consequent defensiveness, inhibit psychological growth. Finally, psychological growth is dependent upon contact with people. It is believed that one reason why the helping relationship provides a powerful growth medium is that special optimum human relationship qualities prevail.

The principle that growth takes place through intimate human contact is highly significant for the helping professions. The relationship techniques discussed in Chapter 7 have the purpose of establishing an environment between the therapist and the troubled client to provide a maximum climate for growth. The capacity to love is perhaps the most important growth ingredient. Fromm, who has written extensively on the topic of love, asserts that, "Analytic therapy is essentially an attempt to help the patient gain or regain his capacity for love" (175, p. 87). He defines love as, ". . . the active concern for the life and growth of that which we love" (171, p. 26). In a similar vein, Sullivan says, "Love begins when a person feels another person's needs to be as important as one's own" (462, p. 246).

A principal quality of mature love is deep concern about the other person's welfare. We postulate that the experiencing of this kind of love from parents or their surrogates is necessary for normal growth. As will be seen in the following discussion of personality development, the experiencing and the expressing of love have special meaning for the psychological growth and health of the individual at every stage from infancy through old age. Paralleling this theme, an effort is made to show how psychological privation and frustration have differing consequences at different age levels.

Some therapists say that man becomes "ill" when the conditions for growth are not fulfilled. But the problems with which the counselor and client struggle are not so much "mental illness" as they are inhibition of normal growth processes. In an individual client, these growth problems may take one or both of two general forms. On the one hand, the person may be experiencing difficulties which are endemic to his particular age level. On the other hand, his problems inhibiting growth may be those which, considering his age and capacity, he should have mastered earlier.

Implicit in the above is the further postulate that the individual is the product of all those experiences which he has had until the time he receives counseling or therapy. Moreover, the experience to which he has been subjected in his early formative years determines, in large part, the type of adjustment that he will make at any later level of development. All individuals have "problems" in growing up. When these are solved successfully and successively, people are well equipped to progress in their psychological development. When the problems have been too threatening or too difficult to resolve, they falter in growth or develop a shield of defensive mechanisms which inhibits or distorts their creative potentials.

A Developmental View

The Dependency Stage (Birth to Two Years). It is largely through the feeding process that an infant interprets the nature of his environment. This is why Freud (168) called the first year of life the "oral period." If the mother's attitude is one of warm acceptance combined with prompt alleviation of the child's hunger, he experiences pleasurable feelings with his food. If he feels rejection or distance in his feeding relationships, he experiences anxiety and displeasure, for example.

The eating-sucking functions thus become closely allied to feelings of security. In this period the child develops a concept of what happens to people who are dependent. These may be lessons in security and love—or in the lack of them. When he is fed regularly and with accompanying warmth and affection, and is weaned gradually, he learns to tolerate frustration without excessive tension. It has become axiomatic in child-development theory that privations should not be too many, too early, or too sudden. When the dependency needs of this period are met and handled properly, the way is paved for natural development in the next stage. Harlow's studies (216) on deprivation of mothering in primates lends support to these generalizations.

For the child who experiences excessive frustration, deprivation, or inconsistency in this early oral period, there may be significant outcomes for personality development (166). Erikson (141) suggests that significant infant learnings of "trust" and "mistrust" grow out of early oral experiences. Buhler (78) refers to the period from birth to eight months as the stage of *mastery* in which the child learns the control of the body and its functions. Oral mastery would be one of these functions. The mastery of the dependency relationship to parents is another form of mastery.

Love at this stage is a primitive, relatively undifferentiated *dependency* need which is largely a matter of *receiving* from others. Thus, the feelings which the child experiences at the time when he is the recipient of food and other need fulfillments are crucial in the development of his personality. Although dependency gratifications predominate at this early oral stage, the seeds of growth problems can be sown if the stage is prolonged. The child must realize even at this early age that he is gradually growing away from the parent. The so-called reality principle needs to be introduced to the child early, in the form of weaning activities. Therefore, the optimum rhythmic balance between physical maturation and personal-social learning is maintained.

The Independence Stage (Two to Three Years). Between the ages of two and three, the child is still helpless in many respects. He has, however, a gradually increasing physical autonomy and begins to develop independence as he learns to walk and to manipulate things with his hands. Not only is he learning control of his movements, he is also beginning to differentiate more of the elements of his environment that are specific to his needs and pleasures; he becomes an explorer to satisfy his growing curiosity. As he senses his power, he begins to rebel more directly against restrictions and wants to make up his own mind about things.

The year from two and one-half to three and one-half is sometimes referred to as the "negative stage"—the "first adolescence." The child feels a growing sense of independence; his concept of selfhood is becoming apparent; adults seem to thwart him at every turn. Aggression and its management become a paramount problem.

Buhler sees the negativistic period as one in which the child "sits up" and tests other people's love. She describes the period from eight months to four years as the period of *relationships*, in which the child experiments or tries out one thing with another. In this period of independence, he tries out his self-determination needs and experiments with independence from mother. The child's first social achievement is to be able to let mother out of sight and to trust in her ability to return. Trust becomes an important growth variable.

Freud called this period the "anal" stage, since the first real clash between the child's need to be autonomous and parental discipline is associated with adult efforts to encourage the child's control of elimination processes. Freud suggested that the superego or conscience (concepts of right and wrong) develops out of this early period. Psychoanalysts suggest that harsh bowel or bladder training may predispose the child toward a rigid or strict conscience (148). Lack of parental assistance in learning these important values may predispose the child to a dearth of "conscience." "Compulsive-giving" in an adult is often traced back to the necessity of conforming during the anal period when the parent makes control of elimination equivalent to loving (148).

The management of aggression becomes a paramount problem at this stage. The parental problem, therefore, is one of channeling the child's aggression so that it is not unduly postponed, disguised, or displaced. Many adults in counseling and psychotherapy have problems in the management of their aggressive feelings because of improper handling by the parents at this early stage of development. For them, psychotherapy provides an outlet for *verbal* expression of hostility without the serious consequences of hurting others. The chronically intrapunitive individual is given opportunity to reevaluate his feelings of unworthiness or self-hate. Psychosomatic reactions, in the form of muscle tightness or illness, to bottled-up anger may be alleviated too. Psychotherapy also may permit the unhappily submissive or dependent person to discover the privilege of owning aggressive feelings and independence.

A goal of psychotherapy is to assist the adult to manage aggressions wisely. Through psychotherapy he can learn that it may be appropriate to express aggressive feelings in selected circumstances. He also can learn to perceive frustration in appropriate proportions. With major annoyances, where basic individuality is threatened, he may learn to channel his aggression into constructive action.

The Role-Taking Stage (Four to Six Years). Between the ages of four and six the child experiences a need for even greater freedom to match his increased motility and mastery of his environment. Curiosity and exploratory activities expand in many directions, and he begins to develop a conscience whose nature is in many crucial respects determined by the manner in which the parents relate to him.

An important development of the role-taking stage is that the child normally accepts his own sex through a process of identification with the sexually similar parent. Parents form the models from which children develop notions of "masculinity" and "femininity." It is natural for boys to develop attachments to the mother and girls to the father.

The important result of this developmental period is that the child emerges with a feeling of value toward, and acceptance of, his own sex. This is most optimally accomplished if the parent of the same sex is a model worthy of imitation. If father is comfortable in his masculine role, the son will want to be a man like his father and will not be afraid of this role. If mother is happy in her feminine role, the little girl can respect, admire, and desire to be like her. Current educational efforts to diversify sex roles and to modify traditional domestic and vocational stereotypes are likely to diminish the potency of traditional parental models.

During this stage of role-playing and extension of initiative, the parents have to exert practical controls which in turn assist the child in the development of a conscience. The kind and quality of these parental controls which are external to the child have important consequences both for the inner controls or conscience which the child develops and for the directions his initiative will take.

Spontaneity and independence are characteristics of the mature person; and if the child is defeated at this early stage in the struggle for freedom, he will very likely have laid the foundations for neurotic submissiveness later in life. As in other areas of life, overprotectiveness and rejective attitudes can complicate the child's progression through this childhood stage.

Buhler (78) sees the period from five to eight years as the *task phase*, in which the child learns to enjoy making things. When there are healthy parental concern and interest, the child develops "task consciousness"— a sense of responsibility to the task. It is for this reason that kindergarten becomes meaningful. Children can create and feel an ethical obligation to their creations as well as for their other activities.

Some Conclusions About Early Childhood Development. In counseling and psychotherapy there appear to be three major developmental problems with which the individual must deal: (1) the expression of affection and dependency; (2) the handling of hostility and aggression; and (3) the management of sexual tensions and sex identity. Each of these has its roots in the first six years of life. Affection has its roots in the dependency stage wherein the child is given love and security and learns that he must rely on others. In this stage it appears that he learns to give affection in kind. In the independence stage the child learns both that he has power and that he can handle his first frustrations. When the parent deals wisely with tantrums and aggressions, the child is given the means of managing acceptably his aggressive tendencies later in life. Finally, in the role-taking stage, patterns are established for effective relationships with the opposite sex so that satisfying heterosexual relationships are possible in later years.

The Conformity Stage (Six to Ten Years). The child enters for the first time a world which is not completely dominated by parents and siblings and is "on his own" for many hours. He is responsible to authorities other than his parents, a fact which may create more problems for the parents than for the child. The youngster is suddenly catapulted by the necessity of going to school into a peer group to which he must learn to conform and with which he must cooperate and share. The selection of friends is no longer restricted to the child's immediate neighborhood, and his intellectual and cultural interests widen as well. A typical nine-year-old's interests are multiple: dolls, bugs, dramatics, crafts, sports, games, and other group activities.

Children of both sexes continue their role-playing and tend to be more interested in the activities of their own sex than in the opposite sex. The differences in sexual roles become more apparent to them, and they strongly emulate the behavior of their friends in this and other areas. In many respects, this is a time in which many more and varied behaviors relative to their sexual role are being explored and learned.

In this conformity stage, the child continues to need love, understanding, and judicious discipline combined with freedom of initiative. As in earlier stages, the parents can provide a rich environment in which the child may learn and experiment with a wide variety of things and human relationships, as well as have a sense of belonging to a wider group than the family. Or the parents, through undue restriction, disinterest, or privation, may force the child into a narrow frustrating orbit in which he senses his difference from others. Hence, his expanding potentialities may be stifled or fixed in a stereotyped sexual role at this developmental stage.

The Transition Stage (Ten to Thirteen Years, Pre-Adolescence). During the pre-adolescent years from ten to thirteen, which Buhler (78) aptly calls the *transition* period, the child's world is shaken up. Two major developments which occur are efforts to break away from family domination and the maturing of sexual functions. The youngster's behavior is often characterized by irritability, restlessness, moodiness, backtalk, and other defiances which try the patience of those around him. He will often talk of running away—a symptom of his efforts to break away from the family. He also begins to experience an increase in heterosexual interests. His capacity to love, which hitherto has been qualified by dependency, identification, and narcissism, begins to change in the direction of mature love as defined earlier in this chapter.

Another important characteristic of this transition period is the remarkable feeling of separateness and individuality which is felt by the typical pre-adolescent. They become more aware of themselves as persons separate from their parents. Parental love at this stage is best expressed by a willingness to give up the child to himself and to respect him for his growing individuality. The fears and guilts which parents retain from their own pre-adolescent years make them fearful for their own children, and so hinder the parents from loosening the cord of emotional control and permitting the child to have his individuality.

The Synthesis Stage (Thirteen to Twenty Years, Adolescence). With the beginning of sexual maturity in the early teens, childhood comes to an end and youth begins. Because of rapid body growth and genital maturation, youth are faced with physiological and psychological revolutions within. Since they are chronologically approaching the age of adult responsibility, they become subject to increasing pressures and restrictions from without. Within this framework, youth relive their early conflicts and experience new conflicts in the struggle to find themselves in life.

Physical growth in adolescence is asynchronous, meaning that there are intra-individual differences in growth rates of various aspects of the body such as height, weight, circumference, hands, feet, and neck. Furthermore, sex differences in growth create special problems. Differential growth peaks are found within each sex. Some boys, for example, reach their peak physical growth as early as twelve years, whereas others may not reach their peak until seventeen years.

These individual and widely variant growth patterns create and complicate many problems. Erikson (141) refers to early adolescence as the "stage of identity" wherein the problem appears to be one of doubt as to one's sexual identity. Intra-individual asynchronous growth of body parts, differential growth peaks within each sex, and sex differences in rates of growth contribute to feelings of uncertainty regarding one's sexual identity. The feelings of inadequacy resulting from the "clumsiness" of uneven growth are well known. Many youngsters are subject to joking remarks from adults as well as from peers. They view their mirror images with alarm as they note any unexpected deviation in growth pattern or complexion. They become fussy and preoccupied with dress and behaviors which help them to identify with their peers. The youngsters who are late developers often resist public showers or other activities involving physical display because of feelings of physical unfitness.

Sex differences in rate of growth tend to drive the sexes apart from their own age groups. Junior high school girls, for example, usually desire the companionship of high school or older boys, because the boys of their same age are still "boys," whereas they in the meantime have developed into young women. The homosexual panic which some male adolescents experience between the ages of twelve and fifteen is related to several factors: (1) anxieties about heterosexuality which often develop at this time; (2) the need to exhibit male prowess, to show off through masturbatory activities; and (3) the opportunities for homosexual exploration which come in gangs.

Counseling can reduce the usual sexual identity anxieties of adolescents and help them realize that they are part of normal development at this period. For example, the problem may be traced to its source to determine in what way masculinity or femininity has not been made attractive, or it may relate back to developmental problems of middle childhood.

Our culture places difficult restrictions on the adolescent:

1. Parents have various forms of legal authority over adolescents until the age of twenty-one, and in some instances age eighteen. Because parents feel a sense of responsibility for the behavior of the adolescent, many tribulations ensue. Adolescents are thus in continued conflict; they want to be dependent, to have their needs cared for, and yet they want all the privileges that come with independence.

2. The adolescent is dependent on parents for economic support and requires help to get an education, a process which is getting longer and more costly.

3. Prohibitions against sexual gratification, alcohol, and drug use are sources of conflict. Boys of eighteen have reached a peak of sexual interest, but much of society frowns on gratification until marriage. Young people desperately want to know the solutions; but they are difficult to give.

With such demands and restrictions, adolescence becomes a natural period of rebellion. Youth need to be independent; they are often obstinate, hoarders, and interested in "dirty stories." They have strong genital interests, masturbate, and are narcissistic and exhibitionistic. It seems that adolescents must declare themselves autonomous even though it causes them and others pain. Both parents and youth need reassurance that the development of autonomy must take place if they are to mature to adulthood. The process can be made much less painful to all concerned if awareness is acquired before misunderstandings develop.

Later adolescence begins the period of adult responsibility with incomplete knowledge for handling that responsibility; consequently, it is a period of "collision" of retrospect and prospect. Buhler (78) describes this period as one of *synthesis* of the first four stages of life. Youths settle down to relating themselves to the larger system of society. They have needs to establish roles in religion, to go beyond the family outlook to a universe perspective, and to realize their own potentials in the world.

Buhler, perhaps more than any other psychologist, has been concerned with adolescence as a period in which one first raises the question, "What is life about, anyway?" For the first time teenagers see their lives as a unit from birth to death. They look backward as well as forward in an autobiographical fashion as a means to gain perspective.

If the question "What for?" makes this time so difficult, intense, and perplexing, it is the answers youth find which carry meaning into the periods of life that follow. Counseling relationships along with institutional relationships in community and youth organizations offer ideal opportunities for youth to work out tentative answers to perplexing questions of life.

Adolescence brings closer to fruition a mature capacity to love in those young people who successfully replace their idealized parental images. Adolescents learn to accept the idea that they can both love and hate the same person, that people have faults as well as assets. If dependency and independency needs assume healthy proportions, young people are in a position to look for partners with whom they can share life on a realistic and satisfying give-and-take basis.

The Experimentation Stage (Twenty to Thirty-Five Years). Buhler sees the ages from twenty-one to thirty as a "second try-out" period, similar to that which occurs between eight months and four years. For the first time, the young adult is completely independent, testing out areas of love and work. Since the selection of a mate and a career are two important decisions one makes, one needs an accumulation of experience to choose wisely. There is often a tendency to settle down too quickly in both of these areas. Parents and counselors can counteract impulsive decisions by assisting young people to experience many friendships and to try out several job opportunities.

During this experimental, or young adult, period of life, young people go through many significant experiences and life crises. The interesting thing about such experiences is that formal education does little to prepare the adult for these significant developmental tasks.

Early adulthood is a period of stress because it is the time of life which marks a transition from an age-graded to a social-status-graded society. Selecting satisfying intimate relationships is one of the most disquieting tasks in the early part of this period. It seems that little help can be given by parents or teachers. However, some assistance is given through courses in family life and through sexuality counseling. Unmarried persons in some cultural subgroups must cope with tremendous social pressure. They can be the objects of unnecessary attention and subtle ridicule, as well as of clumsy attempts at matchmaking. Furthermore, there are the serious problems of dating behavior. Shall one kiss or pet on the first date, for example? When shall one have sexual intercourse? Where can one get help with contraception? Group therapy often helps young people share such mutual problems. Under the leadership of a wise teacher or counselor, such groups often arrive at individually and socially satisfactory answers and tension release.

Preserving a satisfactory couple relationship is a complex problem. An important aspect of this problem is that the partners need to recognize that a contract or a formal marriage is not a fusion of two lives; each should accept the need for the other to maintain a healthy independence. Pregnancy and childbearing are problems not to be taken lightly. There is the question of acceptance or rejection of a pregnancy. Abortion is a frequent topic in psychotherapy. There are many anxieties during pregnancy, such as worry over possible failure to have a normal child, breast-feeding issues, and the anticipated reactions of relatives and friends to the pregnancy.

The current culture has created another problem by providing conflicting roles for a young wife, that of homemaker and career woman. If she desires both roles, she has a most complex challenge to do each task well. Increasingly, men are faced with this conflict as they take on more home responsibilities.

Divorce threats often plague the lives of young married people. Often it is not a solution and simply treats the symptoms of personal maladjustment. The divorcee still has most of the problems of the unmarried person plus many more.

The age of twenty-nine has particular relevance for women in our culture. There is much joking about the fact that women are allowed to stay twenty-nine for ten years. Signs of physical decline have much to do with this concern. Overweight often becomes a problem to which the success of slenderizing organizations bears witness.

The emphasis in our culture on productivity and achievement creates anxiety about performance and competitive concern about masculinity in men. Men of this age take pride in their ability to "take it" and will frequently push themselves to the limit to prove that they are not "weaklings." They hide their illnesses and deny fatigue. Emotions are concealed also.

The problems of young adulthood are largely neglected in the developmental literature. The age period from twenty-five to thirty-five, however, has many problems. It is a lonely period because the most important tasks of life must be accomplished with little attention and support. Because of their intense awareness of problems and the acute pressures for achievement, and because their general education and language development provide the ability to express their ideas cogently, this age group seems able to benefit more than others from counseling.

The Consolidation Stage (Thirty-Five to Fifty Years). About the age of thirty-five, a man enters the second major phase of life. In the first half, his energies, interests, and values have taken direction within his own personal and cultural milieu. The average man has accomplished his vocational goal by the time he reaches his middle thirties and is beginning to be comfortable financially. The woman experiences new freedom as the children begin to reach adolescence, since she no longer has to cope with them so diligently.

When one considers the many competitive demands made on the middle-aged adult, who often has restricted creative potentials and energy with which to meet them, it is no wonder that some unhappy individuals develop a paranoic pattern.

As a man enters the second half of life, it appears basic to his mental health that he recast his energies and values in directions which will reward him and his family to the end of life. He must, as in his early youth, turn inward and ask "What for?"

The dread with which a man anticipates his latter years is exemplified in the phenomenal success of Jack Benny's joking about his being "thirty-nine." The age of thirty-nine for men seems to be as critical as twenty-nine appears to be for women. Men and women at forty feel that they have "crossed the bridge" and are no longer young. Many men and women cannot accept this fact and go through a phase of intensive sexual experimentation and frantic efforts to look and act youthful.

The Involutional Stage (Forty-Five to Sixty Years). Between the ages of forty and fifty in women, and forty-five to sixty in men, a type of depression often develops. It occurs around the menopause or change-of-life in women. Men often experience depression when they are aware of a decline in virility. This reaction is caused not only by endocrine dysfunction, but also by psychological problems associated with this time of life. Buhler (78) likens the menopause period to adolescence. In both stages there is a physical and a psychological metamorphosis of the individual, his or her code of life, and consequent period of intense self-evaluation.

At the involutional stage of life, one may feel that he or she has passed the most productive period and that many ambitions, ideals, and goals will never be attained. Women, especially, feel that their beauty is fading fast, and their inability to bear children sometimes makes them feel that their life is spent. Old conflicts, successfully repressed during maturity, often are felt again.

This middle-adult period in men often is experienced as their "second adolescence." A man begins to feel that he is forgotten, that he is taken for granted as a family provider, and that his business security is threatened by younger competitors. At home, his children have grown to maturity and his wife has moved into the menopause. He worries about health, sexual adequacy, and "success." He defends himself in these situations by projecting to his wife the reasons for his dissatisfaction. She is blamed for his troubles. He believes she never did love or understand him. Often the next step is to find a "girl friend" who will provide for his fancied need for understanding and love.

In addition to family problems, the middle-aged man is concerned about job success. As part of the accelerated process of looking inward that occurs in the late thirties, he begins to evaluate himself as having been a "success" or "failure." Counseling and psychotherapy can help people to see the bases for their evaluations, and to realize that perhaps there are gradations or degrees of what is termed "success."

Erikson refers to this stage of life as "the stage of generativity" (141). By this, Erikson means that the adult can meet the many problems one must face by developing an interest in the leadership of young people and thereby satisfy a need for a parental type of responsibility. Buhler suggests that life can be thought of as increasing in significance and interest if the parent can identify himself "both with his own existence and with that of his offspring" (78, p. 184). For those without children, it appears important at this stage to develop opportunities for a kind of parent-surrogate role.

For one thing, love at this stage of life means being able to *give*, particularly to one's children. One form of giving, however, which should be avoided is that of projection. Parents during this stage often project the problems which they are reliving from their own adolescence onto their children. Even when all seems to go well in family life at this time, living with teenagers creates stresses and doubts about parental competence. In more authoritarian and stable periods in history, parents followed tradition. In this era, parents are understandably confused by uncertain freedom and authority.

For the woman in middle life, it is often suggested that she resume actively the role of *wife*, a role which has been of secondary significance during the years of childbearing. She can give new attention to her husband as a man, meet his needs for affection, understanding, and solitude. She may need to be more concerned about maintaining her own personal attractiveness and charm. The husband also needs to understand the special concerns of his wife as she goes through the menopause. Her condition should increase his genuine courtesy, attentiveness, and regard.

A final developmental task of this age is that of adjusting to aging parents. During this middle-life period, the individual finds himself at the center of a three-generation family. As the children grow to maturity and leave home, the grandparents become older and a charge of the home. They may need financial help or physical care. In general, neither generation wants to live with the other, and unresolved parent-child conflicts often are reactivated whenever two generations are forced to live together.

The Evaluation Stage (Sixty Years to the End of Life). Buhler compares the period from sixty to seventy-five again to adolescence, in which there is preoccupation with the past and the future. The individual is evaluating his life and often is also preoccupied with death.

At the age of 65, now widely recognized to be the age of retirement, the chances are great that the individual will still live another ten years. During this time of life, people usually experience decreased income, loss of spouse by death, or the illnesses of old age. The last item—illness—is a stark reality, since a considerable number of older people must adjust to a period of invalidism or degenerative disease.

Retirement today usually means a marked reduction in income since retirement plans established thirty years ago, when inflation was not present, are now inadequate to provide for comfortable living. This means that the luxuries of leisure, such as membership in fraternal organizations, can no longer be kept up at a time when they are most needed.

Since most women outlive men, by the late sixties there are in the average community as many widows as there are women living with their husbands. Learning to live alone again, to attend to business matters after forty years, is a difficult task to undertake.

According to Erikson, the period of later maturity is one of "ego integrity" or of despair, depending on the individual's adaptation to life. He claims that the possessor of integrity is ready to defend the dignity of his own life style. On the other hand, it is a period of despair if there is fear of death and the feeling that life was spent unwisely. He relates the period of adult integrity to the first stage of infantile trust by saying that "healthy children will not fear life if their parents have integrity enough not to fear death" (141, p. 233).

Buhler's (79) concept of "productivity" is important for the period of adult maturity. She maintains that even though there is biological decline, the personality can continue to grow and experience joyous living as long as the individual can continue to be productive. Productivity is established in these latter years through identifying with the achievements of off-spring, and by evident results of work, play, and community service. It seems, therefore, that old age is enriched by a healthy, retrospective view of life.

There are many examples of people who have forged successful new careers for themselves in their late middle years when they could devote time to things they "really wanted to do." Others have remained active in their chosen profession far past the usual age of retirement. There are many conspicuous examples of outstanding achievement in old age— Titian in art, Lamarck in biology, and Humboldt in philosophy.

Viewing the sunset years from the viewpoint of love, it may be that love between husband and wife during these years can best be expressed by the dimension of *knowledge*. To love a person completely means partly to *know* him, knowledge from the very core of his personality. To make this a developmental task of later maturity would seem to be a way in which the internal mastery principle may be completed. Before death, therefore, man can discover, partially at least, the "secret of life." Man's mature personality is an unfathomable secret; but the penetration into the being of a person whom we love can satisfy this need in a very real way.

Research Dimensions

Any approach to counseling must have an emphasis upon validation of concepts and methods. Otherwise, at best it is an anecdotal accumulation of therapeutic wisdom, and at its worst reverts to the occult and mystical. There are pressing ethical and scientific obligations to validate, with the best experimental means available, the procedures advocated. Unfortunately, scientific methods are not completely adaptable to, nor are many currently known methods always feasible in, counseling settings. We depend upon a rough empirical tryout kind of validation, but we strive for more precise study of concepts and methods through a variety of disciplines. This research orientation to Actualizing Counseling and Psychotherapy was described further in Chapter 2 and is emphasized throughout this book. It is mentioned here only to emphasize the open-ended tentative quality of all systems. One of our current obligations is to state our assumptions, strategies, and expected outcomes in such a way that they can be tested, not only in the rough arena of comparative case experiences, but also in the step-by-step detailed study of process and technique for achieving operationally definable goals of actualization.

We endorse Nevitt Sanford's idea (408) that human problems must be studied from the point of view of culture or social context as well as individual psychology, and that we need a general personality-social theory to guide us. Study of isolated part-function behaviors does not necessarily add to a deeper understanding of complex social behavior, such as clients interacting with counselors or their families. In counseling research we are stymied by methods designed primarily to study elemental rather than holistic behaviors.

Summary

A multidimensional point of view termed Actualizing Counseling and Psychotherapy is described as a process of helping the person to develop his life potentials. It includes philosophical, developmental, structural, dynamic, and research dimensions. Actualizing Counseling and Psycho-therapy is based upon a model of the actualizing person as a developmental goal, rather than a cured state of illness or the mere solution of immediate life problems.

The Process of Counseling
and Psychotherapy

In this chapter we describe process as the steps and changes which take place over time in counseling and therapy. The emphasis, in keeping with the tenor of this book, is on short-term processes. We describe process also in terms of the Actualizing Counseling and Psychotherapy model elaborated in Chapter 3. The basic point of the process of actualizing is that the person moves from a condition characterized by a rigid style of responding to the world, dysfunctional creative and cognitive capacities, and a basically manipulative pattern of response to others. One goal of the Actualizing Counseling and Psychotherapy process is to put the person more in touch with his being, so that he develops a flexible interpersonal response repertoire along the major polarities of existence, becomes more aware of his personal center, becomes more grounded in his body, and functions more effectively and creatively in general. Thus, we will cover two process issues—appropriate process goals for each level of functioning, and the most effective steps and strategies by which those goals are achieved. The following is a list of key process steps.

Step 1: Stating Concerns and Establishing a Need for Help

Step 2: Establishing the Relationship

Step 3: Determining Goals and Structure

Step 4: Working on Problems and Goals

Step 5: Facilitating Awareness

Step 6: Planning a Course of Action

Step 7: Evaluating Outcomes and Terminating

4

Steps in the Process

Step 1: Stating Concerns and Establishing a Need for Help

The process goal at this first step is to enable the client to state his concern, problem, distress, or reason for coming. Many clients have a clear purpose; but some do not. Their presenting statement may or may not imply a recognition of need for help, since clients at this early stage often do not have a strong sense of "ownership" of their problem. Clients may blame others or feel victims of fate. Seldom have they made a firm commitment to work on their problems in a responsible manner. So, a second process goal is to determine the client's recognition of need for help and readiness to commit himself to the process. Much of the first interview is usually devoted to these topics. In terms of our Actualizing model, the main process goal in this step is to work through the facade level resistance.

The process strategy during this first step is to attend to the statements of the client and observe his nonverbal behavior for messages. Clients often come in with vague complaints and goals, and very guarded reasons for coming. Their facade level is often functioning highly effectively to protect them. A second strategy, then, is to help the client clarify the nature of his concern or problem. Further clarification usually is needed regarding the client's expectations and perceptions of the nature of counseling help and his commitment to work under a counseling or therapy model.

Step 2: Establishing the Relationship

The main process goal at this step is to build a relationship which has characteristics of trust based upon openness and honesty of expression. It is important for the counselor to establish credibility as a trustworthy person at this point. A growing body of research (34) supports the idea that how the counselor is perceived in terms of expertness, attractiveness, and trustworthiness determines the effectiveness of counseling.

The process strategy depends largely on how counselors use themselves as persons and the degree of skill they possess in applying relationship techniques, such as listening and reflecting. Additional readiness strategies to be described in the next chapter may be needed to get the relationship off to a productive start.

Step 3: Determining Goals and Structure

The principal goal at this step is to discuss with the client what he would like to get out of the counseling process, especially if his presenting concerns and reasons were vague. This discussion averts the possibility that unrealistic goals and expectations emerge by default, such as counselors having extraordinary power to change client behavior or make people happy. Specific goals are usually discussed along with the kinds of behaviors which would be regarded as successful outcomes. Another goal is to obtain a clear understanding of who is the client. Often in referrals, especially of children, it may be the teacher or the parent who is the "problem" and who possibly should be, therefore, the client. A further process goal at this stage is the determination of the structure, of how the process is going to proceed, of the nature of the goals, and the "contract" regarding ground rules and responsibilities. Further coverage of this topic is given in later chapters.

The strategy at this point involves clear discussion and agreement regarding procedure toward the goals cited above, and negotiating any working agreements.

Step 4: Working on Problems and Goals

The process goals and strategies at this point are determined largely by the nature of the problem, the style and theory of the counselor, and the client's desires and style of communicating. Often this step involves further expression of feeling if the person is distressed or confused. In any case, it often involves further clarification of the problem since the presenting problem often changes with discussion.

Clarifying Nature of the Problem and Choosing Strategies. While defining the nature of the client's problem and refining his goals, an important process goal is to determine the best general strategy to use. A second goal is to be aware of what kind of resources one has as a counselor to facilitate achievement of these goals. In terms of our Actualizing model, at this step the counselor is discussing issues with the client at the actualizing level described in Chapter 3. If the client's problem can be dealt with at this actualizing level by cognitive strategies, there is little use in extending client expectations or making complex commitments for working with the problems at other levels. For example, some clients' needs for information, planning, deciding, or problem-solving require primarily a model such as the following which they can work out at the actualizing level with cognitive resources. An example is planning a career. While there are feeling and valuing elements involving other levels of the personality, it is primarily a process localized in the actualizing level.

Problem-Solving Process Steps

1. Develop a clear statement of the client's problem in terms of a goal to be achieved.

2. Describe the problem-solving or decision-making process.

3. Compile relevant data from interview, case material, and assessment instruments.

4. Discuss data and formulate action alternatives.

5. Apply relevant tests and diagnostic procedures to action alternatives.

6. Develop plan and implementing action steps.

7. Try the plan in simulated or real-life setting.

8. Evaluate outcomes and amend the plan as indicated by data.

These steps are generalizable to a wide range of problems where the use of data and decision-making skills is needed to accomplish the actualizing goals of the person. Even though the counseling process may not focus on these precise steps, the client, faced with the necessity eventually to act, follows formal decision-making steps in a rough way throughout the course of counseling.

Extended Exploration of Feelings. While the nature of the client's problem and goals may be such that formal attention to problem-solving is not indicated at this step, a strategy decision must be made about what to explore further. Typically, with personal problems, feelings are explored in detail to achieve clarity and personal responsibility for them. Rogers (396), for example, views the psychotherapeutic counseling process as a series of ongoing attitudinal changes. His opinion on the manner in which study of the process of psychotherapy should proceed is: First, observe the behavior of the client with as few preconceived notions as possible, or as Rogers states it, ". . . to steep oneself in the *events* . . ." (396, p. 142). Then, from these observations come low-order abstractions and hypotheses which can be tested empirically. Rogers tries to grasp characteristics of the changes in the therapeutic process without thinking of them as fixed or static stages. The seven dynamic stages which he perceives in the process range from an early client condition of threat, resistance to change, and little communication, though a gradual loosening of feelings, assumption of greater personal responsibility for feelings, greater clarity and accuracy of perceiving feelings. Finally, the client experiences his feelings as part of himself. He no longer views himself or his feelings as "objects" or as "problems."

Criteria for Extent of Feeling Exploration. Agency policy or counselor prudence may limit the extent to which the client should be encouraged to explore feelings. To help a counselor determine the depth to which he should allow the client to explore, the following criteria are suggested:

1. The nature and severity of the client's symptoms. For example, prolonged delusional thinking is almost always a sign of psychosis. Hysterical outbursts in which uncontrolled anxiety or hostility is poured forth is another example of a situation which is outside the purview of psychological counseling, and which in most cases is restricted to intensive psychotherapy aided by drug therapy.

2. Length and persistence of symptoms. If a behavior, such as stealing, for example, is persistent and difficult to explain with data at hand, there is a high probability that one is dealing with a pathological process.

3. The nature of the predisposing and precipitating experiences. Some clients, for example, have had a series of severe traumas falling within a short period of time. Deaths in the family, divorces, desertions, plus many small crisis-producing experiences, are examples. These experiences often mobilize more feeling than the client can handle in the interview.

4. Past stability and defensive functioning. A client who desires to express strong feelings and who has a history of stability and adequate defenses generally can be allowed to express his emotions more deeply than the client who has a spotty psychological history.

5. Resistance to psychotherapy. Resistance to further exploration and probing by the counselor is a fairly reliable indicator of the sensitivity of the client's feelings and the rigidity of his defenses.

6. Extent and adequacy of the counselor's or therapist's training. Generally speaking, there is a direct relationship between amount of training and experience in psychotherapy or counseling and the depth at which the process may be pitched.

7. The problems of the counselor or therapist. Often the counselor is unable to handle feelings because the client's feelings touch upon sore spots of his own. This condition should discourage the counselor from delving into similar client feelings.

8. The amount of time available. Time for the counseling or therapy series is significant in that the deeper the involvement in feelings, the more time to work the feelings through must be budgeted. This may mean a hundred or more hours.

9. Institutional policy on doing psychotherapy. Policymakers often dictate to the therapist in general terms how far he can go in probing for feelings and allowing the client to express himself. This is especially true in public school settings where personal counselors have consideration of parental and administrator attitudes as well as numerous technical problems to face.

Values and Limitations of Expressing Feelings. This "ventilation of feelings," as it is sometimes called, has several benefits and limitations. The first value of emotional expression is the feeling of relief it gives from strong physiological tension. A second benefit is the awareness of relief from emotional pressure. A feeling of satisfaction and courage often follows because the client finally could come to admit having feelings which heretofore had been so alien. In addition, he feels a sense of security and freedom from the continuing and often onerous task of defending his feelings. This awareness of security often gives the client courage to solve problems. Thus, new creative energy is released. Previous emotional energy was so tied up with defending himself that the client had little energy available to use constructively. For example, if a client has discussed a fight he had with his father he often will be more ready to discuss other things, such as his own aggressive feelings. A final value of verbalizing feelings is that it prevents "acting out," that is, instead of directing aggression towards others, the client is encouraged to use symbolic means through language.

Intense expression of feeling, called catharsis, has several distinct limitations. If allowed to "ventilate" excessively, the client may feel so good afterward that he will feel it is unnecessary to go on to the causes of his difficulties and the steps necessary to change attitudes and acts. He leaves counseling for the time being with a condition described as a "flight into health." He will stay away then until his anxiety builds up to an intolerable point again. Some anxiety is necessary, however, and the optimal amount necessary for good working motivation is discussed in Chapter 7 under relationship techniques.

Allowing the client to have continuous palliative relief without working into the awareness and action phases of counseling may serve to reinforce his repetitive neurotic patterns. It is as if he has an emotional tranquilizer each week without moving further toward self-understanding. There is little evidence available which might indicate that periodic, emotionally cathartic sessions have much psychotherapeutic value other than the temporary supportive effect of draining off excess tension. Some life experiences, such as confessionals in religious settings, relieve guilt but tend not to produce the type of insight necessary for personality changes. On the other hand, self-confrontation experiences such as those experienced by drug users in programs like Synanon often lead to profound personality change.

Expressing Feelings in the Actualizing Model. Step 4, working on problems and goals, in the Actualizing model involves exploration of feeling at all levels. There is a rhythmic expression of feelings along polar dimensions from the actualizing level to the core and back in the other direction. For example, a client could explore feelings related to his value as a person or his intense fears, loneliness, or rage very early in the process. The client is encouraged to feel anger when he perceives himself as wronged, or to experience love feelings when responded to warmly.

The process goals of the Actualizing model in Step 4 are to encourage the client to explore feelings significant to him in the moment and feelings along the polar dimensions. For example, the counselor may ask a client to exaggerate his hostility so as to become more aware of the basic feeling. The counselor may ask him to express the opposite feelings on the assumption that an excessive use of a manipulative device such as angry domination is a cover for the opposite potential. The extent to which the client responds to such an invitation to express feelings depends on his readiness as well as the conditions of trust established in the relationship. The goal is awareness of wide ranges and types of feelings so that the client can see them in relation to the pattern of his life. Another key goal at this stage is free modulation of affect. The opposite condition of inability to modulate feeling freely is characteristic of seriously disturbed persons, especially those diagnosed as schizophrenic.

Process strategy at this step is to use whatever relationship method works to encourage free expression of feelings along the polar dimensions from actualizing to core levels.

Step 5: Facilitating Awareness

Various terms have been used to describe this step. We prefer achieving "awareness" (of actualizing possibilities). Others have used "working through," achieving "insight" or "understanding." Awareness means self-knowledge from what one sees, hears, and feels. The process involves reexperiencing events and seeing one's life events in a different set with more clarity, integration, and breadth than before. The term "insight" can be defined the same way; but it has a close association with historical "insight therapies."

The concept of "insight" has a varied history. Literally it means to "see into" or understand. In Gestalt psychology the term is used to describe the sudden perceptual reorganization leading to discovery or solution of a problem. An example is Kohler's experiment (270) in which a chimpanzee suddenly discovered how to put various sticks together and pile boxes to reach a much-coveted banana. Insight in counseling and therapy has some of this sudden "aha" or "so that's the way it is" quality to it, in which significant detail stands out from the background. The classical psychoanalytic view of insight includes exploring, analyzing, and clarifying motives and mechanisms for reducing symptoms. Making unconscious motivation more conscious evokes insightful understanding and cures neurotic behaviors. The assumption is that when insight is achieved, the conflict or problem essentially solves itself or disappears.

Ellis (138) contrasts usage of the terms "intellectual" and "emotional" insight. While an intellectual understanding of irrational and self-defeating behaviors is often a prelude to a deeper emotional experiencing of self-awareness, there is wide agreement among therapists that intellectual understanding alone contributes little to behavior change. Ellis emphasizes that emotional insight is a complex process of seeing, believing, thinking, wishing, and practicing. It is different qualitatively in that it involves more forceful committed behavior which leads to constructive action. A long chain of events precedes this state, however, and consists of the client's admitting he is disturbed and is behaving irrationally, that his behavior has antecedent causes, that he is reindoctrinating himself to sustain his disturbance, that he now admits he can change his ideas and patterns of behaving, that he must accept and believe that his previous ideas were false, that he must actively challenge his assumptions by acting in a manner to change them, that his emotions are under his control, and that he realizes that there is no way to remain undisturbed other than through his own efforts.

London (292) is extremely critical of historical "insight therapies." His work is largely an impassioned attack on psychoanalytic views of insight and a defense of "action therapies." The major criticisms of insight approaches are that: therapists are inferring motives when they should be observing behavior to plan behavior changes; symptoms are assumed to disappear when self-knowledge (insight) happens; compared to behavioral (action) therapies, insight approaches take too long and hence are economically less feasible; and finally, the outcomes in insight approaches are more generally stated, whereas in the behavioral approaches they tend to be more specific and limited. To us, the point of London's cogent criticisms is that the counselor cannot depend primarily upon insight approaches, but must look to the best of the action strategies emphasized in Step 6.

The principal process goal of Step 5 is to work from feelings to awareness. An implied goal is to keep the client in counseling long enough to achieve whatever awareness is needed to reach his goals. Three critical points, therefore, must be faced in Step 5. The first relates to the tendency of many clients to leave counseling when they experience discomfort and pain while exploring feelings in Step 4. Occasionally clients experience a feeling of getting worse before things get better, because of the painful self-confrontation. Sometimes the opposite happens when the client feels such relief from the verbalization of feelings that he wants to terminate.

A second critical point is reached when the client has expressed considerable feeling and becomes aware of being defenseless. It is as if the client becomes too aware too fast. While this point is critical from the standpoint that a psychotic process already under way may be accelerated, the vast majority of clients have defenses and actualizing strengths which protect them adequately from various types of psychotic deterioration. The strategy here is to deal with feelings at tolerable levels of intensity. Shneidman, conversing with one of the authors, suggested that this experiencing of intensive feelings was like a basement full of cats waiting to spring out. Uncovering or experiencing too many of the hidden desires, impulses, inhibitions, or thoughts of the past would be like opening the cellar door and letting all the cats out. It would be quite traumatic or even physically catastrophic. The therapist must control the relationship to enable the client to open the cellar door just enough to allow one cat at a time out to be examined and tamed. The succeeding sessions would be occupied with "taming more cats."

A third critical point is reached when the client, having gone through considerable work on feelings, reaches a point of well-being or elation. This experience frequently results in the client's decision to terminate with the conclusion that all's well now because he feels so good. Although there is some logic to the claim that the process properly could be ended when this feeling comes, the client often stops short of commitment to action. It is a difficult professional judgment to know when a client should be encouraged to continue so as to maximize productive outcomes, or let the client terminate whenever he feels ready to do so, or seems unwilling to do something about his problem. The payoff for the hard investment leading toward awareness is what the client does with the awareness.

Process Goals and Strategies in the Actualizing Model. While the general process described above applies to the Actualizing model also, we wish to describe further process events in the special language of the model.

An early process goal is to clue the client to his use of manipulative behaviors, since these forms by definition deviate from actualizing behaviors. The differences are often difficult to determine, as, for example, whether a person is loving or if he is simply pleasing or placating. In addition to one's own rigorous self-analysis, one needs the feedback from a knowledgeable group to distinguish real love from pleasing behavior.

Manipulative Response Patterns. Four illustrative manipulative responses are cited below. The first, *pleasing* and *placating*, is learned early when the child finds that this is an effective means to manipulate parents. This effect is accomplished often through reducing one's own significance by being a "nice guy," or by being "protective" of others, like a solicitous sacrificing mother. We assume that when people engage in these behaviors they are doing the best they know how at the moment. When being "nice," for example, it could be that a person is denying his anger— the polar opposite. Evidence of this condition is found in body responses of rigidity in neck and jaws, for example.

A second typical manipulative response is a *blaming* and *attacking* form. Instead of being angry the person blames or criticizes another. Instead of putting down self, as in placating, he destroys others by attacking. This person also denies tender or loving feelings. It is almost as if loving is to be hurt, so it is safer to attack others first. In extreme form this behavior becomes a struggle for survival. Again, the body reflects this conflict of polarities in the form of tension in vital organs and muscles.

A third pattern is *striving* and *achieving*, expressed through calculating and dictating behaviors. Instead of expressing genuine strength, the person is constantly proving himself, his capacities and superiority. He spends much time managing others for their presumed good. The calculating person is more indirect, getting one to buy his ideas. A father who persuades his children to go to college, for example, may care only about achieving his own goals. Here again, it is assumed that this type of person is denying his opposite dimension of weakness, a point of possible vulnerability.

A fourth manipulative response pattern is showing weakness by *withdrawing* and *avoiding* others (and problem situations). The person says, for example, "I can't . . . You do it." They depend on others to think and act for them. By pleading innocent or weak, they avoid many unpleasant and threatening demands and responsibilities. It is a common and effective control device. Here strength is being denied, and the conflict is often reflected in body dysfunctions.

Character Styles. These styles, as described in the preceding chapter, are extensions of manipulative or controlling styles but are more fixed into the life style of the person and are more remote in the awareness scale. An important process goal, however, is to help the person become aware of these styles so he can become more actualizing or functional in his goal achievement. Some examples of these styles are the *dependent* person who uses denial as his chief mechanism. For example, he seeks love from others and rationalizes his giving in to others' needs as an act of giving and receiving love. He gets some nourishing satisfaction from this action; but it lacks the deeper satisfaction of expressing love from the core of his being. Another style is a masochistic type of *self-attack*, an example of denial of anger and being the nice person. This style blocks not only the expression of anger, but also the polarity of tenderness and love.

The striving, achieving tendencies evolve into a *rigid* character style. To appear strong and confident, for example, the person produces—becomes a "workaholic." The character style of the *schizoid* type is one of coldness and aloofness, but denial of this detachment and demanding understanding and approbation from others is characteristic also. The basic process goal for all of these character and manipulative styles is awareness of how these styles are distortions of basic feelings. The key strategy is interpretation of how these distortions take place in development and how they serve to block the actualizing process in the present. Expressing these basic needs through body work is another fundamental approach to awareness of the denied feelings. Clients are encouraged to give up dysfunctional aspects of a character style, or at least accept their basic profile of character style and its consequences. For more detail on theory and strategy of managing clients with manipulative and character problems, consult Shostrom's *Man, the Manipulator* (434).

Core Goals and Strategies. Since the core is the center of one's existence, a key process goal is to enable the client to get acquainted with his core characteristics as completely as possible. He learns to trust himself rather than external authority. He learns to feel at home with his polar feelings of anger, loneliness, despair, and weakness. A further goal is the release of energies for creative activities from the core. This energy flows in effortless form into many life activities. It means listening to the wisdom of one's center and experiencing its harmonious possibilities.

Strategies for reaching these process goals are many and varied. The principal strategy is release of affect through talk and body work. When one experiences core feelings of rage, longing, terror, or rejection in the safe confines of a supportive relationship, the person is likely to experience feelings of harmony, trust, release, and confidence in himself. The person also experiences a surge of energy which now can be devoted to actualizing tasks.

Various fantasy approaches help the client to get in touch with his center. Numerous meditational styles aid this quest. Journal keeping as described by Assagioli in *Psychosynthesis* (23) and by Progoff in his journal workshop manual (371) provides a means of self-dialogue through writing. Dream analysis is another method to develop awareness of core feelings and symbols. Some of the qualities of the core are tapped in instruments such as the Actualizing Assessment Battery to be described in the next chapter.

The Actualizing Process. The whole point to the preceding discussion is to facilitate the actualizing process and to make this process function at the actualizing level of the person. This means, for example, that the more public functions of the actualizing level are congruent with the more private functions of the core. Actualizing means experiencing the outcomes outlined in the introduction to Chapter 3, which described the actualizing goals of existence.

Step 6: Planning a Course of Action

While some counseling outcomes relate to understanding and comfort alone, most clients are faced with some form of action—deciding, planning, or doing. We do not subscribe to the assumption of most insight therapies that insight or awareness alone is sufficient for action. While there is a natural flow from awareness to action, it is not automatic. Therefore, the main process goal of Step 6 is to help the client to put his newly discovered ideas and awareness into action in real life. In terms of the Actualizing model this means well-functioning processes at the actualizing level to enable the person to move freely along his polar feeling dimensions, utilize his cognitive capacities without interference, live harmoniously with himself at his center, and function effectively in the interpersonal world.

Well-ordered life experiences offer the best therapeutic medium, once the client has sufficient relief from crippling feelings, has achieved some awareness of potential new directions, and has made a commitment to action. Maslow points out this idea very succinctly:

. . . major life experiences can be therapeutic in the fullest sense of the word. A good marriage, success in a suitable job, developing good friendships, having children, facing emergencies, and overcoming difficulties—I have occasionally seen all of these produce deep character changes, get rid of symptoms, *etc.*, without the help of a technical therapist. As a matter of fact, a case could be made for the thesis that good life circumstances are among the *ultimate* therapeutic agents and that technical psychotherapy often has the task only of enabling the individual to take advantage of them (307, p. 311).

It appears from Maslow's thinking above that everything which has been described in the process thus far has been an attempt to prepare the client for therapeutic life experiences. Thus, the counselor or therapist makes himself more and more dispensable through the client's ability to utilize successfully his new skills in self-actualization. Robinson (385) stresses a further point that people can be taught new and higher level life skills much in the same way that dog paddlers can be taught the more efficient Australian crawl.

Step 7: Evaluating Outcomes and Terminating

The principal criterion for successful counseling and the key indicator for termination is the degree to which the client has achieved the goals of counseling. This decision to terminate is a joint effort on the part of counselor and client, although it is the client who is the principal determiner of when his goals have been met. The process goal of termination is not taken seriously enough, in our opinion, since so much of counseling and psychotherapy is structured as open-ended with vaguely defined outcome criteria.

A significant part of the counselor's or therapist's thinking concerns his evaluation of progress toward goals. Some of the questions which go through his thinking are: Did the relationship help the client? In what respects did it help? If it did not help, why not? If the goals were not achieved entirely, what progress was made toward them? Some of the problems in answering these questions revolve around determination of the effect of counseling versus experiences outside of counseling which contribute to change, control of the variables in the counseling process itself, and what is known commonly as the "criterion problem"— reliable standards of change and means to measure them. Current approaches emphasize changes effected by specific variables such as reward, caring, and transference, rather than global approaches such as relationship therapy or rational counseling. Studies of process effectiveness have been done with the *experimental analog* technique and have been reviewed by Zytowski (515). In the laboratory, simulated counselor and client behavior are utilized to study therapeutic variables. For example, stress is induced in a client; a method such as reinforcement of coping behavior is applied; and the results and their transfer to extra-interview behavior are noted. This laboratory analog procedure holds promise for the future, but current studies are not yet sufficiently refined to affect counseling procedure appreciably.

One of the principal difficulties in evaluating counseling and psychotherapy is finding adequate and specific criteria for judging progress. Some of the criteria which have been used in the past are: *opinion* based upon observations of counselor or client that the goals were achieved; *performance* on a standardized test of personality, a projective technique, sociometric study, or a specially constructed test of information or attitude before and after counseling or therapy. Performance in the form of improved grades, occupational stability, job satisfaction, or decreasing numbers of dropouts has been used, but with little success.

2. A second problem in outcome evaluation is to have sensitive instruments and techniques for measuring change as a result of counseling. These are still rudimentary.

3. We also need more knowledge about which counseling procedures will accelerate or retard progress toward the behaviorally defined goals. A troublesome question in counseling has been to explain the lack of positive results from evaluative studies. Often these results have been interpreted as indicating counseling does no good and that longer term therapy is less effective than short term. Eysenck (144) promulgated this view with his widely discussed review on the effects of psychotherapy. Strupp's (461) summary of the numerous critiques of Eysenck's findings on methodological and interpretative grounds leads one to discount his attack on the efficacy of psychotherapy. Eysenck's main criticisms of nineteen studies centered on comparison of treated clients with nontreated. He assumed that the control clients were as disturbed initially as the treated and that recovery criteria were the same for both groups. He concluded that about two-thirds of neurotic patients improved markedly within two years of onset of the difficulty whether they were given psychotherapy or not. He also implied that there was an inverse relationship between intensity of treatment and rate of recovery. He claimed 44 percent of psychoanalytically treated clients improved; 64 percent of eclectically treated clients improved; and those given only general attention by general practitioners, or given custodial care, improved by 72 percent.

Strupp and others have criticized Eysenck severely for procedural fallacies. These center on the unsuitability and noncomparability of untreated control groups, discharge criteria from state hospitals as being certainly different from psychoanalytic clinics, equating neurotic behavior to physical illness, and the difficulty of evaluating so-called spontaneous remissions. Eysenck also classified the dropouts as unimproved. Eysenck updated his basic review in 1960 (145). He contends that Strupp has not produced convincing evidence or arguments that psychotherapy, particularly psychoanalysis, changes people significantly. These comments are presented here to give only a taste of this complicated issue. Interested readers should review Eysenck's original critiques and Strupp's thorough rejoinder.

Sundberg and Tyler (464) also criticize Eysenck's study on grounds of lack of sample comparability, uniformity in defining "improvement," and information on type of therapy administered. This controversy revolving around Eysenck's critique highlights the problems of evaluating the helping process. Evaluation of counseling and therapy must consider comparable *samples* of clients and settings when comparing counseling experiences, definite and *comparable criteria of improvement*, concretely *specified outcomes*, and carefully described *procedures* used in the help-ing process itself.

In a closer look at this entire issue of success and failure, Carkhuff and Truax (91) indicated that some clients are helped and some are hurt by the process. When comparing treatment and control groups, one then finds no differences because the gains and losses cancel each other out. Treatment groups tend to show greater variability than controls in posi-tive and negative personality change. It is a sobering thought that coun-seling may not only retard growth, but be a party to further failure. Research on these growth facilitative and retarding conditions is impera-tive if counseling and psychotherapy are to be dependable helping processes.

The literature on evaluation of counseling and psychotherapy is vast and confusing. The *Annual Review of Psychology* (146) lists the pub-lished evaluative studies for students interested in pursuing the details of this topic. One of the early and extensive and, in our opinion, best of the studies of personality changes in psychotherapeutic counseling is the Rogers and Dymond *Psychotherapy and Personality Change* (400). While all the significant outcome studies cannot be summarized here, a few more illustrative studies will be cited. Campbell (88) performed a massive follow-up study of client counseling twenty-five years earlier where the counseled clients were more satisfied and had higher grades than a non-counseled control group. Using criteria of college achievement and satis-faction, Campbell found that the counseled group years later was less satisfied, more anxious, and had more complaints than a control group. This follow-up kind of study is fraught with many perils. How do you choose comparable control groups, and are counseling groups not full of concerns and problems which send them to counseling? Campbell's study illustrates the typical follow-up, control group type of design and also illustrates the difficulties in assessing effects of counseling. In a report of a ten-year counseling and psychotherapy outcomes project at the Univer-sity of Minnesota Student Counseling Bureau, Volsky, Magoon, Norman, and Hoyt (487) applied the best available evaluative techniques. While it is unjust to summarize this massive study in a few words, its contribu-tion lies in careful specification of counseling outcomes—changes in anxiety, defensiveness, and problem-solving—and use of sensitive meth-ods to assess these outcomes. Hence, this study could serve as a model for other counseling and psychotherapy agencies in evaluating their work. Volsky and associates found that more questions were raised than answers were discovered. While the study did not demonstrate the effectiveness of counseling on their three outcome variables in the college and university setting, hopes were held out for the utility of the approach in counseling research.

Counseling and therapy evaluation studies fall into four major cate-gories: (1) follow-up studies of client attitudes toward their experiences by means of questionnaires or interviews; (2) the opinion of the counselor or therapist about changes which took place in the process and his estimate of the progress made toward the goals; (3) internal process studies based upon close scrutiny of the verbal exchanges interview by interview. This method is best accomplished when the entire transcript is available from a tape. An example of client change would be the decrease in defensiveness exhibited in his remarks, or the signs of increasing client self-directedness manifested by comments such as, "I feel that I can really handle these feelings now," or "I think I can make a decision about what I should do when I graduate." Other studies have used estimates of tension reduction based upon client statements of relief from disabling anxiety through a measure called the "discomfort-relief quotient" of Dollard and Mowrer (126); and (4) external methods based upon objective measures of behavior changes. Examples are using personality tests such as the Minnesota Multiphasic before and after a course of counseling, or studying changes in Rorschach protocols obtained before and after counseling. Shostrom's *Personal Orientation Inventory* (435) is proving to be a useful evaluation instrument for assessing outcomes.

The first two methods of counselor and client opinion of outcomes are based upon observations of the experience shortly afterward and are subject to the usual unreliabilities and biases of reporting. Though the third method, the internal, offers some significant ways of thinking about the changes taking place in counseling processes, it has great limitations for evaluating counseling success. The outcome criteria have a way of becoming the goals for the counseling and they become contaminated with many other changes. There is no effective way of knowing how permanent the changes are and what independent criteria might exist against which to match the internal criteria. The fourth method of using external devices has the limitation of not indicating what changes to attribute to the counseling and what to other life experiences. There is always the problem of the reliability of the instrument and the regression toward the mean phenomenon to consider in such studies using standardized instruments.

Although the field of evaluation criteria and methods at present is very inadequate for the needs of the practicing counselor, he still must strive to develop an attitude of criticizing his work. He must study the developments in the area of evaluating counseling and psychotherapy with the aim of developing his own research design for ascertaining the effectiveness of his work.

Planning a Course of Psychological Counseling

From the preceding discussion the reader will note that the counselor or psychotherapist must make several judgments early in the process. The type and extent of help offered will depend upon the following factors.

Client Needs and Variables

The client has a problem to solve, such as choice of a mate, selection of an occupation, reaching a decision about divorce, or feeling more comfortable with anxiety. These expressions of client need may be construed by the counselor as problems to be solved in counseling and/or symptomatic expressions of deeper personality disturbances. An important first question is, "Who is my client?" The clients may be multiple, as in the case of a family. The general rule is that the client is the person who "owns" the problem, or is most motivated to proceed through the processes just described.

Treatability is another client variable affecting therapeutic planning. Does the client really want help? Is he motivated and ready? Is he capable of profiting from the style of counseling or therapy I am able to offer? Is his character structure and defensive functioning such that he is not likely to change much? The therapist must realize that not every client can be helped. If most of the questions are answered negatively, the only realistic recourse is to judge the client unready to undertake counseling at the present time. The counselor may be able to be of some limited service to such a client, however, in helping him think through the immediate choice he is forced to make or propelling him closer to the ideal of self-actualization.

Which persons should get the most time is often determined by the personal preferences and social values of the counselor. We feel that the main criteria of who should get counseling or therapy should be whether the prospective client can profit from the services offered and whether the counseling is going to help him more than some other person. In other words, the counselor should ask himself whether he thinks the client would be better off with or without the help he can offer. It should be recognized that other agencies operate on such criteria as the greatest good for the greatest number, younger rather than older people, mildly rather than severely disturbed, or those who can make the greatest social contribution.

Clients' knowledge of psychology and the principles of counseling may or may not be an asset. Our opinion is that psychological sophistication can accelerate progress if the knowledge has not been too inextricably tied up in the client's intellectualizing defenses.

Diagnostic formulations regarding the nature and severity of the emotional problems are also factors. These topics are covered in a later section and in the next chapter.

Counselor and Agency Variables

The counselor's or therapist's assessment of the client's needs, problems, and condition for help affect the planning. The counselor's competence determines the level or intensity of counseling. The type of agency in which the counselor or therapist functions also determines level. For example, a counselor working in a high school situation has limits set by the policies controlling psychotherapeutic functions in that agency. The level of counseling may be set at more surface and supportive levels no matter how competent the counselor may be. A counselor functioning in a clinic setting, where there are associates and specialists from other fields with whom he or she can discuss cases and share responsibility, can plan the counseling along broader and more intensive lines.

After considering the client, agency, and counselor-therapist variables, the counselor-therapist and client together must decide whether to proceed at all, the objectives or goals, length of time, and general style to be employed. The counselor-therapist takes the lead in this determination since he or she has primary professional responsibility for the process outcomes.

Length of Psychological Counseling and Therapy

The duration of counseling can be determined generally in the early planning stage by the nature and extent of the goals, whereas the length of psychotherapy is more difficult to predict. The amount of time available for any one client determines the level of involvement and influences the nature of the process goals. The extent to which the client wants to get deeply involved and to stay involved is also a significant determinant of length. Many immediate goals, such as reduction of anxiety, vocational plans formulation, and decisions regarding further education or choice of a mate, may involve just a few hours; whereas the achievement of a general level of awareness necessary to act in a more personally satisfying manner may take many hours.

There is very little research on the relationship between length of therapy and outcome. Morton's study (334) of brief psychotherapy utilized a high degree of interpretation and emphasis on learning principles following Rotter's Social Learning Theory as a framework. Morton concluded that:

We can assume with an extremely high degree of confidence that brief psychotherapy conducted in a rational manner, following a systematic theoretical orientation, and utilizing vehicles appropriate to the theory, will result in striking and lasting changes of adjustment in subjects who were seriously maladjusted (334, p. 17).

Morton's early study was quite restricted in scope and should not be overgeneralized. His study suggests, however, that means can be employed to shorten the process and still obtain some lasting beneficial outcomes.

Morton's process objectives in his experimental therapy sessions were to: (1) test the limits of the resistance; (2) ascertain the nature of the defenses; (3) test the degree of insight in relation to the problems; (4) establish the level of present adequacy in solutions to problems; (5) determine the nature of the potential pathways for satisfaction of needs; (6) determine the level and intensity of interpretation that should be used; and (7) establish a meaningful frame of reference in which the client could organize his approach to problems.

While counselors may feel that they control the duration of a counseling relationship, there is evidence that the interaction and the degree of personality similarity between counselor and client determine length. Mendelsohn (318), using personality test measures in a replication study, found that similarity of counselor and client personality types was related to length in that dissimilar types terminated shortly while similar types had varying length of contact. This kind of study suggests that we need methods for matching clients and counselors.

Research by Muench (343) with college students on time-limited psychotherapy is an example of careful studies on the effect of length on outcome. Muench found with various objective measures and therapists' judgments of change that differences in growth among short term (less than eight interviews), time-limited therapy (terminated at prearranged date from eight to nineteen interviews), and long term (twenty or more) were not significant. Findings were similar when the six most successful therapists were compared to the six least successful. This study suggests that controlled time limits for counseling can be imposed without loss of effectiveness.

Generally speaking, the client should be kept in counseling only as long as he seems to be making satisfactory progress toward the general actualizing goals of the process and toward the solution of his immediate problems. The ethics of counseling make this viewpoint imperative, especially when there are fees involved.

Differences in Psychotherapy with the Mildly and Severely Disturbed

This book was designed for students in counseling and psychotherapy who deal primarily with clients classified as maladjusted normals, mildly disturbed, or neurotic. Some clinical psychologists in clinics and private practice, however, work also with clients having psychotic characteristics. Since the counselor or therapist never knows what kind of client will walk in the door, it is highly important that he be well fortified with information of two types: (1) an understanding of behavior disorders so that he can recognize severely disturbed or psychotic persons; and (2) a clear recognition of his own competence and limitations in dealing with serious disorders both on an emergency and on a referral basis.

The following figure after Klopfer suggests a continuum for normal, neurotic, and psychotic conditions (265, pp. 312, 234). It is noted in Figure 11 that the neurotic exhausts his defenses to the breaking point before his reality-testing functions deteriorate. The average neurotic, before psy-

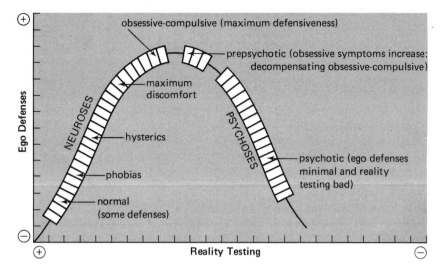

*The Process of
Counseling
and Psychotherapy*

Figure. 11. Normal-Neurotic-Psychotic Ego-Defense Continuum, Adapted from Klopfer.

chotherapy, has a heavy wall of defenses. The psychotic, on the other hand, generally has little defensive strength, and low self-actualizing capacity.

The psychotic often has a rich private world of reality, but his perception of the meaning of his external reality is very distorted, thus giving a delusional quality to his thinking. The neurotic, in contrast, experiences his outer world only photographically (filtered by his defenses), as Fromm (172) points out. The neurotic client is very sensitive to outer stimuli, but is defended staunchly from perceiving his inner world. In Fromm's (172) conception of the healthy personality, both poles are present; inner and outer perceptions are both accurate, thus enabling the client to see the world more objectively and to experience his own thoughts and feelings subjectively without distortion or overreaction.

Summary

In this chapter a summary of the process of Actualizing Counseling and Psychotherapy was presented. The various stages in the process were linked to the levels of awareness in the Actualizing model. Special attention was given to the action approaches at the actualizing level. Critical points in the process were identified and key problems at each stage were described. Counseling and psychotherapy outcomes must be evaluated to determine whether the client was helped or hindered in his search for actualization.

Techniques

part 2

Readiness and Diagnosis in Counseling and Psychotherapy

This chapter covers three topics of concern to counselors and therapists as they begin the counseling process—building readiness for counseling, obtaining data from cases histories and tests, and psychodiagnostic evaluation. These topics concern counselors mainly in the early interviews as they think through questions of involving clients in meaningful, productive relationships, of determining clients' strengths and limitations, and of deciding what data are required for helping clients solve problems. Since so many counselors and psychotherapists work in agency settings where clients are pressured into a counseling relationship, some consideration must be given to readiness.

Readiness

Readiness for learning is a well-known educational concept. The child, for instance, is not "ready" to read until he has achieved a certain level of motivation, maturation, and basic skill development. Readiness for counseling and psychotherapy is similar in that certain conditions must be satisfied before counseling can take place. One of the conclusions from Lipkin's study of client attitudes and therapeutic outcomes was:

Our data strongly suggest that the client who is positively oriented to the counselor and the counseling experience, and who anticipates that his experience in counseling will be a successful and gratifying one, undergoes more change in personality structure than does the client who has reservations about the counseling experience (290, p. 26).

5

The person himself may recognize that something is wrong in his life, but typically he has to have this pointed out to him by someone else or wait for a crisis to emerge. The suggestion that he needs help often provokes resistance—a type of protective defense against change discussed in Chapter 8. It is significant for this discussion because the individual typically comes to counseling with some strong reservations. Counseling and, more particularly, psychotherapy do not begin until the person recognizes a need for change.

Our culture places great emphasis upon ability to solve one's own problems and to stand on one's own feet. Hence, clients frequently perceive a counseling or psychotherapeutic relationship as threatening to their feelings of independence. Even when clients come to counseling voluntarily, they often have feelings of being different from their more "normal" or "adjusted" friends. People in our culture, furthermore, are taught that they should not need help, that they should be logical, and that they should depend on "common sense" to guide their actions. There is a feeling of shame if one cannot "master" one's feelings and solve one's own problems. Some of this feeling is a fear that the psychotherapeutic counselor, particularly, has methods for penetrating one's innermost secrets and for getting one to do and say things against one's better judgment. A concern of this chapter, therefore, will be over methods for getting clients interested in counseling and for working on their problems as expeditiously as possible.

The following discussion is oriented toward readiness principles and techniques, but we wish to stress that sound counseling practice and ethics demand that counseling be voluntary. It is a generally accepted principle that prospective clients should not be persuaded, cajoled, or tricked into a relationship. However, we feel that prospective clients should be given opportunities to learn about the potentialities and limitations of counseling so they can make, from their viewpoint, sound decisions about counseling.

Determining Factors in Readiness

Several factors determine "readiness" of the client for a counseling experience. Present motivation for help is the most important. Other factors are knowledge the client has about counseling, intellectual or conceptualizing ability, present level of insight, expectations of the role the counselor will play, and the general rigidity or fluidity of the client's defense system. An attempt to obtain a more precise measure of counseling readiness was made by Minge (326) with college clients. His study revealed that readiness for change is a useful measure of counseling readiness, and that such readiness for personal counseling can be measured with personality instruments.

Mendelsohn (318) studied characteristics of clients who came for counseling and those who did not seek help. His study was a replication and confirmation of results from earlier studies on this subject which have implications for client readiness. The counseling and noncounseling groups did not differ on pathological dimensions, but differed more on personality traits. Those seeking counseling were more willing to consider change, and to explore themselves through verbal exchanges, and were higher on intuition and perception orientation (on Myers-Briggs scale). The studies on this subject indicate that client personality factors affect the decision to enter counseling, but that client-counselor personality similarity determines decisions to remain in counseling, and for what duration.

Racial and cultural factors determine readiness for counseling. While the controversy rages on whether white counselors can work effectively with black clients and vice versa, the evidence points to acute problems in communication and trust. Cultural and socio-economic differences between persons of the same race create communications chasms difficult to bridge with words. Counselors must work especially hard at the linguistic bases of their profession because of the rapidly changing language patterns of urban youth (Labov 277).

A critical variable in client readiness, apart from cultural differences, is the client's perception of the counselor. This perception is influenced by what the counselor actually does with clients. This reputation factor is verified in several studies, of which Rippee, Harvey, and Parker (383) is an example.

Motivation for counseling is composed of several complex variables which are being clarified increasingly by research. An example is Raskin's study (374) of two sets of male clients matched on age, schooling, and mean ratings on a motivation scale. Of the fifteen variables rated by therapists, five were found to be significantly related to motivation for counseling. Those clients rated high on motivation for counseling had higher educational and occupational levels, were more aware of their psychological difficulties and the type of treatment expected, and were liked by their therapists. This kind of study confirms observations of experienced therapists that their attitudes influence the client's motivation, and also accounts in part for the findings that therapists prefer to work with clients having higher educational, social, and economic status.

A counseling readiness scale to differentiate early terminators from those continuing in counseling has been developed by Heilbrun (220, 221). Premature dropouts tended to get low scores on the scale. A factor found to be related to continuation in productive counseling was described as awareness of the psychological meaningfulness of behavior. This scale is an illustration of the possibilities of developing a set of constructs to predict suitability for counseling.

Obstacles to Readiness

Several factors militate against a client getting off to a good start. The first is the culturally based resistance mentioned above. A second obstacle is the physical setting. Often, privacy and comfort are lacking to such an extent that the client is ill at ease and quite suspicious that others may find out about his being there and what is discussed. Hence, privacy, comfort, and confidentiality are significant "musts" for good counseling readiness.

Previous unpleasant experiences with counselors, competent or incompetent, often start the interview with two strikes against it. The counselor's reputation is a related factor. The fact that he is known for his skill in helping people, or has some of the status symbols such as degrees, titles, certifications, and favorable references helps considerably in the initial phase of counseling.

Lack of clear-cut understanding, on the part of the client, of the nature of counseling and psychotherapy is a widespread source of inadequate readiness to attack problems. It is important that the client know the limitations and possibilities of counseling, as well as certain bits of information such as length of interviews, probable length of the process, or how to make appointments. This element of readiness is handled under the term "structuring," to be discussed in Chapter 7. Intellectual inadequacy is a related readiness obstacle. In psychotherapeutic counseling, for example, Crider's study (112) indicated that the more intellectually able and the more psychologically sophisticated individual had the best chance of therapeutic success. After all, counseling and psychotherapy are primarily verbal enterprises.

Lack of accessibility is another important obstacle to effective counseling readiness. A disturbed client, for example, may come in all set to go to work. He is told he will have to make an appointment for a later date because the counselor is booked up. Often he "cools off" to the point where he does not return. It would seem desirable to have an "intake" system to see each client, even if briefly, when he comes in the first time. This procedure would let him feel something is being done and would ascertain the degree of urgency for psychotherapy, counseling, or referral to specialists. Some counseling services maintain fixed open hours to avoid the intake delays for urgent problems.

A final obstacle in promoting effective readiness is the lack of an overall "climate" of acceptance of counseling within the agency. Some hospitals, schools, and colleges have an administrative policy or an unfortunate history of rumors about counseling or psychotherapy which does not allow even the most skilled counselor to operate effectively. An example is having the counseling function tied in with disciplinary and regulatory activities of a school, which tends to make the counseling function an administrative arm. Students are quick to sense this relationship. This does not mean, however, that counseling services cannot be used effectively as referral resources for a disciplinary officer; but it does mean that the physical proximity and emotional association of the disciplinary and counseling functions must be kept separate, if at all possible.

One way of reaching people with problems is through *talks*. Heads of agencies and counseling service directors report that every time they give a talk to a public group on mental health, family problems, study methods, or child behavior, for example, there are numerous requests for services.

A second method of motivating clients is through creating an *institutional climate conducive to seeking help*. In schools, for example, this is particularly important, since very few student clients seek counseling voluntarily.

A third method for stimulating weakly motivated clients and for building better readiness in those already seeking such services is that of *instructing referral sources*. Counselors constantly must work on sharpening the awareness of referral agents through conferences with physicians, teachers, advisers, ministers, lawyers, personnel directors, and others likely to make the first contact.

A significant principle of referral is that of being honest and sincere about the problem observed. Evasion and embarrassment only complicate a referral. The person making the referral may call the prospective client in and say, "I've noted some things about which you might need or want help." Then he mentions the behavior and suggests the source from which he might obtain such assistance. Unless the client is ready to accept the suggestion and has some awareness of the judgments others are making about him, this approach, too, could be very threatening.

Referral is more difficult when the counselor has worked with the client and then feels obliged to refer him. Again, the sincerity with which the counselor approaches the matter is critical since it is so easy to imply judgment or to have the client feel rejected. The counselor attitude of "I've taken you as far as *I* can go now" or "*You* are too hot to handle" should be avoided. An attitude of "Let's see what other possibilities there might be for help on this problem" would be better.

Referral techniques and resources are complicated and unique to a particular community. The counselor education staff at Michigan State University has published a list of referral guides designed to help school and college counselors particularly, but the list has applicability to all workers and agencies which are faced with referral to another service.

1. Check to see if the school has used all its own available resources in helping the student before looking outside the school for help.

2. Try discussing an incipient problem with an agency or specialist before referral is urgent.

3. Try to discover what persons have had contact with the parent or student in regard to the problem, and what results were obtained from these contacts before making a referral.

4. Designate one person to be responsible in working with the parent and student in developing a referral.

5. Learn whether a community agency is already working with the family, for a consultation with that agency is the proper first step in considering a referral in such cases.

6. It is unwise and impractical to refer a student to community agencies without the knowledge, consent, and cooperation of his parents.

7. Keep in mind when telling students or parents about available services in the school or in the community that the teacher should explain both the functions and the limitations of these services. Do not give the impression that any specialist or agency has all the answers and can work wonders.

8. Do not coach a student or parent regarding how they might "wangle" hard-to-get services.

9. Let the student or his parent make his own arrangements for service whenever possible. Do not "spoon feed" the student by being more "helpful" than necessary.

10. Remember that in some cases, however, help may be needed by very immature, dependent, or ill students or parents in arranging an appointment or even in arranging transportation to the agency.

11. Secure a signed consent from the student's parents before releasing information to a social agency.

12. Help the agency or specialist by indicating which person should be the point of contact representing the school (322).

A fourth device for promoting readiness is to give the prospective client *information about himself*. This is quite easy in a school or college setting compared to private or clinic practice. Generally, test batteries have been given, and personal records are completed routinely and cumulatively. The students are notified that they can come in to discuss the test results. Students in the highest quarter, for example, may be notified of this fact. They come in often expressing surprise at their high aptitude or lack of commensurate achievement. Various workshops in interpersonal effectiveness, assertiveness training, or sexual dysfunction, etc., generate interest in individual counseling.

A fifth significant source of finding motivated clients is through the *educational process* itself. Robinson (385), who has studied the problem of readiness in student counseling, mentions several such sources. The special courses in study methods—English, Reading Techniques, Orientation, Psychology, and Marriage—offer extraordinary opportunities to help people formulate their problems and to coordinate their desires for counseling help. This type of curricular experience not only helps the person with problems to come to grips with them, but also offers excellent opportunities to motivate the better student to achieve what Robinson (385) describes as "higher level adjustment skills." This achievement results in higher efficiency, more productivity, richer emotional experiences, and better health than would be attained by chance or whimsical living habits. Thus, counseling relationships can help the person who is already operating at a high level to improve himself even more.

Survey techniques are a sixth means of finding and motivating potential clients. Inventories such as the Mooney Problem Checklist (332), SRA Youth Inventory (379), Shostrom's *Personal Orientation Inventory* (435), and Berdie's precounseling checklist (43), serve the useful purpose of making people more aware of their problems and possibly motivating them to do something. Robinson (385) found that an average of twenty-five problems were generally checked during routine administrations to students.

Special *precounseling orientation* meetings are a seventh means of giving clients information about counseling and related functions such as testing, helping them formulate realistic expectations about counseling and the counselor's role, acquainting them with the philosophy of the particular counseling service, and reducing anxieties about the anticipated counseling experience. An example is a prevocational counseling readiness meeting which described counseling and related functions (440). Charts were used during the meeting to illustrate the nature of the process, the functions of the counselor, and the goals for vocational counseling. The general aims were to build a realistic "level of expectation" or perceptual "set" for counseling experiences and to begin a relationship with the counselor, who was often present at the precounseling sessions. Another example from Truax and Carkhuff is called "vicarious therapy pretraining" (480), which is used in individual or group therapy. It is a thirty-minute tape illustrating appropriate client interview behavior. It contains excerpts from real interviews showing how clients reveal feelings and explore their psychological environments. Studies by Truax and associates have demonstrated a higher level of intrapersonal exploration by clients with VTP than by those without this pretraining.

Evidence from studies by Stone (457) and Richardson and Borow (382) corroborates the economy values of prevocational counseling orientation when coupled properly with individual counseling. In a study on precounseling orientation, Glazer (195) utilized a questionnaire designed to focus client thinking on assistance desired, to give more accurate perception of the counseling services, and to stimulate thought about counseling outcomes. While the study did not indicate a highly significant result with the questionnaire, the group that took it was judged more ready for counseling than a comparable group that did not do so. Similar tentative results were found earlier in a study by Froehlich on precounseling orientation (170).

Various human potential activities are conducted in groups affiliated with counseling services. These activities serve as resources for referral or as readying experiences for individual counseling.

Readiness Within the Interview

Most of the preceding methods of establishing readiness are concerned with locating and motivating clients. Once the client is in the office, a counselor has a special problem in readiness. Here, attitude, setting, and technique are important factors. Counselors must be able to size up the situation to know if they should apply support techniques to ease clients' anxieties, or whether they should increase client discomfort to get them more emotionally involved and willing to work on their problems.

Counselors can be misled easily by the "facade" phenomenon. The client's resistance may result in opening the relationship on issues such as "no vocational goal," "poor name remembering," "stage fright," or "poor study habits," as the basic problem. We feel that the counselor should start at this level with the client and not jump to the conclusion immediately that this is a "facade" problem. Generally speaking, however, if the counselor's attitudes are appropriate, the client will come forth with a redefinition of his problem shortly. Attitudes which facilitate readiness to discuss problems are elaborated in Chapter 6.

Criteria which the counselor can apply to ascertain the client's readiness to move forward are positive attitudes toward the therapeutic process and a lowered defensiveness which gives an impression of spontaneity and eagerness to talk about problems. Impressions that the client is ready to deal with the emotional implications of his problems, articulateness which enables him to express ideas and feelings directly, and a general acceptance of the therapist's or counselor's role, structure, and style of counseling are further indications of client readiness. The counselor should be alert also to the client who may not be able to articulate problems or feelings directly, but by attitude indicates a desire to go ahead. Similarly the counselor should be wary of the client who is too glib about going ahead, and who uses interview talk as a device to avoid taking responsible action.

The Case History

A case history is a systematic collection of facts about the client's current and past life. This history may take many forms depending upon the style and preference of the counselor or therapist and the type of problem situation. A psychoanalytically oriented therapist, for example, would stress detailed facts of early emotional development through adolescence to present status. The counselor trained in the social work tradition would place considerable emphasis upon the environmental circumstances of the client and would also collect a detailed life history. The career counselor would collect only those items which have a direct bearing upon the client's work of selecting life objectives. A self-theorist would tend to ignore a formal, systematic life history, letting the client select items which were important to him. A counselor in the Rogerian tradition would not ask specific questions to fill in gaps in the story as given by the client because this might tend to throw the responsibility too much on the counselor's shoulders. Some counselors, in addition, feel that it is the client's present perception of his situation that is important, not the accurate systematic reconstruction of the past.

One of the key limitations of the case study method is the overemphasis upon counselor responsibility that is engendered by voluminous data-collecting. The client feels that the therapist is collecting information from which the therapist will later formulate an answer to his "case." Since making a case history generally demands much questioning, it has the frequently unfortunate effect of increasing the client's resistance to help and makes it more difficult for him to help himself later. There appears to be a declining interest in data collecting among counselors. Meehl (316) reported that his study of 168 psychotherapists' opinions revealed that just 17 percent regarded prior personality data collection as accelerating therapy.

Although the method may be limited through the possible danger of using data inaccurately, the danger that a counselor may allow his bias or a priori assumptions to enter, in regard to a particular case, is especially potent when collecting case data. The counselor may find, furthermore, that he collects much irrelevant and unreliable data during a systematic review of the client's life. Skilled counselors know the subtle distortions which often characterize a client's reporting of past events. Preoccupation with case data has the additional disadvantage of being very time-consuming.

In addition to detracting from the job of building the relationship solidly, too much preoccupation with taking a case history may give counselors a false sense of security that they have a meaningful diagnostic and prognostic answer to their clients' problems. Mere data seem to have a morbid and powerful fascination for some counselors to the point that a neat collection of life facts gives the illusion that they understand the client.

Forms of Case Histories

Career Counseling Surveys. Case histories can be obtained in various ways. Career counseling generally requires a highly structured planning survey form designed to be completed by the client. Such a form covers: (1) basic *identifying information* such as name, age, and sex; (2) *educational information* such as school history, scholastic and activity record, subjects liked and disliked, and present educational status and plans; (3) *vocational history* such as part- and full-time jobs held, military experience, present and past occupational choices; and (4) *personal data* including health history, disabilities, parental and marital status, family background with data on socio-economic level, family aspirations, hobbies, personal problems, and the career ideas of the client. To these basic data supplied by the client and often supplemented by the first interview are added the data from *school transcripts, work samples, test profiles* of interest, aptitude, personality, and achievement.

Psychotherapeutic Counseling Histories. With severe emotional problems, the case history may focus more attention upon a systematic social
record such as the family history, and the record of interpersonal relationships with parents, siblings, teachers, and peers. The data are often collected by means of the interview—usually by an "intake worker." This
specialist does not do the psychotherapy but collects information, determines eligibility and suitability for help, and checks with the local
social-service exchange for information on previous agency contacts. The
method is used mostly by multidisciplinary clinics and agencies dealing
especially with children.

In private practice and in school and college counseling agencies, the
data generally are collected by the person doing the counseling. The
authors have found that it serves the best interests of the client to collect
information on a systematic self-report form and to supplement this
with data offered by the client in the course of a statement and elaboration
of the problem. This procedure tends to avoid the pitfalls of the formal
case history mentioned earlier, yet it gives the counselor basic data from
which he must formulate his hypotheses and decisions about the course
of future relationships with this client.

In compiling case data or presenting a report for a staff conference or
supervisor, it is preferable to start with broad general characteristics and
move progressively to the specifics which give flavor to the client's unique
life style. For example, case studies may start with the fact that the client
is white, male, twenty-four years old, married, through more and more
particular descriptive categories to unique characteristics, such as the fact
that he expresses hostility toward dominant women.

The main justification for collecting facts by means of a systematic
case history is to shed light on present problems, their origins, past forms,
and present meanings. The past has different meanings for clients. Some
enjoy preoccupation with details, even those events surrounding traumatic
experiences, perhaps because this preoccupation enables them to escape
responsibility for facing problems in the present. Other clients feel that
the only way they are going to understand the present is to open the past;
hence they become overly occupied with "family skeletons." To avoid
these pitfalls, the counselor must de-emphasize the significance of collecting
information in the interview and use the data only as tools to interpret
material to the client or as a take-off point for discussion and for his
diagnostic formulations. It should be stressed here that concern for collecting systematic data should not interfere with establishing an effective
helping relationship. Thorne (475, p. 87) suggests the following outline as
an aid to a systematic case study. This outline covers the major personality
dimensions which describe the generality and uniqueness of the particular
person being studied.

1. *Genetic.* Hereditary factors where demonstrable.
2. *Constitutional.* The biologic calibre of the organism.

3. *Psychophysiological-supporting functions.* Lower level supports of psychic functions.

4. *Temperament, feelings and emotions.* The affective-impulsive basis for behavior.

5. *Intelligence.* Factors of native ability.

6. *Form of thought.* Perception, symbolic language functions and thinking.

7. *Content of thought.* Ideological composition.

8. *Consciousness and attention.* Orientation and sensorium.

9. *Conditioning and habit formation.* The experiential context.

10. *Self-control.* Voluntary functions in personality.

11. *Attitudes, sentiments and complexes.* "Acting out" behaviors.

12. *Group membership, role and situational determinants.*

13. *Style of life.*

14. *Self, self-concepts and ego development.*

15. *Global dimensions of personality.* General factors.

Occasionally a more detailed study is needed when the existing data are sketchy or unreliable. Lewis's *Outlines for Psychiatric Examination* (288), for example, offers suggestions for a detailed study of the client's past and present life.

Cumulative Records. Most schools and colleges have record systems wherein basic data about the development of the student are maintained. The first step which the counselor must take when a student becomes a client is to check on the recency and reliability of the data already collected.

The fragmentary data of the usual school cumulative record make hasty, superficial judgment a grave temptation. A flagrant example is jumping to conclusions about a client's mental ability from group test scores and course grades. Another problem relative to cumulative records involves the handling of confidential data. The general rule found most suitable for school and college situations is to keep confidential personal notes in a separate highly secure file, with only official notations in the cumulative record. To fulfill school requirements, many states now have laws that give parents, and often students, the right to inspect the student's cumulative record. Many school counselors, for example, can testify that a student can be a "marked" person because of entries made about earlier misconduct. Now it is hazardous legally to do so.

The cumulative record can be a useful counseling tool to facilitate the readiness process. A counselor can formulate hypotheses about problems and can note discrepancies in data, such as the differences between John's test data and teachers' reports on his work. This preliminary exposure to brief case data saves valuable interview time. The counselor can spot possible "trouble" areas in the record, noting that the parents have been divorced recently, that he lists two addresses, and that he is alternately with each parent.

Some counselors prefer to start "with a clean slate." They feel they cannot trust the recorded data or even their own perceptions of data. They are afraid that their biases will affect their relationship with the client adversely. As in most other counseling issues, the value of records hinges on the individual preferences of the counselor and his care and skill in using them.

Case Write-Ups. Counselors and psychotherapists vary in their opinions about keeping notes on clients. Those who take elaborate notes feel they have more material for therapeutic planning, interpretations, and predictions; the main arguments for not keeping extensive notes are that the confidential material might fall into unauthorized hands and the fact that the relationship has been between the counselor and client only. We take the position that some notes are necessary. Certain identifying information and a brief outline of the topics and plans discussed are essential to note trends in the counseling process. With a heavy counseling load, it is easy to get clients mixed up and to forget essential facts. The counselor may wish, or may be required, to put notations in the cumulative or agency records, but confidential material should be kept in the counselor's personal file only and destroyed after the client's termination.

The Autobiography. Client productions are other devices for getting information and for starting them thinking about their current problems in light of their developmental histories. Autobiographies may be of two types. In the systematic form, the client is given general instructions about covering topics such as family, friends, aspirations, and current feelings. The second type is a free response form where no specific topics are mentioned. The client is completely free to develop whatever style and content he wishes. It is like a letter to one's self, and is often called a personal "journal."

The Essay. Here is another example of a personal document from which much rich material can be obtained about client self-perceptions, values, and readiness for psychotherapeutic counseling. In this method the client is assigned a specific topic to write about such as, "What I want to get out of life," "My family," "What I would do on a deserted island," "The most beautiful experience I have ever had." The following is a condensation of an essay voluntarily written by a client on the topic of "What I Want out of Life."

I want to respect tradition such as carrying on the family name. Secondly I want success. I want people to know my name when they hear it. Then I think I want children—to follow the blood line through. I want to write, to travel, to learn. Next, I want to find myself. I want to understand why I do the things I do; why I think the way I do, why I am the way I am. Above all, I want to be happy. Is it perfection, or fulfillment, we sensitive ones are looking for? Is Joe the one I am best suited for, the one I'm better adjusted to? Ideas, talk, writing, thinking, planning, walking together. This is what I wonder about. Have I made a mistake in choosing my mate? or my life career? Just what have I done wrong all along through life? Why must I wait?

Why can't I just dig into whatever I attain, desire, wish, and hope for? Basically what is the matter with me and my relationships with people? Do I really feel inadequate or is it just that I think I should be and feel that way?

I want to make the name of Smith live in the minds of people. It did once and it can again. I am a living organism, I believe, with emotions, love, hate, sorrow, happiness. I do have ambition but I feel that my procrastination is tripping my ambition. I want to overcome it. I need direction. I come to you for it.

Such a document is full of meaning for the therapist and client. This twenty-year-old woman had difficulty getting involved in a psychotherapeutic relationship. It was hypothesized that her "lack of readiness" was due largely to ambivalent feelings about giving up her satisfying defenses and facing up to the pain she was experiencing with other people, her academic failure, and her feelings of inadequacy and guilt over letting the family down. This document gave both counselor and client a fresh start on issues important to her now.

Poetry and Art. Personal productions of verse offer an opportunity for some clients to express feelings when direct oral methods fail. The same is true of drawings and sketches. Descriptions of personal meanings in the interview help the client to verbalize personal messages and offer valuable counselor leads.

The Time Graph. This device combines elements of the abbreviated autobiography with a strict time orientation. The client is instructed, for example, to outline his life by topics such as father, mother, and home location, on the vertical dimension, with the decades or individual years clearly marked on the horizontal dimension. Key life points, past and future, such as marriage, first job, anticipated retirement, and death, are identified. The values of this instrument lie in the perspective and contrasts it offers the clients when they see significant people, places, and events of life outlined in chronological order. It is believed that the autobiographical exposition process itself has therapeutic value. The counselor, too, can more easily pinpoint significant experiences for further elaboration when he has this panorama of the client's life before him.

Psychodiagnosis

The Concepts and Issues

Diagnosis in the medical sense means a process of examining symptoms, inferring causes, integrating observations and fitting them into general categories, and, finally, pinning specific labels on disease entities. Psychiatric or psychological diagnosis is a similar process of ferreting out causation and of naming symptom clusters—schizophrenia, for example, or reading deficiency, or anxiety state; but there is no clearcut psychological analogue to a medical concept like diphtheria or thrombosis, which have definite etiology. In these diseases it is mandatory that various types of medical diagnoses precede treatment.

In the psychological area, however, the diagnostic process takes on several meanings and is not as clear-cut as in medicine. Psychological diagnosis generally means a statement of the problems or present status of the client, probable causes of the difficulty, possible counseling techniques to solve the problems, and a prediction of counseling outcomes or future client behavior. A diagnostic formulation may also include a survey of the strengths of the client.

Types of Diagnoses

Psychodiagnosis has meant historically a descriptive *classification* or taxonomy of problems similar to the psychiatric classifications for neuroses, psychoses, and character disorders. This process is often called "differential diagnosis" wherein the clinician attempts to differentiate one disease entity from another. Various differential classification schemes have been devised for different types of pathological behavior. The American Psychiatric Association's manual on types of psychoses, neuroses, and character disorders is the standard nosological reference for pathology (10).

In looking at nonpathological classifications used in counseling, Williamson (499) proposed a sociological type with five categories: Personality, Educational, Vocational, Financial, and Health Problems. Bordin (59) looked deeper, at the source rather than at the kind of difficulty, and developed five categories: no problem, lack of information, dependence, self-conflict, and choice anxiety. Pepinsky (359) has a similar set of categories for student problems, including lack of assurance, lack of information, lack of skill, dependence, self-conflict (interpersonal, intrapersonal, cultural), and choice anxiety. Robinson (385) has a simple three-category system based on discussion topics: adjustment problems (emotional and nonemotional), skill learning, and lack of maturity. These schemes vary with the times, type of agency, and clientele served. Each agency must develop a classification scheme useful for its own purposes.

Purposes of Diagnosis

Our view of diagnosis is as a general descriptive statement identifying the client's style of life functioning. The purpose of diagnostic descriptions of behavior style is to motivate clients to change their behavior. Clients' confrontation with themselves as self-effacing or manipulative persons, for example, helps motivate them to change. Perls (362) confirms this view from his clinical experience, and Shostrom (434) builds a diagnostic description system around the concept of manipulation of others. Awareness of one's manipulative style is a first step in a client's actualizing process.

Behavioral therapy contributes much to diagnostic thinking with its emphasis upon clear specification of goals. It does little good to identify manipulative style, for example, without having a clear idea of what change is desired and what means are needed to effect the change. A mother, for example, who plays "judge" to her child can be given specific phrases to use instead. She can say, "I want you to," "I'd prefer," "I wish," rather than "You should," or "You must," or "You had better." Mother in these examples is clear and specific about her own feelings and expectations.

Observation skills are the main resource for obtaining the counselor's data. Systematic samples over several interviews where counselors attempt to control their own projections and interpretations are the main source of diagnostic data. Psychometric devices are another source of diagnostic data, but in our opinion the use of psychometrics for diagnostic purposes is diminishing. This issue is discussed in detail later.

The main purpose of diagnostic thinking in counseling and psychotherapy is to plan differential treatment of clients. In the counseling framework the principal exponent of this views is Callis (86, 87), who makes diagnosis central to his planning with clients and research in counseling. The rationale for this kind of thinking is that the counselor must help the client decide whether, for example, he needs information, suffers from lack of experience, or is experiencing distorted perception. Each of these conditions requires a different counselor approach—information-giving, interpretation, or client self-discovery. No one counseling approach is equally efficacious for all behavior changes. Weiner (493) adds evidence to this view with cases illustrating the significance of careful diagnosis in personal problems.

The Missouri Diagnostic Classification Plan is one of the most manageable schemes developed for research reporting purposes (86). It is built upon earlier systematic efforts of many diagnostic thinkers and contains two dimensions: problem-goal and cause. Robinson (384) developed a two-dimensional diagnostic model emphasizing client present and past motivation and response patterns. Robinson suggests a four-step process utilizing his scheme: determine causes to plan differential counseling, determine counselor purpose clearly so efforts are relevant to the task at hand, study case intensively to know client style of response, and select bases for learning best suited to the present purposes.

Since most of the above diagnostic thinking grew out of counseling adults, Byrne (85) proposes a revision of the earlier Bordin-Pepinsky categories, suited to high school clientele and possessing more current psychological relevance. Byrne suggests the following categories for further research: lack of information, lack of insight, lack of assurance, lack of problem-solving skill, immaturity in situation, and dominance by authority person or situation. Byrne's contribution is largely the use of psychologically meaningful categories rather than sociologically descriptive groups.

Diagnostic categorization of counseling clients serves mainly a reporting and research purpose, although the lack of basic agreement on the dimensions of personality and personal problems makes reporting difficult. There has been little effort recently to classify clients or problems according to causes. Pepinsky (359) found that judges of case write-ups agreed with their reliability on classifying clients' problems by his scheme, but they have not proved sufficiently useful in planning differential counseling.

Diagnostic categories may be useful in certain environmental manipulations and for offering specific treatment such as remedial help for slow reading problems, but in their oversimplifications they do not help the counselor very much in understanding a client.

Shorthand labels such as "neurotic" do little to help the counselor, or the client either, since they tend to make the client into a stereotype which may not fit the dynamics of the client in question. If this type of labeling seems necessary, a descriptive phrase rather than a single term is preferable. This type of understanding is merely one basis for applying the most appropriate counseling or therapeutic techniques.

One of the issues in diagnosis, involving diagnostic categories, is reliability of classification. The evidence is conflicting. One study by Ash (21) indicated that the reliability of diagnosing pathological categories was distressingly low, although this study has been severely criticized because of the inadequate categories involved. A later study by Schmidt and Fonda (416) on the reliability of psychiatric categorization revealed a high degree of reliability and met the usual standards of research design. The principal limitation of such studies is semantic in that more sound categories of pathology need to be developed before this issue of diagnostic reliability can be resolved.

A further purpose of diagnosis in counseling is that of *interpreting* case data, sometimes called "structural" diagnosis. Williamson (499) uses the term to mean the "pattern of consistency" which helps to explain or describe the client's behavior. Diagnosis is the step following analysis of the data wherein the counselor selects, from the mass of case data, the relevant facts which form the basis for a prognosis and a plan for later counseling or psychotherapy. By a process of inference, the counselor is enabled to discover new meanings in the data which can be used in the therapeutic planning or which can be interpreted directly to the client. This rationalistic view of diagnosis assumes a certain lawfulness and consistency of behavior, and was developed primarily for student personnel counseling, which is heavily educational-vocational in character.

Klopfer (265) emphasized the importance of collecting descriptive material on defenses used, and strengths and ameliorative factors in personality, as well as pathological signs when making a diagnostic study. This practice is in line with the general trend to make psychodiagnosis a descriptive rather than a classification process.

Thorne (474), looking at the diagnostic problem even more clinically, asserts that an accurate diagnosis must be made before "rational treatment" can be planned and carried out. He gives, therefore, an elaborate rationale and procedure for accomplishing the "act of clinical judgment" in psychotherapy. Thorne, furthermore, depends heavily on tests for diagnostic aid in counseling and psychotherapy.

Thorne (475) built his definition of personality diagnosis around the concept of personality integration, which is a dynamic process of organizing and unifying the behavioral field, as well as a phenomenological trait reflecting the organizational status of the person. The diagnostic process is partly one of understanding the various levels of organization existing at any given moment. In the diagnostic study, the person is examined to see if psychobiological substructures are intact and are supporting higher functions, if deep drives are being satisfied adequately and integrated with environmental demands, and if the person is able to use his personal resources to cope with life. In ascertaining the degree of integration, the diagnostician looks at the various levels of organization which the person uses to deal with his life situation. These levels vary from simple biological processes, such as digestion, all the way to complex learning and the person's style of life.

Cautions in the Diagnostic Point of View

There are dangers in the interpretive point of view of diagnosis described above. The incompleteness or inaccuracy of data, or oversimplification of complex human problems, often causes the counselor to over-extend himself on the diagnosing steps. The evidence cited later in this chapter indicates also that even the best clinical or statistical predictions are not reliable enough to formulate critical decisions.

The second major caution of this interpretive view is that it easily leads the psychotherapeutic counselor to become preoccupied with the client's history, to neglect present attitudes, or to ignore current behavior. The diagnostic process must be rooted in the individual's current psychological milieu to be effective in understanding him.

A third caution is that the clinician is tempted to utilize tests too quickly to aid him in the diagnostic process. This act is likely to lead to a client expectancy of "answers" from the tests rather than from looking inside himself for the causes of his difficulties.

Losing sight of the client's individuality is a fourth difficulty in the diagnostic process. For example, the therapeutic psychologist may possess much comparative data on such things as intelligence measures and MMPI scores, but may lose sight of the subtle distinctions which make the client a unique person responding in his own individual style to common social stimuli.

Since diagnosis has been associated historically with pathology, there is a further danger that the clinician will be preoccupied with morbidity rather than hygiology of behavior. As seen in Chapter 4, there are still too few terms to describe healthy creative personality states which would be comparable to the elaborate terminology of psychopathology. Therapeutic psychologists are devoted to a search for positive characteristics, asking such questions as, "What strengths does this client already possess?" "How much insight does he have now?" "What can we build upon?"

A final objection often cited for the heavily diagnostic approach to psychotherapy is that it leads to a judgmental attitude, a feeling that the therapist is going to "case" the client and then tell him what he ought to do. Responsibility is thus shifted too strongly to the psychotherapist, who is put in the tempting position of pontificating to the client.

Therapists following the Rankian tradition, however, tend to eliminate the early formal diagnostic steps. Rogers (390) seems particularly adamant on the question of diagnosis. He claims that diagnosis, as understood in the preceding light, is an actual detriment to the psychotherapeutic type of counseling. Rogers does not ignore the significance of behavior causation, but he claims that the meaning of behavior lies within the particular way the client perceives his reality. The client, according to Rogers, is really the only one who can know fully the dynamics of his own perceptions and behavior. In order to change client behavior, therefore, a perceptual change must be experienced. Just getting more intellectual data about the client's problem isn't likely to help change his behavior very much.

Rogers feels also that a diagnostic point of view tends to pull the counselor away from the client's frame of reference and make him preoccupied with intellectualizations about the client. Certain counselors would be prone to this overdiagnosing because of their particular judgmental attitudes. Rogers claims, further, that therapy is diagnosis in the sense that it is the client who is experiencing the process and really does the diagnosing in terms of formulating his own experience in meaningful terms.

Another more subtle social danger is seen by Rogers (390) in that too much emphasis upon diagnosis sets up the consequent temptation to make evaluative prescriptions. If clients rely on the "expertness" of the counselor, there is the potential danger of social control and influences where the counselor specifies the goals and makes the value judgments on whether a behavior is appropriate or inappropriate, mature or immature.

Rogers is criticized for his extreme view of diagnosis because he seems to set up a "straw man," in that the understanding of the client in a diagnostic sense is imposing understanding on the client. There seems to be an assumption that if one takes a diagnostic viewpoint, one is automatically judgmental. Bordin (60) points out, also, that the client's perceptual awareness is only part of his experience. He could achieve deeper understanding by making a more active contribution to the process.

Apart from Rogers' criticisms of the diagnostic position, there is another cogent reason or caution. Diagnoses are made partly for purposes of prognosis or prediction of clients' future behavior. Predictions based upon clinical judgment and clinical data are not what they should be, even for modest confidence. Clinical predictions, according to a review by Meehl (315), are less valid than straight actuarial methods in which tests, for example, are used to predict behavior. One of the controversies in the psychological literature is the relative value of clinical and statistical methods for predicting client behavior. While some psychologists express confidence that, under the right experimental conditions, the clinical methods will show up better, the evidence to date is that statistical prediction is superior and that clinical prediction methods have many limitations for counseling.

Clinical prediction is based upon the assumption that the person is consistent within himself. The diagnostician is concerned with ascertaining the person's pattern of consistencies, with which projections can be made about his behavior in the future. Meehl (315) concluded in his review of the problem of clinical and actuarial prediction that the problem can be resolved partly by specifying the conditions under which each method works best. He hopes clinicians will not be forced to think of clinical *versus* statistical methods much longer.

Resolving the Diagnostic Issue

It seems that there is still a third point of view which can be taken on the question of diagnosis. We find it difficult to escape the fact that the therapeutic psychologist must make some decisions, do some therapeutic planning, be alert for pathology to avoid serious mistakes, and be in the position to make some prognoses or predictions. It seems that the therapeutic psychologist is forced to play a delicate role between the Rogerian position of withholding judgment and attempting to stay within the client's frame of reference as much as possible, and at the same time trying to understand the client diagnostically.

It is proposed that this simultaneous "understanding diagnostically" and "understanding therapeutically," to use Porter's (368) terms, be done by the view known as hypothesis or hunch-making. Although counselors may decide to avoid some of the formal diagnostic steps, they are, nevertheless, allowing a series of hypotheses to develop about such questions as: "How serious is this matter from the standpoint of pathology?" "What would be the most appropriate approach to use at this time?" "How far should we attempt to go?" "What seem to be the basic dynamics operating (defenses, dominant needs, symptoms, environmental pressures)?" "What will the likely outcomes be?" The basic diagnostic questions, however, should be: "What is going on?" "How effectively is he responding to demands in his life?"

Hypotheses flowing from attempts to answer the preceding questions are constantly being revised until this client's style of life, basic relationships with people, dominant values, principal defenses, main strengths, and limitations fall into a pattern. This pattern is the inference from observations we have just made. Viewed in this way, the counseling process itself is, according to Pepinsky, a process of ". . . hypothesis formulation and testing, a process of approximation and correction . . ." (360, p. 198). Pepinsky goes further to indicate that what a counselor does with his hypothesis-making is to formulate a hypothetical client with behavioral descriptions in terms of the counselor's basic constructs and assumptions. In other words, the clinician is thinking that if the client with whom he is interacting at the moment behaves like his model, then he can predict how the client is likely to behave in the future. For example, we know from research and experience that depressed clients are potential suicide risks. We have a model of the suicidal person, and as the client tells us more about how he feels and what he has been thinking, we see the client conforming more and more to our model. This starts the prediction process going.

Action questions then come fast. Should I, as his counselor: (1) Refer him immediately to a specialist, a hospital, or contact his relatives; or (2) Would referral upset him even more and should I use some emergency support techniques? (3) Should I decelerate the rate of exploration of feelings, or cut discussion of them completely so he does not become more depressed? (4) Should I stop counseling with him as soon as I can conveniently shift responsibility to another therapist? (5) What other indications of pathology are present and what indications of personality strength does he manifest? (6) Is this a primary personality disorder or a secondary reaction to strong environmental stress? The answers to these questions will be indicated by the predictions made from our model. What the counselor is doing, in effect, is trying to verify a hunch that he has a likely suicide on his hands which requires a swift plan of action.

How the clinician thinks through this hypothesizing process is still quite mysterious and intuitive. Meehl (315) speculates that the process is somewhat as follows: (1) collect data; (2) have a set of assumptions and some general laws about behavior; (3) generate a tentative specific hypothesis about behavior from comparing the case data and the assumptions; (4) collect further facts and compare them to reduce the number of possible hypotheses; (5) juggle the facts and the hypotheses until a meaningful pattern emerges; (6) select through his best judgment the most specific tentative hypotheses; and then (7) make a specific prediction therefrom.

McArthur (299) also reported some research and speculation on the clinical process. He found that successful predictions were made from the model or "clinical construct" each clinician formulated, rather than from a single test, theory, or case datum. The clinicians seemed to be using an inductive method by which they fitted the case data to a model person. From this model they made their prediction as to how the client would likely behave. McArthur indicated that they seemed to be using such a phrase as, "He seems to be the sort of person who . . ." (299, p. 204).

Koester (269) studied the diagnostic process by asking counselors to "think out loud" to a recorder while examining their case materials. He found that instead of a sudden insightful patterning of the data there was a more gradual buildup of the data into a more meaningful understanding of the case. Koester indicated that the steps which the clinicians seemed to follow were similar to a problem-solving procedure described earlier in this chapter: (1) collection and comparison of the data; (2) interpretation of the data; (3) formulation of hypotheses; and (4) evaluation of the hypotheses.

Like McArthur, Koester found that the total formulations were more meaningful when approached openly without the rigidity of a single theory or set. Those counselors who failed to revise their hypotheses because of negative or contradictory data appeared to be the most rigid and single-theory-centered.

An illustration of the use of the clinical diagnosis-prediction process may be had from career counseling. Here, the need to formulate hypotheses about the client's abilities, interests, traits, and experiences in relation to the best model of a successful insurance salesman, home economics teacher, or architect, for example, is particularly important. Clinical prediction methods must be used in career counseling to supplement the actuarial methods which stress test scores and validity coefficients. Career counseling, therefore, illustrates the interplay of clinical and actuarial methods of prediction. It also illustrates the focus of the diagnostic process on prognosis or prediction, and the de-emphasis on some of the problems associated with other connotations of diagnosis.

A third illustration of the diagnostic process and of the utility of a separate diagnostic step can be found in the area of skill deficiencies. A client complaining of reading difficulties must go through a rational diagnostic procedure to determine the most likely combinations of causes such as visual, perceptual, emotional, experiential, or language deficiencies.

The clinical process in the illustrations from psychotherapeutic, career, and skill deficiency areas is going on continuously in the counseling process. Perhaps this is what writers like Rogers mean when they assert that diagnosis blends into the therapeutic process. A further observation on our part is that the further the client's complaint is removed from problems involving cognitive data, such as career plans and learning difficulties, the less distinct the formal diagnostic steps seem to become.

Since the diagnostic problem in career counseling is a little more clear-cut, more might be said about it here. The function of career diagnosis is to achieve thorough understanding by both counselor and client of the client's interests, aptitudes, personality characteristics, aspirations, family history, and work background so that he can match these characteristics with job requirements. Although the preceding process is quite rational and logical, there is a danger in ignoring the attitudes underlying the more cognitive features, such as aptitudes. Just collecting information and collating it with career goals which seem to follow logically is oversimplifying a very complex process. In other words, diagnosis in the sense in which Williamson (499) uses it, as understanding of the meaningful pattern of data, is essential to educational-career counseling. The counselor cannot shift his responsibility as an expert in making this kind of prediction to the client or anyone else.

There is a principal objection to be stressed in this discussion if the diagnosis is made a separate and formal step. It is our conviction that this diagnostic thinking, though generally coming early in the process, tends to blend into the whole counseling process. Furthermore, this diagnostic process is not the precise definitive act which it is in medicine; in counseling it consists of forming and reforming hypotheses for the most appropriate choices. This formulation is then discussed with the client for assimilation and/or amendment. At this point, it generally becomes the client's hypothesis, and all decisions and consequences are his.

As implied earlier in this discussion, the career counselor must make decisions about how emotionally involved he should allow the relationship to become. One of the most difficult things for him to decide is if, and when, he should cap off a persistent effort by the client to force the discussion into a psychotherapeutic relationship. Often the counselor can help reduce anxieties over unsettled plans for the future or difficult relationships with people without implying deep psychotherapeutic assistance. But the diagnostic process comes to the counselor's aid in detecting pathology. This is the reason all counselors, regardless of their assignment or level, must be familiar with the signs of psychopathology or deviant behavior.

The Psychodiagnostic Use of Tests

The Nature and Basic Assumptions of Psychodiagnostic Tests. Tests are one of the therapeutic psychologist's main tools. The discussion to follow will be mainly concerned with their diagnostic use. There are other uses of tests—interpretive, information-giving, evaluative, and predictive—which will be described in later chapters.

The main purpose of all testing is to obtain samples of behavior in a standardized situation devoid of subjective judgment. Test results should represent objective factual material, whereas the subjective element enters into the interpretation of the factual results. Here, the therapeutic psychologist marshals his test data, case experience, and observations, into a series of diagnostic hypotheses about this particular client. In other words, the value of psychometrics in diagnostic assessment is as an *aid to observation*. It may seem paradoxical that we discuss the use of psychometrics in such detail here when we express so much caution and skepticism. Like most aids to observation, we view them as useful, but not as substitutes for careful observations by the counselor. Sundberg and Tyler (464) have reviewed the evidence from many studies. It appears that personality psychometrics in general, and projective methods in particular, are not very useful in diagnosis. Perhaps computer technology will help us with assessment in the future.

Personality characteristics, furthermore, must be studied in their dynamic form, that is, sampled frequently to assess changes. The personal characteristics should be studied also, in their social context, since personality is a product of social interaction. There is good evidence that even some of the difficulties in intellectual functioning, involving thinking, memory, concentration, and perception, have their roots in impaired interpersonal relationships.

A further assumption underlying psychodiagnostic testing is that the unique patterns of thinking and feeling uncovered by the tests are indications of the client's basic character structure. This structure is presumed to be quite stable and consistent.

Uses of Psychodiagnostic Tests: (1) Screening. Although it is beyond the purpose and scope of this book to go into psychodiagnostic testing in detail, it seems important to the authors to describe the diagnostic uses of tests briefly. One of the principal functions of tests for the therapeutic psychologist is as a rough "screen." Earlier in this chapter, the questions of pathology, counseling strategy, and readiness were problems impinging on the counselor. By giving a brief test battery at an appropriate spot early in the process, the counselor can get a clearer picture of the road ahead.

Severe pathology often does not show up until later interviews. By giving a projective technique or a structured test such as the Minnesota Multiphasic Personality Inventory, the counselor often can obtain a more clear understanding of the currently observed pathology, and occasionally he can detect hidden pathology trends earlier.

Similarly, on intellectual variables, the counselor often desires a quick estimate of the client's intellectual capacity and functioning in advance of more definitive data. A short vocabulary test such as the Stanford Binet or Wechsler Adult Scale vocabulary subtests can give these data. In addition, short tests like the Proverbs Test (200) give a quick, even though possibly unreliable, estimate of intellectual functioning. Oral reading tests such as the Gray Paragraphs (203) offer the counselor another quick estimate of intellectual skill-functioning. The studies on culture bias of ability tests, and the rejection of many selection test procedures by the federal government on grounds of bias, lead the counselor to be extremely cautious in their use.

Uses of Psychodiagnostic Tests: (2) Predicting Success of Counseling. Diagnostic screening tests can provide information regarding readiness for counseling, for example. There is support for the statement that the rapidity of achieving successful counseling hinges on ego-strength factors such as response adaptability, capacity to test demands of reality, and undistorted perception, as evidenced by research on the Personal Orientation Inventory. Therefore, the counselor can decide early in the process whether continued counseling with this client would be feasible or desirable.

Uses of Psychodiagnostic Tests: (3) Detailed Information. There is no effective substitute for a diagnostic test in such skill areas as reading and arithmetic. Remedial help and concomitant counseling are often planned around information obtained in diagnostic achievement batteries.

Similarly, in personality trait areas, such tests as the California Test of Personality, the Personal Preference Schedule, or the Personal Orientation Inventory could give the counselor topics which could be explored directly without the circuitous routes of client verbalization. For example, finding through tests that handling feelings of hostility is a problem helps to pinpoint sensitive areas early. This early detection may create less resistance to discussion of the problem later, since the client tends to perceive the test results as "objective evidence."

Counselors working on career planning problems find diagnostic information helpful, but the main focus in career planning is on prognosis. Detailed material on the important prognostic use of tests will be described later.

Uses of Psychodiagnostic Tests: (4) Diagnostic Formulations. Pinpointing pathological types has been and continues to be a major forte of the clinical psychologist. Projective techniques such as the Rorschach and Thematic Apperception Tests have been used along with tests such as the Wechsler Adult Intelligence Scale to give a rounded picture of the perceptual, conceptual, and affective functioning of the client.

Clinic procedure often requires "pigeonholing" into nosological categories of neurosis, psychosis, and character disorders. Here, diagnostic testing is of some assistance, but the evidence for the accuracy of such diagnosing is not very convincing.

Actualizing Assessment Battery

This battery consists of four inventories aimed at assessing aspects of the actualizing process. These inventories are presented here in brief form to illustrate their use with our Actualizing Counseling and Psychotherapy model. This battery is used in promoting client readiness, in diagnosing the presence or absence of key actualizing attitudes and behaviors, and in assessing progress in counseling. These tests aid the assessment of intrapersonal as well as interpersonal dimensions of psychological functioning, just as a thermometer or stethoscope aids the medical practitioner in assessing dimensions of physical functioning. For detailed information about the nature of the battery, its research base, and its use, consult *Actualizing Therapy* (Shostrom, Knapp, and Knapp 432). This reference includes a brief clinical report of a couple's relationship illustrating the application of this battery.

Personal Orientation Inventory (POI). This 150-item inventory is a measure of intrapersonal being. It is based on the theoretical formulations and the research of several humanistic psychologists such as Maslow, May, Perls, and Fromm. Items are grouped into two major scales and ten subscales. One of the major scales assesses inner- versus outer-directedness, while the other is a time-ratio scale assessing the degree to which one is oriented to present, past, and future. The subscales are designed to reveal degrees of self-actualizing, existentiality, feeling reactivity, spontaneity, self-regard, self-acceptance, constructive view of people, synergy, acceptance of aggression, and capacity for intimate contact.

When used in a counseling or clinical setting, the POI provides a fairly objective measure of the client's actualizing level, as well as offering positive guidelines for growth. Scales can be used in combination to assess polarities (such as aggression and contact).

Caring Relationship Inventory (CRI). This is a measure of interpersonal effectiveness applicable to a variety of group and individual counseling settings, especially those involving couples. The focus of the inventory is on the various elements of loving or caring, and is based on views of love by persons such as Fromm, Lewis, Maslow, Nygren, and Perls.

The CRI consists of eighty-three items concerning feelings of one member of a male and female pair toward each other. True-false responses are made, first as applied to the other member of the couple, and second as applied to an "ideal" mate. Two forms exist—one for females to rate males, and one for males to rate females. Development of the CRI was based on responses of criterion groups of successfully married or actualizing couples and of divorced, troubled, or nonactualizing couples.

The scales assess a developmental concept of love from early erotic forms to mature, altruistic, or "agape" forms of love. One of the subscales covers self-love (S)—the ability to accept one's own weaknesses, as well as to appreciate one's unique worth. This concept includes acceptance of one's full range of feelings toward the partner. Deficiency love (D) is a type of exploitative, manipulative love where the other person is regarded for what that person can do for one.

Pair Attraction Inventory (PAI). This inventory is based on a dual theory which emphasizes attraction based on complementary needs and differences. Both complementarity and symmetry are assessed. The basic rationale is based on personality research at the Berkeley Institute of Personality Assessment which emphasized the presence of basic polarities, particularly anger-love and strength-weakness.

Research and usage so far indicate that divorced persons, and those seeking relationships outside marriage, have characteristic patterns and preferences. PAI usage suggests seven basic kinds of unconscious mate choices which operate in pairing relationships: nurturing, supporting, challenging, educating, confronting, accommodating, and actualizing. The actualizing relationship is considered in the context of this book as the preferred one. Some assumptions are that actualizing couples can be strong and weak, angry and caring. The couples can respond also with a freedom and creative rhythm not present in the other types of relationships.

Personal Orientation Dimensions (POD). This is primarily a research instrument at this point. It is designed as an extension and refinement of the POI. Dimensions assessed are: Orientation (time orientation and core-centeredness); Polarities (strength, weakness, anger, love); Integration (synergy, potentiation); and Awareness (being, trust in people, creative living, sense of mission, awareness of manipulation). Preliminary data indicate potential productive use with a variety of populations in colleges, churches, treatment centers, schools, and hospitals.

Summary

Three preparatory concerns face the therapeutic psychologist. First of all, he must face the problems of motivating the reluctant or ignorant client.

The case study is a second concern, expressed in the question: "What are the relevant data needed to help this client?" Various sources of data are available, such as case histories, cumulative records, time graphs, autobiographies, and essays.

A third concern of the therapeutic psychologist, early in the process, is the form and extent of diagnostic formulations. Diagnosis is a process of describing client living style in such a way that it helps him change his behavior in a more actualizing direction. As a means of describing causation and predicting future behavior, the diagnostic thinking process has great limitations. Clinical and statistical predictions are still too limited in validity to be used with confidence. The counselor can, however, look at the diagnostic process as a procedure for formulating increasingly more tenable hypotheses regarding the nature of the client's difficulties. Examples of such questions are, "How much pathology is present?" "How far should I attempt to take this client along the road to mature living?" "In light of the best evidence available, what seem to be the best answers to the client's search for a career or life objective?" Tests and case histories are valuable aids for the diagnostician in making preliminary estimates on the above questions, as well as in executing fine differential psychodiagnoses. The Actualizing Test Battery was described as an illustration of efforts to assess the characteristics of the actualizing person objectively.

The Relationship: Characteristics and Use in Counseling and Crisis Intervention

The heart of the therapeutic process is the relationship established between counselor and client. In the preceding chapter, the importance of client attitudes in approaching counseling was emphasized. In this chapter, further stress is placed upon attitudes of the counselor as a variable in the relationship and how the relationship is used to help the client. In many ways the counselor is a model of how to establish and maintain a relationship.

Before we can describe relationship techniques, which we shall do in Chapter 7, we shall analyze the significance of counselor traits and a rationale in this chapter. Relationship techniques will be presented later because we regard them as *implementations* of the therapist's basic attitudes and of actualizing theory.

The relationship is important in counseling and psychotherapy because it constitutes the principal medium for eliciting, recognizing, and handling significant feelings and ideas which are aimed at changing client behavior. Thus, the quality of the relationship determines not only the nature of the personal exchanges, but also whether counseling will continue at all.

We are becoming more and more convinced that the relationship in psychotherapy and counseling is a helpful agent in its own right. Many people do not have effective interpersonal relationships. The psychotherapist's task, therefore, may be seen as establishing whatever relation the client is able to make, solidifying it, gradually freeing it of unrealities, and teaching the client how to maintain it. This is a positive picture of the therapist's instructional role, as opposed to a more negative, remedial role. This developmental role is also what makes the therapist's own relative freedom from neurotic distortion so centrally important.

6

Before proceeding further, the concept "relationship" should be defined. We prefer Pepinsky's definition of the relationship ". . . as a *hypothetical construct to designate the inferred affective character of the observable interaction* between two individuals" (360, p. 171). It should be noted that in the definition, however, "relationship" refers to the *affective* or emotional elements of the interaction, which can only be inferred from observation of client behavior. The authors feel that a description of the relationship should include additional dimensions, many of which are paradoxical. In actualizing theory terms, a relationship provides the principal vehicle for the actualizing personality level to function interpersonally. Thus, defenses, interpersonal problem-solving skills, and polar feelings find expression in the relationship. While each basic theory has a position on the significance and function of the relationship, recent research on relationship variables indicates that effectiveness of relating in terms of empathy, warmth, and genuineness did not show significant differences among three divergent theorists' interviews (Fischer and Paveza 157).

Characteristics and Dimensions of the Relationship

Uniqueness-Commonality

Though certain general statements can be made about the therapeutic relationship, it is important to remember first that each client-counselor relationship is unique. The factors creating this uniqueness are as diverse as human differences. The unique factors include *counselor* attitudes, behaviors, and physical characteristics, in addition to *client* attitudes, backgrounds, and behaviors discussed in the preceding chapter. This uniqueness makes generalizing about counseling difficult. Each new counseling relationship is a fresh challenge to the counselor. A therapist cannot learn myriads of rules to cover all possible situations, yet we hold the view that he can function effectively in helping people if he knows clearly his own personality and goals, has certain basic attitudes toward people, and is skilled in basic helping functions.

Another aspect of uniqueness in a therapeutic relationship is its distinction from other human relationships. While friends, relatives, and teachers have profound influence on behavior, one unique element of a counseling relationship is its structure, that is, its carefully planned and described process framework. Another unique element distinguishing counseling relationships from others is the counselor's ability to be objective as well as emotionally involved.

Because of its intimate nature, structure, and attitudes, the counseling relationship also has similarities to other human situations, for example, family, friendships, teacher-pupil, doctor-patient, and pastor-parishioner.

In another sense, then, a counseling relationship is an extension of ordinary effective living processes.

Objectivity-Subjectivity

A second way to look at the relationship is in terms of its objectivity-subjectivity balance (352). This balance refers to the degree of emotional intensity of the relationship and the relative weighting of the intellectual and emotional elements. *Objectivity* refers to the more cognitive, scientific, generic aspects of the relationship, wherein the client is regarded as an object of study or as a part of broad suffering humanity. In extreme objectivity, therefore, a counselor would remain psychologically distant and would regard client views and values without personal judgment.

The meaning of objective counselor behavior for the client is that he feels the counselor respects his views, does not force his ideas on the client, and looks at the client's problem rationally and analytically. It is observed often, however, that clients reject such an objective counselor attitude. They want the therapist to get emotionally involved and to be personally concerned about them. This subjective feeling of involvement is one basis for feeling "understood," and seems to offer the reassurance that the counselor knows how the client feels, and that he cares. Therefore, it is our observation that clients tend to be ambivalent about counselor objectivity-subjectivity in the relationship.

Objectivity can have definite meanings and offer security for the counselor, also, since the essence of diagnosis is striving for an objective view of the client's situation. Therapists like to feel that they are aware of their own feelings at all times and that they avoid forcing values and solutions on the client.

The *subjective* elements of the relationship include emotional involvement in the form of human "warmth" and psychological "closeness," as well as intense interest in the particular client and his problems. This element is often described as a feeling of caring. The meaning which subjectivity has for the client is one of feeling understood. Conversely, some clients perceive counselor involvement as threatening, since they are "submitting" to the control of or "revealing" themselves to another person. They experience anxiety, therefore, over feared loss of emotional control. This anxiety is especially strong when a client sees the counselor allied with his externalized or rejected feelings. The client seeing the counselor, for example, as a loving mother becomes fearful of his own uncontrolled dependency needs.

The nature of the emotional interaction appears to be a key variable determining the quality of the relationship, or encounter. The counselor must be *aware of the various levels of his impact* on the client and the client on him. First, the counselor reacts at a friendship level, as one liking certain qualities in the other and experiencing pleasure at the meeting. Secondly, he reacts at a genuine personal encounter level, honestly and directly communicating. Then he reacts at a more intense level of loving concern for the other person's welfare. The counselor must be aware also of possible erotic components of interaction, which if unrecognized may interfere with the counselor's effectiveness at other levels. Rollo May [1] suggests that a real encounter involves all four levels to some degree.

The meaning of the subjective view for counselors is that in some cases they might respond to clients' problems as if they were their own. Yet, the counselor must use his own generalized experiences and feelings as guides to experiencing the client's feelings. For example, how can a counselor really know how it feels to be loving and hostile to a parent simultaneously unless he has experienced this feeling himself and has been aware of the implications? This does not mean that a counselor must have experienced all feeling-situations. He must have recognized in himself, however, those universal human experiences such as anxiety, depression, disillusionment, and self-dismay. He must have worked them through enough to be able to tolerate recognizing and empathizing with them in his clients. One of the key issues in counseling is the extent to which a counselor should reveal himself as a distinct person and how much emotional involvement he should allow himself. This issue will be covered in several contexts in the next few chapters.

The most reasonable goal seems to be that the counselor get emotionally involved to the extent necessary to keep the client emotionally involved; but the counselor's keen interest in helping should be tempered with some reserve and distance so that the counselor can accept attitudes and feelings expressed by the client or confront them objectively with as little counselor projection as possible. If the counselor gets too emotionally involved with the client, it is difficult to be objective about such attitudinal areas as religion, for example, or moral behaviors different from his own which may even disgust him personally. The counselor is objective, or "detached," in the sense that he regards these attitudes and behaviors as important manifestations of the client's personality. The difficulties in maintaining this position will be described later in the discussion of transference and countertransference phenomena.

Thus, it may be inferred that in counseling practice, objectivity and subjectivity are in a harmonic, yet paradoxical, relationship. This means that the counselor operates variously between the two positions and incorporates elements of both. For example, he is deeply and warmly interested in the client, but not in the same sense as lovers would be interested in each other, or parents in children. Objectivity is needed in diagnosing, yet subjectivity is necessary to build the climate to use the diagnostic information to help the client. The term "participant-observer" is used

---

[1] From film "Rollo May and Human Encounter," Psychological Films, Santa Ana, Calif., 1969.

in psychological circles to describe this dual relationship problem. The counselor participates fully in the intricate human interaction; yet, simultaneously, he maintains a detached observer role.

Cognitive-Connotive

Another dimension of the relationship is what Bordin (60) describes as the cognitive-connotive balance. Cognitive elements refer to intellectualizing, such as exchanging information, advising on courses of action, or interpreting, whereas the connotive elements refer to feeling expressions and exchanges. In managing the relationship, the counselor must know when to encourage rational examination and interpretation of the client's problem and when to encourage more exploration of feelings and their ideational connections. Communication is going on at both levels all the time, so it behooves the counselor to be aware of the relative weight of these factors at any given moment. Techniques for handling the connotive aspects of the relationship are described in the following chapter, whereas those techniques for dealing with the more cognitive elements are described in the chapters on interpretation and information-giving.

Grater (201) studied preferences of ninety-five clients for cognitive or affective counselor characteristics. There was a significantly greater focus on personal-social problems in the first interview for clients preferring affective counselors over more cognitively oriented counselors.

Ambiguity-Clarity

The notion of ambiguity and its therapeutic implications, as developed by Bordin (60), is a characteristic of a stimulus situation to which people respond differently and to which no clear-cut response is indicated. The counseling relationship is vague and ambiguous in many ways to the client. The counselor generally defines himself and the situation early by the process known as "structuring"; however, the degree of clarity or vagueness is a profound dimension of the relationship.

Ambiguity serves the function of allowing the client to project his feelings into the ambiguous counseling situation. This is done easily, since humans tend to handle ambiguity stimuli in terms of their unique projected responses. This process of projecting feelings aids the client to become aware and concerned about his feelings, thus enabling the counselor to know and deal with them through counseling techniques.

Too much ambiguity for some clients can allow them to become filled with anxiety in their attempts to make something secure and structured out of the relationship. For example, being too permissive with clients early in the counseling process and encouraging too free exploration of feelings may make them panicky or, in extreme cases, provoke a psychotic episode.

There is some confusion in the relationship if the counselor is too definite a personality to the client or becomes too intimately known as a person by the client. For example, the helper behaves more like a friend than a counselor. Moderate personal ambiguity is necessary so that the client can project any desired role on the counselor. This idea will be explored later under "transference."

The problem is a *social distance* matter and should not be confused with the *emotional distance* discussion under the objectivity-subjectivity section of this chapter. If the counselor is too friendly with the client in the sense that he lets himself be known too early as a well-delineated personality, the counselor will find that he feels compelled to "act himself" too strongly in the interview situation. Thus, the interview might be pushed in the direction of social conversation or intimate friendship. This is a difficult matter to handle in the school situation, for instance, in which counselors frequently meet student clients on social and instructional as well as therapeutic levels.

In a clinical setting the problem of socializing with clients could create relationship problems. Most clinicians, therefore, still consider it unwise to socialize with clients. The expectancies of social relationships tend to be quite different from therapeutic relationships and tend to interfere with an effective counseling relationship. These ideas are changing rapidly, however, since a growing body of therapeutic literature and practice is stressing the importance of the counselor being a natural friendly human being with clients.

Responsibility-Accountability

Accepting a client in a counseling relationship implies a willingness on the part of the counselor to assume some responsibility for the outcomes of counseling and some willingness to share in the client's troubles. Counseling is very serious business and must be matched by a seriousness of purpose and ethical commitment on the counselor's part. It is the client's responsibility as well, which he must assume in great part since it is his problem and behavior which are at stake.

Counselors differ in their interpretation of the proportion of responsibility which each participant must assume. We feel that the counselor does not take responsibility for running the client's life for him or of selecting goals for him. The acceptance of the relationship, nevertheless, places the counselor in a responsible leadership position where he must protect the client and assume certain liabilities for the outcomes because of the influence of his own personality on the relationship. The latter situation holds especially in psychotherapeutic relationships where the client is making such crucial decisions in his life as whether or not to get a divorce, leave home, commit suicide, change jobs, or drop out of school.

It is difficult to reduce the client's responsibility to a formula. The amount of proportional responsibility depends upon such factors as the age of the client, type of problem, type of agency setting, legally designated responsibilities, and professional expectations. There is no question but that the client is responsible for setting the goals of counseling since he or she owns the problem. Usually, if the goals are ethical and feasible, a counselor agrees to facilitate the process of achieving these goals. How accountable the counselor can be for the outcomes is a debatable professional issue. The trend, however, is to hold the counselor increasingly more accountable for outcomes in line with client and agency goals. In other words, counselors increasingly must be able to produce measurable results to demonstrate responsible professional behavior.

Some counselors control the responsibility factors by discouraging clients from making crucial decisions over such matters as divorce while in the counseling relationship. Such counselors claim that the relationship offers them a vehicle for exploring the ramifications of divorce which puts the client in a better position to make a sound decision and to live with it. The writers believe that responsibility cannot be handled so neatly in most cases. The techniques of structuring and contracting described in the next chapter can help both counselor and client to face frankly the problems of allocating exclusive and mutual responsibilities.

Counselors working in an agency setting have a further responsibility to be loyal to the institution for which they work. The preceding discussion emphasized the client's and counselor's responsibilities to each other. Mutual responsibilities of agencies and counselors are controlled somewhat by ethical considerations, but they involve the hard realities of agency responsibility to provide adequate facilities and legal protection, for example. Counselors have responsibilities to their agencies to carry out agency policy. Although this aspect of accountability is not a dimension of the relationship, it has a direct bearing upon it and is occasionally in conflict with client interests.

The counselor's responsibility to the broader society is covered in the next section on ethics.

Ethical Dimensions

A distinctive mark of the professional counselor and psychotherapist is ethical handling of client relationships. The counselor's value system is an important determinant of ethical behavior. Yet, it is difficult to summarize ethical principles based on personal values and to determine the precise nature of ethical behavior. There are typical questions, however, commonly arising in psychotherapy and counseling. The Committee on Ethical Standards of the American Psychological Association has published a *Summary of Ethical Principles* along with periodic modifications (12, 143) to assist counselors and psychotherapists with their ethical decisions. The American Personnel and Guidance Association (142) later published ethical guidelines primarily for school and college counseling settings. The following are illustrations from the APA Code:

1. How can I present my qualifications to my clients realistically and

without misrepresentations? The psychological counselor is bound to maintain the highest standards of excellence and not to claim or imply qualifications which are not possessed. Publicity should be dignified and in the form of announcements to professional persons rather than commercial advertising or announcements directly to prospective clients (12, p. 9).

2. Should I tell the agency of my judgment that this person is potentially dangerous (as in the case of possible homicide or suicide)? Should I tell an instructor, for example, of a client's persistent use of notes in examinations? The Ethical Code (p. 4) indicates that "A cardinal obligation of the psychologist is to respect the integrity and protect the welfare of the client . . . ," and "the psychologist should guard professional confidences as a trust" (p. 5). Yet, the individual's welfare does not always take precedence.

In Section 1 (p. 2) it is stated that "the psychologist's ultimate allegiance is to society, and his professional behavior should demonstrate an awareness of his social responsibilities." Another principle bearing on the question of suicide is stated as follows (Sec. 2c, p. 5): "When information received in confidence reveals clear and imminent danger that the client may do serious harm to himself or to others, intervention by the psychologist may be required." The question of cheating is less clear. The counselor might indicate his suggestion of mentioning the event to another person and seek the client's concurrence. "Otherwise, information obtained in professional work must be kept in confidence, recognizing that the clinical or consulting relationship can develop fully in an atmosphere of trust, and that the psychologist can serve society most effectively by not revealing confidences of antisocial events or intentions, but by helping the individual realize himself as a socially competent person" (p. 5). If the counselor revealed this confidence in a school or college situation, for example, he would jeopardize the future effectiveness of his counseling with other students.

3. If I refer a client, when is my responsibility ended? On this question the code is very explicit. Referral is mandatory when the counselor realizes that he is not competent to deal with the case in question. The following quotation answers the question. "In cases involving referral, the responsibility of the psychologist for the welfare of the client normally continues until this responsibility is assumed by the professional person to whom the client is referred, or until the relationship has been terminated by mutual agreement" (Sec. 2g, p. 8).

4. Are test scores confidential information? Whether test scores are confidential or not depends upon how they were collected. If the client took the tests as part of a college entrance requirement, he knows that the results will be seen by several persons, yet he realizes that the institution will protect them from becoming public knowledge. However, if the client were given a Wechsler-Bellevue as a result of an interview, the information would be classified, generally, as confidential. The same principles as those cited in question 2 apply, namely, that the psycho-

therapeutic counselor must use discretion. If he appears to be too rigid about giving information on his student clients, his superiors or his colleagues perhaps might resent his "ethical purity." But giving results in lunch rooms and hallways might be stretching the limits too far in the other direction, since this atmosphere invites a gossipy tone. It seems to be acceptable practice to convey clinical test information in professional case conferences only. Any further transmittal must be done with the client's permission. Other agencies requesting information usually ask the client to sign a statement authorizing release of clinical data.

5. How can I answer this parent's inquiry regarding problems discussed in the interviews? Counselors in schools and colleges, for example, are plagued with this problem continuously. In most states parents can see their children's records. A teacher asks about a client's problems at lunch. What can the counselor say? In the case of young children who are brought to a psychotherapeutic counselor by the parent, more latitude is allowed in transmitting information. This should be done in an interpretive and recommending manner, however, rather than in a narrative fashion. Thus, the relationship with the child is not jeopardized. With adolescents and adults, the counselor should acknowledge the interest of the parent and question the parent about behaviors he may have observed. Thus, the counselor can use information elicited from the parent to interpret without resorting to interview data. This technique diverts the parent's attention away from the client interviews, yet enables him to gain the information he seeks to help his child. This method also avoids the unpleasantness of forcing the counselor to refuse flatly to discuss the client's interview material. This type of problem offers the psychotherapist an excellent opportunity to observe the parent, both for additional information to help the client and for the opportunity to determine whether it would be wise to suggest that the parent get help with the problem also.

6. Should I tell my client I am recording his interviews? Recording information without the client's knowledge or permission is considered, generally, to be unethical. Clients assume that the interview will be recorded in some form such as notes or summaries. Some hesitate and would prefer not to have recordings made, but they rarely object. Taking a casual attitude towards the whole matter, and refraining from making a big point over permission to record, help immensely. An explanation that this is routine for purposes of later review and learning by the counselor, the reassurance that others will not have access to the record, and that no names will identify the record, usually suffices.

7. Can I mention my client's name in the case conferences with the staff? Whether names are mentioned in case conferences or not hinges largely on the make-up of the conference personnel and the mores of the particular institution. In a situation in which all participants are thoroughly infused with the ethical considerations in handling personal data, using names is considered permissible. The rationale for this view is that the ultimate welfare of the client is to be better served by this conference.

Institutional policies, on the other hand, may lean to the side of strict interpretation in which no mention of names is made in discussing cases in staff conferences. The code states: "The psychologist should present his clinical findings in a manner most likely to serve the best interests of his client. . . . The psychologist should give clinical information about a client only to professional persons whom the client might reasonably expect to consider a party to the psychologist's efforts to help him, and the client's concurrence should be obtained before there is any communication exceeding these customary lines" (Sec. 2e, p. 6).

The preceding questions cover only a small sample of the many which face the psychotherapeutic counselor in everyday practice. Since they involve elements of judgment as well as fact, it would be well if the psychotherapeutic counselor consulted his colleagues concerning questions of ethics in difficult cases. The counselor should look also into his own ethics and areas of bias to find possible sources of doubt and value conflict about the ethical implications of his behavior. Finally, one of the most important safeguards against unethical behavior is knowledge and experience. When in doubt about an ethical problem, it is usual practice to discuss the issues with a group of professional colleagues, using their consensus as a guide.

There are other significant questions to be answered, such as, what causes unethical practice? Is damage or discomfort to the client as a result of ignorance or inadequate training unethical? Schwebel (421) asserts that unsound judgment and ignorance, though dangerous and having important selection and training implications, are not, strictly speaking, unethical. He hypothesizes further that generally it is self-interest which causes unethical practice. By "self-interest" Schwebel means seeking personal profit, self-enhancement, security, and status at the expense of others. Conflicts often arise, therefore, over the infusion of the counselor's values into the process. Recent emphasis on the methods of self-disclosure of counselors in the relationship poses a related ethical problem. While the client's trust may be enhanced by the counselor revealing his true feelings and values, it could have a compelling impact on client values bordering on the unethical. Wrenn (506) stressed the personal values of the counselor as a basis for counseling ethics. He states, in addition, that ethical behavior on the part of a counselor involves more than subscribing to a code of ethics; a feeling of responsibility to relate behavior to ethics is necessary as well.

Characteristics of the Therapeutic Psychologist for Building a Relationship

A principal consideration in building a relationship is the counselor's personality. A counseling follow-up study by Forgy and Black (161) tends to confirm this assumption that the counselor's personality and counseling style are important, although they found that it was the interaction of counselor personality and method which accounted for differences in counseling effectiveness. The changes could not be attributed to counselor personality only, nor to methodology exclusively. Seeman (424), in a study of vocational counseling, concluded that methods are not as important in accounting for differing client reactions as are characteristics of "warmth, interest, and understanding." Fiedler (150) compared three differently oriented groups of experienced therapists with three groups of inexperienced therapists. Fiedler found that for experienced therapists, personalities and experience, rather than different methods, accounted for differences in therapeutic outcomes. Though serious questions have been raised about Fiedler's methodology and interpretation of findings, and though it would be dangerous to ascribe too much importance to the counselor personality at this time, there is sufficient evidence of its importance to warrant an extended discussion.

While Gardner's exhaustive review of relationship variables (179) revealed much research on ideal therapist characteristics and their positive relationship with client progress, research still is not sufficiently definitive on therapist factors for confident counselor candidate selection.

Many of the traits and attitudes to be discussed may seem idealistic; nevertheless, they provide yardsticks against which the counselor can measure himself. What are the characteristics of the effective counselor or therapist? While it had been popular for years to compile lists of characteristics of counselors thought to be significant, we are well along in research on traits of effective and ineffective counselors and therapists. The APA Committee on Training in Clinical Psychology thirty years ago, for example, compiled a list of traits which were difficult to specify behaviorally. Other lists have been compiled by Cox (110), Cutler (116), and Graver (202). Cottle and associates (108, 109), in a series of articles on personality characteristics of counselors, described how they differ from other defined groups, such as teachers. The methods used were largely standardized tests of traits correlated with specific counselor behaviors. This line of investigation was not very productive of useful data about effective counselors. The following discussion of counselor characteristics is derived largely from experimental studies on effective counselor characteristics, as well as from our own experience.

Person-Technician Balance

Counselors and psychotherapists have two strong and balanced components: personal relationship skills and technical qualifications. Clinicians such as Strupp (461) support this view. Our book on Actualizing Counseling is replete with suggested techniques for developing into an effective technician on behavior change. In addition, the counselor must always be in a conscious process of personal growth so his personal actualizing efforts will serve him as well as his methodology. There are abundant data now to validate the view that counseling effectiveness is maximal when the counselor can relate to clients in warm, understanding, and self-revealing ways. In this manner he serves somewhat as a personality model for his client.

While not so clearly established, technical competence in interpretation, information-giving, test usage, and application of rational methods is related to counselor effectiveness also. Several references will be made to the data of Rogers (397), Truax and Carkhuff (480), and Combs (107) on facilitative relationships characteristic of counselors. They found that counselor characteristics of warmth, understanding, positive regard or caring, concreteness of counselor expression, and transparency or realness create conditions for greater client self-exploration. These characteristics in turn result in greater behavior change in a client than if these "facilitative conditions" were not present in optimal amounts. Our problem in counselor selection and training is to find means for assessing these characteristics reliably. Carkhuff's scales on facilitative dimensions have been used extensively in assessment and research (92).

Before describing counselor characteristics further, we wish to reemphasize what we feel to be some focal points of this book:

1. The counselor or therapist is engaged in helping others in a professional capacity. But, more importantly, he is a human being with personal weaknesses and actualizing problems of his own. The therapist has the capacity to grow; as teachers learn from students, likewise therapists learn daily from clients. Counselors must take responsibility for their own constant personal growth through counseling for themselves, group experience, and other self-renewal experiences, such as those described by Gardner (180).

2. The professional counselor is an expert in helping others, but he has no mystical solutions. His technical training can be helpful, but only the continuous attempt to increase his own self-understanding and awareness makes him believe in what he attempts to do with clients. Counseling and therapy are only partly technique; the rest is subtle human effectiveness through personal relationships.

3. Each client with whom one deals is a unique expression of human nature; hence, the textbook generalization never applies completely. Also, the counselor must respect himself as someone who is unique.

4. Thus, counseling and therapy can be viewed as a workshop for the actualizing of both participants. Each client can help a counselor or therapist shed new light on his or her own personal integration.

5. A central emphasis for enlightened counselors or therapists must be, however, the development of a core of valid technique which fits their theory, along with flexibility for learning new ideas each day and for discarding old approaches which no longer seem to apply.

To comprehend the enormous complexity of the human personality and to handle the involved abstractions of counseling theory demand that the counselor be considerably above average in general intelligence. Related to intellectual competence is the requirement of a vast knowledge of the culture acquired through general education and varied living. Intellectual breadth is significant also, since one basis for understanding the client is to have some familiarity with the various cultural environments the client has experienced. While there is no direct evidence on this point of counselor behavior, it is one of those unquestioned "givens."

Counselors have proceeded at times believing that didactically presented knowledge about counseling improves effectiveness. Growing evidence from studies such as Joslin's (249) indicates that, in training situations with school counselors, rated counseling competence has a low relationship to measurable knowledge about the process.

Spontaneity

What was said about spontaneity as a characteristic of the actualizing personality in Chapter 3 applies especially to the counselor. It has been mentioned several times that counseling is not a rigid mechanical application of formulas for producing behavior changes. The counselor's responses to client statements and feelings must be immediate reactions of the counselor's total being at that moment. The counselor must be free to move naturally, quickly, and easily in his thinking and feeling in order to adapt to the subtle nuances of client behavior.

While no concrete suggestions can be offered concerning how this characteristic is acquired, it seems to be a by-product of thorough preparation in counseling theory, attitudes, and methodology plus a nonrigid mature personality relatively free from threat.

Acceptance and Caring

It is questionable how much attitudes can be changed by advice, persuasion, or threats. Client attitudes appear to change most effectively in the presence of other growth-producing attitudes. The client experiences acceptance, for example, as a feeling of being unconditionally understood, loved, and respected. This positive acceptance attitude is the counseling equivalent of a basic form of altruistic love (452). The evidence and logic presented by writers such as Fromm (171), Montague (330), May (312), and Sorokin (452) attest to the therapeutic power of altruistic love. For the past few years counselors looked to philosophy, theology, and anthropology for their concepts of therapeutic love. Psychologists have recently been studying the components of love through ingenious experiments with primates. Harlow's (216) studies of mothering are examples. In the context of long range development studies, Harlow found that primates fed and raised under varying conditions of deprived maternal presence developed maladaptive behaviors which in human terms would be described as neurotic and sociopathic. Examples are infantile sexual behaviors, excessive and inappropriate aggression, and reduced affectional interaction. It was apparent that the deficient quality and quantity of early affectional relationships with the mother or mother surrogates had a profoundly negative effect on their later behavior. Spitz's (454) earlier studies with children in foundling homes further support common sense observations about the powerful qualities of love relationships. Infants not fondled by home personnel had an unusually high mortality rate compared to those who obtained some human attention. Until more evidence is accumulated, however, we should be cautious about overgeneralizing in regard to the curative effect of love.

The counselor is in a position to provoke love relationships in the interview which can have profound constructive or destructive effects on the client's security system and capacity to give and accept love. As long as clients have deep unfulfilled affection needs, the counselor's management of love in counseling will be a crucial therapeutic variable. Observations seem to indicate that the person who has received sufficient love, particularly in early development, learns to be happy with himself and to love adults around him, which, in turn, enables him to direct considerable altruistic concern to all human beings later on.

Some counselors and psychotherapists may have reservations about using the multifaceted term "love" in a counseling context. *Caring* is a term meaning much the same as love, and includes the component of unconditional regard for the client's welfare. This care can be expressed in an aggressive critical fashion as well, as in situations where correction or discipline are involved.

Shostrom's Caring Relationship Inventory (433) is an experimental attempt to measure the essential elements of caring, or love, in couple relationships. It helps the client to discover the spurious, as well as the growth-producing, elements of love in his own person.

Unconditional positive regard is another euphemistic term used by counselors to describe this deep concern for the client's welfare and personhood. Truax (478), for example, found unconditional positive regard as an effective treatment variable in his study of treatment in psychosis.

Nygren (348) contrasts the eros and agape types of love, in which eros refers to the ancient Greek term for a type of self-centered, erotic love which satisfies the organism's desires. Agape refers to a type of love in which a person seeks to assist other people to grow, contributes unequivocally to the welfare of the love object, and allows the loving person to be used for self-enhancement of the loved. Acceptance, as defined in therapeutic terms, has many of the attributes of agape.

Another characteristic of acceptance attitudes is *spontaneous motivation*. The presence of concern for the other person is a natural outgrowth of the basic attitudinal structure of the counselor or therapist personality.

Acceptance is *altruistic* in the sense that the other person's welfare is sought, not exploited.

Acceptance attitudes are *nonjudgmental* in that the counselor holds a "neutral interest" in values held by the client. This appears paradoxical when we assume that the counselor wants to promote the welfare of the client as the counselor views what is best. The counselor tries to say in effect, however, "I neither approve nor disapprove of your behavior and attitudes, but I deeply respect your right to feel as you please and your right to act or feel differently from me." The counselor makes the client feel that no matter how he feels toward the counselor it doesn't matter, and that the counselor won't judge the client for seeking help.

Basic Assumptions Underlying Acceptance. Holding an attitude of acceptance presupposes several basic assumptions. First, acceptance is based on the idea that the individual has *infinite worth and dignity*. In other words, human values are extremely high in the value hierarchy of the counselor. A second basic assumption is that it is the person's *right to make his own decisions* and lead his own life. This assumption is based upon a third even more basic assumption that the client has the capacity or *potential to choose wisely* and *to live a full, self-actualizing, socially useful life*. A fourth related assumption is that each person is *responsible for his own life*. The counselor's value system must be such that he will enhance this sense of self-respect and self-responsibility in clients and in himself. As we indicated earlier in this chapter, while discussing responsibility, counselors must realize that they cannot solve problems for clients.

The basic assumption of many counselors, particularly of those leaning toward the client-centered group, is that there exist within the individual creative growth forces which, when released by the counselor's acceptance, will allow the individual to grow toward the model of the self-actualizing personality. Rogers (390) cites evidence from several fields which appear to support this assumption of growth needs. Allport's concept of "propriate striving" as a positive, goal-directed, motivating force, deep within the personality, is related to this basic assumption (4).

The assumptions and attributes of acceptance mentioned above are rooted deeply in American democratic philosophy, which in turn is based strongly in our Hebraic-Christian cultural traditions. The Leibnitzian philosophical position of viewing the human as an active, growth-motivated organism has contributed much also. The blend of eighteenth-century emphases on universal human rights and values with nineteenth-century views on human uniqueness and individuality has created a rich background for counseling philosophy. Thus, the present cultural and educational climate in the western world appears to favor these assumptions and attitudes. This climate is making it easier for counselors to learn and apply basic attitudes leading to client self-actualization.

A summary definition of acceptance has been stated by Rogers (390) as being a positive attitude toward the individual which views him as a person of worth and dignity with the right to make his own decisions. We have postulated that the major element of this positive attitude is a form of love. Being loved in this accepting sense makes the client more capable of loving himself and others. Perhaps the following is the dynamic of acceptance: When the client has experienced an attitude of acceptance, he is able to take this attitude and experience it in the same way toward himself. Once he has accepted certain characteristics about himself, the client is able to accept those ideas, experiences, and drives which are a part of his basic self, but which, up to now, he has been denying or distorting. Evidence from studies by Truax and Carkhuff (480) support this idea of greater self-confrontation in the presence of warmth and understanding.

Self-Acceptance. There is some evidence for the circular idea that acceptance of others is based on acceptance of one's self, and that self-acceptance is based largely on being accepted by others. Several studies (44, 364, 428, 513) point to the significance of self-acceptance and other positive self-regarding attitudes as basic for acceptance of others. The significance of these findings for a counselor is that he must accept himself before he can accept clients sufficiently well to help them. The significance for a client is that acquisition of self-acceptance and understanding puts him in a position to accept others and to receive social rewards from others. Fromm (171) points out that one great difficulty in this principle is that our culture frowns on self-love yet extols loving others. This difficulty seems to stem from our cultural inability to differentiate "selfishness" from "self-respect."

Values of Acceptance. ⋀·A point of great significance for the acceptance attitude is that *the client gets involved* in the counseling process when the client senses that the counselor really cares about what he thinks and feels, that the counselor can and wants to help him, and that he will not be judged. Counseling then begins in earnest and becomes meaningful. ⫯·A second value of the acceptance attitude is its effect on the *psychological climate* of the interview. By psychological climate is meant the emotional tone resulting from the personality interaction of the client and counselor. The climate may be described, for example, as warm, cold, serious, or frivolous. Conspicuous examples of emotional climates are those surrounding funerals or football games. Porter (367) defines psychological climate more narrowly as those elements of a situation which have implications regarding valuing one's self as a person. In other words, the counselor's attitudes affect the interview climate which, in turn, influences the client's attitudes toward himself—attitudes of confidence, worth, and competence, for example.

The counselor, in addition, tries to keep a fairly consistent or stable attitudinal climate so that the client can express himself freely without expecting disapproval, criticism, argument, or other traditional responses he expects on the basis of his past experience. This accepting climate, and the fact that the counselor does not react toward him as others have reacted, makes a favorable situation, we believe, for learning new responses and extinguishing old nonadaptive behaviors.

3. A third value of acceptance is its salutary effect on *defensive* attitudes. Why does acceptance have such power to counteract defensiveness? A partial answer may be found in the description of personality presented in Chapter 3, which viewed the individual as being protected by a facade of protective mechanisms—mechanisms employed to reduce psychological hurt. Rationalization, denial, justification, projection, and development of symptoms were a few examples.

What happens when a client feels threatened? The defenses, previously learned, are mobilized. He is like the old man in the fable who, when the wind began to blow, wrapped his coat around himself even tighter. You will remember that in the story it was the sun, with its warm rays, which created the atmosphere or climate which made the individual want to take off his coat. Acceptance, similarly, is that attitudinal set of the counselor which seems to create in the client a feeling of being so comfortable in his presence that he need no longer keep his guard or defenses up.

Acceptance—What It Is Not. Because we have endeavored to teach the meaning of acceptance, it has been our experience that many students misconstrue its real meaning. The following are some mistaken notions about acceptance. 1. Approval or agreement is not acceptance. Accepting a person means neither approving nor disapproving of what he says or feels. It means simply taking him as a person with the right to feel and think differently from the way we think and feel, no matter how unfair, absurd, negativistic, wholesome, social, or pleasant his expressions may be. That the client, early in the counseling process, may misinterpret the counselor's acceptance attitudes as agreement with what he says and feels is a real counseling hazard.

2. A second misconception may occur over an attitude of *neutrality*. Acceptance is a *positive*, *active* attitude toward the client. It says in effect, "I *like* you even if I may not necessarily agree personally with all you think or feel." Another way of stating this idea might be, "I see, appreciate, and value these ideas and feelings along with you. You, the essential you, matter more to me than what you say or do."

3. A third distorted notion of acceptance is to equate it with *sympathy*. Sympathy goes much farther than acceptance, in that the counselor actually begins to feel in the way the client does—with a strong empathic response. The counselor actually feels sorry too as he becomes more emotionally involved. Acceptance, however, is more detached. The counselor says in effect, "I understand how badly you feel, although I do not personally feel that way." Sympathy, while intended as a supportive device, has the added disadvantage of tending to *minimize* the feeling of the client. A sympathy attitude says in effect, "You poor person, I feel so sorry

for you since you cannot help yourself; let me give you encouragement and help." The client feels incapable of handling the feelings by himself and feels that he must look to outside support. The net effect is the creation of a psychological climate in which dependent and evasive behavior is learned. When the need in the counselor to offer sympathy is strong, it is suspected that this is an expression of his own dependency needs.

4. A fourth misinterpretation of acceptance is equating it with *tolerance*. Although tolerance may be a desirable social trait, in a counseling relationship it connotes "putting up with." It implies a negative acceptance rather than a positive one, as well as a more superficial kind of respect for personality. The tolerance attitude implies that there is a characteristic, such as race difference, of which the counselor is aware, and about which the client senses he is trying to be tolerant.

Understanding and Empathy

Counseling and therapeutic writings are replete with suggestions to "understand" the client as a special way of being with him, yet the term is seldom defined in behavioral terms. Effective counselors seem to be able to understand their clients more than ineffective counselors can, according to several studies (150, 151, 222). Porter (368) made a useful distinction between understanding diagnostically and understanding therapeutically. *Understanding diagnostically* refers to the intellectualized descriptions of the client's behavior. Examples are the information obtained through testing or observation for making diagnostic judgments for use in career planning. As one would expect, this aspect of understanding enables the counselor to make predictions about the client's overt behavior and of his self-descriptions. The test, then, of the degree of the counselor's diagnostic understanding would be the extent of his ability to describe, interpret, and predict the client's behavior.

Understanding therapeutically refers to feeling reactions on the part of a counselor which enable the client to feel understood, accepted, and empathized with. An attitude of therapeutic understanding emphasizes seeing the client as he sees his experiences. As Gendlin (185) so aptly described it, understanding empathically is sensing the meaning which the client is experiencing so as to help the client focus on that meaning. Raskin (375) studied eighty-three counselors from eight different therapeutic orientations to arrive at a description of the ideal therapist. They agreed highly on the ideal qualities, and most put empathy in the first rank. Yet, when examining the recordings of six expert therapists, Raskin found many short of their ideal. Empathy, even though not a very operational concept, has been studied extensively and has proven to be a key ingredient for obtaining constructive outcomes in classrooms as well as in counseling (Aspy 22).

Therapeutic understanding appears quite unrelated to the counselor's knowledge about the client (153). Effective therapists, although not able to predict their client's self-descriptions much better than the poor therapists (151, 298), were rated significantly better in their ability to establish and maintain a warm, accepting relationship. In this connection, one of Fiedler's significant findings was that there was substantial agreement among skilled therapists of three different schools of therapy as to what constituted an ideal therapeutic relationship. The skilled therapists of different schools agreed more with each other on definitions of the ideal relationship than with the unskilled members of their own school (151). If Fiedler's results can be interpreted at face value, it seems that understanding therapeutically is closely related to therapeutic competence.

The evidence is not all positive, however. Lesser's study (283), although limited in scope to a few counselors and clients, found that the generally accepted idea of empathic understanding being related to client progress did not pertain. Even though all clients in his study made progress as measured by Q-sorts on ideal-self perceptions, this progress was unrelated to measures on an Empathic Understanding Scale.

In a series of studies on the conditions which promoted constructive personality change in college and hospital clients, Truax and Carkhuff (478, 480) found that a sensitive and accurate attempt at therapeutic understanding of the client was very facilitative. This is an empathic response to the client's being, which the client perceives as meaning he has been understood. Truax and Carkhuff found that nonpossessive warmth and counselor genuineness were variables which, in addition to understanding, promoted client growth. The rationale for the effectiveness of these ingredients is stated by the investigators as follows:

The greater the degree of the therapist's accurate empathic understanding of the client, the greater the degree to which the therapist shows unconditional or nonpossessive warmth or integration of the therapist within the relationship, and the more intense and intimate the therapist in the relationship, the greater will be the degree of the client's interpersonal exploration and the greater will be the consequent extent of positive behavior change (480, p. 861).

In other words, if counselor conditions as described above are present in the relationship, clients feel more free to be themselves and face their problems.

The effective counselor apparently needs both diagnostic and therapeutic types of understanding. Yet, he may find that attempting to use both types of understanding is difficult indeed. There is a strong tendency to be preoccupied with the cognitive aspects of the client's difficulties and to overlook the connotive implications of his confusion and indecision. For example, while attempting to see the client's reasons for seeking financial aid, for finding social work more suitable than teaching, or deciding which marital prospect appears most promising, the counselor might tend to ignore the threat to the client's independence involved in the financial aid, or the need to dominate children in the career choice, or the extreme dependency interfering with a marital or occupational choice. In some cases, perhaps, more emphasis needs to be placed on the reality level of the client's occupational choice rather than on the intricate feelings regarding his parents' wishes for success through him. This point is especially pertinent for many school counselors and advisers whose positions are structured around educational-vocational planning. We assume that the really effective therapeutic psychologist has the capacity to keep the understanding emphases in balance and to know when to stress one aspect of understanding over the other.

The Internal Frame of Reference. Another useful concept in understanding the client and in assisting the counselor or psychotherapist to understand the meaning of empathy is that of the internal frame of reference (367, 391). This concept is defined as the attempt by the counselor to perceive the client and his phenomenological world as seen by the client. It means the attempt to think *with*, rather than *for* or *about* the client. By frame of reference is meant simply point of view or the observational vantage point. Rogers cites an example of the counselor's thoughts as he assumes this role:

To be of assistance to you I will put aside myself—the self of ordinary interaction—and enter into your world of perception as completely as I am able. I will become, in a sense, another self for you—an alter ego of your own attitudes and feelings—a safe opportunity for you to discern yourself more clearly, to experience yourself more truly and deeply, to choose more significantly (390, p. 35).

An example of a counselor's thinking from the *external* frame of reference would be, "What is causing this difficulty, and why is he so preoccupied with marital problems?" The counselor thinks, "This fellow is in bad shape; I've got to find out what is wrong and try to help him save his marriage." An example of the *internal* frame of reference thinking would be, "You see this as a very disturbing experience, and you want to do something about it." The counselor thinks, "I must try to understand how he looks at this problem and to help him clarify his own thinking about it so that he can make a decision in line with the best interests of all concerned."

As an aid in conceptualizing the problem of getting within the client's frame of reference, see Figure 12 (440). In stage (1) the client and counselor are in an ordinary social interaction situation where S listens and C talks. The perceptions are formed largely on the basis of the unique past experience of each participant. Each moves down his respective experience lane as in stage (3). Often the counselor, who characteristically assumes the external frame of reference, tries to get the client to come into his lane—to see things his way. Under certain circumstances this may be a legitimate objective, but it does not necessarily help in understanding the client.

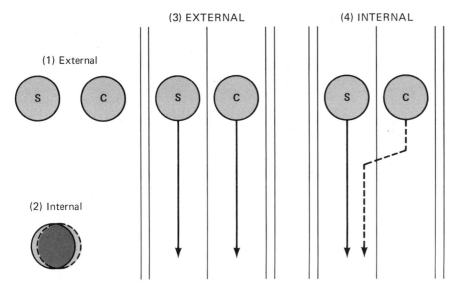

Figure 12.   The Internal and External Frames of Reference

When the counselor assumes the internal frame of reference, however, he tries to make his perceptual framework match that of the client as in stage (2) of Figure 12. Stage (4) illustrates what happens when the counselor tries to get into the client's lane. At least temporarily, he attempts to think and feel the way the client does. We are assuming that this effort is necessary to understand how the client views his situation.

Learning to assume the internal frame of reference and to stay within it seems to be particularly difficult. As one contemplates the reasons for this difficulty, the following examples can be considered.

1 *Language differences* constitute a major obstacle. As the adult tries to understand the adolescent or the child, or as the easterner tries to fathom the particular lingo of the westerner, it seems that the symbols used have different meanings to different people. This is a problem of semantics which has received much attention in the linguistics literature of recent years.

2. *Biological differences* are obviously another barrier. The difficulties experienced as a man tries to assume the feminine frame of reference, and vice versa, can be easily understood.

A current issue in counseling is whether white or black counselors working with clients of a different race can really empathize with their clients since they share so little common experience. It takes unusual empathic ability to transcend these differences.

3. *Socio-economic differences* often cause client and counselor to be in different semantic worlds. Counselors, for example, having from five to eight years of college training, have difficulty assuming the frame of reference of those with little formal education. A thorough understanding of

social class differences and their significance, therefore, should be part of every counselor's training. There is abundant evidence of the need for this type of understanding in studies by Havighurst (219), Warner (490), Postman (369), and Schwebel (420).

Related to cultural differences are *experience differentials*. Counselors, having life experiences different from their clients, can only see the client's world imperfectly in the light of their own frames of reference. Finally, *age differences* influence understanding, in that one who has lived longer often finds it difficult to "see" the significance of the conflicts and frustrations of a much younger person. Teachers, for instance, often forget "how it feels" to be a student.

It was felt that a brief analysis of some of the obstacles to assuming the internal frame of reference would help to punctuate the necessity for striving very hard for broad life experiences, as well as for asking ourselves the questions: "How does he look at this problem?" "How is he thinking and feeling about this matter?" "What is he trying to say?" This attempt at understanding the client by means of assuming the internal frame of reference pays heavy dividends in a better relationship and more appropriate counselor responses to the client's feeling and thinking.

Empathic response is another way of viewing understanding. Empathy is related to the German *einfühlung*, which means "feeling into." An illustration is the response of the crowd as the highjumper clears the bar. All vocalize "umm-mm" and lean forward as the jumper goes up. Bowlers often experience similar feelings when they "empathize" the ball. Similarly, counselors tend to "feel into" the attitudes of the client as they are being expressed. Although this capacity to empathize aids the counselor in maintaining the internal frame of reference, there is a tendency to get overinvolved emotionally, the dangers of which have been described previously.

The question of how a counselor manifests empathic qualities is answered by the quality of verbal responses which capture the essential feeling messages of the client. Reflecting these messages with caring concern leaves the client with a feeling of being warmly understood.

Warmth and Human Encounter

Closely related to therapeutic understanding, caring, and acceptance attitudes is the term "warmth," used to describe an aspect of the relationship. Warmth appears to encompass the sensitive, friendly, considerate, and responsive elements of the counselor personality. "Relating easily to people" is a phrase often used to describe an aspect of warmth. Manifested "warmth" seems basic for an effective relationship. Truax and Carkhuff's research (480) included a warmth scale. They found that nonpossessive warmth was an effective therapeutic ingredient, and that the higher the level of this variable the more evidence of constructive personality change was noted.

The friendly conversation, preceding and interspersed in the process, however, adds little to the progress of counseling. It has been called "sawdust" by Rogers (391), meaning that it helps to maintain a friendly climate but doesn't result in much therapeutic progress.

Consideration for the client is rooted in respect for him as a person, and is another way of manifesting warmth. This counselor attitude conveys a feeling to the client that he is worthy of respect (a feeling which many clients do not have for themselves). Consideration is shown also in the ordinary courtesies of social communication, such as offering a chair and showing concern for the client's comfort. Consideration is shown through the intense interest exhibited in the client so that he feels he is an important, worthwhile person to the counselor, not just another research or practice "guinea pig."

Bugental (75), in describing the mature therapist, uses the term "encounter" to describe the therapist's willingness to "be there with" the client and yet take responsibility only for his own (the therapist's) authentic personhood. The counselor serves as a model for authenticity.

Another external manifestation of warmth in a relationship is the honest smile. This behavior is the test of the genuineness of the counselor's attitudes. Clients can sense when the counselor is "just trying to be nice" and when he experiences genuine pleasure in knowing the client as a person and in spending time with him.

Freedom

This corollary attitude of acceptance characterizes a freedom and lack of authoritarian and judgmental attitudes in the counselor's personality. Permissiveness was a term used in the past to describe therapeutic freedom, but recently accrued negative connotations reduce its descriptive accuracy. The counselor says in effect, "You may discuss anything you wish here without fear of judgment"; hence, he is neither offended nor shocked. He allows the client freedom to be himself and to grow.

A completely *laissez faire* attitude, however, would operate to the disadvantage of the client, since the relationship would be too ambiguous. If allowed too much free expression, the client may fear loss of emotional control and suffer anxiety. As indicated in the discussion of catharsis, too free an expression of feelings may serve to erode the client's defensive structure to the point where he is at the mercy of his feelings and may move toward a psychosis.

A counselor who is too permissive could be extremely cruel to the client who is vulnerable to anxiety. Such a client might flounder without direction. The counselor would abuse his own freedom if he were facetious. An extreme example would be the client who came into the office and announced, "I just killed my mother," to which the counselor replied, "Did you use an axe or a knife?" The client assumes that the counselor takes his professional responsibilities seriously, and responses of this type tend to destroy respect for the counselor.

The counselor's authority role often belies attempts to acquire a permissive attitude. The counselor's personal prestige, specialized knowledge, and professional "halos" make a free expression atmosphere difficult to achieve. The counselor is tempted at most to use his authoritarian status to urge the client toward a definite goal, or at least to select the content of the interview. The desirable amount of authority or direction to be given is the least amount consonant with the goals of the particular counseling case and the least amount which is comfortable for both. Techniques for implementing these attitudes will be clarified later under the subject of structuring. When used appropriately, therapeutic freedom allows the person more spontaneous expression of his feelings, thus allowing him to understand and accept them.

Congruence and Transparency

There is growing evidence that, in order to elicit open, honest self-confrontation by the client, the counselor himself must manifest these qualities. There is little evidence, however, concerning what kind of self-congruent behavior is therapeutic. Does this mean telling the client one's own problems? In a group therapy situation, Branan (65) found that use of the counselor's self-experience did not increase his perceived genuineness significantly; yet Schutz (418) places leader self-revelation in a central place in group work.

Various terms are used to describe the condition of genuineness-realness, congruence, transparency, and authenticity. There is more than just self-awareness and nondenial of feeling in the counselor. He must present himself as a real person in the interview encounter. A common behavior running counter to this idea in counselors is the facade of professionalism —a kind of protective personal distance. In the Truax and Carkhuff studies (480), there was a significant tendency for counselors rated high on the genuineness and self-congruence scales to have clients who were rated most improved or having the most constructive personality change.

The counselor must, above all, be honest and sincere in his attitudes. Counseling cannot be a masquerade. Honesty, as used here, is not perceived in moralistic terms but as a characteristic of "straight-forwardness." The beginning counselor, for example, learns quickly that if he tries to be accepting without truly feeling this way inside, the client does not take long to find it out. It is this quality of honesty which again distinguishes communication in the interview from ordinary social conversation. In much of social communication both parties keep up a "front," hence conversation is often a game of mild deceit. It seems that when the client experiences a relationship in which this deceit is not present and when he feels that the counselor is serious and "on the level" with him, he realizes that he can drop his own facade and can accomplish little by being deceitful himself.

In order to be completely honest, it is necessary that counselors recognize frankly their own errors—that they make errors of judgment and technique. Therapists can more easily recognize and correct errors when they can admit they are present. Their perceptions and humble acceptance of error, however, must be balanced by a mature tolerance for the inevitable mistakes, especially the more trivial ones. Clients seem to have a remarkable tolerance for counselor error providing other aspects of the relationship are adequate. This attitude of alertness to error serves as a useful antidote to counselor complacency, or what is known as the "pedestal syndrome," or the "Jehovah complex." Bugental (75), in describing characteristics of the mature therapist, mentions humility as a consequence of the counselor's awareness of his limited knowledge and the awe he experiences in the presence of potential growth. Bugental mentions further the need to accept normal guilt for being a therapist. This condition results when the sensitive therapist realizes that he is not doing all that can be done for persons who trust their lives to him. These are further illustrations of the need for counselors to face up to the real business of being human in the very sensitive relationship of counseling.

The studies of Truax and Carkhuff on therapeutic variables have been cited often in this chapter. Not only are they models of sound research procedure, but they also give valuable leads for process conceptions and counselor selection. They found that the effective counselor is a person who can sensitively and accurately understand a client, allows himself to express warmth, and who can be genuine and still retain his integrity in the relationship. These conditions encourage the client to manifest the same characteristics, resulting in deepening self-exploration and self-awareness, which then make possible more constructive personality change. They also found that low therapeutic conditions resulted in ratings of client behavior indicating deterioration (91). Thus, counseling can have negative effects; this may help to explain why so many studies of counseling outcomes come out negative, and why so much credence is placed in Eysenck's findings (144) which question the efficacy of therapy. Positive growth indices are canceled out by the deteriorative effects of some counseling conditions.

We feel that, at this point in the discussion of counselor characteristics, it must be mentioned that the counselor is not some sort of inert, bland agent to be manipulated at will by the client. In his attempts to accept the client wholeheartedly and to enter into a close relationship, the counselor or therapist *risks* as much as the client. The counselor, too, must open his facade to make the relationship effective. The risk element involves the possibility of failure or rejection by the client and, if this happens, the counselor may lose part of himself. The counselor accepts this risk as the price of being human.

Flexibility

Carnes' (94) study of counselor flexibility points up the necessity for this vital trait in the counselor's character. The counselor must move easily and quickly from one role to another. For example, a role may be forced upon him of father figure, teacher, or friend. Most of the time he must represent a type of social reality to the client who, as Kelly expressed it, "tries out psychological experiments of test-tube size in the laboratory of the conference room" (257, p. 619).

It is our viewpoint that therapists must be flexible in the use of their counseling techniques as they move along all the dimensions defined at the outset of this chapter. Sometimes they must be objective, and at other times subjective. Often they utilize techniques which are primarily connotive; at other places they are primarily cognitive. For example, they may explain a point about client responsibility to create clarity; at other points they may deliberately promote ambiguity, as will be explained in Chapter 7. Sometimes counselors focus on aspects of client problems which are common to men and women in general. Then again, they may dwell upon the unique problems of particular clients. The essence of the creative synthesis view is flexibility in utilizing all approaches and methods as they seem appropriate and effective in achieving the anticipated outcomes.

Support and Crisis

Nature of Support

The therapeutic relationship, in addition to being the vehicle for the development of awareness and action, serves a broad supportive role. As we have seen earlier, an awareness of anxiety reduction and a feeling of security on the part of the client are the principal results of a suitable emotional response from the counselor. The essence of support, then, is this general feeling of well-being, and satisfaction of "affect hunger," as Levy describes it, which the client experiences in the presence of certain counselor attitudes.

Support may be viewed in four ways. Its implicit form is the supporting nature of the relationship itself. The acceptance, warmth, and other characteristics of the counselor are construed by the client as security-provoking. The client experiences support when the relationship bridge is broadened so that feelings can flow freely from the core to the self- and ego systems, as well as between counselor and client personalities. Rogers, for example, speaking of the counseling relationship says, "It is experienced as basically supporting, but it is in no way supportive. The client does not feel that someone is behind him, that someone approves of him. He does experience the fact that here is someone who respects him *as he is*, and is willing for him to take any direction which he chooses" (390, p. 209). We agree with Rogers in principle, but there appear to be crises when actual support techniques need to be applied. This effort to support a client also may seem contradictory to earlier statements about the use of anxiety and distress for motivating the search for insight. The principles of flexibility and timing, however, make it possible for the therapist to be accepting at times, more supportive at other times, and even threatening at appropriate points.

2. A second type of support experienced by the client takes the form of reassurance, change of environment, and various forms of help which remove environmental or internal pressures. There is a large group of counselors who feel this type of support is necessary with certain types of clients, especially in the early phases of counseling. Thus, whether support is offered explicitly through a medium such as reassurance, or only through the implicit support of the relationship itself, is one of the unresolved issues in psychological counseling. Reassurance techniques will be described in detail in the following chapter.

3. Support may be experienced by the client in a third manner when he feels the counselor assuming more responsibility for leading the interview, carrying the major verbalizing load, and making decisions. While this shift in responsibility may have a supporting effect, it should be viewed as a temporary expedient for reducing anxiety only. *The danger of prolonged support of this type is primarily that of reinforced dependency and reduced capacity to assume responsibility.*

4. A fourth function of support is in the form of crisis intervention, which is described in the next section.

Managing Crises

Crises are produced by two sources of stress—external events such as disasters, death in the family, sudden unemployment, or severe illness, and internal events. Internal sources, while aggravated by external events, are such conditions as suicidal feelings, acute alcoholism, despair, or bad drug trips. Crises are characterized by severe stress, disruption of life routines, acute frustration, and feelings of helplessness. Crises associated with situations such as death are usually of short duration, especially if the normal grief process has ensued. Developmental or existential types of crises, such as going off to school, entering the army, or facing a conflictful choice, usually are more prolonged. In Western societies crises are usually viewed as severe problems to solve; whereas in some Eastern societies—for example, the Chinese—the language symbol for crisis is danger plus opportunity. From an actualizing viewpoint, therefore, counselors need to ask how crisis methods might move the client from comfort and equilibrium to higher levels of growth.

An appropriate supportive relationship provides hope—the best antidote for despair and grief. Currently, helping agencies are experimenting with a multiple impact strategy with families, where several specialists offer immediate and comprehensive help to a family undergoing a crisis. Here, a team of specialists meets the family right at the hospital, in case of severe accident, for example, and provides intensive help to get the family functioning as normally as possible. Crisis centers, run largely by volunteers trained in basic crisis helping skills, are part of almost every large community. Much of the supportive contact work is done by telephone. Skills for managing crises are presented in detail in *The Helping Relationship: Process and Skills* (Brammer 64).

Crisis intervention methodology and strategy has become a specialized helping field. In addition to the usual helping skills, drug therapy may be a useful medical adjunct in severe emotional pain. The goal usually is restoration to precrisis equilibrium. Aguilera and Messick (2) summarized the key steps in crisis intervention as: (1) Assessment of the person and problem (e.g., danger to self or others?); (2) Planning the intervention (e.g., to restore equilibrium); (3) Intervention to explore feelings, gain intellectual understanding, explore coping mechanisms, and reopen the social world; (4) Resolution of the crisis (e.g., reinforce coping mechanisms).

The most common type of crisis is associated with loss, or impending loss, of a loved one, a prized job, health, or physical strength. For example, Kübler-Ross has described the five stages persons facing death go through: denial and isolation, anger, bargaining, depression, and acceptance. Part of the counseling task is to help clients work through these stages.

Values of Support

A supportive relationship has four primary therapeutic values. One of its principal values is that it/]helps to reduce excess anxiety and consequently develops security and comfort. The emotional presence of the therapist enables the client to feel worthy, loved, and respected. This aspect of support waxes and wanes according to the needs of the particular client at various points in the process. Those clients feeling inadequate, grief-stricken, unworthy, uncomfortable, lonely, or fearful about losing control of their feelings are given the specific relationship help they need. For example, the inadequate person is led to feel that here in the therapist is a pillar of strength on which he can lean temporarily while he develops confidence and strength.

He can feel also that for the time being he does not have to be big and strong, mature, and capable. In other words, he feels he can walk before he is expected to run. This may seem, at first, to be promoting dependency, but its value lies in allowing the client to express his security and dependency needs, accept them, and interpret them later. It seems wise to go along with the client's dependency a short while so that he does not feel that the counselor is just another paternalistic adult anxious to push him into maturity.

The grief-stricken or suicide-prone person can feel that here is someone who understands how he feels and with whom he can share troubles. A supportive relationship helps the client who is fearful of his impulses by enabling him to feel that it is all right to have the feelings, to express them, and to feel that they won't get him into trouble. In addition, the counselor may help the client to control his feelings by techniques designed to decrease the emotional intensity of the discussion.

2. A second value of support is the assurance that it gives to the client that he can be helped—for example, that he can make realistic plans, that he can improve his studies, or that he possibly will save his marriage. Clients in a state of anxiety often have a hopeless feeling about their problem, or feel theirs is a unique case. The counselor's calm, accepting, reassuring manner can be a powerful supporting medium for these clients, such that they experience hope and confidence in the future.

3. A third value of support is the awareness it gives the client of his freedom to change his views or behaviors. By fully accepting him, the counselor says in effect that, though he may not agree with the client, he can be receptive to his views at the moment. Thus, the client is not given the reassurance that he is right about his present views. If the client feels overly reassured about having, for example, a picture of himself as a very shy person, he may tend to feel guilty about changing this picture. In other words, he does not feel "caught" in his present attitudes and is able to try out new responses. Support enters again when he tries out the new response which may get him into even greater difficulties temporarily.

4. A fourth value of a supportive relationship is that it prevents the client from accepting abortive solutions to his problems. It encourages the suicidal person, for example, to explore alternatives to suicide. The client can feel that he does not have to take impulsive actions which may get him into even worse trouble. For example, he may see that becoming more settled in his feelings before going ahead with divorce proceedings might save him later regrets. Similarly, hospitalization may support the client until he is better able to work rationally on his problems.

Limitations of Support

Since a counselor is supportive when he helps the client to meet his emotional needs, it is obvious that this condition offers mixed blessings. One liability of oversupport is the resentment or guilt a client may feel when he is aware of his dependence on the counselor. Some clients, in addition, are deeply threatened by too much "warmth" or emotional closeness, possibly because they have not yet learned how to handle a close human relationship. A second limitation is the strong dependency that may develop through prolonged support. This significant counseling condition is discussed in Chapter 8 under the topic of transference.

3. A third limitation or misinterpretation of support is that of sympathy. We have discussed the implication of sympathy earlier in this chapter. It should be emphasized again that liberal use of support may have a ring of insincerity or exaggeration.

4. Resentment against the apparent shallowness and stereotypy of liberal reassurance is a fourth limitation. The attitude that "everything will come out in the wash, so don't worry" has been offered many times by important people in the client's life. He knows that things don't always turn out all

right, so he is threatened by what appears to him to be insincere, stock techniques.

Summary

Psychotherapeutic and counseling relationships have several basic dimensions, such as uniqueness-commonality, objectivity-subjectivity, cognitive-connotive, ambiguity-clarity, and responsibility-accountability. The counselor has the difficult task of recognizing and dealing appropriately with these seemingly paradoxical elements of the relationship.

Since therapeutic effectiveness hinges so much on the quality of the relationship between counselor and client, basic attitudes of the counselor are highly significant. The attitudes of acceptance and understanding have considerable consequences upon the psychological climate of the interview. This climate which these attitudes create holds important implications for the client's evaluation of his own personality. A key to an effective attitudinal climate is the counselor's assuming the internal frame of reference, which is his attempt to understand the client by taking the client's view of his situation and himself as his frame of reference. The counselor must have additional characteristics of warmth, intelligence, flexibility, humility, and a willingness to share the responsibility.

One of the principal functions of the relationship is to provide support for the client, especially in crises. Support is the promotion of comfort and security through the construction of optimal conditions of living. Support is considered generally to be an aim of psychological counseling and is often a condition necessary before more cognitive approaches can be made to solution of the client's broader problems.

Relationship
Strategies

The purpose of this chapter is to present methods for relating easily to clients, promoting client comfort and feelings of being understood, and encouraging client exploration of feelings. In the preceding chapter on counselor attitudes an assumption was made that techniques are limited unless there is full understanding of therapeutic goals, fundamental counselor attitudes, and theoretical assumptions from which the techniques emerge. In other words, there is a danger of becoming too "technique-conscious." One characteristic of a charlatan is blind adherence to pat techniques applied indiscriminately to all clients.

Techniques, on the other hand, are somewhat personal in that counselors develop varying styles and techniques best suited to their own personalities and their estimates of client needs. Techniques are, after all, primarily media for defining and redefining relationships with people. Useful techniques, in addition, have stood the test of time in practice; in many cases, they have been validated experimentally.

Considerable emphasis in this chapter is placed on client-centered techniques. Though we greatly respect Rogers' contributions to these techniques, we differ, in the chapters that follow, with his basic theoretical position. We place more emphasis on variety of technique and flexibility, along with greater acceptance and awareness of the counselor's own attitudes and feelings as he relates to the client. This emphasis fits the broad approach of our Actualizing model. These relationship methods are useful in dealing with problems at the facade level in handling resistance. They also have a modulating effect on feeling awareness and expression at other levels, particularly with feeling polarities. Relationship strategies are especially useful in encouraging expression of feelings along the basic polarities of loving and directing anger, for example. Thus, modulating in this con-

7

text means the process of expressing a full spectrum of feelings along any polarity in a manner which achieves the growth goals of the client.

Keeping the above considerations in mind, we offer the following discussion on methods as possible ways the basic attitudes and concepts of the counselor and psychotherapist might be manifested. We would like to point out also that most of the following methods can be described behaviorally and can be taught as skills.

Opening Techniques

The first task upon meeting a client is to establish a feeling of trust. Earlier books on counseling and psychotherapy speak of building rapport, a condition of mutual understanding and comfort. The counselor establishes this condition by living his accepting, warm attitudes and manifesting deep interest in the client, rather than by applying a kind of technique. Some of the accumulated experience of counselors in beginning the relationship is summarized in the following topics.

The Greeting

If counseling takes place in an office, the counselor's initial interest in a client is manifested by meeting him in the reception room with a firm hand clasp (if socially appropriate to his age level and subculture), greeting him by name, and escorting him courteously into the office. If not in an office, the usual informal greeting customs appropriate to the subculture of the client would prevail. Ordinary human courtesy, therefore, goes far in opening a relationship satisfactorily.

The Topics

Counselors vary in their opinions on how to open an interview. Starting with an urbane or trite conversational topic might result in a more strained relationship than if the client were allowed to state his business frankly and immediately. This problem illustrates an area of artful judgment required of a counselor and reflects his personal style.

Counseling generally deals with problems that are personal and loaded with anxiety. It is often difficult to face these problems squarely and immediately, particularly in the presence of a strange person of uncertain trustworthiness. The counselor must resolve the client's fear and restraint, which is natural in a new setting, by making him moderately comfortable. Sometimes it helps a client to mention a "conversation piece" in the office such as a picture on the desk. Clients often feel comfortable with this conventional way of starting a human relationship. It should be emphasized, however, that such openers are merely "ice breakers" to enable the client to start perceiving the therapeutic attitudes of the counselor.

There is just as much danger that the relationship will get off on a conversational bent as on a "cold," resistive start.

As an additional note of caution, an effective relationship can be established just as easily on a nonverbal basis by a warm and friendly "waiting-for-you, my-time-is-yours" appearance on the counselor's part, and secondly, by competently meeting whatever lead the client gives for a starter. If a client is motivated to seek help, engaging in "small talk" may tend to show a kind of disrespect for this need. Furthermore, too much "small talk" might imply that the counselor needs to protect the client from the reality of the situation. Generally, a lead something like "would you like to tell me what brings you here?" is most realistic and honest. In summary, the first remarks are largely matters of counselor preference or style.

The Physical Arrangements

One of the determinants of a good working relationship is believed to be the physical condition of the room. There is no research on this problem, so we depend upon opinions of counselors. While some counselors work across a desk, we feel this sets up communication barriers. Yet sitting face to face at close range is too threatening for some clients. Each counselor needs to experiment with the most effective arrangement for himself and his clients.

Other physical arrangements would seem to be taken for granted, but it is our experience that often they are overlooked by counselors. It is axiomatic, for example, that the client never be placed in a position where he must face the light. This means that, if it is necessary to face the client toward the window, the blinds or drapes must be closed.

Another consideration is the nature of the client's chair. The possibilities for a good counseling relationship seem to be improved through installation of comfortable chairs for both counselor and client. This represents quite a change from traditional arrangements whereby the counselor is afforded a comfortable swivel chair and the client is given any available straight chair.

The Attitudes

A degree of mysticism seems to surround the client-therapist relationship. Counselors sometimes give the client the impression that therapy is a form of magic and that the therapist is endowed with special powers which make him able to help people. In our experience the relationship bridge is built best on a feeling of the natural human relationship. It is assumed here that counseling is a unique, human interaction which differs only slightly from other human relationships. The counselor may explain that there is nothing mysterious about counseling or psychotherapy, for they are largely processes of planning, relearning, and confronting one's self.

As with all other techniques, building a relationship is rather fruitless unless the counselor possesses the characteristics detailed earlier in Chapter 6. Ethical behavior must prevail. Above all, the confidential nature of the interview must be maintained. Counselors working in colleges and universities often are tempted to use illustrations from their own counseling experiences in classes in counseling, mental hygiene, and psychology. Such procedure is doubtful, yet counselors are apt to follow this practice unless they are aware of the damaging effects this may have on relationships with future clients.

Reflective Relationship Techniques

1. Reflection of Feeling

In the actualizing approach to personality described in Chapter 3, it was emphasized that much of personality is beyond awareness. Reflection technique helps the individual to go beyond the actualizing system to become more aware of obscure feelings of the core and to deal with them more effectively. What seems to happen is that the client talks of his feelings as "it" or "them"—something apart from himself. This tendency of the client to deny ownership of his feelings at first serves a useful defensive function. The reflection technique, however, focuses on the subjective element of what the client says. Reflection emphasizes the pronoun "you" in the phrases, "you feel . . ." and "you think. . . ." Reflection serves a useful purpose in that it leads the client to think of the feelings and ideas being expressed as part of his own personality and not outside of himself. Thus, reflection is a useful intermediate technique to be used after the initial relationship has been built and before the information-giving and interpretation stages in the process are begun.

Reflecting feelings is a skill and, as such, can be learned by understanding and practice. Phillips and Agnew (366) found from their data that reflection is definitely a learned helping skill, and that it is not commonly used in general interpersonal relationships by non-clinically trained, or even able and mature people. With the prevalence of communications training, however, and the emphasis on listening for feelings, reflection of feelings is likely to be more of an everyday occurrence.

The Nature of Reflection

Reflection of feeling is defined as the attempt by the counselor to paraphrase in *fresh* words the essential *attitudes* (not so much the content) expressed by the client. The counselor attempts to mirror the client's attitudes for his better self-understanding and to show the client that he is being understood by the counselor. The word "fresh" is emphasized because, perhaps, the most glaring reflection error of the novice counselor is to express his reflection in words already used by the client. In a humorous anecdote, in which the counselor repeated almost verbatim the client's statement, the client's reply was, "What's wrong with the way I said it?" It is preferable to use sufficiently different words with an air of intense interest and effort to understand, such as "You seem to feel you want to make a decision, yet you find it so hard to do so."

The word "attitudes" is emphasized in the definition of reflection in order to make the counselor aware that he must be able to grasp the underlying feeling about what is being said, not just the content. Therapy is often likened to a river, with the ripples on the surface corresponding to the content. But more important are the undercurrents—the feelings underlying the content. It takes considerable skill to develop the sensitivity necessary to identify these feelings immediately and to mirror them back as soon as the client has completed his statements.

A word of caution about client feelings is worth expressing. A common misconception arising from an emphasis on feeling is that the expression and identification of feelings have in themselves some great intrinsic merit. The conclusion often drawn is that feelings are more important than intellectualizations. Expression of feelings is encouraged by the reflection technique. Its effectiveness, however, seems to reside in the idea that the expression of feeling is a means to self-confrontation, and not an end in counseling.

Feelings are thought by the client to be subjective and not to be trusted. They tell him of danger when there is no danger, of presence of symptoms when he is tired and discouraged. The expression of feeling, therefore, is to make possible the discovery of the idea which underlies or is attached to the feelings. The client should be taught to *trust* the expression of feelings. A person in a panic state, for example, is helped if allowed to express his feelings. The air is cleared of smog and, as a result of the clarification, he can examine and deal with the underlying basis of his insecurity.

The individual, through the aid of his ego system, is the evaluator of his experience. Feelings do not possess evaluational quality; they are not "right" or "wrong." Ideas, however, possess truth or falsity. But evaluation of thought is only possible after feelings have been clarified. This is why reflection of *content* is unwise in the early stages of therapy but appears to have real value in later stages. Thus, clarifying feelings leads to clarification of the *ideas* and *experience* underlying these feelings.

The counselor is interested in helping an individual to change his behavior or his undesirable ways of acting. The route to these changes, however, seems to be through the individual's feelings. The client's feelings, furthermore, are generated by his ideas or perceptions. This means that how he perceives and construes the world determines how he feels about his world. This process seems to work in a cyclical fashion also, since feelings, in turn, appear to influence perceptions and so determine what and how the client sees. His past experiences, feelings, and basic needs, therefore, are at the roots of his behavior. Feelings in particular can be described as the road to the deeper levels of ideas and experiences which constitute the individual's core system.

2. Reflection of Nonverbal Experience

A form of reflection in actualizing counseling which goes beyond reflection of verbalized feeling is reflection of experience—a method of "reading" behavior. This is a technique where a counselor observes the posture, gesture, tone of voice, and eyes of the client. The counselor reflects back to him not just his intended *feelings*, but also the message from his *observed nonverbal behavior*. Our actualizing therapy view states that much of our expressive potential is projected in our posture, movement, and voice. Actualizing counseling assists the individual to discover and use directly the energy that was expended in these projections.

Reflection of experience technique confronts the contradiction of *what* the client says he feels and what the counselor *sees or observes his total organism saying*. Some examples follow:

C: You say that you are angry but your eyes appear to say to me that you are hurting inside.

C: You say that you hate me but I seem to hear caring in your voice.

C: You say that you love her but every time you talk about her your fists clench.

The actualizing counselor must have the courage to reflect his own percepts of the client as well as to state the client's intended or stated feelings. This requires confidence in one's ability to observe what is going on in the here and now of this situation.

3. Sharing of Experience

Actualizing therapy holds that the relationship between client and counselor is a key dimension of the therapeutic process. This relationship may be thought of as being expressed on a *continuum of personal responsiveness* with *reflection of feeling* at the one end, with *reflection of experience* in the center, and with *sharing of experience* at the opposite end. By *sharing of experience* is meant the honest effort of the counselor to share his own experience in the moment with the client. Thus, *sharing of experience* is *"modeling"* for the client in the behavior frame of reference, to encourage clients to share their experience. The therapist is modeling for his client how to be a person and is not simply a technician mirroring the client's verbalizations. This requires risking and a willingness to share with the client the therapist's personal feelings at the moment. The following are examples:

1. *TH*: "It makes me angry when you let her get to you like that."

2. *TH*: "I get uncomfortable when you *always* hurt and never let yourself feel any other feelings."

3. *TH*: "Your intellectualizing is boring me and I am getting sleepy."

In teaching the technique of reflection to new counselors, it has been found helpful to categorize the nature of human feelings so as to assist the novice in the immediate recognition of the feeling expressed. Reid and Snyder (378) found considerable variation among counselors in their ability to name feelings expressed by clients. There was high agreement among counselors rated as good, however. This implies that ability to reflect is partly a matter of general counseling skill and experience.

In general, it may be said that feelings fall into three broad categories: positive, negative, and ambivalent.[1] Positive feelings are those which are ego-constructive and self-actualizing, while[2] negative feelings are generally ego-destroying.[3] Ambivalence refers to the presence of two or more contrasting or conflicting feelings expressed or implied at the same time toward the same object. In clinical counseling, it is found that such feelings underlie a great many interpersonal relationships; therefore, it is particularly important for the counselor to spot these apparent contradictions and to reflect them to the client. It is important for the client to see and to accept seemingly contradictory attitudes toward the same person, for this can be a source of great intrapersonal tension. One of the goals of psychotherapeutic counseling is to realize that we can both love and hate the same person at the same time.

The following list gives some examples of labels which fall into the two arbitrary categories of positive and negative feelings.

Positive		Negative	
Happiness	Self-worth	Guilt	Disgust
Security	Love	Resentment	Antagonism
Gratitude	Optimism	Fear	Rebellion
Self-confidence	Contentment	Depression	Rejection
	Warmth		Hostility

A beginning counselor who can observe and identify common feelings will find it easier to reflect these feelings more quickly and confidently. The ability to sense fine shades of client feeling is dependent largely on the empathic capacities of the counselor.

Difficulties in Reflecting

Stereotypy. A common error is made in reflection when the counselor uses a stereotyped introductory phrase, such as, "You feel. . . ." This procedure, if it is not varied, will tend to arouse client feelings of resentment and attempts to analyze the process hypercritically. The following variations are suggested:

Use of the word that expresses the feeling; for example: "You were mad (sorry, confused, etc.) when that happened."

"You think . . . ."

"You believe . . . ."

"It seems to you . . . ."

"As I get it, you felt that . . . ."

"In other words . . . ."

". . . is that it?"

"I gather that . . . ."

Inflection—intonation of various words to express the reflection; for example:

C1: "It really hurt me to hit her."

C: "It *really* hurt." (Note: This is an exception to the general rule of not reflecting content.)

Timing. Another error which the novice counselor seems to make is that of waiting for the client to stop his comments before reflecting. When much content and little feeling are expressed by the client, this is not serious. As counseling develops, however, a great many feelings may come rapidly. This condition often necessitates interrupting the client so as to focus on significant feelings that might have been overlooked. It is easy to make the opposite error of interrupting the client too soon and completing the client's sentence for him.

Selection of Feeling. When Rogers introduced this reflection technique it became associated with the Rogerian label, "nondirective." A cursory examination of the technique suggested that since the counselor was only repeating feelings which already had been expressed by the client, the counselor, therefore, was not "directive." A closer scrutiny of this technique reveals, however, that any reflection requires that the counselor *choose* from the verbalizations of the client those elements which he feels have greatest quality of feeling and are in greatest need of clarification. This means that the counselor, in a sense, is highly direct and confrontative in using this technique, since every time he reflects he must choose from the variety of material presented to him by the client. This is a significant argument against indiscriminate use of this technique by untrained people. Damage could be done by failing to reflect accurately or by reflecting accurately and then not working through the feelings properly.

Porter (367) made a significant contribution to the use of reflection technique when he suggested that the counselor must learn to avoid the "four common errors of reflection." A paraphrased and illustrated summary is presented below.

Content. "Reflecting content" is an error in counseling which consists of reflecting back to the client his statement in essentially the same words that the client used. When the counselor does this, he does not convey understanding, but merely repeats blindly what has already been said. His reflection, moreover, is generally met with denial rather than acceptance.

C1: I've always just considered medicine because my father always dictated to all us boys what we should be.

C: You've always sort of considered medicine because your father dictated to you and your brothers what you should be.

A counselor who uses these techniques is fortunate if the first interview lasts over five minutes. The counselor who has a "knowledge-of-acquaintance" in reflecting techniques might reflect in the following manner:

C: You just went along with him since you never thought of disagreeing with him?

This is an attempt by the counselor to get below the surface and to touch on the undercurrent of feeling expressed by the student. The counselor disregards the words of the student in favor of the feelings being expressed.

2. *Depth.* The counselor who fails to respond to the same degree of depth in feeling as expressed by the client is also not reflecting accurately. Some counselors are consistently too shallow in their reflections. Others are consistently too deep, and the reflection becomes an interpretation. An illustration follows:

C1: I want to be an engineer, but I just can't drive myself for four long years without her. . . . I just can't do it. . . .

C: You'd like to be an engineer, but you'd also like to get married.

The reflection obviously is too shallow. A more accurate reflection might have been:

C: It's just too long a grind without her.

Or, the counselor might have reflected:

C: You just wouldn't be able to live without her for four years.

This reflection perhaps is "too deep" and might be met with denial or by a change of subject on the part of the client.

3. *Meaning.* It is also important that the counselor not *add to* or *take away from* the meaning of the client's statement. An illustration of such procedure is as follows:

C1: I just can't see myself as an accountant sitting at a desk all day.

C: You don't think you'd like the idea of having to balance budgets, and making profit-and-loss statements, day in and day out.

It is obvious that the client did not say all that the counselor did. The counselor has read much more meaning into his statement. The counselor might have taken away meaning by a reflection of the nature of the following:

C: You just don't like indoor work.

To be accurate in reflecting the proper meaning on the surface appears easy, but too often the counselor responds from his own frame of reference rather than from the client's frame of reference.

4 .*Language.* Experience by many trained counselers indicates that the counselor should always use the language most appropriate to the situation. Here is an example of a poor use of language:

C1: I just seem to be shy with girls. I just can't be friendly.

C: This inferiority complex seems to be extremely active in these heterosexual relations.

The errors the counselor made in the reflection are mainly overinterpretation and pedantry as well as absence of feeling.

It should be emphasized that although reflections should be accurate, an inaccurate remark may still promote interview progress if the client perceives that the counselor is trying to understand him. For example, the counselor may say, "So you resent your father for doing this?" The client responds, "Oh no, I actually admire him for it." While inaccurate from the client's viewpoint, the remark may still be effective since the client feels compelled to clarify his feelings and correct the counselor. The net effect often is progress in the interview.

Types of Reflection

Immediate Reflection. This type consists of reiterating a feeling immediately after it has been stated by the client.

Summary Reflection. This involves "tying together" several feelings. This summary method is diagrammed in Figure 13. The summary reflection is a method of bringing together in one statement several feelings expressed previously. An illustration is, "From your descriptions of your family relationships, school experiences, and now your new job, you seem to have strong feelings of personal failure in all of them."

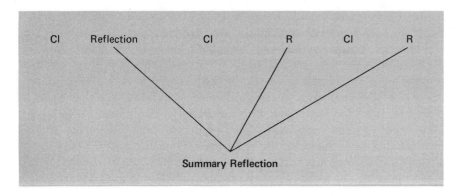

Figure 13. The Summary Reflection

Terminal Reflection. This is a technique of summarizing the important aspects of the entire counseling hour. Terminal reflection may also include certain content material which summarizes the proceedings of the hour.

Reasons for Effectiveness of Reflection

It seems appropriate in the discussion of this technique to examine some of the possible reasons for its effectiveness in achieving the goals of counseling.

Reflection helps the individual to feel *deeply understood*. Most disturbed clients are defensive and feel misunderstood. When confronted with this technique their fear of feeling misunderstood is overcome. For the first time in the lives of many of them, the clarity with which the counselor reflects their deepest unverbalized feelings causes disturbed clients to feel deeply understood. Thus, reflection serves a supportive function and is used most effectively in the early and middle phases of counseling.

The reflection technique helps to break the so-called neurotic cycle, often manifested in marital counseling and expressed by such phrases as, "She won't understand me and therefore I won't understand her." The counselor, relying on the reflection technique, helps break this tenaciously held line of reasoning.

Reflection impresses clients with the inference that *feelings are causes of behavior.* Perhaps the most significant contribution that reflection of feeling makes to the counseling process is that it affords a vehicle for conveying understanding of causes. Feelings are elusive and often uncontrollable. Frequently we feel that we do not understand ourselves because of the emergence of strange or unwanted *feelings.* When another human being tries so genuinely to understand us, and appears so capable of clarifying for us the elements of our own experience which are cloudy and fearful, this human being comes to be valued by us. Reflection serves, therefore, as a clarifying and simplifying function.

Reflection causes the *locus of evaluation* to be in the client. Another reason that reflection so effectively challenges the individual to take responsibility for himself is because it subtly suggests that a value system is not something inherent in any experience or object, but that value is placed on it by the individual. Bombardment of the individual with such phrases as "you feel" and "you think" and "you believe" teaches the individual that he is the evaluator of his own experience and that values are alterable. The client sees that values are judgments made by the individual, based upon his experience. Values are also alterable if and when new experience gives new evidence. The term "locus of evaluation" is helpful here. In the early phases of therapy the client tends to put the locus of evaluation of his behavior *outside* of himself in parents, friends, or social groups. Toward the end of counseling, the individual finds that he can place and must place this evaluation of behavior in himself. Clients learn that they own their feelings.

Proper reflection gives him the feeling that he has the *power of choice*. A current tendency in our culture has been to shy away from assuming personal responsibility and to trust the "expert." The specialist is expected to tell us how to rear our children, to advise us on marriage or divorce, to choose our career, to advise in matters of love-making, budgeting, *ad infinitum*. In matters of personal concern, the result is a continuous cycle of helplessness. The more the expert is consulted, the greater the feeling of helplessness, the greater the need for further advising. In counseling, the aim should be to create self-direction in the client. The reflection technique along with the lack of advice on these matters encourages the individual to achieve this end.

Reflection *clarifies the client's thinking* so that he can see the situation more objectively. Reflection technique by its very nature involves an attempt by the counselor to draw out essential elements of the client's conversation for his reconsideration. The natural result of such a procedure is to mirror to the client high points of his thinking, and to enable him to clarify his present situation and to see it in a more objective and focused fashion. Robinson (385) describes a special type of content reflection which he calls "clarification." Clarification, which summarizes the substance of the client's verbalization, is designed to accelerate insight development through simplification of his wandering and scattered responses without his feeling he is being "pushed."

Another reason why reflection seems to be such a useful technique is that it helps communicate to the client the idea that *the counselor does not regard him as unique* and different. The phrase, "you feel . . . ," conveys the impression that the counselor is never shocked into inability to understand. Indirectly, therefore, the reflection technique serves a further supportive function in that it gives clients the feeling that they are "normal" and not weird or different.

Reflection helps clients to *examine their deep motives.* When the counselor concentrates on the individual's feelings rather than the ideational content of his remarks, he is reaching the individual at a deep motivational level. This observation is illustrated by the common question with which all of us have been faced: "Why did you do that?" The answer may have been, "Because I felt like it." People often do things just because they "feel like it." Feelings are manifestations of the needs and drives which compel us to act. Careful scrutiny of our feelings leads us to examine the motivating forces underlying these feelings. This process is illustrated by the comment, "Well I felt like it because. . . ." The word "because" often leads us right to the core motive or experience.

Acceptance Techniques

Nature and Value of Acceptance Techniques

This is a simple technique of responding mainly with short phrases, such as, "mm-hm," "Yes, go on," which imply attitudes of attention and acceptance. It is employed particularly in the early stages of counseling when much content or narrative material is produced, often without much associated feeling. Acceptance techniques are employed also in the later stages when the client is delving deeply into himself and is painfully bringing out significant material. It is simply a verbalization of the attitudes of acceptance of the counselor which say in effect: "Go on, it's safe, you needn't be ashamed of expressing how you really feel."

The value of expressions like, "I see," "Uh huh," are that they reinforce discussion along the same lines. Another value is the transitional bridging effect between ideas, which gives a smooth forward-moving feeling to the discussion units.

Elements of Acceptance Technique

Simple acceptance technique has at least four major observable elements. The first is simple *attending behavior,* largely maintaining eye contact. Eyes are very expressive for most people and are a key vehicle for counselors to express acceptance and caring. Second is the *facial expression* and nodding of the counselor. The counselor must convey genuine interest in his face. The counselor who puts on a feigned expression of interest will be discovered by the sensitive client.

Third, *tone of voice* and inflection tell the client whether the counselor is accepting, even if he uses conceptually meaningless vocalizations such as "mm" instead of words. Of course, the counselor who speaks so quietly that the client must strain to hear him hampers the process by conveying an impression of disinterest. But the counselor who speaks with an overbearing voice conveys an impression of dulled sensitivity to the expressions of the client or is exhibiting his own needs for controlling the interview.

4. *Distance and posture* make up the fourth consideration in acceptance. If the counselor leans over and sits comfortably close to the client, the client will infer a friendly attitude on his part. This conveying of an attitude of "towardness" as opposed to "away-from-ness" by posture is important, since the former attitude conveys the qualities of openness and sincerity of the counselor. Many clients are hypersensitive to cues like those mentioned above. They may interpret, therefore, the slightest negative gesture of the counselor as rejection or disinterest. Yawning, crossing and recrossing of legs, grasping the arms of the chair tightly are examples of negative cues which are easily discerned by the client and often interpreted as disinterest.

Ellis (134), in surveying the literature on couch and face-to-face therapy positions of clients, concluded that face-to-face therapy was preferable, partly because acceptance techniques could operate more effectively. In terms of a microcounseling approach, the above acceptance methods have come to be known as attending behaviors (241).

Structuring Techniques

Nature and Value of Structuring

Structuring technique is the counselor's definition of the nature, conditions, limits, and goals of the process. In other words, structuring provides the client with a framework or orientation for therapy. He then feels that the relationship has a rational plan. Structure provides him with a counseling road map and with a dossier of his responsibilities for using the road map, thus reducing the ambiguity of the relationship. The client should know *where* he is, *who* the interviewer is, and *why* he is there. Thus, the structure of counseling has three elements, the first being the 1.implicit element in which the very setting and known role of the counselor automatically set limits that are generally understood by the client. The second element, formal structuring, consists of the 2.counselor's purposeful statements to explain and limit the counseling process. The third, or 3.contracting element, is described later in this chapter.

The use of May's analogy (311) to illustrate the nature of implicit structuring may be helpful: Each person is traveling through life as though he were in a boat going down a river. Without the structure of the river bank the water would flow in all directions. The banks of the river provide the limiting factors which guide the boat and give it added power to go down stream. The individual, likewise, is free to make his own choices, but always there seems to be a frame of reference which limits and gives direction to choice.

Another illustration of the directional value of structuring is provided by a former client: "It was kind of like going down the highway on a foggy night. I drove my own car but the counselor provided the illuminated white line in the middle of the road for me."

Bixler's survey (51) on the therapeutic value of setting limits may be distilled to the following general principles: (1) limits should be *minimal,* consonant with the security of the client and therapist; (2) limits should be applied nonpunitively; (3) limits should be *well-defined* in regard to such things as action, time, and number of appointments; and (4) limits should be structured *at the proper time.* Too early or too rigid structuring may destroy a relationship.

Dangers in Lack or Inadequacy of Structuring

It appears that the therapeutic process is a miniature social condition in which the individual should utilize his freedom, but in which he must simultaneously accept the limits imposed by that freedom. The counselor who fails to provide structure would be unfair to many of the clients who have no notion of what counseling is all about. Curran stresses this point:

A confused person is likely to approach the first interview feeling a minimum of responsibility for himself and a maximum of fear, insecurity and defensiveness. Continued miscues on the part of the counselor in structuring the relationship seem to cause the client to depend on the counselor and to feel rejected and hostile if the counselor refuses to solve his problems, and finally in defensiveness and fear to flee the interviews and not keep subsequent appointments (115, p. 189).

Structuring, therefore, has value in preventing such early misconceptions about counseling as magical cures, fast help, single causes, advice-giving, smooth sailing, inevitability of cure, and counselor responsibility. By focusing on the positive learnings and roles of client and counselor, and the reasonable expectations of the process, many misconceptions can be offset. This aspect of structuring, by the way, must be a continuous process.

Rogers tends to feel that the structure of therapy can be provided for the individual at the nonverbal level; that is, the client will "get the idea" as he participates in the process. This may be true with highly sophisticated clients, but does not seem to be adequate for average clients.

Ingham and Love suggest that undesirable insecurity develops when structuring is not provided:

The patient may at first feel that his task is unorganized and formless and that there are no rules. Then he experiences a strange feeling of helplessness and dissatisfaction. It is as though the therapist did not care what he talked about or how he spoke of it (238, p. 81).

Lack of structuring might arouse anxiety in the client and perhaps account for a counseling failure. It is important, therefore, that the structure be made a *means* to enhance the security of the relationship and not an *end* in itself. Otherwise, permissiveness and acceptance values are lost. Structuring in the beginning phases of counseling must be approached with caution, since there is a danger of conveying a feeling that the counselor has a definite preconceived way of doing things which the client had better follow as an ultimatum. Another danger is that the counselor might convey an impression of how the client ought to feel rather than encouraging him to feel the way he *does* feel.

Sherman (428) found that failure to structure, so as to leave the client too much on his own resources early in the process, results in strong resistance. A feeling for the right amount of structure for each individual client is a paramount counseling skill. If structuring is done badly, it can be a relationship barrier. Similarly, if it is ignored in institutional settings, the results may be equally tragic, since the client may build unreal expectations about the outcomes. Structuring has a positive value if it reduces the anxiety of the client who is not cognizant of the dual roles of his counselor or is not aware of situational limits which exist. An example is the counselor who has instructional or administrative relationships with a student. The counselor must point out that these relationships are different from his relationship as a counselor. Thus, authoritarian imputations will not spill into the counseling.

Robinson (385) cautions, however, that the counselor's compulsion to structure frequently, to set the client straight, may be a symptom of his lack of assurance. Another caution in structuring is the tendency to imply that the relationship will continue with this particular client. It may turn out that the counselor will decide not to work with this client or that the client may not be suitable for this counselor. Hence, the client or the counselor may feel too committed to the relationship if it has been over-structured.

Types of Structure and Contracts

In earlier definitions the authors described structuring as the technique which defines the limits and potentialities of the process. Paradoxical as it may seem, the provision of clear-cut limits provides the client with the power to move forward in therapy. Structuring methods extend to contracting, which is an agreement on how and when counseling goals are to be achieved.

Contracts. Several approaches to counseling use the term "contract" to describe extended structuring agreements. Some contracts, especially with young clients, take on a formal character. They list privileges extended, responsibilities incurred, bonuses or sanctions, how and by whom the contract is to be monitored. Contracts have characteristics of *specificity*, that is, the client knows exactly what is expected of him, and *feasibility*, meaning it is within the capabilities of the client to carry out. Contracting works most effectively when the client is acquiring or getting rid of a specific behavior, such as smoking or excess eating. The key value of a contractual form of structure is that a counselor knows when he has been successful—i.e., when the client reaches the goals he agreed to work on, and in the way both agreed. Contracts tend to focus on expected *outcomes*.

Time Limits. Perhaps the time limit is paramount in school counseling, in which only a limited amount of time can be given for each interview. The counselor, therefore, must explain at the onset of the interview just how much time is available. We suggest that when time limits are presented, clients very often hasten the therapeutic processes in an effort to accomplish as much as possible in the time available. This applies to short five- or ten-minute interviews as well as those lasting longer. An example is, "We have forty-five minutes; let's see what we can accomplish."

A second aspect of time limits concerns the time required for the process as a whole. It appears that one of the contributing factors to the success of psychoanalytic therapy, for example, is that the analyst emphasize very carefully to the patient that the process might take two to three years and will be costly. It is admitted that many clients cannot accept this, but at the same time, for the clients who can, the process seems to be facilitated. The counselor, in similar fashion, indicates that to reach the agreed goals, several sessions will be required. The counselor is careful to point out, however, that no commitments can be made as to specific outcome. For example, a counselor might say, "Ordinarily we get together a couple of times to go over the test data and other material collected, then we spend a session or two helping you plan a specific course of action. In all, it should take four or five hours to get where we want."

In more emotional problems the counselor may feel that he does not want to become committed to a long term therapeutic relationship. Structuring may help him prevent misunderstanding with the client, as the following example shows:

C: We have been talking about "first-aid" methods for a while. Perhaps we had better talk a bit about where we go from here. As you realize, we cannot become committed to a major personality overhaul (pause).

C1: I see, more of a tune-up job then.

In structuring time limits the counselor must guard against being over-anxious for the client by making promises or raising false hope, or even by stating that counseling "is a good investment." Promising success violates one of the ethics of psychotherapy. A positive attitude, however, on the part of the counselor, which creates confidence in himself, his client, and the process, can assist greatly an insecure and anxious client to begin working confidently. This attitude, combined with clear contractual agreements on respective responsibilities, can go a long way toward realizing the desired outcomes.

Although it is difficult for the counselor to make definite long-range time commitments to a client, he should discuss fees very clearly early in the first interview. Phone calls and missed appointments, generally, are not charged for, though the counselor who does not charge for long phone calls and uncanceled missed appointments plays into the manipulative client's hands. Also, it is not sound therapeutically because it does not take cognizance of the *reality* of the relationship. A clear contract should help on these issues.

Action Limits. There are also what might be termed action limits. The counselor does not limit verbal expression, no matter how absurd, unfair, or foolish it sounds; but there are certain feelings which cannot be permitted direct expression in *action*. A younger client, for example, cannot break windows, or destroy furniture and equipment. He can say he does not like the therapist, but he cannot physically attack him. As Rogers (391) points out, hurting the therapist may arouse the child's deep guilt and anxiety in relation to the only person who can help him. Fear of retaliation and the threat of withdrawal of this unique kind of supporting relationship may destroy the possibility of therapy.

Role Limits. In educational, industrial, religious, or medical settings we find that the counselor often has dual roles: teacher-counselor, supervisor-counselor, administrator-counselor, minister-counselor, and physician-counselor. This means that these people also have a role of authority in the life of the client, as well as the role of nonjudgmental listener. These roles must be so structured. The teacher, after a hearing, must ultimately point out for Johnny that he must take certain prescribed courses whether he wants to or not. Thus, one role of the advisor is to maintain the school structure. A foreman, counseling one of his men, cannot permit him to come and go on the job whenever he wishes. A teacher cannot permit a student client to avoid handing in class work. These are limits defined by the *role of authority* which these people also have.

In situations which make it necessary for the counselor to take dual roles, the use of the "coat analogy" is often helpful. The following is an example of how it may be used:

C: Well, Jack, before we start I want to clarify my role with you. You might say I wear two coats around here—my teacher's coat and my counselor's coat. When I wear my teacher's coat, I have to be evaluating and judging to a certain degree in order to state your progress as a student. When I see you personally, however, in a relationship such as this, I am wearing my counselor's coat. This means that you can feel free to talk about anything you like and I won't hold it against you or make judgments about you. O.K.?

Procedural or Process Limits.   If counseling is to be successful, the client must accept the nature of the process. In the first place, the client must accept his *responsibility* for carrying on the major share of the interview. There are certain things he must know to utilize the process most effectively. Ingham and Love (238, pp. 79–81) suggest six basic process values which must be conveyed to the client in the early structuring remarks and through basic attitudes.

1. ". . . *that it is appropriate and good to investigate ourselves.*" This means facing his disturbing problems as much and as fast as he is comfortably able. This value suggests that there are causes of his difficulties which can be known and understood.

2. ". . . *that it is better to investigate than to blame.*" This approach conveys the idea that there is a difference between a "bad" person and the "bad" act. The counselor stresses that he is trying to understand, not blame him. Thus, he will be better able to accept what he discovers within himself.

3. ". . . *to regard emotion as a real and important thing. . . .*" This value stresses the idea that emotions and their free expression are important realities and not signs of weakness.

4. ". . . *that there must be relatively complete freedom of expression.*" The idea emphasized here is that the emotional importance of a topic, not its social acceptability, is the criterion of topic choice. This means that swearing, sex topics, and unconventional ideas are acceptable.

5. ". . . *the use of investigation of the past in developing an understanding of the present. . . .*" This focus on the past is a controversial value among counselors and therapists.

6. A series of process *values centering about the client's present view of his world* are often mentioned in structuring. These are his capacity for human relationships, his own individual importance, and his own life values and morals as a basis for further changes through counseling. A keen interest in the client's basic style of life is indicated.

Structuring Process Values.   It should be emphasized that all of the aforementioned process values need not be made explicit. Clients have differing needs for explanations about how counseling proceeds. Generally, the counselor lets the client bring up his own topics, and as it becomes apparent that he has misconceptions, or feels bewildered, helpless, or dissatisfied with this new experience, the counselor aids him through structuring. The counselor should start counseling on grounds familiar to the client and get him involved in the main job of counseling as quickly and comfortably as possible.

A second important use of structuring as a means of describing the process comes in the *handling of direct requests for advice*. In general,

197

the authors recommend reflecting the feeling underlying this request first. This often allows the client to continue and to see his dependency needs as a problem. It is often necessary, however, actually to define this limit, as given by the following example:

C1: Can't we do something about this? The tension is really getting me. Can you tell me what to do? It might help both of us.

C: I can understand how desperate you feel; but we have found that there are certain answers that only the individual can give himself. By working together I think that we can arrive at some answers for you.

Unfortunately, it is easy to give the client a feeling of getting the "brushoff" with a response like this. The anxious, dependent client tends to miss the structuring and reassuring intent of the counselor's response and may interpret it as, "So you are another one who doesn't want to help me."

A third use of process structuring is to present to the client the philosophy underlying the method of counseling. Porter (367, p. 60) gives an example of this method:

Counselor: "I don't believe I know much about why you are here. The Dean mentioned you some time ago, but I know very little about it."

Frank: "Well, the Dean and Professor R. wanted me to see you. They said you were a good psychologist, and that if you studied me you might be able to diagnose my adjustment. They think I'm not getting along very well and if you diagnosed what was the matter, you would be able to help me."

Counselor: "They think you need some help, and you are trying to do what they wish?"

Frank: "Well, they say I'm not doing as well as I should, and if you studied me, you could say why."

Counselor: "Well, now I'll tell you, Frank, I really haven't had much luck helping students with problems that the Dean thinks they have. I don't know whether I can be of help to you along that line or not. When a student is concerned about some problem that *he* thinks he has, then frequently we can work out something together, but otherwise, I don't believe I get very far. I wonder, quite aside from what the Dean thinks about you, whether you feel there is anything about your situation that is causing you concern?"

Frank: "Well, I don't know—I suppose I don't live up to my ability."

Counselor: "That is something you feel a little concerned about?"

Frank: "Yes, I don't know, I guess I procrastinate; I just don't get things done on time. I don't see why. I've thought about that a lot and tried to analyze it but I don't seem to have helped it."

Counselor: "So you feel you really do procrastinate, and that you've been unable to do anything about it."

A cardinal principle of structuring is that it is a continuous process, although the specific bits of content must be given at the right times. With some clients who demand more structure or seem to be confused, formal structuring of the process must necessarily come early. With others, the formal structuring must come later when attempts to shift the "locus of evaluation" to the counselor are made. With other clients who seem to take to the process easily, a very minimum of formal structuring is necessary in the beginning. In fact, if too many structuring remarks preface counseling, the client may interpret and resist them as ultimatums. Most sophisticated clients expect that the structure will grow out of the relationship rather than be dictated to them in a formal, instructional manner.

Additional structuring is done from time to time during the course of counseling when the client strays too far from the counselor's conception of the direction in which he should go, or if the client seems confused about the goals or process.

From this presentation the reader may rightly infer that structuring is a controversial issue in counseling practice. Some writers emphasize the value of the technique while others minimize its value and stress its limitations. We have attempted to present various sides of current views so the counselor can develop a style most effective for him.

Listening as a Technique

Listening is an active attending process with little or no verbalization. It may seem strange, at first glance, to give prominence to listening as a technique of counseling. It is our conviction, however, that therapeutic listening is a technique which must be learned. Perhaps this is so because the ethics of social conversation in our culture discourage silence. Hence, we have learned to become uncomfortable with silences and to regard long pauses as synonymous with a social vacuum. Beginning counselors, perhaps, often feel that when pauses are long they are not doing enough for the client. The appropriate mix of counselor response and listening is one of the most difficult counselor behaviors to learn.

The Meaning and Handling of Client Silence

In evaluating the significance of a pause, the time of its occurrence and whether it was initiated by client or counselor are significant. A long pause initiated by the client early in the initial interview conveys a different meaning to the counselor from one occurring later in the process. Pauses made by the client early in the interview may reflect embarrassment or resistance. As the counseling progresses, silence gradually comes to be a vibrant communicative medium for support, emotional expression, and thought.

In addition, it should be emphasized that counseling interviews are characterized by pauses of varying lengths from a few seconds to several minutes. It is difficult to assess the meaning of all pauses and no attempt is made here to catalogue these possibilities. The following are offered merely as suggestions for interpreting and handling interview silences initiated by either counselor or client.

Any discussion of silence requires that recognition be given to two types: negative or rejecting, and positive or accepting. Socially, we often use the "silent treatment" as a form of rejection, defiance, or condemnation. In social situations, when we argue with a person we are saying in effect that we respect him enough to want to change him. The negative silent treatment, however, says coldly in effect that the other person is not even worth talking to. Unfortunately, before a proper counseling relationship is established, it is possible for a client to interpret early silence in the interview as being this negative or rejecting type. This is true particularly when the client is still afraid of what the counselor is thinking about him. Appropriate acceptance techniques frequently have a reassuring effect, so that the client feels he does not have to impress the counselor.

A second meaning of silence is that the client or counselor has reached the end of an idea and is merely wondering what to say next. An extended pause may mean, also, that both have lost their way temporarily and that the interview has become confusing to both. The client may realize also that he has come to the end of the conversational period and must get down to work. Characteristically, there is an extended silence before getting down to serious work. The counselor can help the client over this hump by saying something like, "It is sort of hard to get down to serious business." The counselor's silence points up dramatically the transparency of small talk in later interviews. If the pause is of this "thought-collecting" type, it is considered wise not to interrupt. Tindall and Robinson (477) found in study-improvement interviews that this type of contemplative silence accounted for half the pauses.

A third meaning of silence is that of hostility-motivated resistance or anxiety-motivated embarrassment. This is true particularly when the client has been called for or sent in. At first, the client may be waiting cautiously for the counselor to make all the first moves and may answer or comment in short words or phrases followed by a long expectant pause. This kind of silence is an effective client manipulative device.

The pause with a fourth meaning may be the signal that the client is experiencing some particularly painful feeling which he is not ready to verbalize, whereas consciously he may want to express the feeling desperately. The counselor may say something like, "It is all right if you want to wait until words come along," or "It seems hard to say what you want at times, doesn't it?" Without pushing the client, the counselor might say, "Perhaps if you gave me some hint where your thoughts are moving, maybe I can help you put them into words." We have facilitated expression in this type of client by handing him a pencil and paper without comment so that he can write what he wants to say as a starter.

In the resistive type of silence the participants may appear to be engaging in a contest to see who can outwait the other, like children trying to stare one another down. This may be owing to a preconceived notion of counseling in which the client expects the counselor to ask questions, or has a cautious "wait and see" attitude. This silent response may indicate to the counselor that there is a need for structuring or for a brief exploration of some case history items to get the client talking. The counselor may provoke the hostility-motivated client to talk by making a disarming reflection, "You don't feel like talking just now, do you?" Another way is to ask him to interpret his silence, "What do you think has brought this about?" However, the client may consider that the counselor who takes the attitude of, "Well, I'll wait until you decide to talk," or who pauses too long, is rejecting him.

If shyness seems to be the difficulty, it might be overcome if the counselor starts with some items from the client's life history, for example, "Here we've spent quite a bit of time together and you haven't mentioned your mother (pause)."

A fifth meaning of silence might be labeled as "anticipatory," wherein the client pauses expecting something from the counselor—some reassurance, information, or interpretation. Tindall and Robinson (477) found that counselors were quite sensitive in assessing and responding appropriately to this type of pause.

A sixth meaning of a client's pausing is that he may be thinking over what he has just said. In this case interruption of the pause may be inappropriate, since it might destroy the client's train of thought and may throw the interview off the client's main theme.

Finally, a pause may mean that the client is merely recovering from the fatigue of a previous emotional expression. Here again, quiet acceptance of the silence is probably the best approach.

The problem for the counselor in the preceding illustrations might be simply stated as follows: Shall I interrupt the pause or shall I wait and let the client go on? In general, our view is to let the client assume responsibility for going on when he was responsible for pausing originally. This avoids interfering with a forward-moving activity. Yet, the counselor must be alert to those situations in which it seems best to support the client over rough places rather than to force him to face his problems, feelings, and responsibilities before he is ready. Problems of handling the negative silence are treated in the following chapter under "resistance," which will be defined and illustrated. In any case, the counselor is asking himself continually during the silences, "What is going on?"

It is one of our basic assumptions that listening of the positive and accepting type is a most promising counseling technique. The counselor's silence forces the client to talk. Similarly, being in the presence of another silent person often moves the client's attention to the task at hand—his problems. Silence on the part of the counselor then can have the value of focusing responsibility on the client.

A second value, emphasized from research with the Rorschach technique, indicates that introversive persons may be deeply creative individuals, with rich inner lives. They should not necessarily be seen as people inferior to the more socially valued extroverted individual. In counseling, the client discovers that he can be a silent person and still be liked. Perhaps it is this acceptance of silence in the client which gives the less articulate person a feeling of worth and thereby helps the individual to accept himself for what he is. By feeling accepted as a shy and quiet person, he is able then to experience this same attitude toward himself. The following case comments by Rogers suggest the therapeutic value of silence.

I have just completed the strangest counseling case I've ever had. I think you might be interested in it.

Joan was one of my very first clients when I started counseling one half-day each week at the local high school. She told the girls' adviser, "I feel so shy I couldn't even tell her what my problem is. Will you tell her for me?" So the adviser told me before I saw Joan that she worried about having no friends. The adviser added that she had noticed that Joan seemed always to be so alone.

The first time I saw Joan she talked a little about her problem and quite a bit about her parents of whom she seemed to be quite fond. There were, however, long pauses. The next four interviews could be recorded verbatim on this small piece of paper. By the middle of November Joan remarked that "things are going pretty good." No elaboration on that. Meanwhile the adviser commented that the teachers had noticed that Joan was now smiling a friendly greeting when they met her in the halls. This was unheard of before. However, the adviser had seen little of Joan and could say nothing of her contacts with other students. In December there was one interview during which Joan talked freely; the others were characterized by silence while she sat, apparently in deep thought, occasionally looking up with a grin. More silence through the next two and one-half months. Then I received word that she had been elected "woman of the month" by the girls of the high school! The basis for that election is always sportsmanship and popularity with other girls. At the same time I got a message from Joan, "I don't think I need to see you any more." No, apparently she doesn't, but why? What happened in those hours of silence? My faith in the capacity of the client was sorely tested. I'm glad it did not waver (390, pp. 158–59).

Apparently the therapeutic value of spending time with someone who understood her and who had faith in her ability to solve her problem was helpful even though little was said.

A third value of counselor listening is that, after a significant expression of feeling, the client is allowed to think and to come up with a profound insight. Had the counselor forced continued exploration or verbalized too much, the awareness might not have followed. The client often uses silence to delve deeply into feelings, to struggle with alternative courses of action, or to weigh a decision. He wants to feel that the counselor approves of his doing this, and that he is not letting the counselor down by this behavior. In fact, one extreme style of therapy, called the silent interview method, consists almost entirely of this nonverbal type of communication wherein the therapist conveys to the client his understanding that he is struggling with deep, difficult feelings. Hence, one value of silence is that it forces depth of client penetration into his own feelings.

A fourth value of counselor listening is that it reduces the pace of the interview. Often the counselor senses that the client is rushing, or that he feels himself compelled to push too hard. He can reduce the intensity and pace to a more tolerable level for both participants by making the pauses longer. The counselor says in effect, "We are not in a hurry; take it easy." Thus, counselor silence in later interviews tends to have a beneficially calming effect on the client.

In a study of counselor pauses, Tindall and Robinson (477) classified the pauses of the counselor giving educational skills counseling into three types: deliberate (for emphasis), organizational (for transitions), and natural termination (to close counseling). Organizational pauses, in the vast majority of cases, helped most to clarify the subject discussed and prepared the way for information to be given by the counselor. Clients generally responded only after a deliberate or natural terminal pause. It is apparent, however, from Tindall's and Robinson's study that pauses have many different meanings to clients, and that counselors must use them naturally.

Difficulties in Using Listening Techniques

In the training of counseling psychologists, we have found that it has been necessary to teach toleration of client silence without embarrassment. To the untried therapist a minute of silence seems like an hour. He has, consequently, an overwhelming desire to interrupt the client's thought. Porter (367) suggests that one of the errors of reflection is that of completing sentences for the client. Many clients find it difficult to state what they mean precisely without fumbling for words. Therefore, a very common error that inexperienced counselors make is to put words into the client's mouth, or in some way to take the conversational initiative away from the client.

Using listening technique does not mean being passive or uncommunicative, however. There has been a growing conviction among counselors, arising from studies and clinical experience, that activity level of the counselor is a significant variable in client response, and indeed affects whether the client stays in counseling. It is difficult to do conclusive studies on such a variable as counselor activity-passivity, but Heller, Davis, and Myers (223) surveyed the literature and conducted a laboratory-type study on effects of interview style. They suggest that clients verbalize much more actively, rate counselors as more friendly, and continue in counseling when counselors are more active than passive and silent. While these terms need more definition to be useful as guides to counselors, such evidence contradicts long-standing views that interviews should start with low structure and a more passive stance to allow the client to do more projecting and talking.

One of the most difficult aspects of using the listening technique is keeping silent when the client wants to talk. A greater proportion of client talk, however, is not necessarily an indicator of a more effective working relationship. Carnes and Robinson (95) analyzed 353 discussion units from four types of counseling interviews. They concluded that ". . . a high talk ratio is not necessary to a good working relationship but it is good insurance" (95, p. 639).

The relationships between insight and talk ratio in the above study were inconclusive; although, with study skill interviews, insight tended to be associated with low frequency of client talk. In other words, when the counselor explained things in study skill interviews, the client apparently gained more insight than he did if he, himself, talked. For therapeutic problems, Carnes and Robinson found that it was not the amount of client talk per se which was related to awareness, but rather the relative amount of client talk within the framework of a particular counseling style. In other words, keeping silent and just getting the client to talk more will not necessarily lead to more insight. A counselor can talk too much or too little at the wrong times.

The most definitive relationship in the Carnes and Robinson study cited above was found between client talk and amount of client responsibility assumed for discussion unit progress. (The discussion unit is the verbal exchange between client and counselor on a discrete subject.) When clients felt primarily responsible for interview progress they talked more. It is interesting to note also that Carnes and Robinson found that the stronger the counselor's lead, the less the client talk. The general conclusions of Carnes' and Robinson's study are that the causal relationships between desired interview outcomes and amount of client talk are not clear, and that it is not possible, therefore, to use the amount of client talk as a measure of counseling effectiveness.

Leading Techniques

General Principles and Values of Leads

The term "lead" is used with two meanings. One usage refers to the extent to which the counselor is ahead or behind the client's thinking, and the extent to which the counselor directs the client's thinking or "pushes" the client into accepting the counselor's remark (94). Bugental (76) uses the term "impact" to describe the counselor's influence on the client and the interviewing process. Counselor questions, for example, would have a high impact compared to the accepting vocalization "mm." Silence would have a lower impact or lead.

Robinson (385) uses "lead" in a different, but related, sense. He construes leading in counseling to mean "a teamlike working together in which the counselor's remarks seem to the client to state the next point he is ready to accept" (385, p. 66). In addition, Robinson compares leading to the act of passing a football down the field so that the receiver's path passes the flight path of the ball at the same time. All techniques can be rated according to degree of lead involved, but in the present discussion the topic will be limited to general leading as a technique by itself.

The value of leading is that the counselor is enabled to retain or delegate varying amounts of responsibility for counselor-client talk and to generate more client responses.

Using Leads

Three general usages of leading are recommended. One principle is to lead *only as much as the client can tolerate* at his present level of ability and understanding. Enough old material must be mentioned to form a bridge of understanding to the next new idea. Robinson (385) uses a ladder analogy to indicate that the counselor is not more than one rung ahead of the client, hence, close to his needs and interests. A lead too far ahead of the client generally arouses resistance to counseling. Similarly, too little lead may annoy clients who feel that the counselor should carry more of the responsibility for the interview talk.

The second general principle of leading is to *vary the lead*. The amount of lead changes from topic to topic or within a discussion unit so as to match the pace and lead of the client.

A third principle is *to start the counseling process with little lead*. For example, begin the counseling process with relationship techniques which have low lead, until the relationship is well established. Then increase the lead as needed with information and interpretation, which are useful in developing awareness.

The *indirect lead* may be used to help the client elaborate upon a topic of his choice. Examples are, "Would you explain that a little more?" "How do you mean that?" This type of lead is used also in the form of general questions to start an exploration, such as "What would you like to talk about today?" "Is there anything more you would like to discuss?"

The *direct lead* indicates the area of discussion desired from the client and is akin to the probing techniques discussed in Chapter 5. Examples of the direct leads are: "Tell me more about your father"; "Suppose we explore more fully the idea of teaching"; "What do you think that means?" Asking the client a question, whether rhetorical or for information, is a means of shifting responsibility to the client. Conversely, if the client asks many questions of the counselor it may indicate more than a desire for information or interpretation; it may mean he is expressing his need to shift responsibility to the counselor.

Interpretive techniques which are described in Chapter 8 employ various degrees of lead. Leading utilizes Robinson's (385) principle of moving ahead of the client just enough to stimulate his growth. The concept of lead is introduced in this chapter, however, to emphasize that some degree of lead is always present in the relationship techniques which the counselor uses. Even silence is a leading technique, since lack of verbal response on the counselor's part causes the client to make a judgment about the significance of the material he has just presented. Thus the counselor, through his manipulation of the pauses, often is responsible for the direction of the interview.

Reassurance Methods

Nature and Values of Reassurance

One relationship technique which has wide utility for conveying support is reassurance. In Chapter 6 the concept of support was introduced as a necessary ingredient of the counseling and psychotherapeutic relationship. The nature of reassurance is essentially a type of reward which has a reinforcing effect on behavior and builds expectancies for future rewards. The counselor says directly, or in effect, that, "You are a capable person; you can be consistent; you can be reasonable; you can be organized; you can feel better; you can solve this problem."

Reassurance also is a process of fitting counseling to the client's present belief system. Reassurance encourages exploration of new ideas or tryout of different behaviors. In this capacity reassurance is a temporary expedient to keep the client in the relationship. Kelly (257) compares reassurance to the proverbial string and baling wire which is used to hold structures together until more solid or productive work can be done. Reassurance also prevents fragmentation of the client's ideas, even though eventually he may want to change his maladaptive responses.

A second value of reassurance is the means it provides to reduce anxiety and insecurity directly. Although anxiety in the proper amount is a positive motivating force to keep the person in counseling, and is a useful guide to indicate where the trouble lies, excess amounts interfere with the therapeutic process. Reassurance tends to keep the anxiety generated by the counseling process itself under control by assuring the client that he doesn't have to explore his feelings too fast. This use of reassurance is particularly valuable in controlling anxiety outside the relationship, for example, over weekends and vacations. An example is offering simple suggestions to a mother who is having problems with her child, such that weekend crises are lessened.

A third value of reassurance is the reinforcing effect it has on new patterns of behavior. It is often difficult to launch a new course of action, even after significant insights have been achieved. The client often feels discouragement, leading to loss of confidence, which arises from small failures to make his planned adjustments. An example is the student who is attempting to improve his failing grades. Reassurance in the form of praise for his attempts, assurances that he will pull through the temporary setbacks, and the encouragement of confident attitudes generally help him to retain or regain his new behaviors.

Reassurance is thus a form of expressing implied counselor value, a form of promising improvement which we feel is wholly consistent with an eclectic frame of reference that places value on the counselor's honest expression of his own feelings as well as those of the client. This expression of counselor feelings must be consonant with client welfare, however. We feel that the counselor's failure to express reassurance when he honestly feels it is a form of therapeutic dishonesty. A counseling relationship which does not allow any expression of feeling puts the counselor in a form of emotional strait jacket which may be harmful to the relationship.

Use of Reassurance

The *approval or acquiescence remark* is one means of reassurance. Its purpose is to give the client some feeling of security about the ideas or feelings he is expressing. Expressing approval of the client's remarks tends to have a reinforcing effect also. An example is:

C1: It seems that people resent being criticized or told they are wrong.

C: That's right; a very interesting observation and a good rule about personality.

This technique goes beyond acceptance; it is actual agreement with the client. Though generally reassuring, it may be hazardous, because the client may feel he cannot change position without admitting error. Thus, the approval technique tends to have the unfortunate effect of rigidifying the client's thinking. The client may be communicating feeling on a different meaning level also, so a reassuring counselor response may be disruptive.

The counselor who suggests that there are other ways of thinking and acting builds expectations of success in his client. For example, the counselor assures his client that he can change himself and that counseling can be an effective means to help him change.

Prediction of outcomes is a phrase used by Kelly (257) to describe the consequences of counseling or psychotherapy over the following few days. Avoiding sweeping predictions, the counselor makes a limited forecast about how the client is likely to feel between conferences. An example is: "We've been talking about your problems in a more intensive fashion. You will probably find that you will be more uncomfortable and moody the next few days. Don't be alarmed, because this is part of the process. You will be able to handle it all right."

Postdiction of outcomes is a related reassuring technique, also described by Kelly. An example is, "It is my guess that during the last few days things have been tougher for you to handle. We opened up many sensitive areas last time which have upset you during the week. Is this correct?" Another example is, "Perhaps you were disturbed by our session last time; but this is a normal part of the process." The reassuring value of such comments comes from the impression the client gets that his behavior makes sense to the counselor and is predictable.

The *interview conditions* tend to be reassuring. As we pointed out in our earlier discussion of support, it is the acceptance, structured limits, attention, affectional warmth, and outward signs of friendship in the counselor which have a powerful reassuring effect. This is true particularly with children, whose behaviors can often be drastically changed through the reassuring effect of emotional support. Thus, meeting specific emotional needs of the client is one of the key uses of reassurance.

Factual reassurance can be given to the client who feels his problem is unique. When he knows that many other people suffer from the same feelings, his fearful bewilderment may subside. Related to this point is the reassurance that his problem has a solution and that the cause of his difficulty is known. Thus, a person can tolerate anxiety and annoying symptoms when he knows that they are, very likely, temporary reactions to his basic problem. He can also feel reassured that he can reach specific objectives, such as achieving an educational goal, formulating a vocational plan, getting better grades, or saving his marriage.

Often, the counselor's reassurance of his client that he does not have to feel ashamed, guilty, or alarmed about his problem helps. The client can feel that the problem does not have to be viewed moralistically, but as a personal problem to be solved in an objective way.

Reassurance that the best of help available to science will be given to a client is an often successful means that the counselor can employ to reduce the client's anxiety about the efficacy of treatment. Sharing diagnostic and prognostic formulations with the client when they are favorable is a very convincing type of reassurance.

Reinstating defenses is another psychotherapeutic "first-aid" method. The client may be using a defense, such as vigorous sarcasm, to handle his hostilities. In the course of counseling, the client sees the inappropriateness of his extrapunitive tendencies. But he has not worked them through sufficiently, so he develops incapacitating migraine headaches which appear to be manifestations of intrapunitive hostility. The client is better off if he is "given back" his former defensive mechanisms through being encouraged to express his hostilities more outwardly— the social consequences of which are less severe than the personal consequences of repressed hostility.

Limitations and Cautions

This section is not intended to discourage the student from utilizing reassurance techniques. However, these limitations are mentioned in the following paragraphs in order to acquaint the student with the fact that reassurance is a two-edged sword in many ways. It can be most helpful when utilized properly as a reinforcer in the situations described, and most detrimental when used indiscriminately.

Reassurance is a technique which is particularly vulnerable to misfiring. Reassurance is so easy to use that there is a temptation to be over-liberal. It is a vehicle so common in everyday human relationships that it may be stated fairly that reassurance is much overused in counseling. A frequent misuse of reassurance, for example, is in false concealment of the true nature of a serious situation. This is an ethical problem as well as a procedural concern.

Reassurance is used crudely in the approach that "everything will come out in the wash." The "just relax, everything will come out all right" attitude and the old aphorisms, such as "every cloud has a silver lining," serve only to create resentment in clients.

Reassurance might be interpreted by a very disturbed person as artificial and insincere sympathy. Reassurance, at best, is a temporary expedient and the counselor must be reconciled to the possible slowing of progress if he uses it. There is the obvious limitation that the whole relationship can be put in jeopardy because subsequent events do not bear out the optimistic predictions of the counselor.

Reassurance has the additional liability of promoting a dependency relationship between client and counselor. The periodic need for reassurance is a type of substitute satisfaction for real accomplishment. The responses reinforced by reassurance tend to become fixed learnings, and the client feels a strong need to get reassurance from this particular person. Some clients use reassurance as an excuse not to change their behavior.

If clients interpret reassurance as agreement, they may limit themselves in the sense that they will feel guilty about changing their behavior or experimenting with new methods of viewing their problems. In other words, they may feel trapped in their present efforts and may think that they can't find any solutions to their problems.

It has been stated earlier that reassurance is most valuable in supporting the anxious, distressed client. It can be grossly misused if given to the client who is already overly aggressive or self-confident. This type of client needs discouragement of his often insensitive, rigid, egocentric behavior, rather than support for it.

Terminating Skills

The effective termination of counseling is as important for counseling success as is the establishment of the relationship. How neatly the counselor "settles his dust" or "ties up his package" determines the ease with which the client can assume complete responsibility for himself and the extent to which his progress can be consolidated.

Since the problems and procedures for closing interviews and changing discussion units during the counseling process are related to techniques for terminating, these are considered together in the following discussion.

Terminating a Discussion Unit

A discussion unit can be closed by the summary reflection described earlier, wherein the counselor ties together the loose ends of several related ideas. The net effect of this summary is to give a feeling of closure and progress to the client, whereupon he generally proceeds to another topic. The counselor must sense when the client is ready for such a summary, knowing that its application will result in a change of topic.

A second device for ending the discussion unit is a *capping technique*. This consists of shutting off the flow of talk or feeling in such a way that the client does not stop talking or feel rejected. Frequently the counselor senses that the more the person delves into his feelings the more uncomfortable he becomes, or the more dissociated he seems to get. When the counselor feels that the client's defenses are not sufficiently functional to protect himself, he helps the client regain his defensive armor through capping techniques. He does this with the hope that it is a temporary expedient, and that the client will be more ready to attack the conflict at a later time.

Capping techniques consist of *changing the subject* to something less intense. The subject can be changed back to a topic previously discussed, the original symptoms, or a new and less loaded topic. Reducing the *length of counselor lead* and the general *pace* of the interview often reduces the client's discomfort, resistance, or undesired feelings toward the counselor. The counselor can help to decelerate the pace by *pausing* longer and more frequently. In order to cap exploration which has become too intense, he can *reduce the frequency of interviews*. It is well known in counseling and psychotherapeutic practice that the intensity of the relationship varies directly with the frequency of interviews per week. The counselor, for example, may suggest meeting every two weeks instead of once a week. Sometimes reassurance that there is plenty of time to work through the problems helps to take feelings of pressure off the client. Increasing the amount of *counselor talk* has a "shutting off" effect on client communication, thus preventing his delving deeper into his problems.

There may be times, also, when the quality of the relationship is such that the counselor can use *direct interpretation* to terminate a topic. An example is, "You are getting quite disturbed about this. Suppose we drop it for a while and go on about your plans after graduation." The client may need further explanation for changing the subject and reassurance that he can come back to this topic at a later time.

Terminating an Interview

The counseling literature contains very little information about the nature of skills for terminating an interview. Yet, most counselors would agree that it is important that the interview be drawn to a definite close and not be left hanging in mid-air, with the client feeling that nothing has been accomplished. Beginning counselors report that ending an interview is one of the most difficult tasks they face. The following are some "tricks of the trade." The reader should note that detailing of such methods can be carried to the point of misleading absurdity. Ordinary natural courtesies common to our culture are the best guides.

Reference to time limits is one natural way to remind the client that the hour is up. No matter what the length of the interview, it is important that the counselor inform the client at the beginning of the interview that he has a fixed length of time. In a clinical setting, a forty-five- or fifty-minute period is usually standard. In other settings, such as public schools, a much shorter time may be more appropriate. Interview time is a matter of agency policy, case load, and the purpose of the interview.

Generally, it is felt that a minimum of forty-five minutes is needed to deal with a client's most pressing problems. This allows the client a few minutes for "warmup," wherein he moves slowly into the main content of the interview and picks up the loose threads from the preceding session, and gives him a few minutes at the end of the hour to "pull himself together." This is especially necessary after a therapeutic counseling session which delved deeply into feelings.

In school counseling, however, time and case load pressures often force the problem to be stated and analyzed in interviews of ten or fifteen minutes. In any case, as long as the time limit is set, the successful conclusion of the interview can be more assured. At the end of the interview, for example, the time limit can again be brought up by such a statement as, "Our time is nearly up; when would you like to come back again?" or "Well, that does it for today" or "It seems we've reached the end of the hour." This provides an easy transition to the calendar, the door, or the receptionist.

Summarizing is a second means of terminating the interview. This can be done by the counselor, the client, or as a collaborative act. When the counselor sees that the interview is drawing short, he can summarize the essential factors of the interview himself. Again, the terminal reflection technique can be used if the counselor is disposed to summarizing the essential feelings which have been expressed by the client during the interview. A topical summary to reflect the major content of the interview would be in order also.

From the counseling literature it appears that client summaries are used widely. The counselor asks the client for a summarization of key feelings and ideas as follows: "Tell me how you think the situation looks now," or "Now suppose you tell me what you think you have accomplished in this interview."

The counselor usually precedes the collaborative summary with such a phrase as, "Suppose now we take a look at what we have done today. As I see it, we have said. . . . Perhaps you could state how you have seen it."

Reference to the future is a third and graceful way for the counselor to terminate an interview; at the same time, an indication of his desire to maintain the relationship is made by the use of a statement which would refer to subsequent meetings with the client. Such a statement would be as follows: "I am sorry our time is about up today. When would you like to come in again?" or "Would you like to make it at the same time next week?" or "I have Thursday at three and Friday at two open. Which would you prefer?" It is important to end in a warm positive tone, following the setting of the exact date and time, with a parting phrase such as, "Fine, I'll be expecting you then at two next Friday," rather than a doubtful "Then you'll come next week at two?"

Fourthly, *standing up* is frequently a persuasive technique for ending the interview. With particularly difficult clients, such as obsessive-compulsive people who do not wish to terminate the contact, it may be necessary for the counselor to stand up as a more blunt means of indicating that the interview is finished. This can be done gracefully at a "low point" before the client has a chance to delve into another topic of conversation. In more formal situations, especially with adults and at the end of first interviews, the offering of the hand as a parting gesture is helpful too.

Subtle gestures are a fifth category of cues to close the interview. While most counseling contacts close naturally at the fixed time, some clients continue to chat on. Most counselors develop certain gestures to indicate that the interview is to be terminated and that it is time for the client to depart. Examples of counselor cues which even the most obtuse client can perceive are to glance at his watch or desk clock, and lean forward. It should be mentioned that the counselor should be alert to and evaluate the wisdom of common devices such as fidgeting, distractibility, irritability, and shuffling desk papers to cue clients that the hour is up.

Ushering the client to the door and opening it for him could aid a graceful and prompt departure. Ordinary courtesy demands that the counselor rise with the client and walk to the door with him. This makes it much easier for the client to leave than it would be if the counselor left the whole burden for terminating the interview upon the client.

Summary notes are a sixth useful aid to terminating interviews. In certain types of counseling where decisions are being made, some counselors find it useful to jot down notes while the interview is in process. They may have another sheet with carbon between so that at the end of the interview the client is handed the carbon of the counselor's notes. This is especially important in career planning, where data are profuse and significant. Many counselors feel that the client will remember the interview if they make a concrete summary of the salient features of the interview. Other counselors encourage the client to make his own notes, thus encouraging independent action in the client.

The *"homework"* or *"prescription" method* can be utilized as a terminating device. Herzberg (225) suggests the use of the "social task"—doing something like joining a folk-dance group before the next interview. Sullivan (463) also suggests giving the client something to do between interviews. Examples would be: "Before you leave I'd like to suggest a little 'homework' . . ." or "I wonder if you could give some thought to these questions which have arisen in our conversation today (mention items)." Ellis (134) utilizes homework as a prominent feature of his rational-emotive approach.

Related to the activity approach is the *arrangement for tests* or *occupational reading* if the problem is primarily educational or vocational. This is another natural way to end the interview. It should be stressed that endings are arrived at cooperatively and by counselor suggestion; they are not coerced.

It is important that the interview end on a note of positive planning in that the client knows exactly what he is going to do. If the counselor is ambiguous about plans or expectations concerning the client, he may arouse insecurity and consequent anxiety and disillusionment.

One of the rules in terminating an interview is to start *tapering off* in intensity a few minutes before the scheduled end. A counselor should never let a client leave without allowing him to pull himself together again and to reduce the feelings stirred up by the interview. Yet this very condition makes it difficult for the client to leave. He tends to relax when he feels the pressure is off. The client often becomes very spontaneous, and will try to detain the counselor with new and interesting material. The counselor can hold to his structure or he can use the "five-minutes-more" technique. This technique is ushered in as follows: "I have a few minutes between the interviews. I'll share them with you. You may have five minutes more if you wish. Then we will have to close for today."

The counselor may decide that the material coming out is so significant that it warrants using the "extra hour" device if by chance he has the next hour free. He says, "I have this next hour free; I gather this is a significant area for you. Suppose we take more time, then, while the matter is still hot." This hour may be extremely productive since the usual defenses may not be prepared for it. The client is likely, therefore, to be exceedingly spontaneous. It is our experience that material often comes out in this hour which very likely would not arise in interviews for which the client is more "set."

One danger of the "extra hour" technique should be mentioned. Once an extra hour has been given to a manipulative client, he may try to get extra hours again and again. His approach would be "You helped me then—why don't you again?" It may also result in the client remaining superficial in the first hours as his defenses get re-set. In any case, this technique is useful if used with discretion.

Regardless of the device used to end the interview and to get the client out the door, the interview should end on a positive and friendly note. The counselor should not adopt a cold, neutral attitude, in an effort, perhaps, to avoid deciding for the client whether he will continue and when he will return.

Techniques for terminating interviews, in summary, should be planned in advance, and should be friendly, definite, and collaborative. These characteristics are necessary in order to help the client feel wanted, to know what he has accomplished, to know what to do next, and to realize that he participated cooperatively with the counselor in solving his problems.

Case Termination

The Problems. Practically speaking, no case is ever closed in the sense that the problem is "solved." Effective counseling opens possibilities of client growth which are never finished. Yet there comes a time in the process where either client or counselor feels that the client should be placed completely on his own resources. How does the counselor tell when closure has been reached? The client often gives cues that his expectations of counseling have been satisfied or that he has hopes of reaching his goals on his own efforts, such as, "Well, I guess this answers my questions," or "I feel much better about it now."

Generally, the counseling process tends to terminate spontaneously when the client's goals have been reached. A series of elaborate studies of the counseling process indicate that client responses tend to become more positive and self-directive toward the end of counseling (424).

There are other cues which the counselor can use to effect closure. A crucial factor is fulfillment of the counseling contract. Reference should be made to the goals set in the first interviews and the contractual agreements which were negotiated. Were the expected outcomes achieved and to what degree? Counselors can watch for indices that the general goals of counseling have been accomplished. The client's goals might be understanding of himself and his problems, an intellectual awareness of solution and direction to the problem, diminution of such symptoms as anxiety, and, most importantly, behavior improvement. The counselor must be wary, however, of the "hello-goodbye" and "flight into health" phenomena. Clients often experience feelings of euphoria and completion after an interview or two. They may feel that their problem is solved when their symptoms subside after a cathartic interview. They feel better and frequently wish to terminate counseling. Yet, the counselor realizes that no lasting insight has been achieved and that the client will be back as soon as another little decision or crisis upsets him.

A distinction must be made between termination of the process by the client and by the counselor. Clients terminate counseling for many reasons. There may be completion according to the structure or contract. They might stop because of a disruption caused by resistance, ignorance about counseling, trauma, impasse, time, finances, or a feeling that the counselor is no longer needed.

The question naturally arises as to why clients leave therapy rather than become addicted to it. In addition to the cost in time, and sometimes in money also, the client may experience pain and humiliation at having to face further personality change or to achieve a higher stage of self-actualization. Or, in the successful case, the functions which were once located in the counselor are now the client's property. The client no longer has a "need" for counseling since what he has learned in the process has now become part of himself and his way of life.

The counselor terminates counseling, in contrast, when he feels that the goals of counseling have been achieved, or when lack of progress on the formal or implied contract does not warrant, in his opinion, continuation of the relationship. Many counselors, once the problem is delimited, structure the time limits of the process in such a way that when this limit is reached closure proceedings are begun. For example, the counselor starts the closure by saying something like, "Well, here we are nearing the end of the term when we said we would try to finish off our counseling. Suppose we examine where we have been, where we are now, and our next steps." This method of terminating at fixed limits has great drawbacks and some danger in that the person may not be ready to terminate, or may be ready long before the structured limit. However, it is felt that the client's anxiety, which often accompanies lengthy counseling, is alleviated when he can anticipate the approximate time of closure.

Often the counselor's skill and patience are tried by the dependent client who resists assuming personal responsibility for his life. The counselor can only have faith in the client's capacity for and interest in personal growth. It is assumed here that lingering feelings of dependence upon, affection for, or resentment against the counselor (to be defined under "transference" in the next chapter) have been resolved. These feelings may show in relatively short informational or supportive types of counseling too, if a client, lonely or dependent, simply cannot face the deprivation of the counseling relationship, even though his most pressing problems have been resolved. A useful procedure with this type of client is to space interviews in increasingly longer intervals prior to final closure.

Steps and Methods of Closure. The first step to close the interviews is *verbal preparation*. The client is reminded of the time limits agreed upon in the initial interview. For example, "Well, this is our fourth and last interview. . . ." Statements of client growth as a lead to termination of contacts may be expressed as follows: "You seem to have achieved some important awareness about yourself, and some realistic plans; do you think you can go it alone from here?" Other examples are: "It seems we have come to a point where you can work this out by yourself," or "You seem to feel that you can carry on from here without further help from me. . . ."

The counselor should then work out a *final summary statement* with the client. This may be a general review of accomplishments, arrangements for referral or follow-up, or preparation of a plan or written summary. An example of written summaries made during counseling on careers is the "Life Planning" brochure described by Shostrom and Brammer (440) or the workbook by Borow and Lindsay (62). This brochure contains the client's tentative objectives with educational plans to match. Supporting data from occupational research, test results, and interview conclusions are often included. This step corresponds to Sullivan's "prescription of action" in his terminating technique (463). We prefer not to use the term "prescription" in this context; it is important, nevertheless, that the client knows what he is going to do next and that he leaves with clear notions about the goals, results, possible courses of action, and limitations of the interviews.

Another step the counselor may take is to leave the door open for possible *follow-ups*. This is especially necessary in short-term, highly structured interview series. Abruptness is avoided when the counselor can say something like, "Drop in to see me when you are around campus," or "When you try it alone for a while you may wish to drop in to review how things are going." It is debatable how much this type of "open-door" policy should be encouraged, since it has possibilities of renewing the dependency of the client and of laying the counselor wide open for attempts to reconstitute the relationship. However, with a younger client in a school situation, the counselor may wish to establish a "standby" contact to observe his development or to give him further information. An interest inventory may be used in the case, for example, "It is a good idea to take inventory of your developing interests occasionally. . . ." This type of statement generally has a reassuring effect on clients and permits continuous observation without an intensive relationship.

A variation on the third step is possible *referral*. If the counselor has gone as far as he feels capable of going, or if another type of therapist or agency is going to take responsibility for the relationship, referral technique is used. Here it is important that the counselor structure the nature of the referral in order to pave the way for easy transition to the new relationship without revealing the nature of that new relationship in advance. As indicated in Chapter 5, reasons for the referral should be discussed carefully with the client so he does not get the "run-around" feeling. The client must convince himself that the referral is necessary or helpful. If the counselor were to say, "I think you ought to see a psychiatrist about this," the client would be likely to be resistive or frightened. To avoid these possible negative responses the counselor might say, "Our psychiatrist might be able to help us on this problem. Would you care to make an appointment?" These same principles apply whether referral is to the school librarian, a social agency, the speech therapist, employment agency, or physician.

Another consideration the counselor should keep in mind in making referrals to outside persons is the desirability of mentioning two or three names, say of physicians, from which the client may choose. It is assumed, of course, that the counselor is familiar with the intake and eligibility policies and conditions of the agencies to which he refers clients, as well as the policies of his own institution regarding referral channels and procedures. Schools, for example, have definite channels established for handling relationships with social agencies, courts, and professional persons in private practice.

The fourth step is the *formal leave-taking*. What was said about concluding the final phase of the individual interview applies here, with emphasis upon parting with a cordial and confident tone. It should be recognized by the counselor that the steps just cited do not always unfold smoothly. The client may make several abortive attempts to operate alone with his newly discovered insights, only to be forced to return to the same or another counselor.

Before leaving this topic of termination, the authors would like to examine Thorne's concepts of overtreatment and undertreatment (474). Thorne places the responsibility for determining the safety and appropriateness of termination squarely with the counselor. Some of the attitudes counselors have which tend, according to Thorne, to result in undertreatment are: [1] "therapeutic nihilism," in which the counselor has a pessimistic attitude that his counseling will not work with this client, as a result of which he gives up; [2] "diagnostic failures," wherein the counselor fails to find or deal adequately with pathological processes and so terminates counseling prematurely; [3] "passive methods," with which a counselor fails to deal actively enough with client problems; [4] "lack of confidence" in attempting to counsel difficult cases; [5] "lenience" in not following up clients persistently; and [6] "overwork" of the counselor from taking too many cases, which results in rushing through appointments, or becoming "stale."

Though these dangers may be valid for certain cases, Thorne cautions that the counselor may err on the side of "overtreating" also. By this he means that a counselor might carry the client beyond the point of ethical treatment, or beyond the point of his competence. Some overtreatment may result from a conscientious attempt to be thorough, thus perhaps reinforcing the dependent client's need for constant support. However, a loose type of relationship over an extended period may have a prophylactic effect which would prevent further deterioration of the client's problem-solving ability. As in so many other areas of counseling methodology, the counselor must assess the situation, weigh the advantages and disadvantages of a course of action, and then use his best judgment.

Summary

The techniques for implementing the basic principles of relationship in the preceding chapter have been classified into eight categories—opening, reflecting, accepting, structuring, listening, leading, reassuring, and terminating. Each method has its unique values, as well as limitations for creating the optimal kind of relationship necessary for the development of insight and self-actualization. In the next chapter, some of the conditions which present difficulties in building and maintaining an optimum relationship and applying relationship techniques will be explored.

Barriers to Actualizing Relationships

Counseling and psychotherapy are interpersonal processes which have identifiable barriers. The purpose of this chapter is to identify these barriers to building and maintaining a relationship, whether formal counseling or friendship. Transference, countertransference, and resistance are three conditions which may help or hinder the relating process, depending on how they are expressed and handled. Some sensitive therapists feel that use of these terms intellectualizes a very personal relationship too much. Describing warm feelings toward a client, for example, as countertransference depreciates the deeply human quality of the relationship. Students wishing to understand conceptually the subtle interplay of feelings in counseling relationships, however, need some thinking tools. This objective approach need not interfere with appreciation of the more nonrational and subtle interpersonal events. This point is emphasized to reassure the counselor that he is dealing with normal feelings and that he need not feel guilty in having genuine and varied feelings toward clients and for experiencing normal gratifications from the helping process. Similarly, he should not be disturbed when clients possess strong and varied feelings toward him.

The three terms above are central to psychoanalytic technique, which is where they originated. Since these concepts are so significant for general psychotherapy and of such considerable consequence for counseling, they will be described and illustrated in detail.

8

Transference-Type Barriers

The Nature and Origin of Transference Feelings

After examining the original writings of Freud and the elaborations of Fenichel, Fromm-Reichmann, Alexander, French, and others, it appears there are several meanings of the term "transference." In a broad sense, the term refers to any feelings expressed or felt by the client toward the therapist, whether a rational reaction to the personality of the therapist or the unconscious projection of earlier attitudes and stereotypes.

We favor the view of the existential therapists (310). The neurotic client does not really "transfer" his feelings about family members to the therapist. Instead, as May says, ". . . the neurotic is one who in certain areas never developed beyond the limited and restricted forms of experience characteristic of the infant. Hence in later years he perceives wife or therapist through the same restricted, distorted 'spectacles' as he perceived father or mother" (310, p. 79). Hence, the problem of transference for the neurotic client is primarily one of delayed development and his perception of the present situation through the colored glasses of past experience. May (313) further cautions that too much dependence on a traditional view of transference as the re-creation of personal relationships from the past leads to a diminished significance of the present encounter with the therapist. It can rob the client of personal responsibility for his feelings in this moment, and it can serve the therapist as a protective screen to avoid the threat of a direct encounter with the client. This positive approach to transference emphasizing encounter is a significant characteristic of actualizing counseling.

Psychoanalytically, transference means the process whereby client attitudes formerly expressed or felt toward another person important to the client are unconsciously "transferred" or projected to the counselor. For example, feelings of love, hate, ambivalence, or dependence at one time directed toward a parent are now irrationally repeated with the psychotherapist as the object.

An intensive development of the transference process is called the "transference neurosis" by psychoanalysts. Colby (103) describes three usages of the term transference neurosis: a person with a severe neurotic condition exhibiting transference feelings, a simple transference condition, and a severe form in which a heavy proportion of the client's infantile problems are focused on the therapist. Transference is a necessary component of the analytic process wherein the person transfers his intrapsychic conflicts into the interpersonal relationship between therapist and client in such a way that it replicates other neurotic relationships past and present. The analyst then uses the transference as a vehicle of therapy.

Transactionally, transference and countertransference can be viewed as interaction problems of ego states. For example, the client's natural child ego state may be rebelling against the amount of responsibility demanded by the therapist, who is speaking from his or her adult ego state. Interaction problems can also be viewed as "games" between counselor and client. A client, for example, may play "the stupid game," manifested as resistance to perceiving strong reality pressures clearly. A behavioral therapist might construe this same example as learned avoidance behavior.

In the therapeutic use of the transference neurosis, the therapist does not view transference as a *problem*, but rather as a fortunate circumstance making the neurosis available in miniature. In existential terms, the transference feelings expressed by the client give the therapist valuable information on how he perceives and manipulates his world. Strupp (461) is convinced that the transference relationship is not only a rich source of interpersonal data but has a validity of its own and should be studied more intensively.

Sometimes the term transference is used as a synonym for relationship, as in the phrase, "The transference was established early. . . ." We feel that this usage is too loose. In this sense, the psychotherapeutic relationship described in earlier chapters could be considered as a type of transference because of the mutual attraction feelings which are present. An equally vague usage is to regard transference as any expression of feeling toward another person.

Rogers (390) states that transference feelings develop when the client perceives that the other person understands him better than he understands himself. The way of viewing transference, whether as hostility or dependency, depends largely on the degree of threat involved.

We prefer to view transference as a concept midway between the classical Freudian view, with emphasis on the past, and the position that all feelings currently expressed toward the counselor are transference. In other words, transference is viewed as a type of projection of the client's past or present unresolved and unrecognized attitudes toward authority figures and love objects—toward the therapist. This projection is done in such a way that the client responds to the therapist in a manner similar to the way he responds to other love objects. Clients build certain expectations of therapists and their roles through this transference process. The client may expect the therapist, for example, to be supporting; or he may expect him to be a punishing or controlling agent. In other words, transference is a term describing how the client construes the therapist and how the client behaves toward the therapist.

Intensive transference, commonly found in psychotherapy, is regarded as a type of relationship which goes beyond that considered desirable or optimal for counseling. A concept of degrees of transference relationship is illustrated in Figure 14. The client, in Figure 14, enters the counselor's presence with the usual mixed feelings people have as they meet strangers. Since counselors and therapists generally are cordial and emotionally warm, the relationship bridge begins to widen and client feeling flows more freely toward the counselor. At this point, the transference relationship begins. Clients with strong affection or dependency needs may project these so

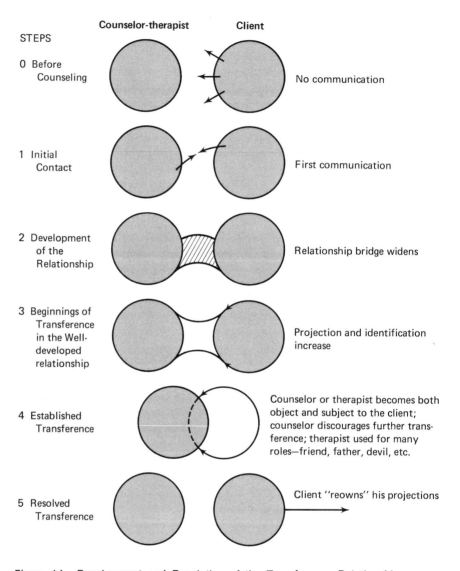

STEPS

Counselor-therapist   **Client**

0 Before Counseling — No communication

1 Initial Contact — First communication

2 Development of the Relationship — Relationship bridge widens

3 Beginnings of Transference in the Well-developed relationship — Projection and identification increase

4 Established Transference — Counselor or therapist becomes both object and subject to the client; counselor discourages further transference; therapist used for many roles—friend, father, devil, etc.

5 Resolved Transference — Client "reowns" his projections

Figure 14. Development and Resolution of the Transference Relationship

intensively at times that the client's perception of the counselor is grossly distorted. An extreme example of this idea is the unusual client who literally hugs or throws himself upon the psychotherapist. Often, clients with weak actualizing capacities must "use" the therapist's strength. In this sense, transference may be a necessary prelude to building the client's own actualizing strength.

Parenthetically, we believe that Step 4 of Figure 14 illustrates a fundamental distinction between counseling and psychotherapy. The counselor develops a close personal relationship with his client, but he does not encourage or allow strong transference feelings as does the the psychotherapist.

The resolved or broken transference relationship is conceptualized in Figure 14 as a complete emotional detachment, with the vectors of the client's feeling moving away from the counselor as a person and in the direction of investing feeling in other mature human relationships.

Transferences may be designated as positive or negative. A positive transference would be made by the client when he projected his feelings of affection or dependency to the counselor, perhaps perceiving him as a loving, helpful father. A negative transference would be made by the client when he projected his feelings of hostility and aggression. These transference feelings change form, sometimes quite suddenly. For example, a client may experience warm feelings toward the counselor while describing his problem, yet feel fearful and resentful for having told "all" or for having exposed his perceived "weaknesses." Often the client's positive transference will change to negative feelings when the counselor doesn't give him all the reassurance or advice he expects. Sometimes a client responds to the counselor in a manner similar to that used during childhood "confessions" to his real parents.

Origins of Transference Feelings. As we explained in the preceding material, transference feelings have their roots in the client's life experiences. The counselor's personal reactions to the client or his institutional role (minister, dean, or physician, for example) arouse selective feelings in the client. The counselor should be aware of feelings which he might elicit from the client. These feelings might be very normal social reactions to what the counselor is, says, or does. As illustrated in Chapter 7 on the nature of the relationship, the more ambiguous the counselor personality, the more opportunity the client has of projecting his inner needs and attitudes rather than of responding socially and rationally to the situation. The nature of the physical setting of the counselor's office also seems to have a pronounced effect on the client's emotional responses to the counselor, although little is known about this phenomenon.

Implications of Transference for Counseling and Psychotherapy

Since the counselor depends primarily upon a relationship of mutual trust and acceptance, a strong transference, especially of the negative or hostile type, tends to interfere with his counseling effectiveness.

The psychotherapist, on the other hand, does not necessarily view transference as an interference. He uses transference-type feelings to help his client recognize what he is trying to do with the relationship to the therapist—for example, how he may be trying to manipulate the therapist. The client's demands help the therapist to understand what sort of person the client is trying to be or wants to be. The transference relationship, therefore, provides valuable clues for later interpretations to the client on how his interpersonal relationship mechanisms are functioning.

Counselors recognize also that, though they do not depend upon a transference relationship for effective therapy, transference feelings are present in varying amounts. For example, there are the clients who fear counselors, depend on them, love them, or expect varying roles of them. These responses may be projected self-regarding attitudes and may be related to earlier experiences with parents; nevertheless, they must be recognized and handled effectively to maintain client involvement.

Clients are often aware of these feelings and express them openly. Wood (505) analyzed five completely recorded client-centered counseling cases. He found only sixty-one out of the total of 1,900 client responses dealing directly with a discussion of the relationship. Qualitatively, however, there were a number of responses which indicated a deep emotional involvement with the counselor. The following excerpts are illustrations:

(Second interview) ". . . it seemed to me that as we were talking along, that you, not only as a counselor, but you as an individual, were getting sort of excited about this thing too, just as I was. And that, well, at times, you were no longer a counselor to me, but you were just another person that I was talking over this problem with" (505, p. 74).

(Fourth interview) "As a matter of fact, a peculiar thing—I hate to admit it —(laughs) is that, except in the last two interviews, I don't believe I've been much concerned with your reflections. You probably realize I've been moving pretty fast, and somewhat running up the middle of your spine at times without, uh, knowing it, desiring to go ahead. A sort of manic euphoria (laughs). But I guess I've done enough to you today" (505, p. 74).

Client-centered or phenomenological counselors, in particular, do not regard a transference situation as a significant therapeutic problem. The result is that persons using the client-centered style of counseling rarely confront intensive transferences, and they reflect it as they would any other feeling. Rogers' writings suggest this procedure:

In client-centered therapy, however, this involved and persistent dependent transference relationship does not tend to develop. Thousands of clients have been dealt with by counselors with whom the writer has had personal contact. In only a small minority of cases handled in a client-centered fashion has the client developed a relationship which could in any way be matched to Freud's terms. In most instances the description of the relationship would be quite different (390, p. 201).

Another cause of low-intensity transference phenomena in counseling might be the counselor's approach to a transference feeling. He does not usually try to analyze deeply the manifold ways in which the client manipulates his life relationships. Instead, the counselor utilizes reflection and acceptance techniques which aid the client to see that the transference feelings reside within his own inadequate perception, and not within the counselor.

The counselor tends to regard the expressions of negativism, hostility, and guilt more as manifestations of resistance in an incomplete growing-up process. The psychotherapist generally handles transference feelings with interpretation of the unconscious impulsive nature of the feelings, whereas the counselor, dealing with the same feelings at a more superficial level, tends to use a variety of responses, including a more oblique approach through reflection of feelings. The counselor, furthermore, looks upon the task as a continuation of the maturation process which has been incompletely guided by the client's natural parents. The counselor tries to help the client to understand and accept his feelings and to see what he has been trying to accomplish with his attitude. After gaining a more rational understanding, he can take his projections on the counselor back to himself, so that, for example, he can be less dependent. The client also is helped to understand in which ways his former behavior was ineffective in reaching his goals of effective living.

Often, the client persistently tests the counselor's or therapist's sincerity through repeated criticisms, unrealistic expectations, aggressiveness, resistance, and irritability. Gradually, however, the client feels "safe" in dropping his defensiveness and changing his perception of himself and the counselor. The client, for example, finds himself able to reconstruct satisfactory relationships with others as well as with the counselor, since he learns he may not always expect counteraggressive acts when he is hostile to others.

Negative transferences often follow positive transferences. When the client suddenly realizes he has been idealizing or has been depending upon the counselor, he begins to perceive the counselor as he really is rather than in the client's "God-like" image. This is the counselor's welcomed cue of client growth. The counselor must help the client work through these feelings of disillusionment, however, by "giving him back" his projections. The situation is analogous to "falling out of love." The lover, in fairness to his former beloved, returns her projections of idealized images (romantic love) so that her actualizing mechanisms are restored to their former state.

Not all negative feelings expressed in the interview are transference feelings. Instead of being projected to the counselor, they may be directed inward. Intrapunitive hostility or guilt, for example, can lead to depression. Though the counselor must be alert to pathological forms of depression which should have more extensive treatment, he can interpret anxious and mildly depressed feelings as a sign that the client is struggling with important feelings. For example, the counselor says in effect, "If we stick together, we can make use of these feelings because they show us that we are very close to something which is important."

Therapeutic Functions of Transference Feelings for Counselors. While strong transferences toward the counselor often complicate his task, it should be recognized that this process serves significant functions for the client. The awareness of freedom to express previously repressed irrational feelings is a unique experience which often reduces anxiety.

Transference serves to build the relationship by allowing the client to express distorted feelings without the usual counterdefensive responses. For example, a client with a "chip on his shoulder" expects his irritability to arouse counterhostility from others. When the counselor does not react as expected (by getting irritated), the client can safely reduce his defensiveness and, hence, has less need to feel guilty because of hostile impulses, and less need to project his hostility on others. This refusal of the counselor to respond according to the client's projections is one of the main vehicles for accomplishing therapeutic goals. For example, if the client's former human relationships have been characterized by rejection or devaluation, the counselor is very accepting and warm. If the client has felt exploited and abused, the counselor is careful in making demands upon the client. The general principle here is that the counselor should not fit himself into the client's projections so as to satisfy the client's neurotic needs. If the counselor fulfills the client's expectations, there is the possibility they will be perpetuated by virtue of having been reinforced.

A second function of transference, implied above, is to promote the client's confidence in the counselor through his wise handling of transference feelings. Such feelings also have the net effect of amplifying the client's emotional involvement with his problem, thereby enabling him to stay in counseling.

A third function of transference is to enable the client to become aware of the origin and significance of these feelings in his present life through interpretation of his feelings. The transferred feelings, along with their maladaptive behaviors, tend to disappear with insight so that he can establish more satisfying and mature relationships with people.

Working Through Transference Feelings and Preventing Deep Transference Relationships. The counselor's main task in this regard is to encourage free expression of feelings while simultaneously keeping the transference attitudes from developing into a deep transference relationship. In psychotherapy an intense transference relationship often develops, and the therapist is faced with a long and arduous task of working through the transference feelings. Several general suggestions for handling and resolving transference feelings follow.

1. A primary technique for resolving transference feeling is by means of *simple acceptance,* as one would handle any type of client feeling. This procedure enables the client to "live out" his feelings, "take back" his projected feelings, or continue to express them more freely in the interview. The client recognizes, then, that transference feelings reside in himself and not in the counselor.

2. The therapist may ask *clarifying questions* regarding the forms of anxiety which the client seems to be manifesting. An example would be, "You seem to be unloading on me today. Why do you suppose this is happening?" This statement is a prelude to the interpretation likely to follow, but it explores the client's attitude first and gives him the opportunity to do his own interpreting.

3. The transference feeling in the client's statement may be *reflected*. For example, the therapist might state, "You feel that we shouldn't discuss this because it may make *me* uncomfortable."

4. The therapist may *interpret* the transference feelings directly. For example, "Sometimes when people feel they have been telling too much, they get insecure about their relationship with that person. Do you suppose this is happening here?" You will note that, even with the use of interpretation, the therapist seeks the feeling response of the client, since it is his distortion of human relationships and feelings which very likely are at the root of his difficulties. The main goal of transference interpretation, then, is to clarify the relationship between the client's earlier interpersonal experiences and his present behavior. A second goal is to reassure the client that these feelings and their resolution are a normal part of the process.

The interpretations generally emphasize present problems and crises and do not dwell on earlier experiences. Interpretations also come relatively late in the process so as to allow the therapist to accumulate data from which to make valid interpretations. Sometimes interpretations come as "shock treatment" where the therapist says in effect, "Congratulations; you are now able to take these projections and see them as existing in yourself." (The counselor then may go on to explain the nature and function of transference feelings.)

As the client becomes comfortable with the counselor, a common question on transference would be, "Toward whom else have you had these feelings you are feeling toward me?" Such a question suggests to the client that feelings toward the therapist may be directed genuinely toward him, but that they should be considered in terms of the idea that feelings at the moment are often attempts to relate past expectations to the present.

5. The following suggestion by May that the counselor should focus on *what* is going on now in client feelings rather than *why* provides a most fruitful technique for the handling of the difficult problem of transference:

In existential therapy "transference" gets placed in the new context of *an event occurring in a real relationship between two people.* . . . The only thing that will grasp the patient, and in the long run make it possible for her to change, is to experience fully and deeply that she is doing precisely this to a real person, myself, in this real moment. . . . Part of this *sense of timing* . . . consists of letting the patient experience *what* he or she is doing until the experience really grasps him. Then and only then will the explanation of *why* help.

This is a point the phenomenologists make consistently, namely, that to know fully *what* we are doing, to feel it, to experience it all through our being, is much more important than to know *why*. For, they hold, if we fully know the *what*, the *why* will come along by itself (310, pp. 83–84).

The general principle here is that not all feelings automatically need be construed as transferred from the past, but may be the result of genuine interaction between therapist and client, or between client and client in a group, in the here and now.

6. In general, calling attention to the transference causes the client to react in the opposite manner. Therefore, therapists usually adhere to the principle of calling attention to negative transference feelings, but not calling attention to the positive transference unless it has reached a level where it is interfering with therapeutic movement.

7. A common method for handling transference is to regard it as a form of *projection*. The therapist can test this idea by asking the client to reverse the projection, and to encourage repetition until the statement is felt by the client as that which he is really feeling. The following is an example:

Cl: I have the feeling that you don't like me.

C: Can you reverse that statement?

Cl: You mean, I don't like you?

C: Yes, can you say that again louder?

Cl: I don't like you!

C: Say it again louder.

Cl: I don't like you!

C: True or not true?

Cl: I guess that's true!

8. The therapist may also interpret transference feelings as expressions of "being deficiency" in which the client is seeking environmental support instead of simply seeing the feeling as a transference from the past. An example using a role reversal method follows:

Cl: You don't help me.

C: What do you want me to do?

Cl: To say something helpful.

C: You be me and say something helpful.

Cl: OK, Gloria, you ought to stand on your own two feet and think for yourself.

C: Now be yourself and answer.

Cl: You are right!

9. The counselor may *refer* the client to a therapist qualified to give more extensive psychotherapy if the relationship develops to an intensity which is beyond the competence and responsibility of the counselor.

Types of Transference Feelings

The following discussion covers more problems on transference and illustrates the use of the principles discussed above.

Ambivalent *authority* feelings are commonly transferred to the counselor. In middle class society, which provides the bulk of the psychological counselor's clientele, authority feelings are exceedingly mixed. The client, in addition to having possibly both dependent and hostile feelings about authority figures, becomes anxious when he divulges personal information to the counselor. The emotional material may come up too fast for him to handle, resulting in anxiety and a possible breakdown of control mechanisms. His feelings may change suddenly to hostility directed toward the counselor for allowing him to tell so much.

The following excerpt illustrates an authority-type of feeling transfer (the client is a nineteen-year-old single woman who has spent two previous interviews describing her feelings of inadequacy and hostility toward her father):

C1: I just can't talk any more.

C: You feel run down like a clock spring?

C1: No, I'm just finding it harder and harder to talk to *you*.

C: You feel that I as a person am making it harder for you?

C1: Well, yes, I mean (long pause and signs of distress).

C: You mean that somehow I remind you of someone—like your father perhaps?

C1: Yes, I never thought of it that way; but I guess most men do; but you just sitting there looking at me (pause) bothers me.

C: When you think of me as a man, you get the same mixed up feelings as you do when you think of your father. Is that it?

C1: When I really think about it, I know I haven't any real reason to (pause) well, to think of you as my father. It seems silly, but it makes me feel better to know why I feel this way.

(Followed by further discussion of relationships with father.) The counselor in the excerpt tried to maintain an attitude of understanding and acceptance. He had listened to her outpouring of feelings for two sessions. Mild interpretation from the counselor led her to see that her growing difficulties in expressing herself were not due to the counselor's austere paternalistic attitude, but were more the projections of her own feelings. She realized that she could be secure and that she had no palpable reason for feeling that the counselor was censuring her or that he represented father to her. This re-perceiving experience, as well as the intellectual awareness of projection, tended to reduce her defensiveness. Thus, she could perceive the counselor as he really tried to be—a personality who understands and accepts rather than evaluates. Rogers emphasizes the value of the above perceptual change in clients:

> The whole relationship is composed of the self of the client, the counselor being depersonalized for purpose of therapy into being "the client's other self." It is this warm willingness on the part of the counselor to lay his own self temporarily aside, in order to enter into the experience of the client, which makes the experience a completely unique one, unlike anything in the client's previous experience (390, p. 208).

The following example illustrates a type of transference feeling involving *dependency* (this is a first interview with a nineteen-year-old woman):

C1: I'm not doing so well in school.

C: Mm-hm.

C1: I thought you could help me by telling me what I'm doing wrong.

C: You are confident that I can help you improve your school work possibly by analyzing your procedures?

C1: Well, yes; I've heard you have tests and things.
(After further structuring the role of the counselor and client and further elaboration of the problem, the client is still thinking along dependent lines.)

C1: I certainly hope these tests give me the answers. I know they aren't very accurate; but with your experience with them, you should be able to tell me what I should do.

C: While you recognize the limitations of tests, you still feel I will be able to suggest a definite course of action. However, I will interpret the results to you and discuss them with you in such a way that you will be better able to decide.

C1: Well, I guess that is what you are here for, aren't you?

In the preceding example, it became clear that the client was depending on the counselor to solve her problem. In spite of the counselor's patient acceptance and later interpretation of her dependency, the client continued to look for further support without much evidence of awareness. The counselor's effort to shift responsibility gently back to her was met with a negative transference remark. The counselor, realizing that his own personality or technique might be arousing this aggressive transference, finally decided that continuation of this relationship would merely reinforce the client's dependency and would very likely arouse some countertransference feelings. He utilized the "capping" technique to ease out of the counseling relationship and to refer her to a psychotherapist more able to work with this type of client.

While hostile or affectional transference feelings seem to be more ade-quately resolved by counselors, it is this persistent form of dependency which gives them most difficulty. The dependent client insists that the counselor take over the decisions and self-management. This dependent attitude generally shows up early in counseling, so that the counselor can decide whether his skills can cope with the alternating apathy and aggres-sion often accompanying the dependency. The client frequently does not obtain the solutions and support he seeks; hence, he becomes defen-sive. The resulting aggression severely tests the counselor's judgment whether to inhibit his own negative feelings and maintain an attitude of acceptance and understanding, or to react more openly with his feelings.

Another danger in dependency transference is that the client's desires to solve his problem may be outweighed by his wishes to prolong the counseling. It is often necessary to put a "brake" on the regressive-dependent type of transference feeling early in the process, before it be-comes a persistent response.

Rogers (390) offers the hypothesis that a dependent transference arises when the client feels he is being evaluated and that the evaluation has more accuracy than his own estimate of himself. The net effect is to decrease self-confidence and to increase dependency. Use of techniques, such as interpreting a test score, or reassuring expressions such as, "It is normal to feel that way," or interpretive remarks such as, "Maybe you do not resent her as much as you thought you did," convey the idea that the counselor has a high degree of omniscience; hence, the client feels relieved to place responsibility for his decisions on the counselor. In psychotherapy situations, the therapist is not afraid of assuming responsi-bility toward the client for a prolonged period before working through the unconscious emotional aspects of the transference.

In amplifying the hypothesis in the preceding paragraph, Rogers (390) suggests that as the client explores his feelings more deeply, he becomes more threatened. Then there generally is a tendency to displace or project these threatening feelings to the counselor. This feeling of threat and its accompanying anxiety often result in more dependence, which only the psychotherapist is willing to deal with on a long-term basis.

Schuldt's data (417) suggest that clients discussed dependency themes if counselors approached this topic, and, conversely, clients tended to avoid the topic if the counselor did so. In studying the dependency theme over the total process, he found significantly more client dependency responses during the early stages than the later stages, although the coun-selor approaches to these dependency responses remained consistent throughout the process. Schuldt's data suggest that amount of dependency expressed is related to many complex therapeutic variables, but that the counselor's approach-avoidance manner is a likely contributor to the degree of client-expressed dependency.

A third common type of transference attitude is that of *affection*. This feeling is elicited largely as a function of the understanding and accepting attitude of the counselor. A client with strong needs for love and attention will often respond to the counselor's or therapist's "warmth" with feelings ranging from friendly interest to intense erotic love.

Since this interview may be the first relationship in which the client has experienced genuine acceptance and in which he shares his deepest feelings, it is easy to understand how intense positive feelings, even of intimacy, may develop. This development of feeling, unless recognized, becomes increasingly more difficult to handle by both client and counselor. It was this type of situation which, in the early days of formal psychotherapy, produced so many rumors of irregularities in the conduct of therapists. This is another reason for counselors to limit the buildup of strong transferences. However, these positive feelings elicited by a therapist's accepting attitude can be utilized to create understanding of need deprivations.

Three classes of feelings—hostility, dependency, and affection—were utilized here for expository purposes. You are reminded, however, that feelings exist in a vast array of types and combinations, although the basic techniques for all are similar.

In the concluding phases of counseling or therapy, it is necessary that any strong residual transference feelings be discussed frankly with the client and broadly interpreted. He must be made aware, for example, that he must become less dependent on the counseling or therapy relationship as well as on the counselor, since the present relationship is about to terminate. The affection felt toward the counselor or therapist, in addition, must be generalized to include all human beings. Any resentments lingering toward the counselor must be completely understood by the client in light of the total psychotherapeutic discussion of parents, siblings, and so on. Thus, the client is not left struggling with unresolved feelings dredged up during the counseling.

In counseling, the diminution of transference feelings is due to increased client awareness of previously unaccepted, distorted, or partially known experiences. In psychotherapy, there is usually a more pronounced personality change, and the decreases in transference problems run parallel to personality changes.

Summary of Transference Discussion

In this section, transference was described as a largely irrational part of the counseling process wherein the client projects to the counselor self-regarding attitudes and unresolved feelings from earlier human relationships. Intensity of transference seems to be a function of the type of client involved, setting, length of counseling, extent of emotional involvement, counselor personality, and counselor technique. Although the expression and working through of transference feelings has therapeutic values, it is the intense feeling or involved relationships that create counseling problems. In psychotherapy, however, the development and working through of transferences are considered to be a significant part of long-term personality change.

The resolution or working through of transference feelings is accomplished if the counselor maintains an attitude of acceptance and understanding, if he applies reflection, questioning, and interpretive techniques appropriately, and if he is willing to share some of his own feeling reactions to the client's transference. In any case, transference is a normal condition of every relationship.

Countertransference-Type Barriers

The Nature of Countertransference Feelings

The following section also applies to counseling and psychotherapy, so the more general term, counselor, will be utilized for both.

The reader may have deduced from the previous discussion that countertransference refers to the emotional reactions and projections of the counselor toward the client. In an extensive review of the writings on countertransference, Cohen (102) concluded that, although the term transference has fairly standard meaning, countertransference has not. Winnicott's (502) "objective countertransference," wherein the counselor's resentment of the client, for example, is based upon some objective antisocial or psychotic behavior which would be objectionable to any human being, is on one end of the continuum. Fromm-Reichmann (176) separates the type Winnicott mentions from the more subtle unconscious forms—especially the counselor reactions to client transference feelings. Alexander and French (3) include all attitudes of the counselor toward the client. Other writers include only affectionate or libidinous feelings under countertransference.

We view countertransference broadly to include conscious and unconscious attitudes of the counselor toward real or imagined client attitudes or overt behavior. It is the expression of the counselor's humanness. It may be simply a feeling of the moment which is a genuine response between two human beings; it also may be a form of therapist projection. Examples follow:

1. Genuine expression:

   C: You are very pretty.

   Cl: Thank you very much.

   C: You're welcome.

2. Projection:

   C: You are very pretty.

   Cl: Thank you very much.

   C: I suppose you react that way to all men who say that?

One of the qualifications mentioned in Chapter 6 was that the counselor have insight into his own immaturities, prejudices, objects of disgust, anxieties, and punitive tendencies. No counselor is free of these feelings. Unless he has an awareness of his attitudes, however, his responses to client statements will all too frequently be tainted with his own feelings. These negative attitudes tend to have a deleterious effect on the relationship by arousing negative transference feelings in the client. Positive countertransferences, made by the counselor, can be even more deleterious, since he is less apt to recognize them and the client is more upset when they are withdrawn.

There are positive and helpful countertransference attitudes in the form of facilitating counselor traits described in Chapter 6. Attitudes of acceptance are essential in building a therapeutic relationship. The counselor, furthermore, must decide how much of a "real person" he must be to the client.

Since handling client feelings is reported to be one of their principal difficulties, countertransference complicates the problems of beginning counselors. These counselors are relieved to know that it is commonplace to have some mixed feelings about the client. In addition, the client is an overvalued person in the beginning counselor's life because of his own strong desires to succeed in counseling.

There are few studies with implications for the subject of countertransference, but Chance (98) studied the attitudes of therapists toward their clients and found that, as therapy progresses, the clients become more alike in the therapist's eyes. The results of this study suggest that as psychotherapists anticipate client progress, clients become more like the therapist's projected "generalized client," rather than more sharply differentiated people.

Sources of Countertransference Feelings

Cohen (102) hypothesizes that anxiety, either felt or defended by the counselor, is the prime source of countertransference behaviors. The counseling relationship mobilizes anxiety from former relationships in a manner similar to transference. The anxiety patterns in the counselor may be classified into three types: unresolved personal problems of the counselor, situational pressures, and communication of the client's feeling to the counselor by empathic means.

The first category, the counselor's unresolved personal problems as a source of interview difficulties, needs little explanation. The main solution here is counseling for the counselor. Even after having had personal therapy, counselors must increase self-awareness so as to avoid countertransferences.

The category of situational pressures is tied in with the counselor's problems but may aggravate latent feelings. An illustration follows: The counselor had just come from a fatiguing meeting. He had to wait a few minutes for a late client who, noting the austere facial expressions of the counselor, apologized profusely. He felt that the counselor was provoked with him, when in reality it was the emotional exhaustion and frustration experienced by the counselor in a previous hour which caused him to respond so severely to the client.

Situational pressures exist for the counselor in the form of his feeling responsibility to see that the client improves, or feeling that his professional reputation is at stake if he fails with this client. As a result, the counselor "tries too hard," by pushing the client, and thereby may defeat his own purposes. The counselor must be on guard so that his anxious feelings of frustration when a client does not improve are not transmitted to the client.

Related to situational pressures are heavy case loads and long counseling hours which result in excessive fatigue. Prolonged efforts of this kind, or just the boredom of months of counseling without breaks, lead to a condition called by many counselors the "burnout effect." This is a condition of chronic fatigue, apathy, mild depression, and loss of motivation. In severe and persistent form, it has led counselors to leave the field of counseling.

3. A third category of countertransference sources is communication of client feelings to the counselor. When the counselor tends to be overly sympathetic, is it because he has unwittingly responded to a strong bid for sympathy and attention? When the counselor feels himself becoming anxious or resentful, is it owing to the contagion of the client's anxious feelings? That this happens frequently is possibly on account of the counselor's special training in alertness to client feelings. The counselor then responds empathically to minimal cues, such as changes in posture, voice, and manner. The counselor may not be aware that the stiff jerky walk from the reception room to the office, the grating voice, or the loud aggressive talk of the client generate tensions in him.

Counselor responses to client hostility were studied by Gamsky and Farwell (178) in an experimental situation. They found that counselors reacted in a negative manner when the hostility was directed at them. Counselors so threatened reacted with significantly more reassurance, suggestions, and information than at other times. Experienced counselors handled the hostility better than the less experienced.

It should not be overlooked, perhaps, that in addition to the empathic explanation, the preceding behaviors are also related to the counselor's past personal problems. One of the ways the counselor manifests his anxiety is to emit impulsively a verbalization of his own—a question, comment, or change of subject which may not technically be relevant to the counseling process at the moment. The net effect is often disastrous from the standpoint of stopping or diverting the flow of client feelings, throwing him off the loaded topic, or creating more transference feelings. An example is the counselor who has difficulty working with teenage youth because his own unresolved teenage problems are reenacted.

235

In addition, the counselor may reveal his anxiety by feelings of uneasiness. Reusch and Prestwood (380) studied the transmission of feelings in an experiment which involved psychiatrists listening to recordings of therapeutic interviews. The investigators found that the emotional tone of the listeners varied significantly with the rate of speech, use of personal pronouns, and frequency of expression of feeling. A relaxed client resulted in a relaxed listener. Those interviews heavily laden with anxiety resulted in listener reports varying from being ill at ease to being angry or disturbed.

Any discussion of the source of countertransference attitudes would not be complete without mentioning the counselor's value structure again. As indicated in earlier chapters, the very nature of the relationship puts the counselor in a position of influencing the client. This happens even though he claims to be objective and nonjudgmental. It is difficult for a counselor to avoid conveying the feeling that he regards emotional maturity, for example, as an important goal for counseling. It is quite easy for the client to guess by emotional implication, if not verbally, the values which the counselor holds after a discussion of moral problems.

The counselor conveys two types of values to the client—those relating to how he should live, and those concerned with how he should behave in counseling. There is no question professionally that a counselor can convey counseling process values which facilitate counseling. Examples are: "It is important to express how you really feel here." "It is all right to tell me how much you resent your aunt."

There is considerable question as to how far a counselor should go in promoting his own moral concepts or styles of life in the interview. On the one hand, it may be desirable to help a racially prejudiced client to perceive others in a less rigid manner consonant with his capacity for insight; on the other hand, it might lead to unfortunate consequences to specify a particular type of religious faith.

There are two reasons for restricting value projection. One is that the counselor might succeed. We cannot safely trust even a sophisticated counselor to be a type of "cultural high priest" where he poses as the best judge about right and wrong or appropriate or inappropriate beliefs. If it is felt that the client needs more information and clarification in the area of religious values, for example, it is preferable in our opinion to refer him to a reliable minister from whom there is clear understanding that he will receive instruction in values consonant with his needs and subculture identity.

Another reason for restricting this activity is that the counselor's deliberate efforts to influence the client's values might fail. The unsuccessful attempt might interfere with a good therapeutic relationship by promoting an unwanted negative transference attitude. Yet, a counselor is an expert in the process of living. There are so many commonly accepted behaviors in the area of legal conformity, marriage, and generally mature behavior which the counselor can feel justified in espousing. He cannot use his own or society's frame of reference on value completely, however. The counselor constantly must be aware of the client's personal standards and beliefs. He must try to see these values as the client sees them and help the client utilize them for his own benefit. The counselor must keep up with the fast-changing value scene in society at large and in extreme subcultures so he can help his client gain perspective.

Ingham and Love suggest a technique for handling the instances where the client is aware of the counselor's values. The counselor explains the situation by saying, for example, "You've picked up something of my feeling about marriage. I don't mind your knowing what I think about it, but it doesn't mean that you should follow my ideas" (238, p. 78). Here the counselor admits he has given his values and allows the client to accept or reject them, yet does not refute his own feelings.

Signs of Countertransference Feelings

The following checklist of illustrative signs is offered to the counselor to test himself. Hopefully, it will help to distinguish positive therapeutic feelings from anxious or defensive countertransference involvement with clients.

1. Finds himself getting sleepy, or not listening or paying attention as well as he might, not hearing client's messages clearly.

2. Sees himself denying the presence of anxiety and thinks to himself, "I feel all right about this topic and should feel upset; but I don't." (If there were no anxiety present, why would the counselor even think about it?)

3. Finds it difficult to shift positions or feels himself "tighten up."

4. Feels himself becoming sympathetic rather than empathic or becoming over-emotional in face of client's troubles.

5. Selects certain material to reflect or interpret and wonders afterward why he selected this material rather than some other material.

6. Finds himself consistently reflecting or interpreting too soon or incorrectly (and the result cannot be accounted for on client resistance grounds only).

7. Finds that he underestimates or misses the client's depth of feeling consistently.

8. Has unreasoning dislike or attraction for the client. He gets angry at the "unappreciative" client.

9. Finds he cannot identify with the client. For example, when the client feels upset, the counselor feels no emotional response.

10. Overidentifies himself with the client, as in becoming aggressively sympathetic when the client cites maltreatment by an authority figure.

11. Discovers a tendency to argue with the client, becomes defensive, or is otherwise vulnerable to client criticism.

12. Feels that this is his "best" or "worst" client.

13. Finds himself preoccupied with the client in fantasy between sessions, even to the extent of thinking of responses to be made.

14. Realizes that he is habitually late in starting interviews or runs over the hour with certain clients.

15. Attempts to elicit some strong affect from the client by making dramatic statements.

16. Finds himself overconcerned about confidential nature of work with the client.

17. Feels the compulsion to do something active; hence, makes too strong an impact with "shotgun" interpretations and suggestions.

18. Dreams about the client.

19. Is too "busy" to see the client or may complain of "administrative duties."

20. Works excessively hard with clients to point of fatigue, then complains of overwork.

An insidious form of countertransference expression is compulsive advice-giving. This "if I were you" approach is so exceedingly common in everyday human relations that it tends to spill into counseling relationships. The counselor may feel the need to convince the client that the course of action discussed is best for him; yet the advice, persuasion, or reassurance is motivated more by the counselor's personal needs. A possible motive for advice-giving is extrapunitive hostility. It is a way of controlling others, depreciating them, and elevating one's self to a dominating role. There are conditions, however, where *information* and *opinions* can be offered. These conditions are discussed in Chapter 10 on information techniques.

A common form of countertransference feeling is the idea that the client must somehow like the counselor and that the counselor must please the client. Though the relationship is built upon mutual trust and cordiality, there are times when the counselor must risk this client admiration. For example, sometimes the therapist must help the client see that he must give up important things, and that removal of pleasing behaviors is sometimes painful.

Fiedler (152) found in his studies of the factors in the counseling relationships that the poor, or nonexpert, counselors had the tendency to "not hear," "ignore," or communicate poorly with clients. The expert counselors had these tendencies significantly less often. This study suggests that such countertransference signs, as Fiedler found, are not a great problem for experienced therapists.

For the counselor who feels that he is not vulnerable to countertransference tendencies, a revealing and sobering exploratory study by Fiedler is cited. He found that there was a high relationship between therapeutic competence and lack of negative countertransference attitudes. Fiedler's method consisted of comparing the similarity of the counselor's and the client's self-descriptions. The counselor's "ideal" description, then, was used to determine the nature and intensity of countertransference feelings. An implication of this study is that, as the counselor grows in counseling experience and personal understanding, his harmful countertransference attitudes diminish.

Resolving Countertransference Feelings

Although little research has been done in the area of resolving a countertransference, there is a body of clinical experience which may be useful to the counselor in handling his feelings toward the client. Increasingly, encounter group experiences are helping not only beginning, but experienced counselors to become more aware of their feelings toward clients.

1. *Locating Sources of Feelings:* After awareness of the feelings the first step consists of the therapist asking himself, "I wonder why this is so?" This question is precipitated by the feeling that the counselor is not communicating with his client. The following list of questions should give every counselor additional reasons to ponder his countertransference attitudes.

A Counselor's Guide to Self-Criticism [1]

Why did I make this particular response to this student's remark? What was behind it?

What was I reacting to when making this remark?

What was I endeavoring to convey to the client?

Why did I ask that question?

Was it really asked for purposes related to helping the client?

Was I merely curious?

Was I really being judgmental by asking that question?

Why did I feel impelled at this point to give advice?

Was it because I felt that the client expected me to have all the answers?

And did I respond by being all-wise?

Why did I become so emotionally involved with the client who felt so unloved and insecure?

Could it be that basically I too still feel unloved and unlovable?

Why did I want (or did I not want) to bring the parent, husband, or wife of this client into counseling?

Can it be that I have overidentified with the client and have already rejected the spouse? (or the parent?)

Why in this first interview did I talk so much instead of letting the client tell his story?

Was it because I felt I had to impress the client with my own knowledge so he would return?

[1] Adapted from Johnson (248).

Why does it upset me when appointments are broken?

Is it because I am really insecure and uncertain concerning my skill?

Why am I so reluctant to "let go" when the counseling with a client has reached a good termination point, or when I know the client should be referred for a different kind of help?

Am I using the client for my needs or am I letting him use me?

Each counselor must accept the fact that he has varied feelings about the client and that he will be changed somewhat by the counseling experience. The counselor must also be aware that he has anxieties coming from insecurity in the counseling role and the client's expression of anxiety.

The counselor must control his tendencies to give reassurance to the client because of his own needs for reassurance. For example:

C1: Sometimes I feel like screaming out loud in a quiet place like the library. In fact, I feel so tensed up at times I feel like wringing somebody's neck till he dies.

C: It is all right to feel that way. After all, thinking of killing isn't the same as murder.

This counselor response is likely to arouse more anxiety in the client, whereas the following response would recognize his feeling, tend to tone down the reassurance, and yet not show the counselor's anxiety (even if the counselor realistically pictures himself as a possible object of the client's homicidal feelings):

C: Sometimes these feelings do seem hard to control and we feel an urge to let them go at times. Perhaps you would like to mention some experiences with other people or situations which make you feel this way.

The counselor controls his anxiety through the knowledge that non-psychotic clients rarely assault counselors, and that the hostile, threatening language is often a clever device used by disturbed clients to frighten counselors and therapists.

2. *Supervisory Assistance*: First of all, every counselor who feels uneasy about his responses to a client should admit to the possibility that his comments are a form of his own projections. All that may be necessary is to admit to this possibility frankly with a supervisor or colleague and attempt to change. There are times in the professional life of every counselor when he must admit that certain types of personalities make him defensive or are beyond his level of competence. He can handle this problem by assessing the client as a case "too hot to handle" and referring him to another therapist. An additional recourse is the supervisor or a colleague with whom he can discuss, with considerable candor, the feelings involved without breaching the confidences of the relationship.

For example, a counselor may recognize that he has trouble with hostile, aggressive women; hence, he might suggest that such a client change counselors. Again, discussing this problem in a counseling relationship with a supervisor helps the counselor resolve his own feelings.

3. *Discussion With the Client:* Though there is no objective evidence to indicate that it is expedient to discuss countertransference feelings with the client, we have found a mild reassuring and interpretive reference occasionally helpful in allaying anxiety. For example (this is a second interview with a thirty-three-year-old married woman, after a discussion about an involved marital problem):

C1: Well, there it is—straight from the shoulder.

C: You feel you have told the story quite frankly. Perhaps you have noticed that there are times when things you say may seem to disturb me a bit. I trust though that you will not hold back any feelings for fear of disturbing me.

C1: I appreciate your telling me this. It might make it easier to talk to you.

Another example wherein the counselor rationalizes his unwarranted intrusion follows: The counselor has just interrupted the client and says, "I'm sorry; I didn't intend to stop you. Sometimes we are so eager to help we interrupt your train of thought."

4. *Counselor Growth:* The counselor can use his own awareness of himself as reflected through the therapeutic process to enhance his own growth and resolve his difficulties. Cohen (101) cites an example of a psychotherapist who doubted his own intellectual adequacy and habitually overrated and competed with his more intellectual clients. This situation made it difficult for the counselor to help the clients who use intellectualized defenses against their own anxieties. Similarly, the "burnout effect" cited earlier can be allayed or avoided by careful attention to a personal growth program of renewal, rest, and recreation.

5. *Referral to Group Counseling or Therapy:* Another technique for handling a countertransference is to require that the client discuss his problem in group therapy. For example, if it is obvious that a woman client has strong affectionate feelings toward the therapist, he can ask that she talk about this matter in a group therapy situation. This procedure depersonalizes the problem and removes much of the possibility of any undesirable countertransference reaction.

6. *Exemplary Encounter:* If, instead of seeing the client-therapist relationship as one which is active on the part of the client and passive on the part of the therapist, the dialogue is seen as an *encounter,* then the therapist will not be afraid of expressing and introjecting his own feelings of anger and frustration. His awareness of countertransference dangers, and his willingness to admit that "this may be my problem," provide the client with an open model of humanness and expression which will help him more than an overcautious counselor who is constricted because of his countertransference fears.

7. *Analysis of Tapes and Videotapes:* An additional source of counter-transference awareness is through use of audio- and videotape recordings. A frank discussion with fellow staff members of the countertransference aspects of their work samples will reduce the danger of introjection of the counselor's projections into therapeutic work.

Summary of the Countertransference Section

The purpose of this section is to impress upon the reader the significance of the counselor's irrational attitudinal responses. Another purpose is to suggest ways of resolving these feelings. We support the hypothesis that the counselor's attitudes are one of the most important determinants of interview climate. A counselor can resolve his feelings toward the client by recognizing that he has countertransference feelings, by examining himself concerning why the feelings exist, possibly admitting that he should not work with this client, and by using the recognition of countertransference feelings as information to enhance his own personal growth outside the interviews through counseling or encounter group work himself.

The next section contains a consideration of the phenomenon of resistance, which draws upon elements of the transference and counter-transference discussion; yet, the resistance phenomenon has unique characteristics of its own.

Resistance-Type Barriers

The Nature of Resistance

One of the principal realities of building and maintaining an effective counseling relationship is the presence of resistance. Resistance may be viewed as a special defensive form of transference and a key function of the facade level. The term resistance, as we use it, refers to a characteristic of the client's defense system which opposes the purposes of counseling or therapy.

The term resistance was introduced by psychoanalysts to indicate unconscious opposition toward bringing unconscious material into consciousness, as well as the mobilization of repressive and protective functions of the ego (168). Transactional theorists would construe resistance as an elaborate "game" with definite "payoffs."

The existentialist view of resistance is stated by May as follows:

. . . this is an outworking of the tendency of the patient to . . . renounce the particular unique and original potentiality which is his. This "social conformity" is a general form of resistance to life; and even the patient's acceptance of the doctrines and interpretations of the therapist may itself be an expression of resistance (310, p. 79).

Perls states cogently from the Gestalt viewpoint that all resistance represents the client's refusal to be self-supportive. Therefore, he has to be confronted with the "gain" he gets from such resistance. An example as Perls would respond follows:

C: What does it do for you just to sit there?

C1: Then I don't have to work.

C: You really don't want to help yourself?

C1: Well, yes and no.

C: Be the yes and no!

C1: Well, the no self says, "I enjoy frustrating you." The yes self says, "but I've got to do it myself."

Resistance, like transference, has different implications for counseling as opposed to psychotherapy. In general, counselors see resistance as something which opposes progress in problem-solving and therefore is something which the counselor tries to reduce as much as possible. The therapist, in contrast, sees resistance as an important phenomenon for intensive analysis. If he can understand the client's unique form of resistance, then he will more likely be able to help the client understand and change his personality. The aim of psychotherapy, therefore, is not just to ascertain the client's defensive system or to "find out his secret." Rather, it is the significant question, "How does the client hide his secret?" A significant part of psychotherapy, therefore, involves the intensive awareness and study of resistance and transference feelings.

Resistance exists in varying amounts in all interviews and may be viewed as being at the opposite end of a continuum from free emotional expression. Daulton (118) and Sherman's (428) data appear to support this thesis of a continuum relationship. Haigh (214) found a significant inverse relationship between defensiveness in early interviews and later expressions of positive attitude.

Resistance may vary from rejection of counseling and overt antagonism, on the one hand, to subtle forms, such as hesitation and inattention, on the other. Clients may say: "I know what I want to say, but I can't say it"; "I'll have to leave early today since I want to study for a test"; "I don't think that applies in my case"; "I'm sorry I'm late, but I almost forgot about our interviews"; "I thought you were supposed to be the expert." An obvious form of resistance is *embarrassment*—the tendency to make contact and retreat at the same time. *Blocking* or blank spots may be interpreted as restraining oneself and taking responsibility for it. *Not seeing or hearing* are tendencies which definitely can be labeled as resistance.

Although resistance is present in some degree in all interviews, it is seldom recognized by the client. Hence, resistance exists largely as an unconscious phenomenon and is manifested by an ambivalent attitude toward counseling. He wants help, yet he resists the very help he seeks. This ambivalent client attitude is one of the most baffling situations confronting the inexperienced counselor. Even experienced counselors occasionally cite resistance as an excuse for not establishing an effective relationship.

Freud emphasized that the ambivalent and paradoxical attitude is a normal state of affairs in therapy. Many psychotherapists typically regard resistance as a normal mechanism which functions independently of therapy, to prevent disturbing feelings from coming to awareness.

The degree to which it is necessary to focus upon resistance to reach the goals of therapy illustrates, further, the differences between counseling and psychotherapy, as indicated in the following examples:

1. *Counseling:*
   C1: I can't seem to be successful as a salesman—I just can't get along with other people.

   C: You've pretty well ruled out selling then? Have you considered some of the other occupations on which you score high on the Strong Test?

   Psychotherapy:
   C: Why do you find it necessary to keep people distant from you?

2. *Counseling:*
   C1: I can't seem to get along with my supervisor.

   C: Since this seems such an obstacle, let's look at some techniques for getting along with such people.

   Psychotherapy:
   C: You seem to have much resistance to working with persons in authority.

Sources of Resistance

There appears to be general agreement among counselors that resistance arises when the client perceives the counselor, topic, or situation as threatening. Since anxiety is present in response to threat, the client is compelled to defend himself further against the anxiety through behaviors which are resistive in nature.

Resistance can be classified conveniently as "internal" or "external" in origin. Internal resistance comes from within the personality structure of the client and is a generalized response to threat; external resistance is provoked as a result of the counseling setting, the impact of counselor technique, or countertransference attitudes.

Internal Resistance. One common source of internal resistance is the tendency of anxious clients to retreat from usually painful attempts to explore or alter patterns of behavior or of personality structure. It represents a fear of growing, or not wishing to be self-supportive.

There seems to be anxiety associated with change in life status or attitude. Clients fear the expression of anxious or hostile feelings because they have learned to anticipate judgmental labels such as "immature," "lazy," or "neurotic." These feelings seem to be most manifest when the client is expressing feelings too fast, in which case he feels that he is exposing himself to the anxiety of ego-relevant stimuli faster than he can judge the safety of these stimuli. Crider (112), in his study of the hostile personality, found repressed hostility, especially in persons fearing expression of aggressive feelings, to be a prominent source of resistance.

Margolies (306) uses the term "facade" to describe another form of *internal* resistance. Facade refers to the initial statement made by a student client—for example, to explain his poor showing in college. Examples are: "I guess I hang around with the gang too much"; "I must be in the wrong major"; or "The Army is going to get me soon"; "My study habits are no good." Although these statements serve a useful function as reference points for further discussion, they are very often rationalizations and expressions of resistance. The client seems so captivated by the simple logic of his statements that he often finds little motivation to overcome his resistance and explore the situation further.

Another phenomenon creating resistance is reification anxiety; that is, the client's fear that to put his feelings into words will make the condition real. An example of this basis for resistance is reluctance to express anxieties about having cancer, of death, or of losing love.

External Resistance. Some counselors are convinced that external resistance grows out of poor technique. Rogers, in his earlier work on counseling, offers the hypothesis that resistance is not necessarily ". . . an inevitable part of psychotherapy, nor a desirable part . . . ," and that what resistance is present appears to come from attempts to accelerate or to cut the process of therapy short (391, p. 151).

An illustration of *external* resistance is the case where the counselor has made modest suggestions about improving study efficiency. The client may be anxious about carrying them out because of a supposed feeling of closeness or obligation to the counselor. He may resent being "drawn in" to this type of relationship at this stage of development, or he may have experienced a family relationship where children were obligated to return helpful favors in kind. The counselor's suggestions here create a negative transference which interferes with counseling effectiveness.

Another illustration of counselor technique which arouses resistance is a situation where the counselor gets too far ahead of the client, and reveals it by reflecting an implied feeling or offering a premature interpretation.

C1: "My parents are always criticizing me and threaten to stop giving me money for school."

C: "You resent your parents for these things they say and threaten to do."

C1: "No, not exactly, I don't dislike my parents for it, I think they are right in lots of ways; I'm wasting my time here at college, really . . . I shouldn't be talking about them like this."

Here, reflection and interpretation, although very likely accurate, pinpointed feelings which could not be recognized and accepted at this stage.

Another cause of external resistance is related to lack of proper readiness. The client may misunderstand the counselor's role or he may not have faith in the value of verbalization. The client may not realize that counseling takes time; therefore, he may resent spending the time which he could devote to other less threatening activities. The client may be embarrassed to admit that he has a problem which he is unable to solve by himself.

The counseling relationship itself presents a paradoxical situation to the client. The accepting atmosphere encourages free expression of feeling, yet the client often is neither ready to express nor prepared to accept his own feelings. The relationship tends to force the premature examination of his own feelings, thus creating a source of considerable resistance. A common device clients use for manifesting this type of resistance is to talk about someone else's problems. An example is the case of a mother who worried about her fourteen-year-old daughter's behavior. The mother felt guilty, in addition to having intense feelings of failure. When the counselor encouraged the mother to talk about her own feelings, she felt compelled to continue discussing her daughter's difficulties.

English (140) cites further examples of situational anxiety as an obstacle to an optimal therapeutic relationship. He found that using lead techniques low in intensity early in the interview left the client dominated by his anxieties. English indicated that he found it necessary very often to reduce some of the anxiety temporarily by taking a greater lead and giving more support.

Mixed Sources of Resistance. In addition to the client's perception of threat in the interview or anxiety concerning his own impulses, other conditions exist as causes of resistance. Such conditions as fatigue, disease, mental deficiency, foreign language barriers, and psychoses cause resistance. The schizophrenic, from one point of view, exemplifies his resistance through withdrawal into hallucinations, muteness, or general negativism and projection. The neurotic may manifest resistance defensively through rigidity, concern over details, irritation, argumentation, or playing "stupid."

Knowing the sources of resistance, particularly the internal type, should be reassuring to the counselor who tends to feel personally responsible for the resistance he encounters. On the other hand, since counselor manner is the trigger for so much resistance, one must study continually one's techniques and professional setting in order to reduce external resistance cues.

In addition to the protective or defensive functions of resistance for the client, there are valuable clues which resistance provides for the counselor. A principal value of resistance for the counselor is that it gives an indication of general interview progress and the basis for diagnostic and prognostic formulations. Noting resistance symptoms is the first step toward taking appropriate measures to ignore, reduce, or utilize them.

A second function of resistance is the glimpse into the client's defensive structure which it affords. The presence of resistance tells the counselor that the client does not wish to explore these particular feelings further at this moment. Areas involving morals and deeply held beliefs are usually defended rigidly. Hence, resistance symptoms inform the counselor when he is treading temporarily in taboo territory. When these areas of threat become known, therefore, they offer the counselor much valuable interpretive information. Resistance is the counselor's cue that perhaps his usefulness has ended as a therapeutic agent and that counseling should be formally terminated. Rogers (392) comments that clients often change their feelings of warmth and acceptance toward the counselor to resentment when they no longer feel the need of the relationship. This manifestation, therefore, may be a healthy indication for terminating the relationship.

Resistance acts as a protective mechanism for the client through keeping acute anxiety under control, and through avoiding disintegration of his defensive structure prior to establishment of new constructive behaviors. In this sense, resistance often serves a useful decelerating function for the early stages in the counseling process.

Manifestations and Classifications of Resistance

Although it is futile to attempt to list the myriad forms of resistance, it may be helpful to indicate some of the subtle as well as glaring examples of resistance. We feel that a distinguishing mark of the experienced counselor is his ability to recognize resistance and deal with it appropriately.

Resistance may manifest itself in a number of negativistic ways. For example, the client criticizes the counselor, expresses dissatisfaction with the results of counseling, fails to hear or to understand the counselor, comes late or fails to keep appointments, remains silent, forgets the fee, engages in intellectual discussion using complex psychological terms, expresses negative attitudes toward psychology, desires to end counseling prematurely, is unproductive in associations or with unfamiliar material, introduces irrelevant topics, makes unreasonable demands on the counselor, is pessimistic about counseling, or expresses skepticism about interpretations.

The client's resistance may take less aggressive forms as, for example, agreeing unequivocally with everything the counselor says, refusing to get emotionally involved, being overly cooperative, prolonging a dependency transference, maintaining persistent facetiousness, forcing the process into a semantic wilderness of abstractions and philosophical notions, pressing the limits of the relationship by asking for overtime, perhaps, and expressing strong interest in the counselor's personal life. Shostrom's concept of manipulation (434) is useful in helping a client define ways he manipulates others, including counselors, in order to resist changing himself. Berne's (47) concept of client "games" is a further illustration of client avoidance of emotional realities.

Two scales for organizing signs of resistance, and one study on scaling signs in order of intensity, have been reported in the counseling literature. From a hypothetical base line of ideal free expression, Bugental (76) postulates five levels of symptom intensity varying from *lagging* through *inertia, tentative resistance, (true) resistance,* to *rejection.* The headings used by Bugental are illustrative of the behavior he is describing.

At the *lagging* level, the client shunts responsibility to the counselor, is sluggish in response, distractible, and concerned with intellectualization rather than emotional content. Understanding is difficult for the client, who must ask for frequent clarification from the counselor.

The *inertia* level contains more pronounced disinterest manifested by short answers, disregard of counselor leads, and fatigue.

3, *Tentative resistance* includes indications that the client is unwilling to continue the interview. Some indications are: arguing, excessive qualifying, showing physical tension, and inhibiting expression of hostility, anxiety, and guilt feelings. Bugental regards this type as temporary, but of crucial importance in the interview, since it is while he is manifesting tentative resistance that the client vacillates between more active resistance and cooperation.

4, *True resistance* is described as an intensification of the tentative type with more open and direct attack or withdrawal behaviors, such as making vague or diffuse answers to counselor questions, remaining silent, assuming a hostile attitude to counselor leads, questioning the competence of the counselor, or using vituperative language.

5. The most extreme form of resistance in Bugental's framework is described as *rejection.* The forms are generally extreme, such as terminating the interview by direct request, making hostile remarks about the counselor or institution, or refusing to communicate sufficiently.

Sherman developed a similar five-point scale on which interview units may be rated for amount of resistance.

1. Definitely resistive—rejects counselor point of view or manner of structuring interview in a somewhat belligerent manner, refuses to talk about a real problem, or attempts to close interview.
2. Somewhat resistive—rejects counselor point of view or suggestions but in a

polite manner, does not talk freely, or may show a tendency to contradict counselor.

3. Apathetic—takes no initiative, but accepts counselor suggestions usually in a noncommittal fashion.

4. Counselor and client work together fairly well—talk together rather freely, although there may be some friendly parrying to advance points.

5. Counselor and client work together on a real problem—talk very freely, feeling of mutual respect is marked (428, pp. 57–61).

Daulton (118), extending the work of Sherman, studied forty-eight interviews of twenty counselors. She found that the most frequent and intense forms of resistance were rejection of counselor suggestions and denial of counselor statements. Reticence in expressing feelings was rated as frequent but not intense. It seems that these findings would indict counselor technique as a potent source of resistance.

The counselor must evaluate the significance of resistance signs in light of the individual client's expressed feelings. Some clients exhibit many verbal symptoms of resistance because of a less inhibited personality and a strong verbal fluency; in contrast, others are excessively cautious or suffer acute distress before they actually verbalize their resistance. In other words, the signs and symptoms cited above do not have the same meaning for all clients. The "life style" of the client and apparent voluntary control over resistance determine the significance to be attached. As Thorne has stated, "Many clients, particularly in the higher intelligence groups, conduct their human relations as they would a game of chess. Every move is more or less deliberately calculated" (474, p. 238).

Research on resistance phenomena is meager. In addition to the studies cited above, Mowrer (340) produced a series of studies on the relationship between two parameters of the therapeutic process—psychological and physiological tension. Hypotheses that increases and decreases in resistance are associated with measurable tension changes have been studied. The principal techniques used to prove these hypotheses have been subjective ratings by subjects on "tension" and "happiness," palmar sweating, and discomfort-relief quotients derived from analysis of interview recordings. The tentative results indicate these approaches to be valuable means of studying observable changes in tension as a result of therapy.

Techniques for Handling Resistance

In one sense, all of the readiness and relationship techniques mentioned in preceding chapters are designed to build a relationship and, consequently, to reduce or to prevent resistance. How this is accomplished is an intensely practical problem for the counselor, because the resistance variable determines to a considerable extent whether a client will leave counseling or continue. We assume at this point that the main aim for the moment is to keep the client in counseling and to prevent his loss of confidence in the counselor.

Davis and Robinson (119) studied the resistance-handling techniques of experienced counselors and found great variation in frequency of use and type. Those techniques used most often by counselors, according to the study, were questions, personal reference, approval, reassurance, nonpersonal illustration, and humor. Davis and Robinson had little to offer on the evaluation of the differential effectiveness of these techniques and indicated that frequency was not necessarily a measure of effectiveness. These authors found frequent use of personal reference techniques, such as, "I think . . ." and "I would do this. . . ." However, the frequency finding should not be construed as endorsement of this dubious device.

In the same study, Davis and Robinson found that counselors were strongly tempted, when encountering resistance, to use techniques of sympathy, reassurance, approval, humor, research citations, personal experience, anecdotes, and rhetorical questions. The investigators concluded that these techniques alone were not sufficiently effective to close discussion units effectively. The only exception was approval techniques (a support device) which was associated with high rapport in discussion units on vocational problems. A discussion unit is a discrete interview topic in Robinson's (385) research designs.

The counselor's first step in dealing with resistance is to become aware of possible external causes in himself and the influence of the amount of lead in his techniques. The counselor then can take judicious steps according to the following suggestions.

1. The *noting-but-disregarding technique* consists largely of ignoring the symptoms, but it includes alertness to increased resistance. Mere presence of mild resistance does not mean the counselor should do something about it. The content of the discussion unit which arouses resistance is examined for possible adjustments in lead. The counselor realizes that this type of resistance is a normal artifact of counseling. Instead of blaming himself or the client, the counselor concentrates on understanding the unique defensive style or security operations of the client. Resistance indicates to the counselor that the psychic balance in the client is in favor of repression and anxiety control rather than expression.

2. *Minor adaptations technique* is applied by the counselor when he feels that he must do something actively to reduce the client's resistance if it has reached the second level in Bugental's and Sherman's systems (pronounced inertia, with an outward appearance of cooperation). Obviously, there are no rigid rules about the most efficacious thing to do. The main goal is to reduce the client's defensiveness and to maintain exploration of his problem. Generally, at this level, no attempt is made to change the topic.

One of the minor adaptations which counselors use is *lessening the emotional impact* of the discussion by moving to a more intellectually loaded aspect of the topic which has aroused the resistance. This tends to reduce the pressure felt by the client. Examples are referring to test results, using a nonpersonal illustration, or asking a question which can be answered in a matter-of-fact casual way. Rhetorical questions can be especially useful when anticipating resistance during the interpretation of personality-appraisal results.

A second minor adaptation technique is a *change of pace* effected by lessening the length of counselor lead, pausing, or shifting posture to a more relaxed state.

A third minor adaptation technique counselors can rely upon is the *judicious use of humor,* which often eases the tension felt by the client. This must be a natural and spontaneous act, however, since a strained or awkward use of humor, or use with an implication which makes the client appear ridiculous, will "backfire" on the counselor in the form of increased resistance.

Supportive and accepting techniques, as described in the preceding chapter, are often the keys to reduction of resistance, particularly when the client can accept the counselor.

3. The *temporary diversion technique* involves re-direction of interview content to less threatening areas when it appears that the client cannot protect himself adequately by his own defenses. The strategy is to return to the painful subject at a later time. This technique is used with resistance which is hindering, but not yet obstructing interview progress.

The principal element of diversion technique is changing the subject gently. Secondly, the counselor limits his own ego involvement in the process by assuming a more detached and disinterested attitude. This device has the effect of taking pressure off the client by reducing the speed and intensity of the interview. Korner (271) speaks of a "disengagement" technique wherein the counselor examines his own ego involvement in the interview and personal threat in the presence of resistance. In applying this technique, the counselor changes the tone of the feeling of the interview rather than the topic; hence, it is difficult to cite illustrations. The counselor assumes a more reserved and cautious bearing, limits interpretation, or reduces the speed and intensity of the interview.

A third diversion technique is the citation of related research findings, illustrations, a suggested test, or bibliotherapeutic reading matter. These devices often provide the needed change of pace without straying too far from the subject.

4. *Direct manipulation techniques* are used when the client appears to be aware of his feelings of resistance. Their use assumes a fairly effective working relationship and a well-structured interview. Because these conditions take time to build, direct manipulation techniques are more useful in later interviews. The counselor says, for example, "You have been spending a great deal of time talking about things you wanted to talk about; now let's talk about those things you don't want to talk about."

Interpretation of the resistance, a principal direct technique, involves an explanation of what the client is doing to resist. This technique helps the client develop a tolerance and acceptance of his own resistance, as well as an intellectual understanding of its uses and the difficulties caused when resistance gets out of hand. The counselor expresses his own acceptance of the resistance along with the interpretation. This acceptance helps to decrease the likelihood that the client will take offense at the interpretation. Examples are:

C1: I just can't talk about it.

C: You feel that sex is a topic to be avoided. Perhaps you can see that this tendency is serving some useful purpose which we cannot yet understand.

C1: Yes, that makes me feel a little better about it.

An example of interpretation of a transference-type problem follows:

C: (replying after the client has made a series of skeptical comments about the counselor after a preliminary exploration of family relationships) Do you see that your feelings toward this relationship of ours are possibly related to your feelings about your father? You felt you couldn't trust him and now you unconsciously see your father in me.

C1: I never looked at it quite that way before. I'll have to think about that.

Reflection of the feelings of resistance often is effective as a direct technique when the client appears to have an intense feeling, such as guilt, about resisting. It is an effective technique in the earlier interviews where interpretation might be premature.

Referral techniques are needed occasionally when intensive resistance is encountered. The counselor should assess his own therepeutic competence carefully before penetrating the defenses of a highly resistant client. Sometimes, if he shifts the client to another counselor he can remove the source of external resistance which has been inhibiting therapeutic progress.

Threats in veiled form, though a last resort, are useful occasionally in a high-risk attempt to motivate a resistive client to change his behavior. This situation would be apparent where the counselor's role included, in addition, that of dean, personnel manager, or other authoritarian position. For example, a student client having academic difficulties has been resisting discussion of his problem. The counselor may say, "If you don't want to work this out, I suggest we stop getting together."

5. *Direct confrontation* or direct questioning in depth around the resistance theme may be required. For example: "What is your objection to . . . ," or "You are now playing the protection game. What is it you are protecting?" A more extreme position a therapist may take is, "So you don't want to play the therapy game? It makes you happy to frustrate me, and so you win the battle with me and lose the war with yourself?"

Since one of the counselor's key professional problems is helping clients to overcome resistance, this section was devoted to a discussion of the nature of resistance, illustrating and classifying its manifestations, and suggesting appropriate methods of handling the resistance. Resistance was regarded as a normal part of the counseling process.

Summary

Although transference, countertransference, and resistance are ever-present phenomena in the counseling process, the counselor must deal judiciously with these conditions to keep the process moving toward satisfactory termination. Transference feelings, the projections of stereotypes from the past to a counselor, have an ambiguous status in counseling. Transference feelings can be useful psychological data. They also can hinder counseling progress. Countertransference, the transference feelings of the counselor, is a tendency which must be recognized and resolved by a counselor before counseling can progress satisfactorily. Resistance is the natural blocking of interview progress and must be resolved by a number of counseling techniques—from ignoring the resistance to direct interpretation. Resistance signs serve as useful cues concerning sensitive personality areas, general interview progress, and the nature of the client's defensive structure.

Interpretation and Body Awareness Strategies

The purpose of this chapter is to present strategies for developing understanding through interpreting and body awareness methods. Interpretive illustrations for the different levels in the Actualizing Counseling and Therapy model are presented.

Nature of Interpretation

It is difficult to formulate a neat set of principles about interpretation of personality data because the style and content are determined by the assumptions one makes about behavior change and personality function. Therefore, several illustrative styles are presented early in this chapter with some generally applicable principles and cautions cited later. Levy (285), in his extensive treatment of the general questions on interpretation, emphasizes that the interpretive process involves translation of observational data in the framework of a theory which then is used to make further propositions about the observed behavior consistent with the theory.

The kinds of data which may be interpreted to a client are usually classified by psychologists into two broad categories. Some data are derived from test results presented and explained to clients in terms of statistical expectancies or, as in the case of projective techniques, as hypotheses for further consideration. Interpretation of such objective data will be discussed in Chapter 10.

The data in the second category are derived from intrapersonal data revealed during the counseling process. Interpretations of these data have the purposes of making the client more aware of relationships among his personal experiences and of transforming dysfunctional feelings and behaviors into actualizing behaviors.

Definitions of Interpretation

Interpretation has been defined as an attempt by the counselor to impart meaning to the client. Interpretation means presenting the client with a *hypothesis* about *relationships* or *meanings* among his behaviors. Interpretation from this viewpoint gives the client more freedom in the resolution of his problems. Interpretation varies with one's theoretical viewpoint because, in part, it is a process of *imposing meaning* on events. It is not a quest for some mythical true meaning of an event. Interpretation merely brings a fresh look at the behavior in the forms of different language, new frame of reference, or revised theoretical outlook. The ultimate criterion of interpretive effectiveness is whether it facilitates behavior change in the direction desired by the client.

Interpretation, like so many psychotherapeutic terms, is construed differently by therapists. A classical psychoanalyst, for example, would label many of the techniques described in the previous chapter as interpretation. Remarks intended to confront the client with the nature of his resistance would be considered interpretation by some therapists as well.

Interpretation techniques are used by psychotherapists of most theory views. Client-centered therapists generally do not favor techniques defined above and appear to restrict their methods primarily to clarification and reflection of feelings. The client-centered view holds that interpretation fosters resistance and puts too much therapeutic responsibility on the counselor. We believe, however, that most reflections of feelings are really mild or conservative interpretations. Whenever the counselor reflects feeling, he must always *select* from the material which the client has presented to him. These feelings are emotionally toned ideas which the counselor judges to be the most significant of all that have been expressed. Therefore, reflection of feeling is interpretive in the sense that the counselor's judgment of significance is involved. The counselor, through additional efforts to clarify feeling, generally adds more meaning than the client did originally. On this issue, a client-centered counselor would claim that he is not interpreting because he tries to remain completely within the client's meaning framework. The evidence and opinions are contradictory. While client-centered groups emphasize the liabilities of overintellectualizing, studies such as Dittman (124) report improvement with intellectual interpretive techniques.

It is posited, therefore, that there is a continuum of differences between reflection of feeling and interpretation, with much blending of the two. It seems, furthermore, that the alternatives are not either interpretation or reflection, but rather *what kind* and *degree* of interpretive-reflective response the therapist chooses to use. This is not a new concept since this view of the interpretive continuum has been described earlier by Bordin (60) and Collier (105).

A Continuum of Interpretive Methods

Reflection. In the chapter on relationship techniques, great emphasis was placed upon reflection of feeling. The key idea underlying reflection of feeling is that the therapist goes no further than the client has already *explicitly* gone in his verbal productions, although the counselor is selective in what he reflects.

Clarification. A technique which goes beyond this just slightly is called "clarification," which means clarifying to the client what is *implicit* in what he has just said. Clarification, therefore, reflects relationships or meanings for the client which are *suggested* or *implied* in the feelings or ideas brought out by the client's actual responses. Clarification deals with material which, in the judgment of the counselor, is just beyond the awareness of the client. Clarification requires knowledge of psychodynamics and mechanisms of which the client is usually not aware. The counselor adds strong cognitive elements to his reflection of feelings. It gives the client a feeling of forward movement in that it verbalizes material which the client may have felt only vaguely. It is analogous to the pacing of a young racehorse by a more mature one. The counselor goes far enough beyond the client's conscious verbalizations to stimulate further thinking, but not so far that he loses him.

Confrontation. A third point on the interpretive continuum is a technique called "confrontation." Here the counselor brings to the attention of the client ideas and feelings which are *implicit* but of which the client is unaware or which he refuses to acknowledge. In using this technique, the therapist confronts the client with his own words, but relates past to present, pointing out similarities, differences, and discrepancies of which the client is unaware at that moment.

Depth Interpretation. Finally, in depth interpretation, the therapist introduces new concepts, relationships, and associations which are rooted in the client's experience, but which are considerably beyond his awareness.
Some examples of the above levels of interpretation follow:

C1: Last night I was really bothered by a wet dream I had which involved a little seven-year-old girl who looked partly like my baby sister and partly like my little daughter. .

1. Reflection:
"It was really disturbing to have such a dream."

2. Clarification:

"It bothered you to have an experience which suggested erotic impulses toward your daughter or sister."

3. Confrontation:

"You apparently have similar erotic impulses toward your daughter as you reported you had toward your little sister."

4. Interpretation:

"You are becoming more free to admit your past and present impulses toward those whom you love, even though it is disturbing to express feelings that are so strictly forbidden in our society."

Clarification Methods

Associative Type. The counselor presents a hypothesis which draws together or makes associations between the client's explicit or implicit thoughts or feelings. Four major forms of association can be distinguished:

1. *Similarity.* The counselor may draw together two ideas with similar content as follows: "What you are saying now about your wife appears to be very closely related to the feelings which you expressed about your mother a few weeks ago. Would you say that is a fair statement?"

2. *Contrast.* The counselor may associate two dissimilar ideas. An example of this form would be: "I gather, from what you said, your feelings about your father are almost the opposite of those you have about your mother."

3. *Contiguity.* The counselor may associate ideas which are close in space and time. For example, "You seem to get these feelings of tension whenever you come into the biology laboratory?"

4. *Distance.* The counselor may associate ideas or feelings which are far apart in space and time. For instance: "You seem to have many of the feelings toward this person that you had toward your mother several years ago under similar circumstances."

The counselor may relate feelings or ideas to each other which have been evident in prior sessions and which seem to have some relevance to the client's present expressions. The counselor may thus be said to reduce the distance in time and space between the client's feelings and thoughts in order to make them more comprehensible, to stimulate finer differentiations, or to promote integration of feelings and ideas.

Suggestive Type. In this type, the counselor suggests to the client certain ideas and feelings which are related to material already presented. Suggestive clarification verbalizes this connection. An example is, "You seem to understand that your feelings of hostility might be at the root of your social difficulties."

Suggestive clarification differs from general interpretation in that nothing new is brought out in the interview except that which is only dimly in awareness or, by remote implication, suggested by the client's comments.

In contrast, by the general interpretation method, hypotheses or meanings are imparted to the client which may or may not be thought by the counselor to be suggested by the client.

Curran (115) uses the term "forking response" to describe a situation where it is important, in the counselor's opinion, to bridge superficial problems in order to reach deeper concerns. The counselor accepts the client's feeling that perhaps the problem goes beyond the one he has just stated, and he broadens his reflective response to include references to the deeper problem. For example, a client is describing at length his scholastic difficulties and has included a few references to girl problems implying a lack of information on sex. The counselor responds, "School work has been difficult for you and it seems to have been complicated by problems with girls. I gather that sex is part of the difficulty. You seem to feel that all of these things are tied together." This response opens the way for the client to talk about his more emotionally involved concerns and is an open invitation to move away from the topic of scholastic difficulties to the underlying problems.

Suggestive clarifications can be classified into five general categories:

1. Pacing Clarification. Here the counselor words his statements in a manner which will pace the client. In other words, the counselor moves out just a little ahead of the client's thinking, but in the direction which he believes the client is going. An example follows:

Cl: It's difficult to talk about these things.

C: They are painful to you. (Implying that growth is often painful.)

Cl: You might put it that way—and yet I need to face them.

C: It's painful, and you feel it necessary to discuss it; yet would you say it is a relief too? After you talk about them you feel better? (Introduces a clinical principle.)

Cl: Yeah. Once I get it out it doesn't seem so strong any more.

C: It's like an internal cleansing process.

2. Selective Clarification. Using this form, the counselor selectively emphasizes feelings or ideas expressed by the client which the counselor judges to be of therapeutic significance even though these feelings or ideas have not yet been given this weight by the client. An example follows:

Cl: I just feel so all alone. I have no one. I guess I'm just weak. You don't like me either, do you?

C: You don't think much of yourself? (Relates to self-concepts.)

Cl: No I don't. Oh, I guess I'm not that bad—there are some things about me which I like.

C: Some good, some bad, and some between. (Reflects ambivalent self-regard.)

It may be noted here that material relative to the client's self-concept is suggested to him directly.

Should the counselor select the most important feeling to comment on, or should he reflect all those that have been stated? Though it may be desirable to give summary reflections in later interviews, it is our opinion that responses should be short in the first interviews because of the client's need to get release.

3. *Labeling Clarification.* Here the counselor utilizes some of the common psychological labels which may assist the client in understanding his situation more concisely.

C1: I just can't seem to get to the things which really bother me. I keep talking about all kinds of irrelevant things.

C: Let's learn a new word today. Would you say that you are kind of "resisting" the process?

C1: Yes, that's it.

One danger of this method is that the discussion may become too abstract and may sound like the table of contents from a textbook.

4. *Clarification of Unhealthy or Untenable Attitudes.* Many adjustment problems of normal people relate to unhealthy or untenable attitudes which are acquired in experience. Sometimes this takes the form of "canned thinking," where people act or believe certain assumptions about human behavior which they have learned from people without psychological sophistication. Bugental suggests other ways in which clients have crystallized their attitudes in unhealthy neurotic thinking. Many of these perceptions have come from general cultural attitudes and not from the personal experience of the client. He gives the following as examples:

Something is wrong with a person who feels both love and hate toward the opposite sex; you should be devoted to your spouse, and if anyone else interests you, it shows you are fickle or over-sexed. It is childish to want something you can't have. If you've once given up a habit, you should never feel any desire to practice it again. If one doesn't try to be the best in whatever he does, he's giving up, a quitter. The easy way is, *ipso facto,* the wrong way. If you have to *learn* how to get along better with people, it isn't natural. Normal people (or, other people) know why they do anything and want to do whatever they do. If I were only in the right field, I would want to work hard and wouldn't have to force myself (74, p. 5).

The counselor should be sensitive to ideas, beliefs, or attitudes such as those given in the examples and suggest their fallaciousness through clarification. The following is an example:

C1: I hate my father. And there's no reason for it. It makes me feel awful because it's a sin to hate your father—especially if there's no reason for it.

C: You feel that a person just shouldn't hate his parents, especially if there is no reason for it?

Cl: Yes, don't you think so?

C: Many people do have such feelings; we call them ambivalent feelings—feeling both ways about the same person. I gather, however, that this is objectionable to you.

5. Humorous Clarification. This type employs the use of humor by the counselor to help the client to regard his situation more light-heartedly. Crying and laughing seem to be fraternal twins. Adlai Stevenson's comment upon losing an election in 1952 is an illustration: "It hurts too much to laugh and I'm too old to cry." Psychotherapy is not a laughing matter, but there are times when the introduction of humor may facilitate the growth process. Humor seems to help the client gain perspective and makes bearable the anxiety which often destroys decision-making powers.

Cl: I hate this place, and everybody in it; including you. You make me so damn mad just sitting there.

C: Boy, you're really giving me both barrels today, eh?

Cl: Yes, damn it; real shotgun barrels, too.

C: I guess this is the season for counselors.

Humor in this instance implies acceptance of the client's feelings and may serve to reduce guilt feelings. The counselor can also use it to reduce or put in perspective a client's strong feelings. It can also be a kind of "capping off" effect.

It should be mentioned that the use of humor in therapy, although many times effective, should be done with caution. It certainly should not be used to satisfy the counselor's basic needs, nor should it be used with anxious, guilt-ridden clients. Generally, humor should not be used until the relationship is well established.

General Guidelines for Interpretation

Although there are no universally valid rules for interpretation, there are some guidelines which, if individualized and applied judiciously by the counselor, can help the client toward awareness.

What to Interpret. The content of interpretation is determined by the particular stage in the counseling process. In the early interviews it may be necessary for the counselor to interpret attitudes toward counseling and the meaning of resisting efforts. He keeps interpretations very general and tentative at first, the main purposes being to explain the process to the client and to open up new areas for consideration.

Later, interpretations take the form of explanations of how defenses function to keep us from becoming aware. Here, in the middle of the process, the counselor makes interpretations more specific in terms of his basic theory. Toward the end of counseling, he makes the interpretations more general and vague to encourage the client to do his own interpreting. He also has the goal of closing issues, rather than stirring up new problems. So, interpretations become fewer and more general toward the end of the process.

When to Interpret. Perhaps the most important consideration in the use of interpretation is that of timing. In general, interpretations are made very cautiously and, in the counselor's judgment, not until the client is ready to accept them. Freud has stated many times that an interpretation should be given only when the client is at the point where he can almost formulate it himself.

It is wise for the counselor to interpret, or to elicit interpretations from the client, after he has gained some awareness of the subject area of the proposed interpretation. In other words, interpretations should rarely be offered "blindly." There are occasions when clients may be accelerated by a thoughtful "shot in the dark," but this should be regarded as a high-risk technique.

As a general rule, reflection of feeling dominates the early phase of counseling, followed by the tentative formulations of clarifications. In the later stages, when awareness must be expanded and insights tested, general interpretation in terms of a specific theory, as illustrated later in this chapter, is appropriate. Figure 15 illustrates the time relationships of technique to the counseling process.

Interpretation according to a specific theory is usually reserved for later interviews, when the relationship is well established. The counselor's interpretations must be based upon and verified by the information obtained in earlier interviews. This avoids making the client feel that he is being treated as a stereotype rather than as an individual. He may feel, rightly, that the counselor is way off base when he gives him explanations with little supportive evidence.

The counselor, generally, should not offer interpretations unless he has an extensive picture of his client's personality, and a well-thought-out rationale for his interpretations.

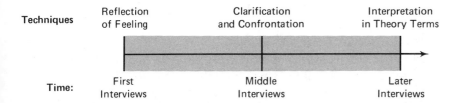

Figure 15. Process Timing of Interpretations

It should be made explicit that many times an interpretation may be appropriate because the client's fear is operating to keep a threatening emotional linkage out of awareness. For the counselor to interpret without assessing the client's readiness and ability to cope with the interpretation is to risk breaking a dam that has served the psychic economy and may flood the client with truly destructive anxiety.

Often the counselor will make interpretations early in the interview so there will be sufficient time for him to work through the client's reactions. This is especially true when potentially threatening interpretations have to be made. When such interpretations are made late in the interview, the client may become panicky before the next counseling session or may build up resistances to facing this issue in later sessions.

There is an occasion when interpretations are given more appropriately toward the end of the interview. Then it is necessary to prepare the client carefully for the interpretation and to collect current documentation to support the interpretation. There are also occasions when the counselor should plant interpretations in the form of suggestions at the end of the interview to stimulate the client's thinking between sessions.

When the counselor offers an interpretation, however, the elaboration should come from the client. This takes time. A useful technique, in this connection, is to let the client describe his problem and then encourage him to get off and look at it. For example, the client has just given a long description of a family problem. The counselor responds, "Now that you have described your feelings about your parents, what do you think this means? How does it seem to you?"

Another method is role-playing. The client is asked to be the counselor while the counselor takes the client's role.

General Methods of Interpretation

Tentative Approach. Counselors frequently are critical of their more active colleagues because they feel that their interpretations are given dogmatically and without finesse. This is a gross misconception, because even the highly direct cognitive counselor generally suggests interpretations rather than stating them harshly. He does not say, "This is the way it is"; but rather, "This appears to be this," or "This seems to be this way with you." This method is similar to Robinson's "tentative analysis" technique (385) wherein the counselor suggests a fresh approach to the problem.

Free Association. Especially in the early stages of interpretations, it is important for the counselor to stay *with* the client and not to get too far ahead. The counselor should not give the impression he is a detective trying stealthily to observe, diagnose, and influence the client. One of his main goals is to help the client become aware and to do his own interpreting. This is done through a process of loosening his thinking so that new relationships become more apparent to him. Loosening is facilitated by encouraging more free association. For example, the counselor reminds the client to "say whatever comes into your mind"; "Let yourself go"; "Don't try to be consistent and logical"; "Just give me parts of ideas"; "Say it, even if it seems vague or unimportant to you."

Free association is a fundamental technique of psychoanalysis which was introduced by Freud. As Sullivan suggests, however, "trying to tell patients what is meant by free association, and trying to get them to do it, can be quite a problem" (463, p. 83). He recommends that the best way to handle this problem is for the counselor to demonstrate it to the client by having him associate to a particular question which may arise in the interview, for which he has no answer. For the counselor to ask him at that time to talk at random about the question often gives a convincing demonstration of the effectiveness of this technique. An example might be:

C: You seem to be stuck on this question of the importance of your mother's influence on you. Suppose you try stating the word "Mother" and then follow it with as many words as come to your mind in rapid-fire order. Get it?

C1: I think so . . . Mother—nice—soft—does things—silly—mad—stupid—damn her.

C: You really resent her doing so many things for you, and yet you like it too?

This fragmentation and association of ideas often lead to relationships which the client might never have discovered. When the free association leads to significant areas, the counselor may then accelerate the re-integration process again by using short-lead interpretations, such as questions. An example would be, "This discussion reminds you, then, of how your past ways of looking at your parents and your present feelings are similar?" One of the goals of the counselor here is to move among the different levels of client thinking, pointing out parallels and contrasts.

A cardinal goal of all counselors is assisting clients toward *self-interpretation*. The client must get the insight, not the counselor. Karpman (253) developed a self-interpretation method which he has labeled "objective psychotherapy." Here the client gives the counselor the preliminary case data from which the counselor formulates questions. The client takes the questions home to write out answers and weave in materials from his reading. When the client returns, he and the counselor discuss the written materials and do further interpretation. From this discussion, an additional set of questions is formulated. At certain places in the process the psychotherapist gives the client interpretive memoranda which the client comments upon in writing.

Because so much written material is involved, the Karpman technique appears to require more than average intelligence, cooperation, and persistence from the client. It is offered here as an additional device to encourage client participation in the interpretation process. The ultimate usefulness of this device, however, must depend upon the adequacy of interpretations made both by the client and counselor, and upon an evaluation of whether this intellectualized approach reinforces defensive intellectualization—a form of avoiding confrontation of feelings.

Phrasing Interpretations. Phrasing is a significant element of interpretation. It is suggested that counselors use "soft" words which imply tentativeness rather than certainty, such as "perhaps; will you; it's possible; do you suppose; I wonder if; would you buy this; does this seem to fit." These carefully chosen words tend to minimize resistance.

Thorne (474, p. 301) suggests some acceptable phrasing for interpretations and suggestions:

"Would you buy this idea. . . ."
"Is this a fair statement. . . ."
"What would you think of. . . ."
"For what it's worth. . . ."
"You feel this is the only solution. . . ."
"Ben Franklin had a saying. . . ."

The best interpretations are phrased in the client's own terms and constructions. The counselor does not have to use the exact words of the client, but he should maintain the same general style and concept level.

Thorne (474, p. 302) suggests some *unacceptable* phrases which are often cited in criticisms of interpretation:

"I think you should. . . ."
"The only thing for you to do is. . . ."
"If I were you I would. . . ."
"I'm going to tell you what to do. . . ."
"There's only one right way to do it. . . ."
"I want you to do this. . . ."
"There is a better way to do it. . . ."
"You must try to do this. . . ."
"If you don't do this you may be sorry. . . ."

Counselor Insecurity and Hostility. Interpretations should not be made on the basis of projected personal experience of the counselor. Neither should the counselor reason that "this worked in another case; so it should apply here." If the counselor feels insecure about an interpretation, he would do well to avoid it.

Hostility from clients is encountered frequently and should not disturb the counselor or tempt him into an argument with the client. Interpretive techniques occasionally provoke client hostility, and the fact that this feeling is aroused and that the interpretation is not accepted gives the counselor valuable data. Perhaps it would be better if the interpretation were dropped and raised again at a more opportune time.

Repetition.   Repetition is an important interpretive principle. Since a useful and valid interpretation may be resisted, it may be necessary for the counselor to repeat the interpretation at appropriate times, in different forms, and with additional supporting evidence. The client often achieves understanding after this concerted effort which he might not after one early interpretation.

Although repetition is an important learning principle, it should be mentioned that the counselor would do well to reexamine his interpretive hypothesis and try to understand the evidence pro and con on it, rather than blindly pushing it again and again on his client. One of the best checks in therapeutic work is to test whether the therapist's hypothesized model of the client's dynamics can explain the *resistance* to the interpretation as well as the interpretation itself.

Interpretive Questions.   Interpretations are hunches or hypotheses based upon client observation more than they are declarative statements of fact. The question, therefore, is a common format for a confrontative type of interpretation. These questions vary from general leads such as, "Would you care to discuss this idea a little further?" through moderately structured questions such as, "How do you mean that?" "What does this mean?" "Wouldn't you like to talk about it?" "How did that make you feel?" to highly structured interpretive questions such as, "Do you think, then, that perhaps you distrust men because your father did not treat you well?"

In a special approach to questioning, Boileau (58) suggests that often the client is endeavoring through some behavior to satisfy a certain basic need. His mode of expression or way of satisfying this need may be inappropriate. The problem, therefore, is not the need, but is more the manner of expression. He recommends that the counselor simply ask the client, "What's wrong with that?" This starts the client exploring his behavior to determine the root need. The client typically reacts with all of the social moralizing which prohibits such behavior. The implication of the question, however, is that he can go on with this type of "acting out" if he so desires. However, continued questioning of this type usually leads him to an evaluation wherein he determines whether or not this behavior is to his greatest interest and advantage. The main limitation of this technique is the danger of incurring client resistance. The following example illustrates Boileau's method:

C1: I just have to buy new clothes all the time.

C: What's wrong with that?

C1: Well, you just can't spend all your money that way.

C: Why not?

C1: You wouldn't have any money left.

C: So——

C1: You'd starve!

C: Oh?

C1: I know, there are other needs that we have to satisfy, besides being pretty.

Another approach to the utilization of questions in psychotherapy is the idea that therapy is not so much a process of giving quick and easy answers as it is a process of assisting the client to ask himself appropriate questions. An example of a basic question that needs to be faced squarely by any client is: "Shouldn't you be concerned about yourself too?" As several writers, notably Rogers (390) and Snygg and Combs (451), have suggested, the preservation and enhancement of the self is a most important need. Fromm (171) suggests the importance of recognizing the significance of self-love and respect. As indicated in Chapter 7, each client, from our experience, must cope with this basic problem of self-love. By the use of appropriate questions, the counselor can assist the client to ask himself some of the basic questions which lead to answers needed for self-acceptance and a healthy personality.

Limitations of Interpretation

Although much has been written about the value of interpretation for promoting awareness, there have been strong arguments and some data advanced against the overuse of the technique. The principal limitations cited are that interpretation is threatening; hence, resistance is aroused which blocks spontaneous new perceptions and understandings. Interpretation may have the effect of reducing client self-explorations. Bergman (46), for example, in studying recorded interviews, found that when counselors interpreted at the client's request for evaluation, there was a significant drop in further self-exploratory responses.

Interpretation technique may tend to overintellectualize the client's problems prematurely, thus encouraging the use of interpretation as a type of defense mechanism. This happens because the client is searching for all means possible to keep his feelings from awareness. He isn't ready to invest responsibility for control of feelings in the counselor.

Utilizing Interpretation to Facilitate Emotional Involvement

On the other side of the above argument, it should be emphasized that there is a tendency on the part of many counselors to think that interpretation is simply intellectual. This is not so, because many counselors and therapists are most effective in utilizing interpretation to get *emotional involvement*. The following response is an example:

C: "You've told me about your family as though you were a disinterested observer; what do you feel when you are with them?"

Another example:

C: "You've several times lost the train of thought as you got around to the topic of your mother's death; I wonder if you're hesitant to show how deeply it still affects you?"

Illustrative Styles of Interpretation

Interpretation Methods in the Actualizing Model

The methods to be described in this section usually come later in the process when the relationship is well established and the counselor has enough data. The goal of all interpretive actions in this section is to encourage transformation of manipulative and character styles into actualizing behavior styles—the most functional in the hierarchy of behaviors. The following discussion is based on the Actualizing Counseling and Therapy model described in Chapters 3 and 4.

Interpreting Manipulative Styles. As people grow they need to feel loved; but life experiences threaten this feeling as people are manipulated by parents and significant others. Through these experiences, they learn to avoid the pain and to manipulate for survival. Manipulations are basically patterns of survival by which people adapt to their environment without the necessity of feeling. Figure 16 shows some manipulative patterns of the basic polarities with eight illustrative manipulative styles.

Manipulation Analysis. Description of primary manipulation is the first step in manipulation analysis. As the client talks, the therapist begins to see a pattern emerging in which the individual is utilizing one or two of the basic manipulative patterns shown in Figure 16. For example, the client may continuously resort to the patterns of helplessness and stupidity, or he may utilize power plays and blackmailing techniques. Once the pattern becomes clear, the counselor *describes* to the client what seems to be his primary manipulative game or style. Manipulations are then analyzed from the standpoint of "gains" or payoffs. The active manipulations are seen to have possible *coercive* controlling values, and the passive manipulations to have possible *seductive* values. Gains are analyzed from a short-range, as well as from a long-range, viewpoint. The client is asked to state what he sees as the short-range gains received from the particular manipulation. For example, manipulations are most often used for control of others, exploiting others, avoiding situations, structuring time, and seducing others to work for one. From the long-range point of view, however, they can be shown to be self-defeating, because they alienate

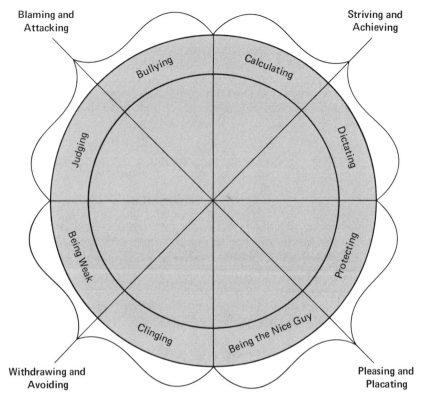

Figure 16. The Manipulative Processes. From E. L. Shostrom, L. Knapp, and R. Knapp, *Actualizing Therapy* (432, p. 139).

the individual from others and keep him immature and dependent, rather than mature and self-supporting.

Restoring inner balance is the second concern in manipulation analysis. The principle of inner balance is illustrated by the rhythmic loops seen in Chapter 3 which showed movement between the polarities of anger-love and strength-weakness. At any given time, a client might be at any one point on either of these polarities. If, for example, a client is mildly angry, the therapist will facilitate his expression in one of two ways: by encouraging *exaggeration* of the expression of anger, or by encouraging *reversal*—the expression of the opposite polar dimension. In the latter case, he is likely to encounter some resistance from the client, since this is not where the client is at this moment. Thus, it may be more appropriate for the therapist to encourage the intensification of the feeling of anger. The therapist's purpose in asking the client to exaggerate the manipulative tendency is to allow him to experience its apparent foolishness when expressed to such an extreme. The therapist may ask the client to express the opposite pole of the manipulative pattern he is demonstrating. For example, a person who is playing weak may be asked to try to play a dictator. The reason for this technique is the fundamental hypothesis that the exaggerated expression of any manipulative pattern is indicative of the underdevelopment of the opposite pattern. For example, playing weak by expressing hurt is usually indicative of covering up a strong need to express the vindictiveness that a dictator-type might feel. Expression of dependency is covering a deeper need to control others. Playing the role of a nice guy, a person may attempt to make others feel guilty for contesting him. He is often covering a need to express his hostility. The protecting person, in his need to feel responsibility for others, is often covering his need to be omnipotent. The therapist, in using this method, however, must constantly be aware of the principle of resistance and not *demand* the expression of any feeling but rather *encourage* feeling expression.

Integration, the final step in manipulation analysis, involves merging both active and passive dimensions into a unified working whole. In order to do this, the therapist continues to encourage the client to express all of his active and passive potentials, so that he might appreciate that actualizing involves the integration of all his polar styles into a unified whole. The actualizing person is like an ice skater who skates freely from one potential to another, creatively employing each in his movement through life.

In this connection, the client must realize that *self-defeating* manipulative behavior may be naturally transformed into more self-fulfilling actualizing behavior. Dictating can be transformed into leading, playing weak can be transformed into empathizing, and so on, as illustrated in Figure 17.

Character Style Interpretation. Character styles have their roots in early manipulations by parents and significant others. Character styles are basic ways of responding to the world. The relationship between manipulative and character styles is as follows:

1. Pleasing and placating often are transformed into an *oral character*. The oral person needs *love*, but he feels abandoned by parents or significant others. He feels dependent and fears isolation.

2. Blaming and attacking often turn into a *masochistic character*, who has been hurt by parents or others. He feels burdened by their demands, but fears expressing anger because he fears losing others.

3. Striving and achieving having failed, a *rigid character* develops. He needs to *love others*. His strength and independence have tended to become a substitute for his real need to love someone.

4. Since withdrawing and avoiding have not worked, the *schizoid character* contracts further and seeks solace in his illusion that his being is his *mind*. He avoids relationships; but he still has needs to *exist*.

As the therapist and client discuss the client's present and past relationships, manipulative and character styles are uncovered. The client

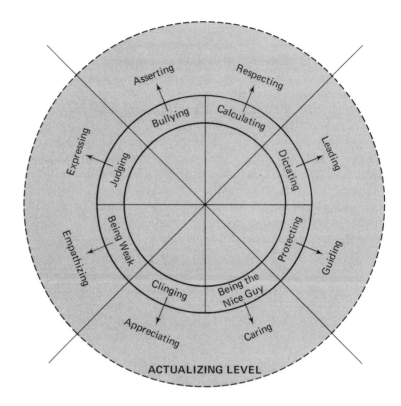

Figure 17. Manipulating Styles to Actualizing Styles. From E. L. Shostrom, L. Knapp, and R. Knapp, *Actualizing Therapy* (432, p. 142).

becomes aware of his primary manipulative patterns and learns to understand the muscular character styles that reinforce his manipulative patterns. Character problems tend to be expressed in taut musculature. His body expresses the feelings of distrust and hostility in three ways, according to Kirsh (262): 1) *Holding*—tight, spastic muscles bind feelings inside the body; 2) *Flaccidity*—flaccid, unusually flexible muscles also bind feelings; and 3) *Hyperactivity*—muscles become hyperactive so there is an inability to maintain feelings.

Each of the three basic personality levels has unique ways of dealing with feelings. At the level of manipulation, feelings are *avoided;* whereas they become *defensive* or *hostile* at the character level. Finally, at the core, these feelings merge into pain and hurt. When clients experience these feelings, they become aware of muscle tightness.

The Character Dialogue. This strategy has a heavy confrontational quality designed to elicit and deal with strong feelings and bodily action. Most clients will respond to all four basic character styles, but they will respond in particular to the ones that seem most characteristic of those they experienced with their parents. Once the therapist hears that certain parental admonitions obtain responses, he tends to focus on them.

The therapist, using the technique of *character dialogue*, "plays" the role of parents and significant others, expressing the negativity, abandonment, and rejection that they used to manipulate the client earlier in life. This process releases angry feeling, *character feelings* which in earlier years the client probably handled with tantrums. Part of the current procedure is to encourage body involvement in the form of kicking, pounding, or screaming "No!" repeatedly as refutation of parental patterns of behavior. Illustrations of character interpretations may be obtained in *Actualizing Therapy* (432).

Body Awareness Techniques

Introduction to Body and Feelings. One of the ways for people to get in touch with their bodies is to help them become aware of expressions that express body messages. The following phrases illustrate this awareness of the body: "You *rub* me the wrong way." "I feel *touched* by that." "You get under my *skin*." "Get off my *back*." "I can't *stomach* this." "You give me a pain in the *neck*." "I can't *stand* that." "I don't have the *guts* to do it." "You *depress* me." Everyone has heard or used these expressions many times, and yet most people are not usually aware of the significance and accuracy of the body as a vehicle of expression.

A here-and-now approach to living suggests continuous attention to the body and what it is expressing at every moment. This assumes that one's body can be trusted as a reliable indicator of one's feelings. The recent body therapies—in particular, the Reichian and Bioenergetic—make this important assumption. Alexander Lowen says:

A person experiences the reality of the world only through his body. The external environment impresses him because it impinges upon his body and affects his senses. . . . If the body is relatively unalive, a person's impressions and responses are diminished. The more alive the body is, the more vividly does he perceive reality and the more actively does he respond. . . . The aliveness of the body denotes its capacity for feeling. In the absence of feeling the body goes "dead." . . . The emotionally dead person is turned inward: thoughts and fantasies replace feelings and actions. Despite this mental activity, his emotional deadness is manifested physically. We shall find that his body looks "dead" or unalive. (296, pp. 5–6)

Lowen further describes the therapeutic task and the relating of the body to feeling:

Looking at the body and listening to it is a continuous process. A patient's tone of voice tells me where he is, not his words. His words can lie. The body doesn't lie. The eyes may lack feeling, i.e., be dull or vacant, but that says something. His voice may be a monotone and that, too, is a sign. The lack of movement is as revealing as movement itself. But of even greater importance is the way a person holds himself, i.e., his psychological character structure. (297, p. 4)

Some Eastern approaches to problems of living, such as the Zen form of Buddhism or Yoga, stress attention to natural body processes. Proper breathing is central to Zen and Yoga meditational forms, since focusing on the body aids "turning off" cognitive processes and slowing down metabolic processes. Part of the effectiveness of meditational methods used increasingly in the Western hemisphere, such as Transcendental Meditation, is due to attention to the body. A growing collection of empirical findings supports the claims of slowed physiological processes which accompany a subjective awareness of well-being. Relaxation routines used by counselors and psychotherapists of many theoretical persuasions utilize body approaches, particularly breathing exercises.

Relaxation methods are significant adjuncts to counseling and therapy skills. While various forms for inducing a relaxed state exist, some on tapes and records, the basic form is adapted from Jacobson's early physiological research (242). It is a progressive form of alternating tensing-releasing of muscles with relaxation messages to muscle groups. For example, one begins with the top of the head and moves progressively through muscle groups until one's whole body is relaxed. Once clients have learned this method thoroughly, they can relax in a few seconds with auto-suggestive messages to "relax." In the action strategies, the relaxation skill is basic to anxiety reduction since the aim is to substitute relaxation responses for anxiety feelings in the presence of cues which have set off the learned anxious behavior.

To be able to feel fully requires that one get in touch with one's body both through sensory awareness and proper breathing. Holding one's breath is associated commonly with anxiety. Breathing opens up one's excitatory processes and helps one to feel anger, for example. Since breathing is associated with energy metabolism, proper breathing helps one to release feelings. By breathing exercises one also gets in touch with the muscular tensions and rigidities in the body. When a client becomes aware of his body, he gradually becomes aware of feelings; and when he is aware of feelings, he becomes more aware of the possibilities of actualizing behavior, rather than tying his energy to defensive and manipulative behaviors.

As with the lowly amoeba, human beings are constantly expanding and contracting, observed most easily in the pulse beat and in respiration. People are either reaching toward the environment or withdrawing from it. Emotions, similarly, can be thought of as either expansive or contractile. Anger, for example, is expansive, as blood sugar and energy flow to one's muscles. Anxiety, or fear, tends to be a contracting emotion. Sadness is also a constrictive emotion, the withdrawal seeming to take place in one's arms and chest. When withdrawal becomes a permanent style, the emotions become bound up in muscle contractions, and the normal expansion and contraction process is stopped. This event happens to many people who have been hurt by the environment and by others.

Maintaining a rhythm of contact and withdrawal requires an understanding of one's self and one's body, of the fact that people *are* their bodies. It also requires hearing, touching, and seeing other people. Such contact is not possible without an awareness of physiological processes that make human contact possible.

Breathing Methods. First, clients must learn to breathe correctly, since breathing is one means by which a person feels excitement and identification with his or her body. Since most people, when they are anxious or afraid, hold their breath to some degree, they should try to breathe as a baby breathes, from the diaphragm. In doing the exercises that follow, therefore, one should breathe from the diaphragm, by thinking of the diaphragm as a balloon that collapses when exhaling and expands when inhaling.

Expressing the Anger Dimension. One of the easiest ways to begin expression of anger is simply to have a "family argument." One person is asked to say "Yes" to another, and the other is asked to respond "No," while at the same time reflecting on past experiences of being required to do something he did not want to do. The technique is to go back and forth, "Yes," "No," gradually increasing the volume and bodily participation. The exercise puts the participants in touch with their anger and their wants. Standing up to the other person, even making a fist, increases bodily involvement. It has been suggested that the jaw is the place where repressed hostility seems to center, so people are encouraged to stick out their jaws to one another in such a "fight." This also facilitates awareness of anger in the whole body.

A second way to get in touch with anger or hostile feelings is for two participants to turn back to back and begin pushing each other, gently "fighting" each other with their buttocks. During such an exercise one can easily discover feelings of anger. Although some people feel rather childish and foolish at first, these feelings, too, serve the purpose of the exercise, which is to help reactivate a more basic, childlike approach to one's feelings.

A third method for getting in touch with anger is for two people to interlock hands and push each other. If they can find a rhythm in their pushing and in allowing themselves to be pushed, they can discover the "joy" that comes from being able to communicate anger. It is joyful to feel one's capacity to relate rhythmically.

Expressing the Love Dimension. The opposite end of the anger dimension is the caring dimension. In exercises for expressing this dimension, two participants, working together, can begin to feel their caring for one another by both saying "Yes," instead of saying "Yes" and "No." Saying "Yes" to each other warmly can help two people begin to discover their caring. Then, turning their backs to one another, they can rub each other's backs—this time, tenderly. Each begins to feel warmth—a loving, caring feeling—that can be expressed and received in a physical way.

Another effective caring exercise is the "facial touch." Most people, as children, were touched often by their parents. One way for people to discover their ability to care for one another is to touch each other facially as a parent might touch a child. For example, one person may say to another, "I'd like you to close your eyes now and I'm going to touch your face. I'd like you to feel that I'm your father (or mother)." Then he or she may go through a touching and talking sequence something like this: "This is your hair, and it's very soft. This is your forehead, and beneath your forehead is one eyebrow, which comes down here and goes up there, and the other one goes up like this and down like this. And these are your eyes (touching the eyes very softly). Your eyes are soft, delicate, wonderful. One eyelash comes out here and one eyelash comes out over here. And this is your nose, the bridge of your nose comes out to a very nice point and then goes out here toward your cheeks. Your cheeks are red and soft and beautiful. Below your cheeks are your lips. This is your upper lip, and it's soft and red and very lovely, and below your upper lip is your lower lip, and it's very nice and soft and beautiful. Below your lips is your chin, and your whole face comes down like this toward your chin and is very, very pretty."

Simply to say this to another person while touching him or her often brings tears to the person's eyes. This may seem a simple exercise, but if one is willing to take the risk of going through it, this physical expression of tenderness can be a very meaningful demonstration of the importance of caring.

Expressing the Strength Dimension. Stamping one's feet firmly on the ground, for example, gives a real sense of feeling one's strength, for the lower half of the body is where people get their support. In this series of exercises, people try to get in touch with their own strength. If one *stamps his feet* firmly into the ground until he begins to feel the muscle strain in his calves and thighs, his feet will seem to become firmly planted in the ground, like the roots of a tree. This helps one feel a sense of strength and self-support.

A second exercise, helpful to developing strong resistance to manipulation in one's environment, is to lie on a bed with both knees up and to pound the bed with both fists and say, "I won't give up." Both movement and voice should express conviction. In this experience, clients often move to the opposite polar dimension and cry.

A third method for feeling strength is for the client to hold the weight of someone's head in his hands. The client's partner sits or lies down, and the client then lifts his or her head. In lifting or holding the partner's head, one begins to feel the strength of being trusted by another.

Expressing the Weakness Dimension. Just as holding another person's head enables one to feel his strength, the ability to put one's head into another's hands helps one feel weakness or vulnerability. The person playing the weak role in this exercise lies on the floor and pretends to be a child again, perhaps only six months old and still not able to get out of his crib. The other person acts as his parent, and tries to make the "infant" feel his vulnerability, his weakness, as he lies on the floor. When the "infant" is ready, he raises his hands, reaching for the "parent" and saying to him, "Will you help me?" It is important that this be a plea, not a demand. It should express great need: "I want you to help me, I need your help, will you please help me?" When this exercise is done seriously, it often brings tears to the eyes of the person playing the weak role. It also brings a feeling of strength and worth to the parent figure, who experiences having another person reach out to him. In the last part of this exercise, the "infant" reaches for the "parent" and allows himself to be lifted up. As he is lifted off the floor, he can rest in the arms of the parent figure—rest his weight on his body. In doing so, the "infant" experiences, more fully than in any other exercise, his own weakness, vulnerability, and need. Conversely, the parent figure feels great strength, capacity, and ability to cope.

A second technique for getting in touch with one's weakness is to stand with one's back to a couch, bent forward, with all weight on one's feet. The feet should be approximately fifteen inches apart, with toes turned in slightly. The fingers touch the floor out in front for balance. The knees are bent forward, and then slowly brought back so that a tremor in the legs begins. The vibration is accompanied by a tingling sensation in the feet and legs. Respiration now begins to deepen. When standing this way becomes painful, the client is instructed to fall backward onto the couch. He is usually in tears by this time, and group members are instructed to touch and comfort him. The point of the exercise is to experience falling and surrendering to one's weakness and vulnerability. This exercise is illustrated in the film *Three Approaches to Group Therapy* (438).

In a third exercise to get in touch with one's vulnerability or weakness, the client is asked to stand with his feet about thirty inches apart, toes inward, knees bent as much as possible, back arched, and hands on hips. The therapist then grasps the client's arms at the elbow and pushes him forward and down. As the client slowly lets himself down to the floor, he experiences deep feelings of vulnerability and surrender.

The ability to get in touch with and surrender to one's feelings of weakness and vulnerability is a central aim of Actualizing Counseling and Therapy. Everyone is afraid to give in to his feelings; but, in particular, people are afraid of being weak. They feel they must be in control at all times. To surrender is to accept one's losses. The fear of falling is related to the fear of surrendering to another, especially parents and others who have manipulated one. As individuals overcome their fear of falling, they give in more readily to their bodies and their feelings.

Gendlin's Focusing

Gendlin (184) has developed a procedure whereby one can understand and integrate the relationships among thought, feeling, and bodily sensation. He calls this process "experiential focusing." His hypothesis is that words come from feelings and that feelings lead to freshly sensing one's bodily feelings. The following verbal exchange illustrates how a focus on feeling experience is achieved:

Cl: I don't care about getting close to anyone. It makes me uncomfortable. (*Intellectualizing*)

Th: What is "it"?

Cl: I'm afraid when I get too close to anybody. (*Feeling*)

Th: How do you mean?

Cl: I get *really scared* of closeness! (*Deeper Feeling*)

Th: What makes that happen?

Cl: I've been hurt too many times. (*Whole Problem*) My body becomes tight and freezes up in any intimate relationship. (*Bodily Response*)

Gendlin supports the goal of bringing together thinking, feeling, and bodily responses in therapy. He believes that sequences like the above illustrate that all therapeutic interactions are part of a *loosening process* that leads to freedom of expression.

Kelly's Personal Construct Interpretation

Kelly (257) considers the material of interpretation to be the personal construct, which he defines as an anticipatory concept or predictive idea which the individual utilizes in dealing with the events or experiences of his life. Kelly, therefore, sees interpretation as a process in which events of life are compared and contrasted with one's constructs. A client makes a generalization about himself which he utilizes as a construct to predict his life events and behavior. For example, he might have feelings of inadequacy which would result in his predicting failure at a task. Unless this construct is related to the events of life, it is meaningless. The interested reader will find Kelly's system of constructs elaborated in his two-volume work (257). It is too detailed to present a complete picture of his methods here.

A prominent feature of the interpretive phase of counseling and psychotherapy is an emphasis on rational processes. In this tradition, Ellis has evolved a point of view for psychotherapy which he calls "rational-emotive psychotherapy" (135). We believe that this system has value for certain types of clients, particularly for those who are bright and flexible in their thinking. Because the Ellis approach has implications for our discussion of interpretive techniques, we are including a summary of his views here.

Rational psychotherapy "is based on the assumption that human beings normally become emotionally disturbed through acquiring irrational and illogical thoughts, philosophies, or attitudes" (139, p. 3). The therapist analyzes the client's feelings of hurt, anger, fear, and guilt, and shows ". . . him that these emotions arise not from past events or external situations but from his present irrational attitudes or illogical fears about these events or situations" (139, p. 3). To Ellis, therefore, "Emotion itself is conceived of as *largely being a certain kind, a biased, prejudiced kind of thought*" (139, p. 3).

Some of the major illogical ideas or philosophies which have been learned and believed by troubled individuals in Western culture are described by Ellis in the following excerpts. We quote them in full so the reader can get a more complete picture of the kinds of values and ideas which Ellis suggests as replacements for what is often regarded as irrational thinking. The following excerpts illustrate the problem of broadening the client's value possibilities and perceptions of his world so as to find the most effective means of construing his life circumstances.

1. The idea that it is a dire necessity for an adult to be loved or approved by everyone for everything he does—instead of his concentrating on his own self-respect, on winning approval for necessary purposes (such as job advancement), and on loving rather than being loved.

2. The idea that certain acts are wrong, or wicked, or villainous, and that people who perform such acts should be severely punished—instead of the idea that certain acts are inappropriate or antisocial, and that people who perform such acts are invariably stupid, ignorant, or emotionally disturbed.

3. The idea that it is terrible, horrible, and catastrophic when things are not the way one would like them to be—instead of the idea that it is too bad when things are not the way one would like them to be, and one should certainly try to change or control conditions so that they become more satisfactory, but that if changing or controlling uncomfortable situations is impossible, one had better become resigned to their existence and stop telling oneself how awful they are.

4. The idea that much human unhappiness is externally caused and is forced on one by outside people and events—instead of the idea that virtually all human unhappiness is caused or sustained by the view one takes of things rather than the things themselves.

5. The idea that if something is or may be dangerous or fearsome one should be terribly concerned about it—instead of the idea that if something is or may be dangerous or fearsome one should frankly face it and try to render it nondangerous and, when that is impossible, think of other things and stop telling oneself what a terrible situation one is or may be in.

6. The idea that it is easier to avoid than to face life difficulties and self-responsibilities—instead of the idea that the so-called easy way is invariably the much harder way in the long run and that the only way to solve difficult problems is to face them squarely.

7. The idea that one needs something other or stronger or greater than oneself on which to rely—instead of the idea that it is usually far better to stand on one's own feet and gain faith in oneself and one's ability to meet difficult circumstances of living.

8. The idea that one should be thoroughly competent, adequate, intelligent, and achieving in all possible respects—instead of the idea that one should *do* rather than always try to do *well* and that one should accept oneself as a quite imperfect creature, who has general human limitations and specific fallibilities.

9. The idea that because something once strongly affected one's life, it should indefinitely affect it—instead of the idea that one should learn from one's past experiences but not be overly attached to or prejudiced by them.

10. The idea that it is vitally important to our existence what other people do, and that we should make great efforts to change them in the direction we would like them to be—instead of the idea that other people's deficiencies are largely *their* problems and that putting pressure on them to change is usually least likely to help them do so.

11. The idea that human happiness can be achieved by inertia and inaction—instead of the idea that humans tend to be happiest when they are actively and vitally absorbed in creative pursuits, or when they are devoting themselves to people or projects outside themselves.

12. The idea that one has virtually no control over one's emotions and that one cannot help feeling certain things—instead of the idea that one has enormous control over one's emotions if one chooses to work at controlling them and to practice saying the right kinds of sentences to oneself (135, pp. 40–41).

Ellis adds that there is more to therapy than changing some beliefs, but Ellis does not seem to believe that it is necessary, as in psychoanalysis, to focus on historical events to show the client how he *became* disturbed or to depend on relationship variables for behavior change. Rather, he feels that after any necessary support or ventilation of feelings, emphasis should be placed on *attacking* the client's irrational beliefs and on showing how he is *sustaining* his neurosis by still believing them. He then teaches him how to *re-verbalize* and *re-think* these ideas in a more logical, self-helping way. Finally, he encourages the client to engage in *activity* which will prove the validity of his newly formed and valid assumptions about life.

Gestalt therapy, especially as interpreted by Perls (361), is concerned with producing awareness through focusing on the here and now. Perls asks "what" questions, such as, "What are you doing now?" This method draws attention to immediate behaviors and avoids the distant intellectualizing that sometimes goes on when "why" or "cause" questions are posed. He draws attention to discrepancies in behavior such as, "You say you are afraid, but you are smiling. A frightened person does not smile." The client is thus forced to do his own interpretation when his behavior, or disjointed fragments of behavior, are brought into focus in the present. This confrontative strategy also helps the client to recognize and "take back" his projected feelings to objects and persons.

Gestalt theory suggests also that learning through interpretation means discovery learning. The person has a new experience. He is made aware of his press for environmental support through various manipulations—playing stupid, using flattery, or being helpless. He is led to lean on his own resources and to assume responsibility for his own behavior.

The key interpretive problem in Gestalt counseling is to work through what Perls calls the "existential impasse." This is the critical point where the client's environmental support has diminished and he feels he has not reached the point where he can cope with life by himself. The counselor's interpretive problem is to help the client get over the impasse and to take responsible risks. In the "safe emergency" of the relationship he discovers that his exaggerations and catastrophic expectations exist in his imagination. Finally, he sees the total Gestalt of his life in his actualizing efforts.

Menninger's Neo-Analytic Methods

Interpretation is an important method in psychoanalytic therapy. Karl Menninger (319) presents an interesting scheme for identifying various types of interpretation in terms of the time sequence and theoretical constructs of analysis.

1. Preparation for interpretation:

Having identified some connections, or certain common elements, in a considerable number of events in the patient's life, . . . the next step is to further the preparation for real interpretation (319, p. 136).

2. Real (content) interpretation:

Sooner or later, the therapist is in a position to say something like this: "This thing, then—(this trick, this experience, this defense, this defeat)—happens to you repeatedly; it seems to happen especially to you. You seem to have something to do with its happening. Perhaps it doesn't just *happen*, possibly you actually do it. You have done it before. Perhaps you have some hidden purpose behind it, a purpose which was once valid but which is no longer valid. This can be seen as what Fate does to you; but let us look at what you do with your Fate!" (319, pp. 136–37).

As Menninger recognizes too, such interpretations tend to be hard blows to the client. He will attempt to justify, to "not get it," to theorize, to digress, to dawdle at some of these interpretations.

3. Interpretation of resistance:

Instead of rubbing his nose in it, so to speak, one proceeds to the interpretation of the resistance. One says in substance "You do not want to see this for certain reasons." First, one points out that such resistance exists, then one points out how it manifests itself; then one points out its obvious purpose (and, of course, if one doesn't know what its obvious purpose is, then the patient's cooperation has to be enlisted in that search). In general, of course, the purpose is to avoid seeing the unpleasant truth (319, p. 137).

4. Transference interpretation:

It (the real interpretation) may be further obscured by various transference patterns and purposes; the patient may be bribing, defying, or seducing the analyst (319, p. 137).

It may be seen, above, that transference, as we have already mentioned, is a form of resistance to real interpretation which is yet too painful to accept.

5. "Working through" or repeat interpretations:

. . . Resistance will often cover with the same obliviousness the repetition of the same old pattern, so that all that was won by painstaking labor seems to be forgotten. . . . We have to begin (over and over) again from the beginning (319, p. 138).

This necessity for "working through," for the analyst to repeat interpretations until they are taken hold of is a reflection of the extension of the neurosis into many different aspects of or events of the patient's life. His defensive structure isolates these events from one another, so that he is not aware of the common tendency running through them. In the language of some learning theorists, the "transfer" or "spread of effect" of the insight from one situation to other situations is limited or blocked. In Freud's words "One must allow the patient to get to know his resistance. . . ." Hence the necessity of repeating the interpretations as the patient repeats his neurotic behavior in different contexts (319, p. 138).

Grossman's Hyperbolic Approach

A type of value reorientation approach to interpretation is described by Grossman (209) as hyperbolic therapy. This is an effort to adopt an exaggerated form of the client's defenses, impulses, and conscience. These vary from a rational supportive stance to a "devil's advocate" approach using humor, sarcasm, and ridicule when appropriate. The rationale is to shock or press the client so that he sees himself in more clear relief. The counselor does this by being more like the client than the client is himself.

Special Interpretive Adjuncts

Written Communications

Written communciations have become an accepted adjunctive method for individual counseling. Pearson and his contributors (357) have reviewed the advantages, disadvantages, and future uses of various documents such as diaries, letters, creative writing, and notebooks on fantasies and dreams. While many counselors are skeptical about the value of such materials and their use in avoiding interpersonal contact, many others are experimenting with written communications as an adjunct to counseling and have become enthusiasts for the method.

Fantasy and Metaphors

Another stylized way of introducing an interpretation is to put it in the form of a fantasy (daydream), even using picture language like a metaphor. An example is, "I have a fantasy about what you have just said. I picture you walking down a path in the woods, coming to a fork in the path, and being undecided which one to choose. You unconcernedly flip a coin and run joyfully down the path chosen by the coin. How does this fit?" Hopefully, the fantasy is close to the client's awareness and triggers new ways of perceiving himself through further discussion. The limitation is that in using this skill the counselor shifts all the way into the client's frame of reference, thus forcing the client to deal with him (or his fantasy). Sometimes it is useful just to give one's reaction in the form of a metaphor, such as, "Most of the time I perceive you as a great big soft teddy bear who stays in any position he is placed."

Drugs, Hypnosis, Dream Analysis

The scope of therapeutic psychology, as outlined in Chapter 1, includes major techniques of counseling and psychotherapy, but does not include a detailed focus on such specialized psychotherapeutic techniques as dream interpretation and hypnotherapy, or the use of drugs such as sodium pentothal or lysurgic acid in collaboration with medical specialists. The student who specializes in long-term psychotherapy will want to explore these techniques further.

Dreams, for example, can be regarded as coded messages from the unconscious. Special study and training are required to become an effective

dream analyst. A similar statement can be made for hypnosis as a therapeutic technique. Fromm's work, *The Forgotten Language*, is recommended as an introduction to dream interpretation. LeCron and Bordeaux
present an informative introduction to hypnosis in *Hypnotism Today*.
Wolberg's *Hypnoanalysis* is also a fruitful source. Psychologists who work
with drug-induced therapy always work in collaboration with a medical
specialist, and the procedures utilized are beyond the scope of this volume.
It is interesting to note, however, that an increasing number of psychologists in private practice are utilizing collaborative drug therapy.

Summary

This chapter includes a variety of interpretive approaches and illustrations
along with selected body awareness methods. Interpretation is the principal technique the counselor uses during the awareness phase of the counseling process. The major goal of interpretive techniques is to promote
client understanding and self-interpretation that lead to mature self-
actualizing action. A number of theoretical approaches to interpretation
are presented, with special attention to dealing with feelings in the
Actualizing Counseling and Therapy model.

Information, Tests, and Action Strategies

This chapter is concerned with two basic strategies: (1) the use of data as an interaction medium between client and counselor and as a tool for counselors focusing on planning and decision-making problems; and (2) the use of behavior changing approaches that mobilize clients into action.

Advice and Information-Giving Strategies

To the man in the street, counseling and psychotherapy are almost synonymous with giving advice. Offering "common-sense advice" in a friendly manner is probably the oldest form of counseling, the aim being to offer substitute attitudes and behaviors for those the client holds. It is an appeal to the client's intellectual powers through logical reasoning and evaluation of his experience.

Advice-giving generally is accompanied by a heavy dose of persuasion because the counselor, in giving the advice, often has a personal interest in seeing that the client follows it. This point is valid, particularly when a teacher-counselor's value to colleagues or superiors, for example, is judged by the behavior changes he effects in student clients. Although professional counselors give valid information when it seems appropriate, they seldom use advice of the "Here is what I think you ought to do" variety, mainly because it is a projection of the counselor's own values and styles. The importance of using proper informational techniques, however, was emphasized in Yalom's study of groups (511), where information-giving was one of the ten most significant methods of promoting constructive change.

10

Persuasive advice-giving is a standard technique used by unsophisticated persons. Nevertheless, there are occasions when advice in the form of suggested alternate courses of action for the client to follow might be indicated. The word "suggested" should be emphasized so as to leave the evaluation and decision about the course of action with the client. Examples are those situations when a parent is exploring possible ways in which she has been mishandling her young child, or when a client feels caught on the horns of a dilemma about which occupation to select, and for which the counselor suggests additional possibilities.

Sullivan (463) distinguishes between "prescriptions for action" (suggestions), which he advocates, and outright "advice," which he condemns. He claims that good advice is usually an elaboration of the obvious and an insult to most clients; advice based on incomplete or faulty data is often dangerous.

The use of suggestion and opinion is most appropriate when it is known in advance that the contact will be short and where a relatively inconsequential life decision must be made quickly. The counselor recognizes that this is a superficial, intellectualized approach which generally does not affect basic attitudes. If used sparingly and cautiously on normal people with situational problems and with minor decisions to be made, little risk is involved. Normal people generally are capable of evaluating suggestions and rejecting them when not acceptable.

Thorne (474) suggests the use of persuasive advice in crisis situations where cooperative action of several people must be secured to prepare clients for major readjustments and to prevent emotional trauma. Examples are situations where reorganization of families is undertaken in cases of hospitalization, divorce, imprisonment, loss of job, or financial crisis. Complex classroom changes in school situations, for another example, usually require the concerted efforts of several people, obtained through the medium of persuasive recommendations.

Experiments in short-term counseling have been made from time to time. These studies often involve persuasive informational techniques. An example is given by Herzberg (225), who uses persuasion and intellectual appeals to change behavior by manipulating the inhibitory powers of the personality. Much research is needed on the rationale and techniques of persuasion, suggestion, and advice-giving before these methods can be advocated unequivocally as effective short-term counseling techniques.

In family counseling much use is made of suggestions, such as on child behavior management, to try out during the week. These interventions are not offered as advice, although they might be so interpreted by clients. The important question is, does the intervention result in positive behavior changes in the client?

One of the greatest limitations of advice-giving for counselors is the temptation to use it indiscriminately and profusely. If they give advice excessively it may court strong resistance from clients, even to the point of causing them to terminate the relationship. Strong dependency relationships may be built up when the counselor meets demanding overtures for solutions to a dependent client's problems.

A chief danger, however, is that a counselor may be tempted to give advice which is not in the client's best interests, because it is a projection of the counselor's needs, problems, and values. This is known as the "If I were you . . ." approach. The client may take the counselor's advice and suggestions, then, later, find that they are not valid. Bach (27) observed that in group therapy, advice-giving originated when the person giving the advice perceived the problems brought up by another as consciously or unconsciously his own. In other words, interest in giving advice is aroused when we identify with the person having problems similar to our own. Bach asserts that objective advice-giving is rare except when it is attempted in professional psychotherapy, where, he too claims, it has limited utility.

Even if a counselor's values permitted direct advice-giving, he cannot know enough about a person's situation to decide what that person should do concerning such questions as, "Should I get a divorce?" or "What occupation should I enter?" If the client follows the counselor's advice, the client's situation may change so that the original opinion is obsolete, perhaps even dangerous. There is also the risk that the counselor will be blamed if things do not work out right. In any case, jeopardy to the relationship hardly warrants the risk involved in choosing sides in the client's conflicts.

Counselors using the client-centered approach to counseling are critical of advice-giving on the grounds that its use shifts the responsibility for solutions to the client's problems onto the counselor, and limits the client's opportunities to make his own changes in fundamental self-evaluative attitudes.

The issue on the use of suggestive advice boils down to the old problem of good judgment on the counselor's part. The weight of counselor opinion, however, seems to be against the use of straight, opinionated advice. It certainly has gross limitations for extensive psychotherapeutic types of counseling. A distinction must be made, furthermore, between giving valid information and offering opinionated advice of the personal projection variety. Methods for presenting information to a client are offered in the following sections.

Case Management Skills

The management of cases often involves suggestions which might be classed as advice. Occasionally the counselor must advise referral, hospitalization, or some other significant move which, in his professional judgment, would be in the best interests of the client. Counselors or therapists constantly must evaluate themselves in terms of what they can do with clients. They must also assess client life circumstances in light of their ability to profit from counselor services. Finally, the institutional setting must be appraised in terms of what kinds of services can be safely and legitimately offered. Often, the conclusions drawn from appraisal of these factors must be communicated to the client in the form of suggestions of steps to be taken next. The principal issue here is what is the extent of accountability assumed or assigned?

Testing and Observing Strategies

It is assumed that students and practitioners reading this volume are familiar with basic principles of measurement and are acquainted, also, with commonly used tests. This section will cover some of the questions involved in the functions and choice of tests, as well as in the use of tests in counseling. Tests are viewed in this chapter as tools to be used in the therapeutic process and not as central emphases. We feel that tests have been used too profusely in counseling in the past, largely because they have been a convenient "screen" to hide a lack of counseling knowledge, and an "escape" from facing the real problems of facilitating client growth. Clients have reinforced this practice in their frequently stated reason for counseling, that is, "to take some tests."

One of the key contributions to clinical practice is the predictive use of tests to help clients make decisions and plans. There is also a continuing trend in the therapeutic use of tests, in addition to their traditional diagnostic use of helping the counselor formulate hypotheses about his client.

Functions of Tests

Tests help the counselor in surveying and diagnosing personality characteristics and problems with the aim of giving the client useful information about his own personality. A counselor who locates problem areas by means of personality inventories, problem checklists, and temperament tests often accelerates the client's exploration of problems and economizes exploratory interview time.

Clients come to psychotherapeutic and vocational counselors expecting to take tests to find out more about themselves; hence, they expect direct and useful answers from the tests. For the psychologist in a clinic setting, in contrast, the survey function of testing may be important for helping the counselor obtain hypotheses or to verify some of his hunches about the functioning of the client's personality. Here, the client takes tests without necessarily expecting to have the results given to him. In fact, some of the interpretations under clinical conditions frequently would prove very mystifying and threatening to the client.

Testing, especially personality appraisal, for personnel selection and upgrading purposes is under fire. Accusations of bias toward minorities and the poor, as well as invasion of privacy, have curtailed the use of tests for all purposes. The American Psychological Association has published a set of standards for use of psychological tests to reduce misuses and abuses of psychometrics (17).

The diagnostic function of tests with children is well recognized. Counselors rely extensively upon tests for assaying reading and learning difficulties, for example, where several hours of interviewing would be needed to get the same information.

Bordin (60) proposes that an important area which the counselor may analyze with tests is the client's sense of reality, by having the client try out his self-expectations through his own behavior samples on tests. Just as one tests his abilities in athletics through tryout experiences, the client can test perceptions of his abilities and traits through the medium of testing. A by-product for the client of this reality-testing experience is the development of a desire to explore his motivations and capacities further.

Discovery of interest and value clusters is another use of tests and inventories in counseling. Clients generally know their manifest interests well, but they have little idea of how they compare with individuals in known groups, such as men in general or college women. It is this relative standing on definitive norm tables which gives tests their value for appraising the client's interests, aptitudes, achievement, and other personality variables. Thus, an important question which tests help to answer for the client is, "How do I compare to others with whom I will be competing?"

A third significant function of tests is the prediction of behavior. Aptitude tests are examples of instruments which take behavior samples from which the counselor can make inferences about the client's ability to pursue a particular educational or vocational plan. Predictions are made in terms of probabilities of success in a given program. The probabilities are directly related to the specific validities of the tests used.

Selection of Tests

In many clinical situations, standard batteries of tests are administered, such as Wechsler or Stanford Binet, Rorschach or MMPI, and the Actualizing Assessment Battery. Yet, for many clients, tests must be selected to bear more appropriately upon age and unique problems. In career planning, selection of tests is especially important because of special needs for accurate prediction.

Most often a counselor selects the tests which he thinks would be most useful from a standard checklist, much in the same fashion that a physician writes a prescription. This method puts the responsibility upon the counselor. Being, of course, the expert in the matter of appraisal, the counselor should have the prerogative of determining the tests to be used.

The counselor should suggest tests when the client reaches the point of feeling a need for more data about himself for the decision at hand. A client may wish to know, for example, whether he has enough scholastic aptitude to succeed in college. He also may desire an interest inventory to help ascertain the major most likely to give him satisfaction. This principle of timing in test selection is especially important in counseling. If the counselor proposes personality tests at the outset, the client may come to overvalue them as a means for suggesting solutions to personal problems, rather than coming to depend upon the relationship to reach self-actualizing goals. If the counselor suggests them too far along in the process, it is very likely that the client may tend to feel that the counselor is baffled by his case or that it is more serious than was thought at first. The counselor must sense the most appropriate point early in the process when tests can be given and when it can be explained to the client that this procedure is routine.

When the client expresses a desire for more data, the counselor may then bring up the topic of tests and suggest specific types which would give the kind of answers sought. At this point, the counselor would do well to explain that sometimes tests can give helpful data on the problem and sometimes not. It should be stressed, however, that the client should have a genuine desire to take the tests as an outgrowth of his feeling the need for more data. There is some evidence from studies by Bordin and Bixler (61), Seeman (422), and Shostrom and Brammer (440) that client participation in test selection tends to facilitate the client's development of self-direction or self-actualization more than when the counselor alone prescribes tests.

The client-participation method of test selection presupposes some readiness of the type described in Chapter 5. Before counselors allow clients to participate in the selection of tests, they should inform clients about the values and limitations of tests as well as the various types available. Thus, the process to be described assumes that the client has some test sophistication plus the verbal ability to comprehend fundamental principles of testing. Generally, selection of tests proceeds as follows (440): (1) The client and counselor decide from their discussion what types of data are needed to help solve his problem; (2) the counselor describes the various categories into which tests are classified; (3) the counselor recommends those specific tests which will give the kinds of data sought by the client and recommends against testing in areas where there are already sufficient data or where tests would not help much; (4) the counselor allows the client to react to the selections so that any doubts or negative feelings about tests can be worked through; (5) arrangements are made for the tests to be administered.

The degree of client participation would depend largely upon his maturity and sophistication. The authors participated in a study (440) in which it was found that superior college freshmen could do an adequate job of selecting their own test batteries with the technical assistance of the counselor. It was felt that this tended to get the client more involved in the process and to reduce, somewhat, the tendency to view test assignment as a prescription. This tendency to lean on the expert judgment of the counselor could lead the client to gain an exaggerated confidence that tests somehow would give him the answers he needed, hence, reduce responsibility for choices he made.

Counselors who oppose giving clients responsibility in the test selection process use the analogy that physicians as technical experts do not ask their patient's opinions about taking laboratory tests to help in the diagnosis of the problem. One difference between a physician and a psychological counselor in this situation is that the physician assumes a large share of the medical responsibility for the patient's recovery, whereas the counselor does not assume similar responsibility for the choices made by the client. The psychological counselor, though assuming some professional responsibility for what the client does in his relationship, does not attempt to make a definitive diagnosis on the basis of his fallible tests. He does not attempt to make final prognoses or prescriptions about the course of the client's behavior since he recognizes the unreliability of the instruments. The counselor, then, takes responsibility only for giving the most reliable information possible, with interpretations and explanations to the client commensurate with the known reliability and validity of the instruments. In our opinion, the counselor must leave responsibility for decisions to the client. As part of the preparation for these decisions, furthermore, the counselor should keep the client involved in all phases of the process, including the selection of any tests.

At this point it should be emphasized, however, that tests given in clinical or hospital settings by a clinical psychologist largely for the purposes of diagnostic evaluation involve considerations different from those required in counseling. The data generally are gathered for a psychotherapist who evaluates the psychometric data along with much other case material and assumes responsibility for the use of the data.

Principles of Using Tests in Counseling

Until recently, test interpretations have been performed in interviews. A number of studies have been carried out with school-age clients comparing group and individual methods of test interpretation. On understanding and memory of test scores the results have consistently shown no differences between group and interview settings. A replication study by Walker (488) revealed that with high school clients there were no significant differences in ability to recall scores in group and individual settings, but personal acceptance of test scores was significantly higher with individual procedure. In the same study, different methods of presentation were used, and effects on students of varying mental ability observed. A further conclusion was that no approach is equally satisfactory for all clients and that a variety of test interpretation methods must be utilized.

Presentation of test results by means of programmed materials has supporting studies to substantiate its effectiveness. Forster (162), using a prepared program manual with college freshmen clients, found that such methods were effective in promoting accurate self-estimations from tests without emotional reactions often associated with low scores. Forster's results demonstrated significantly greater gains in self-estimation with programmed materials than with counseling interviews. The Gilbert and Ewing study of programmed counseling (191) cited in Chapter 2 utilized information in program form and had findings similar to Forster's study. These studies suggest that test interpretations might be done more economically and more effectively by means of carefully prepared programmed materials than in conventional test interpretation interviews.

The following principles of interpretation were developed from best-known practices and research at the present time.

1. The first rule of test use is to *know the test thoroughly.* This means more than knowing just the manual. The test should have been taken by the counselor himself and should have been investigated in the journals and in such collections of critiques as Buros' *Mental Measurement Year-books* (83). The weaknesses and limitations, as well as the strengths, of the test should be known to the counselor.

2. Exploration of the client's reasons for wanting tests and past experience with tests is undertaken. The client's expectations are important data to be considered, since he may be expecting much more than tests can reasonably be expected to perform. Some clients have been to several counselors and have taken tests with each, yet they are still searching for the magic answer which they hope tests will reveal. Further testing adds little to these situations, and more of a psychotherapeutic approach is needed to help them understand their compulsive searching.

Clients have often been traumatized by tests made earlier in school. They may regard them with deep suspicion, skepticism, or outright hostility. As a first step, the counselor should determine the client's feelings about the threatening aspects of testing to avoid distortion of the results of the interpretation and possibly failure of the counseling itself. Adults, especially, seem to feel threatened by any kind of testing, whereas adolescents have had so many tests in school that most of them seem to take tests without emotional difficulty.

Hills and Williams (226) studied the effects of interpreted test scores on client self-knowledge and self-acceptance in educational-vocational counseling. Clients who did not get results which corresponded with their ideas about themselves did not experience increases in self-acceptance and self-understanding. This kind of study emphasizes the need for counselors to be keenly aware of the emotional impact of test scores.

3. Structuring of the test interpretation session is especially important to prepare the client for meaningful, undistorted information. The counselor must ascertain the client's knowledge of the limitations of testing as well as the values for giving various self-information. An example is a discussion of the fact that tests do not give answers to problems. This is done in a casual manner to allow the client to ask questions and react to the counselor's introduction to the test interpretations. Test interpretation should grow out of the general discussion of the client's problem, with the counselor stressing how tests add to the pool of data about the client's personality.

4. The *meaning* of the scores should be established early in the discussion. That is, the client should know clearly what type of measure is being discussed—interest, aptitude, achievement, or personality. Most counselors probably could cite instances when they have been annoyed or embarrassed later by having a client interpret his Kuder Preference Record scores to a parent or friend as abilities.

5. The *frame of reference* of the test results should be specified clearly. That is, the client must know at all times which norm group is being used so that he has some yardstick for judging how high a high score really is. In helping a client to estimate his chances of success in a liberal arts college program, for example, it makes a tremendous difference whether he is being compared to high school seniors or college freshmen at the institution of his choice.

6. *Test results*, not scores, should be given to clients. If tests are given to a client with his expectation that he will be informed of the results, he is entitled to know the outcomes. Numerical scores are merely technical symbols for use by the counselor. Clients generally have just enough information about the meaning of numbers, such as I.Q.'s and percentile scores, that they tend to fix on the single score as "their score." Numbers are thus subject to the distortions which reflect the client's stereotyped meanings. Perception is focused, then, on the score symbol instead of on the meaning behind the symbol.

The counselor would do well to use trait terms and descriptive phrases such as, "Your high capacity to use language and to do verbal reasoning . . . ," instead of, "Your high scores on the scholastic aptitude test. . . ."

A corollary to this rule is to avoid using exact scores in interpretation. The lack of sufficiently high reliability in most tests indicates that the score symbol reported by the psychometrist represents a range or band of possible scores about the reported score. Brief mention of this phenomenon to clients often dispels their tendency to repeat requests to be told their reported scores.

Although counselors and psychotherapists are familiar with standard errors of measurement, it would be well for every counselor to pause periodically to examine data on reliability and the fact that it must be very high for the test to be useful. It should be noted, for example, that a typical correlation of .50 between scholastic aptitude tests and grades reduces the error of prediction over chance by only 13 percent. A correlation must be around .70 before error reduction reaches 30 percent and half the variance can be accounted for. The correlation must be almost .90 before the percentage of error reduction is 50 percent.

A third important point, relative to interpretation, concerns the language used to convey the relative significance of test results. In light of a lack of research on the matter, there seems to be a consensus that the counselor should use broad categories in presenting the client's relative rank. For example, if the client's rank is in the middle range of the distribution, the terms "average," "high average," "low average," or "middle range" are meaningful. If around the 70th to 85th percentile range, the phrase "high" or "upper quarter," or "upper 15 percent" is descriptive, although the term "high" has unfortunate value connotations for many clients. The terms "low" and "below average" certainly have negative associations for many clients. Phrases implying rankings for low scores, such as "lowest 10 percent of machinist apprentices," are meaningful without stirring negative self-regard feelings.

7. Test results should always be *verified*. Another way of stating this principle is that test results should be presented with an air of tentativeness. This cautiousness is especially important until further data are collected to verify the test results. Again, knowledge of all the various sources of unreliability in test administration and reporting leads counselors to the position that they should never accept test scores at face value.

There are many ways to check the reliability of a test score. Comparison of the score with past academic achievement gives a rough check on scholastic aptitude scores, although grades themselves are notoriously unreliable. Giving an additional test, especially an individually administered form, is desirable when the results are suspect. Interest inventory scores can be checked from case data on hobbies, reading, and activity interests.

As a corollary to the principle of verification, the counselor should never use a score in *isolation*. Test results should be woven in with other case data to check on the validity as well as the reliability of the test score. Decisions which people make as a result of counseling interviews are most often too consequential for the counselor to risk making predictions on skimpy and unconfirmed data.

8. *Counselor neutrality* in imparting test results is important since it is so easy to slip into evaluative phraseology. Examples of evaluative phraseology are: "You did extremely well on this test." "The results look pretty good; I think you will be pleased." "I think this test means that. . . ."

The test results should speak for themselves without the counselor's personal value projections. Clients, in addition, should formulate the evaluations for themselves. It would be preferable for the counselor to avoid overpersonalizing scores by indicating something like, "Adults with results like these seem to find college work quite easy," or "People with

results like these would very likely find engineering training very difficult."

9. Meaningful and clear interpretations should be the counselor's constant aim. Clients should make their own evaluations, as indicated in the
previous principle. However, they should not have raw data thrust at them
for interpretation. Neither should the counselor explain the meaning of
test results in technical language. Ambiguous reporting of test results
invites distortion of the interpretations, since clients can more easily
project their own meaning into the results.

If the counselor is overcautious in making interpretations, however,
he encourages the client to become overanxious and, consequently, to
distort them. Though the counselor should not go beyond his data, he
should be willing to state his predictions with forthrightness when reasonably certain that the client would be able to accomplish a planned
course of action, such as attending college.

Diagrams and profiles aid the counselor in giving meaningful interpretations. Counselors vary in their opinions on the appropriateness of
showing a profile to a client, because the client tends to look for identifying labels and specifics. Unless used properly, the profile may be very misleading, as in the case where several tests are reported on one graph, yet
each has differing standardization groups. Tests having comparable scores
because of a common standardization population, such as some of the
recently developed aptitude batteries or standard interest test profiles,
can be presented on a single graph so that comparisons among tests in the
battery would have meaning relative to each other.

Shostrom and Brammer (440) report a procedure for presenting test
results to clients in career counseling interviews. A normal curve was
used with one hundred schematic figures drawn on it. A few reference
points, in percentile terms, were indicated to give the client some idea of
how he compared to the norm group. The counselor proceeded somewhat
as follows: "Your scores fall approximately above the point indicated by
the red arrow," whereupon the counselor drew a small arrow under the
diagram to indicate the approximate range of all scores.

We usually sketch a diagram to indicate the idea of a distribution of
scores and what it means to fall in a certain area under the curve. Since
most college student clients have been exposed to the idea of the normal
curve and score distributions in their school work, this is an easy concept
to grasp. With high school students and adult clients, who do not have
this specialized knowledge, it is doubtful how wise it would be to make
a long discussion of scores, distributions, and normal curves.

Programs for interpretation of test results, such as Forster's "A Programmed Interpretation of Test Results" (162), are another example of
a graphic presentation of test results which has had experimental validation.

10. Accurate prediction is the principal aim of testing. Test results should be stated in terms of statistical predictions. This rule hits at the heart of the testing problem—that of validity. So few test batteries have been developed sufficiently, or standardized according to the local population, that the counselor has the principal difficulty of giving probability figures to his clients. It would be fine if the counselor could say, "Three out of four students with results like these succeed in law," "A person with results like these has a 60 percent chance of succeeding in engineering." In spite of the general absence of these more exact probability figures, the counselor can still rely on probability language in which to couch his interpretations. A counselor may say, for example, "With results like these the chances are very high that one could succeed in a liberal arts program."

11. Client participation and evaluation is another aim in the test interpretation phase. Interaction between client and counselor is valuable because it gives the counselor constant information regarding how the client is receiving the interpretation. In a study by Dressel (130) it was found that more self-understanding and satisfaction was associated with high client participation. Asking the client an occasional question, or asking if he has questions, often prevents the counselor from going off into long didactic soliloquies concerning test data. Pausing occasionally to allow the client to react serves to increase his assimiliation of the results. Perceptual research by Kelly (256), interpretation studies by the Bixlers (52), and studies of memory by Bartlett (35) point out clearly the tendencies of clients to hear selectively and distort and forget what they hear. So much of the research growing out of the Gestalt psychology approach, such as Wulf's studies (510), bears out the tendencies to reproduce figures more in line with the "good gestalt." Clients, then, unconsciously distort their perceptions in ways which make their sensory data more understandable and meaningful. There is the presumption here that this perceptual distortion phenomenon also takes place in test scores which are laden with threat potential. The counselor must be alert to these tendencies so he can help the client perceive the results as accurately as possible, and see the distorting effects of the counselor's own motivational structure.

12. The interpretation of *low scores* to normal clients is one of the most difficult problems the counselor must face. We have found from experience that it is best to start the interpretation period with the client's high scores. This tends to build the confidence which is so helpful to acceptance of low scores later.

A second helpful device the counselor may use is to test the client's readiness to accept low scores by asking the client to predict what he thinks his relative ranking might be on the trait in question. Clients often have a good hunch of how they rank. The counselor then makes a statement confirming the hunch with the test results. However, if the client does not have a clear idea of how he ranks, and if he is emotionally ready for the results, the counselor should present the results factually and wait for the reaction. The counselor should be ready for whatever feelings may be elicited—surprise, disappointment, pleasure—and be prepared to reflect these and help the client work them through.

The counselor should be especially cautious and tentative in giving low scores, since they may be fallible. The client who achieves scores which do not seem to be confirmed by other case data should be questioned to discover the cause. That is, the counselor should determine if his client suffered from excessive fatigue, test anxiety, misunderstood directions, or improper test readiness. The counselor should entertain the possibility that unreliability due to the test itself might be a factor.

13. *The appropriate conceptual level* for phrasing test interpretations is very significant if the client is to understand test results. If the counselor uses phrases such as "scholastic aptitude" or "linguistic aptitude" with many clients, for example, he conjures up a stereotype of foreign language ability. It would be much more appropriate for him to use the client's symbols and to speak in terms of "ability to use words." Asking questions to test the client's understanding of the interpretation is one technique to help the counselor stay on the most appropriate conceptual level.

Specific Informational Uses of Tests, Inventories, and Projective Techniques

Paper-and-Pencil Personality Inventories. These inventories are divided into three general categories—those which propose to measure presence and strength of such traits as dominance or submission, presence and strength of emotional problems, and, finally, the extent to which the client has feelings and problems similar to a standard diagnostic category such as hysteria.

Paper-and-pencil tests of the trait-measurement type have little utility in counseling because they do not give the counselor clear information with which to assess discrete traits or trait clusters. In our opinion, the tests have a second limitation because the counselor could not relate the tenuous traits to anything meaningful, even if he could find them. Few useful validity coefficients have been worked out using trait-type inventories.

The Actualizing Assessment Battery (435) is an example of paper-and-pencil approaches to measuring self-actualization. These tests, which now have been used in many validity studies, emphasize mentally healthy and actualizing qualities rather than pathological characteristics. Clients can be given this battery, particularly the POI, at the beginning of counseling to measure their self-actualization. Then it can be given again at the end of counseling and compared with the original as an indication of growth toward self-actualization.

So-called adjustment inventories, which purport to inventory personal problems, are useful in providing an opening wedge for discussion of the client's problem. Adolescent clients, especially, have resistance mechanisms which can be modified by personality test results because they are so curious about their own personalities. However, the questionnaire type of adjustment inventory often is unreliable, and its use tends to divert the client from real problems to a defensive preoccupation with test results.

The third type of personality inventory, which measures the degree to which a client has symptoms judged similar to psychiatric categories, is mainly useful in rough-screening. The Minnesota Multiphasic Personality Inventory (217) is an example. It has a "can opener" function also, to help clients get to the descriptive level of their adjustment problems more quickly. The MMPI helps the counselor make his diagnostic formulations, although he must exercise great caution in using the diagnostic categories of the instrument literally.

Projective Techniques. Another category of personality appraisal devices is the projective technique group which allows the client to project his own unique perceptions upon ambiguous stimuli in the form of ink blots, pictures, and three-dimensional objects.

Projective techniques are useful to help a psychotherapeutic counselor make diagnostic formulations, as well as to give him leads for counseling. There are some indications that projective techniques are also useful in making predictions for career counseling.

A picture-story type of instrument, such as the Thematic Apperception Test, is used in counseling or therapy principally for client self-interpretation. Several studies by Bettleheim (49), Deabler (120), Jacques (243), and Morton (335) indicate the usefulness of having clients interpret their own stories. Morton found the TAT an especially useful device to expedite brief psychotherapy, since the themes and their interpretations tended to center the client's attention upon immediately pressing problems and their solution. One of the strategies of short-term psychotherapeutic counseling is to get the client to talk about present perceptions of his problems, the nature of his defenses and goals, rather than to dwell at length upon past events.

Deabler (120) uses the TAT as a device to reflect back important client attitudes so that further expression of feeling is facilitated. The client then suggests his own interpretations, thereby generating insights more quickly than he would if the counselor were to use direct methods of interpretation.

Rorschach protocols can also be used to get immediate data for therapeutic purposes. Although the Rorschach cannot be used by clients in self-interpretation, as can the TAT, the findings from the content and the psychogram can be used to stimulate much therapeutically valuable material from the client in the early phases of counseling, or to get him off a resistance "plateau" later. For example, the counselor may interpret the life-style elements of the Rorschach psychogram as follows: "As this instrument is interpreted, you give the picture of a person who has difficulties establishing satisfactory interpersonal relationships, or as we say, relating to others. Does this fit with your estimates of yourself?" Often, if the counselor makes this type of interpretation early in the interview, he can pinpoint the defensive areas faster than if he allowed the client, himself, to approach them through the often tortuous channels of free conversation and resistance.

Pepinsky (358) describes more informal projective methods for counseling through use of common objects, such as room furnishings. For example, Pepinsky, referring to a landscape picture on the wall, would casually ask clients how they felt about it. One typical response was given, as follows, when a bright client was describing her disturbances over her failing midterm reports:

C: You would like to relax. Would it help you to look at my picture here? (Points to picture on wall.)

C1: (After a brief pause.) I'm looking at it, but I don't like it.

C: Can you tell me more about that?

C1: (Clenching her fists.) The branches of that tree—they seem to be clutching for something they never reach—just like me. (Bursts into tears.)

Pepinsky summarized the values of the picture device as allowing the client to feel at ease in dealing with a stimulus which seemed external, thus enabling the counselor to get more verifying data with which to firm up his diagnostic formulation. A further value was that of keeping the responsibility for analyzing the problems directly on the client.

There seem to be many implications and many promising leads in the use of projective devices in counseling. A few examples are given here of some of the possible uses. Serious clinical students have access to many books on projective techniques which will enable them to go far beyond the brief introduction made here. The whole area of the use of projective tests in psychotherapy, however, needs more study before definite statements can be made of the utility of the methods.

Expressive Movement. Observation of the posture, speech, artistic productions, and gestures of clients has always been a rich source of data for counselors to make inferences about their internal world. Fidgeting and sweating are especially valuable nonverbal indicators of the general state of tension in the client. An essential skill of counselors is ability to read nonverbal body messages accurately.

Interest and Value Inventories. Inventories in this category have utility primarily in educational and career counseling situations. They help the client to compare his casually stated or manifest interests with his solicited opinions on an inventory. According to his measured interests, the client is compared to other groups having known interest patterns, such as boys in general, or engineers. By helping the client to see that the various approaches to interests corroborate each other and that his interest patterns are consistent, the inventories serve a supportive function in counseling. Conversely, inventories help to point out indeterminate or immature interest patterns. If a counselor should find that one of his adult clients has no dominant interests, it may have much clinical significance, suggesting that the dynamics of his personality should be investigated. A lack of interests may mean, for example, that the client is incapable of identifying with a group, that he has general emotional immaturity, or that he is inexperienced. Patterson (356) indicates that the emotionally disturbed client tends to be interested in creative talent and social-service types of occupations, which may be interpreted as escape into the arts or into service activities.

A second value of interest and value inventories in counseling is that they shed light on client self-concepts.

As a third use, interest inventories may be used by the counselor to predict the amount of satisfaction a client will derive from a given occupational area. Strong's research (459) on the value of interest inventories in predicting later vocational choices and work satisfaction is illustrative of this function. Inventories of interest are limited largely to mature adolescents and older clients who have more stable interest patterns than younger clients. Sometimes, however, a general inventory made early in adolescence can give the client a general idea of the relative strengths of his interests, according to such broad areas as mechanical and clerical.

The problem of the use of specific tests in counseling is a vast topic and beyond the scope of this volume. It is assumed that the general reader is familiar with tests commonly used. If not, we recommend Super and Crites' *Appraising Vocational Fitness* (465) as a good source.

Aptitude and Achievement Tests. There is extensive literature on aptitude and achievement testing. The purpose of this section is only to point out some of the principal informational uses of this type of test in the counseling relationship.

One function of aptitude and achievement tests is to give the client support. Frequently clients feel "stupid" or "inadequate" without factual bases for such feelings. If used along with psychotherapeutic techniques, a test of aptitude for scholastic work, for example, can help to give clients a more realistic indication of approximately where they would stand relative to the group in which they would compete. This group may be the general population, college freshmen, engineering freshmen, art students, or other groups for which the test is normed. It is often reassuring to clients to have more accurate knowledge of where they stand so that more realistic planning can be undertaken.

A second function of aptitude and achievement tests in counseling is to give the counselor a basis upon which to make predictions of the possible success of a client in a given general or specific effort. Examples are predicting success for a client in engineering training, a college liberal arts program, or a teacher selection program. Validities of tests and pre- diction tables are not as useful as counselors would like, though such tests are better than choices based upon whimsy.

Aptitude testing often serves a third, but oblique, function in counseling. If the client is threatened easily by judgmental situations, doubts his ability, or has discrepancies between his ability and his ambition, the testing program catapults these anxieties forcefully into the relationship, where the counselor can deal with them psychotherapeutically.

The main purpose of all testing in counseling is to provide the client with reliable and valid information about himself so he will be able to make wise choices.

Action Strategies

Since a key client goal is to act in some way to solve a personal problem, counselors need methods to help clients move from insight, awareness, or understanding to action (deciding, choosing, planning, and doing). We do not assume, as some theorists do, that awareness or insight is sufficient for the client to act appropriately. We will describe some illustrative methods in two basic strategies—one a general problem-solving model, and the other a cluster of skills for changing specific behaviors. These action approaches, furthermore, are some specific things a counselor can do to bring about mastery and behavior change goals at the actualizing level of our theory. The theoretical and experimental base is social learning theory, especially as advanced by Bandura (30).

It is assumed also that the action strategies discussed below are carried out in the framework of an effective relationship as described in earlier chapters. Mickelson and Stevic (323) found, for example, that client information-seeking behavior was more effective when the action methods were conducted by counselors manifesting high-level facilitative conditions of warmth, empathy, and genuineness than by counselors skilled in action methods but low on facilitative conditions.

Problem-Solving Process and Skills

Process. The steps below follow general problem-solving sequences and are applied to many problems, but most of the illustrations are in the area of educational and career planning as exemplified by Krumboltz and Sheppard (274). These general steps are:

1. Establish a *relationship* and get the client *involved*. The client must be interested in the process and have hope that he has the power to make decisions that will influence his life profoundly.

2. State and clarify the *problem* and determine *goals*.

3. Determine and explore *alternatives* to the apparent solutions.

4. Gather relevant *information*. This may take the form of active seeking and reading, statements of fact by the counselor, simulation games, films, or tests.

5. Explore *implications* of information and *consequences* of the alternatives.

6. Clarify *values* that underlie personal choices. Clients must know what they desire and the order in which they value those desires. The counselor leads the client into exploration of his interests, competencies, family circumstances, social expectations, and realities.

7. *Reexamine the goals*, alternative choices, risks, and consequences. A final check on understanding the information and implications is made before the final decision.

8. *Decide* on one of the alternatives and formulate a *plan* or course of action implementing that decision.

9. *Generalize* the process to new life situations.

10. *Try out* the plan for implementing the decision with periodic *reevaluation* in light of new information and changing circumstances.

Most people, particularly young ones, have limited life experiences in making decisions and are generally unfamiliar with this rational process. Therefore, many clients must be taught this process through problem-solving interviews, direct trial-and-error experiences, and through simulations, such as "Career Games," "Marriage Games," and "War Games." Young clients often ask outright, "What shall I do?" "What course should I take?" "Should I try drugs?" "What career should I choose?" "What college should I apply to?" Instead of giving advice or opinions it is preferable to say, "I can't tell you because I don't know what is best for you; but I can help you decide for yourself what to do. Would you like to learn how?" There is abundant evidence in guidance studies that school-age youth make poor-quality decisions about many areas of their lives.

Decisions in the areas of interpersonal problems, such as sexual behavior involving previously learned response patterns, are more complicated. Solutions to these problems involve relearning methods, as well as rational problem-solving described above. Adult clients who face difficult choices, such as what to do with rebellious children, dependent relatives, errant spouses, or changes of work locale, must be taught this same problem-solving process as a substitute for acting on impulses, stereotypes, or advice.

Skills. Most problem-solving skills are combinations of those described in other contexts: problem identification, goal setting, informing, interpreting, diagnosing, and evaluating feedback. There is a skill applicable to Step 3, generating and weighing alternatives, called "force field" analysis. This skill utilizes physics concepts of fields of force and polarized valences. It is a method of comparing personal and social forces which are propelling the client toward his goal and distracting him from it at the same time. Force field skills are applicable to many kinds of decision-making situations. The client's goal is stated briefly at the top of Figure 18, and the direction of solution is indicated by an arrow. The forces pushing him toward his alternative goal (in this simple illustration, to reduce weight by three pounds a week for six weeks) are indicated by a plus sign, and those working against him by a minus sign. After listing the + and − forces, he can see more clearly where he is in relation to the feasibility of his goal. He can then rank the forces on their strength by rating each from 1 to 3. Now the client can decide on a strategy of strengthening the + forces or weakening the − forces. If it is a conflict-of-choice problem, each alternative goal can be analyzed and then compared.

Goal statements are derived from problem statements and have characteristics of specificity and clarity of expected outcome. A client says, for example, "My problem is that I'm lonely; it really hurts." The skill of stating goals comes in when deciding the best time to urge the client to stop talking about loneliness and start talking about a goal which can be achieved. Restated, the goal might be to relieve some of the loneliness by making two new acquaintances during the coming week and exploring common interests with them. While making new friends often doesn't relieve the loneliness totally, at least it is a tangible start. So, counselor and client can work on specific actualizing behaviors which will reach these goals.

GOAL: Reducing weight by three pounds a week for six weeks.

+	Rank	−	Rank
Spouse likes me thinner	1	Like rich food	3
Better for my health	2	Dislike diets and diet foods	1
Live longer	3	Lack knowledge of low calorie foods	2
Clothes will fit better	1	Will smoke instead of eat	2
Less fatigue	3	Three pounds seems too much in a week	1

Balance Point for Forces

Figure 18.   Illustration of Force Field Analysis. From L. M. Brammer, *The Helping Relationship: Process and Skills* (64, p. 145).

Modeling. Modeling is a method of learning by vicarious experience or imitation, such as watching the performance of others. The research evidence (Bandura 30) suggests that a wide variety of behavior can be changed through modeling. Common sense experience attests to the power of examples also. Clients tend to do what the counselor does. If the counselor uses colorful street language to express himself, so will the client; if the counselor discloses personal data about himself, the client will be more inclined to do so also. One of the problems in helping interviews is that clients do not know what to do, and verbal explanations often do not help. If the counselor models expression of feeling, this gives the client a clearer picture of what behavior is expected. Another problem is that the counselor's behavior must be at a higher level of functioning than the client's performance so that he has a behavioral model to work up to (Carkhuff 92).

Role playing is another example of vicarious behavior where the client can see, through roles performed by others, what is expected. If he is fearful of approaching an employer about a job, for example, the counselor can perform the role of an applicant (the client), while the client acts as the employer. The two then continue until the client sees other ways of acting in an employment interview. Then the client tries on the new behavior himself through reversing roles and having them critiqued repeatedly until he learns the new behavior to his satisfaction.

A third example of modeling effectiveness is the removal of fears by observing fearless behavior in a model, acquiring information about the feared object, and, finally, having a direct experience with the threatening object with no ill effects. This type of situation would be effective with fears of snakes or of making speeches, for example.

Modeling seems to be most effective when the model has characteristics of credibility, competence, knowledge, and influence. If the models possess qualities similar to counselors, they are effective. Advertising methods take advantage of these facts. An implication of these findings for counselors is to discover which qualities are most attractive to clients and then use them as guidelines for selecting models.

Modeling can be done by live, filmed, or taped methods. Although live methods have some advantages, such as maintenance of interest, filmed versions allow for more careful emphasis on the behaviors that one wants to model. An example of a helping situation with delinquent boys, which utilized live college-age models, is the work of Sarason (409). Adolescent boys observed special modeling of the following situations: (1) career planning; (2) motivation and interests; (3) attitudes toward work and education; and (4) utility of socially appropriate behavior. When the boys observed socially acceptable models, they improved their own planning skills and ability to think in socially positive terms. The models were attractive to the boys, and role-playing methods sustained their interest.

Filmed models have also been used with effectiveness. Hosford and Sorenson (235) used audio tape and filmed models successfully with fourth-to-sixth graders who wanted to speak up more in class. Motivating teenage students to do the investigational work necessary to career planning is a problem also. Stewart (456), using group models on audio tape, found that students improved their interest in career information and more actively explored sources of information after listening to the tapes.

General principles of using modeling are:

1. Determine which features of a model would be most *attractive* to the client.
2. Decide upon the *objectives* of the modeling.
3. Choose *believable models* similar to the clients in age, sex, and race.
4. Decide if *live or simulated modeling* would be more appropriate and practical.
5. Design a *modeling format*, script, or role-playing sequence.
6. Conduct the *modeling exercise*.
7. Discuss the *client's reactions* in terms of feelings, learnings, and suggestions.
8. Recognize that *informally we are modeling behaviors constantly* for clients.

Rewarding. At several points in this book we have described the reinforcing, or rewarding, effect of various helping procedures. This section will develop this idea as a consciously applied skill. The basic idea is that rewarded behavior tends to be repeated. Another striking characteristic of rewards is that a wide variety of events can have reinforcing functions. We can use reinforcement: (1) to overcome behavior deficiencies (as in encouraging a client to plan ahead); (2) to change undesirable behavior (as in chronic stealing); and (3) to maintain present responses (as in encouraging statements of feeling).

Although the idea of using rewards to shape behavior is a simple one, there are some pitfalls. Most of the principles of reinforcement have come from animal learning studies in which animals were deprived of food and water, which then became the reinforcers. Since human responses are so much more complex, rewards have varied meanings. In helping situations we depend mainly on words, which have different effects depending on the cultural background of the client. Praise words, such as "good job," for example, are used commonly, but soon lose their effect because of overuse, and because they have differing levels of potency for different people. Verbal rewards are most effective when the counselor and client are working toward common goals. They are resented as blatant manipulation when used to influence the client in ways that are not in his apparent best interests.

Some *general principles* in using reinforcement as a skill are that the reward, or incentive system, must be capable of maintaining a high level of action over a *long period*. In other words, we want the learning to be lasting. Secondly, we want the reward to be dependent on the appearance of the behavior we want. We want the *desired behavior rewarded*, which is difficult in ordinary life situations because the reward is often badly timed or is given haphazardly. As a result, the undesired behavior is rewarded. Finally, the reward must be *strong* enough and given *often* enough for the desired behavior to be repeated. We also want the behavior to *generalize* to similar situations when the rewards are not present, as in being able to solve problems in other contexts. This reinforcement process is aided by using natural settings, varying the reward, and rewarding conditions systematically.

The *general strategy* for using rewards is to plan them selectively in a pattern so that the desired behavior is emitted in the form and sequence desired. This is a *reinforcement schedule* or *contingency*. We apply these stimuli (such as praise) in the appropriate strength and frequency until the appearance of the desired behavior is as strong and as frequent as required. With children, tangible reinforcers such as toys and candy are used. Adults respond to money, usually. The strategy begins with finding the *appropriate type* and *strength* of reinforcing agent.

Using tangible reinforcers is very controversial since some claim it to be similar to bribing. This argument is not relevant here because bribery is "pay" before the act, whereas reinforcers are given after the act is performed. Tangible reinforcers have a place if they are *not* used: (1) to *control* others; (2) to reward an act required in *daily living*; (3) to stop undesirable behavior (such as giving ice cream to stop crying); (4) to *replace* intrinsic rewards (such as self-satisfaction); (5) to *affect* others *adversely* (such as favoritism with rewards). When tangible reinforcers are used, it is understood that they are an expedient to get the desired behavior more fixed and that they should be reduced as soon as possible. It is hoped that more *intrinsic* personal rewards will take their place and that people of all ages will outgrow their dependence on "gold stars." We must recognize, however, that people seemingly never outgrow their need for praise and affection, so these usually remain through life as powerful reinforcers in the helping process.

Generally, it is desirable not to use "if-statements" to get desired results, because they imply doubt about the person's willingness or ability to do the task. For example, one could say, "If you learn this vocabulary list, you can eat lunch." A preferred method is to say, "When you have completed this task, you can go outside."

A final word on strategy of reward is to *praise the action, not the person*. An example is, "I liked the way you helped Bob this morning, Jim," rather than, "You are a good boy, Jim, the way you help others."

This process may sound very mechanical and manipulative, but we are describing a behavior change technique used in an ethical context where these methods are used with the client's knowledge and consent. If we are interested in the effects of these methods on the group, we can use these same principles at a social system level. Individual performance can be made contingent on the group performance and vice versa. We may design double reinforcement contingencies for the person and the group. For example, we can influence the degree of support, cohesiveness, productivity, and level of responsible behavior in individuals and groups by planning a suitable system of rewards.

There are many opportunities to use rewards in helping interviews or groups. If we want the client, for example, to focus on feeling expression, our attention to these expressions, as well as overt praise, will tend to increase this behavior. If initiative in seeking information to solve his problems is important, there are many ways to show approval in a reinforcing manner. This discussion of reward should make us more aware of all aspects of our counselor behavior which have a reinforcing effect on the client's behavior.

Reinforcement has a decided effect on client interview behavior, as demonstrated by Ryan and Krumboltz (406). Using verbal reinforcers, such as "good" and "fine," and approval nods in decision-making interviews, they were able to effect significant increases in client deliberation and decision responses. Similarly, a study of rural youth in group settings done by Meyer, Strowig, and Hosford (320) revealed that information-seeking behavior can be increased considerably in eleventh graders by reinforcement methods. They found also that counselors could be taught to use these skills very quickly.

A summary of rewarding skills in the helping process follows:

1. *Reward performance*, not the person.
2. Determine the reward most *appropriate* to the client, considering unique interests, age, and setting.
3. Utilize *social* rather than tangible reinforcers.
4. Apply the reinforcer as *soon* after appearance of the desired behavior as possible.
5. As an *ethical* matter, obtain the understanding and permission of the client when using rewarding methods.

Extinguishing. Extinguishing skills are closely related to reinforcing methods since behavior gradually subsides and eventually disappears when it is not reinforced. Thus, the skill element for the counselor is applying extinction in systematic ways. Behavior can be changed by discontinuing the rewards. If the client wants to change an undesirable behavior, for example, the counselor assists him to identify the conditions that are reinforcing it and then removing or weakening them.

Characteristics of extinction are that: (1) *rates* of extinction are *variable* and depend upon the regularity of reinforcement, the effort required to perform, perceived changes in the reinforcement pattern, and the availability of alternate responses; (2) *avoidance behaviors* can be extinguished by prevention of punishing consequences; (3) behavior is *displaced* rather than lost since it can be reinstated quickly through reestablishing the reward schedule; (4) using extinction does *not guarantee* that more desirable behavior patterns will emerge.

Usually, after extinction of the undesirable behavior, efforts to elicit and reward desired behavior need to be undertaken. Behavior changes can be brought about most effectively by a *combination strategy* of extinguishing undesirable behavior along with modeling and reinforcing desirable behavior.

Methods of extinction include: (1) simple *removal of reinforcing conditions* (as in not attending to an overly talkative client); and (2) gradually *changing the external stimulus* for an undesirable behavior, for example, by exposing the person in small increments to a fearsome situation, where the fear is minimally elicited and the fear response is blocked. Gradually, the fear will be neutralized. One method for doing this is through "behavior rehearsal," a kind of role playing. The counselor and client play scenes from actual problem situations. The method works well with clients who want to be more assertive. In this case, the counselor poses problems for the client involving asking favors, making complaints, or refusing a request, in a gradual way, until the most difficult situations are encountered. Time is taken for critiquing the experience and for occasional modeling where the counselor takes the role of the client. The client is urged to try the new techniques under conditions where anxiety arousal is least probable. The advantage of this behavior-rehearsal method is that it involves the client in actively solving a close-to-life problem.

The main implication of extinction phenomena is to know how to change undesirable client behavior by removing the rewarding conditions. Does intense attending behavior, for example, always reward the desired client behavior? Are there some behaviors, such as tendencies to over-intellectualize, or to talk to the floor, that we would like to extinguish by altering the reinforcing stimuli? In summary, then, counselors can use extinction by showing the client how he can remove rewarding conditions for unwanted behavior. He can help, also, by neutralizing undesirable emotional behaviors, such as fear of crowds, by gradually exposing the client to fearsome situations and by helping him to avoid punishing consequences.

Aversive Control. This skill related to reinforcement and extinction involves a process of removing undesired behaviors through use of "punishing" or "aversive" stimuli. The principal theory of how aversive control works is that the punishing effect results in a conditioned fear which has an inhibiting or suppressing effect. Aversive control is used to help reduce undesirable and persistent responses which are self-reinforcing. Examples are self-punishing activities in children, and unwanted smoking, overeating, and drinking in adults. To be used successfully, however, aversive methods should be paired with a positive reinforcement program for desired behaviors. Usually, other forms of help are needed, since aversive control methods deprive the client of much pleasure. He must be unusually cooperative and desire behavior change intensely.

Elements of aversive control are: (1) Introduce an aversive stimulus at the *time the person is engaging in the unwanted behavior*. Standard efforts for problem drinkers, for example, have been to combine an emetic with the drink so as to cause nausea and vomiting. Dire warnings of impending cancer are given to smokers when they light up. Temporary banishment from the group is effected for stealing property. (2) Develop a *positive reinforcing schedule for new behaviors* when the noxious behavior has ceased. (3) Be alert to *undesirable side effects* such as excessive fear arousal or unwanted negative attitudes toward the counselor who suggested or administered the aversive stimulus.

Sometimes aversive consequences can be imagined with desirable effects. The client is asked to create the situation in his fantasy which is like the one he faces. For example, the client is having great trouble fighting with his demanding mother. He wants to avoid his strong responses, so with the aid of the counselor he can imagine his demanding mother and work out alternative responses to her.

Desensitization. Desensitization is a method of reducing the emotional responsiveness to threatening or unpleasant stimuli by introducing an activity which is incompatible with the threat response. Sometimes this process is known as "counterconditioning." For example, fear of speaking up in class is associated with an incompatible pleasant and relaxed feeling. The unpleasant response (fear) cannot be experienced when the pleasant response (relaxation) is present. Most desensitization activities are concerned with introducing relaxation in the imaginary presence of anxiety, although they have been used with feelings of anger and guilt also. Occasionally, desensitization is used in combination with modeling and reinforcement.

Desensitization methods were developed initially by Wolpe (504) and were refined by him and numerous other behavioral scientists. There are several steps in desensitization procedure: (1) discussion of conditions under which the problem occurs; (2) explanation of the method and its rationale, as a learning process, to the client; (3) relaxation training; (4) construction of an anxiety hierarchy; and (5) working through the hierarchy.

Steps 1 and 2 are straightforward explanation. Step 3, relaxation training, follows any of the various methods, such as Jacobson (242), for inducing relaxation. Step 4, hierarchy construction, is conducted at the same time as the relaxation training takes place. Essentially, the hierarchy is a list of twelve to fourteen anxiety-producing situations around the same theme, such as taking tests. These situations are ranked by the client from lowest anxiety at the top to highest anxiety at the bottom. It is desirable to go over the list with the client to determine the strength of each and the equality of intervals between items. They should be evenly spaced as to their potency in arousing anxiety. In the "fear of testing" example, they would be arranged from "waking up on the morning of the test" all the way to "opening the cover page of the test booklet."

The items in the hierarchy should be similar to, or represent, the client's real life experiences. They should be sufficiently detailed to help him imagine a clear image of the incident. Items should include a broad sample of situations where the feared incident, for example, might take place. The client should be able to see himself as actively involved rather than passively observing.

After the hierarchy is constructed and checked, the working-through process (Step 5) is begun. In the relaxed state, the client is asked to imagine a few neutral scenes, such as a path in the forest. Then, he is asked to project himself into the real problem and is given the top item in the hierarchy (lowest in anxiety). He is asked to indicate with a signal, such as raising an index finger, if he feels any anxiety. If so, relaxation exercises are undertaken again briefly. Then the counselor returns to the hierarchy, reading the same item, and proceeding in the same manner through the hierarchy. If successful, the client should still feel generally relaxed even after imagining the most potent anxiety-provoking situation on his list.

The following list is a summary of desensitizing skill utilization:

1. Discuss *problem* with the client.

2. Decide if desensitization is *applicable*. (Desensitization might be indicated when a special isolated fear situation needs to be faced.)

3. Teach *relaxation* routines.

4. Construct *hierarchy* with the client.

5. *Test hierarchy* for rank order of *potency* and *evenness* of intervals between items by asking client, "Which is more anxiety-provoking, A or B?"

6. Conduct *desensitization* by reading from the list, the least potent first, in about thirty-minute sessions.

7. Check for relaxation and *repeat items* from the hierarchy until relaxed— stop and go back to relaxation methods if the client cannot go on without anxiety.

8. Complete *entire hierarchy* (usually twelve to twenty items).

Semantic Analysis Strategies

Semantic analysis in counseling is more an approach to problems of communication than a series of techniques. The basic postulate of the semantics approach is that emotional disturbances arise largely from misuse of words, lack of clear understandings, and distorted meanings caused by malfunctioning of the client's symbolic processes. Through the use of clarification, restatement, and interpretive techniques, the client is helped to correct his faulty language habits. Ellis's rational psychotherapy (135) uses this technique heavily.

By using the semantic approach in discussions with client, counselors can correct faulty thinking clients may have concerning unrealistic ideals. The counselor, thereby, can prevent the frustration and disappointment which result from the client's efforts to achieve "success." Johnson (248) called the tendency to set unrealistic goals, the "IFD disease"—idealization, frustration, and demoralization. Enabling a client to define goals more accurately helps to avoid this semantic pitfall.

Clients who have difficulty in assigning accurate symbols to feelings and ideas present another type of problem in communication. One of the principal values of counseling is that it provides a verbal structure for emotions. The client becomes able to verbalize ambivalent feelings, for example, and to see that it is possible to construe one's self as having two opposing feelings toward the same person at the same time.

Counselors may use semantic analysis to correct loose thinking—another problem in communication. Loose thinking is generally accompanied by "ververbalization" and characterized by a frantic search for meaning. The individual who ververbalizes is really avoiding thinking. The counselor can encourage tighter thinking by asking the client frequently what he means by his statements, or by attempting to restate and clarify the ideas just stated by the client, or by encouraging longer pauses.

Sometimes rigid thinking, along with underverbalization, is symptomatic of semantic difficulties. The use of stereotypes, prejudice, dogmatism, single causes, absolutism, and "either-or" are examples of thinking difficulties of this type. The counselor can help clients to see, for example, that human traits are not dichotomous, but exist in all shades and combinations. Ellis's (136) rational approach to helping clients ferret out the faulty assumptions they make about themselves helps clients correct inaccurate conclusions about themselves. An example is, "I make mistakes; therefore, I am an incompetent person."

Semantic analysis, then, is an approach to the problem of expressing feelings by describing them accurately so that the client can handle them in a problem-solving manner, and so that he can see the relationship between his feelings and his thoughts. Semantic analysis also helps the counselor clarify meaning, tighten thinking, analyze assumptions, and make the client aware of his tendency to abstract and to confuse symbols with reality. Thus, the client can move closer to self-actualization when he stops asking vague questions and stops accepting ambiguous answers.

Bibliotherapy Strategies

The use of literature to help people with problems is a very old practice. Reading is used for two purposes in counseling—information and psychotherapy (commonly called bibliotherapy).

The Informational Use of Reading

The informational use of library materials covers such situations as educational and occupational study in career counseling, sex and marital education in family and marriage counseling, and religious instruction in pastoral counseling. Reading materials are used in these situations mainly to economize time in the counseling hour. The client is given the responsibility, for example, to look up material on training institutions for law or to read occupational pamphlets related to law as a career.

The counselor's suggestions for relevant reading are generally accepted without question by clients, although he must include some motivational factors to stimulate the client's independent exploration of the materials. The suggestions for reading are introduced at a time when the client seems to exhibit a need for information. Principles for using specific types of informational material will be covered in Part III on their applications to various human problems. It should be noted that many of the principles using bibliotherapeutic materials apply to general informational reading matter.

The key use of outside readings is to promote the idea of self-help, that is, that the client has capacities for developing his own problem-solving methods and generating solutions on his own initiative. This is not to say that reading about a problem leads to effective action regarding it; but it is a start.

The Bibliotherapeutic Function of Reading

In his review of the literature on bibliotherapy, Brower (71) indicated that there is little data bearing on the usefulness of bibliotherapeutic techniques. Many psychotherapeutic counselors, however, attest to its usefulness with certain types of clients. The intelligent client seems to make most use of this device.

There are two types of bibliotherapeutic literature. One type—fiction, biography, and inspirational literature—offers much in the way of varied expressions of human experience. Shrodes (442), for example, edited a volume entitled *Psychology Through Literature*, which is a compilation of excerpts from well-known literary works. The materials are classified into sections devoted to such topics as family life, economic pressures, and emotional conflicts. This approach to reading about human problems through literature helps the client to broaden his understanding of human motivation and culture conflicts. It is claimed also that literature offers the client the opportunity to share experience, which can be therapeutic. Many clients find that reading the Bible and other religious literature provides them with much emotional support.

The other type of bibliotherapeutic literature, on personal growth, is designed to give useful information for solving human problems and covers practical principles and facts on adjustment problems.

One of the values claimed for bibliotherapy in counseling is the time-saving feature. Reading materials, appropriate to the problem, serve as a device to start the client thinking about related features of his feelings. Often clients are so eager for information that the counselor may resist giving it to prevent the relationship from starting on a too highly intellectualized basis. Suggesting some special reading, however, satisfies the client's need for specific information, yet enables the counselor to avoid the tendency to get involved in a question-answer sequence. Such efforts are frequently resistance devices of the client.

A second value of therapeutic reading is that it provides the client with more familiarity with the terminology of testing, mental hygiene, defenses, and emotions in general. The semantics values for the client of finding more exact language to express ideas and feelings seem to be encouraged by proper reading.

A third value of therapeutic reading is that it stimulates thinking. The client runs across ideas which may increase his awareness. A mother, for example, finds that while she has been telling her child that she loves him, she has not been accepting many of his characteristics. The child, in turn, interprets the mother's behavior not as loving but as rejecting. Reading about such ideas encourages clients to do their own interpreting.

Bibliotherapy, as a final value, enables the counselor to give support. When a client is anxious about his problems it may help to read about such problems. He finds that others have the same feelings and same problems. He discovers that his marital difficulties, for example, are not as unique as he thought.

Limitations of Bibliotherapy

We have pointed out some of the functions of bibliotherapy which are cited by psychotherapists as being helpful for some clients. Bibliotherapy has apparent limitations as well. One of the foremost is based on the fact that people tend to rationalize their problems when they read about them. Hence, any readiness for counseling which they may have had could be reduced, and their neurotic defenses could tend to become aggravated rather than diminished. Reading would become a type of resistance to, or even substitute for, going ahead with a plan of psychotherapeutic counseling.

A second limitation of bibliotherapy is that it encourages the client to think that the reading is helping him to solve his problems. Unless the reading is carefully described as being an aid to counseling, the client may substitute the vicarious participation and pseudo-insight he gains from the reading for the painful experience of genuine growth to be gained from the counseling relationship itself. It is estimated that few behaviors are changed through reading. It is feared also that too many of the so-called insights achieved through reading turn out to be as ineffective and elusive as the New Year's resolution.

There are, in addition, the clients whose anxieties are reinforced by reading about emotional problems. They see themselves in every case and, if suggestible, acquire more symptoms for their defense repertoire. This personalizing tendency is particularly acute in paranoid individuals and in clients with weak defense systems.

Principles in Using Bibliotherapy

Knowledge of the books the counselor recommends is a first principle. The counselor who refers clients to books with which he is not familiar runs the risk of misleading them and might fail to meet their needs or their level of sophistication. Missing the client's level of understanding could have deleterious effects on rapport. This principle puts a severe burden on a counselor to keep abreast of literature and to keep the titles in his immediate memory. This familiarity enables him to suggest books not only appropriate from a content standpoint but also for age, experience, and language level.

The counselor should *evidence confidence* in the suggested reading to interest the client in it and to make sure that he considers the ideas presented in it. Readings are *suggested* rather than prescribed.

Timing is a third significant principle the counselor must consider to ensure that his client properly understands and accepts the idea of reading. The counselor does not want to convey the idea that the client's problem is so simple it can be solved by reading a book rather than working it out through the counseling process. Neither does the counselor want to convey by poorly timed suggestions that he can no longer help the client and that reading might be a way out of the therapeutic impasse. A significant timing principle is to make the suggestions during a period of low resistance. The counselor who suggests readings at a time when the client is struggling with a feeling or when he is rolling toward insight will annoy him and be considered as lacking understanding.

Discussion of the results of the client's reading is important to ascertain the effect the reading had upon him. The client can ask questions and point out ideas which were especially valuable. Often, related passages can be read aloud for clarity. It is very important that distortions and misunderstandings be corrected at this point and that a realistic evaluation of the ideas is made. Some significant questions are: How authoritative was the writer? How recent is the material? Some books written in the twenties and thirties do not reflect current psychological thought. Are opinion and fact clearly differentiated? So many popular writers are not scrupulous about the factual bases of their opinions.

Lists of suggested readings and mimeographed tables of contents can be used to stimulate reading. Books and pamphlets, often with passages underlined, can be left in the waiting room for clients to browse through and to borrow. Often the browsing itself directs a client's thought process and produces significant material for the counseling hour. The following is an example:

C1: I was reading an article in one of the journals in the waiting room. It discussed reasons why people are apt to create marital problems for themselves. I don't believe that writer had all the answers. I could think of some reasons that the author didn't mention.

Smaller doses of reading seem to be more helpful than larger amounts. A pithy article or pamphlet is often more helpful than a book. It is easier for the counselor to pinpoint his suggestion in a short work, since so much material extraneous to the client's immediate concern may distract him and dilute the emphasis desired.

Summary

Information and action strategies are important to counseling. The use of advice and suggestion is appropriate under some counseling conditions. The principal danger in advice-giving is that it often becomes a projection of the counselor's needs and values. Procedures designed to solve problems and change behavior directly through self-helping methods are suggested. Tests of personality, interest, aptitude, and achievement are widely used informational tools designed to give the client information about himself with which he can make wiser decisions. Tests are highly technical devices necessitating special training in their careful selection and use. Semantics principles help the client to sharpen his ability to think about his problems and to communicate more clearly. Informational reading and bibliotherapy are techniques designed to give the client valid ideas for use in planning his future and solving his present problems. Methods for helping a client move from awareness to action are covered.

Group Principles
and Methods

The Human Potential Framework

In 1968 Carl Rogers wrote of the burgeoning group movement:

> The Encounter Group is perhaps the most significant social invention of this century. The demand for it is utterly beyond belief. It is one of the most rapidly growing social phenomena in the United States. It has permeated industry, is coming into education, is reaching families, professionals in the helping fields, and many other individuals. (398, p. 3)

In this chapter we deal with this significant social invention, as well as with more traditional group therapy methods. Group methods are part of the larger Human Potential movement, consisting of a variety of interpersonal and intrapersonal growth methods for developing individual potential. The Association for Humanistic Psychology and the Division of Humanistic Psychology of the American Psychological Association are two key organizations spearheading this movement.

Group methods are growing in popularity, not so much as clinical methods to help the seriously disturbed, but as media for assisting the already functional person to achieve higher levels of functioning and awareness. This awareness in turn can lead to increased effectiveness, greater humanness, and further actualizing of his or her potentials. Present trends indicate group approaches may largely supplant individual counseling and psychotherapy because of their effectiveness in leading to behavior change. The increased attendance at group events has removed much of the social stigma of any kind of help, since groups appeal to people already functioning effectively. Groups are perceived as laboratories for trying

11

314

out new behaviors and styles of interactions. Group techniques are used widely in collaboration with individual approaches, however, and are not designed to supplant individual work entirely.

Task groups, in contrast with growth groups, focus on problem-solving and specific agenda functions, such as committees. In this chapter we deal with growth groups only. Organizational development, which focuses on the organization as the client system, deals with group issues of problem-solving, goal-setting, communicating, and leadership development. These group functions in the organizational context are also beyond the scope of this book.

Distinctions between counseling and psychotherapy cited in Chapter 1 hold for multiple counseling and group psychotherapy. The term "multiple counseling" seems to have wider usage than group counseling in educational settings. The focus is on group dynamic and interpersonal skills rather than on basic personality changes. The T-group is a special educational group form where the members focus on improving their communication skills and interaction styles in the laboratory atmosphere of the group. The Bradford, Gibb, and Benne collection of papers (63) presents a rich fare of theory and practice with T-groups. "Group psychotherapy," conversely, has been a standard term for many years for a problem-centered, crisis-oriented method of clinic and private practice settings. The most significant differences between the two terms are intensity of emotional involvement and agency setting. Multiple counseling groups, which are generally conducted in schools, work on a common theme, interest, or problem area, such as academic achievement or getting along with parents. Multiple counseling deals more with present attitudes and behaviors and less with past difficulties and intrapersonal problems. Exploration of feeling usually is more controlled during multiple counseling than in group psychotherapy, which not only permits, but encourages, members to express intensive core feelings. For example, during group therapy a member would elaborate on such feelings as his intense hatred of women in his past and present life, or his deep anxieties about loneliness. This intensive therapeutic approach is more applicable to clinics and private practice settings, although, as counselors in educational agencies gain more skill and public acceptance, these distinctions will tend to disappear. Family group therapy activities in some schools are examples of a breakthrough.

A number of additional terms are used commonly in group literature. Group dynamics refers to the general principles of group interaction and communication. Groups are described variously as "sensitivity" training (largely obsolete), "T-groups" (mentioned above), "encounter" groups (from existential viewpoints), and "conjoint" family groups. Applications of group principles stressing openness with feelings, leading to self-awareness and improved human relations, have been made to industrial, educational, governmental, clinical, church, and family settings. These general approaches emphasize personal growth for people already functioning well, rather than solving intense personal problems. They also differ from counseling and therapy groups in their emphasis on the "here and now" of present group interaction and communication skills, rather than on problems and feelings of the past. The spread of the T-group model for improving human relationships has great portent for the future. If many people can become skilled group leaders in family, community, and work settings, and if the trend toward greater public acceptance of human relations training continues, there is the likelihood of a "chain reaction" toward improved human relations. This, hopefully, will lead to confidence in people helping one another and using experts mainly as teachers of leaders and as monitors of group development experiences. This development could be a potent force in counteracting the alienation, fractionation, and dehumanization felt particularly by persons living in cities and working in large organizations.

Developments in Group Work

Actualization Groups

Developments in group work such as the Actualization Group, Assertiveness Training, Consciousness Raising, and Life Planning are focused extensions of basic group work. These intensive group experiences are conducted for periods as long as twelve weeks or as short as a two-day weekend. There is a dual emphasis—didactic (lectures, films, demonstrations), and experiential (exercises and encounter groups). An example of an actualization group in action is the "Actualization Group" film (439).

A fundamental theory of actualization groups and workshops proposed by Shostrom (434) is: "The group is the individual turned inside out." By understanding the various manipulative patterns shown by members of a group, they learn to see potentials that exist within themselves. Shostrom and Satir describe four manipulative response forms—avoiding, blaming, conniving, and placating. The basic theory of group change is to create an actualizing person with characteristics of contacting, affirming, confronting, and engaging.

The Actualizing Model Applied to Group Work

This approach draws heavily from the group encounter and group therapy literature of the past twenty years. We try to synthesize these varied approaches into a model for the actualizing group. For example: the feeling emphasis of the client-centered approach is prominent; the interpersonal skills element of the National Training Laboratory T-group model is a strong feature; the confrontational strategy of Perls' Gestalt approach is evident; the body methods of Lowen are included; and the open encounter emphases of Schutz are part of the Actualizing model. A unique feature of the Actualizing model, however, is its emphasis on evaluation and measurement strategies to assess outcomes through instruments, such as the Actualizing Assessment Battery.

Goals of Actualizing Groups. The goals of actualizing group work cover broad outcomes to match the Actualizing model values cited in Chapter 3, as well as the specific outcomes expected by individual participants. While Freud stressed that the general goals of psychoanalysis were to love more deeply and hate more wisely, we believe that one can love more deeply and be angry more appropriately. One can be strongly self-expressive, and yet be responsive to one's perceived weaknesses. We see the group process as providing a unique learning setting for growth on these broad polarities. Because of the emphasis on individuality and actualizing for each person, the focus must also be on the specific growth goals each person brings to the group.

Working with Polarities in the Group. This section is based upon the discussion of the Actualizing model of Chapter 3 and is linked to the theory in the following manner. The basic polarities functioning within each person are represented as the intersecting whorls in each circle (representing each group member) in Figure 19. Within the person there is a rhythm between his own primary polarities and the polarities of other members of the group, represented by the lines linking the individual circles in Figure 19. This process broadens each person's perspective of the group and the various roles developing for each.

Group Energy. The group has its special energy system, much more complex than the dyadic relationship in individual work. This energy field in a group is experienced by the perceptive members; but it is a difficult phenomenon to capture and study in any reliable manner. Yet, experienced leaders have known about the group energy phenomenon for some time. In a small group of eight to ten persons, each person seems to radiate an energy field up to several feet. This common experience is illustrated when a prominent or particularly powerful person enters a room. John Kennedy is reputed to have had this effect on people. His energy was perceived immediately. In terms of implications for group work strategy, Schutz (419) emphasizes the importance of assessing and following the energy of the group. Signs of such energy are the postural and voice cues exhibiting stress or enthusiasm, for example. Contrast this phenomenon with the low level of energy associated with intellectual discussion of problems or outside issues.

Power. Another issue to be perceived and dealt with effectively in the actualizing group is how power and influence are used. They may be used in manipulative or actualizing ways and can have enormous influence on a group in either direction. For more details on managing manipulative in-

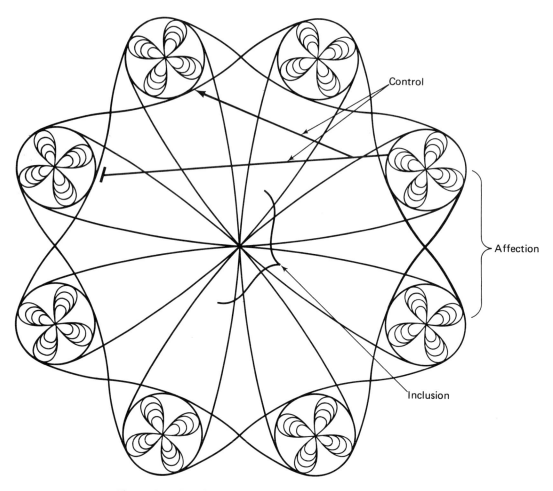

Figure 19. Polarities in the Actualizing Group. Adapted from E. L. Shostrom, L. Knapp, and R. Knapp, *Actualizing Therapy* (432, p. 192).

fluence in a group and developing more balance in active and passive participation, consult *Actualizing Therapy* (432). For example, one implication of balancing power roles in a group is the practice of selecting group members, sometimes called "hawks," who have strong aggressive influence already, and less assertive and influential members, sometimes called "doves." The potential awareness of these polarities in individual members with this kind of selection offers, for example, greater opportunities for individual growth along this polarity.

Expression of Interpersonal Needs in the Group. Three basic interpersonal needs have been identified by Schutz (419)—inclusion, control, and affection. We use them to help understand the interactions of the group and the individual needs of the members. These dimensions are identified in Figure 19. By inclusion is meant feelings of being prominent, significant, or worthwhile as a group member. It manifests itself, as indicated in Figure 19, as a reaching out and focusing of energy toward the center of the group. It means searching for togetherness, belongingness, attention, and response. This may take manipulative forms, if thwarted, as if the person were saying to himself, "I'll make them pay attention to me in any way I can."

The second need to be concerned about in actualizing groups is control —the need to manipulate others, have authority over them, or dominate them. It may be expressed as a polarity in the form of need to be dominated or manipulated. These polarities are represented in Figure 19 as the attack ($\leftarrow$) or push ($\vdash$) symbols. Confronting behaviors such as blaming, attacking, controlling, and conniving are examples.

The third need is affection, for close relationships between group members. It usually takes place in pairs (dyads), rather than in some global group-loving sense. It is expressed in the symbolic form of the embrace ($\times$) in Figure 19. Again, polarities are involved as expressions of affection directly or avoidance of closeness.

General Stages of Group Growth. Inclusion: These same need dimensions cited above describe Schutz's (419) conceptions of group growth. Inclusion is the first stage, where new members express concern about how much in or out of the process they see themselves. It is a time of decision on how much commitment to the group one is going to make. It is a time of keen concern about how each member sees himself in relationship to the total group, that is, where he fits in. This anxiety is expressed, for example, in overtalking, withdrawal, exhibitionistic behaviors, or telling descriptive stories about previous group experiences.

Control. When the group has become somewhat established, concerns are expressed about who is in charge, who administers the sanctions and rewards, how much power does a member have. Manipulations through both strength and weakness strategies become apparent. Attacks on the leader (often in the form of questioning his competence) become evident, as examples, at this stage.

Affection. When issues of control are resolved, affection concerns become prominent. Positive feelings, as well as hostility, are expressed to one another. Jealousies and pairings become evident. There is heightened emotional expression generally.

The tire-changing metaphor is useful here. Just as the mechanic tightens each wheel nut enough to keep the wheel in place, so each person in the group is attended to "once over lightly" early in the process in terms of his feelings. Then the bolts are tightened further until the wheel is firmly in place. Similarly, each member's needs for inclusion, control, and affection are worked through until they are satisfied.

Separation. In most groups this is a critical stage of development. For continuous groups, where members leave one at a time, this is not a key issue; but the weekend encounter group, or the ten-week group, must face termination feelings. As groups terminate, they tend to resolve their affection, control, and inclusion needs in reverse fashion. First, personal feelings (positive and negative) are dealt with. Next, discussion often focuses on the leader and how the group members have rebelled at or complied with his methods. Finally, the group discusses the feelings of termination and the possibilities of continuing the group. Sometimes the "fantasy reunion" phenomenon occurs here when the group makes elaborate plans to come together at a future time, names and addresses are exchanged, but the future meeting rarely occurs.

Family Groups

Group methods with families have become very popular with agencies and private practitioners. Some school systems described by Zwetschke and Grenfell (514) have developed family counseling programs as a means of helping children make a better adaptation to the learning environment through improved home environments. Whole families come to the sessions, sometimes for one to three days over a weekend. McGregor (299) reports such a successful family counseling venture with a combination of group and individual interviews over a three-day period. Usually a crisis precipitates the process, and the family can change quickly under conditions of high motivation.

Satir's system of conjoint family therapy (413) is a particularly significant development in group methods. According to Satir, most individual therapy deals with an "identified patient." But to treat him alone is impossible without understanding his role and status, as well as the values and norms of the interpersonal group from which he comes.

A family is an individualized system of feeders and the fed, directors and the directed, supporters and the supported. A client is someone having a problem of growth in the family. His problem in part is deciding what he needs to do to survive in this system. A symptom is a behavior which is considered sick, bad, stupid, or crazy by members of the family system. It always takes at least two people to make a behavior: the feeder and the one fed.

Satir stresses that group communication is always at two levels: the literal and the metacommunicative. This second level is the message about the message, since it covers feelings and intentions toward the receiver. Family therapy deals largely with these message levels and patterns.

Satir classifies communication patterns in five groups or targets:

1. Where the literal message is one of *agreement*
   Where the affective message is *pleasing and placating*
2. Where the literal message is *disagreement*
   Where the affective message is *blaming and attacking*

3. Where the literal message is *changing the subject*
   Where the affective message is *being irrelevant or withdrawing*
4. Where the literal message is *being reasonable*
   Where the affective message is *conniving*
5. Where the literal message is *reporting oneself*
   Where the affective message is *making a place for others*

Family therapy is an attempt to get families into pattern or target 5 above. This process of actualizing communication is illustrated in the film "Target 5" (414). Typically, according to Satir, when Father plays the "pleaser" (pattern 1), Mother plays the "blamer" (pattern 2), and child plays "irrelevant" and withdraws (pattern 3), we may have a schizophrenic family! Often, the child's communication "games" evolve from the interaction that he sees and hears in the family. In effect, the child is conditioned to behave with certain communicative patterns as he grows up. Thus, family therapy is a form of de-conditioning/malfunctioning communication patterns.

Satir utilizes behavior therapy techniques in the following ways:

1. Many of the communication patterns of family members reflect fear. Even psychiatric labels are reflections of fear communication patterns. The paranoid, for example, is constantly fearful that the senders are criticizing him. Clients with schizoid tendencies garble their messages out of fear of being understood! Thus, one of the basic techniques of good therapy, and especially family therapy, is that technique of *de-conditioning fears.*

2. Therapeutic methods are also very supportive, especially of the younger family members. Therapeutic support is a companion method for de-conditioning.

3. Communication patterns which are clear and direct instead of phony and manipulative are *rewarded.*

4. Finally, the leader behaves in the family group session as a *model,* doing and saying that which will encourage similar behavior in the family.

Satir suggests a definition of transference as it relates to the interpersonal system of the family, *viz.,* relating to another in terms of certain *expectations* from one's past. For example, if there were no anger allowed to be expressed in his family, the client would transfer this same expectation to the therapist. Patients in mental hospitals have been known to improve greatly while there because that was the expectation of the therapeutic community. Then, when they return to the family system, the expectation is that they will flop, which they often do!

This discussion of transference reemphasizes the importance of family therapy. If the client's behavior toward the therapist is characteristic of his communications with mother and father, why not help the client deal with the family more *directly* by seeing the client and family together? This removes the burden of change from the identified client only. He

*Group Principles
and Methods*

can be seen as someone who is already trying to change his family's system of behaving. If he is seen alone and is urged to increase his efforts by himself, he often receives more intense criticism from his family.

Communication training is considered by Satir as a central feature of family therapy. She differentiates between the functional and the dysfunctional communicator. The functional communicator:

1. Firmly states his case.
2. Clarifies and qualifies.
3. Asks for feedback.
4. Considers feedback.

Dysfunctional communicators are vague and send incomplete messages. They use pronouns vaguely, such as "it," "we," and so on. They often do not send messages at all and then behave as if they have.

According to Satir, *all messages are requests.* Whenever a person is communicating he is not only making a statement, he is also trying to influence the receiver, or to ask something of him. The receiver, in turn, must respond, because people cannot avoid communicating. Family therapy, therefore, is a workshop on message-sending and message-receiving skills in a family setting.

Marathon Groups

Intensive group work is known as "marathon therapy." This development has been described by a number of writers, especially Bach (28). It is an intensive, living-in kind of therapeutic experience with a group of about twelve, a therapist, and a co-therapist or two. It may go on for twenty-four hours or more, with little time taken for vital functions. The total honesty and free expression of feelings over an intensive and extensive period of time results in greater transparency of feelings for some than would more spaced sessions. Marathon groups are not necessarily "one-shot" sessions, since follow-up sessions are conducted frequently. Sometimes a weekend is spent, with three intensive sessions interspersed with short sleep periods. Most evaluative data are in the form of personal testimonials about how one's life style has changed. Few data are available about the permanence of changes when participants return to Monday morning routines without reinforcement for new-found gains. One criticism is that current practitioners do not screen candidates for marathon groups with sufficient care; a person with weak defenses or latent emotional crises would be especially vulnerable.

Research on Groups

Abundant research comparing group and individual methods with controls has appeared in the last few years. Results are conflicting because of the difficulty in specifying the methods of the counselor. Some groups are more effective and some individual counselors are more effective, depending on the peculiar characteristics of the counselor. Combinations of methods appear to be most efficacious in behavior change. A study by Katahn, Strenger, and Cherry (254) is an example. They used group counseling with a form of systematic desensitization with test-anxious college students. Results indicated a significant rise in grade average and a reduction of measurable anxiety.

Questions for additional research are: What personality changes are effected by group process? How do these changes affect behavior and how permanent are they? What undesired "side effects" of group process take place? Are group experiences deleterious to the welfare of some persons? What are the best combinations of individual and group experience to maximize growth? What are the best time intervals and lengths of sessions for maximum growth? Are marathon sessions more effective than spaced sessions? What kinds of persons can profit most by group experiences? How can trust conditions be accelerated in groups? Are certain group experiences, such as T-groups, more effective in changing attitudes and traits than other types of educational experiences? What is the effect of leadership style on group outcomes?

A productive application of group methods is to use the group leader as a change agent in a social system. More research is needed on organizational development and planned change through group process. Productivity of small leaderless groups compared to more structured groups is also a continuing subject of research. See Bradford, Gibb, and Benne (63) and Havelock's change agent's guide (218).

Group Effectiveness. The question whether group techniques do, in fact, yield enduring positive personality change (Gibb 188), or actually result in psychological damage in some cases (Yalom, Lieberman, and Miles 511) has only recently been subjected to objectively quantified assessment. After analyzing 106 studies, as well as examining 123 additional studies and 24 recent doctoral disserations, Gibb stated, "The evidence is strong that intensive group training experiences have therapeutic effects. . . . Changes do occur in sensitivity, ability to manage feelings, directionality of motivation, attitudes toward the self, attitudes toward others, and interdependence" (in 389, p. 117). The term "interdependence" refers to interpersonal competence, teamwork in problem-solving, and effectiveness as a group member. Because interdependence is also one of the chief goals of Actualizing Counseling and Therapy, we believe Gibb's research summary is significant.

Yalom, Lieberman, and Miles conducted a study of encounter groups in which 210 Stanford undergraduates were divided randomly into seventeen different groups. Two of the groups were led only by tape-recorded instructions, and the others were led by professionals whose philosophical approaches included Gestalt, Transactional Analysis, Synanon games, "Esalen eclectic," and others. In contrast to Gibb, the Stanford researchers found the rate of casualties to be an "alarming and unacceptable" 10 percent. Casualties were defined in terms of psychiatric problems such as severe depression. Chances of "clear, positive benefit" proved to be about one in three. Only 16 percent of the participants had "peak experiences" during the course of the groups. Gimmicks and structured exercises did not prove especially valuable. In conclusion, Yalom, Lieberman, and Miles emphasize that it is important to keep deep respect for the self-preservatory functions of defenses, and that to encourage attack in an effort to dislodge a person from familiar defenses is cruel and often counterproductive. The Yalom study also has implications for leadership style. Those leaders with either a strong, confrontative style or a pronounced laissez faire, low-key style were least effective and had the largest number of group "casualties."

The results of the Yalom study confirm certain tenets of Actualizing Counseling and Therapy. Expressing anger is good, but sustained levels of anger are unproductive and need to be balanced by love and support. Furthermore, the study concludes that both feeling *and* thinking need to be expressed in the group, in contrast to the Rogerian emphasis on feeling only. The results also refute the layman's myth that one should use only his head and deny his feelings and body signals.

Outcome Studies with the Personal Orientation Inventory (POI). The Personal Orientation Inventory has been a major instrument used in studies on group effectiveness. In a recently published review of instruments in human relations training, Pfeiffer and Heslin have noted:

> The POI, perhaps more than any other instrument described in this book, measures the things talked about by people in human relations training. For this reason it is an excellent training device. It awakens people to important dimensions of life and ways of viewing the world and themselves that they may well not have considered previously (363, p. 100).

Many of the early studies considered here contained a number of methodological shortcomings, but because of the importance of objective data in this area, a review and integration of findings to date seems appropriate.

The POI has been successful particularly in measuring the effectiveness of group work in a variety of settings. For example, of fifteen studies reviewed by Knapp (432), seven dealt with adult samples, seven with college student samples, and one with high school student samples. Eight of these fifteen studies incorporated a control group. Sample sizes, an important factor in statistical interpretation, ranged from 14 to 135, with results in four of these studies being based on responses from fewer than 30 subjects. Perhaps of greatest importance in the review of these studies, however, are the effects of such variables as length of time over which the changes are evaluated and comparisons of the effects of different encounter techniques. Before undertaking studies evaluating effects of such variables upon outcome of the encounter group experience, adequate measurement techniques are required. As mentioned, the availability of the POI has accelerated research in this area.

A number of studies have demonstrated changes in self-actualizing following encounter group experience. A summary of the results of these major studies is presented in Shostrom (432).

To examine the effects of a program of Transcendental Meditation on self-actualizing, Seeman, Nidich, and Banta (423) administered the POI to an experimental group of twenty college students, and to a control group of twenty, prior to the initiation of the program and two months following completion of the program. The mean difference for the experimental group on the Outer/Inner support dimension was significantly higher than that for the control group. Significant mean changes in the positive direction were also obtained on five other scales.

A number of controlled studies using the POI as a criterion have demonstrated significant changes, immediately and after three months, as a result of human relations training (Alperson, Alperson, and Levine 7, Banmen and Capelle 32 and 33, Bebout and Gordon 39, Byrd 84, and Reddy 376). These representative studies cover high school student, high school teacher, church professional, and general adult populations. In the area of military drug treatment programs, Knapp and Fitzgerald (268) report significant before and after changes on five scales of the POI.

The studies reported above are based on the criterion of self-report of changes taking place as a result of group experience. While the POI has been demonstrated to be a sensitive instrument with which to systematize and assess these self-reports, there is always the big question of what these perceptual changes mean in behavior. Does the participant in an actualizing group really move into actualizing behaviors?

The question of "faking" to look better on a post-test looms large also. This issue has been studied with the POI. While knowing the concepts and rationale of the POI makes it possible to improve one's score, it is fairly resistant to efforts to make a good impression (Braun and LaFaro 67, Wareheim, Routh, and Foulds 489).

Group Dynamics Principles

The principles which underlie groups at work may be classified into three categories: leader behaviors, discussant behaviors, and content analysis. Students of group dynamics can utilize the following outline for analyzing group behavior in terms of the three categories.

Typical Leader Behaviors

Groups may function with varying degrees of leadership ranging from leaderless to a strong professional group leader. Berzon and Solomon (48) present a series of studies illustrating the growing interest in leaderless group methods for encounter and therapy groups. Under some circumstances, self-directed groups using prepared program materials were feasible and effective in changing behavior.

The importance of leadership style for producing destructive as well as constructive outcomes was emphasized in the Yalom study cited above. This study found that leaders who were extremely active or passive had the least constructive outcomes. Implicit in the Actualizing model is a leader behavior characterized by more active participation and responsibility than the more nondirective style of leadership. Yet, the leader does not dominate the group. He tries to "read the group" in a sensitive manner and does what appears most appropriate to achieve the actualizing goals of the group. He leads actively in terms of giving information, making process observations, or using confrontative or supportive interventions as indicated. He tries to model actualizing behavior as much as possible himself without setting himself up as a paragon of such growth. The following list is suggestive of the various possible group maintenance functions performed by a facilitator of an actualizing group. These are general process behaviors. More specific strategies and methods are presented later in the chapter.

Problem Setting. In a problem- or issue-oriented group, the leader states the issue or question to which the group is to address itself. This may occur at the outset or at various points in the discussion. The statement is made without indication of what solution should be reached or which side the leader favors.

Process Moderating. The leader calls on some members or asks others to withhold comment; he may ask for order or attention. This category has nothing to do with content of the discussion but only with the process.

Sentiment Testing. The leader seeks to learn the balance of opinion in the group. He may call for a show of hands or he may simply state his impression of the trend of opinion and ask for confirmation.

Idea Developing. The leader seeks to aid in the clarification and development of ideas before the group by restating, summarizing, or contrasting them. He does not inject new material, but, by his handling of what has been said, seeks to make issues more clear or to insure more general understanding.

Monitoring. The leader reminds the group of limits and constraints under which it is operating (for example, time limits, authority bounds, ground rules).

Energizing. The leader seeks to motivate the group to its self-assigned task. He may cite reasons for its work or simply enjoin the group to greater activity or chide it for inactivity.

Group Serving. The leader may perform service functions for the group (for example, keeping notes, recording on a blackboard, distributing paper, adjusting lighting). There may be no verbal aspect to this function.

Content Participating. The leader takes part in the discussion, as another member, without exercising his leadership functions in any way.

Leaders also utilize certain *process facilitation techniques* with a view toward carrying forward the discussion of their group. The following list is a partial compilation of such techniques:

Initiating. The leader proposes new ideas, procedures, or orientation. Major content is not derived from previous work of the group but mainly from "within" the current speakers.

Amending. The leader develops ideas already before the group. He may add new "twists," but basically he modifies more than he initiates.

Supporting. The leader lends emphasis, reason, or other aid to ideas already before the group. He does not seek to change them, but only to accelerate their acceptance.

Opposing. The leader may question, challenge, or detract from ideas before the group. He may seek to change them and to influence the group to reject them.

Summarizing. The leader brings out common or contrasting ideas before the group, reduces issues to essentials, and focuses or clarifies points.

Controlling. The leader may seek to control who will talk, when, or how much; he may intercede for less vocal members.

Informing. The leader provides information to the group (sometimes in response to a question), often simply to supply data, but he may have a secondary intent to influence the group. However, the main aspect of this function is to transmit facts or what are offered as facts.

Member Behaviors

Although members often utilize some of the foregoing techniques also, it is possible to identify certain unique characteristics of member behavior.

Frequency and Volume. Occasionally groups are concerned about participation norms. Here a process observer can perform a useful function. Participant frequency of each group member can be found simply by tallying each of the group member's responses. When a member speaks for a longer than average period, the tally can be underlined. When the volume is particularly loud, the tally can be blackened so as to indicate the strength of the response.

Types of Appeal. In any discussion, the speaker's appeals and group influence can be determined. Sometimes this influence will be grossly explicit and sometimes more subtle. Some examples follow:

Appeal to reason and logic . . . . "it seems only reasonable"
Appeal to interest . . . . "should be interesting"
Appeal to sanity . . . . "don't be foolish"
Appeal to decorum and good taste . . . . "not in mixed company"
Appeal to enjoyment . . . . "might be fun to . . ."
Appeal to a need, such as dependence . . . . "would help us to . . ."

Indirect Influences. Many influences on group members are implicit and indirect, since they are not a part of the topic or discussion content. Some examples are: personal characteristics (sex differences, age differences, physical-size differences); status characteristics (vocation, position, community or civic activity, educational background, experience); and nonverbal "signaling" techniques (contrasting voice volume, pounding the table, sex appeal, fidgeting and restlessness, silence followed by strong activity, staring). In making these observations, it is useful to watch for individuals whose behaviors are at variance with those of the group as a whole—for example, those who make a soft-spoken response when everybody else has been shouting. Thus, though one may watch a particular individual, it is well to be aware of the whole group as a frame of reference.

Influence Patterns. Certain persons in the group seem to have the power to be "addressed to" more than others. Some group members seem to draw and often monopolize the attention and expressions of the group.

Some process observations focus on *content* of the group's work. The following are examples:

Topical Development. In listening to a discussion, particular attention can be given to the "life history" of the topics. Though it is not possible or necessarily desirable to be highly precise about this historical analysis, nevertheless, the following scheme can help: How does the topic arise—from one individual, from the interactions of several members, from some other topic? How does the group work with the topic—by arguing contrasting aspects of it, by illustrations and examples, by emotional appeals, by responding to the influence of particular members? What changes occur in the topic as the group works on it—a part gradually displaces the topic as a whole, it is expanded and generalized, it is gradually lost sight of, it is thoroughly examined and concluded? What is the eventual fate of the topic—it is dropped, it becomes a part of the group's product, it is blended with other topics?

Topical Concurrence. By concurrence is meant the degree to which a second speaker seems to understand, accept, and extend the subject matter of the first speaker. The second speaker does not necessarily agree with the first, but he stays with the same general ideas. Often he builds on the previous idea. Following is a scale demonstrating four types of concurrence:

1. Concurring: No new content areas are opened; there is direct agreement or disagreement or repetition.

Speaker A: "I think we should try to get more time to do the job."

Speaker B: "I agree"; or "I don't think we need any more time"; or "Yeah, we don't have enough time."

2. Expanding: The same basic content area is covered, but it is expanded, developed, amplified, or illustrated. The next logical step is taken, or a direct challenge to the preceding remarks is made without bringing in a new focus of attention.

Speaker A: "I think we should try to get more time to do the job."

Speaker B: "If they want more than a hasty piece of work, we certainly need more time"; or "There's no use seeking more time until we've seen what we can do as it is"; or "Look, if we've got to plan the next meeting, arrange for the speaker, and do all those other things, then we've got to have more time."

3. Altering: The topic as covered by the first speaker is only generally the same as that covered by the new speaker; a major change of emphasis or application is made; the ideas previously expressed are given quite a different turn.

Speaker A: "I think we should try to get more time to do the job."

Speaker B: "Yeah, we certainly need it to settle this question about whether to have a lecture or a film. If we're going to use a film, we have to decide which one. I think it should be . . ."; or "No, it isn't more time we need; it's more good ideas; time won't help us until we start really producing. . . ."

4. Changing: The previously expressed ideas are ignored or given only a perfunctory recognition in what is essentially a new topical development.

Speaker A: "I think we should try to get more time to do the job."

Speaker B: "Yes, that's a good idea. Now about those films we were talking about. It seems to me that . . ."; or "What's the name of that film we saw last week?"

General Considerations in Group Therapy Procedure

While the preceding discussion pertained to general group functions, the following material applies especially to growth and therapy groups. Usually when the client comes for therapy, he is seen individually by the therapist first, so that the therapist knows the client well before he places him in a group. A group is selected which seems to meet the needs of the client, as well as the client's meeting the needs of the group. The client may then continue to meet his therapist individually once a week and also work in his group once a week. He may reduce the number of individual visits, depending on the setting and problem.

In multiple counseling, clients are usually selected because of common characteristics, such as underachievement or behavior problems. They usually do not obtain collateral individual counseling.

Selection of Group Members

Background. One of the first questions that usually arises is, "Who should be in a group?" For a long time, counselors and therapists suggested that members be selected according to diagnostic problem categories. Joel and Shapiro (246) contend that problems and dynamics should be relatively similar, but that diagnostic categories should be forgotten. Winder (501) holds that, whenever possible, the members should be chosen so as to have fairly homogeneous backgrounds. This opinion is shared by Coffey (99). Cohen (102), however, feels that a calculated attempt should be made to include varied personality types in the composition of each group: for example, one or two outspoken or aggressive individuals, several mature and stable personalities, and several depressed, anxious members. From experiments with grouping of individuals for therapy, Glatzer (194) found that judicious groupings of varied personalities was important for optimum therapeutic movement. Powdermaker and Frank (370) concluded from their research that, except for alcoholism, none of the attributes usually considered in grouping—age, intelligence, education, marital status, clinical diagnosis—are significant in themselves, either in determining which clients are suitable for group therapy or in selecting those to be treated in the same group. Similarities or differences in any one of these factors may be important in a particular group under special circumstances, but their effects can be understood only in terms of their importance to the issue with which the clients are concerned at the time. Bach (27) states that the selection of an individual client is really meaningful only in relation to the factors of group dynamics in the particular group for which membership is being considered. A focus on family remarriage problems, for example, determines group composition by age and sex. Type of problem is also a factor. The success of the Synanon movement with persons addicted to hallucinogenic drugs is an example. Alcoholics Anonymous is another.

Bach has introduced a theory of grouping which he calls the "Nuclear Expansion Theory." Here, the group is started with two or three members, and the expansion is made according to the identification and similarity needs of these particular individuals. We tend to subscribe to Bach's point of view on selection of members.

Maintaining Group Balance. Fundamental to the decision of placement is the concept of "role" vacancies in a group. A key strategy in forming actualizing groups is to select, or to add, persons with balanced polar opposites. This means, for example, including persons with various traits, such as love and anger, dominance and submission, to give variety to the group and to enable persons to have models and growth stimuli for traits opposite to their own. In other words, it is not desirable to have all angry types, or all bullies, or all nice guys. This selection not only promotes more effective interaction (such as energizing the group), but it also facilitates growth along each polarity. It is felt by most group therapists that groups should have a balance of roles represented. These various personality types give the group material to provoke discussion of common human problems and transference relationships. Some of the many possible role needs for a mixed group are illustrated in the following examples:

1. Father figure or "critical parent."
2. Mother figure or "mother hen."
3. Sex object or "sweetheart."
4. The prodder or facilitator of discussion.
5. The "warm, understanding" member.
6. The adolescent or "delinquent" member.
7. The referee or "compromiser."
8. The religious, "self-righteous," or moralizing member.
9. The "devil," Don Juan, or "wolf."
10. The "snob."
11. The "good wife."
12. The "bad wife."
13. The "good husband."
14. The "bad husband."
15. The "executive" or "very important person."
16. The "woman-hater."
17. The "man-hater."
18. The "masculine" woman.
19. The "feminine" man.
20. The "learned scholar" or "professor."

21. The "working man."
22. The "castrating female."

Placement in a particular group, therefore, would be determined partly by role vacancies which exist in a group.

A further consideration in role placement is that of the individual needs of the client. Placement is often made when the new member is expected to identify with, or will feel close to, other members. Predicted hostility to other members can be a criterion for placement also.

Sex and Age Composition. The most common group is composed of mixed sexes, unless there is a definite reason for like-sex grouping. If one assumes, however, that the group therapy or multiple counseling situation must be viewed as a part of the transference phenomena, then, as Slavson indicates (449), a mixed group may favor the tendency to act out problems in a therapeutic fashion. Slavson states that during certain stages in the treatment process, clients develop libidinal desires directed toward the psychotherapist as a parent surrogate. These can be displaced or retransferred upon fellow group members who resemble parental images.

When considering the age composition of a group, Joel and Shapiro (246) feel that mixed groups are most natural. Older persons offer more significant transference and identification opportunities for younger members, and vice versa. Bach (27), who uses the principle of heterogeneity in the selection of his clients, contends that it is desirable not to mix very young adults having had little sexual and social experience with more experienced adults. Conversely, in educational institutions, the older experienced persons would tend to be excluded because of their scarcity in the school and college populations.

Criteria for Exclusion of Members from Groups. When selecting certain members for groups, Hobbs (228) has found that there are several types of persons who tend to disrupt or hinder group progress. They are: (1) psychologically sophisticated persons who use knowledge of psychodynamics cruelly on others; (2) extremely aggressive or hostile people who destroy the atmosphere of acceptance and freedom essential to the success of the group; and (3) people who are continuously in close contact with each other outside of the group.

Bach uses four personality criteria for exclusion of members from groups: (1) insufficient reality contact; (2) extremes of culturally tabooed or illegal behavior; (3) the dominant character who would be a chronic monopolist of discussion; and (4) those with psychopathic defenses and impulsiveness (27, pp. 18–22).

Size of Groups. In organizing an actualizing group, the question usually arises as to how many persons should be included. Size is important because it can be a barrier to effectiveness of communication. A suggested minimum number for an effective social unit is three to five. Ten to twelve would be the maximum. It is generally agreed by group therapists, however, that eight is an optimum number. Loeser, for example, has several properties which he feels are characteristic of the therapy group with four to eight members:

1. It is large enough to dilute basic drives to safe and easily handled levels.

2. It is large enough to provide a variety of intragroup transference potentialities to suit the needs of each person at any given time.

3. It is large enough to avoid the strong positive and negative polarity of reaction of the dyad (two-member group) and triad (three-member group) and hence is more enduring. It cannot be destroyed by one or even two people.

4. It is large enough to permit heterogeneity and diversification of psychodynamic types and thus implement the group interaction process.

5. It is large enough to permit acting out in a diluted and workable manner.

6. On the other hand, it is small enough to be handled by a therapist with a minimum of leadership and control. The therapist can maintain his uncritical, permissive, and passive role, all of which are necessary for effective therapy.

7. It is small enough to operate without strong or numerous rules or regulations. Beyond a few simple rules such as hours, meeting places, etc., very few regulations need to be introduced.

8. It is small enough to permit each member a reasonable amount of attention and time, but large enough to remove the tensions of face-to-face talking. The passive individual can remain inconspicuous until his confidence is built up before he need take on an active role (291, pp. 11–12).

Hobbs (228) and Joel and Shapiro (246) contend that more interaction is obtained if the group is not large, since discussions led from within the group can operate more effectively. Such discussions are desirable, because leadership from within the group seems to be preferable to therapist leadership for controlling monopolists and for drawing out shy members. The "Post-Session Technique," described later, is essentially such a discussion which operates most effectively when the number of members is small.

Seating and Physical Setting

The group is arranged in such a way that all participate in an easy and informal manner. For effective participation, the group members must be able to see and hear each other easily. The circle arrangement seems to facilitate participation better than rectangular table arrangements. The use of a table should be avoided, for it can serve as a psychological barrier to free interaction. If there are co-therapists in the group, they should sit several seats away from the therapist in order to avoid having the focus of leadership in one area. Another factor of importance is that each client should have the opportunity to choose his own chair.

The physical settings in the room must be conducive to group processes. It is desirable that the room be furnished to some degree like a comfortable living room.

Session Length and Time Interval

The length of the sessions and the time interval between them have been found to be as important in group therapy and counseling as in individual work. The number of sessions and the length of each vary according to the particular therapist. Some counselors and psychotherapists contend that as many as three meetings a week are preferable, because continuity and intensity of personal interaction are facilitated by the greater frequency of meetings. If three meetings are held, they generally continue for one hour (Joel and Shapiro 246). Other groups will agree to have only one or two meetings a week, with one-and-a-half to two hours of actual work (27, 228). Generally, multiple counseling sessions are held once a week for an hour to an hour-and-a-half to keep the emotional involvement factor under control. Marathon approaches emphasize fewer but longer and more intensive sessions.

Hinckley (227) found that the majority of group members from the Student Mental Hygiene Clinic at Minnesota preferred meeting one hour a week. Sessions longer than one hour were tried but were found to be unsatisfactory. Usually the first hour was very active and productive, but the succeeding hour was much less productive. In general, it may be said that therapists differ in their opinions about length of session, but group therapy meetings usually last from one to two hours in length and are conducted about once a week.

Role of the Co-Therapist in Group Therapy

It is not uncommon for groups to employ the services of two therapists. The second therapist acts as an interpreter-observer in many instances, or he may remain quite passive. The question often arises whether or not two therapists in the same group setting are conducive to group progress. In our experience, it is most helpful to have co-therapists. The facilitative role is then performed by one therapist, the interpreter-summarizer role by the other. The co-therapist role also permits a training situation to exist, wherein trainees can function in this real leadership role.

From psychoanalytic theory one might hold that the co-therapist is better played by a female, so that both "mother" and "father" roles are played by the therapists. In terms of Fromm's theory, however, one therapist can play the mother role of being accepting and permissive, while the interpreter-summarizer role is more akin to Fromm's idea of father love, that is, love with expectations and demands (171). Joel and Shapiro (246) contend from their experience that the presence of two therapists, especially if they are of the opposite sex, more readily revives the family situation.

Group Principles and Methods

Closed and Continuous Groups

There are two kinds of groups—closed and continuous. In the closed group, the same members are maintained throughout the life span of the group. This is often the case in educational settings where groups run the length of the academic semester. In the continuous group, replacements are made when a member leaves.

There is some degree of speculation among certain therapists whether closed groups offer more advantages than continuous groups. Some think that the closed group has more advantages because data can be accumulated and the group composition kept constant. If members drop out, however, because of an unavoidable circumstance, it may make the group unduly small. An advantage of an open group is that a new member, who has just come to the group, sometimes fosters a reworking of rivalries and competition in the group. Also, a new member may help therapeutic movement through a consolidation of group feeling. New members may reduce their defensiveness by identifying with other members who have already overcome theirs. The presence of less-advanced group members appears to have some actualizing potential for the older members, since the older members gain therapeutically through the experience of sharing and helping new clients adjust to the group.

Strategies of Group Therapy and Multiple Counseling

The leader should be, first of all, competent in individual counseling and therapy techniques. In group therapy he uses all of the relationship, interpretive, and informational techniques discussed earlier in this volume. In addition, he must use other techniques which are unique to, or which must be adapted to, group work. Some of the strategies and techniques mentioned are illustrative only. This topic is so broad and is developing so rapidly that intensive study and co-leader training experience are necessary to become competent as a group facilitator. These techniques are presented in the following sections.

Structuring and Contracting

Although there are many theories of group psychotherapy and multiple counseling, most practitioners agree with Frank and Asher (164) that the group provides support, stimulation, and reality-testing opportunities. In the group setting, clients have an opportunity to express themselves freely. Support is provided for the member by the reassuring social climate of the group, in which each member feels safe in saying what he wants to say. The therapist, however, often initiates group discussion by some type of structuring in the first session. Hinckley (227) gives examples of this method, as follows: One therapist explains, "We are here to learn about ourselves and to help each other manage our natural feelings in more comfortable ways. Now, my name is ———, as most of you already know. Perhaps the simplest way of beginning is for each of us to introduce ourselves and to say something about ourselves." Another therapist comments, "In group sessions we come together to talk over some of the feelings we have which may be causing us discomfort. By finding out how much we are like other people, we sometimes feel better. Also, we may learn how other people handle some of their worries." A third therapist states, ". . . and there will be times in our meetings when it will be very hard to talk about our feelings because they may be painful to us. No one need talk of his troubles, though, until he is ready." A fourth therapist says, "Most of us can feel a little better when we learn to share, that is, talk out some of our troubles. This is possible in here. When we are able to get along comfortably in a small section of society like this group, perhaps later we will feel comfortable in larger groups. Shall we introduce ourselves now and begin by telling a little about ourselves? We don't have to speak of painful matters immediately."

In the structuring process the therapist should make it clear why the clients have come together. The members should be aware of the fact that conflicting feelings and attitudes are the basic reason for the formation of the group. It is also appropriate to state some advantages of group therapy so that clients can anticipate realistic results. It should also be stressed that what goes on in the group is strictly confidential.

The reassurance of structure is needed because group therapy is generally a new experience for clients. Further reasons and techniques of structuring are covered in Chapter 7.

As an aid to helping clients form a realistic "set" toward the group experience, the authors use the following guidelines for communicating in actualizing therapy groups:

1. Always use "I," never "them," "they," "we," "you," "us," and so on.
"I feel."
"I think."
"I am."

2. Avoid "but," "although," "because."
"I feel hurt today"—*not* ". . . because I was hurt by my husband."
"I don't like you"—*not* ". . . but I don't like people like you."

3. Attempt to verbalize your feelings and thoughts in the *here and now* situation. Even past and future experiences should be expressed in the present: "I am going to group today and I feel tense"—*not* "I was driving here today and felt terrible." Feel terrible *now*!

4. When addressing a fellow group member, talk to him directly, eye-to-eye

contact, and *don't* use the third person when relating to him. "I like you"—
not "I like him."

5. Be constantly aware of what your body wisdom is saying to you (listen
to your tensions, boredom, joys, and so on, and communicate these to the
group). This is best done by listening to your voice.

6. When you are spoken to, *listen* intently and try to *hear* what is said and with
what feeling it is being expressed.

7. The one question that should not be asked is "Why?" For example, if
someone expresses caring for you, please don't ask why! Be responsive to the
other person. How do you feel when this person cares for you?

Bach (27, pp. 29–30) has prepared a group therapy contract on which
six procedural principles are structured for the new group member. The
new member signs this sheet when he accepts group membership. We
have modified this preparation sheet for use in our practice and present it
as an example.

New Group Member Contract

1. Size of group:
The group's size is limited to a minimum number of six and a maximum number of ten clients.

2. Admission of new members:
When an old member leaves the group, his or her place in the group will be
filled by a new member. The selection is made on two bases: (a) which group
is best for the prospective member, and (b) which prospective member is best
for the group.

3. Extraoffice meetings:
The regular office meetings of the group with the therapist, while of central
therapeutic importance, are only part of the total program. Experiences during
the post-session between members of the group provide important material for
self-observation and analysis. No extraoffice meetings other than post-session
meetings are allowed.

4. Sharing of mutual experiences:
Group members usually adhere to the principle that everything anybody says,
thinks, or does which involves another member of the group is subject to open
discussion in the group. In other words, the emotionally important experiences
of any member are shared by all members. There are no secrets *inside* the group.

5. Ethical confidence:
In contrast to Principle Number 4, everything that goes on within the group
—everything!—must remain an absolute secret as far as any outsider (non-
member) is concerned. Anyone participating in group therapy automatically
assumes the same professional ethics of absolute discretion which bind professional therapists.

6. The group's goal:
The group goal is free communication on a nondefensive, personal, and emotional level. This goal can be reached only by the group effort. Experience

shows that the official therapists cannot "push" the group; the group has to progress by its own efforts. Each member will get out of the group what he puts into it. As every member communicates to the group his feelings and perceptions and associations of the moment as openly as he can and as often as he can, the group will become a therapeutically effective medium. The goal of free communication is freedom to be oneself most fully and comfortably. I have read the above and agree to cooperate fully.

Signed: _____

The "Going-Around" Technique

The going-around technique is often used as a warm-up device by the therapist to pitch the communication at a more emotional and less intellectual level. Each member describes his feelings about how every other member in the group affects him emotionally. This is usually done from neighbor to neighbor, "going around" the group circle. This technique is particularly useful in situations involving "newcomers." Older group members give their first impression to the newcomer in a casual manner. Then the newcomer has an opportunity to do likewise with the group members.

The Communication-Training Technique

Since a basic process goal of all groups is to promote communication among group members, the facilitator presents (at appropriate times) the following communication rules:

1. The principle of *direct communication* is stated to the group as follows: "We never withhold feelings that we have about another person in the group. When we communicate these feelings we look directly at the person to whom we are talking, and we use his name or the pronoun *you.*" A poor example would be (talking to group in general): "I think Bill is not facing this problem with his wife." A better example would be (talking directly to Bill): "Bill, I think you are not facing this problem with your wife."

2. Making statements is preferable to asking questions. The principle of *question analysis* is stated as follows: "Whenever we ask a question, we must state the hypothesis behind our question." A poor example is: "What was your wife's reaction?" A better example is: "I was curious about your wife's reaction because I wondered if she reacts like my wife does."

3. The principle of *advice analysis* proceeds as follows: "There is a strong tendency to project our needs, wants, perceptions, and meanings to others. Whenever we give advice we must speculate on what it was in our own life experience which has made us so alert to this particular advice." A poor example is: "Why don't you leave your wife?" A better example is: "I think you ought to leave your wife, since you have the same situation which caused me to leave my first wife."

The role-playing technique permits the client to apply playful acting-out of his problems as a serious attempt to understand his conflicts. The value of this method lies in the fact that participants reveal feelings and tensions without the burden of shame. It facilitates presenting a situation with fewer words and with greater clarity than can be achieved with the ordinary discussion methods. Driver (131) claims that role-playing is an effective alternative for talk and is an excellent warm-up device for discussion.

Role-playing as a counseling technique often helps a client to gain a better perspective of himself and others. It can be used, for example, to practice social situations which are difficult for the client. Even when it is used in a group situation by qualified workers, emphasis should be placed on the fact that many complications can arise if it is not used properly. Bach (27) warns of the possible traumatic effect of premature externalizing of threatening materials through role-playing.

Some of the major types of psychodramatic procedures in a group therapy setting, as adapted from Del Torto and Cornyetz (121), are described below.

1. Role reversal is a procedure which allows two individuals to exchange roles. Role reversal is used in the following example: Mother and daughter figures might be discussing what would be a reasonable hour for the latter to come home from a date. The daughter could exchange roles with the mother to see her side. Conversely, the parent could be afforded the frame of reference of the daughter.

2. The double technique allows a second individual to assume the identity of the subject. This is a technique whereby two identities may seem merged into one. Functions of the double are illustrated in a situation in which one individual has to make a decision. For example, when meditating over whether or not to buy a new car, one might be in doubt about its being a good buy. A double ego, in this situation, would function as the subject's conscience and desire, and would verbalize the conflict in a low tone of voice at the same time the subject was verbalizing his dilemma.

3. The soliloquy is a technique to make known "hidden" thoughts of role-playing participants. Another purpose of the soliloquy is to clarify and fix newly gained insights. For example, in a conference, each individual is allowed to speak his piece. Then, as the scene is "frozen," each is asked to soliloquize or to speak out what feelings are going on in his mind which he is not expressing. For example, he is asked, "What thought occurred? How do you really feel about the other person?"

4. The mirror technique is an attempt to allow the subject to see himself. It is used when it is thought to be helpful to see himself in action. For example, a subject may wish to observe himself at a given task, such as a job interview. The person serving as the substitute ego is placed across from the subject and mimics his behavior.

5. *Periodic stimuli technique* is a method used to test the client's range of expansiveness within the role. It is designed also to test his spontaneous adaptation to surprise elements. For example, a situation might be created where the subject is an artist working in his studio. At periodic intervals the director may send in a landlord demanding rent, his complaining sponsor, or a cantankerous model. The basic situation is not changed; only the stimuli are varied.

6. *The hidden theme technique* brings out the subject's ability to perceive a behavioral theme in a social situation and to create an appropriate role to deal with it. For example, a subject is sent out of the room. He is told beforehand that, when he returns, a social situation will be in progress and that he should relate himself meaningfully to the situation that is going on.

7. *The mute technique* is used to reveal nonverbal resources for communication and expression. A theme is given to the subject and other clients with instructions that they communicate by gestures and bodily movements. An example would be a card game involving four people who are allowed to communicate only by gestures.

Expression of Polarities

Primary emphases of Actualizing Counseling and Therapy are awareness and expression of inner polarities so as to achieve ultimate integration and actualization. The actualizing counselor, therefore, does not simply role-play in the Moreno interpersonal sense. Instead, with the counselor's help he role-plays the polarities within himself and the differences between himself and others in fantasy. The following are examples (434):

C: Be your lonesome self.

C1: I feel so blue and unhappy; I just need people.

C: Now be your strong opposite self.

C1: Oh, quit being such a weakling. You know that you don't need anybody else but me.

C: Now be the weak one again.

C1: What good are you?

C: Now be the strong one and answer.

C1: Without me you're a machine with only one wheel; but with me we drive the machine together.

C: Now be the weak one and answer.

C1: Gosh, I never thought of that. I guess we can be strong when we work together.

The above is an example of an individual *listening* to both weak and strong sides of himself. Through the conflict, antagonistic poles become complementary. When both sides of ourselves are accepted, integration comes more easily.

The Summary Interpretation Technique

Usually after forty or forty-five minutes of the therapeutic hour have elapsed, the group therapist or co-therapist finds it propitious to make a summary interpretation of what has happened in the hour. We feel that this summary task is best performed by a co-therapist, rather than by the therapist himself. The latter usually has a facilitative or management role, and would find it difficult psychologically to perform both the summary interpretation and the facilitative role.

The interpretation technique has been found helpful in giving the group a picture of what has happened during the hour. We have found the following types of summaries to be useful:

1. "Theme" summaries: Hobbs (228) suggests that group therapy is much like a musical composition, in that there are certain "themes" which run through group conversation. The co-therapist identifies these themes in the summary. An example is: "Tonight we have been talking about competition. Sally and Jack see themselves as always running away from it. In the area of romance, Bill says he just gives up, or disposes of the possibility of winning. In interpersonal competition, we have decided that we have to define the problem clearly. This means defining the assets and liabilities of our competitors and then defining our own assets and liabilities. We can then decide on which techniques we ought to use. Doreen is competing now with another woman for her husband. One thing she can do better than this other woman is to be a good mother to her children and a good wife to her husband. She has decided this is one of her chief assets which she can develop. We have also discussed the idea of 'shooting against our own par'—that is, competition with oneself is one of the best ways for improvement. This method doesn't hurt anybody in the process. Jim does this in his golf game—and we can do it here too."

2. Individual analysis summaries: Sometimes the discussions of a group do not center on a particular theme, but the individual group members discuss their own unique problems. The co-therapist then summarizes more individually, as for example: "Our discussion tonight has focused on four people, and I'd like to say something about each of them. We might call these people by certain pseudonyms.

"Alex here is Accepting Alex. He wants to be so accepting of everybody, because he has learned that this is what good psychologists do. But this is only half the story. Before we can really accept others, we first must learn to accept ourselves—both the negative and positive parts of ourselves. When Alex is able to do this completely, he'll not have trouble accepting others' positive and negative sides too.

"Doreen we might call Doormat Doreen. She has spent seventeen years being a doormat for her husband, and now she wants to change. She has been thinking that one way to do that is to take off from teaching this year so that her husband will not have the money she makes to depend on. But Les and Sam are in agreement that a better way would be to continue teaching, since just sitting around might make her more depressed and tired than before. Les found that out in his own experience. Furthermore, we know that most of us get more tired from underwork than overwork. If Doreen then continued to teach, she could keep her own money and really be selfish for once in her life.

"Will we might call Un-Warm Uncle Will. He just doesn't want to admit he is warm, and yet Doreen has shown us that he really is. He doesn't want to be this way, and for the first time tonight has asked us to pull him down from his stand-offish position. He has humbled himself to do this, and I think we can help him."

3. *Interpersonal dynamic summaries:* Instead of focusing on the individual problems of clients, the therapist can describe the interpersonal dynamics of feelings which have been taking place in the hour. An example is: "We have had many feelings shown here tonight. Some of them have been obvious, others not so obvious. Pete and Ted have both openly expressed their warm feelings toward Connie. Jack has expressed hostility by saying that he doesn't like her because she is so pretty, that everyone likes her, and that rejection is good for such a person. But after analyzing this feeling we find that Jack is saying this because he fears that if he were to express his real feelings of warmth to Connie, she might reject him, so he takes the offensive instead by rejecting her first. But he finds that this isn't very satisfying, because it leaves him feeling, as he says, lousy."

These methods of interpretation may be combined in summarizing the session; they are presented separately above for purposes of clarity in exposition.

The Post-Session Technique

One of the techniques recommended by Bach (27) is the post-session technique. This is a procedure of allowing the group to remain after the therapeutic hour for the purposes of integrating the accomplishments of the hour and for the purpose of preparing one another for further therapeutic work. Bach sees the following goals for post-session work: (1) therapeutic reinforcement of insight gained in the work session of the group; (2) preparation to deal with difficult and resistance-evoking material through the development of social alliances; (3) opportunity to release pent-up tensions that were instigated but remained unleashed in the clinical work session; and (4) provision of experiential data on neurotic set-up (acted out transference) behavior for later working through.

There are several basic rules which must be observed with the post-session technique. First, the group members must stay together as a group. There must be no post-session pairing off and departing from the group.

Group members are told that, other than in the post-session, they must not socialize outside the group. Furthermore, all material discussed in the post-session should be brought out ultimately in the regular session. Clients are encouraged in their individual sessions with their counselors to discuss what happened in the post-session.

Nonverbal and Body Awareness Techniques

Since words are often difficult means for expressing experiences, group leaders use various exercises designed to increase self-awareness and mobilize energy. Schutz of Esalen Institute, for example, has developed a program of group fantasy, bodily movement, physical release, and drama as media for expressing and increasing awareness of feelings. To accomplish these goals, encounter groups make use of a number of exercises in relaxation, stretching, touching, pushing, and striking. Sensory awareness, or "awakening," is developed through activities such as dancing and art work, with the goal of increased pleasure and joy. Interpersonal relationships are enhanced through exercises emphasizing touching, competitive activities, and physically breaking into the group circle. In the ensuing discussion, members become more aware of their impact on others and the meaning of their own feelings.

Summary

Group techniques to develop interpersonal as well as intrapersonal dimensions have been presented. General considerations for development of groups, such as selection, composition, size, physical setting, time, facilitator roles, and closed versus continuous groups, have been outlined. Research, particularly on learning outcomes, has been a prominent group development.

It was suggested that the effective group facilitator must be familiar with all the individual techniques presented in this book. In addition, certain supplementary group strategies were presented. Some of these techniques are: structuring, "going-around," communication training, psychodrama, group summary and interpretation, and post-session meetings.

Special Areas
of Application

part 3

Counseling and Psychotherapy with Couples and Families

Counseling with Couples

Couples counseling is tied closely to therapeutic psychology; however, it has a unique history. In the past, couples counseling was performed, for the most part, by clergymen and social workers in churches, public welfare agencies, and family-service organizations. Counseling of couples has become such a specialized activity that some states, such as California, require a special license to advertise as a marriage and family counselor. This category includes persons from varied professional backgrounds. In addition to their respective basic professional organizations, many marriage and family counselors belong to the American Association of Sex Educators and Counselors or the National Council on Family Relations.

Historically, social workers have worked mainly in agencies with low-income families who have not been able to seek professional help on a private basis. More recently, however, social agencies have begun to develop services designed for the middle-income group (159). Family-service agencies have become part of almost all large community-service rosters. This service gives total family counseling, as well as marriage counseling, to middle- and low-income groups. Numerous psychiatrists, psychologists, and social workers perform these services in private practice also.

The development of marriage assistance as a specialty dates back to such pioneer work as that of Stone, who established the first marriage consultation center in New York in 1929, and of Popenoe, who established the Institute of Family Relations in 1930. Much pioneer work has been done by Emily Mudd since 1932, when she established the Philadelphia Marriage Council. These people established marriage counseling as a specialty separate from family casework.

12

The clergy is another profession that has been associated with marital counseling and particularly premarital counseling.

The family physician has also played a particular role in premarital counseling, since professional medical men are necessarily involved in the establishment of healthy attitudes toward sex and contraception.

Lawyers, because of their special role in relation to divorce, find themselves doing marital counseling by the very act of accepting or refusing a client. In any case, the highly specialized area of legal information and rules makes the lawyer an important partner in marital counseling. Courts are paying increasing attention to the part they can play in bringing about reconciliation rather than granting divorce. Judge Louis Burke founded the Conciliation Court of Los Angeles, in which psychologists and social workers give reconciliation counseling. This development emphasizes the need for, and effectiveness of, interdisciplinary approaches to marriage problems. More recently, with the advent of clinical and counseling psychology established on a private practice basis, psychologists are applying their psychotherapeutic techniques and are making special applications to the field of marriage and legal problems.

Specialists in working with sex problems and sexual enrichment in couples have become popular on the individual counseling and group scene. Sexuality topics in couples counseling and special workshops have become widespread owing largely to development of several strategies of sexual dysfunction treatment in addition to increasing public awareness of enrichment potential and admission of sexual problems. Some of these strategies are aimed at sexual enrichment primarily through educational media and sensory awareness. Other strategies, such as sensate focus, apply mainly to partners with some kind of sexual dysfunction, such as impotence. Masters and Johnson (309) have done the basic research and development on treatment of sexual disorders. While their methods focus on sexual functioning, they view their work in the broader perspectives of caring relationships and pleasure outcomes. A key method is sexual enrichment through "sensate focus"—a method designed to reawaken pleasurable bodily sensations and feelings through touch activities and clear emotional communication.

Issues in Couples Counseling

Philosophical Issues. We take the position that a counselor or therapist does not have the right to decide whether or not divorce is the best solution for those who seek marital counseling. Marriage counselors can assist in the actualizing progress of the persons concerned, whether or not divorce is a part of the solution.

The counselor should recognize that there are some couples whose emotional separation has been of such long duration, with so much bitterness, that reconciliation is not likely. Where great personality damage has been done to one or both individuals, reconciliation may be a dubious answer anyway. This does not mean that divorce is the only solution. A couple may be helped to live together in relative harmony and security even though the goal of a close marriage is impossible.

In some instances, a separation is the only means by which a marriage can be saved. Frequently this leads to final dissolution of the marriage. However, separation may help individuals face the realities of living instead of blaming each other for their problems. If a counselor can help the couple to stop quarreling over petty issues, it may be possible for one or both of them to do some basic growing. Later, they may be able to cope with complex marital interactions on a more constructive basis. Separation is seldom instigated by the counselor. Usually it is one reality factor to be considered in a particular counseling situation.

Effects of Disruptions on Children.   Sometimes a separation is a necessary transition to final divorce. It can facilitate reasonably amicable post-divorce relations and minimize unnecessary bitterness that likely will react unfavorably on the children caught in the middle. Thus, one of the most common considerations in divorce is the effect it will have on the children involved. Despert, in an analysis of the effects of divorce on children, says: "Divorce is not the costliest experience possible to a child. Unhappy marriage without divorce—what we shall call emotional divorce—can be far more destructive to him than divorce" (123, p. 18).

Mahler and Rabinovitch, among others, list ways in which marital conflict may affect a child's development adversely. The following list is an adaptation of their discussion of marital conflict and children:

1. The child is made a buffer between parents; either or both turn to the child for satisfactions not obtained from the partner.
2. The child is made a pawn—something planned for, conceived, and used to cement a marriage already in jeopardy.
3. The child is made a confidant to either or both parents who are hostile to each other, thus burdening him emotionally beyond his capacity.
4. The child is hurt by impulsive actions, such as confronting him with major decisions or changes.
5. The child is subjected to recurrent or violent scenes, sometimes alternating with periods of false peace.
6. The child is exposed to protracted subtle discord, such as "the predivorce uncertainty."
7. The resolution of the oedipal phase is made difficult, since it is accomplished through identification with the parent of the same sex.
8. The child's period of dependency on mother is prolonged, since his dependency phase has been arrested at this level (304, pp. 50–54).

When divorce takes place, the counselor frequently can help clients assist their children through this difficult period. Despert (123, p. 42) thinks that the child of estranged parents needs to know that: (1) he is not to blame; (2) his parents still love him; (3) something is wrong—but not, as he fears, everything; (4) parents are not gods but human beings who have made mistakes.

Unfortunately, bickering families not only tend to diminish actualizing behaviors, but they also tend to perpetuate their unhealthy patterns in the marriages of the next generation. Marital counseling, in many instances, is the most direct and suitable approach to breaking this vicious circle. The conclusion is that there is no one best way to solve marital difficulties for the best interests of the children.

If divorce does take place, the effects on the children are further complicated by the now common occurrence of the remarriage of one or both parents. If marital or family counseling is needed, the counseling is affected by the complex interrelationships of the new marriage, as indicated in Figure 20. Children, jealous of the attention given by a parent to a new spouse, very often become difficult; step-parents, seeking love from their

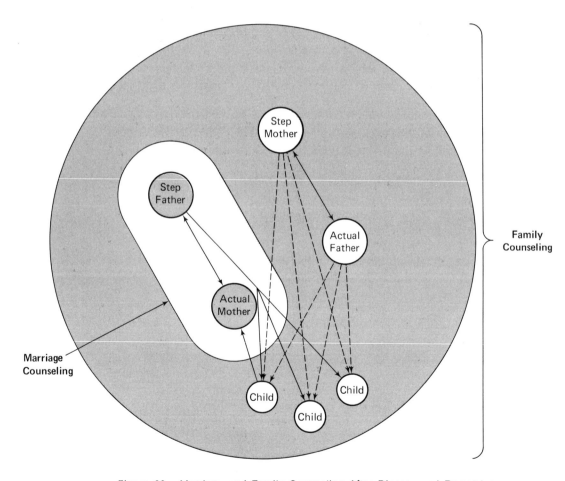

Figure 20. Marriage and Family Counseling After Divorce and Remarriage

new spouses, often see the children as interfering with the new relationship; the obligation to include children in the total family decision-making
process often creates many problems. Children of the two families become
part of the marriage counseling, and the marital problems of one couple
affect the family of the other couple.

The discussion above has suggested the complexity and consequences
of the problem and has implied that it is frequently impossible that any
solution will be absolutely constructive for everyone concerned. The following discussion can only outline some of the major problems in the
complex area of marital counseling and suggest some techniques for
handling them.

Models of Couples Counseling

Couples counseling differs from other types of counseling in that one or
both of the partners seeks help because he or she believes that their relationship is in difficulty. It is this emphasis on the problems of the relationship itself, at least in the early stages of the counseling process, which
makes couples counseling a specialty.

Foster (163, p. 213) has contrasted individual psychotherapy and marriage counseling in the two figures which follow. In Figure 21, illustrating
psychotherapy, the therapist is directly connected with the client, who, in
turn, is concerned directly with his symptoms, developmental history,
character structure, and reality.

In Figure 22 Foster (163, p. 214) shows a direct, individual connection
between the separate entities of marital counselor, husband, wife, and the
marriage. In addition to the symptoms, developmental history, and reality
with which husband and wife are individually concerned, the marriage
substitutes its own conflict patterns for the individual character structures.
Thus, it is important to note that individual psychotherapy is very much
a part of marriage counseling; but to this is added the emphasis on conflict patterns within the marriage, as well as the marriage symptoms and
developmental histories. This means seeing both partners at the same time
in most cases.

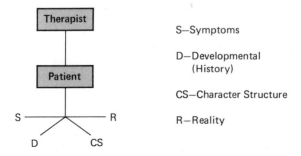

S—Symptoms

D—Developmental
    (History)

CS—Character Structure

R—Reality

Figure 21.   The Individual Psychotherapy Model. Adapted from Foster.

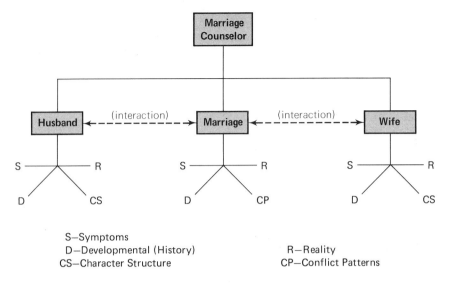

S—Symptoms
D—Developmental (History)   R—Reality
CS—Character Structure   CP—Conflict Patterns

Figure 22. The Marriage Counseling Model. Adapted from Foster.

Foster distinguishes marriage counseling from psychotherapy in that the former must deal with a third element, the marriage relationship, as well as with the individual histories and conflicts of husband and wife. However, he does not make clear the dynamic relationships among these three elements. The naive or inexperienced marriage counselor tends to focus on the *relationship* in marriage counseling only, concentrating on such problems or symptoms as bickering and unkindness. Consequently, he attempts to smooth out the relationship between husband and wife. The result, generally, is superficial. Marital psychotherapy usually means that the therapist begins with the individual spouses themselves and their unique problems. Thus, the marriage therapist works with the individual first and then with the relationship. Marriage counseling does both but tends to focus on relationship problems and seeing the couple together.

Finney (156) describes a "partnership psychotherapy," which consists of interviewing two clients at the same time. These may be a couple or persons of the same sex and age but total strangers to each other. Sharing and mutual stimulation draw on the advantages of group therapy while retaining the personal focus of individual interviews. Finney found this method had not only economy values but additional therapeutic outcomes as well.

Infidelity Problems

An analysis of marital conflicts leads to the conclusion that a basic problem is lack of healthy self-regard in one or both partners. Infidelity is often a symptom of not having achieved this major actualizing goal. The typical spouse, not feeling a sense of personal worth or love from husband or wife, may seek to prove lovableness by engaging in an extramarital affair. Counselors find, however, that simply eliminating the third person in a triangle does not help. What is required is a type of therapy that helps the individual to develop feelings of worth and adequacy. Once this is achieved, he will be able to see the neurotic need that is being met by an affair and to express his hostility to his spouse for not having loved him more. The spouse responds typically by recognizing the dependence on the errant spouse. Finally, with these unexpressed and unrecognized dependencies having been worked through in an actualizing fashion, the relationship is likely to improve.

Horney describes the multiple factors involved in reactions to infidelity. The counselor often must deal with the spouse not involved in the infidelity also. Her discussion illustrates the meaning of such problems from the viewpoint of this other spouse.

There are a number of reasons that might explain why she feels and acts in this way, quite apart from a genuine hurt about the breach of confidence. (1) It may have hurt her pride that the husband could be attached to anyone but herself. (2) It may be intolerable to her that her husband could slip out from her control and domination. (3) The incident may have touched off a dread of desertion. (4) She may be discontented with the marriage for reasons of which she is not aware, and she may use this conspicuous occurrence as an excuse for expressing all her repressed grievances, thus engaging merely in an unconscious campaign of revenge. (5) She may have felt attracted toward another man and resent the fact that her husband indulged in a freedom that she had not allowed herself (234, pp. 283–84).

The Reconciliation Decision

The course of reconciliation in marital counseling may be diagrammed as in Figure 23. What is suggested here is that, initially, marital counseling

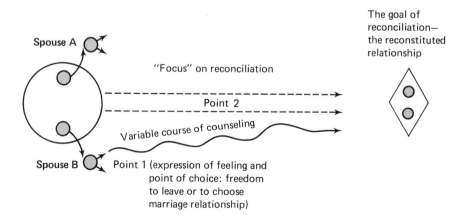

Figure 23. The Process of Marital Counseling

causes the marital relationship to get worse rather than better. Thus, the general idea developed in Chapter 4 that "you often get worse before you get better" holds true here also. In Figure 23 the course of marital therapy suggests that, at first, the spouses seem to separate psychologically. For this reason, it is unwise in the initial phases to focus on reconciliation, as indicated at Point 2. To do this would be to limit the necessary expression of hostile feelings toward one's spouse. Counseling brings out these hostile feelings, many of which have remained dormant for years. The expression of such negative feelings enables the client to come to the end of Point 1—decision—more easily. Here he comes to regard himself as a person of worth and dignity who does not need to stay with the marriage at any cost. This is the "brink of disaster" point, as far as the marriage is concerned.

Awareness of these facts, however, leads the client to make a choice. He can be free of the marriage; but he is free also to *choose* marriage and not be neurotically bound to it. When he makes the latter choice, he is able to relate effectively to his partner for the first time. Parenthetically, this means that it may be unwise for the client or counselor to focus consciously on "saving the marriage at all costs" if the process is to run its course.

In light of the above discussion, it is asserted, therefore, that the area of marriage counseling is but a special application of Actualizing Counseling and Therapy. Marriage counseling is more extensive in scope, however, since it deals with multiple relationships, as well as with the personalities of the persons involved.

Premarital Counseling and Planning

Until recently the main problems of young people as far as partnerships and sex were concerned were whether to get married or not, and whether to have sexual relationships before marriage or not. Now the choices are so many with the advent of the "pill" and the presence of widely variant values on sexual relationships. There are basic choices to be made among various forms of partnerships—the temporary marriage or "trial marriage," just "living together," homosexual relationships, premarital communes, "swinging" in various forms, in addition to conventional marriage. Even after the marriage choice is made, there are forms of group marriage, communal living groups, and various swinging options for the marrieds. This state of affairs makes counseling, of an informal type at least, all the more attractive for those persons faced with these decisions on what is best for them.

Skidmore and Garrett indicate that the "basic aim of premarital counseling is to assist the prospective partners to gain a better understanding of themselves, of each other, and of what marriage entails" (446, p. 323). It is most difficult to categorize certain problem areas as being unique to premarital counseling. However, there are a number of considerations that are basic to this subject, relating to counseling young people.

The Problem of Partner Choice

A basic consideration in premarital counseling is the obvious question of partner choice. Psychologists have pointed out that many choices are based on some form of neurotic attraction. Mittleman, for example, lists some common types of neurotic attraction, fitting in with our model of manipulation described in Chapter 3.

1. One aggressive and sadistic versus one dependent and submissive.
2. One self-sufficient through emotional detachment versus one demanding love.
3. Mutual attempts at domination.
4. One neurotically ill versus one extremely considerate.
5. One with fluctuating helplessness and assertiveness versus one fluctuating in responsibility and disappointed desire for love (329, pp. 82–83).

One of the major jobs in premarital counseling is to help young people determine the extent to which their choice of partner is actualizing for them or not. Fromm (171) suggests the criterion that to love someone because you "need" him is neurotic; to need him because you love him is healthy. Fromm points out also that love in this sense is both an emotional feeling and a decision.

Maslow (307) suggests also that marriage between self-actualizing people is a merging of feelings and intellectual choices. The choice is *felt* to be right. Their cognitive acts confirm their feelings, or vice versa. This reciprocal confirmation and convergence process takes place in varied ways with the individuals involved.

The Nature of Love and Commitment

A second area of prime concern in premarital counseling is dealing with the meaning of love. Few people have ever taken time to develop any clear concept of love, much less to evaluate what that love means to them as individuals. When asked, most people are likely to say that they married for love; but often they cannot verbalize what they meant, or what they mean now when they say they love or do not love their mates.

Frequently a person's concept of love does not distinguish between "romantic love" and "mature love" between man and woman. Romantic love has cultural roots in the past; but it survives in the present, nurtured by an endless barrage of fairy tales in movies, magazines, novels, and on television. The media cater to the susceptible daydreams of the immature and tend to make them addicts of romantic emotionalism. This happens because in their immaturity they appear unable to understand, let alone grow into, mature love relationships without assistance.

A counselor needs to be familiar with common psychological interpretations of love and the processes of loving. Although a thorough analysis cannot be made here, certain generally accepted ideas concerning love will be described as they affect the problem of premarital counseling. In our earlier discussions, caring was expressed as a way of manifesting love. Shostrom's "Caring Relationship Inventory" (433), described in Chapter 5, identifies some of its dimensions. The CRI includes seven concepts of love. *Affection* reflects the capacity of the client to feel a sense of unconditional concern for another. It is charitable, compassionate, and appreciative. Its potential liability, however, lies in the overintense expression of these affectionate feelings such that a vague perception of ownership of the other person develops, or a feeling of obligation is incurred. Whether in parent-child or partner relationships, this manipulative tendency (in our Actualizing model terms) needs to be recognized and changed. In an actualizing relationship, the sincere valuing of the other is a helpful antidote to regarding the other as a thing to be manipulated.

Friendship is another level of caring in the form of unconditional acceptance of the personhood of the other. It involves feelings of mutuality, equality, and appreciation. Again, the danger is that with manipulative twists this quality becomes exploitative.

The *eros* form of love and caring is characterized by romantic and erotic qualities. It is closely associated with sensory qualities from physical contact. It can be expressed in a manipulative form also as seduction or using the body of the other without much concern for the feelings of the other.

Empathy forms in the CRI reflect the capacity to feel for another, as described in earlier chapters on the nature of the counseling relationship. It is based on mutual appreciations, commitments, and common interests. Its manipulative form is pretense that one is empathizing, but then one does the opposite. An example is a spouse saying, "I know how badly you feel when I'm gone so much." Then he does nothing about it.

Self-love is appreciating one's individuality, feeling a strong sense of personal worth, and accepting one's weaknesses. Self-love moves into the manipulative category when one treats one's self as an object, prostitutes one's self, or allows others to exploit one.

Being love is a type of admiring, respecting feeling which does not extract conditions or reservations. *Deficiency love*, on the other hand, views the other for what he can do for one. Love is viewed as a means to gain other ends than solely being with the person.

Romantic love is a special form of the eros type described above. It needs to be faced honestly by prospective partners. It is defined as the projection of an individual's emotional needs onto a love object. Romantic love is the search for the ideal mate. This ideal mate personifies all the perfection and divine attributes that the individual feels he himself lacks or needs. Mature love, by contrast, comes only after a knowledge of and experience with the loved partner. It may follow a "period of disillusionment" associated with romantic love. "Falling out of romantic love" results from a shattering of the idealized, romantic love illusion. One "falls out of love" because one does not work through the period of disillusionment to a new conception of love based not on projected needs, but on a realistic appraisal and deep valuing of each other as unique persons.

"Counterfeit" or "profane" love are terms referring to manipulative forms not uncommon in marriage conflict. Counterfeit love can be recognized when the relationship is degrading, exploitative, possessive, violent, antisocial, irresponsible, sadistic, or masochistic. These are the symptoms that point to the need for more actualizing before a normal love relationship can be developed.

Fromm lists the following distorted ideas that many people have in regard to love: (1) They "see the problem of love primarily as that of *being loved* rather than that of *loving*." (2) They "think that to *love* is simple," whereas to find the correct love object is difficult. (3) They feel that love is beyond understanding, and they cannot learn how to love (171, pp. 1–4).

Fromm states, furthermore, that mature love includes four basic elements: (1) ". . . the *active concern for the life and growth of that which we love*." (2) *Responsibility* for the needs, physical and psychic, of the other. (3) *Respect* for the other, the ability to see a person as he is, to be aware of his unique individuality. (4) *Knowledge* of self, of the other, and of the nature of love (171, p. 26).

Many other psychologists and philosophers emphasize that loving involves learning to give and receive love and that the needs of the other must be considered at least as important as one's own; otherwise love, mature love, does not exist. Maslow, for example, expresses it as follows: "One person feels another's needs as if they were his own and for that matter also feels his own needs to some extent as if they belonged to the other" (307, p. 249).

Gibran emphasized that mature love requires "spaces in your togetherness." "Stand together yet not too near together: For the pillars of the temple stand apart, and the oak tree and the cypress grow not in each other's shadow" (189, pp. 16–17). The idea that love is not possession, incorporation, or destruction was further described by Gibran when he said, "Love gives naught but itself and takes naught but from itself. Love possesses not nor would be possessed. For love is sufficient unto love" (p. 14). "Love between man and woman may be defined," Blanton writes, "as a relationship in which each helps the other to preserve and enlarge the life of the other" (54, p. 83). According to Overstreet, "Love of a person implies not the possession of that person, but the affirmation of that person. It means granting him, gladly, the full right to his unique manhood" (353, p. 103).

The nature and expression of *commitment* are key issues here. We see three types: a commitment of *concern* which is much like caring described above, a commitment of *obligation* based on promises and pledges, and a commitment to *growth* which is mutual assistance toward personal development. Masters and Johnson (309) describe one kind of commitment based on agreed, or implied, responsibilities to care for each other or to give each other pleasure. There is a kind of give-and-get norm established. They use the term "commitment of concern" (p. 235) to describe a contrasting type of commitment where the partners feel a mutual obligation to each other, not out of compulsion, but from free choice. Masters and Johnson see this mutual concern about each other's welfare as the basis for pleasure, especially sexual pleasure, in a relationship. We emphasize an additional quality of commitment, *viz.,* the mutual feeling of desire to enhance the actualizing growth of the other.

There is no blueprint for telling how a counselor can help clients understand and feel the meaning of these concepts. Each individual must discover what love means and how he can become lovable and loving in his own way. However, an awareness and a willingness on the part of the counselor to interpret these formulations on the meanings of love can greatly assist the client in his search for understanding and expressing love.

Sex

Fromm suggests that the neurotic individual often seeks to establish intimacy with another by sexual contact rather than through a gradual association. "Such experiences of sudden intimacy are usually short-lived and unsatisfying" (171, p. 53). Sexual desire is often mistaken for love, and frequently sexual desire is motivated by other character needs. Fromm suggests four: (1) the anxiety of aloneness; (2) the wish to conquer or be conquered; (3) vanity; (4) the wish to hurt or even to destroy (171, p. 54).

Faulty sex education or nonactualizing sex attitudes learned in childhood are frequent sources of trouble. The client is often helped by facing the feelings that these early experiences developed within him. Frequently, if the counselor gives specific sex information, he can rectify problems based on misinformation or lack of knowledge. In the process of sex education, the counselor can be reassuring and helpful by giving specific information, although it is important that he make the client realize that it is not faulty information but distorted attitudes that are the seat of the real trouble. If not used carefully, the "sex manual" approach can be grossly misleading.

It is important that during premarital counseling the counselor impart an understanding of the relation of sex to love. In order to complete a human relationship, it may be said that biological desire must be joined with love as it has been described heretofore. Masters and Johnson (309) describe a process of building relationships consisting of attraction, caring, commitment, pleasure, more caring and commitment, and more pleasure (and so on in an ever intensifying and renewing pattern). They are using pleasure largely, but not exclusively, in a sexual sense. A common social value we have inherited through our Hebraic-Christian tradition is that sex is one means of expressing love. This means that unless both elements are present, there is a "psychic prostitution." Parenthetically, this interpretation suggests that there is often much of this type of prostitution in many marriage relationships. When present, it tends to have a destructive effect on the personalities involved.

Differences Between Men and Women

Closely related to understanding the love relationship in marriage is understanding that the differences between men and women are more than physiological. Again, the client may need help in understanding how his attitudes toward his own sex role and that of the opposite sex developed. His early lack of proper sex-role identification or his early resentments relating to sibling rivalries may be the source of much hostility in marriage. He may need considerable assistance in learning to understand, on an emotional level, just what his responsibilities and privileges are in regard to marriage.

Jung was a great exponent of psychic sex differences. He pointed out that women operate in terms of the "Eros Principle" and are basically feeling or intuitive in their approach to life. Men operate on the "Logos Principle" and tend to be more intellectual, systematic, and power-centered in their approach (252). Fromm, too, suggests some basic character differences in men and women. The masculine character he describes by such terms as "penetration, guidance, activity, discipline, and adventurousness." The feminine character he describes in terms of "productive receptiveness, protection, realism, endurance, and motherliness" (171, pp. 36–37).

Cultural stereotypes of masculinity and femininity have been in a considerable state of flux. Consequently, what it means to be a man or a woman has been changing so much that it is difficult to maintain a distinctive role identity other than child-bearing. The Freudian stereotypes of the Victorian era and the Hebraic-Christian mandates on women's roles especially have diminished in influence. Maleness and femaleness were defined largely in cultural terms of fatherhood as protective and aggressive, and motherhood as nourishing and receptive. The "feminine" man or the "masculine" woman was considered a curious aberration. Such stereotypes now seem chauvinistic, arrogant, and rigid. Actualizing Counseling and Therapy is concerned with helping each person discover his or her most comfortable and effective male-female role behavior. This process often involves choices of when to blend with cultural expectations, when to flout them, and when assertively to change them. The range of choices is now far greater than it has ever been before. The price, however, is increasing choice anxiety.

The main therapeutic implication of the preceding opinions is that each individual needs to recognize that his partner has different needs, has had different experiences, and of necessity looks at life differently, and reacts to life's demands in a different manner. This area of psychological sex differences illustrates why a counselor probably will have little success in helping the client develop new attitudes if he relies solely on authority. Actually, the conflict between a man and a woman needs to be understood in terms of the two unique personalities. What is *this* woman like? What is the personality pattern of *this* man?

A further counseling implication is that an understanding of cultural and physiological forces at work can take some of the sting out of the conflict between the sexes; but essentially each human being must learn to accept and develop his own sex role in relation to his past experiences, his present situation, and his future goals. In practice, it is noted that once the client has been helped to understand, accept, and enjoy his own role, he can then be helped to accept the fact that the differences of his mate need not be a source of hostility. He can see that they are an important basis for enriching his marriage and his personal life. He sees that learning to value differences is a measure of personal and marital maturity. Consciousness-raising groups have great potential for helping men and women appreciate what it is like to be of the opposite sex. Typically, this goal is accomplished in a small group setting with either same or opposite sex membership going through exercises which force a confrontation with one's attitudes toward one's own and the opposite sex.

Empathy

Although the subject of empathy was discussed at length in Chapter 6, its relevance for marriage counseling will be elaborated here. Murphy makes the following distinction between empathy and sympathy: "Empathy is 'direct' apprehension of the state of mind of another person, without, as in sympathy, feeling as that other person does. In sympathy shared attitude is the chief matter" (344, p. 985). It is important that the counselor, building on an understanding of the differences between men and women, as well as on the basic concept that each personality is unique, help the marital client to develop insight into the personality, feelings, and behavior of his partner, that is, to have *empathy* for his partner.

Too frequently an individual's background has not prepared him for any further stage in human relationships than a sympathetic role. When empathy is not experienced, such an individual often feels there is no basis for the relationship. Consequently, the marriage appears doomed, unless mutual empathy can be developed. Skidmore (445, p. 69) lists empathy as one of the four major bases for building confidence and security in a marriage.

"I would never do that," "How can he feel that," "I can't understand why she would ever say such a thing," are all attitudes that may be approached from the viewpoint of developing empathy. Of course, the counselor's own ability to empathize with the client frequently can be used as a meaningful starting point for the client. The client knows, or can be helped to realize, that the counselor's acceptance is not the same as approval or sympathy. Having received an empathic response, the client then may be more ready to show empathy for others.

Experiencing empathic responses from a counselor sometimes suffices to stimulate a client's potential growth. In other cases, the counselor can demonstrate to a client his stubborn resistance to empathy and can use himself as model to lead the client to deeper understanding of his defenses and development. Without empathy there can be little basic acceptance between human beings. Growing empathy between husband and wife can be a measure of improvement in their marriage relationship.

Communication

In some marriages, one or both individuals have such distorted means of communication or undeveloped skills in communication that even in casual conversation they misinterpret simple facts. Poor communication, then, becomes a focal point of many quarrels. The individual first may reduce exaggerated expressions of hostility standing in the way of his understanding the more basic causes of his conflict by learning to recognize precisely what others mean or what they feel.

Accurate communication in a marriage not only can reduce hostility based upon misunderstanding, but it can also be a basis for developing a feeling of closeness or oneness within the marriage. It is a practical means for alleviating the loneliness that so many people feel in our society. Practical steps to improve communication do not obviate the need for awareness, but they are ways in which the client can consolidate the progress he is making and can encourage him toward further growth. Following are examples of skills to be learned and used cautiously for improving communication:

1. Repeat what the first person says. Try to rephrase it in your own words and try to see the other person's frame of reference. (See Chapter 7 on reflection techniques.)
   a. Ask, "When you say so and so, do you mean this and that?"
   Example: "When you say I am too strict with the children, you mean I shouldn't have punished Bobby for taking the cookie?"
   b. Ask, "What do you mean by such and such?"
   Example: "In what ways do you mean I am uncooperative?"
2. Learn to recognize that people express themselves differently.
   a. Some people express affection or any other emotion by words—some by behavior.
   Example: Some people say "I love you"; others bring a bunch of violets; and others keep the house in tiptop repair without being asked.
   b. Just because something isn't expressed verbally doesn't mean it isn't felt.
   Example: The individual who is "never" hostile outwardly may express it by illness, sarcastic jokes, or sly innuendoes.

3. Reduce generalities to a minimum.

Examples: "You *never* smile when I come home." "*All* men make life miserable for their wives."

4. State your own feelings clearly first before expecting your partner to express his feelings. Make clear "I . . ." statements.

Negative Example: "Do you think we ought to move now?"

Positive Example: "I think we ought to move . . . for the following reasons. . . ."

5. Distinguish the *situation* from the *person:*

Example: "I would like to talk to you longer, but I have someone in the office and I can't *now.*"

6. Set aside time for communication regularly, even when there is no particular problem to resolve. Use communication as a preventive measure to head off incipient problems.

Hayakawa's [1] theorem is pertinent here: "Misinformation breeds in an information vacuum." An example follows: If communication between persons A and B is bad, A then makes guesses. The longer the time that elapses, the less A's "information vacuum" resembles reality. For example, John is expected home at seven o'clock. As the time elapses past this hour, his wife begins to make more and more false assumptions: "Has he been in an accident, or is he drunk, or has he been killed?"

Partnership Problems

Once a partnership agreement has been consummated, two basic types of problems may arise: (1) those involving the individual personality adjustment of the partners, and (2) those more related to the marriage or partnership itself.

Special Personality Adjustment Problems in Marriage

There are several deep characterological problems that often are seriously aggravated by marriage. These problems include alcoholism, gambling, extreme jealousy, compulsive nagging, chronic complaining, and violent temper. Moralistic admonitions to do the "right thing" will not help these individuals. In most instances, they need considerable individual help to move from a basically manipulative and exploitative approach to people toward a more actualizing state.

In addition, the partner of a client with these types of problems frequently can be a deciding factor in the outcome of therapy. The "innocent" partner needs help in understanding the reasons for his original marital choice, the underlying dynamics of his reactions to his partner's

[1] From personal communication with Dr. S. I. Hayakawa.

present symptoms, how he has aggravated the problem, and finally how he can realistically help his partner.

Special Areas of Conflict in the Marriage Relationship

It would be presumptuous and unwise to suggest specific answers to problems that commonly arise in the marriage relationship. Nevertheless, the practicing counselor must be aware of these problems and, as suggested earlier, he must know the right questions to ask. The following list concerns problems on which there must be some consensus in marriage. It must be remembered, however, that disagreement is only symptomatic of a poor relationship, and that before the relationship is dealt with, individual therapy on pertinent personal conflicts generally must be handled by the counselor.

1. *Finances.* Is an inability to agree on finances a cover-up for more basic disagreements? Which partner (or is it both) is immature in handling finances? Are financial difficulties a symptom of overall immaturity? What significance does money have for this individual and his partner?

2. *Social Life.* Do these individuals actually have different social aims? Are they temperamentally different in terms of sociability? Is each lacking in an understanding of the other's social needs? Why is one of them placing great emphasis on social life? Is there basic dissatisfaction with the demands of family living generally or of this marriage specifically?

3. *Parent-Child Relationships.* Is there basic disagreement in regard to discipline? Has either of these individuals a distorted idea of discipline? Is there overidentification with a child or the children by either parent? Is there jealousy of one parent's closeness to a child? Is the parent-child difficulty a displacement of hostility? Is there a resentment of the responsibilities of marriage expressing itself through parent-child difficulties?

4. *Religious and Life Values.* Are differences in religion being used as a cover-up for other differences? Why did this couple marry in the first place? Why is this couple now having difficulty with a difference they evidently felt could be resolved before marriage? What does religion mean to each of these individuals? How much real effort have they made to resolve this difference? How important were religion and other general life values to these clients while they were growing up?

5. *In-Laws.* Are the in-laws the problem or is it the client's attitude toward them? If there is not unity in handling this problem, how much unity is there on other problems? Is jealousy a major issue? Is one client complaining about his in-laws because his own parents are his problem? How mature is this individual in terms of maintaining his own independence?

6. *In-Family Triangle.* Why is this individual alarmed by his partner's having close ties with someone else in the family? Was this ever a close

marriage? Is this client basically possessive? Is the partner expressing hostility by overdevotion to some other family member?

7. Extramarital Relationship. How has this client failed to build a marriage that meets the needs of his partner? Is he overly hostile or overly forgiving in his attitude? Is this client really interested in reestablishing the marriage? Or is this client playing the martyr role? If this is the client who has "strayed," is he overly repentant or overly defiant? What was he trying to accomplish, in terms of his own needs, by extramarital entanglement? What kind of individual did he pick to make the triangle, and why did he pick this individual?

8. Job pressures. Why are job pressures impinging upon the marriage? Is the individual really in a dead-end job or the wrong type of work? Does one or both have resentment or shame in regard to the job's prestige or income level? Are the hours of work really excessively long or is the job used as an escape from the home? What goals did this couple have originally in regard to economic status? Is the wife jealous of the husband's career?

9. Inadequate Self-Actualization. Is this individual really bogged down with too much responsibility and too many pressures? Does he really want to help himself or does he want some magic solution? Is this client unprepared for the responsibilities of family living? Are there practical things that could be done to give this individual some opportunity for creative activity that he has not tried? Is this client really trying to pull away from the marriage?

10. Different Cultural Background. What part did defiance of family play in the original choice of each other? Is one enjoying basically what he considers a superior role? What does this couple have in common? Is one using cultural differences to cover up more basic dissatisfactions?

It should be emphasized, of course, that the counselor must not ask the client these questions directly. Rather, he should use them to develop his own awareness of what is behind the client's problems. It might be well to reemphasize here the importance of the counselor's periodic analysis of his own reactions to the client's problems. He must remember that his own standards will not necessarily serve as a solution for this particular client's problems.

Going one step further, it should be understood that these questions about cultural backgrounds may be a means whereby the counselor can lead the client from a superficial approach to consideration of deeper problems. The goal is to make the client understand how the problem developed, what underlying attitude is reflected, and what it symbolizes in the marriage. Knowing the client's cultural background will help the counselor to decide which of the client's remarks he will choose for reflection.

11. Sexual Conflict. Though mentioned in the introductory paragraphs as a problem in marital relationships, sexual conflict is considered again here to emphasize its importance as being an especially difficult problem.

Clients eventually report sexual adjustment problems, although at first they obscure them by many resistive types of rationalizations. Marriage counselors generally work on the underlying psychological problems of the couples rather than directly on the sexual problems, since the sexual maladjustment is so often merely symptomatic. There are situations, however, where problems of inadequate knowledge and technique contribute to the difficulty, or where physiological problems are present. The latter problems should be investigated and dealt with first by specialists competent to diagnose and treat them.

There is considerable variation in the client's willingness to go beneath the surface of the problem confronting him. The client should be the main person to determine the length of marital therapy and the depth of insight to be achieved. Frequently, the manner in which the counselor helps the client to think about the problem, even on a superficial level, will make the client seek deeper counseling. It is not a matter of forcing the client against his desires, but of planting ideas that can come to fruition later when the client is more ready. For this reason, the counselor's understanding of the broad implications of presenting symptoms is an important facet of his proficiency.

Strategies and Issues in Marital Counseling

Therapeutic techniques having particular application to marital counseling are:

Structuring: In the beginning phases of marital therapy, this technique is frequently very important, particularly with unsophisticated clients who know very little about the process.

There are several basic attitudes that are important for the counselor to structure to the client early. Following are some of the basic counselor attitudes that must be communicated verbally to the couple. The therapist does not tell the couple how to run their lives. He does not function as an arbitrator, telling the couple who is right and who is wrong. He does not act like a top sergeant or parent substitute, telling them what to do. He is not a tattletale. He does not place blame, nor is his goal to give approval. He plays no favorites, but is equally interested in helping each client to realize more satisfaction from the marriage.

However, the therapist may structure the process by telling the couple that he has had training and experience in helping people to understand themselves and their partners. His purpose is to help them to understand how others have solved similar problems. The counselor hopes that by helping his clients understand how their problems originated, they will develop insight and techniques for handling present and future difficulties.

Frequently, only one marriage partner is willing to be counseled. The other may come to the counselor but he usually does not participate beyond the most superficial discussion. In such cases, the counselor can structure the relationship by suggesting that marriages often have been helped when one partner takes the initiative. The cooperative client can learn to build a better life for himself within the marriage as well as to improve the marriage itself. It is not unusual for the noncooperative client to change as a result of the observable changes actuated by the cooperative client.

Fee Problems: With the low-income family, finances are likely to be one facet of the family's problems. For this reason, the low-income group traditionally has received counseling in a social agency where a casework approach and financial aid were most appropriate.

In the middle-income group, high fees can aggravate a marginal problem. In many instances, this condition shortens the counseling process to a few sessions, thus jeopardizing the effectiveness of the work.

The best generalization that can be made concerning fees seems to be that it is desirable for the client to pay a fee reasonable for his income level. A broad definition of a reasonable fee is one that does not substantially increase the client's problems. The fee does, however, put enough pressure upon him to work at his problems conscientiously.

Handling Information and Building Skills: In the third element of marital counseling, concerning the marriage itself, information is more important than in some other types of counseling. The counselor must exercise as much skill when giving information as when performing other forms of counseling, and it is often the crucial factor in improvement. Basic to successful information-giving is the attitude with which the counselor presents data. When information is given suggestively as a basis for the exploration of ideas, and not pontifically or as reinforcement for preconceived ways of thinking, the client can be helped to grow.

Skill-building in areas of communication or sexual technique is a key intervention strategy. This is not usually done in a counseling relationship itself, but more in a workshop setting with several couples. Communication exercises take the form of practicing the kinds of rules cited in the previous section, in addition to learning how to express resentments and appreciations more clearly. In the sexual area, the methods of "sensate focus" described in the introduction to this chapter are examples. Films are used commonly in this process to show models of sexual practices and to increase awareness. Many sex technique films are available, but few on the intricacies of relating in a caring manner exist. "Touching: Importance for Human Growth," produced by Shostrom (437), is an examination by Ashley Montague (331) of the importance of human touch in human development.

Referrals in Marital Counseling: The marital counselor frequently finds it necessary to make special referrals. Ideally, he should be well informed about, and have direct contact with, the available resources in the community.

Some clients may, in the counselor's opinion, need a complete referral.

The individual may be so seriously dysfunctional that custodial medical care may be indicated. Finance or other broad family problems may suggest a social-casework approach; hence, a complete referral to a social agency would be preferable.

At times, the counselor may continue to work with the client under a partial referral arrangement. If there are physical symptoms, such as headaches or stomach ailments, it is essential that a physician decide if they require medical care, or at least whether counseling and medical care can be carried on simultaneously.

The establishment of a working relationship between a psychologist and an attorney makes for the facilitation of cross-referral between psychologist and attorney. In marital counseling, it is often necessary for the psychologist to refer clients to an attorney for pertinent information concerning marital laws, adoption, and annulment, for example. If it were necessary to refer the client to an attorney located some distance from the counselor's office, the client might not accept referral readily. However, if the attorney can be summoned into the psychologist's office at the critical time, or if the psychologist can be brought into the attorney's office at a time when psychological help is suggested, referral is facilitated.

Clients with a marriage problem are often in trouble legally as well as psychologically. One client, for example, revealed that she had completely repressed a former marriage. Skillful legal help assisted her in dissolving the first marriage without social incident or involved legal maneuvers. Another young man was assisted immeasurably during premarital counseling by an attorney when the legal problems surrounding a premarital pregnancy came up in the therapy.

Similar arrangements are made for collaboration with ministers and physicians where close office association is made for purposes of easy cross-referral. In institutions such as schools and colleges, this collaboration is made quite easily except for legal services, which generally are nonexistent.

Multiple-Counseling: Whether one or two counselors should handle one marriage is a question that cannot be answered definitely at the present time. It depends on the couple, the counselor, and the setting in which the counseling is done. We have used both methods, although research is needed on this point to help decide on the most efficacious procedure.

The following material explores the arguments for and against relying on more than one therapist. A general rule seems to hold that if the problem involves intensive psychotherapy for each partner, two therapists would probably be indicated. If the problem were primarily one of marital counseling on relationship problems, one therapist or counselor would probably be sufficient and satisfactory.

The counselor who sees both partners in a marital dispute has the advantage of participating in a relationship with both and seeing the likely reality or distortion of the material each presents to him. Mittelman (329, p. 93) feels that the advantages of one counselor working with a married couple are as follows: (1) The counselor secures information that makes him more able to perceive accurately the problems of both partners. (2) The counselor can see the distortions or omissions in the material from one or both of the partners. (3) During times of stress for one of the partners, the counselor can modify the behavior of the other, which was complicating the problems of the partner.

Even in cases where one counselor is definitely indicated, the counselor has a difficult role to play. Mace (303, p. 136) thinks that, "As a rule the relationship between the two individuals with whom he is counseling is initiated by conflict. In the presence of mutual hostility and recrimination, the marriage counselor must remain impartial and maintain the confidence of both husband and wife." In many instances, this is not an easy task.

Mittelman (329) points out that special transference problems may develop where one counselor sees both husband and wife. This transference is expressed by one partner in the form of concern over whether or not the therapist agrees with his evaluation of his partner, fear that the therapist is siding with the other partner, and wish-fulfillment fantasies that the therapist will change his partner by magic, thus saving the need for working out his own conflicts.

Mittelman (329) states, furthermore, that the counselor who handles both marital partners needs a reliable memory to know from which partner he got what information, the capacity to withstand the usually sustained rivalry and attack of both partners, the ability to be impartial but not neutral, and the courage to take a clear-cut stand in critical situations concerning who contributed what to a dispute. In other words, the therapist should behave like a benevolent, impartial, and firm parent to keep quarrels from getting out of hand.

Sometimes the counselor may find that what he says (or doesn't say) is so distorted or misinterpreted by one or both that the marital conflicts become exaggerated beyond repair. Under these circumstances, two counselors, particularly if they can work in close collaboration, can do more effective counseling than one.

Mittelman (329) suggests two reasons against using one counselor with both parties: If one of the partners seems paranoidal in the sense of blaming everyone for his problems, and therefore would probably blame the therapist for the termination of his marriage, it would seem more wise to have two therapists work with the partners. Secondly, if one spouse objects to working with the same therapist as the other, or if such a client were advised to go to the same therapist, he or she might refuse to be treated at all and might hide all resistance to help behind the cloak of objections to concurrent therapy.

One of the advantages of having separate counselors for each of the parties in a marital conflict is that the transference and memory problems suggested by Mittelman above are avoided. Each partner perceives his problems in a unique way; and to get into the frame of reference of just one of the perceivers of a marital dispute often is much easier. Furthermore, since the counselor does not have to remember who said what, he does not have the problem of keeping confidences.

If each partner has his or her own therapist, the therapists should confer at regular intervals in order that they may cooperate in the therapy. It is important for each of them to remember that he received the information from the conference. Martin and Bird (486) suggest the importance and value of this cross-communication approach. By this they mean that therapists should meet regularly for the purpose of comparing their ideas on the problems of their respective, concurrently counseled clients. They may approach the problem by having one therapist present the picture of some event that took place in the life of the married couple in the frame of reference of his own client. The other therapist would then report on the same incident as he reconstructed it from his client's presentation. The two perceptions would finally be placed side by side, leading to the fusion effect of a stereopticon, hence the term "stereoscopic technique." The ability to discover distortions of reality on the part of one or both partners is most valuable. We feel, also, that this method leads to the recognition of ego defenses and impulses.

Some advantages of the dual approach are that it frees the therapist from distortions due to his single observation; it saves time in a quicker recognition of the client's distortion of reality; and it cuts through the therapist's and his colleague's countertransference.

Some disadvantages of the dual-counselor approach are that it is more time-consuming and complicated, since it demands regularly planned conferences between therapists.

In the later stages of counseling, separate therapists and "joint sessions" or multiple-counseling can be introduced. As counseling continues, husbands' and wives' perceptions of their relationship become more congruent. Then counseling of both partners at the same time by two counselors may be helpful. The two counselors may rely upon a profitable technique, at this time, of appearing particularly understanding of their respective client's partner.

Another technique is that of requiring one spouse to interpret what the other has just said to his satisfaction before he is allowed to state his own views.

Group therapy, as an adjunct to individual psychotherapy, can be of immeasurable help in overcoming marital problems. We have developed two principles for utilizing supplementary group methods: husbands and wives are always placed in different groups; communication between them on what happens in their own groups is not allowed.

Eitzen [1] has developed a unique therapy technique for marital counseling. The program is arranged on a twelve-week-series basis. During the

[1] Dr. David Eitzen, from personal conversation.

first four weeks, only spouses of the same sex are placed together. During the second four weeks, they participate in a mixed group, but not with their own spouses. Finally, husband and wife are assigned to the same group. After the first eight weeks, they are more ready to understand each other.

Vincent (486) suggests some ways in which group therapy can be helpful: loss of the feeling of being isolated, different, or inadequate; catharsis and reassurance from talking without disapproval or condemnation; development of communicative skills and their transference to husband-wife discussions at home; awareness of the roots of sexual maladjustment in early experiences; insight into the many factors that militate against a complete sexual response; and breaking down of previously unrealistic sexual expectations.

Appraisal: The specialist in marital counseling sometimes uses personality appraisal devices. If the marital partners are interested, a comparison of personality profiles can be a useful therapeutic technique.

The Sex Knowledge Inventory (302) is the result of many years of research on pertinent sex information for marriage preparation as well as for successful marital relationships. The client may take the test, consisting of eighty multiple-choice questions, and then review the answers with the counselor.

Sometimes each partner takes a test such as the Allport-Vernon-Lindzey *Study of Values.* In addition to completing a blank on how he responds to the questions, each partner completes a blank on how he thinks the spouse would respond. Comparative profiles can then be drawn and shared. The Actualizing Test Battery (435), described in Chapter 5, is a further example of an instrument useful in marriage counseling.

Counseling with Families

There is a long history of therapy with children in individual sessions, but only recently have methods been developed for prevention as well as for intensive treatment of family problems through natural family groups or groups of families. In Chapter 11 the principal group approaches applicable to family problems were discussed. The purposes of this section are to review the main strategies for working with families and then to focus on special counseling issues in working with children and adolescents.

A body of methodology around family group work has developed. Satir (413) teaches what she calls "conjoint family therapy," discussed in Chapter 11, which emphasizes treatment of the whole family as a unit and may include several family units in a unitary therapy group. It has become a standard method of dealing with dysfunctional and distintegrating family units. Diagnostic and treatment methods are combined to give the therapist maximum information to use in interpretation without destroying individual responsibility. There is an emphasis on appreciation of differences among family members, an effort to open communication, and a reconstruction of the flow of family life chronology through discrete questioning.

There is a widespread style of family therapy known as Adlerian, after basic principles propounded by Alfred Adler earlier in this century. While there are many derivatives from his basic work, one of the modern developers was Dreikers (128), who advocated simple methods which parents could try with children to give them responsibility for their own behavior. His strategy was to see family members separately, then together, to work out ways of meeting the power and influence needs of all. A key part of the therapy is to anticipate and work out the special needs of children due to their ordinal birth position in the family.

Much family therapy procedure was developed around problems of fairly intact middle-income families. The problems of low-income families are quite different. Minuchin (327) has developed a series of techniques called "conflict resolution family therapy," specifically designed for the special multiple problems of low socioeconomic families. It takes into account the psychological restriction and impoverishment of children from these families and their characteristic ways of handling conflict.

There are experiments in intensive marathon types of family treatment where families are assembled for weekends of continuous confrontation. Families can take advantage of the motivation of the family crisis and learn to stay in the situation long enough to work through the stress. An example is described by McGregor (300) under the title "multiple impact therapy." Here a family is brought together for intensive study and treatment by the guidance team for two days. As a result of working through problems at the height of the crisis, more dramatic changes can be effected. Group sessions are supplemented with intensive individual counseling interviews. Sometimes the therapist brings his own family to these intensive weekends to add to the naturalness of the human interaction.

Most family therapy methods have been developed in clinical or non-school agency settings. There is a trend to involve families within the circle of school counseling functions. An example is the Oregon approach, described by Zwetschke and Grenfell (514), and later amplified by Fullmer and Bernard (177). They have developed an adjunct to individual counseling called "family group consultation." It is an effort to improve communication within families and to develop more awareness of mutual impact on various family members. Three or four families are included in one group, and families more experienced with the method are used to help new families introduced to the group.

Counseling Children

When a therapist is working with children rather than adults, it becomes necessary to modify counseling techniques to meet their particular problems of youth and immaturity. The first section below is devoted to problems of counseling young children and their parents. The second section discusses the problems of counseling adolescents and their parents.

Evaluating results of counseling and psychotherapy with children is difficult. Levitt (284) concluded, after reviewing the earlier treatment literature on psychotherapy with children, that untreated children improve about as much as treated children over time. These results, similar to Eysenck's analysis of adult therapy, suggest that we must be cautious in claiming results for psychotherapeutic methods with disturbed children. On the other hand, the data are too inconclusive to be pessimistic about helping methods with children; there may be a cancellation phenomenon operating also when results of various studies are averaged. As in adult cases, some are helped and some are actually hindered in their growth by formal therapy. Evaluation studies then indicate an averaging effect, which hides the actual and true growth of individuals.

Special Counseling Problems with Children

The most apparent difference between child and adult is in the level of communication they use. The dependence of the child on adults forces the counselor to consider the needs of these close adults along with those of the child. Because children are pliable, and because their defenses are not as entrenched as are the adult's, there seems to be less stability in therapy. This condition makes it impossible to predict any permanency in the changes that take place. Because of these difficulties, the counselor must accept more responsibility for directing and protecting the client (Watson 491).

Communication. Poor communication is a difficult obstacle for a therapist to overcome when counseling a child. Such a child is restricted in his ability to communicate for two reasons. The child's capacities to differentiate and integrate his outer world with his inner feelings are incompletely developed. His conceptual thinking and verbalizing abilities are at a relatively primitive level, with many gaps, inaccuracies, and elements of magical thinking present. The second reason is that the child has had so little practice communicating that his conversation is not a reliable or even intelligible bridge between himself and the therapist.

Because of the child's limitations, the counselor must rely on a behavioral rather than a verbal medium for a solution to the difficult problem of achieving adequate communication between himself and the child. For this reason, the use of play therapy as a communication medium and a therapeutic technique has been given impetus. The therapist, in addition, must be skilled in reading the child's bodily nonverbal communication.

Dependency. Because of the child's dependency, some adult is always involved in a child's therapy. The importance of the role of the adult depends on the age of the child and the adult's sense of responsibility toward the child. A close adult, usually the mother, is frequently the *informant* through whom the therapist is able to obtain a preliminary history of the child and to obtain assistance in the therapeutic planning. The conference with the mother also gives the counselor an opportunity to evaluate the mother's role in the child's problems, her own emotional disturbances, and some idea of the family relationship. Also, it is an opportunity to establish a good working relationship with the mother, which is especially important if the child is to remain in the home. Without the assistance of the parents, the child is not likely either to progress or to be kept in therapy.

Help for Parents. Since the child's difficulties are tied up with those of the adults who created his problems, it is often wise for the counselor to insist that one or both parents cooperate to the extent of entering therapy themselves. There is increasing evidence from the therapeutic experience, especially that of psychoanalysis, that disordered behavior in the child has frequently been taught unconsciously as a result of observing the parents act out their repressed feelings and impulses. This approach assists the parent to create better personality growth conditions in the home.

Parental attitudes and behaviors are decisive in determining the developmental progress of their children. Thus, therapy for a parent can play a decisive role in changing the child's environment from one of unmanageable threat to one of security and love. Beverly (50) implies that parents often see things in their children that are not there and try to force attitudes on the child that are impossible to accept. Occasionally it will be impossible to persuade the adult to participate in any form of therapy. When this happens, the counselor may gain some measure of reassurance from Axline (26), who reports several instances of successful child therapy in which no adult was counseled.

Skills-training for parenting is a commonly used strategy for dealing with parental problems. Some approaches, such as Gordon's Parent Effectiveness Training (199), are highly concentrated communication skills packages and programs. The program focuses on methods of active listening, for example, and ways of managing conflict so that both parent and child end the confrontation as "winners."

Therapist Responsibility. Since the child is less able to absorb stress than the adult and has very little control over his environment, the therapist must often assume a greater responsibility for the welfare of the child by giving direct help. Strang (458) maintains that the first step in treating an emotionally disturbed child is to change his environment so he can handle it more comfortably. As he experiences success where he had formerly only experienced failure, he will begin to realize that the world is not as hostile and defeating as he thought. Sometimes a summer camp experience or a new school will provide this change. The therapist may act specifically as a child advocate by arranging a transfer to a new school or by reporting maltreatment of a child to the proper authorities.

Awareness of Need for Help. In contrast with the adult, the child is less aware of a need for help because his limited experience tells him "this is the way things are." He seldom refers himself for therapy; instead, he is usually brought or sent in because he has displeased some adult. Consequently, he seldom comes to the therapist with a conscious desire for self-exploration as do most adults. The child will usually say that he "has no problem," but that his parent or teacher thinks he has. Axline reports the case of a disobedient twelve-year-old boy who enters the playroom and says, "Well, here I am. I just came because . . . I can't understand what mother was talking about. She said that you would help me with my problems, but I don't have any problems" (26, p. 30). In spite of this beginning, the boy had told the counselor of his troubles with his stepfather, the substitute teacher, and his peers at school before the end of the first session. He had also selected a medium (puppets) through which he could act out his problem. After this first session, the child usually looked forward to returning to the playroom.

It is often more difficult for the therapist to establish a common purpose with a child than an adult. The child is less able to understand the role of the therapist. His past experience conditions him to think of adults as authority figures who deal out rewards and punishments. The child's expectation of reward may make him try to please the therapist by acting the way he thinks a good boy should and by avoiding expressions of hostility. Fear of punishment may increase his anxiety so that his emotions become even more diffused.

Environmental Management. In addition to the helping environment created in the interview, specific steps must be taken frequently to order the broader environment in helpful ways. This may take the form of "milieu management," such as arranging for a private sleeping room at home, or it may be a type of behavior modification, such as keeping track of reinforcing conditions provided by parents. The main point is that interview strategies usually have limited success with children, whereas environmental management is a very powerful behavior-changing intervention.

Immaturity. The child's immaturity leads to greater fluidity in therapy than does the adult's comparatively greater maturity. One reason for this is that the child often mixes fantasy with reality. He has difficulty distinguishing the real from the imagined and may often relate a mixture of fantasy material with real events. Fluidity may also have a longitudinal dimension. For example, a child who at one session may be working through a deep emotional conflict may at the next session merely wish to act out something from TV or play a game of checkers. Because of this fluidity there is greater unpredictability in working with children than with adults.

Voluntariness. The child cannot discontinue therapy when he wishes. Even though the therapist maintains that it should be up to the child to decide to continue or to quit therapy, in reality a parent or teacher may insist that the child continue until certain unacceptable behaviors are changed.

Group Therapy with Children. Axline (26) and Moustakas (337) found it helpful for the child to experience peer relationships within group therapy. Slavson (448) found also that many children can be helped toward insight in a group situation. He reported that children substitute the therapist for their parents rather than develop a transference relationship in the adult sense. Their ties to their parents are still primary and intense, so that other adults are subsidiary. Many of the family techniques described earlier apply specifically to children.

Counseling Goals and Strategies with Children

In developing a relationship with children, the counselor must be aware of the techniques mentioned in Chapters 6 and 7, but he must adapt these methods to the maturity level of the child. He must respond to the child's feelings just as he does to adult feelings. Because of the real communication barrier imposed by the child's immaturity, the therapist frequently has to develop other means of understanding and interpreting feelings and behaviors to the child.

In the counseling of adults, the therapist is frequently assisted in his understanding of the client by inferences drawn from observing facial expressions, mannerisms, gestures, and other body movements. In children, such behavioral expressions are frequently the principal conveyance of the child's feelings. Therefore, the success of the therapist depends in large degree on his ability to observe, understand, and interpret the child in action. Since children use gestures as a means of expression to a much greater degree than adults, and in turn give personalized meanings to the gestures of others, the counselor must be mindful of his own facial and body movements and the interpretation the child might give to them. For example, if the counselor should suddenly raise his hand in an explanatory gesture, he might frighten the child. Likewise, raising his voice or even prolonging silence might be interpreted as anger. From such reactions, the counselor may infer some of the principal learnings of the child, as well as how he, the therapist, may best convey accepting, loving attitudes to the child.

Some counselors suggest using the same words the very small child uses to avoid talking over his head. Axline mentions the value of reflecting the gestures of the small child. For example, if the child stamps his foot, the counselor stamps his foot, or if the child shakes his head, the counselor does likewise. Other therapists feel that what one says is not important as long as the reflection conveys an honest empathy of feelings.

However, there are a few general suggestions that apply to all children. The therapist's responses should be brief, relaxed, and natural. Care must be taken also to avoid talking down to the child, acting like an authority figure, or engaging in baby talk.

It is often helpful for the counselor to sit on a low chair or on the floor so that he is at eye level with the child. This seems to help create a "we" feeling that adds to the rapport of the counseling session.

The counselor must at all times be aware of the sensitivity of the child to the sincerity of adults. One often hears the comment "You can't fool a child or a dog," with the implication that they are able to sense the true intentions of adults through their pretended intentions. The aphorism "What you are speaks so loudly I can't hear what you say" is a strong reminder to the counselor.

In summary, the counselor can help to overcome communication barriers by paying attention to the expressive movements of the child and himself. His verbal responses should reflect the attitudes and feelings of the child in simple, relaxed, natural phrases and gestures. By keeping his responses simple and sincere, he helps to build understanding and a relationship bridge that will permit the child to change his attitudes and behavior.

Goals of Child Therapy

Primary goals of child therapy are to help the child develop centering and actualizing strength so that he can cope more successfully with himself and his environment. One hypothesis here is that these goals come about when the child is exposed to a good therapeutic relationship. A second hypothesis is that to facilitate behavior change the environment must be managed so as to produce actualizing outcomes. As the child gains awareness, he learns to grow emotionally and to gain faith in himself as a responsible individual. Moustakas (337) suggests that there are three basic attitudes inherent in this good relationship: faith, acceptance, and self-respect.

The attitude of faith is intangible. It is reflected when a child considers himself to be an important person—one having something important to offer himself and others. If he comes from a home in which the emotional climate is negative and critical, however, he isn't as likely to have such faith in himself. Jourard and Remy (251) suggest that a person's self-appraisal is closely related to his perception of his parents' appraisal of him. To overcome the often negative effects of parental judgments, the therapist must believe sincerely in the child's ability for self-growth. This belief can be expressed to the child with such remarks as "What do you think?" or "I'm sure you know more about that" or "How you feel is the important thing."

If the counselor is able to build a relationship of faith and acceptance, self-respect is not difficult to achieve. When the child realizes that his feelings and interests are understood by the counselor, he believes that the counselor is sincerely interested in him. For example, the counselor's attitude might be as Moustakas has stated it: "These are your feelings and you have a right to them. I shall not try to take them away from you, to divert you from them, or to deny them to you, for they are a part of you, and I shall honor them as I do all aspects of yourself" (337, p. 5). The counselor should accept the fact that the child feels that his parents have mistreated him without making him feel guilty or ashamed for not "honoring" his parents. The child must believe that he is still a person of worth, even though he has many feelings that society considers "bad." The respect of the counselor thus goes a step beyond acceptance because he implies, through his respect, that the child has the freedom to express negative feelings. He is also implying that the child does not become an inferior person because he holds "bad" feelings (Baruch 36).

The therapeutic process in play therapy seems to pass through three definite stages, similar to the process discussed in Chapter 4. At first, the emotions of disturbed children are diffused, undifferentiated, and very negative in expression. They are angry and afraid of everyone because they have lost contact with the source of their frustrations and fears. In the playroom, they either want to destroy everything indiscriminately or they wish to retreat in silence and be left alone.

As the relationship between the therapist and the child grows, the child is able to express his anger more specifically. Pounding, smashing, and the desire to kill may still be present, but it is likely to be directed toward a particular person, such as a parent or sibling. In this second stage, the child releases and expresses his negative feelings directly toward the people in his environment who have made him feel inadequate. It is assumed, of course, that the parent has been prepared for these events. As the child releases negative feelings and as they are accepted, he begins to feel himself a more worthy person. Hence, he is able to express more constructive feelings (36). He is free to explore the polarities of his existence.

The child shows a great deal of ambivalence in the third stage. He still expresses specific anger, yet at the same time he shows kindness. He will love and fondle the doll one moment and spank it harshly the next moment. These ambivalent reactions are often intense in the beginning;

but gradually, as the more positive feelings emerge, the child enters the final stage of the therapeutic process. Now, he sees himself and his environment more realistically. For example, a seven-year-old boy said of his five-year-old sister, "She's pretty cute sometimes, even if she *is* a spoiled brat."

During the growth process, then, the child's anger and fear move from a diffused feeling to a focused and specific feeling, which he is able to express verbally or in play. As the child learns to express these negative feelings specifically, he begins to express positive attitudes occasionally. Finally he is able to separate more realistically his positive and negative attitudes toward his environment. This process of actualizing combined with the environmental management strategies described below provides the child counselor with a wide range of behavior-changing intervention methods.

Even though awareness is limited to the maturity level of the child, it is conceded that such awareness can be gained by the small child without verbalization (25). The behavior of the child changes as a result of his experiences in play therapy. The bully becomes a helper without explanation. Just as a chimpanzee can learn to solve his problem of reaching food by putting two sticks together, so the small child is able to bring together different ideas from his experience that help him solve his problem. This therapeutic process does not occur automatically in a play situation. It is made possible by the counselor's responding with constant sensitivity to the child's feelings, accepting his attitudes, and conveying a consistent and sincere belief in the child's worth as an individual.

Play Therapy

The techniques of play therapy evolved because the child is unable to express himself adequately on a verbal level. Play seems to help the child develop more elaborate and effective techniques for controlling his environment and appears to give him an opportunity to interact with an adult who takes a different attitude toward his person (491). The purpose of this section is to provide the reader with enough description to get a solid feeling of play therapy methods.

History of Play Therapy. The use of play therapy as a technique dates back to the analytic movement, when Anna Freud (492) used play to win children's friendship and when Klein (263) developed a "Play Analysis," which in principle was true to the psychoanalytic tradition. Taft and Allen contributed to the movement with a modification of Rank's theories on relationship to the therapist. Rogers, although not the first to state it, hypothesized that the individual had a strong capacity for self-direction and growth. Axline (26) then applied Rogers' client-centered philosophy to children at play. Axline cites examples that imply that immature and

dependent children have the capacity for self-direction and growth. The
parents of some of her children would not enter therapy. Others of her
children came from public institutions, and the adult supervisors were
not directly concerned with them. Despite these limitations, the children
apparently were able to overcome traumatizing experiences. This is possible
because as a child undergoes a personality change, however slight, his
environment is no longer the same. The child's stimulus value to others
changes, and as a consequence he is perceived and reacted to in a different
way.

Room and Materials. Play therapy requires a playroom and materials.
The room should be brightly colored, cheerful, and soundproof if possible. The walls and floors should be of a type easily cleaned and of a
material that will withstand clay, paint, and mallet attacks. A washroom
with hot and cold water should be accessible. For research and teaching
purposes, the therapy room can be wired for tape recordings. Also, if the
room is provided with a one-way mirror and is wired for sound, observations can be made without the child being aware of the observer. If
observations and recordings are made, it is assumed that the ethical requirements have been met.

The list of materials used successfully in play therapy grows each year.
Klein (263) used only a few primitive toys laid out on a low table. Axline
(26) suggests a long list of "acceptable toys." Many other toys have been
used with success. The success of Lebo (281) in using toys that had not
been recommended by any other therapist suggests that there are no
apparent limitations with respect to play devices that may assist a child
in working out his problems. It seems wise to select a wide variety so that
the child may find a personally convenient medium for expressing his
particular feelings.

Some Techniques. Many experiments have been reported in which dolls
provided a highly adequate means for working through problems. Dolls
generally appealing to young children are simple as well as suitable for
exploring many different problem areas. Since the child's problems stem
frequently from family relationships, a complete family of dolls—father,
mother, brother, sister, and baby—is essential. Dolls can help the child
to work through sex anxieties and to accept sex differences. Dolls and a
bottle with a nipple are a must for the small child who is working through
dependency needs.

Toys that are used often by children in expressing aggression are guns,
trucks, soldiers, masks, and inflated plastic figures. Axline found it convenient to use a sandbox placed flat on the floor as a background for the
doll house, furniture, and family. She found that sand was a good medium
for expressing aggressive feelings. The child buries toys in it or uses it to
represent rain, snow, bombs, or any number of other imaginative symbols. Puppets are very popular with older children between the ages of

six and twelve. They provide a helpful means for role-playing with readily identifiable figures, such as hero, villain, mischievous monkey, horrible alligator, or giants (494).

Finger and easel painting are very popular with some therapists. Shaw (426) and Alschuler (8) have had success with these media and hypothesize that color offers many clues to the nature and degree of emotional life of the child. Messing materials, such as finger paints and clay or sand and water, are popular with children who are having difficulty working through early training conflicts.

Controlled Versus Free Play. There is a difference of opinion as to whether play should be controlled or free. Levy (494) controls the play by selecting definite toys that he feels the child can use to work out his particular conflicts. Levy seems to make no attempt to point out feelings to the child, to develop transference, or to promote changes in behavior; yet, he has been highly successful in therapy with children between the ages of two and ten.

From the child's history, Levy decides the probable cause of the child's present problem. For example, a boy of seven had nightmares of being bound and tortured. He would awaken with cries of pain. Levy learned that two weeks previously some of his classmates had tied him to a tree and pretended to torture him. A little later, a story had been read in school about two knights who nailed an innkeeper to the door of the inn. These two experiences were highly threatening because of their strong similarity to a traumatic experience the boy had a few years earlier when he had been wrapped in blankets for the puncture of his eardrums without anesthesia. Levy set up the playroom with dolls to represent a knight, a doctor, and boys. There were toys to represent the inn, rope, tree, and blankets. Using the toys, the boy worked through his experiences, and the symptoms were removed in four sessions (494). This illustration does not imply that a rapid solution is usual. Most problems require many more sessions for satisfactory resolution.

Levy finds that children under six are helped apparently without their knowing why they were sent to the clinic and without perceiving any relationship between their play and their behavior at home. There is a possibility that Levy's success reflects the fact that fantasy and reality are not strictly differentiated at the younger age levels (494). The success of Mann, using a similar process, supports this hypothesis (305).

Axline (26) and Moustakas (337) insist on a free choice of materials. They set the playroom up in the same way for all children and with all equipment available for the child to use as he pleases. Spontaneous choice of materials is less artificial; the child selects his own media and proceeds at his own speed. The therapist may not even know the problem that the child is working through. Axline reports a little girl who would make a limping clay man, punch holes in him, tear him to pieces, and finally bury him. She continued to make and destroy the clay man at each session for several weeks. Not until after the girl was dismissed did the therapist learn that the mother was considering marriage to a crippled man.

Special play techniques for dealing with child frustration have been presented in films such as those produced by Vassar and Sarah Lawrence colleges. These techniques, developed by the late Eugene Lerner, suggest that an individual may react in many different ways to a frustrating situation according to his present needs. It is suggested that as a child learns to overcome these obstacles in play, he gains insight into the solving of other frustrations in his life.

In the film, several children in succession play with an adult who presents a series of play obstacles. The child is first presented with a situation in which the adult's and the child's car meet on a narrow track. The adult says, "We meet in the middle. How can my car pass?" The child's verbal or action response gives the counselor an idea as to the child's dependency, aggressiveness, or fear of authority. Ruch suggests three responses the child may make to this question (403, pp. 474–75). The child may turn his car around and go back so the adult's car may proceed; he may poke at the adult's car or hit the adult's hand; or he may coyly answer the adult's question in the negative and then slowly ease the adult's car back out of the way of his own car.

The adult had his doll stop the child's car. What happens? Is the adult's doll run over or asked to ride? In play with the cars, the adult says, "Let's see who can get there first." The therapist observes if the child must always be first or if he must never win. Does the child permit the cars to crash, and if so, does he seem to enjoy the crash or does he appear frightened?

When playing house, the adult asks, "May my doll come into your house?" After a short time the role is reversed. When the child's doll wishes to enter the house, the therapist says no and notes the child's reactions. A wide variety of situations similar to Lerner's may be used to explore the child's feelings and reactions.

Both free and controlled play seem to have merits in assisting the child to work out his problems. The success of the various methods, as used by different therapists, suggests that the counselor can be versatile and use discretion, either selecting the media himself or allowing the child to do it. It should be pointed out that there does not appear to be an adequate rationale for explaining the success of play therapy. Just as in adult therapy, there are many hypotheses springing from the various theoretical positions.

Limits of Play Therapy. It is important that the child be permitted great latitude of self-expression in the playroom, with fewer restrictions than he experiences outside. However, it appears equally important that the child observe certain limits if therapy is to progress. These limits must be well defined and concrete but need not be mentioned to the child until he threatens to break them. In this way, he learns what he is permitted to do as he explores the relationship with the therapist. He becomes aware of his manipulative efforts with adults and the effects of manipulative adults on him.

Well-defined limits within the therapeutic framework have as their purpose the preservation of reality, the psychological security of the child, and his health and safety.

The first element of reality to be considered is time. There must be a definite time to begin and to end the session, regardless of how interesting the play may be. This is a necessary consideration for the counselor who works on a schedule, and the child learns that freedom is not unlimited and is encouraged to focus his activities within a definite time limit. Another element to be considered is the rule that materials may only be used inside the playroom and cannot be taken home. However, the counselor may permit the child to take home the pictures he paints or simple toys that he constructs of paper or clay if this seems important to increase his feelings of worth. In such situations, it is wise for the counselor to instruct the parents regarding how they should react. Parents can demonstrate interest by asking the child to tell them about his handiwork and taking time to listen to his story.

The child should not be permitted to destroy irreplaceable items or to throw a toy through the window. Giving the child unlimited freedom with property does nothing to teach him the reality value of possessions or help him channel his feelings into less aggressive and destructive behaviors. Too much freedom very likely will increase his anxiety.

Most therapists follow the general rule of forbidding the child to hit the therapist, since striking an important person in his life may create guilt feelings or reinforce openly destructive behaviors.

Health and safety considerations rule out any behavior that will harm the child. For example, should he wish to break a glass bottle against the wall, drink the paint water, or throw sand in someone's face, the therapist would stop him.

Bixler (51) suggests three mechanisms for enforcing limits: (1) The therapist may reflect the child's desire or attitude, for example, "You are very angry—you would like to hit me." (2) The therapist may verbally express the limitation, for example, "You can't hit me but you may hit Bobo." (3) The therapist may control the child by physical means, perhaps holding his hands or sitting him firmly in a chair and saying, "You may pound with this mallet." If the child continues to try to fight, the therapist must put him outside the playroom for the remainder of the session. The therapist must not be punitive in his attitude but must carry out exactly everything he says he will. If he does not, he invites more aggressive behavior. However, in his firmness he must make the child understand that his actions are being rejected and not he himself. Bixler suggests that limits in the playroom may be as important for progress as acceptance of the attitudes that provoke the behavior. This is similar to the idea on acceptance discussed in Chapters 6 and 7 on permissiveness and structuring in adult counseling.

The playroom with its equipment is but an aid to the attainment of a primary goal of child therapy—helping the child establish a working relationship with a permissive adult. When the therapist can act as a permissive parent, he creates an emotional climate that stimulates the child to verbalize and dramatize his conflicts in play. This helps the child to extend himself, to expect warmth from an adult, and thus to learn that all adults are not punitive.

Behavior Management

This section contains an overview of the behavior-changing strategy known as behavior modification. It is a method widely used by parents, teachers, and community agencies to control and change children's behavior. Behavior modification is based upon the experimental work done by Pavlov on conditioning and later work by Skinner on operant behaviors. It assumes our environment controls our behavior through providing and withholding reinforcements, or rewards. Therefore, if one wants to help another person change his behavior, or change it for him if this seems indicated, as in the case of hyperactive children, then one must control the contingencies, or reinforcements, in the environment. Paying attention to a child while he is doing an approved act, or giving him a treat after he performs a reading lesson satisfactorily, are examples. These reinforcements tend to insure that the behavior will return, although the schedule for reinforcing must be planned to insure this repetition. The assumptions and methods are similar to those described for behavioral counseling in Chapter 2. Bandura's work (30) is an excellent overview of the principles and research in this area.

While behavior modification methods involve a complex technology and vocabulary too extensive to deal with here, our purpose is to point out that this strategy is widespread and effective for changing child behavior. The key limitations cited for the methods are that they work too well, in that they are easily subject to abuse in the form of controlling behavior. To obtain conformity, for example, a parent, teacher, or counselor may manage the environment to the point where spontaneity, initiative, and risk-taking could be controlled to the detriment of the child's actualizing. While depending on environmental management, one de-emphasizes free and responsible choice by the client. Many adults are fearful that these methods will diminish responsibility and other actualizing capabilities in people. Therapists, and collaborating parents, need to understand that behavior modification is a technology which can be used for enhancement of, or as a detriment to, the actualizing process.

Counseling Parents of Young Children

General Principles

Since parents are largely responsible for the happiness of their children, one way of changing the child's environment is to change the behavior of the parents. For this reason, the child counselor often insists that parents enter therapy as well. Modern American parents suffer considerable confusion over child-rearing, an intensity of confusion not shared with past generations. Earlier parents were guided by traditional child-rearing practices not available to modern parents, who are bombarded with multiple and conflicting principles of parenting. The "child experts" don't seem to have consistent answers either, so parents are understandably confused and deficient in self-confidence and knowledge.

Parents have two broad and overlapping kinds of problems. First, the parent may have anxieties and problems not strictly related to the child, but which are passed on to the child through attitudes of tension, emotional inconsistency, strictness, thoughtlessness, and the like. In such cases, the procedures are the same as for adult counseling, but with efforts to help the parent understand the effects of his or her behavior on the child.

Secondly, the parent may be well intentioned but inadequate through ignorance of a developmental perspective to understand that everyone passes through certain physical, mental, and emotional phases in growing from infancy to adulthood. This knowledge is usually very reassuring to parents and helps them anticipate and meet problems of development with more confidence. Children's behavior must be evaluated in terms of the norm for particular age levels. Reference to a work such as Gesell's (186) is helpful in this regard, although parents need to be cautioned about the atypical samples and overgeneralization. The developmental approach gives parents a framework in which limits can be set. Parental guilt, anxiety, and primitive attitudes can then be reduced or eliminated. Parents want accurate information on normative behavior.

Some of the persistent developmental problems encountered by a counselor working with parents of young children are aggressiveness, sexual tensions, elimination problems, and relating to other children. Specific ideas for parents in dealing with these problems are beyond the scope of this book, but abundant literature exists on child-rearing and research on child development.

Manipulative and Actualizing Parent Models

Just as children learn many ways to control and manipulate their parents, so parents apply a wide range of manipulative techniques to their children. Creating guilt through emphasizing "shoulds" is one of these. The manner in which love is given or withheld is another example. One of the principal counseling approaches used with parents is to help them perceive these manipulative ways of managing their children's behavior and to move to more actualizing forms of communication.

The actualized parent emphasizes self-responsibility in his or her child and is aware of the child's need for autonomy even though painful to the parent. He or she is willing to "let the child go," even at great risk, to become an actualizing person in his own right. Counseling with parents emphasizes the problem of shifting responsibility for choices from parent to child and of helping the parent interpret the limits of freedom to the child.

Counseling Adolescents and Their Parents

The adolescent is too mature for play therapy techniques, but since he or she is still a dependent with special developmental problems, some techniques additional to those used with adults are applicable. The developmental outlook assists adults in understanding the adolescent as well as other age groups. At the same time, a counselor should believe in the adolescent's potential to solve his own problems and actualize himself when he understands himself and his particular problem. Counselors are asked by parents and teachers to be of help with certain typical adolescent concerns. Some of these typical developmental concerns are choosing a career, deciding on higher education, relating effectively to peers, finding a place in society or deciding to change it, managing sexual tensions, finding a satisfactory relationship with parents on a host of issues, and, finally —emancipation from home. High school counselors find that this developmental period is a specialty in itself.

A characteristic difficulty in working with adolescents, and one which makes it difficult to keep them in therapy, is their impatience. They want the answers right now. Since adolescence is a transition stage from childhood to adulthood, it is usual to find conflicts and confusion relative to long-term satisfactions versus immediate pleasures. The counselor can assist the adolescent to realize that his impatience is part of this conflict and help him make realistic choices. A further characteristic is dependence on peers for help rather than seeking adult assistance. The suspicion growing out of perceptions of adults as untrustworthy and not "with it" is an obstacle to counseling.

Counseling Parents of Teenagers

Goals in counseling parents of an adolescent are to help them channel his or her feelings into constructive activities and to understand his or her behavior. A parent is often reassured to learn that rebellious behavior is a necessary part of growth and emancipation from parents. This phase of development can be less painful for the parents and the adolescents if awareness of the growth process is gained before serious misunderstanding develops.

Baruch (36) suggests that parents need to give their adolescents three things—*understanding, practical sex information,* and *help in becoming an independent person.* Adolescents should be encouraged to express their feelings without fear, and parents should attempt to accept their right to express hostile feelings. This view may be very threatening to a parent, which suggests that the parent can't understand the child's feelings unless he understands his own feelings. This parental lack of insight is one of the reasons why it is so necessary that parents enter therapy with the adolescent. As the parent learns to talk out his true feelings with his child, he learns to understand himself and his child better.

The parents can be assured that the youth needs their help in learning to express feelings and to control impulsive actions. Baruch (36, p. 69) suggests five ways of channeling negative feelings into socially acceptable actions: (1) verbalizing the grievance; (2) writing out the bad feelings; (3) drawing pictures of the hated person; (4) painting, modeling, and dramatizing; and (5) playing games, such as tennis, golf, checkers, or chess, in order to work out family or peer battles.

To understand their adolescents, parents must realize that their children's present and past feelings cause them to act the way they do. Behind unacceptable actions are negative feelings that may have had their origins in early childhood. These feelings not only result from what actually happened but are also tied up with the child's fantasy of what happened. This fantasy also plays a part in the imagined attitude of the parent toward the youth (36). If a child felt a lack of love, of trust, or of a sense of belonging in his early life, he or she will tend to find it difficult in adolescence to feel at home with his or her peers. Therapy with the adolescent must uncover basic feelings from childhood that are causing ineffective actions in adolescence.

The parent needs assistance in learning to help the child avoid dangerous behavior and still allow him or her optimal personal freedom. This may be accomplished in two ways. First, the parent may anticipate certain interests and provide opportunities for the needed activity with a structured environment. Ball leagues, hot-rod clubs, camping, and fishing and hunting trips are examples. Secondly, the parent can be taught to accept the youth's negative feelings and verbalize them back to him. If the parent can accept the negative feelings, it is easier for the adolescent to accept them and thus eliminate his or her guilt feelings. Finally, parents must realize that there is the "generation gap" and that customs, entertainments, and mores are changing rapidly.

Parents often complain, "What about me? I have feelings too." They need assurance that it is sometimes necessary for them to express feelings also. They should express anger, and then, if they have regrets, say so in sincere humility. Usually, the parent is surprised at her adolescent's understanding and acceptance when she, as a parent, admits a problem too.

This de-idolization goes a long way toward building rapport between parents and children and toward building teenagers' respect for parents' feelings.

Parents need assurance that limits on adolescent behavior are still necessary. Youth must accept the necessity of following certain customs and rules. Baruch suggests three reasons for limits which can be understood by the adolescent: "This is important for health and safety. This is important to protect property. This is important because of law and order and social acceptability" (36, p. 11).

Dynamics of Parent-Adolescent Relationships

The problem, from the therapist's point of view, is to help the adolescent secure as much freedom as he or she is able to handle and to help parents accept the risks of this freedom. There are certain difficulties that make it hard to achieve this goal, even if the therapist has tried. The following devices, derived largely from Wickes (497), are suggestive of the numerous maladaptive ways parents use to control adolescents.

1. Utilizing love as a dominating and holding force to satisfy personal needs in the parent that "may happen when the parent is disappointed in other human relations and, pouring out all the pent-up emotion on the child, also feeds himself upon the child's love" (497, p. 90).

2. "Placing the youth under a burden of gratitude and sense of duty because of values received" (497, p. 90).

3. Treating youth as emotional toys; thus, not allowing the child to reach for greater maturity.

4. Prolonging one's own youth beyond its rightful time. "Daughters are kept the little girls; the son begins to assume the place of the youthful lover" (497, p. 96).

5. Being overstern and authoritarian on the parents' part and refusing to allow the child to break the submissive role.

6. Being too weak and too ready to yield, on the part of the father, and being unable to accept his responsibilities. "This may inspire only contempt in the son; thus the adolescent problem of freeing himself becomes too easy, and his contemptuous attitude is carried over toward all the struggles of life. A weak and acquiescent son, having a similar identification, may gravitate toward failure—even as his father has done. He is inclined to present his father-identification as an excuse for his own failure to meet life" (497, p. 99).

7. If mother is the stronger parent, she represents not only love but authority, thus making it more difficult for the son to break away and establish independence. He may now fear the power of women, as he may acquiesce and lose his masculine attitude. Furthermore, he may break the bond completely and consistently undervalue women in an effort to deny their power.

8. Being suspicious and unreasonable, on the part of the mother, toward

the father may create a similar unconscious attitude toward men on the part of the daughter.

9. Holding inappropriate attitudes, on the part of the father, may furnish the daughter similarly inappropriate expectations toward men in general. For example, if he is too fond of her, there is a danger that the daughter will find herself unable to break the close bond for marriage. She goes through life looking for her father's image in a prospective husband. If he is too dominatingly devoted, the daughter may repudiate his overinsistent demands and repudiate him. "She is frequently suspicious of men and their demands upon her. She senses sexual motives where none really exists, or if they do exist she refuses to see their normal aspect in adult life" (497, p. 106).

Conversely, indifference and neglect on the part of the father may cause feelings of inferiority and may motivate the daughter to go about looking for a father surrogate who will give her the fatherly devotion she has missed. Other girls may feel only hatred and resentment toward such a father. Lacking the proper discipline, which is a part of development, she is torn by a conflict between rebellious aggressiveness and a desire for submissiveness.

It is the counselor's job to become thoroughly acquainted with dynamic patterns such as those illustrated above and to place them in the perspective of the child's and parent's lives. As a result, both can see more clearly what is operating among all family members. All the counseling skills described in earlier sections of this book are needed to do this job well.

Summary

Couples counseling is a term applied to helping both partners in an intimate relationship. The case for interdisciplinary collaboration is illustrated. Premarital issues are explored in sexuality and relationships.

Some of the basic problems in counseling and psychotherapy with children, young adolescents, and parents revolve around achieving accurate communication, handling dependency feelings, working with the whole family, and helping clients to become aware of their need for help, while still keeping the relationship voluntary. Play has been found to be one of the best media for therapy with children. The principal goal of individual and group therapy with children is to help them achieve strong egos so they can cope with their environmental demands and their own inner pressures. Behavioral strategies are compared to play therapy. Counseling with parents involves many problems common to the development of young children, such as sexual and elimination problems, excessive aggressiveness, and unresolved dependency. Adolescents have their unique problems also, in the form of vocational choices, sexual adjustment, and relationships with parents and peers.

Counseling on Life Style, Careers, and Rehabilitation

Choosing a satisfying life style is one of the principal developmental tasks of life. In terms of our Actualizing model, it involves all levels of awareness in the person, from values clarification at the core level, analysis of basic character styles, and development of rational choice methods at the actualizing level. This life style choice incorporates what was once called vocational planning, but now this choice includes a much broader range of choices covering type of community life, desired family structure, avocational activities, as well as range and kinds of friendships and partnerships. It is considered an integrated process involving many values and choices. This state of affairs offers a great challenge to Actualizing Counseling and Therapy to provide a range of counseling methods and the most appropriate kind of relationships to help people make responsible choices and plans. Life style counseling, combined with group experiences where values are explored, strengths and resources are inventoried, problems are examined, and plans are formulated, offers such a comprehensive approach.

Since a significant part of life planning involves productive work, a large part of this chapter will be devoted to careers and to the companion topic of educational planning. Since handicapped persons have special problems of actualizing in the career area, this topic will receive attention as well.

The social consequences of career choices are considerable. The principal values of professional career counseling services to society are the discovery, utilization, and conservation of human talent as a humanistic goal. Appropriate career choice is especially significant in view of the multiple career changes people now make in a lifetime to keep up with rapid changes on the job scene, as well as to match their careers to their

13

evolving life style. Career counseling for the handicapped is wise social policy also.

Counseling, and the collateral area of appraisal, cannot become manipulative tools or instruments of national policy, however, since this would violate our highly valued freedom. Therapeutic psychology seeks to help a client become aware of his assets, limitations, and opportunities in all possible areas so that he will make wise choices and will use his unique talents if he cares to do so. We believe that when individuals know their talents and use them in ways of their own choosing, the effects ultimately will be best for the society in which they live. In addition, counseling serves broad social purposes through helping individuals overcome obstacles to effective learning and achievement by means of remedial and rehabilitative planning and action.

Career Counseling

Our Point of View

Career choice has been regarded historically as vocational guidance—a process of helping the client to choose, prepare for, and succeed in a given occupation. This process was centered around counseling, which consisted largely of examining data about the client and looking over the occupational possibilities to find a specific career goal, whereupon an educational plan was formulated to reach that goal. Although this rationale is still basic, there have been recent changes in the perception of the significance and scope of career counseling. A significant change is from *occupational* guidance, oriented to a group of possible entry choices, to *career* guidance emphasizing the process of progressing from one level to another. Another change is the concept of continuous career planning over life. The data about rapid professional obsolescence, for example, emphasizes the need for continuing education. For many persons this means massive retooling in midlife for a vastly changed job classification or for a wholly new career. It is commonplace now for a person to anticipate three or four major career changes in his or her lifetime. Another significant development is support for career education and counseling by the United States Congress. This has become part of a national manpower and education policy. This career education commitment has resulted in large-scale financial support for training, research, and development programs in career counseling.

One of the principal changes is the perception of career counseling as part of general counseling, or in our terminology, a task of therapeutic psychology. Vocational psychology cannot be singled out as a special branch of counseling and psychotherapy, largely because career counseling must be accomplished in the context of the individual's total life style and in relationship to the client's subculture. Optimally effective career counseling, therefore, cannot be an isolated and mechanical process of matching people and jobs.

A broad clinical approach to career counseling has had much attention in recent years, especially as choice-making is seen as a developmental process. An example is Forer's (160) framework for clinical techniques, wherein he reviews the psychology of work, projective personality appraisal, and the psychodynamics of career choice. The clinical approach stresses a comprehensive personal assessment in conjunction with the usual vocational assessment with specialized tests.

Career counseling goals can be construed in several ways. First, and most commonly, career counseling is a process of confirming the choice already made by the client. Many clients have done a fair job of assessing themselves and their opportunities and of making tentative choices, as a result of other life experiences with parents and teachers. Second, career counseling is a process of clarifying vocational objectives. People are collecting information about careers and their personalities all the time, but they have difficulty interpreting the meaning of the data and stating the choice problem precisely and in the context of life style planning. Counselors can help this type of client perceive his problem in clearer terms. The third manner in which career counseling is helpful to clients is that it allows them to discover facts about themselves and the working world that they had not known before. The most revelatory aspects are those in which occupational choice limits are broadened to include many which the client had not considered in his original career formulations.

Therapeutic psychology is uniquely suited to accomplish this broad goal of effective career planning as part of life planning. The techniques described in earlier chapters, plus some special tools uniquely suited to educational-vocational planning, are the principal requirements for effective career choice. It was pointed out in Chapter 4 on the counseling process that planning problems differed somewhat from other types of personal problems because there is more emphasis on rational problem-solving methods and more involvement of the actualizing level functions. It should be emphasized, however, that any career counseling worth its salt includes considerations of the client's polar attitudes, aspirations, and core feelings. Career choice, from the research results reported to date, is not a strictly rational process. Neither is it a process of choice-making on the basis of a few interviews with a counselor. Research supports the idea that career decisions are the product of a long series of life experiences and learnings that come to a focus in the interviews with the counselor.

Theories of Choice

Prior to examining problems and procedures in helping clients to make career choices, some of the principal theories on how such choices are made will be presented.

Psychoanalysts view the origin of interests as a response to an ego need for recognition and status satisfactions. Explanations are made along the lines of expression of unconscious needs, as illustrated by the person with aggressive, sadistic tendencies wanting to be a policeman. There is little research evidence to support this point of view.

Roe (386) has formulated a series of hypotheses to account for the early determinants of interest. These determinants are basic human needs and early family experiences of acceptance, avoidance, and emotional concentration. These early experiences influence the general orientation of the child toward things or people. Roe has classified occupations according to eight clusters, such as service, technology, and entertainment. She also classifies them in levels from professional to unskilled. Roe hypothesizes that the clusters can be identified in terms of major orientations toward people and objects and that the early life experiences of the child predispose him toward certain major occupational groups.

Ginzberg (192) viewed career choice as a process covering three developmental periods—the fantasy (six–eleven), the tentative (twelve–seventeen), and the realistic choice (eighteen up). Ginzberg indicated that he thought the process was largely irreversible, a result of many compromises of values and opportunities, and a function of the person's perception of the job rather than a realistic view of work. Criticisms of Ginzberg's study center around the inadequate design, the lack of description of the compromise process, and the fact that he ignored the phenomenon of occupational mobility.

Carter (96) claimed that the individual's vocational attitudes develop from efforts to adapt to direct family and social pressures and to his own perceptions of his needs and capacities. His interests develop from identification with an occupation and are confirmed through try-outs in that career field. Eventually, the individual incorporates the occupational demands into his self-concepts and the occupational interest becomes relatively stabilized. Others, such as Bordin (60), feel that occupational interests are by-products of personality traits and self-concepts in particular. Interests shift when the self changes or when the individual's stereotype of the particular occupation changes.

One of the most comprehensive and data-supported theories of occupational choice was formulated by Super (468). The gist of his theory is that occupational choices are implementations of the self-concept. According to his theory: a person is qualified for many occupations; each occupation requires a characteristic pattern of abilities and traits (with wide tolerances); since individual self-concepts and social situations change, the process of choice is continuous due to growth, exploration, establishment, maintenance, and decline; the career pattern (level, sequence, and duration of occupations) hinges on parental socioeconomic level, ability, personality, and opportunity; vocational development is mainly that of developing and implementing a self-concept that is the product of interacting heredity, physical factors, opportunity for various roles, and the extent of approval from superiors and peers; compromises between individual and environmental variables, between self-concepts and reality demands, are made through role-playing opportunities in fantasy, counseling, school, or work; satisfaction depends on the extent of adequate outlets for personality needs, a work situation in which a congenial and appropriate role can be played. Super is verifying his theories through a Career-Pattern Study (466), consisting of longitudinal and horizontal research on how children and adolescents make their career choices. Super is using actuarial, life-history, and career-pattern-analysis methods to study the career choices of youth.

Holland (230) has formulated a developmental theory of vocational development with a final focus on six personal types—realistic, intellectual, social, conventional, enterprising, and artistic—from empirical goal, role preference, activities, and self-concept summaries of each group. The realistic person, for example, prefers physical and technical activities, holds conventional economic values, and holds social and esthetic values in low importance. He sees himself as a masculine, practical, conventional, submissive, and uncreative kind of person. This developmental theory helps the person facing a career choice to consider the complex personality dimensions of occupations in a systematic and realistic manner.

Appraisal and Diagnosis

For didactic purposes, the career counseling process will be divided into three elements: appraisal and diagnosis, information methods, and counseling techniques. The methods and areas of appraisal are summarized in Figure 24. The various methods of appraisal in career counseling are listed in the outer circle, and the matching areas to be appraised are indicated in the inner circle.

Most of the methods listed in Figure 24 are designed for appraising the personality characteristics that are close to the surface and to aid in diagnosis of the more manifest vocational problems. Hence, this discussion will focus on those personality levels that are related to the problem of career choice and adjustment.

The diagnostic process in career counseling follows the principles of diagnostic thinking cited in Chapter 5 and is designed to clarify the client's choice problem. The following material illustrates some of the diagnostic formulations built on appraisal instruments. Detailed use of specific tests will not be discussed because there is so much information available elsewhere.

Aptitude Appraisal. One of the counselor's first diagnostic tasks is to note the congruence or discrepancy between the client's aspirations and aptitudes. The first step a counselor should take to accomplish this goal is to ascertain the client's vocational aspirations and knowledge. General mental-ability tests, along with special aptitude measures, then, are ad-

Figure 24. Areas and Methods of Appraisal in Career Counseling

ministered to infer the client's relative capacity to perform job functions or his potential to succeed in specified tasks or curricula. This procedure may be applied to many individuals, such as the seventeen-year-old boy who wants to be a lawyer but for whom reliable and valid aptitude measures indicate he is in the lowest 10 percent of the college freshman population on scholastic aptitude.

Aptitude measures may be applied as well to the student who is performing beyond a comfortable level of achievement. This student is called, in educational terms, an "overachiever." Although it is desirable, perhaps, to emphasize high achievement, experienced teachers note that many clients of this type achieve above their rated aptitudes even though performance is not emphasized. Many of these clients experience much anxiety about status and failure; some even pay the heavy price of emotional distress later as a result of allowing their inordinate ambition to outstrip their capacities.

Aptitude tests may be applied to a third type of client—the so-called underachiever. This client has known aptitudes but ones he is not using to the fullest. He may not be using his aptitude to the utmost because of a deep-seated motivational difficulty, educational-skill deficiency, or health problem. For this type of client, a more refined diagnostic process must be initiated.

Aptitude discovery is a further problem in appraisal. A client, for example, finds that as a result of the aptitude survey he has potentialities in the area of numerical reasoning and arithmetic problem-solving that he did not know existed in vocationally significant strength.

Two additional types of clients confronted are those without tangible aptitudes and those with many high aptitudes. For the former, career counseling is difficult because training and placement of such clients is a problem. The problem is made even more difficult if the client or his parents have unrealistic aspirations for a certain occupational pursuit. For the latter type with multiple aptitudes, the counselor's difficulty often boils down to his determining which of the high aptitudes fits other factors of the client's interests and opportunities.

Interests, Attitudes, and Values. Although aptitude appraisal is a matter of capacity and vocational performance, interest and value measurement are concerned with vocational satisfaction. Various measures purporting to appraise interest are correlated closely with measures of job satisfaction. Aptitude is not so related as far as we know now.

The client with a conflict between interests and measured aptitudes— that is, with a diagnostic problem in the interest and value area—is confronted often in counseling. Such a client, for example, may have much interest in science but little aptitude necessary for work in that area. A counselor may note, however, the existence of artistic talents. The counselor may reconcile the discrepancy by suggesting that the client consider, perhaps, becoming a scientific illustrator.

Another type of client, presenting a diagnostic problem to the counselor, has measured interests not related to stated interests or ambitions. For example, the client says he wants to be an engineer because he likes to manipulate and repair mechanical objects. However, the pattern he gives on a standard interest test is that of social service with no measured interests in common with persons in engineering.

The client who has no well-defined interest patterns is another type the counselor encounters. He may lack interest maturity as a cause of his condition, especially if he is an adolescent. There may be no dominant pattern nor even an above-average interest area. His life experiences, out of which interests develop, may have been constricted. The solution may lie mainly in waiting a few years until a crystallized pattern develops. Strong (459, 460), for example, found considerable instability of interests in men younger than twenty-five. This lack of significant career interests may have some clinical meaning in that the client cannot get interested in anything or identify with a particular family of occupations because of some more involved value commitment issues.

Counselors occasionally meet clients who have unused or undiscovered interest patterns that are revealed by inventories. This condition creates counseling problems since the discovered interest pattern may be related to a field that the client cannot enter because of limited finances, family, religion, or some other socially constricting circumstance.

Part of the diagnostic picture in career counseling is the relationship between interests and values. Values are prime motivating characteristics that should be explored in any career counseling process. Their importance for career planning is contained in fundamental questions such as, "What is my philosophy of life?" "How do I feel I want to use my life?" "What is important to me?" These questions are closely bound up with occupational choice, but there is little research to indicate the ways in which material related to these fundamental questions can be used effectively in career counseling. The counselor must depend on his skill in helping the client clarify his attitudes about these important questions and in helping him find activities that fulfill the demands of his philosophy. Some instruments, such as the Allport-Vernon-Lindzey study of values, are useful to the counselor to help clients identify their dominant value clusters.

Physical and Emotional Adjustment. Counselors make attempts to appraise emotional factors related to vocational predictions, but not very much is known concerning the influence of these factors. There are few validity studies of personality traits or styles of life related to specific occupations. Apparently, there is considerable intraoccupational variability on such personality traits. Emotional problems, however, have a direct bearing on occupational success, in that attitudes toward authority, hypochondriacal tendencies, and other emotional adjustment problems, involving neurotic and psychotic characteristics, affect the client's ability to obtain and hold employment.

Physical factors play an important part in the counselor's diagnosis of occupational problems. These factors will be considered later under rehabilitation problems. As noted in Figure 24, there are many other considerations that must be made in career planning—finances, family situation, opportunities, and pressures from teachers, relatives, and friends.

Although we covered the general topic of using information in counseling in Chapter 10, there are several types and sources of information especially useful in counseling on career problems.

Types of Occupational Information. Occupational information covers quantitative data, such as the number of people employed in certain occupations, and qualitative data, such as the structure and description of occupations. The several types of information that a career counselor must know are occupational structures, facts, and trends. These data serve two general purposes in counseling—exploration and verification (405). The exploratory function is performed in the early phases of counseling before the client makes a career decision. Browsing through occupational readings, seeing occupational films, evaluating part-time jobs, and watching selected television programs offer direct or vicarious tryout experiences. Rusalem (405) points out how these exploratory experiences are emotionally toned and how they become part of the self-concept. Clients, during this exploratory phase, must get "the feel" of a career in addition to the usual stereotypes.

The verification function of occupational information comes late in the process when the client observes or reads about occupational material to verify his tentative choices. He may actually try out the occupation to test the congruence of work reality with his expectations and self-concepts. For example, a prospective medical student obtains summer work as an orderly to check on the reality of his perceptions of medical environments.

The United States Employment Service is conducting continual occupational research designed to keep up with the changing job scene (154). Classification is based on the assumption that workers are involved to varying degrees with things, data, and people. It is focused, therefore, on what the worker does on the job. Jobs are broken down into eight components, some of which are: interest, aptitude, temperament, educational development, and work performed. Twenty-six worker functions, such as computing, analyzing, serving, and copying, are weighted and organized into a hierarchy according to requirements for each job and not according to skill level. For example, a plumber is given a weighting of 6 on precision working, 3 on computing, and 1 on taking instructions (154). This line of research has shown great promise in career counseling, particularly for those occupations requiring specific on-the-job training rather than broad general types of advanced education.

Occupational classification schemes are useful to the counselor as a means of orienting the client concerning his career objectives, on a level which the client can understand. They are valuable, in addition, because they suggest occupational goals that might otherwise have been over-looked in a systematic search for suitable occupations.

The counselor needs all the facts on various occupations his client is considering in order to describe to the client what demands each occupation will make on him. It is apparent from Ginzberg's (192), Holland's (230), and Super's (468) research that it is not the external objective reality of the occupation that enters into career choice as much as the client's subjective perception or idealization of that occupation. Hence, there is much need for transmitting accurate and comprehensive job facts to clients. Most of this information is obtained in job analysis surveys performed primarily by the U. S. Bureau of Labor Statistics. The specific kinds of career information needed in career counseling are as follows: opportunities (current and long-range), compensation (salary or wages and supplemental benefits), hours (number and regularity), entry levels, and related jobs, qualifications, and restrictions (physical characteristics, marital status, memberships, licenses, certifications, examinations, and special personal qualities and training requirements).

Sources of Occupational Facts

Occupational facts found in thousands of occupational books and pamphlets are usually classified according to characteristics considered important for persons entering the occupation, or characteristics and duties of the jobs. There are three main sources of such information: federal agencies, commercial publishers, and trade associations. The Bureau of Labor Statistics and the Bureau of the Census generally do the basic research. This is published in a variety of government pamphlets. Many of these occupational data are written up in attractive format and style by commercial publishing firms. Trade associations publish a plethora of occupational information, mainly of the recruitment type.

The counselor should note the *source* of the data in estimating the reliability and usefulness of the information for his client. He should note also the *date* of the publication and of the underlying basic research, since out-of-date occupational data can be very misleading. Data on salaries, which have changed very rapidly, become out-of-date quickly as well. However, most descriptive information remains valid over a long period of time.

Agencies in which career counseling is performed compile the occupational data in libraries called in most places "career centers." The data are classified by an alphabetical or numerical scheme such as that of the *Dictionary of Occupational Titles* (484). Often a specialist librarian is employed to locate information for clients and to perform the monumental chore of keeping the information current. Several bibliographic sources contain compilations of current publications of value in career counseling. State departments of education often have special services for counselors in the location and dissemination of occupational literature. A current development is computerized information which is retrieved directly by the client. Printouts from the system contain the most compatible career options, and supporting data, which match data about the client. Career development centers often join a network which provides the printout terminal services and maintains the system.

The study of occupational trends is another source of useful data to indicate future prospects of occupations. The numbers of farmers and laborers, for example, have declined considerably and clerks, technicians, and semi-skilled workers have increased greatly. As in the case of occupational-structure information, these quantitative data are useful mainly for the general orientation of counselor and client. A client, for example, would not desist from choosing farming as an occupation merely because the national trend for employment of farmers was way down. Local occupational trends, however, might influence very much the choice of an occupation if the client were planning to stay in the local community. The principal problem here is that local data are most often nonexistent or outdated. School or community college counseling directors sometimes take leadership in conducting a community survey of local economic, population, and job trends with the aim of predicting employment opportunities for young workers entering the labor market.

The Occupational Outlook Service of the Department of Labor is one of the best sources of information on national occupational trends. A significant tool for the counselor is the *Occupational Outlook Handbook* (485) and its supplements, which contain trends and other pertinent data on occupations and are revised frequently.

National economic trends are useful data for counselors since they give clues to areas of potential employment. An example is the increased need for atomic energy for power purposes and rocket propulsion for transportation, which, in turn, requires the reorganization and building of entire communities around atomic and rocket industries. These industries call for new skills and training in the research, development, manufacture, and operation of novel machines and processes. The phenomenon of population mobility demands that the counselor keep up with national, state, and regional occupational trends, as well as those in his local community.

In the preceding paragraphs it was emphasized that a counselor working with career planning problems must have a vast array of occupational data at his fingertips. In Figure 25 we have summarized the types and major sources of occupational data for use in counseling. The sources of the occupational facts are listed in the outer ring, and information from those sources is located in the inner ring.

Counseling Methods for Career Planning

Career counseling is more than a rational process of matching an appraisal of the individual and appropriate occupational information into a

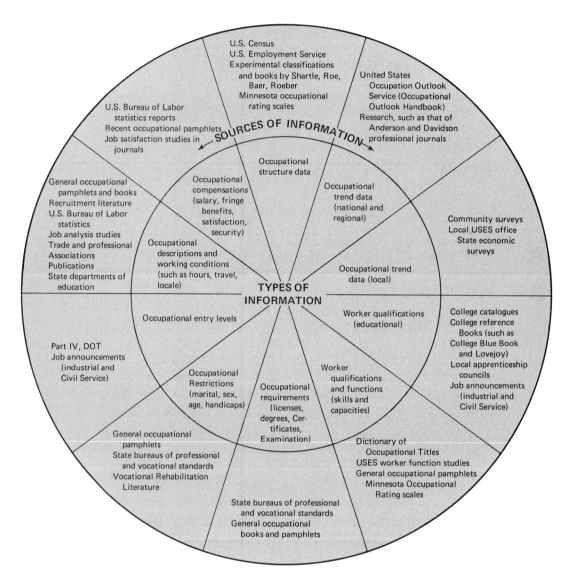

Figure 25. A Summary of Types and Sources of Occupational Data Needed in Career Counseling

career plan. This process involves careful integration with a life style which may be planned, or which evolves without much formal choice. Career counseling, according to Super (468), is largely the implementation of the client's self-concept. This means that the client perceives himself as behaving in a certain manner, with status, pleasures, social contacts, and other values satisfied through his occupation. This is why career counseling cannot be a simple process of fitting "a square peg to a square hole." Williamson (500), writing generally about career counseling, emphasizes that such counseling is a process of expanding the freedom and range of choices for the person.

Survey and Evaluation Interviews.   Early in the career counseling process, the counselor collects data on the client from which he makes predictions about probabilities of the client's success in training or work. Data are collected largely from the interview, a personal-data summary blank, case records, and test instruments. The data are weighted informally by the counselor from his experience and are then put in a type of multiple regression equation by means of which he makes his predictions. This process was described more in the diagnosis discussion of Chapter 5.

Newer methods of thinking about prediction problems, such as Information and Decision Theory (113), include the application of logic and mathematics to the interaction of predictor variables and their relation to the final decision to be made. Much information and more useful theories are needed on how career predictions are made. It seems that the best that can be done at present is for the counselor to make the most accurate hypotheses possible on the basis of the most valid and reliable clinical data, and utilize the best of the present statistical prediction methods with tests.

Use of computers promises changes in prediction procedures in the future. The early work of Tiedeman's Harvard project on Information Systems for Vocational Decisions (476) and Loughary's project in Oregon (293) were examples. Computers can be programmed with necessary educational-occupational data and information about a specific client in such a manner that the best "fit" can be decided by the computer. Certainly, as a preliminary screening process to pick out likely educational and occupational choices, computer technology has great promise as a counseling adjunct. It is conceivable that every school counseling facility eventually will have a teletype console connected to a remote data center which students can use to obtain preliminary suggestions before going to a counselor for final decision-making. The system could be designed to supplement a counseling relationship by doing the more routine work of giving the student current information to match his or her interests and capacities. The computer could not only provide selected information on training, conditions, salary, and outlook, but could also often give printouts of suggested jobs matching the student's interests and abilities. The student could then seek more information in depth, and he would at all times remain in control of the amount and type of information he received. The San Diego County Career Information Center and the States of Oregon and Indiana have computerized systems designed to give students up-to-date national, regional, and local occupational information.

Early interviews in career counseling are marked by preoccupation with the reliability and validity of data from interviews, surveys, records, and tests. The counselor is asking himself constantly what kinds of criteria (successful educational plans and vocational pursuits) are related to all the data being collected. The counselor should also ask himself how he can bring the client more closely into this predicting, decision-making process. Gustad (212) points out eloquently how research of the future must take into account the interactive process between counselor and client in the prediction process.

The Synthesis Interview. The counselor reviews material from the first interviews, examines the personal data summary, reviews test data, and compiles relevant occupational information. The client considers the interpreted test data, reviews his own values and feelings, and collates findings with the results of his independent occupational study. The client and counselor discuss these data in the synthesis or decision-making phase of the process. The synthesis interview ordinarily consists of the test interpretation, a discussion of occupational data, and then a discussion of these and earlier data. Counseling techniques mentioned in earlier chapters are used throughout the process.

Establishing the Occupational Objective. Prior to the synthesis interview the client has done his own occupational study. This study may have been performed as part of a class, or it may have been accomplished specifically for this interview. The client is aided greatly, of course, if there is a handy career center which concentrates occupational literature in one place. A guide or outline of relevant facts that should be observed about occupations is a great aid also.

From the synthesis interview a career plan is formulated. Generally, this takes the form of specifying the general areas of greatest promise, such as science, service, or business. Then, depending on the client's age and need to be specific, goals of a more exact nature, such as machinist, typist, engineer, or elementary teacher are specified. This more specific selection usually is the culmination of a long process of vocational exploration and study, so that the choice naturally evolves out of the data. Often, however, the choice must be made in a short time to prepare for a training program or immediate employment. Such was the case with many veterans seeking career counseling. Typically, the counselor administered several tests, made his "shotgun" predictions, and then came up with several specific objectives in preferential order so as to formulate an immediate training plan. Similar "crash" decisions tend to be made in rehabilitation and employment, settings where time is a factor in moving heavy case loads. This "short-circuiting" of the career choice process is to be regarded as an expedient when viewed from a broad actualizing viewpoint. Career counseling should have built-in arrangements for follow-ups. Furthermore, there should be a thorough understanding with the client that a specific choice made in such a short time is strictly tentative.

Counselors must be aware of the rapid changes in occupations. Conventional occupations are disappearing and new ones arrive daily. Clients must be helped to think of career fields rather than specific occupations. Data are accumulating to indicate that the present high school student will change careers many times in his life. Even if his chosen occupation retains its general form and function, the obsolescence factor requires that he retrain every few years. This fact must be considered when making long-term educational and career plans with school-age youth.

The process of formulating an occupational objective is characterized by the counselor suggesting career ideas for further exploration. The client makes his own decisions on the objective. The counselor may give specific occupational data from his knowledge and experience, but it behooves him to be right. It is preferable, therefore, that he use the source of the data verbatim to avoid distortion. There is evidence, such as that of Speer and Jasper (453), which indicates that it is the counselor's presentation of occupational data that is most effective in selecting suitable goals. Independent reading on the part of the client, in itself, was not of much value in selecting suitable career goals. Counselors, therefore, must take a more active role in presenting occupational facts and guiding client readings. Counselors should point out that occupational information is more than just facts about jobs. It should be presented in terms of a way of life, of a relationship between worker and job, and relationships among workers. Fine (154), for example, points out how persons planning careers "fit in" to the jobs performed. In family and school environments a person can be creative, be himself, be expansive and spontaneous. Most jobs, however, are dull and require that he conform to expectations, that he be a team member. Fine emphasizes how lack of understanding of this fundamental principle leads to frustration, hostility, and general job dissatisfaction. In other words, the counselor must consider career planning in terms of the values, life experiences, and expectations of the client. It is for these reasons that the career counselor must have a thorough understanding of therapeutic psychology and must place career planning in the broader context of choosing life styles.

The counselor has an additional responsibility to show the client how his occupational objective does or does not *fit the data*. The counselor then must let the client come to his own conclusions. The counselor can show the client how his tentative objective fits into organizational patterns and job families. The counselor may have organizational charts of typical industries related to the client's interest to show how a geologist, for example, fits into the organizational structure, or how a school psychologist fits into a public school administrative organization.

An important principle in presenting occupational information is *timing*. The client should be ready. Generally, he is ready when he is aware of his characteristics from the appraisal phases, and is wondering what relationship they have to career choices. The counselor judges that the client is ready, for the most part, when he begins to ask for information.

The Educational Plan. After the client has selected the general occupational area and made some specific occupational choices in preferential order, a plan is made for obtaining the necessary education to achieve the objective. This education may take the form of college, trade school, or on-the-job training. Methods and tools for accomplishing this plan are discussed in the next section under educational counseling.

Many counselors prefer to have the client leave with some kind of plan on paper. Hence, various career and life-plan brochures can be made that list the client's principal career choices, educational plans, and general profiles of test results. An example of such a life-plan brochure is described in Shostrom and Brammer (440). In a process as complicated as career and educational planning, distortions of the life plan take place over a period of time; hence, a summary of the results would tend to reduce distortion, at least in the factual elements of the program.

Tryouts and Follow-ups. It is necessary to convey to clients the idea that general area choices, specific objectives, and training plans are tentative until confirmed by tryout. This can be done without undermining the client's security. It is deemed unwise and unethical for the counselor to imply that, after taking some tests and talking things over for a few hours, the client has found the answers to his life plans.

Because of the process nature of career counseling, it is necessary to try the plan and reevaluate the objectives in light of the educational or occupational tryout. Follow-up interviews are arranged to check on the adequacy of the objectives and the preceding counseling.

Educational Counseling

Educational counseling consists of two distinct types of counseling assistance: educational planning and remedial help. Educational counseling has acquired special social significance in light of talent searches and encouragement of the academically able student.

Educational Planning

Selecting a Training Institution. This type of counseling is aimed essentially at helping clients select the most suitable educational goals and the best fit of educational institutions. Several factors must be considered in helping a client select an educational institution: scholastic aptitude sufficient for admission and retention, financial capacity, and suitability of the college program to the client's interests, general educational needs, and career goals. There are several characteristics about an educational institution that a client must consider also. Does it have suitable living facilities? What is the reputation of its faculty? What is the placement record for its graduates? Is it accredited by the regional accrediting agencies and by the professional associations for the particular curriculum being considered? Other factors, varying in significance from person to person, must be considered, such as the size of the institution, and extracurricular programs. Research on college environments is providing accurate comparative descriptions of colleges to help students choose wisely; but the rapid changes in higher education and patterns of attendance are making these studies obsolete quickly.

Some of the standard references the client may rely on to make a thorough study of educational institutions are: the *College Blue Book* (82), *American Junior Colleges* (57), *Lovejoy's College Guide* (294), and *Junior Colleges and Specialized Schools and Colleges* (410). These references are used to supplement information from the catalogues of the individual colleges. All students planning to take educational counseling must be familiar with them.

References for other types of educational institutions are *American Trade Schools Directory* (114) and *Lovejoy's Vocational School Guide* (295) for trade schools, the *Home Study Blue Book* (346) for correspondence schools, and *Private Independent Schools* (81), *Handbook of Private Schools* (411) for the numerous private pre-college educational institutions.

Predicting Success in Training and Education. One of the principal problems a counselor must face in educational planning is making predictions of probable success in a given college. Many institutions have predictive indices, or at least a validity coefficient based on a correlation between a standard aptitude measure and grades in that college or curriculum. These validity coefficents generally fall in the low fifties for Pearson correlations. For the counselor making predictions about training success, the previous grades of the client in high school are still the best reference since grades generally have higher validity than a standard scholastic-aptitude test. For example, the counselor can fairly accurately predict success in the first year of engineering training in college relying on high school grades, mathematics achievement tests, and general scholastic-aptitude tests (Layton 278). There has been a strong trend toward grade inflation among colleges and high schools, however. This tendency to constrict the range of grades given has changed the predictive accuracy of earlier grades.

So far, studies in the area of predictions indicate that it is much easier to predict success in training for an occupation than to predict success in that occupation. There are more definite criteria of success in training, such as grades and completion of the program. Obtaining criteria of success in many professional occupations is very difficult. Hoyt (236) surveyed the cumulative evidence from studies predicting occupational success on the basis of grades. He found very low correlations generally between college grades and various criteria of occupational success, which suggests that factors other than scholastic ability enter into the criteria of success.

Financing Training. An important consideration in college planning is finance. Major sources of tuition, besides parental subsidies and savings, are scholarships, fellowships, and loans. Private and governmental sources of such aids are becoming more plentiful. Counselors working in areas of educational planning should have financial-aid bulletins of the major colleges and should have access to such reference volumes as Feingold's *Scholarships, Fellowships, and Loans* (147). The current procedure used by colleges in awarding financial aids is the package plan. This is a mix of loans, tuition waivers, scholarships, and part-time work experiences suited to the needs of the student and the financial condition of the family. Financial status of families is determined by the College Scholarship Service, a national nonprofit organization that compiles detailed financial statements from parents and forwards this information to colleges at the parents' request.

Remedial Assistance. Although overcoming educational deficiencies is more an instructional than a counseling responsibility, the counselor practicing in an educational institution comes face to face with this problem frequently. We take the position that the counselor must be able to diagnose remediation problems in order to recommend steps to remedy deficiencies, or to make suitable referrals to remedial specialists. The availability of diagnostic testing instruments for assessing the achievement level and the precise areas of difficulty, as well as a dearth of experts in remedial assistance, make such diagnostic studies by counselors feasible and necessary. Appraisal instruments, along with supplementary diagnostic interviewing, often can be used to indicate to a client where the causes of his difficulties lie.

Diagnostic Skills. Knowledge of diagnostic procedures in basic skills is of value to both the counselor working in educational institutions and to the private practitioner. Achievement problems are a key reason for referral in a school or college. In private practice, the psychologist spends much of his time with clients having difficulties in schools. The psychologist is in a key position to work with problems of educational achievement also, because of the complex psychological factors usually operating in cases of low achievement. There may be combinations of emotional problems, educational-skill deficiency, low motivation, physiological handicaps, or lack of practice in the basic skill. A thorough diagnostic and remedial program, therefore, calls on the skills of many specialists. The psychologist often is selected to coordinate the various specialists' diagnostic studies and to make recommendations to the tutors, teachers, or remedial specialists.

Although it is beyond the scope of this book to describe educational diagnostic methods in detail, some of the areas to be investigated are mentioned to give the counselor without orientation in these skills some background. There are two areas of investigation—general study methods and reading. Several inventories exist for diagnosing study difficulties. Examples are the Wrenn "Study Habits Inventory" (509) and the Brown-Holtzman "Survey of Study Habits and Attitudes" (73). Though inventories identify problem areas, they do not differentiate between habits of good and poor students. A well-conducted study at Ohio State University revealed that even superior students used widely variable and unrecommended study procedures. The students apparently were superior in spite of their study methods (117).

Diagnosis of educational problems should start with a good *physical examination* with particular attention to sensory and metabolic factors. Secondly, a close look at *motivational factors*, with special emphasis on personal problems, should be taken. There are generally many complicating factors in achievement deficiencies; however, attitudinal difficulties are often at the root of the problem. One should not overlook the possibility that emotional problems are the result as much as the cause of educational achievement problems. Achievement problems often reveal some deep-seated hostility toward parents or a confusion of values. These problems indicate therapeutic counseling perhaps more than remedial educational techniques.

The counselor should examine *basic skills* and *knowledge,* which underlie achievement. Some of these are rate and flexibility of reading; level of comprehension and vocabulary; interest; quantity of reading; and interfering habits such as finger tracing, word reading, regression, and vocalization. These diagnostic data enable the educational counselor to formulate the client's problem more accurately than the usual "I can't concentrate" or "I can't read fast" type of offhand symptomatic statement of the client. This diagnostic survey enables the counselor either to make a referral to a remedial specialist or to offer some suggestions from his general knowledge in the field of remediation.

Remediation. Generally speaking, counselors do not perform remedial instruction since individual tutoring is so time consuming. Counselors can spend their time so much more profitably in other types of services. Most agencies offer remedial-type courses, which give the client an opportunity to learn basic skills over a fixed period of time in a group or clinic setting. Though there are many books and pamphlets available for self-help on educational problems, there is no evidence to indicate that a person improves his skills substantially by reading a pamphlet. The educational counselor may use the pamphlet-reading technique on a prescription basis, however, to give the client some background for later conferences on specific learning and study skills. The pamphlets and time-study schedules are useful as diagnostic devices to help a client find areas of weakness. Pamphlets are useful when a lack of learning techniques is not at the core of the achievement problem, but something more basic in attitude and approach to learning tasks.

Counseling on Problems of Academic Deficiency. There seems to be considerable folklore among educational counselors about the efficacy of short counseling interviews with poor students. Klingelhofer (264) performed one of the few studies indicating that short-term, direct-suggestion counseling with such clients has value in raising course grades. His study suggested that organized counseling was associated with improved scholastic performance, although the differential amounts of counseling given the groups did not seem to effect similar differences in grades. The same achievement level was attained whether the student received one or four hours of directive counseling.

Margolies (306) points out the heavy resistance encountered from poor scholarship students who are called by the counselor for discussion of their achievement. He points out the necessity for looking behind the "facade" of the student's resistance and logic-tight rationalizations. The purpose is to look for dynamic factors and points where the awareness process might be started.

Rehabilitation Counseling

Basic Concepts

Rehabilitation is a process of restoring the client with handicaps to the fullest possible usefulness to himself and society. It is estimated that there are in the United States over three million disabled or severely handicapped persons in the productive years between fourteen and sixty-four (482). Of these, two million come within the scope of services offered by vocational rehabilitation programs. Most of these two million could achieve happy and productive lives through suitable work. Vocational rehabilitation services offered through the states and assisted by the United States Government have been working with this group since 1918. These programs have been able to help clients overcome their dependency and contribute to their society. The programs, furthermore, have enabled clients to achieve personal satisfactions, which come from engaging in productive work and avoiding the stigma of social and economic liability.

The Vocational Rehabilitation Act of 1965 and the Rehabilitation Act of 1973 broadened the concept of rehabilitation from original legislation in 1920 to include any person who has been hurt by life. This includes not only the physically and mentally handicapped, but also the culturally deprived and the socially handicapped, such as released prisoners. Counseling plays a vital part in this rehabilitation process. Counseling techniques for handicapped persons are little different from counseling for the able-bodied. Occupational distribution of the handicapped is roughly similar to that of persons who are not disabled. State bureaus of vocational rehabilitation employ special counselors, many with master's degrees in counseling, who are trained in the rehabilitation process. The U. S. Veterans Administration employs counseling psychologists to perform similar rehabilitative functions in veterans hospitals, with more stress, however, being placed on the counseling function.

The vocational-rehabilitation process covers many services to the handicapped client. In addition to the diagnostic and vocational counseling techniques described in this book, there are orderly sequences of services, such as physical restoration, training, psychiatric treatment, provision of training materials, maintenance while training, placement, license acquisition, and furnishing of equipment, such as vending stands, to establish a business under the supervision of the agency.

Generally, the process proceeds according to well-established steps, beginning with the *intake interview*, which includes orientation to the service and determination of eligibility, assignment to a counselor and the *initial interview*, the *case study, psychological evaluation, counseling*, formulating the *rehabilitation plan, training* and/or *placement*, and *follow-up* (482). These steps are aimed at promoting maximum vocational usefulness as soon as possible.

Existential ideas have been infused into the rehabilitation process. Easton and Krippner (133) point out the special existential problems of the handicapped in areas of apathy and meaning, motivation to assume responsibility for choice and action, and the meaning of pain. It takes the client beyond mere adjustment to a more creative approach to life with his disability.

Interest in professional counseling organizations has grown rapidly in rehabilitation circles during the past few years. In 1957, the American Rehabilitation Counselors Association was organized as a division in the American Personnel and Guidance Association. Division 17, Counseling Psychology, of the American Psychological Association also has many psychologists working primarily in vocational rehabilitation. The National Rehabilitation Association is another professional group available to rehabilitation counselors. To meet rising expectations for standards of service, a Council on Rehabilitation Counselor Certification establishes experience and educational requirements and also administers a competency examination for the certificate. This council is composed of representatives of the major professional rehabilitation counselor organizations.

The Rehabilitation Counselor

The vocational rehabilitation counselor must have the same skills and knowledge that persons in other helping professions must have. He is a professional caseworker since he usually handles the client's problems from the first interview to satisfactory placement and follow-up. His counseling functions are very much like those described in this book, with special emphasis on psychometrics and career counseling. He must be conversant with medical and psychiatric terminology and must be familiar with community service agencies and educational institutions. In state agencies, he is an expediter and a coordinator of many services to clients.

The vocational rehabilitation counselor, therefore, must be a versatile person. Many lists have been drawn up to indicate what he should know to do his job well. Cantrell (90) studied the matter of training rehabilitation counselors by asking a large number of counselors in the Veterans Administration, officials of state vocational rehabilitation centers, and counselors in private practice what they felt was important in training and how they would rank the material in usefulness. Though there were some disagreements in rankings among the three groups of practitioners, the average rankings, from first to last choice in significance, for their work as vocational rehabilitation counselors were as follows:

1. Counseling theory, principles, and practice.
2. Professional activities, including ethics, duties, interprofessional teamwork, professional growth, and public relations.
3. Supervised field work, including visits to agencies.
4. Psychological information, including developmental, abnormal, personality theory, and effect of disability on personality.
5. Testing principles and practice.
6. Occupational information.
7. Casework history, principles, and method.
8. Rehabilitation, including history, philosophy, legal, and administrative aspects.
9. Social and community resource information.
10. Medical and related information, including knowledge of physical restoration resources.
11. Research and statistics methods.

It was noteworthy in Cantrell's study that the practicing counselors considered counseling the very center of the process of rehabilitation and felt that the major emphasis in training should be on counseling. The other areas, such as medical information and case methods, were considered necessary supportive elements to the counseling relationship.

The problems of defining rehabilitation counselor tasks and evaluating counseling performance have been investigated by Muthard and Miller (345). This kind of research is limited by the varying conceptions of counselor role and by differing views of evaluating successful rehabilitation counseling in qualitative terms as well as number of case files closed. On the one hand, pressures for agency accountability stress the number of people placed in jobs and the closure of the case; on the other hand, the quality of life and general coping capacity of the client requiring more extended counseling are contrary pressures.

Summary

Life-planning involves a broad approach to choices of life style, partners, living locale, and careers. Therapeutic psychologists often specialize, or become involved at some point, in problems of career choice, educational planning, diagnosis on remediation problems, and rehabilitation counseling of the handicapped. Though there are various theories on how vocational choices are made, there is much agreement among counselors that suitable career choices have profound consequences for individual actualizing and for society. Educational and vocational counseling draw heavily on appraisal and diagnosis functions, yet retain counseling techniques as the core of the process. The principal sources of data used in educational-vocational-rehabilitation counseling are tests, case histories, client self-evaluations, clinical observations, occupational information materials, training directories, and tryout work experience.

Counseling on Problems of Values

The question of what I am going to do with my life is raised frequently in Actualizing Counseling and Psychotherapy. It comes in the form of choices of life style or of value conflict. Terms such as "human revolution," "human potential," and "human declaration" put this basic question of purpose and meaning in a broad social context. The main purpose of this chapter is to examine the place of basic human values in therapy and how counselors and psychotherapists manage value choice issues and methods.

Psychology as a science and a profession has become more concerned about values, including the value assumptions underlying science itself. The term *value* in this context is defined as a firm, conscious or unconscious belief in the worth of an idea or feeling. For the purposes of this chapter, the philosophical problem of the origin of values and the question of the absoluteness or relativity of values will be treated only incidentally.

Values in Therapeutic Psychology

Another purpose of this chapter is to examine some of the value relationships between therapeutic psychology and religious counseling. We shall use Wrenn's description of the two approaches: ". . . religion and psychology complement each other. Psychology contributes to an understanding of the *nature* of self and of one's relationships with others, religion to an understanding of the meaning and purpose in life, and the *significance* of these same relationships. Both may contribute to more effective living" (506, p. 331).

In Actualizing Counseling and Psychotherapy terms, the valuing process takes place primarily in the core of the person with the rational choice-

14

making largely an actualizing function. This means that the person looks inward toward the core for value guidelines. He is "inner-directed" rather than "outer-directed," to use Rotter's terms. The outer-directed person seeks answers for value questions largely outside of himself; he values expert opinion on these matters; he looks to authority and tradition for answers to difficult life questions. He attempts to please others through manipulative behaviors and operates largely at a facade level. One goal, then, of the actualizing process is to encourage the actualizing person to look within for cues and guidelines and to learn to trust what he uncovers. This does not mean turning inward for answers exclusively, but to find the best balance between inner and outer criteria of evaluation. The Actualizing model offers a wide spectrum of methods to deal with this search for awareness and inner support as well as for decision-making skills in acting out value choices. The research bases for these views may be found in Shostrom (432).

In the psychological literature generally, there appears to be an awakening interest in philosophical problems underlying the psychological study of man. Mowrer, for example, states that psychology perhaps ought to examine its long-fostered assumption that the nonphysical elements of personality (conceived popularly as man's mind or spirit) serve the body (341). Although personality grows out of needs to serve the body, Mowrer wonders whether the "mind" has its peculiar needs, characteristics, and survival demands also. He realizes that this is a disturbing question since the topic moves from the traditional pale of naturalistic observation to the area of the "spirit"—a traditionally religious subject. Yet, psychologists are becoming increasingly concerned about the subject of values clarification, psychological "survival," and the "human tragedy." Human problems, especially, have become such an acute social concern that practicing psychologists are willing to examine all available means of helping clients to survive psychologically. Apparently, they are willing to do this even if it means going beyond traditional laboratory and strictly behavioristic methods of studying and helping man.

It is a truism that psychotherapists and personal counselors deal with fundamental problems of actualized living, namely loving, becoming an independent person, handling normal guilt, and gaining a mature perspective on the frustrating and tragic incidents of everyday life. We are aware of the difficulties in approaching the topic of values in the context of therapeutic psychology. This chapter is offered as a starting point for the student who may not have done much previous reading or thinking about the numerous value problems confronting client and counselor or therapist.

Psychological counselors have been reluctant to face the possibility that they might have functions and responsibilities that could be termed broadly as "religious." This reluctance has been due to the empirical tradition, basic philosophical differences between social science and theology, alleged emotional extremes and hypocrisy in much of organized religious behavior, and the counselor's own spiritual ignorance or conflict. More psychological counselors are recognizing, however, that religious sentiments and feelings become powerful positive or negative motives in their client's lives.

Traditionally, psychology has been biologically oriented. The early models and scientific procedures of the late nineteenth century were based on physiology and physics. Darwinian philosophy had considerable influence on psychologists' view of man as a continuation of the animal world and subject to the same natural laws. Early American psychology added a functional note to the biological models imported from Germany. There was a very strong effort to divorce psychology from its earlier philosophical roots and to make the understanding of behavior a strictly scientific venture.

We do not advocate a return to rationalistic and other philosophical methods as a substitute for careful observation and rigorous experimentation. Psychology as a science must remain firmly planted in scientific methods and critical thinking. We are in accord, however, with the trend in psychological services to examine the methods and assumptions of psychology in regard to their adequacy for understanding man's basic problems and helping him to deal with them more effectively. Part of the difficulty is that the hunger for knowledge about man and efforts to assist him with his problems is making premature and unrealistic demands on such an infant endeavor as scientific psychology. Nevertheless, the therapeutic psychologist is faced with the practical reality (or at least the pressure) for looking beyond scientific methods and psychological techniques to help clients with values beyond the process itself.

The assumption that it is necessary to go beyond empirically validated psychological techniques in helping clients with value problems puts the therapeutic psychologist squarely in the area of traditional religious concern. Here again, the history of psychology at some points has run counter to formal religion. Freud, for example, is well known for his indictment of organized religious endeavors in his work, *The Future of an Illusion* (167), wherein he asserts that so much of religious dogma and behavior are projections of unconscious wishes. In addition to the maligning of, or indifference toward, formal religious belief, there has been an attitude of suspicion toward professional psychologists who had any strong personal religious beliefs. They were automatically suspect because of the assumed interference these beliefs had with an attitude of objectivity so necessary for their psychology.

Jung's attitude toward religion was that the client's present belief system should be used in such a way that it would hasten his recovery of healthy attitudes. This view was a radical departure from the Freudian position, which, as described above, tended to regard much of formal religion as a form of abnormality. Jung is reputed to have advocated finding God within experience as part of the individuation process (196). The "God within" the racial unconscious of the Jungian system is then equated by many persons with a transcendental "God without." Jung admits that it is not the business of the psychologist to establish or even investigate objective truth regarding the existence of God. He states, furthermore, that neither is it the psychologist's business to construct a pseudo-religion out of primitive yearnings or myths. Jung tries to stay close to empirical facts in this realm and to concentrate on the oak rather than on the acorn (252).

White (496), a priest as well as a psychologist, approached the problem of God and the psychology of the unconscious in a spirit of compromise. He attempted to tie together the idea of an external reality, called God, with the inner nature and psychological realities of man. Kunkel (276), a psychiatrist, also made efforts toward reconciliation of the two realms into a "religious psychology." The elements of this collaborative relationship are naturalistic observation and depth psychology. They are used to help understand behavior on the one hand, and to give purpose and direction to behavior on the other. Kunkel feels that a human helping relationship such as therapy and the goals of maturity need both approaches working together.

Efforts were made even earlier to tie more closely psychotherapeutic methods and assumptions to those of religion. Putnam, a New England physician of the early twentieth century, tried very hard to encourage his psychoanalytic colleagues to join him in efforts to broaden the base of psychoanalysis so as to include problems of the larger community and the cosmos. His proposals to tie a religiously oriented metaphysics to psychoanalysis met with strong resistance and some outright rejection in both Europe and America. This resistance persisted until such contemporary writers as Fromm (175), Mowrer (341), White (496), and May (312) reopened the question without suggesting that psychology compromise on its scientific bases.

A Point of View

We are discussing values in this book because clients often confront counselors with problems concerned with value conflicts, such as handling guilt over immoral behavior, meeting crises, overcoming deep-seated anxieties, feeling worthwhile, and relating to something significant. The counselor is often put in a difficult position when the client expects more of him than help in gaining awareness or comfort. Many clients, in effect, beg the counselor to tell them how to live, what kind of person they should be, how they can meet the vicissitudes and seeming meaninglessness of life. Frequently, clients expect the counselor to relieve them of basic anxieties such as fear of nonbeing, or death.

We are not proposing that counselors set themselves up as authorities on such questions, nor that they should yield to client demands for answers to basic questions by giving their personal philosophies. What is being suggested, though, is that counselors be very much aware of this problem and be cognizant of temptations to pontificate on philosophical and religious questions.

It seems that one must recognize that religious and psychological concepts are not mutually exclusive. One must not assume that either religious concern or psychological interpretation is the total solution to, or explanation of, man's problems. Many people put this proposition into the form of an uncomfortable dichotomy. They feel inclined either to reject psychological interpretations and explanations of behavior or to reject their religious belief system. There seems to be a third position for clients to take, which we would like to explore. This view is that there is considerable overlap and congruence as well as conflict between the psychological and theological views of man. One should recognize these points of overlap and conflict and then look assiduously for areas where the meanings are congruent and seem to give greater combined insight into man's existence and the solution of human problems.

We think that it is important to encourage colleagues to ponder questions on the relationships among scientific psychology, philosophy, and religion. If such an endeavor is successful, a "breakthrough" might be achieved that would be of great benefit to counselors and clients struggling with these interdisciplinary problems, many of which are presently outside the scope of scientific and professional psychology.

There are some compelling social reasons why such a breakthrough is needed. As we mentioned earlier in this chapter, the problem of improving the human condition is bound to questions of life philosophy or *Weltanschauung*. Mowrer (341) thinks that we need a type of development program for twentieth-century man that will have genuine psychological survival value, something over and above the concern for mastery of his natural environment. Such an approach appears to be needed to prevent mass emotional disturbances. A means must be found, in addition to formal religion, to help clients with feelings of disillusionment, depersonalization, being unloved and abandoned, and of being a "thing" unscrupulously manipulated by other people. Development of such a philosophy may help clients to cope with gnawing free-floating anxiety, guilt over real or imagined misdeeds, and feelings of helplessness and resentment during periods of crisis. These are questions with which the average psychological counselor feels quite inadequate to cope, other than to use general techniques of psychological support and relatedness offered through a warm therapeutic relationship.

Several groups are searching for interrelationships between psychology and religion. The Academy of Religion and Mental Health is an example of such a group. The Society for the Scientific Study of Religion is another group designed to facilitate intercommunication between students of religion and social science.

Professional meetings of psychological and counseling groups have an increasing number of sections devoted to value concerns. There are committees within the American Psychological Association and the American

Psychiatric Association devoted to this problem of relationship to values and formal religion. Educational agencies and growth centers sponsor popular value-clarification workshops and rap sessions. The pastoral-counseling movement has grown rapidly also, and is being accelerated through the clinical training of student clergymen.

Pastoral Psychology

Pastoral counselors are ordained clergymen trained in psychological counseling to deal with problems of belief, morals, guilt, and life crises. Such counselors assist parishioners with a wide range of human problems from marital conflicts through child-rearing. The family clergyman and the family physician have been the traditional helpers in most communities, and this special training in therapeutic psychology expands their range of help. The average minister has had three years of general professional education leading to the B.D. degree. In pursuit of this degree, he is given general classes in personality and counseling theory, as well as supervised experience in a clinical setting for six weeks to a year in residence.

The term "Pastoral Psychology" refers to a more extensive graduate specialization. Such leaders as Hiltner, Wise, Johnson, and Eitzen have developed curricula leading to a doctorate in this specialty. These graduates usually serve as therapeutic counselors in pastoral-counseling or church-growth centers as part of a collective effort of various churches in a city, or as teachers on the college or seminary level.

To assist in establishing a frame of reference for pastoral counseling, various levels described by Oates (349) are cited. Most of the pastoral functions listed below have some counseling aspects:

1. Level of friendship (rapport).
2. Level of comfort (support).
3. Level of confession (cathartic).
4. Level of teaching (informational).
5. Level of pastoral counseling (psychotherapeutic).
6. Level of referral.

The act of affirmation or loving, in the broad "agape" sense, is involved in pastoral counseling too. Pastoral counselors generally subscribe to the view that man's love for man is rooted in God's love for man. The religious counselor ties in this client acceptance of himself and his fellow man with God's love for man as the principal source of attaining insight, freedom, security, maturity, and similar therapeutic goals. The counseling relationship is often construed as a quest for the "kingdom of God" in man. These positions do not necessarily militate against an optimal counseling relationship unless they are accompanied by a judgmental and authoritarian attitude.

The religious counselor, particularly one in the Christian tradition, often

417

begins with a different set of assumptions about anthropology and psychology from that of the professional psychologist. The central values of the pastoral counselor reside in what is called divine law. It is difficult to generalize or be categorical about the teleological assumptions of theologians since they seem to hold many views depending on their unique perceptual vantage points and training. For example, some theologians do not see the traditional dichotomy between God and man since they view God and man in a common relationship. In any event, the view one holds about the nature, purpose, and origin of man influences his approach to counseling problems.

The psychologist, in contrast, generally operates on the more humanistic assumption that ultimate values are rationally determined and are found in man himself. Herein lies, in our opinion, the central issue between pastoral counseling and nontheologically oriented counseling. It is possible, however, to resolve this issue, somewhat, at the technique level, since both are concerned with helping suffering humanity. Psychologists can evaluate the techniques they use on the criterion of effectiveness in reaching limited goals quite apart from the basic philosophical assumptions and basic purposes involved.

For an extensive and fair analysis of the comparative assumptions underlying psychological science and Christianity the reader is referred to the volume *What, Then, Is Man* (317), which is a symposium report on the unique and interrelated features of two basic ways of construing man.

There are many things clergymen can do to promote the same growth goals as therapeutic psychology. It must be recognized that the religious leader is concerned about many more aspects of his parishioners' lives than their mental health, and that mental health is defined variously; but this is one area for which people look to him for leadership, albeit under a variety of guises. The pastoral counselor should recognize that the recent surge of religious interest and church attendance is probably more than a simple desire to renew the ties of childhood to a community institution, or to escape from tension. It may be viewed also as a deep expression of man's search for a moral and spiritual framework for life, and a foundation on which to build a rich and satisfying life. It should be recognized that throughout history social crises have produced such great surges of religious interest.

So often a client's deep psychological problems come in the guise of moral or spiritual problems. The clergyman must have the skill with which to distinguish the basically spiritual problem from one involving pathology in the personality. He must know, also, his own limitations in dealing with problems construed by the client as "spiritual," since one can put this type of interpretation on almost all human difficulties.

The Pastoral Counselor's Role in Relation to Other Specialists.   The pastoral counselor's principal role, as far as psychological counseling is concerned, would seem to be to explore the client's initial problem to see where it touches upon areas of spiritual concern and knowledge, and where emotional conditions would warrant the services of a therapeutic psychologist, psychiatrist, or social worker. The principal techniques employed would be supportive and informational. Delving into unconscious motives could lead to a relationship fraught with deep transference and countertransference feelings, expectations of unrealistic accomplishments, or aggravation of a developing psychosis.

Personal problems may be approached from an interdisciplinary point of view in which the pastoral counselor and the psychologist or psychiatrist work together, and where cross-referral can be accomplished easily. Practically, however, this is difficult to achieve because remnants of mutual suspicion exist among practitioners, and clients often become confused when working with two similar types of specialists. This type of cross-referral among pastors and psychologists can work satisfactorily, but only under conditions where the primary responsibility is invested in one of the two specialists.

Contributions of Therapeutic Psychology to Pastoral Counseling. The tools of therapeutic psychology are useful to the pastoral counselor in many ways. The application of relationship techniques, such as listening, accepting, and reflecting, for example, can go far in overcoming the traditional authoritarian advice-giving role into which the clergyman is so often cast. The understanding of unconscious motivation in behavior and human culture can go a long way to gaining an understanding of defensiveness and emotional problems as a type of ignorance, rather than thinking of these behaviors in traditional moralistic terms so destructive to a good counseling relationship. Greater knowledge of human motivation should help the clergyman deal with concepts of freedom of the will, moral responsibility, guilt, and responsible action more understandingly.

Possibilities and Limitations of the Ministerial Role in Counseling. A clergyman can take advantage of a strategic helping relationship with clients that is based on a traditional "pastor" perception of the clergy. He has an advantage over other helping professionals in that he is perceived by the family as a helper. He can deal with the whole family as a casework problem, which is often as important as dealing with a selected individual. However, he suffers from the client's aforementioned perception of him as an authoritarian figure, a teacher, or as the symbol of moralistic judgment. Yet, in counseling it is imperative that the counselor be perceived as an understanding person. The traditional exhortational or advice-giving role is inimical to the general goals of present-day counseling.

The pastoral counselor is in a unique position to assist clients in confronting profound life problems, such as developing a philosophy of life. He is in a strategic position to discuss moral problems also. Even here, a cultural anthropology frame of reference is helpful in ascertaining more clearly the areas of right, wrong, and neutral. When the religious dogma is not clearly interpretable in a given case, it is useful to know the mores of the culture and how these are distinguished from clearly delineated religious codes or conduct. For example, a behavior which a client may regard as "sinful," and from which he suffers considerable anxiety and guilt, may be more a deviation from the cultural norms than a violation of the moral code of his religion or denomination.

The minister familiar with therapeutic psychology can utilize group techniques to help create a climate of growth in his parish. These groups encourage mutual support and honest confrontation of personal problems.

Actualizing Churches. A church, synagogue, or temple traditionally has been a community of people enhancing one another's growth, but critics of current highly institutionalized churches feel that this "koinonia," or fellowship of persons, has been lost. The actualizing approach described in earlier chapters is one approach to recapturing this spirit. Actualization groups conducted by ministers and/or understanding therapeutic psychologists can provide a vehicle for members to experience the rewards of peace, joy, and a renewed sense of community and commitment. Each participant has possibilities for reexamination of his values, rediscovery and enhancement of his human dignity and worth, and respect for the "thou-ness" of others. Actualization groups in churches are more, therefore, than conventional sensitivity training or encounter groups.

In a major study of the American Catholic priesthood, Greeley (204) has reported a number of significant relationships between priests' levels of self-actualizing and amounts of perceived institutional support. In responding to questions concerning conflict between real and ideal distribution of power in the Church, the more actualizing priests perceived a greater conflict and expressed a greater need to reform the Church. Higher levels of actualizing, as defined by the Personal Orientation Inventory (POI), appeared to be negatively related to adherence to traditional values within the Church, and positively associated with general dissatisfaction with the Church. The correlation between self-actualizing, as measured by the POI Inner-Direction scale, and professed plans to stay in the priesthood was significant and negative.

Mowrer (342) has shown that the original Christian Church was a small-group movement. The faithful would meet secretly in caves to discuss their mutual concerns. The modern church must revitalize the spirit of the small-group sharing if it is to remain relevant for modern man. It is our thesis that the actualizing process is a way to recapture this spirit.

Introduction of the actualizing process through encounter group techniques has produced results in several church-affiliated studies. Reddy (377) has reported the effects of a five-day residential human relations training program for forty interdenominational missionaries preparing for foreign service. He found significant increases in self-actualizing behaviors as defined by the POI. Knapp and Fitzgerald (268) showed gains in actualizing behaviors with the Navy Chaplain Corps in an eclectic transgenerational workshop program with navy personnel. This program was established with the particular objective of building an increased sense of community among those persons whose feelings of alienation had led to such unsatisfactory behavioral expressions as drug abuse or alcohol addiction. Again, results from administration of the POI before and after the workshop demonstrate the positive effectiveness of programs of this type. Through such experiences, conducted by trained and sensitive clergymen, each participant had the opportunity to reexamine his personal values to rediscover and enhance his dignity and worth, and to regain his respect for others.

Value Problems Confronted by Therapeutic Psychologists

The therapeutic psychologist must be aware of the dangers of becoming a spiritual counselor. The therapeutic psychologist, for example, generally does not give a client answers to direct questions on values. His principal role is to help a client to clarify his thinking and to discover feelings and thoughts regarding questions of values in his own personality. When such values are lacking, are considered by the client to be inadequate, or are not discoverable with the usual therapeutic techniques, then the psychologist may present various cultural viewpoints and trends on the problem in question or refer the client to religious specialists for more detailed information. There he can obtain ideas in a type of setting characterized by teaching. These ideas can be discussed further in the psychotherapeutic interviews, where he can scrutinize his belief system and religious experiences. Finally, through counseling, the client can integrate his new discoveries smoothly into his personality core.

The therapeutic psychologist generally does not attempt consciously to influence a client's basic life values. Yet, it would be pure sophistry to presume that, in the deeply human relationship of counseling, the counselor does not influence the client's values. It is often quite apparent how the counselor feels about marriage and divorce, extramarital sex, the existence of God, and similar values without his expressing himself directly on the questions. For the manifold problems in this area of values projection, the reader is referred to the countertransference discussion in Chapter 8.

Perhaps the transmission of personal values is unavoidable in the close human relationship of psychotherapeutic counseling. Sullivan (462) even went so far as to claim that the therapist's personal values and attitudes toward life influence his professional work as much as his skills and training. If this statement is as valid as it seems on the surface, then there are many implications here for the selection and training of therapeutic psychologists and for referrals to psychological specialists.

However, there are counselors working in therapeutic psychology, or related areas, whose own personal problems are so well worked through in the value area that they are in a strategic position to help clients work through their value problems. Some therapists and counselors have particular interests and skills in working with basic value problems, just as they might have interests and abilities in marriage or career choice problems. For counselors with such interests, the following sections are included as samples of some counseling problems on value questions.

Our position on the question of transmitting counselor values is that if a counselor's own problems in the value areas are worked out to his satisfaction, if he is not aware of a need to "clear up" or "reform" the client's thinking, and if he is aware of his tendencies to project his own needs and problems, then he could work with clients having basic value problems. If such help, however, involves information or interpretation of dogma, this should be done by a reliable minister on referral or through bibliotherapeutic references. If these conditions still do not allow a comfortable relationship, or they are doing violence to his own belief system, the counselor then must face the issue frankly and refer the client to another counselor.

Developing a Philosophy of Life

An assumption of this section is that each individual has a life philosophy, a life style, a set of religious beliefs, even though they are implicit and not consciously known or felt by the person. A companion assumption is that behavior is an expression of a person's basic philosophy. When the behavior and the basic philosophy of life are at odds, the person usually is in trouble. A person's philosophy of life usually includes his beliefs about the origin and nature of truth, the purpose and significance of his particular life, the nature of reality, including the possibility of a personal God. Further elements of his philosophy would include the nature and the hierarchy of values he holds, the origin and destiny of man, and the relative functions of reason and faith in the knowing process. His beliefs are sets of assumptions about these philosophical areas.

The process of learning, projecting, and incorporating values into a mature belief system or philosophy of life, as we see it, is diagrammed in Figure 26. The beliefs in the core level (a) are learned during the growing-up process from values held by parents and others close to the person. These internalized external values (b) are reperceived later as external to the person since they are projections of previously learned values.

During this projection process (c), the core and the rational processes of the actualizing level modify the projected values so that there is no one-to-one relationship between the core values and the projected values. For example, a person may project his security value system to external objects in such a way that he builds his security around a bank account, a family member, or an ideology.

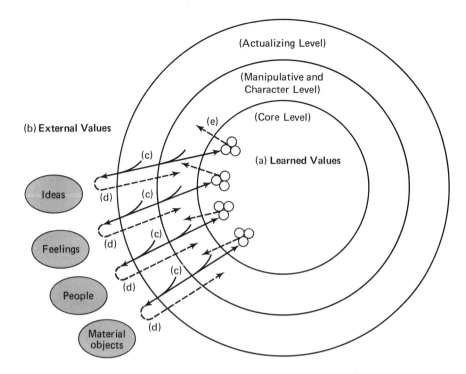

(Actualizing Level)

(Manipulative and
Character Level)

(Core Level)

(b) **External Values**

(e)

(c)

(a) **Learned Values**

Ideas

(d)   (c)

Feelings

(c)

(d)

People

(c)

(d)

Material
objects

(d)

Figure 26.   The Process of Developing a Philosophy of Life

The therapeutic task seems to consist of helping the client to examine his implicit beliefs, to know how he is projecting these core values, and then to see how he is perceiving external values. This phase of counseling leads him to reinvest these projected perceptions of external values into his core and character levels, as in (d) of Figure 26. He can see how his core values are influencing his character also. Armed with this rationally derived knowledge and insight, he can proceed to the development of a trustworthy and unified core value structure, which is no longer focused on external values. As a result, he should no longer be a blind slave to his core needs and values, nor a victim of an externally imposed value system. He need not, for example, depend as heavily upon the ideas, feelings, people, and objects about him since he now has a reconstituted, but cohesive and independent, value structure uniquely his own.

The role of the counselor in helping the client achieve a mature philosophy of life appears to us as diagrammed in Figure 27. At the beginning of counseling (a), the main task is to become aware of and to clarify the client's current value system. The second task (b) is to accomplish the phases associated with the previous discussion of Figure 26 covering the process of developing a mature philosophy. These phases usually take place during the later stages of the total counseling process. Here the

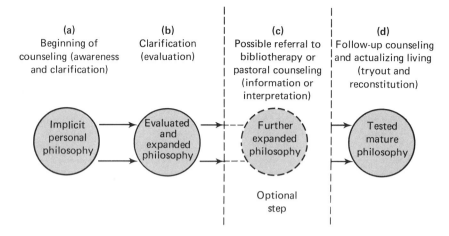

Figure 27. The Role of Therapeutic Counseling in Value Problems

client evaluates the effectiveness of his beliefs and explores ways of implementing them. Out of this effort often comes a more mature, expanded, unified, and effective world and life view.

If the preceding steps do not seem effective, it may be that the client either is not ready, or needs more specialized information which the counselor cannot provide or declines to give. This condition may necessitate referral (c) for information and interpretation through resources such as bibliotherapy, pastoral counseling, or instruction in a belief system.

Finally, if all goes well in the process, the client reaches a point (d) where he works out a tested personal philosophy adequate for his times and circumstances.

Though it is not the purpose of this section to set up a model philosophy of life, we consider it to be important to point out some of the problems clients face in developing or changing a philosophy of life. There seems to be evidence of a need for each person to work out a philosophy to fit his times and circumstances. If he does not have such a philosophy, he generally suffers from feelings of drifting, pessimism, loneliness, disillusionment, and possibly even disintegration. Having a satisfying philosophy appears to build personal strength and to make more possible the goals of actualizing.

Meaning Problems. It is common knowledge that one's personal beliefs about the fundamental questions cited in the introduction to this section are personal and vary widely according to cultural backgrounds and denominational dogma. As recommended earlier, this type of problem is considered from a therapeutic standpoint to be primarily one of instruction and clarification by a specialist in theological matters.

Belief conflicts, however, are at the root of many client anxieties. Most counselors, for example, are familiar with the typical late-adolescent problem of discovering that one's familial beliefs brought along from childhood suddenly seem to deteriorate into a morass of confusion and disillusionment. An example is the student who comes to college from the sheltered life of a small community with a cohesive theistic world-view and is thrust suddenly into an intellectual atmosphere of naturalism, rationalism, scientism, humanism, and many other "isms" that pose threats to his neat childhood belief-structure. This conflict and disillusionment may result in an even more rigid adherence to his childhood beliefs, or the conflicts may lead to a type of agnosticism where he refuses to take a position on the significant questions. As a third possibility, he may reject his former beliefs as revealed by violent emotional and educational upheavals. Out of these upheavals often comes an allegiance to a different system offering similar satisfactions, such as political movements, science, or philosophy.

If the client chooses one of the theistic views of life, he bases his search for meaning on faith in God and builds his world-view about the central idea of God's existence. One way of viewing the so-called "human quandary" is man's perception of his estrangement from God and later expressed needs for reconciliation. He would take the position that man has a transcendental self to be associated ultimately with God. He would feel that man is not alone in a universe that is not indifferent to his fate. He believes he is a creature of God, responsible to God, and with the hope of reconciliation and reunion with God. A significant problem for him is how to be his true self within the tragic framework and disorder of his society.

The Christian view emphasizes man's alienation from God, and man's realization of this estrangement results in much basic anxiety. Klann, in a symposium on psychology and Christianity, stated the view as follows:

Man's anxiety is the product of his sinfulness, that state of alienation or contradiction which exists between him and God, between man's will (taken as the expression of his being) and God's will. Because man's being is derived from God, as had been stated before, man in contradiction to God has good reason to feel himself threatened in his existence. It is the consequence of the threat upon his disobedience: "Thou shalt surely die" (Genesis 2:17) (317, p. 55).

The redemption and conversion doctrines of Christianity provide the means whereby man is reconciled to God. The interested reader is referred to Klann's summary in *What, Then, Is Man* (317).

Basic to a theistic view of life, then, is the existence of a personal God. Some clinicians, such as the Viennese neurologist Viktor Frankl, postulate a strong need for God, similar to the biologically based needs of hunger and thirst (165). He postulates this need because of man's striving to attach meaning to his life. Frankl asserts that the human personality (*Das Geistige*) has laws that go beyond psychological laws and are concerned with man's ideals and responsible behaviors. He calls the methods of helping man to become more aware of his ideals and to focus on the awareness of his responsibilities "logotherapy." This is a form of therapy devoted to discovering the central purpose and meaning of life. The "existential analysis" methods of logotherapy do not determine which values the client will choose, but they impress on him the fact that he must make a choice. The methods of logotherapy are claimed to be especially suitable for conditions that an individual must accept, such as invalidism and suffering.

Mowrer is representative of a slowly expanding group of psychologists who are becoming alarmed about the notion (spreading rapidly during the past four decades) that, fundamentally, neuroses and psychoses are illnesses. The sickness concept of emotional disorders, and the troubles of normal persons also, implies that the states of irresponsibility, narcissism, dependency, and extreme aggression, for example, are not one's own fault. The sickness view indicates that the person can hardly be "blamed" for his condition. He can place the blame conveniently on parental behaviors, environmental deprivation, or other factors outside his control or personal responsibility. Mowrer indicates that we need to examine this sickness concept of emotional problems very carefully, even to the point of exploring the theological doctrine of sin as an explanatory concept for personality disorder. Emotional disorder, then, according to this latter view, is a type of moral problem emphasizing *personal responsibility* for behavior.

Mowrer proffers the idea that perhaps clergymen also are becoming too bedazzled by the sickness concept of personality disorder and with psychoanalytic explanations of human problems. At this writing we are not prepared to comment on this trend, except to say that this moral construction of the human predicament bears serious study and close watching during the next few years.

A second major philosophical choice, or focus of belief, is that position broadly described as humanism. The basic value of this view is man's own existence. Two fundamental postulates are that man is alone in a morally neutral universe and that man is his own moral referent. His troubles are believed to be of his own making. He is limited in his achievements only by his nature. Man's quandary is solved within himself by a process of reason and the methods of self-discovery involved in psychotherapeutic or educational methods. There is a strong belief in man's powers of growth and positive motivation to solve his own and society's problems. Conditions like death, for example, must be accepted as human fact with no necessary implications for further life.

Erich Fromm is selected as an example of an "existential humanist" who attempts to bridge the chasm between these divergent views. The humanist position has its roots in the philosophical upheavals that took place during the enlightenment period of the seventeenth century. Fromm's view of human problem, which we trust is fair and typical of his ideas, is summarized in the following excerpts:

Humanistic religion . . . is centered around man and his strength. Man must develop his power of reason in order to understand himself, his relationship to his fellow men and his position in the universe. He must recognize the truth, both with regard to his limitations and his potentialities. He must develop his powers of love for others as well as for himself and experience the solidarity of all living beings. He must have principles and norms to guide him in this aim. Religious experience in this kind of religion is the experience of oneness with the All, based on one's relatedness to the world as it is grasped with thought and with love. Man's aim in humanistic religion is to achieve the greatest strength, not the greatest powerlessness; virtue is self-realization, not obedience. Faith is certainty of conviction based on one's experience of thought and feeling, not assent to propositions on credit of the proposer. The prevailing mood is that of joy, while the prevailing mood in authoritarian religion is that of sorrow and guilt.

Inasmuch as humanistic religions are theistic, God is a symbol of *man's own powers* which he tries to realize in his life, and is not a symbol of force and domination, having *power over man* [italics ours] (175, p. 37).

Fromm indicates in another source that:

There is only one solution to his problem: to face the truth, to acknowledge his fundamental aloneness and solitude in a universe indifferent to his fate, to recognize that there is no power transcending him which can solve his problems for him. . . . If he faces the truth without panic he will recognize that there is no meaning to life except the meaning man gives his life by the unfolding of his powers, by living productively (173, pp. 44–45).

An essential point in the humanistic position is that man lives in a confused human situation. He must face up to the incongruities in this human situation through his own powers. He must discover his own values within himself and lean heavily on consensus and cultural norms. His possibilities and troubles are largely of his own making.

There are many individuals who are trying to construct a "bridge" between these two basic views of man's situation in this universe. Clients often express anxieties about such problems, and it behooves the therapeutic psychologist to be aware of the basic philosophical assumptions underlying various belief systems. The counselor can aid the client to see discrepancies and contradictions in his system and can help him to a more clear definition of his life values. Lifton, for example, applies three criteria of counselor effectiveness in helping clients to more clear ideas in the area of religious belief:

(1) The client's feelings of achieving a satisfactory solution to his problem; (2) the counselor's feeling that the client is doing what the counselor believes

is most appropriate; and (3) the degree to which the client's solution coincides with the approved answer in terms of mores of his society (289, p. 367).

We agree most closely with criterion one. There is much potential danger in the counselor projecting too many of his own values into the discussion, as in criterion two. Criterion three in Lifton's list again is primarily the client's own concern, provided the implications of his religious beliefs do not threaten the welfare of others. The religious counselor probably would feel obliged to take a view different from these criteria because of his particular sectarian commitments.

Existentialist views are having an increasing influence on American counseling and psychotherapy. These views, imported from Europe, grew rather spontaneously and simultaneously in several centers. Existential views do not constitute a new school or new set of theories, but rather a fresh way of looking at human existence. The two basic problems in understanding the Existential movement are the variety of ideas, some contradictory, which have come under its semantic cloak, and the difficulties in finding English language for the experiences and concepts developed within the existential framework.

Essentially, the existential approach seeks to avoid the usual subject-object approaches of studying human behavior, wherein man is broken into segmental "essences," by looking beneath these characteristics (May 310). It is an effort to understand the essential nature of a particular man, in addition to the usual objective approaches of science. In psychotherapy, for example, attempts are made to help the client experience his essential being, or humanness. Counseling and psychotherapy experiences are especially appropriate to this task because one finds this essential being in periods of crisis and distress that often characterize clients in the course of a therapeutic relationship. In fact, Existentialism is a view of man as being in a perpetual process of becoming through continuous crisis.

Since Existentialism is not a philosophy or a way of life with palpable goals and identifiable axioms, but an effort to grasp reality, the reader is enjoined to investigate some of the original sources through writings of Kierkegaard, Jaspers, Heidegger, Tillich, Binswanger, and Buber, for example. May (310) has written a summary and edited a collection of papers on Existentialism and therapy that will serve the reader as an introduction.

Eastern views have had an impact on the thinking of many persons in the West. These include Zen forms of Buddhism, Kundalini Yoga, and Taoism. The central attractive features are their emphases upon viewing one's being as a part of nature, of grounding existence in the body through basic breathing exercises, and letting the meaning of life emerge naturally without strain. The life of meditation and quiet is especially attractive to Westerners tired of the pressures and dehumanizing effects of strong achievement drives. The growing popularity of Transcendental Meditation training and practice is an example.

The Counselor's and Therapist's Role in Belief Problems. What can the counselor, *as a counselor,* do with client questions of religious belief? First, he can recognize the significance of religious sentiments and beliefs in personality development in general and in the life of this particular client. Secondly, the counselor should know how to handle his own religious problems, which are precipitated by the client's problems. He should work them through to the point where he does not project them and where they do not interfere with an optimal relationship. Also, he should know his own faith well enough so that he can be accepting without jeopardizing that faith through the empathy process. Thirdly, he can regard problems of religious belief in much the same manner as he would treat any other affect-laden problem concerning marriage, job, children, or sex.

The counselor should have certain knowledge about the client, such as the origin of his beliefs. Were they derived from Sunday school, movies, life crisis, or family instruction? It would be well to note the client's social background, such as parental beliefs and church background, and their effects on his religious beliefs and practice. Finally, if the counselor finds his techniques and relationship are not meeting the client's needs, then something else, in the form of religious counseling by a specialist, or a human potential group experience, may be needed.

Problems of Relatedness

To feel at home in the universe, to be valued as a person, and to feel close to someone are deep personal needs. Counselors are impressed by this overpowering need for relatedness, or more broadly speaking—love. The problems of giving and receiving love have been discussed at length elsewhere in this volume. The purpose of including the topic at this juncture, however, is to consider the gyroscopic effect of relatedness and love on a human life.

One of the appeals of membership in and identification with broad social, political, and religious movements is the feeling of close belonging and of being important to a significant cause. One's group affiliations, then, play a significant part in developing feelings of relatedness. It should be stressed that the relatedness must involve a high degree of intimacy—close friendships, comradeship, work organization, or marriage. Of these, marriage provides opportunity for the greatest satisfaction of the relatedness need because in marriage there is at least one other person who cares deeply about one's self.

Work provides further outlets for such feelings, but work is a paradox in several respects. Though work offers relatedness satisfaction, it often gives the individual the feeling that he is being manipulated and that he is regarded as a "marketable product." The specter of the "company man," for example, frightens many thoughtful people.

A second problem in connection with work relatedness is the common picture of the business executive or professional man who derives most of the satisfaction for his feelings of relatedness in his work. Frequently, he obtains little satisfaction from, or contributes little of himself to, the family or community. Counselors and therapists often observe the phenomenon of the "vicious circle" of the individual gaining decreasing satisfactions from family life and increasing his searches for satisfaction from work. This cycle can lead to other signs of personality deterioration such as alcoholism or infidelity. Shoben (431) has analyzed the problem neatly in the less severe cases where the client's feelings of self-worth are sought increasingly in his occupational pursuits or in tangential social or sexual activities.

Many men and women feel they must choose between their intimate relationships and their work. The balance of these two features in a person's life is again a personal affair not to be dictated by a counselor. There seems to be an optimally proportionate emphasis on work and home, however, that leads to maximum satisfaction and productivity for all concerned. Freud is reputed to have answered the query on what a person must do to be mature with the reply, *"Lieben und arbeiten."* The mature, well-functioning person in our society must be able to both love and work in the proper balance.

Counselors must be ready for problems originating in underemployment. Satisfactions are so closely tied to work that the prospects of no work or being paid not to work have anxious implications. Counselors will have great service opportunities for actualizing counseling as people have increasing leisure and opportunity to look inward.

The main therapeutic implication here is that often client symptoms appear in the form of a basic management problem—such as finding the optimal balance among work, family, play, and civic participation. Such clients, furthermore, tend not to find their need satisfactions for relatedness and self-worth in the activities they currently employ. The counselor may be requested by the client to help him find some person or group to which he might relate. This bid needs to be assessed and interpreted in light of possible dependency reinforcement, and the extent to which the counselor feels he can afford to be maneuvered into the role of an "agent" for the client. The therapist definitely can help the client to understand his deep-seated needs for security and self-worth, which might be attainable through a more satisfying human relationship.

There are conditions where the counselor may need to help the client accept the limitations of his current situation through awareness and support. Examples of such situations would be the low probability of marriage for a chronic invalid, or the loneliness felt by new widows and divorcees, where such individuals may need to develop inner resources to cope with the lack of intimate relationships. Sometimes such clients can find compensations through small group relationships in their community.

Closely related to the relatedness-loneliness problem is that of depersonalization. We are not speaking so much of the type of detachment or splitting of affect and cognition that occurs in the psychotic, but of the normal person's feelings of being an "object" to be manipulated, bought and sold, traded, seduced, or used. Fromm (174) warns of the damage that may result in personalities when they are led to feel like a "thing," a marketable commodity, rather than a person.

The counselor can help such clients through helping them to establish points of relatedness to people. The principal vehicle is the therapeutic relationship where the client can see his defenses more clearly, especially those that alienate him from other people. He will be less likely also to regard other people as "things" to be manipulated, used, or exploited when he discovers the defensive distortions in his own personality.

Meeting Life Crises

While the main discussion of crisis management was presented in Chapter 6, a more extended presentation on value choice crises is given here.

Medical and pastoral counselors generally confront clients in severe life crises more than psychological counselors. There are occasions, however, where problems associated with losing a job, death, divorce, disability, or financial disaster are brought to the psychologist for the purpose of working through the feelings associated with the crisis. Kunkel (275) has developed a point of view on handling real or projected crises that seems to be valuable for the therapeutic psychologist.

Often the crisis is due to a misperception of a situation, although the experience of anxiety or dread from the projected problem can be just as intense as the more objective kinds of crises. An example is the individual who had taken an examination for entry into a much-coveted position. A clerk made a remark to the candidate that was interpreted by the man to mean that he had failed. He brooded at length and finally moved into a mild depression and headaches for the next three days prior to receiving word of his standing. He heard that he had passed the examination and that he would very likely be appointed in the near future. The clerk's remark was then reperceived as being a warning that passing the examination did not necessarily mean employment in the desired position. The emotional effect, however, persisted for several days.

Kunkel's thesis is that people learn to face large crises later in life by a process of meeting minor life crises from early childhood on through development. He sees human life as one "unending chain of crises" (275, p. 150). Old behavior patterns are disrupted and discarded for the new patterns required by the crises. The feelings of creativity and confidence that come out of a crisis solution constitute, according to Kunkel, an important part of personality growth. He feels that the client's experience of desperation and helplessness is the prelude to critical examination and transformation of his defenses. Suffering is regarded as a facilitative force in the growth process.

Crises require judgments. The process of making judgments that propel the person forward in his mastery of life draws on many elements of personality and demands a high level of functioning. Each life crisis, according to Kunkel, has rich potentiality for building spiritual strength in the mature personality. Therefore, we feel that counseling on matters of life crises is within the province and skills of the therapeutic psychologist.

What can be said about the person with feelings of inadequacy, failure, and incapacity to meet crises? If this problem is construed as being in the realm of therapeutic psychology, then surely more must be considered than the aforementioned feelings. The whole problem of the client's life style, creative potential, life philosophy, and religious outlook must be considered. In addition, the therapeutic psychologist must allow the client to explore his deeper feelings and relationships to parents in early life experiences. This is done to throw further light on why he lacks the personal resources to meet life crises. Through counseling, clients may obtain insight into their defense mechanisms and their problems of developing spiritual strength for meeting life crises. An example is the case where a client projected to God certain expectations of the help provided by his mother. When the crisis came and mother was not nearby to nurse his hurts, he blamed God, who had become equated psychologically with mother. He began to see that his inadequacies in meeting life demands and crises were not failure of his God, but the results of his own immaturity and fear of psychological and spiritual creativity. The therapeutic psychologist, in short, utilizes the life crisis problem to help the client gain insight and to make progress along the road to self-actualization.

A critical factor in achieving these objectives, as indicated so many times in this volume, is the therapeutic relationship itself. The opportunity to face feelings of doubt, inadequacy, insecurity, and defeat in the presence of a warm and accepting counselor is what seems to us to be the primary factor in drawing from a client new powers to meet life's challenges. This phenomenon of discovering either within or without his person this feeling of confidence and creative power is what Kunkel has called the "miraculous center of every constructive crisis" (275, p. 163). The alternatives to this creative experience are continued feelings of discouragement, defeat, and emptiness, often leading to personality deterioration.

Moral Problems

Moral problems are related to religious concerns in that formal religions incorporate an ethical and moral code and use the weight of religious authority to enforce the code. Moral problems, defined broadly as behavior contradictory to the established mores of the social order, can exist apart from problems of religious belief. The therapeutic psychologist's principal concern in the moral area is over the feeling of guilt associated with immoral behavior and the defensive function that immoral behavior performs for the personality. The psychologist is concerned also about the enhancing or damaging effects of moral and immoral behavior on clients and others affected by their behavior.

As background for the discussion of therapeutic counseling on moral problems, some conceptions of morality are described briefly. One viewpoint stresses the dual and simultaneous presence of the "good" and the "bad" in man. For example, he is said to be sinful and destructive, yet potentially virtuous and loving too. The problem then becomes how to help the individual seek victory of the "good" over the "evil." This view may presuppose either an inherent knowledge of good and evil or a learned series of attitudes and behaviors. A contrary view is held also that "good" and "bad," used as nouns, are social artifacts and that man is neither by nature. When used as adjectives, they imply an arbitrary standard to be meaningful.

The view that man is by nature a sinful being (hence, by definition bad and reprehensible) is commonly held by the Hebraic-Christian world. This sinful-nature conception of man's moral condition is accompanied by a belief that there is potential good in man expressed in such terms as man's capacity to be kind, loving, conscientious, and to hold similar virtues. The "sinful nature" and "total depravity" concepts refer to man's condition from God's viewpoint. From a human standpoint, classical Judaism and Christianity both hold that man has great potential for either goodness or evil.

Certainly not all persons in the Hebraic-Christian moral framework subscribe strictly to this fundamental position; however, it is representative of the majority. To some extent, this view of innate evil is common to the Freudian group also. The main implication here is that this innate evil conception of moral behavior leads to the attitude that human nature cannot be trusted, must be restrained by external forces, or transformed by a mystical process.

That man has basically a heredity of socially constructive forces in his nature is a third view of the moral nature of man. This is a faith in the basic "goodness" of man. The main implication is that man's principal moral problem is to create conditions where the "good" can be brought out and the "bad" learnings extinguished.

Horney holds a growth and personal responsibility view of morality described briefly as follows:

. . . the problem of morality is again different when we believe that inherent in man are evolutionary constructive forces, which urge him to realize his given potentialities. This belief does not mean that man is essentially good—which would presuppose a given knowledge of what is good or bad. It means that man, by his very nature and of his own accord, strives toward self-realization, and that his set of values evolves from such striving. Apparently he cannot, for example, develop his full human potentialities unless he is truthful to himself; unless he is active and productive; unless he relates himself to others in the spirit of mutuality. Apparently he cannot grow if he . . . consistently attributes all his own shortcomings to the deficiencies of others. He can grow, in the true sense, only if he assumes responsibility for himself (231, pp. 14–15).

Kirkendall presents the hypothesis that immoral behavior is that which destroys self-respect and heightens difficulties in interpersonal relationships:

The obvious concern of students in classes in marriage and family life for values and principles of moral living has led me to the formulation of a concept useful in making decisions on right and wrong. The concept is that moral decision and conduct are those which result in improving the capacity of people to work together with trust and understanding. The outreach of individuals and groups toward others should be constantly furthered, and individual self-respect should be heightened by moral living. Immoral or wrong conduct is that which creates distrust and suspicion, produces withdrawal, and a decline in self-respect (261, p. 5).

On college campuses particularly, there is much talk about the "sex revolution." This appears to mean that a strong rational relative values point of view is guiding student behavior. Visits to campuses by persons such as Nathaniel Branden (66), who reflects views on "objectivist ethics" of Ayn Rand, are reinforcing this position. Objectivist ethics emphasizes rational, responsible moral choices that consider human values, and human survival particularly, as the standard of value. Branden feels these views have strong implications for psychotherapy, because so much human misery and hypocrisy are due to irrational moral positions.

We are indebted to Hugh Bell for many illustrations in this discussion on moral behavior and counseling (41). Bell illustrates the variety of forms through which moral problems are brought to the psychological counselor. The most common problems are sexual ones, which take the form of anxieties about promiscuity, homosexuality, infidelity, masturbation, and exhibitionism. A second type concerns accuracy of reporting, which involves occasional dishonesty and lying all the way to gross and habitual deception and cheating.

Disturbing the property and personal rights of others is another area of morals that involves the occasional client. Disturbing others' rights often creates guilt and anxiety when the acts are committed impulsively or under the influence of a narcotic.

There is another category of moral behavior surrounding the classification of psychopathic or inadequate personality. This group includes those persons classified as delinquents, alcoholics, vagrants, truants, and drug addicts. Their acts of hostility, though directed against themselves sometimes, are mainly expressed against others. Their feelings, rather than their acts, however, are the principal concern of the therapeutic psychologist.

Most of the problems of the psychopath involve some legal action against him. In this discussion we will not cover the legal, moralistic, or disciplinary implications of these behaviors but will attempt to suggest therapeutic roles and techniques for dealing with the feelings associated

with problems that are judged by the client or society to be moral problems. The therapeutic psychologist is not concerned, then, with the concept of the "goodness-badness" dichotomy so commonly thrust on human
behavior. He is interested primarily in a rehabilitative approach, although
he is interested also in the diagnostic problem of the meaning the immoral behavior has for the client and what some of the causes leading to
this behavior might be. The therapeutic psychologist is interested also
in the ethical problem of protecting the client and others who might be
influenced by his behavior.

The Problem of Guilt. A striking characteristic of a client coming for
help on a moral problem is the feeling described as guilt. The term *guilt*
has two meanings in the present discussion. The first is a broad pervasive
feeling of "wrongness." The client often feels a vague sense of "something
is wrong with me; I'm not really doing what I should be doing; I should
be something better." This feeling is closely related to feelings of inadequacy and fears of failure. Even persons successful by the usual social
standards often have such feelings, which seem to come from early experiences and learned ways of handling hostile and dependent feelings, especially toward parents. The child experiences, very early, strong love and
hostility feelings toward parents. Such ambivalent feelings may be distorted
and experienced later as guilt. It seems that this type of normal guilt is an
intimate condition of human life and may even perform protective functions for the individual and his society. Therefore, it may not necessarily
be a personal liability.

A second type of guilt feeling is that experienced as an acute emotional
reaction to a specific behavior. For example, breaking rules against lying,
cheating an associate, or stealing property may arouse strong subjective
feelings of having done something reprehensible, which can be described
as guilt. One is very much aware of having broken a social rule, a religious
injunction, or a moral "law." These feelings seem to be characteristic of
most cultures in the forms of awareness that one is being watched and will
be held accountable for his acts. Fromm summarizes the origin and consequences of the preceding type of guilt feeling as follows:

The problem of guilt plays no less a role in psychoanalytic procedure than it
does in religion. Sometimes it is presented by the patient as one of his main
symptoms. He feels guilty for not loving his parents as he should, for failing
to do his work satisfactorily, for having hurt somebody's feelings. The feeling
of guilt has overpowered some patients' minds and they react with a sense of
inferiority, of depravity, and often with a conscious or unconscious desire for
punishment. It is usually not difficult to discover that this all-pervasive guilt
reaction stems from an authoritarian orientation. They would give a more
correct expression to their feeling if instead of saying that they feel guilty they
said that they are afraid—afraid of punishment, or more often, of not being
loved any more by those authorities whom they have disobeyed. In the analytic
process such a patient will slowly recognize that behind his authoritarian sense

of guilt is another feeling of guilt which stems from his own voice, from his conscience in the humanistic sense. Assume that a patient feels guilty for leading a promiscuous life. The first step in analyzing this guilt feeling will be to discover that he really feels afraid of being found out and criticized by his parents, by his wife, by public opinion, by the church—briefly, by anyone who represents authority to him. Only then will he be able to recognize that behind this authoritarian feeling of guilt is another feeling. He will recognize that his "love" affairs are in reality expressions of his fear of love, of his inability to love anyone, to commit himself to any close and responsible relationship. He will recognize that his sin is against himself, the sin of letting his power to love go to waste (175, pp. 90–91).

It seems to us that Fromm, in the quotation, is pointing out the distinction between normal and neurotic guilt, which is developed later in this section.

Meehl and his symposium co-workers presented a distinction between valid and displaced guilt. Valid guilt is claimed to be present when man realizes that his relationship with God is not proper. His feeling is manifested by an awareness of anxiety, or even dread. The symposium described valid guilt as follows:

. . . we have been suggesting that man's objective sinful and alienated relation to God, with its attendant effects upon his relation to his fellows, gives rise to a psychological state of valid guilt (317, p. 221).

Displaced guilt, however, is that feeling of guilt that is detached from the original idea (the alienation phenomenon described above) and appears in the individual's awareness as a different idea, such as remorse over some small act or a haunting fear that he has done something reprehensible like injuring someone with his automobile.

Conscience. There is considerable difference of opinion concerning the validity and origin of the concept "conscience." In common usage, the term "conscience" connotes three quite different things: (1) involuntary submission to external authorities with the concomitant fear of discovery and punishment; (2) condemnatory self-accusations; and (3) discontent with self in a constructive sense (232).

The classical religious conception of conscience from the western Christian point of view is that man is born with a rudimentary, though very imperfect, knowledge of right and wrong. This rudimentary conscience is sharpened through religious training by means of the following rationale: God created man with a certain nature; man is obligated to live according to that nature; God revealed how he wants man to behave; if man disobeys, he has made an offense against God and, hence, is estranged from God. The result is that he feels guilty; this feeling of guilt creates a need for God's forgiveness and ultimately brings him back to God. This is an oversimplification, of course, but it points out the basic rationale for the development of conscience and guilt feelings from one religious point of view.

The Freudian view of the superego development, in contrast, is typical of psychological viewpoints on conscience. It is considered a learned concept arising largely out of internalization, or "introjection," as Freud called it, of parental prohibitions, threats, and values. These internalized values are picked up through the process of incidental learning during early childhood. Punishments rather than rewards seem to be the decisive determinants. The child learns to "hear" the parental voice of authority whenever he comes against similar circumstances, and he suffers painful feelings when he transgresses.

In the Freudian framework, personality problems are caused, to a great extent, by a severe superego overwhelming the ego and forcing it to repress the biologically based primitive impulses of the id. Mowrer (338) feels that a more correct view of the Freudian model would be that disturbances in personality are caused by the id and the ego joining forces against the superego. The latter is a type of guilt theory where the ego functions are immature and, under the influence of the id, have done things of which the superego disapproves. In this sense, the person with a diminutive superego and an immature ego would tend toward anti-social, criminal acts; whereas the person with the overdeveloped superego would tend toward oversocialization and rigidity which would place severe demands on the ego and restraint on the id. According to Mowrer (338), a dual task of the counselor is to help the client develop a stronger ego that is able to escape control by the id, and to develop a working relationship with the superego.

The preceding elaboration of Freudian superego or conscience theory, and its implications for counseling and psychotherapy, is an oversimplification of a very complex metaphorical system. We sketched it here because it is such a commonly held point of view in therapeutic psychology. A humanistic view of conscience is popular among counselors. If the child grows up feeling that this conscience is somehow absolute and synonymous with divine or cosmic law, the child may go through life trying to live up to these expectations, justifying his actions, and forever feeling guilty that he should be doing something he isn't doing or not doing something he is doing. The psychological viewpoint (largely psychoanalytic in origin) is that the client must be helped to recognize the relativity of value systems and must be helped to develop his own frame of value reference suited to his times, unique circumstances, and needs. This is a basic humanistic view that sees man as his own moral referent.

Allport (4) asserts that the preceding explanation helps to account for childhood conscience, but it does not explain the adult conscience adequately. He postulates a shift from *ad hoc* habits of obedience built up through conditioning and punishments to broader permeation of the personality. The shift is from fear of punishment to feelings of obligation. In other words, the person has incorporated his former learnings into a value structure in the core and character levels of our system. He changes his view from must to ought and from compulsion to obligation.

Normal or healthy guilt, in the mature adult, becomes a feeling of having violated the integrity of core values, a feeling of self-hostility for not achieving the ideal of the actualized person. Thus, a more voluntary and seemingly purposeful ethical act is substituted for the conditioned habit and fear of punishment. The habit of obedience in the adult, according to Allport, gives way to self-guidance based on a "broad schemata of values that confer direction upon conduct" (4, p. 73). The child, in developing this mature schemata of values, sees that restraint and ideals have purposes other than merely pleasing one's parents. Horney emphasizes this approach to normal guilt or the mature conscience, too, in her term "constructive discontent with self" (231).

We believe that the preceding theory of conscience results in more permanence and flexibility than the views stressing internalization of parental authority or the theories of genetic origins. We feel also that conscience can be a positive creative force in interpersonal relationships, as well as an inhibiting, guilt-provoking force. According to May's (312) view of conscience, learnings from past experience become blended with present experiences so that one's ethical sensitivity is sharpened and one's level of awareness is deepened. The actualizing conscience then becomes a device for tapping one's enlarged experience and for developing one's valuing center in the core level.

In Figure 28, we present our views on the development of a mature conscience, beginning with the rudimentary awareness of social values resulting from demands and punishments of parents. As the child grows, parental demands become internalized into feelings of "rightness" and "wrongness." Conditioning plays a significant part here also, since rewards and punishments are important. As the child grows into adolescence, he acquires a self-picture as a moral person, with the mores a part of his developing core value system. This value system is based on earlier learned values, a growing self-awareness, and a rationally determined view of the mores. As a mature adult, he makes more selective and rational responses

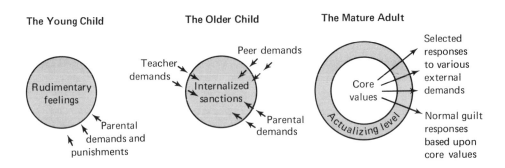

Figure 28. The Development of a Mature Conscience

to environmental demands. He still feels guilt, but it is *normal* guilt, which helps him to reduce the gap between actualizing self-values and inappropriate behavior.

Regardless of the position taken on the nature and origin of conscience, psychologists tend to agree that the phenomenon of conscience is a profound factor in the control of impulsive behavior and opportunism. They believe that it has a significant long-range influence on goals and values also. A key therapeutic implication here is that one of the roles of counseling is facilitating the transformation of a blind, impulsive, infantile conscience into a mature value structure. A second implication is the possibility of helping the client whose childhood conscience is overly severe or fixated at a childhood level. The counselor may help to modify the compulsive demands and consequent neurotic guilt feelings of such conscience while the mature value system is developing.

Therapeutic Handling of Guilt and Conscience Problems

The handling of guilt in therapy is a most critical problem. A summary of methods for dealing with this significant problem in the therapeutic interview follows.

The counselor's first step is to release his client's tensions within a relationship characterized by acceptance on the counselor's part. A nonjudgmental attitude of a counselor is especially important to encourage free expression of guilt feelings. When the working-through phase of the process is reached, a client can be helped to see and understand the origins of his guilt and conscience problems.

According to May (310) guilt is best understood if a differentiation is made between normal and neurotic guilt. Normal guilt is universal and is of three basic types: guilt against one's self for not fulfilling one's potentialities; guilt against one's fellow man for not meeting his needs; and guilt against nature or God and a feeling of separateness or alienation therefrom. Neurotic guilt is defined as unaccepted and repressed normal guilt. Therapy, therefore, consists of assisting the client to accept and face his neurotic guilt and to turn it into normal guilt. This is in sharp contrast to the view that therapy should water down, expunge, or neutralize guilt entirely. The following steps are suggested for changing neurotic to normal guilt. The counselor should:

1. Help the client to *admit* what he has done to feel guilty.
2. Help him to become aware of the *motives* underlying his guilt feelings, especially those of destruction and hatred.
3. Cut through the *rationalizations*. This implies taking *responsibility* for what one does.
4. Transform neurotic (unfaced) guilt to *normal guilt* by assisting the client to see that it can be tolerated and constructive. When the client is able to experience normal guilt, he can utilize the gap between his self-image and what he actually is for further growth.

439

Traumatic incidents can be desensitized so that the intense suffering associated with neurotic guilt can be minimized and understood. Neurotic suffering, for example, can be understood as a kind of atonement that the severe conscience is exacting for real or imagined misdeeds. Suffering from normal guilt can be used as a springboard to awareness, as indicated in the earlier discussion on crises.

The client can be helped to understand the defenses he has used to handle his guilt feelings. Sometimes this takes the form of physical symptoms and requires the collaboration of a physician. Often, the defense takes the form of projection where others are blamed for the very behaviors for which the client feels guilty. This development comes later in the working-through process, however, since it presupposes considerable ego strength to tolerate the loss of defensive strength. Another illustrative projective mechanism is that of the overdeveloped conscience, which expresses itself in a paranoid delusion. This type of client projects his guilt feelings to others whom he accuses of criticizing or blaming him. This projection may involve the belief that his deity is constantly condemning and punishing him also.

A related defense often seen in guilt cases is the pharisaically self-righteous client who defends his guilt feelings stoutly by means of a superior demeanor and condemnation of others.

Counseling or therapy on guilt might involve referral. If the traditional rituals and methods of formal religious experiences are meaningful and acceptable to the client, perhaps referral to a church group or pastoral counselor would assist in both the emergency reduction and in the long-term resolution of his guilt feelings.

When it comes to the action phase of the process, the counselor frequently is in a dilemma. If the client has acquired some insight but his actualizing capabilities are still quite weak, he may not follow through with responsible behavior. Should the therapist assume a very authoritarian role and use shock techniques to assist clients to feel personally responsible for their behavior? An example is the case of a married man with a family, who is concerned about dating a young woman. Should the counselor depend on the relationship and the client's maturation potential to develop a conventional solution to the problem? The answers would depend greatly on the counselor's basic orientation to therapy as well as the degree of confidence he feels in his own value system. We feel that with some types of clients, direct methods can often effect drastic behavior changes. The limitations, however, are that without considerable awareness the changes will be temporary at best. In any case, it is very important for the counselor to assist the client to feel a sense of decision and responsibility for his own behavior. Therapy consists of assisting the client to make a decision even if it turns out to be a wrong decision.

The overall goal of counseling on moral problems is to help the client to develop greater feelings of responsibility to his core feelings, especially if his problem is one of too little anxiety about his behavior. The counselor also may suggest that the client having too much anxiety about his moral behavior develop a more stable and mature value structure, which consequently can lead to a greater degree of internal direction for his behavior. A positive self-regard manifested by strong actualizing capabilities appears to us to be the most dependable route to moral behavior.

In addition to individual counseling, the actualizing group provides a potent resource for the person to express and share his feelings of guilt with fellow humans. Ancient values of group "confession" are being rediscovered in the actualizing group experience.

As the client learns to trust his innermost feelings about himself, he learns that such trust will help him to make more wise decisions. As he learns to listen to all these feelings, both positive and negative, his core feelings will be found to be trustworthy for aiding decisions that will be beneficial not only to himself, but to society as well.

Summary

In the science and profession of psychology, keen interest is being exhibited in problems of value. This chapter included some of the implications of value problems, such as developing an effective philosophy of life and working out feelings associated with moral problems. The therapeutic psychologist has a role to perform in each of these areas that is different from, but overlapping with, that of the pastoral counselor. The pastoral counselor has a unique role, yet in many ways it is similar to that of the therapeutic psychologist. A principal task of the therapeutic psychologist is helping the client to transform neurotic guilt into normal guilt and to help the client trust his core feelings.

References

1. Adams, D. K., et al. *Learning Theory, Personality Theory, and Clinical Research: The Kentucky Symposium.* New York: John Wiley, 1954.

2. Aguilera, D. C., and J. M. Messick. *Crisis Intervention: Theory and Methodology,* 2nd ed. St. Louis: C. V. Mosby, 1974.

3. Alexander, F., and T. M. French. *Psychoanalytic Therapy.* New York: Ronald Press, 1946.

4. Allport, G. W. *Becoming: Basic Considerations for a Psychology of Personality.* New Haven: Yale University Press, 1955.

5. Allport, G. W. *Personality: A Psychological Interpretation.* New York: Holt, 1937.

6. Allport, G. W. Psychological models for guidance. *Harvard Educ. Rev.,* 1962, *4,* 373–81.

7. Alperson, B. L., E. D. Alperson, and R. Levine. Growth effects of high school marathons. *Experimental Publications System,* 1971, 2 (Ms. No. 369-56).

8. Alschuler, R. H., and L. W. Hattwick. *Painting and Personality: Study of Young Children.* Chicago: University of Chicago Press, 1947.

9. American Board of Examiners in Professional Psychology. Annual report. *Amer. Psychologist,* 1954, *9,* 766–70.

10. American Psychiatric Association. *Diagnostic and Statistical Manual of Mental Disorders.* Washington, D.C.: American Psychological Association, 1952.

11. American Psychological Association. Bylaws for the American Psychological Association. *Directory American Psychological Association.* Washington, D.C.: American Psychological Association, 1954.

12. American Psychological Association. Standards of ethical behavior for

psychologists. *Amer. Psychologist,* 1958, *13,* 266–71, and as revised in proposals of 1975.

13. American Psychological Association. *Psychology and Its Relations with Other Professions.* Washington, D.C.: American Psychological Association, 1954.

14. American Psychological Association. The scope and standards of preparation in psychology for school counselors. *Amer. Psychologist,* 1962, *17,* 149–52.

15. American Psychological Association Committee on Counselor Training. Recommended standards for training counseling psychologists at the doctorate level. *Amer. Psychologist,* 1952, 7, 175–81.

16. American Psychological Association Committee on Training in Clinical Psychology. Recommended graduate training program in clinical psychology. *Amer. Psychologist,* 1947, 2, 539–58.

17. American Psychological Association Standards for Educational and Psychological Tests and Manuals. Washington, D.C.: American Psychological Association, 1966.

18. American Psychological Association Subcommittee on Counselor Trainee Selection. Annual report. *Counseling News and Views,* 1953–54, 6.

19. American School Counselors' Association. Tentative statement of policy for secondary school counselors. *Pers. and Guid. J.,* 1963, *42,* 194–98.

20. Ansbacher, R., and H. Ansbacher. *The Individual Psychology of Alfred Adler.* New York: Basic Books, 1956.

21. Ash, P. The reliability of psychiatric diagnosis. *J. abnorm. soc. Psychol.,* 1949, *44,* 272–76.

22. Aspy, D. N. Empathy. *The Counseling Psychologist,* 1975, *5,* 10–14.

23. Assagioli, R. *Psychosynthesis.* New York: Viking Press, 1965.

24. Association for Counselor Education and Supervision. Standards for counselor education in the preparation of secondary school counselors. *Pers. and Guid. J.,* 1964, *42,* 1061–73.

25. Axline, V. Mental deficiency: Symptom or disease. *J. consult. Psychol.,* 1949, *13,* 313–27.

26. Axline, V. *Play Therapy.* Boston: Houghton Mifflin, 1947.

27. Bach, G. R. *Intensive Group Psychotherapy.* New York: Ronald Press, 1954.

28. Bach, G. R. The marathon group: intensive practice of intimate interaction. *Psychological Reports,* 1966, *18,* 995–1002.

29. Baer, M. F., and E. C. Roeber. *Occupational Information: Its Nature and Use.* Chicago: Science Research Associates, 1951.

30. Bandura, A. *Principles of Behavior Modification.* New York: Holt, Rinehart & Winston, 1969.

31. Bandura, A., and R. H. Walters. *Social Learning and Personality Development.* New York: Holt, Rinehart & Winston, 1963.

32. Banmen, J., and R. Capelle. Human relations training in three rural Manitoba high schools. Paper presented at the Convention of the National Council on Human Relations. Winnipeg, Canada, April 1971.

33. Banmen, J., and R. Capelle. Human relations training in three rural Manitoba high schools: A three-month follow-up. *Canadian Counsellor*, 1972, *6*, 260–70.

34. Barak, A., and M. La Crosse. Multidimensional perception of counselor behavior. *J. counsel. Psychol.*, 1975, *22*, 471–76.

35. Bartlett, F. C. *Remembering*. Cambridge: Cambridge University Press, 1932.

36. Baruch, D. *How to Live with Your Teenager*. New York: McGraw-Hill, 1953.

37. Baruch, D. *New Ways in Discipline*. New York: McGraw-Hill, 1949.

38. Baruch, D. *One Little Boy*. New York: Julian Press, 1952.

39. Bebout, J., and B. Gordon. The value of encounter. In L. N. Solomon and B. Berzon (eds.), *New Perspectives on Encounter Groups*. San Francisco: Jossey-Bass, 1972.

40. Bell, H. M. *The Adjustment Inventory*. Stanford, Calif.: Stanford University Press, 1938.

41. Bell, H. M. Counseling Students with Moral and Religious Problems. Chico, Calif.: Chico State General Lectures, 1952.

42. Bem, S. Fluffy women and chesty men. *Psychology Today*, 1975, *9*, 58–60.

43. Berdie, R. F. An aid to student counselors. *Educ. psychol. Measmt.*, 1952, *2*, 281–90.

44. Berger, E. M. The relation between expressed acceptance of self and expressed acceptance of others. *J. abnorm. soc. Psychol.*, 1952, *47*, 778–82.

45. Bergler, E. *The Revolt of the Middle-Aged Man*. New York: A. A. Wyn, 1954.

46. Bergman, D. V. Counseling method and client responses. *J. consult. Psychol.*, 1951, *15*, 216–24.

47. Berne, E. *Transactional Analysis*. New York: Grove Press, 1961.

48. Berzon, B., and L. Solomon. The self directed therapeutic group: three studies. *J. counsel. Psychol.*, 1966, *13*, 491–97.

49. Bettleheim, B. Self-interpretation of fantasy: the thematic apperception test as an educational and therapeutic device. *Amer. J. Orthopsychiat.*, 1947, *17*, 80–100.

50. Beverly, B. *In Defense of Children*. New York: Day, 1941.

51. Bixler, R. H. Limits are Therapy. *J. consult. Psychol.*, 1949, *13*, 1–11.

52. Bixler, R. H. and V. H. Bixler. Test interpretation in vocational counseling. *Educ. psychol. Measmt.*, 1946, *6*, 145–55.

53. Black, J. D. Common factors of the patient-therapist relationship in diverse psychotherapies. *J. clin. Psychol.*, 1952, *8*, 302–6.

54. Blanton, S. *Love or Perish*. New York: Simon & Schuster, 1956.

55. Blocher, D. H. *Developmental Counseling*. New York: Ronald Press, 1966.

56. Blos, P. Psychological counseling of college students. *Amer. J. Orthopsychiat.*, 1946, *16*, 571–80.

57. Bogue, J. P. (ed.) *American Junior Colleges*, 6th ed. Washington, D.C.: American Council on Education, 1963.

58. Boileau, V. New techniques in brief psychotherapy. *Psychological Reports*, Monogr. Suppl. #7, 1958.

59. Bordin, E. S. Diagnosis in counseling and psychotherapy. *Educ. psychol. Measmt.*, 1946, *6*, 169–84.

60. Bordin, E. S. *Psychological Counseling*. New York: Appleton-Century-Crofts, 1955.

61. Bordin, E. S. and R. H. Bixler. Test selection: A process of counseling. *Educ. psychol. Measmt.*, 1946, *6*, 361–74.

62. Borow, H., and R. V. Lindsey. *Vocational Planning for College Students*. Englewood Cliffs, N. J.: Prentice-Hall, 1959.

63. Bradford, L. P., J. R. Gibb, and K. D. Benne. *T-group Theory and Laboratory Method: Innovation in Re-education*. New York: John Wiley, 1964.

64. Brammer, L. M. *The Helping Relationship: Process and Skills*. Englewood Cliffs, N. J.: Prentice-Hall, 1973.

65. Branan, J. M. Client reaction to counselor's use of self-experience. *Pers. and Guid. J.*, 1967, *45*, 568–72.

66. Branden, N. Psychotherapy and the objectivist ethics. Paper delivered before the Michigan Society of Consulting Psychologists, Nov. 24, 1965.

67. Braun, J. R., and D. A. LaFaro. Further study on the fakability of the Personal Orientation Inventory. *J. clin. Psychol.*, 1969, *25*, 296–99.

68. Brayfield, A. H. Counseling psychology, in *Annual Review of Psychology*, Volume 14. Palo Alto, Calif.: Annual Reviews, Inc., 1963.

69. Brayfield, A. H. Counseling psychology: Some dilemmas of the graduate school. *J. counsel. Psychol.*, 1961, *8*, 17–19.

70. Brewer, J. M. *History of Vocational Guidance*. New York: Harper, 1942.

71. Brower, D. *Progress in Clinical Psychology*, Vol. VI. New York: Grune & Stratton, 1952.

72. Brown, J. F. *Psychodynamics of Abnormal Behavior*. New York: McGraw-Hill, 1940.

73. Brown, W. F., and W. H. Holtzman. *Survey of Study Habits and Attitudes*. New York: Psychological Corporation, 1955.

74. Bugental, J. F. T. *A Phenomenological Hypothesis of Neurotic Determinants and Their Therapy*. Unpublished paper. Los Angeles: Psychological Service Associates.

75. Bugental, J. F. T. The person who is the psychotherapist. *J. consult. Psychol.*, 1964, *28*, 272–77.

76. Bugental, J. F. T. Psychological Interviewing. Unpublished manuscript, 1952.

77. Bugental, J. F. T. *The Search for Authenticity; an Existential-Analytic Approach to Psychotherapy.* New York: Holt, Rinehart & Winston, 1965.

78. Buhler, C. Maturation and motivation. *J. Pers.*, 1951, *1*, 184–211.

79. Buhler, C. Personal communication with the authors.

80. Buhler, C. Unpublished paper presented before Group Psychotherapy Association of Southern California, June 1958.

81. Bunting, J. E. (ed.) *Private Independent Schools*, 19th ed. Wallingford, Conn.: Editor, 1966.

82. Burckel, C. E. *The College Blue Book*, 11th ed. New York: Author, 1962.

83. Buros, O. K. *The Third Mental Measurements Yearbook.* New Brunswick, N. J.: Rutgers University Press, 1949.

84. Byrd, R. E. Training in a non-group. *J. humanistic Psychol.*, 1967, *25*, 296–99.

85. Byrne, R. H. Proposed revision of the Bordin-Pepinsky diagnostic constructs. *J. counsel. Psychol.*, 1958, *5*, 184–87.

86. Callis, R. A. Diagnostic classification as a research tool, *J. counsel. Psychol.*, 1965, *12*, 238–43.

87. Callis, R. A. Toward an integrated theory of counseling. *J. of College Student Pers.*, 1960, *1*, 2–9.

88. Campbell, D. *The Results of Counseling: Twenty-Five Years Later.* Philadelphia: W. B. Saunders, 1965.

89. California State Department of Education. *The preparation and training of pupil personnel workers.* Bulletin Series, 1952, No. 5, Vol. 21, Chap. 1, p. 15.

90. Cantrell, D. Training the rehabilitation counselor. *Pers. and Guid. J.*, 1958, *36*, 382–87.

91. Carkhuff, R. and C. Truax. Toward explaining success and failure in interpersonal learning experiences. *Pers. and Guid. J.*, 1966, *44*, 723–28.

92. Carkhuff, R. *Helping and Human Relations.* New York: Holt, Rinehart & Winston, 1969.

93. Carmichael, L. *Child Psychology.* New York: John Wiley, 1954.

94. Carnes, E. F. Counselor flexibility: Its extent, and its relationship to other factors in the interview. Unpublished doctoral dissertation, Ohio State University, 1949.

95. Carnes, E. F., and F. P. Robinson. The role of client talk in the counseling interview. *Educ. psychol. Measmt.*, 1948, *8*, 635–44.

96. Carter, H. D. Vocational interests and job orientation. *Appl. Psychol. Monogr.*, 1944, *2*.

97. Cattell, R. B. *Personality.* New York: McGraw-Hill, 1950.

98. Chance, E. Measuring the anticipations of therapists about their patients. Unpublished paper, 1958.

99. Coffey, H. S. Group Psychotherapy, in Berg, I. A., and Pennington, L. A. (eds.), *An Introduction to Clinical Psychology*. New York: Ronald Press, 1948.

100. Cogswell, J. F., and D. P. Estavan. Computer simulation of a counselor in student appraisal and in the educational planning interview. SDC document SP-1944. March 10, 1965.

101. Cohen, M. B. Countertransference and anxiety. *Psychiatry*, 1952, *15*, 231–43.

102. Cohen, R. C. Military group psychotherapy. *Mental Hygiene*, 1947, *31*, 94–103.

103. Colby, K. M. A *Primer for Psychotherapists*. New York. Ronald Press, 1951.

104. Cole, L., *Psychology of Adolescence*. New York: Holt, 1956.

105. Collier, R. M. A basis for integration rather than fragmentation in psychotherapy. *J. consult. Psychol.*, 1950, *14*, 199–205.

106. Combs, A. W. Counseling as a learning process. *J. clin. Psychol.*, 1954, *1*, 31–36.

107. Combs, A. W. *Florida Studies in the Helping Professions*. Gainsville, Fla.: University of Florida Press, 1969.

108. Cottle, W. C. Personal characteristics of counselors: I. *Pers. and Guid. J.*, 1953, *31*, 445–50.

109. Cottle, W. C., and W. W. Lewis, Jr. Personality characteristics of counselors: II. Male counselor responses to the MMPI and GZTS. *J. counsel. Psychol.*, 1954, *1*, 27–30.

110. Cox, R. D. *Counselors and Their Work*. Philadelphia: University of Pennsylvania Press, 1945.

111. Crampton, W. How U. S. Men Can Live Longer. *This Week*, Feb. 20, 1955, 7–26. Also printed in C. Solomon and R. Brooks (eds.), *How to Enjoy Good Health*. New York: Random House, 1955.

112. Crider, B. The hostility pattern. *J. clin. Psychol.*, 1946, *2*, 267–73.

113. Cronbach, L. J. Counselor's problems from the perspective of communication theory, in Hewer, V. H. (ed.), New Perspectives in Counseling. *Minnesota Studies in Student Personnel Work, No. 7*. Minneapolis: University of Minnesota Press, 1955.

114. Croner, U. *American Trade Schools Directory*. New York: Croner, 1961.

115. Curran, C. A. Structuring the counseling relationship: A case report. *J. abnorm. soc. Psychol.*, 1944, *39*, 189–216.

116. Cutler, R. L., The relationship between the therapist's personality and certain aspects of psychotherapy. Ph.D. dissertation, University of Michigan, 1954.

117. Danskin, D. G., and C. W. Burnett. Those superior students. *Pers. and Guid. J.*, 1952, *31*, 181–86.

118. Daulton, J. A study of factors relating to resistance in the interview. M. A. thesis, Ohio State University, 1947.

119. Davis, S. E., and F. P. Robinson. A study of the use of certain techniques for reducing resistance during the counseling interview. *Educ. psychol. Measmt.*, 1949, 9, 297–306.

120. Deabler, H. L. The psychotherapeutic use of the thematic apperception test. *J. clin. Psychol.*, 1947, 8, 246–52.

121. Del Torto, J., and P. Cornyetz. Psychodrama as an Expressive and Projection Technique, in J. L. Moreno (ed.), *Psychodrama Monograph #14.* Boston: Beacon Press, 1945.

122. Dept. of Vocational Education, Pennsylvania State University, *Computer Assisted Occupational Guidance.* Brochure published by Pennsylvania State University, University Park, Pennsylvania, 1966.

123. Despert, J. L. *Children of Divorce.* New York: Doubleday, 1953.

124. Dittman, A. T. The interpersonal process in psychotherapy: development of a research method. *J. abnorm. soc. Psychol.*, 1952, 47, 236–44.

125. Dollard, J., and N. E. Miller. *Personality and Psychotherapy.* New York: McGraw-Hill, 1950.

126. Dollard, J., and O. H. Mowrer. A method of measuring tension in written documents. *J. abnorm. soc. Psychol.*, 1947, 42, 3–33.

127. Dorfman, E. Chap. 6 in C. R. Rogers (ed.), *Client Centered Therapy.* Boston: Houghton Mifflin, 1951.

128. Dreikers, R. *Challenge of Parenthood.* New York: Duell, Sloan, and Pearce, 1948.

129. Dressel, P. L. Implications of recent research for counseling. *J. counsel. Psychol.*, 1954, 1, 100–105.

130. Dressel, P. L. and R. W. Matteson. The effect of client participation on test interpretation. *Educ. psychol. Measmt.*, 1950, 10, 693–706.

131. Driver, H. I. *Multiple Counseling: A Small Group Discussion Method for Personal Growth.* Madison, Wis.: Monona, 1954.

132. Durnall, E. J., J. F. Moynihan, and C. G. Wrenn. Symposium: The counselor and his religion. *Pers. and Guid. J.*, 1958, 36, 326–34.

133. Easton, H. and S. Krippner. Disability, rehabilitation, and existentialism. *Pers. and Guid. J.*, 1964, 43, 230–34.

134. Ellis, A. New approaches to psychotherapy. *J. clin. Psychol.*, Monogr. Suppl., 1955, 11.

135. Ellis, A. Rational psychotherapy. *J. Gen. Psychol.*, 1958, 59, 35–49.

136. Ellis, A. *Reason and Emotion in Psychotherapy.* New York: Lyle Stuart, 1962.

137. Ellis, A. The sexual element in non-sexual crimes. *Psychological Newsletter*, 1957, 8, 122–25.

138. Ellis, A. Toward a more precise definition of emotional and intellectual insight. *Psychological Reports*, 1963, 13, 125–26.

139. Ellis, A. The treatment of a psychopath with rational psychotherapy, published in Italian, *Quaderni di Criminologia Clinica*, 1949, 2, 1-11.

140. English, H. B. The counseling situation as an obstacle to nondirective therapy. *J. consult. Psychol.*, 1948, *12*, 217–22.

141. Erikson, E. H. *Childhood and Society.* New York: Norton, 1950.

142. Ethical standards, American Personnel and Guidance Association. *Pers. and Guid. J.*, 1961, *40*, 206–9.

143. Ethical standards of psychologists. *Amer. Psychologist*, 1963, *18*, 56–60.

144. Eysenck, H. The effects of psychotherapy: an evaluation. *J. consult. Psychol.*, 1952, *16*, 319–24.

145. Eysenck, H. (ed.) *Handbook of Abnormal Psychology.* London: Pitman, 1960.

146. Farnsworth, P. R. *Annual Reviews of Psychology*, Vol. 1–17, Stanford, Calif.: Annual Reviews, 1950–1967.

147. Feingold, S. N. *Scholarships, Fellowships, and Loans.* Boston: Bellman, 1955.

148. Fenichel, O. *The Psychoanalytic Theory of Neurosis.* New York: Norton, 1945.

149. Fensterheim, H., and M. E. Tresselt. The influence of value systems on the perception of people. *J. abnorm. soc. Psychol.*, 1953, *48*, 93–98.

150. Fiedler, F. E. A comparison of psychoanalytic, nondirective, and Adlerian therapeutic relationships. *J. consult. Psychol.*, 1950, *14*, 436–45.

151. Fiedler, F. E. The concept of an ideal therapeutic relationship. *J. consult. Psychol.*, 1950, *14*, 339–45.

152. Fiedler, F. E. Method of objective quantification of certain countertransference attitudes. *J. clin. Psychol.*, 1951, *7*, 101–7.

153. Fiedler, F. E., and K. Senior. An exploratory study of unconscious feeling reactions in fifteen patient-therapist pairs. *J. abnorm. soc. Psychol.*, 1952, *47*, 446–53.

154. Fine, S. A. A structure of worker function. *Pers. and Guid. J.*, 1955, *34*, 66–73.

155. Fine, S. A. What is occupational information? *Pers. and Guid. J.*, 1955, *33*, 504–9.

156. Finney, B. C. Partnership psychotherapy: a new technique. Unpublished manuscript, San Jose State College, 1964.

157. Fischer, J., and G. Paveza. The relationship between theoretical orientation and therapists' empathy, warmth, and genuineness. *J. counsel. Psychol.*, 1975, *22*, 399–403.

158. Fisher, J. A *Few Buttons Missing.* Philadelphia: Lippincott, 1951.

159. Fizdale, R. A new look at fee charging. *Social Casework*, 1957, *38*, 60–65.

160. Forer, B. R. Framework for the use of clinical techniques in vocational counseling. *Pers. and Guid. J.*, 1965, *43*, 868–72.

161. Forgy, E. W., and J. D. Black. A follow-up after three years of clients counseled by two methods. *J. counsel. Psychol.*, 1954, *1*, 1–8.

162. Forster, J. R. An investigation of the effects of two feedback methods when communicating psychological information. Ph.D. dissertation, University of Minnesota, 1966.

163. Foster, R. G. A point of view in marriage counseling. *J. counsel. Psychol.*, 1956, 3, 210–16.

164. Frank, J. D., and E. Asher. Corrective emotional experiences in group therapy. *Amer. J. Psychiat.*, 1951, 108, 126–31.

165. Frankl, V. E. *Ärtzliche Seelsorge.* Vienna: Franz Deuticke Verlag, 1946.

166. Freud, S. *The Basic Writing of Sigmund Freud.* Translated and edited by A. A. Brill. New York: Modern Library, 1938.

167. Freud, S. *The Future of an Illusion.* New York: Liveright, 1928.

168. Freud, S. *A General Introduction to Psychoanalysis.* New York: Liveright, 1935.

169. Freud, S. *An Outline of Psychoanalysis.* New York: Norton, 1949.

170. Froehlich, C. P. An investigation of precounseling orientation. *Vocational guid. Quart.*, 1956, 4, 103–5.

171. Fromm, E. *The Art of Loving.* New York: Harper, 1956.

172. Fromm, E. *Escape from Freedom.* New York: Farrar and Rinehart, 1941.

173. Fromm, E. *Man for Himself.* New York: Farrar and Rinehart, 1947.

174. Fromm, E. Man is not a thing. *Saturday Review*, March 1957, 9–11.

175. Fromm, E. *Psychoanalysis and Religion.* New Haven: Yale University Press, 1950.

176. Fromm-Reichmann, F. *Principles of Intensive Psychotherapy.* Chicago: University of Chicago Press, 1950.

177. Fullmer, D., and H. Bernard. *Family Consultation.* Boston: Houghton Mifflin, 1968.

178. Gamsky, N. R. and G. F. Farwell. Counselor verbal behavior as a function of client hostility. *J. counsel. Psychol.*, 1966, 13, 184–90.

179. Gardner, G. The psychotherapeutic relationship. *Psychol. Bull.*, 1964, 61, 426–37.

180. Gardner, J. *Self Renewal.* New York: Harper & Row, 1965.

181. Garfield, S. L., and R. Kurtz. Clinical psychologists: a survey of selected attitudes and views. *Clinical Psychologist*, 1975, 28(3), 4–7.

182. Garrison, K. C. *Psychology of Adolescence.* Englewood Cliffs, N.J.: Prentice-Hall, 1956.

183. Gelatt, H. B. Decision-making: A conceptual frame of reference for counseling. *J. counsel. Psychol.*, 1962, 9, 240–45.

184. Gendlin, E. Focussing. *Psychotherapy: Research and Practice*, 1969, 6, 1–12.

185. Gendlin, E. *Experiencing and the Creation of Meaning.* New York: Free Press, 1962.

186. Gesell, A. *Child Development*. New York: Harper, 1949.

187. Gesell, A., F. L. Ilg, and L. B. Ames. *Youth: The Years from 10 to 16*. New York: Harper & Row, 1956.

188. Gibb, J. R. Sensitivity training as a medium for personal growth and improved personal relationship. In G. Egan (ed.), *Encounter Groups: Basic Readings*. Belmont, Calif.: Wadsworth, 1971.

189. Gibran, K. *The Prophet*. New York: Knopf, 1923.

190. Gilbert, J. G. *Understanding Old Age*. New York: Ronald Press, 1952.

191. Gilbert, W. M., and T. N. Ewing. An investigation of the importance of the personal relationship and associated factors in teaching machine procedures. A study under Title VII of National Defense Education Act of 1958. Mimeographed. University of Illinois, 1965.

192. Ginzberg, E. *Occupational Choice, an Approach to General Theory*. New York: Columbia University Press, 1951.

193. Glasser, W. *Reality Therapy*. New York: Harper & Row, 1965.

194. Glatzer, H. The relative effectiveness of clinically homogeneous and heterogeneous psychotherapy groups. *Int. J. group Psychother.*, 1956, 6, 258.

195. Glazer, S. H. An open-ended questionnaire for precounseling orientation. *Vocational guid. Quart.*, 1956, 5, 15–17.

196. Glover, E. *Freud or Jung*. New York: Norton, 1950.

197. Goldstein, K. *Human Nature in the Light of Psychopathology*. Cambridge: Harvard University Press, 1940.

198. Gonyea, G. G. The ideal therapeutic relationship and counseling outcome. *J. clin. Psychol.*, 1963, 19, 481–87.

199. Gordon, T. *Parent Effectiveness Training*. New York: John Wiley, 1971.

200. Gorham, D. R. Proverbs test. Missoula, Mont.: Psychological Test Specialists, 1954.

201. Grater, H. A. Client preference for affective or cognitive counselor characteristics and first interview behavior. *J. counsel. Psychol.*, 1964, 11, 248–50.

202. Graver, P. A. A study of counselors in selected industrial, education, and social service institutes. Ph.D. dissertation, Northwestern University, 1948.

203. Gray, W. S. Gray oral reading paragraphs test. Bloomington, Ill.: Public School Publishing Company, 1923.

204. Greeley, A. Personal communication, December 1970.

205. Green, A. W. Social values and psychotherapy. *J. Pers.*, 1946, 14, 199–228.

206. Greenleaf, W. J. *Occupations and Careers*. New York: McGraw-Hill, 1955.

207. Greenwald, H. *Decision Therapy*. New York: Peter H. Wyden, 1973.

208. Grossberg, J. M. Behavior therapy. *Psychol. Bull.*, 1964, 62, 73–88.

209. Grossman, D. Ego-activating approaches to psychotherapy. *Psychoanalytic Rev.*, 1964, *51*, 65–88.

210. Grummon, D. L. Client-centered Theory. In Stefflre, B. (ed.), *Theories of Counseling*. New York: McGraw-Hill, 1965.

211. Gustad, J. W. The Definition of Counseling. In Berdie, R. F. (ed.), *Roles and Relationships in Counseling*. Minneapolis: University of Minnesota Press, 1953.

212. Gustad, J. W. The evaluation interview in vocational counseling. *Pers. and Guid. J.*, 1957, *36*, 242–50.

213. Hahn, M. E., and M. S. McLean. *General Clinical Counseling*. New York: McGraw-Hill, 1950.

214. Haigh, G. Defensive behavior in client-centered therapy. *J. consult. Psychol.*, 1949, *13*, 181–89.

215. Harlow, H. F. The formation of learning sets. *Psychol. Rev.*, 1949, *56*, 51–65.

216. Harlow, H. F. Nature of love. *Amer. Psychologist*, 1958, *13*, 673–85.

217. Hathaway, S. R., and J. C. McKinley. *The Minnesota Multiphasic Personality Inventory*. New York: Psychological Corporation, 1942.

218. Havelock, R. G. *The Change Agent's Guide to Innovation in Education*. Englewood Cliffs, N.J.: Educational Technology Publications, 1973.

219. Havighurst, R. J. *Human Development and Education*. New York: Longmans, 1953.

220. Heilbrun, A. B. Counseling readiness: a treatment specific or general factor. *J. counsel. Psychol.*, 1965, *12*, 87–90.

221. Heilbrun, A. B. Psychological factors related to counseling readiness and implications for counseling behavior. *J. counsel. Psychol.*, 1962, *9*, 353–58.

222. Heine, R. W. An investigation of the relationship between change in personality from psychotherapy as reported by patients and the factors seen by patients as producing change. Ph.D. dissertation, University of Chicago, 1950.

223. Heller, K., J. D. Davis, and R. A. Myers. The effects of interviewer style in a standardized interview. *J. consult. Psychol.*, 1966, *30*, 501–8.

224. Herman, R. The "going steady" complex. *Marriage and Family*, 1955, *17*, 26–40.

225. Herzberg, A. *Active Psychotherapy*. New York: Grune & Stratton, 1945.

226. Hills, D. A., and J. E. Williams. Effects of test information upon self evaluation in brief educational-vocational counseling. *J. counsel. Psychol.*, 1965, *12*, 275–81.

227. Hinckley, G., and L. Hermann. *Group Treatment in Psychotherapy*. Minneapolis: University of Minnesota Press, 1951.

228. Hobbs, N. Group-Centered Psychotherapy. In Rogers, C. R. (ed.), *Client-Centered Therapy*. Boston: Houghton-Mifflin, 1951.

229. Hogan, R. A. Theory of threat and defense. *J. consult. Psychol.*, 1952, *16*, 417–24.

230. Holland, J. L. *The Psychology of Vocational Choice*. Waltham, Mass.: Blaisdell Co., 1966.

231. Horney, K. *Neurosis and Human Growth*. New York: Norton, 1950.

232. Horney, K. *The Neurotic Personality of Our Time*. New York: Norton, 1937.

233. Horney, K. *New Ways in Psychoanalysis*. New York: Norton, 1939.

234. Horney, K. *Self-Analysis*. New York: Norton, 1942.

235. Hosford, R., and D. Sorenson. Participating in classroom discussions. Chap. 24 in Krumboltz, J., and Thoreson, C., *Behavioral Counseling*. New York: Holt, Rinehart & Winston, 1969.

236. Hoyt, D. P. College Grades and Adult Achievement. *Ed. Rec.*, 1966, 47, 70–75.

237. Hughes, E. C. Psychology: Science and/or profession. *Amer. Psychologist*, 1952, 7, 441–43.

238. Ingham, H. V., and L. R. Love. *The Process of Psychotherapy*. New York: McGraw-Hill, 1954.

239. Irwin, M. (ed.). *American Universities and Colleges*, 9th ed. Washington, D.C.: American Council on Education, 1964.

240. Ivey, A., and J. Leppaluoto. Changes ahead! Implications of the Vail Conference. *Pers. and Guid. J.*, 1975, 53, 747–53.

241. Ivey, A. *Microcounseling: Interviewing Skills Manual*. Springfield, Ill.: Charles C Thomas, 1972.

242. Jacobson, E. *Progressive Relaxation*, 2nd ed. Chicago: University of Chicago Press, 1938.

243. Jacques, E. The clinical use of the TAT with soldiers. *J. abnorm. soc. Psychol.*, 1945, 4, 363–75.

244. Jahoda, M. *Current Concepts of Positive Mental Health*. New York: Basic Books, 1958.

245. Janowitz, M. Some observations on the ideology of professional psychologists. *Amer. Psychologist*, 1954, 9, 528–32.

246. Joel, W., and D. Shapiro. Some principles and procedures for group psychotherapy. *J. Psychol.*, 1950, 29, 77–88.

247. Johnson, D. Understanding and use of the self in counseling. *Bulletin of the Menninger Clinic*, 1953, 17, 29–35.

248. Johnson, W. *People in Quandaries*. New York: Harper, 1946.

249. Joslin, L. C. Knowledge and counseling competence. *Pers. and Guid. J.*, 1965, 43, 790–95.

250. Jourard, S. M. *Personal Adjustment*. New York: Macmillan, 1958.

251. Jourard, S. M., and R. Remy. Perceived parental attitudes, the self and security. *J. consult. Psychol.*, 1955, 19, 364–66.

252. Jung, C. G. *Modern Man in Search of a Soul*. New York: Harcourt, Brace, 1933.

453

253. Karpman, B. Objective psychotherapy. Clinical Psychology Monographs, No. 6, *J. clin. Psychol.*, 1960.

254. Katahn, M., S. Strenger, and N. Cherry. Group counseling and behavior therapy with test-anxious college students. *J. consult. Psychol.*, 1966, 30, 544–49.

255. Keet, C. D. Two verbal techniques in a miniature counseling situation. *Psychol. Monogr.*, 1948, 7.

256. Kelly, E. C. *Education for What is Real.* New York: Harper, 1947.

257. Kelly, G. A. *The Psychology of Personal Constructs*, vols. 1 and 2. New York: Norton, 1955.

258. Kelly, G. A. *Verbal Communication in Psychotherapy.* Unpublished manuscript of lectures presented to a postdoctoral institute of the Los Angeles Society of Clinical Psychologists in Private Practice, January 17–18, 1959.

259. Kinsey, A. C., W. B. Pomeroy, and C. E. Martin. *Sexual Behavior in the Human Female.* Philadelphia: Saunders, 1953.

260. Kinsey, A. C., W. B. Pomeroy, and C. E. Martin. *Sexual Behavior in the Human Male.* Philadelphia: Saunders, 1948.

261. Kirkendall, L. A. Implications for college teaching of a concept of morality. Unpublished paper, Oregon State College.

262. Kirsh, C. The role of affect expression and defense in the character. Unpublished manuscript, 1973.

263. Klein, M. *The Psychoanalysis of Children.* New York: Hogarth, 1949.

264. Klingelhofer, E. L. The relationship between academic advisement and the scholastic performance of failing college students. *J. counsel. Psychol.*, 1954, 1, 125–31.

265. Klopfer, B. *Developments in the Rorschach Technique*, vol. 2. Yonkers, N. Y.: World Book, 1956.

266. Klopfer, B. Personal communication, 1958.

267. Klopfer, B. Rorschach clinical diagnosis. Unpublished mimeographed paper, p. 4.

268. Knapp, R. R., and O. R. Fitzgerald. Comparative validity for the Personal Orientation Inventory. *Educ. psychol. Measmt.*, 1973, 33, 971–76.

269. Koester, G. A. A study of the diagnostic process. *Educ. psychol. Measmt.*, 1954, 14, 473–86.

270. Kohler, W. *The Mentality of Apes.* Translated by E. Winter. New York: Harcourt, 1925.

271. Korner, I. N. Ego involvement and the process of disengagement. *J. consult. Psychol.*, 1950, 14, 206–9.

272. Krasner, L., and L. P. Ullmann. *Research in Behavior Modification.* New York: Holt, Rinehart & Winston, 1965.

273. Krumboltz, J. Behavioral goals for counseling. *J. couns. Psychol.*, 1966, 13, 153–59.

274. Krumboltz, J., and L. Sheppard. Vocational Problem Solving Experiences. In Krumboltz, J., and C. Thoreson, *Behavioral Counseling*. New York: Holt, Rinehart & Winston, 1969.

275. Kunkel, F. Growth through Crises. In Doniger, S. (ed.), *Religion and Human Behavior*. New York: Association Press, 1954.

276. Kunkel, F. *In Search of Maturity*. New York: Scribner, 1955.

277. Labov, W. Language Change and Human Understanding. John Danz lecture, University of Washington, Oct. 6, 1975.

278. Layton, W. L. Selection and counseling of students in engineering. *Minnesota Studies in Personnel Work No. 4*, 1954.

279. Lazarus, A. In support of technical eclecticism. *Psychological Reports*, 1967, *21*, 415–16.

280. Leary, T. *Interpersonal Diagnosis of Personality*. New York: Ronald Press, 1957, p. 65.

281. Lebo, D. The expressive value of toys recommended for nondirective play therapy. *J. clin. Psychol.*, 1955, *11*, 144–48.

282. Lee, A. M. Social pressures and the values of psychologists. *Amer. Psychologist*, 1954, *9*, 516–22.

283. Lesser, W. M. The relationship between counseling progress and empathic understanding. *J. counsel. Psychol.*, 1961, *8*, 330–36.

284. Levitt, E. E. The inefficacy of therapeutic processes with children. *J. consult. Psychol.*, 1957, *21*, 189–96.

285. Levy, L. H. *Psychological Interpretation*. New York: Holt, Rinehart & Winston, 1963.

286. Lewin, K. *Principles of Topological Psychology*. New York: McGraw-Hill, 1936.

287. Lewis, J., and M. Lewis. *Community Counseling: A Human Services Approach*. New York: John Wiley, 1976.

288. Lewis, N. D. C. *Outlines for Psychiatric Examinations*. Albany, New York: New York State Department of Mental Hygiene, 1943.

289. Lifton, W. M. Counseling and the religious view of man. *Pers. and Guid. J.*, 1953, *31*, 366–67.

290. Lipkin, S. Clients' feelings and attitudes in relation to the outcomes on client-centered therapy. *Psychol. Monogr.*, 1954, *68*, p. 372.

291. Loeser, L. H. Some aspects of group dynamics. *Int. J. Group Psychother.*, 1957, *7*, 5–19.

292. London, P. *The Modes and Morals of Psychotherapy*. New York: Holt, Rinehart & Winston, 1964.

293. Loughary, J., D. Friesen, and R. Hurst. Autocoun: A computer-based automated counseling simulation system. *Pers. and Guid. J.*, 1966, *45*, 6–15.

294. Lovejoy, C. E. *Lovejoy's College Guide*. New York: Simon & Schuster, 1965–66.

295. Lovejoy, C. E. *Lovejoy's Vocational School Guide*. New York: Simon & Schuster, 1955.

296. Lowen, A. *Betrayal of the Body*. New York: Macmillan, 1967.

297. Lowen, A. *Training Manual in Bioenergetics*. Unpublished manuscript, 1972.

298. Luft, J. Implicit hypotheses and clinical predictions. *J. abnorm. soc. Psychol.*, 1950, *45*, 756–59.

299. McArthur, C. C. Analyzing the clinical process. *J. counsel. Psychol.*, 1954, *1*, 203–8.

300. McGregor, R. Multiple impact therapy with families. *Family Process*, 1962, *1*, 15–29.

301. McGregor, R., A. M. Ritchie, A. C. Serrano, F. P. Shuster, E. C. McDonald, and H. A. Goolishian. *Multiple Impact Therapy With Families*. New York: McGraw-Hill, 1964.

302. McHugh, G. *The Sex Knowledge Inventory*. North Carolina: Duke University Press, 1950.

303. Mace, D. Your marriage today. *Women's Home Companion*, April 1956, 29–33.

304. Mahler, M., and R. Rabinovitch. The Effects of Marital Conflict on Child Development. In V. Eisenstein (ed.), *Neurotic Interaction in Marriage*. New York: Basic Books, 1956.

305. Mann, L. Persuasive doll play: A technique of directive psychotherapy for use with children. *J. clin. Psychol.*, 1957, *13*, 14–19.

306. Margolies, B. D. The problem of "facade" in the counseling of low scholarship students. *J. consult. Psychol.*, 1945, *9*, 138–41.

307. Maslow, A. H. *Motivation and Personality*. New York: Harper & Row, 1954.

308. Maslow, A. H. *The Psychology of Science*. New York: Harper & Row, 1966.

309. Masters, W. H., and V. E. Johnson. *The Pleasure Bond*. Boston: Little, Brown, 1974.

310. May, R., E. Angel, and H. Ellenberger. *Existence*. New York: Basic Books, 1958.

311. May, R. *The Art of Counseling*. New York: Abingdon-Cokesbury, 1939.

312. May, R. *Man's Search for Himself*. New York: Norton, 1953.

313. May, R. *Psychology and the Human Dilemma*. Princeton: D. Van Nostrand, 1967.

314. Mead, M. *Ladies Home Journal Treasury*. New York: Simon & Schuster, 1956.

315. Meehl, P. E. *Clinical Versus Statistical Prediction*. Minneapolis: University of Minnesota, 1954.

316. Meehl, P. E. The cognitive activity of the clinician. *Amer. Psychologist,* 1960, *15,* 19–27.

317. Meehl, P. E., et al. *What, Then, is Man?* St. Louis: Concordia, 1958.

318. Mendelsohn, G. A. Effects of client personality and client-counselor similarity on the duration of counseling: a replication and extension. *J. counsel. Psychol.,* 1966, *13,* 228–34.

319. Menninger, K. *The Theory of Psychoanalytic Technique,* Menninger Clinical Monograph Series 12. New York: Basic Books, 1958.

320. Meyer, J., W. Strowig, and R. Hosford. Behavioral reinforcement with rural high school youth. *J. counsel. Psychol.,* 1970, *17,* 127–32.

321. Michael, J., and L. Meyerson. A behavioral approach to counseling and guidance. *Harvard Educ. Rev.,* 1962, *32,* 382–402.

322. Michigan State University. *How to Make Referrals.* East Lansing, Mich.: Guidance and Counselor Training, College of Education, Michigan State University, 1956.

323. Mickelson, D., and R. Stevic. Differential effects of facilitative and non-facilitative behavioral counselors. *J. counsel. Psychol.,* 1971, *18,* 127–32.

324. Miller, J. G. General behavior systems theory and summary (Part 3, Behavior theories and a counseling case: A symposium). *J. counsel. Psychol.,* 1956, *3,* 120–24.

325. Miller, J. G. Toward a general theory for the behavioral sciences. *Amer. Psychologist,* 1955, *10,* pp. 513, 531.

326. Minge, M. R. Counseling readiness as readiness for change. *J. College Student Pers.,* 1966, *7,* 197–202.

327. Minuchin, S. Conflict Resolution in Family Therapy. In G. E. Stollak (ed.), *Psychotherapy Research: Selected Readings.* Chicago: Rand McNally, 1966.

328. Mischel, W. Toward a cognitive social learning reconceptualization of personality. *Psychol. Rev.,* 1973, *80,* 252–83.

329. Mittelmann, B. Analysis of Reciprocal Neurotic Patterns in Family Relationships. In V. W. Eisenstein (ed.), *Neurotic Interaction in Marriage.* New York: Basic Books, 1956.

330. Montague, A. *On Being Human.* New York: H. Schuman, 1950.

331. Montague, A. *Touching.* New York: Harper & Row, 1971.

332. Mooney, R. L. *Mooney Problem Checklist.* New York: Psychological Corporation, 1950.

333. Moore, B. V., and L. Bouthilet. The V. A. program for counseling psychologists. *Amer. Psychologist,* 1952, *7,* 684–85.

334. Morton, R. B. A controlled experiment in psychotherapy based on Rotter's social learning theory of personality. Ph.D. dissertation, Ohio State University, 1949.

335. Morton, R. B. An experiment in social psychotherapy. *Psychol. Monogr.,* 1955, *69,* 1–17.

336. Mosier, H. P., W. Dublin, and I. M. Shelsky. A proposed modification of the Roe Occupational Classification. *J. consult. Psychol.*, 1956, 8, 27–31.

337. Moustakas, C. E. *Children in Play Therapy.* New York: McGraw-Hill, 1953.

338. Mowrer, O. H. Anxiety Theory as a Basis for Distinguishing between Counseling and Psychotherapy. In R. Berdie (ed.), *Concepts and Programs of Counseling.* Minneapolis: University of Minnesota Press, 1951.

339. Mowrer, O. H. *Learning Theory and Personality Dynamics.* New York: Ronald Press, 1950.

340. Mowrer, O. H. Tension Changes During Psychotherapy with Special Reference to Resistance. In *Psychotherapy: Theory and Research.* New York: Ronald Press, 1953.

341. Mowrer, O. H. Some philosophical problems in psychological counseling. *J. counsel. Psychol.*, 1957, 4, 103–11.

342. Mowrer, O. H. *The New Group Therapy.* Princeton, N.J.: D. Van Nostrand, 1964.

343. Muench, G. An investigation of the efficacy of time-limited psychotherapy. *J. counsel. Psychol.*, 1965, 12, 294–98.

344. Murphy, G. *Personality: A Biosocial Approach to Origins and Structure.* New York: Harper, 1947.

345. Muthard, J. E. and L. A. Miller. *The criterion problem in rehabilitation counseling.* Iowa City: College of Education, 1966.

346. National Home Study Council. *Home Study Blue Book.* Washington, D.C.: National Home Study Council, 1956.

347. National Vocational Guidance Association. *Counselor Preparation.* Washington, D.C.: National Vocational Guidance Association, 1949.

348. Nygren, A. *Agape and Eros.* London: SPCK, 1953.

349. Oates, W. E. *The Christian Pastor.* Philadelphia: Westminster, 1951.

350. Ohlsen, M. M. Interpretation of test scores. Chap. 12 in *The Impact and Improvement of School Testing Programs*, NSSE Yearbook. Chicago: University of Chicago Press, 1963.

351. O'Kelly, L. I., and F. A. Muckler. *Introduction to Psychopathology*, 2nd ed. Englewood Cliffs, N. J.: Prentice-Hall, 1955.

352. Oppenheimer, O. Some counseling theory: Objectivity and subjectivity. *J. counsel. Psychol.*, 1954, 1, 184–87.

353. Overstreet, H. *The Mature Mind.* New York: Norton, 1949.

354. Parsons, F. *Choosing a Vocation.* Boston: Houghton, 1909.

355. Paterson, D. G., C. d'A. Gerken, and M. E. Hahn. Revised Minnesota Occupational Rating Scales. In E. G. Williamson (ed.), *Minnesota Studies in Student Personnel Work, No. 2.* Minneapolis: University of Minnesota Press, 1953.

356. Patterson, C. H. Interest tests and the emotionally disturbed client. *Educ. psychol. Measmt.*, 1957, 17, 264–80.

357. Pearson, L. (ed.). *The Use of Written Communications in Psychotherapy.* Springfield, Ill.: Charles C Thomas, 1965.

358. Pepinsky, H. B. Application of informal projective methods in the counseling interview. *Educ. psychol. Measmt.*, 1947, 7, 135–40.

359. Pepinsky, H. B. The selection and use of diagnostic categories in clinical counseling. *Appl. Psychol. Monogr.*, 1948, No. 15.

360. Pepinsky, H. B., and P. N. Pepinsky. *Counseling Theory and Practice.* New York: Ronald Press, 1954.

361. Perls, F. *Gestalt Therapy Verbatim.* Lafayette, Calif.: Real People Press, 1969.

362. Perls, L. P., P. Goodman, and H. Hefferline. *Gestalt Therapy—Excitement and Growth in Human Personality.* New York: Julian Press, 1951.

363. Pfeiffer, J. W., and R. Heslin. *Instrumentation in Human Relations Training.* San Diego: University Associates, 1973.

364. Phillips, E. L. Attitudes toward self and others; a brief questionnaire report. *J. consult. Psychol.*, 1951, 15, 79–81.

365. Phillips, E. L. *Psychotherapy; a Modern Theory and Practice.* Englewood Cliffs, N.J.: Prentice-Hall, 1956.

366. Phillips, E. L., and J. W. Agnew, Jr. A study of Rogers' "reflection" hypothesis. *J. clin. Psychol.*, 1953, 9, 281–84.

367. Porter, E. H., Jr. *An Introduction to Therapeutic Counseling.* Boston: Houghton Mifflin, 1950.

368. Porter, E. H., Jr. Understanding Diagnostically and Understanding Therapeutically. In E. G. Williamson (ed.), *Trends in Student Personnel Work.* Minneapolis: University of Minnesota Press, 1949, 113–19.

369. Postman, L., J. S. Bruner, and E. McGinnies. Personal values as selective factors in perception. *J. abnorm. soc. Psychol.*, 1948, 43, 142–54.

370. Powdermaker, F., and J. Frank. *Group Psychotherapy.* Cambridge: Harvard University Press, 1953.

371. Progoff, I. *At a Journal Workshop.* New York: Dialogue House Library, 1975.

372. Raimy, V. *Misunderstanding of the Self.* San Francisco: Jossey-Bass, 1975.

373. Rand, A. *Atlas Shrugged.* New York: Random House, 1957.

374. Raskin, A. Factors therapists associate with motivation to enter psychotherapy. *J. clin. Psychol.*, 1961, 17, 62–65.

375. Raskin, N. *Studies on Psychotherapeutic Orientation.* AAP Psychotherapy Research monograph. Orlando, Florida: American Academy of Psychotherapy, 1974.

376. Reddy, W. B. The impact of sensitivity training on self-actualization: A one-year follow-up. *Comparative Group Studies*, in press.

377. Reddy, W. B. On affection, group composition, and self-actualization in sensitivity training. *J. consul. and clin. Psychol.*, 1972, 38, 211–14.

378. Reid, D. K., and W. U. Snyder. Experiment on "recognition of feeling" in non-directive psychotherapy. *J. clin. Psychol.*, 1947, *3*, 128–35.

379. Remmers, H. H., A. J. Drucker, and B. Shimberg. *SRA Youth Inventory.* Chicago: Science Research Associates, 1948.

380. Reusch, J., and A. R. Prestwood. Anxiety. *Arch. Neurol. Psychiat.*, 1949, *62*, 1–24.

381. Ribble, M. *The Personality of the Young Child.* New York: Columbia University Press, 1955.

382. Richardson, H., and H. Borow. Evaluation of technique of group orientation for vocational counseling. *Educ. psychol. Measmt.*, 1952, *12*, 587–97.

383. Rippee, B. D., W. E. Harvey, and C. A. Parker. The influence of counseling on the perception of counselor role. *Pers. and Guid. J.*, 1965, *43*, 600–606.

384. Robinson, F. P. Modern approach to counseling diagnosis. *J. counsel. Psychol.*, 1963, *10*, 325–33.

385. Robinson, F. P. *Principles and Procedures in Student Counseling.* New York: Harper, 1950.

386. Roe, A. *The Psychology of Occupations.* New York: John Wiley, 1956.

387. Rogers, C. R. *Becoming a Person.* Oberlin, Ohio: Board of Trustees, Oberlin College, 1954.

388. Rogers, C. R. *On Becoming a Person.* Boston: Houghton Mifflin, 1961.

389. Rogers, C. R. *Carl Rogers on Encounter Groups.* New York: Harper & Row, 1970.

390. Rogers, C. R. *Client-Centered Therapy.* Boston: Houghton Mifflin, 1951.

391. Rogers, C. R. *Counseling and Psychotherapy.* Boston: Houghton Mifflin, 1942.

392. Rogers, C. R. *Counseling with Returned Service Men.* New York: McGraw-Hill, 1946.

393. Rogers, C. R. The fully functioning personality. Unpublished paper.

394. Rogers, C. R. A personal view of some issues facing psychologists. *Amer. Psychologist*, 1955, *10*, 247–49.

395. Rogers, C. R. Persons or science? A philosophical question. *Amer. Psychologist*, 1955, *10*, 267–78.

396. Rogers, C. R. A process conception of psychotherapy. *Amer. Psychologist*, 1958, *13*, 142–49.

397. Rogers, C. R. Some Directions and End Points in Therapy. In O. H. Mowrer (ed.), *Psychotherapy: Theory and Research.* New York: Ronald Press, 1953.

398. Rogers, C. R. Interpersonal relationships. *J. Applied Behavioral Science*, 1968, *4*, 1–12.

399. Rogers, C. R. A therapist's view of the good life. *The Humanist*, 1957, *5*, 291–300, American Humanist Association, Yellow Springs, Ohio.

400. Rogers, C. R., and R. F. Dymond. *Psychotherapy and Personality Change.* Chicago: University of Chicago Press, 1954.

401. Rosensweig, S. An Outline of Frustration Theory. Chap. 11 in J. McV. Hunt (ed.), *Personality and the Behavior Disorders.* New York: Ronald Press, 1944.

402. Rotter, J. B. *Social Learning and Clinical Psychology.* Englewood Cliffs, N. J.: Prentice-Hall, 1954.

403. Ruch, F. L. *Psychology and Life.* Chicago: Scott, 1948.

404. Rudikoff, L. C., and B. A. Kirk. Goals of counseling: mobilizing the counselee. *J. counsel. Psychol.,* 1961, 8, 381–84.

405. Rusalem, H. New insights on the role of occupational information in counseling. *J. counsel. Psychol.,* 1954, 1, 84–88.

406. Ryan, T. A., and J. Krumboltz. Effect of planned reinforcement counseling on client decision making behavior. *J. counsel. Psychol.,* 1964, 11, 315–23.

407. Salter, A. *Conditioned Reflex Therapy.* New York: Capricorn Books, 1961.

408. Sanford, N. *Self and Society.* New York: Atherton, 1966.

409. Sarason, I. Verbal learning modeling and juvenile delinquency. *Amer. Psychologist,* 1968, 23, 254–66.

410. Sargent, P. *Junior Colleges and Specialized Schools and Colleges,* 2nd ed. Boston: Porter Sargent, 1955.

411. Sargent, P. *The Handbook of Private Schools,* 37th ed. Boston: Porter Sargent, 1956.

412. Szasz, T. S. The myth of mental illness. *Amer. Psychologist,* 1960, 15, 113–18.

413. Satir, V. *Conjoint Family Therapy.* Palo Alto, Calif.: Science and Behavior Books, 1966.

414. Satir, V. Target Five. 16 mm. film. Santa Ana, Calif.: Psychological Films, 1967.

415. Schafer, R. *Psychoanalytic Interpretation in Rorschach Testing.* New York: Grune & Stratton, 1954.

416. Schmidt, H. O., and C. P. Fonda. The reliability of psychiatric diagnosis: a new look. *J. abnorm. soc. Psychol.,* 1956, 52, 262–67.

417. Schuldt, J. W. Psychotherapists' approach-avoidance responses and clients' expressions of dependency. *J. counsel. Psychol.,* 1966, 13, 178–83.

418. Schutz, W. C. *Here Comes Everybody.* New York: Harper & Row, 1971.

419. Schutz, W. C. *Elements of Encounter.* New York: Bantam, 1975.

420. Schwebel, M. Learning and the socially deprived. *Pers. and Guid. J.,* 1965, 43, 646–53.

421. Schwebel, M. Why unethical practice? *J. counsel. Psychol.,* 1955, 2, 122–27.

422. Seeman, J. A. A study of client self-selection of tests in vocational counseling. *Educ. psychol. Measmt.*, 1948, 8, 327–46.

423. Seeman, W., S. Nidich, and T. Banta. Influence of transcendental meditation on a measure of self-actualization. *J. counsel. Psychol.*, 1972, 19, 184–87.

424. Seeman, J. A., et al. A coordinated research in psychotherapy. *J. consult. Psychol.*, 1949, 13, 154–95.

425. Shaw, F. J. Some postulates concerning psychotherapy. *J. consult. Psychol.*, 1939, 12, 426–32.

426. Shaw, R. *Finger Painting*. Boston: Little, Brown, 1934.

427. Sheerer, E. T. An analysis of the relationship between acceptance of and respect for self and acceptance of and respect for others in ten counseling cases. *Amer. Psychologist*, 1948, 3, p. 285.

428. Sherman, D. An analysis of the dynamic relationships between counselor techniques and outcomes in larger units of the interview situation. Ph.D. dissertation, Ohio State University, 1945.

429. Shoben, E. J. Psychotherapy as a problem in learning theory. *Psychol. Bull.*, 1949, 46, 366–92.

430. Shoben, E. J. Special review: Some recent books on counseling and adjustment. *Psychol. Bull.*, 1955, 52, 251–62.

431. Shoben, E. J. Work, love and maturity. *Pers. and Guid. J.*, 1956, 34, 326–32.

432. Shostrom, E. L., L. Knapp, and R. Knapp. *Actualizing Therapy: Foundations for a Scientific Ethic*. San Diego: EDITS Book Co., 1976.

433. Shostrom, E. L. *Caring Relationship Inventory*. San Diego: Educational and Industrial Testing Service, 1966.

434. Shostrom, E. L. *Man, the Manipulator*. Nashville: Abingdon, 1967.

435. Shostrom, E. L. *Personal Orientation Inventory*. San Diego: Educational and Industrial Testing Service, 1963.

436. Shostrom, E. L. Three approaches to psychotherapy. Films of Rogers, Perls, and Ellis. Santa Ana, Calif.: Psychological Films, 1966.

437. Shostrom, E. L. Touching: Importance for Human Growth. Film. Santa Ana, Calif.: Psychological Films, 1974.

438. Shostrom, E. L. Three Approaches to Group Therapy. 16 mm color films. Santa Ana, Calif.: Psychological Films, 1974.

439. Shostrom, E. L., and N. W. Ferry. The Actualization Group. Series of 16 mm films. Santa Ana, Calif.: Psychological Films, 1968.

440. Shostrom, E. L., and L. M. Brammer. *The Dynamics of the Counseling Process*. New York: McGraw-Hill, 1952.

441. Shostrom, E. L., and C. M. D. Riley. Parametric analysis of psychotherapy. *J. consult. and clin. Psychol.*, 1968, 32, 628–32.

442. Shrodes, C. (ed.). *Psychology through Literature, an Anthology*. New York: Oxford Book Co., 1943.

443. Shuttleworth, F. K. *The physical and mental growth of girls and boys age six to nineteen in relation to age at maximum growth.* Washington, D.C.: National Research Council, 1939.

444. Silberman, H. F., and L. F. Carter. "The systems approach, technology, and the school," in Educational Testing Service Conference proceedings. *New Approaches to Individualizing Instruction.* Princeton, N. J., May 11, 1965.

445. Skidmore, R. A., et al. *Marriage Consulting.* New York: Harper, 1956.

446. Skidmore, R. A., and H. Garrett. Joint interview in marriage counseling. *Marriage and Family Living,* 1955, *17,* 320–24.

447. Skinner, B. F. *Science and Human Behavior.* New York: Macmillan, 1953.

448. Slavson, S. R. *Analytic Group Psychotherapy with Children, Adolescents and Adults.* New York: Columbia University Press, 1950.

449. Slavson, S. R. *The Practice of Group Psychotherapy.* New York: International Universities Press, 1947.

450. Smith, H. L. The value context of psychology. *Amer. Psychologist,* 1954, *9,* 532–35.

451. Snygg, D., and A. W. Combs. *Individual Behavior: A New Frame of Reference for Psychology.* New York: Harper, 1949.

452. Sorokin, P. A. *Explorations in Altruistic Love and Behavior.* Boston: Beacon Press, 1950.

453. Speer, G. S., and L. Jasper. The influence of occupational information on occupational goals. *Occupations,* 1949, *28,* 15–17.

454. Spitz, R. A. Role of ecological factors in emotional development of infants. *Child Devel.,* 1949, *76,* 145–46.

455. Steiner, L. R. *Where Do People Take Their Troubles?* Boston: Houghton Mifflin, 1954.

456. Stewart, N. Exploring and processing information. Chap. 26 in Krumboltz, J., and Thoreson, C., *Behavioral Counseling.* New York: Holt, Rinehart & Winston, 1969.

457. Stone, C. H. Are vocational orientation courses worth their salt? *Educ. psychol. Measmt.,* 1948, *8,* 161–81.

458. Strang, R. *Child Study.* New York: Macmillan, 1954.

459. Strong, E. K. *Vocational Interests Eighteen Years After College.* Minneapolis: University of Minnesota Press, 1955.

460. Strong, E. K. *Vocational Interests of Men and Women.* Stanford, Calif.: Stanford University Press, 1943.

461. Strupp, H. H. The outcome problem in psychotherapy revisited. *Psychotherapy: Res. and Pract.,* 1963, *1,* 1–13.

462. Sullivan, H. S. *The Interpersonal Theory of Psychiatry.* New York: Norton, 1953.

463. Sullivan, H. S. *The Psychiatric Interview.* New York: Norton, 1954.

464. Sundberg, N. D. and L. E. Tyler. *Clinical Psychology.* New York: Appleton-Century-Crofts, 1962.

465. Super, D. E., and J. O. Crites. *Appraising Vocational Fitness by Means of Psychological Testing.* New York: Harper & Row, 1962.

466. Super, D. E. Career patterns as a basis for vocational counseling. *J. counsel. Psychol.*, 1954, *1*, 12–19.

467. Super, D. E. Transition from vocational guidance to counseling psychology. *J. counsel. Psychol.*, 1955, 2, 3–9.

468. Super, D. E. Vocational adjustment: Implementing a self concept. *Occupations*, 1951, *30*, 88–92.

469. Symonds, P. M. *Dynamics of Psychotherapy*, vol. I, New York: Grune, Stratton, 1956.

470. Symonds, P. M. *Dynamics of Psychotherapy*, vol. II. New York: Grune, Stratton, 1957.

471. Thompson, A. S., and D. E. Super. *The Professional Preparation of Counseling Psychologists.* New York: Bureau of Publications, Columbia University, 1964.

472. Thoreson, C., and M. Mahoney. *Behavioral Self Control.* New York: Holt, Rinehart & Winston, 1974.

473. Thoreson, C. The counselor as an applied behavioral scientist. *Pers. and Guid. J.*, 1969, *47*, 841–48.

474. Thorne, F. C. Principles of Personality Counseling. Brandon, Vt.: Clinical Psychology Monograph, 1950.

475. Thorne, F. C. Principles of psychological examining. Clinical Psychology Monograph. *J. clin. Psychol.*, 1955.

476. Tiedeman, D. V., and R. P. O'Hara. *Career Development: Choice and Adjustment.* New York: College Entrance Examination Board, 1963.

477. Tindall, R. H., and F. P. Robinson. The use of silence as a technique in counseling. *J. clin. Psychol.*, 1947, *3*, 136–41.

478. Truax, C. B. Effective ingredients in psychotherapy. *J. counsel. Psychol.*, 1963, *10*, 256–63.

479. Truax, C. B., and R. R. Carkhuff. For better or for worse. In *Recent advances in the study of behavior change.* Montreal: McGill University Department of Psychology, June 1963.

480. Truax, C. B., and R. R. Carkhuff. The old and the new: theory and research in counseling and psychotherapy. *Pers. and Guid. J.*, 1964, *42*, 860–66.

481. Tyler, L. E. *The Work of the Counselor*, 3rd ed. New York: Appleton-Century-Crofts, 1969.

482. U. S. Department of Health, Education and Welfare. *Annual Report.* Washington, D.C.: U. S. Government Printing Office, 1963.

483. U. S. Department of Health, Education and Welfare. *Orientation Training for Vocational Rehabilitation Counselors.* Mimeographed. Rehabilitation Service Reports #832. Washington, D.C., 1955.

484. U. S. Employment Service. *Dictionary of Occupational Titles*, 3rd ed. Washington, D.C.: U. S. Government Printing Office, 1965.

485. U. S. Government Occupational Outlook Service. *Occupational Outlook Handbook.* Washington, D.C.: U. S. Government Printing Office, 1966–67.

486. Vincent, C. E. (ed.). *Readings in Marriage Counseling.* New York: Crowell, 1957.

487. Volsky, T., T. Magoon, W. Norman, and D. Hoyt. *The Outcomes of Counseling and Psychotherapy.* Minneapolis: University of Minnesota Press, 1965.

488. Walker, J. L. Four methods of interpreting test scores compared. *Pers. and Guid. J.,* 1965, *44,* 402–4.

489. Wareheim, R. G., D. K. Routh, and M. L. Foulds. Knowledge about self-actualization and the presentation of self as self-actualized. *J. pers. and soc. Psychol.,* 1974, *30,* 155–62.

490. Warner, W. L., M. Meeker, and K. Ells. *Social Class in America.* Chicago: Science Research Associates, 1949.

491. Watson, R. I. *The Clinical Method in Psychology.* New York: Harper & Row, 1951.

492. Watson, R. I. *Psychology as a Profession.* New York: Random House, 1954.

493. Weiner, I. B. The role of diagnosis in a university counseling center. *J. counsel. Psychol.,* 1959, *6,* 110–15.

494. White, R. W. *The Abnormal Personality.* New York: Ronald Press, 1948.

495. White, R. W. *The Abnormal Personality,* 2nd ed. New York: Ronald Press, 1956.

496. White, V. *God and the Unconscious.* Chicago: Henry Regnery, 1953.

497. Wickes, F. *The Inner World of Childhood.* New York: Appleton-Century-Crofts, 1927.

498. Williamson, E. G. Counseling and the Minnesota point of view. *Educ. psychol. Measmt.,* 1947, *7,* 141–56.

499. Williamson, E. G. *How to Counsel Students.* New York: McGraw-Hill, 1939.

500. Williamson, E. G. *Vocational Counseling.* New York: McGraw-Hill, 1965.

501. Winder, L. Group Psychotherapy. In J. L. Moreno (ed.). *Group Psychotherapy—A Symposium.* New York: Beacon, 1945.

502. Winnicott, D. W. Hate in the countertransference. *Int. J. Psychoanal.,* 1949, *30,* 69–74.

503. Wolberg, L. R. *The Technique of Psychotherapy.* New York: Grune, Stratton, 1954.

504. Wolpe, J. *Psychotherapy by Reciprocal Inhibition.* Stanford, Calif.: Stanford University Press, 1958.

505. Wood, A. B. Transference in client-centered therapy and in psychoanalysis. *J. consult. Psychol.,* 1951, *15,* 72–75.

506. Wrenn, C. G. Psychology, Religion, and values for the counselor, Part III, in the symposium, The Counselor and His Religion. *Pers. and Guid. J.,* 1958, *36,* 326–34.

507. Wrenn, C. G. *The Counselor in a Changing World.* Washington, D.C.: American Personnel and Guidance Association, 1962.

508. Wrenn, C. G. The ethics of counseling. *Educ. psychol. Measmt.,* 1952, *12,* 161–77.

509. Wrenn, C. G. *Wrenn Study Habits Inventory.* Stanford, Calif.: Stanford University Press, 1931.

510. Wulf, F. Uber die Veränderung von Vorstellangen. *Psychol. Forsch.,* 1922, *1,* 333–73.

511. Yalom, I. D., M. A. Lieberman, and M. M. Miles. A study of encounter group casualties. *Archives of General Psychiatry,* 1971, *25,* 16–30.

512. Yamamoto, K. Counseling psychologists—who are they? *J. counsel. Psychol.,* 1963, *10,* 211–21.

513. Zelen, S. L. Acceptance and acceptability. *J. consult. Psychol.,* 1954, *18,* 316.

514. Zwetschke, C. T., and J. E. Grenfell. Family group consultation: a description and a rationale. *Pers. and Guid. J.,* 1965, *43,* 974–80.

515. Zytowski, D. The study of therapy outcomes via experimental analogs: a review. *J. counsel. Psychol.,* 1966, *13,* 235–41.